D1570697

WJ III CLINICAL USE AND INTERPRETATION

Scientist–Practitioner Perspectives

WJ III CLINICAL USE AND INTERPRETATION

Scientist–Practitioner Perspectives

Edited by

FREDRICK A. SCHRANK

The Woodcock-Muñoz Foundation
Olympia, Washington

DAWN P. FLANAGAN

Department of Psychology
St. John's University
Jamaica, New York

ACADEMIC PRESS

An imprint of Elsevier

Amsterdam   Boston   Heidelberg   London   New York   Oxford
Paris   San Diego   San Francisco   Singapore   Sydney   Tokyo

Academic Press
An Imprint of Elsevier
525 B Street, Suite 1900, San Diego, California 92101-4495, USA
http://www.academicpress.com

Academic Press
84 Theobald's Road, London WCIX 8RR, UK
http://www.academicpress.com

Library of Congress Catalog Card Number: 2003103959

ISBN-13: 978-0-12-628982-4

International Standard Book Number: 0-12-628982-4

PRINTED IN THE UNITED STATES OF AMERICA
08 09 10 11 12   7 6 5 4 3

CONTENTS

1

INTERPRETATION OF THE *WOODCOCK–JOHNSON III TESTS OF COGNITIVE ABILITIES:* ACTING ON EVIDENCE

RANDY GRANVILLE FLOYD, RENEE B. SHAVER, AND KEVIN S. MCGREW

2

QUALITATIVE ANALYSIS OF WOODCOCK–JOHNSON III TEST PERFORMANCE

BARBARA G. READ AND FREDRICK A. SCHRANK

3

INSTRUCTIONAL IMPLICATIONS FROM THE WOODCOCK–JOHNSON III

NANCY MATHER AND BARBARA J. WENDLING

4

USE OF THE WOODCOCK–JOHNSON III IN THE DIAGNOSIS OF LEARNING DISABILITIES

NOËL GREGG, CHRIS COLEMAN, AND DEBORAH KNIGHT

5

USING THE WOODCOCK–JOHNSON III DISCREPANCY
PROCEDURES FOR DIAGNOSING LEARNING DISABILITIES

NANCY MATHER AND FREDRICK A. SCHRANK

6

USE OF THE WOODCOCK–JOHNSON III
WITHIN THE CONTEXT OF A MODERN OPERATIONAL
DEFINITION OF LEARNING DISABILITY

DAWN P. FLANAGAN

7

USING THE *WOODCOCK–JOHNSON III* TESTS OF *ACHIEVEMENT* WITH THE WISC-III AND WAIS-III TO DETERMINE A SPECIFIC LEARNING DISABILITY

LEADELLE PHELPS AND KEVIN S. MCGREW

8

ASSESSMENT WITH THE WOODCOCK–JOHNSON III AND YOUNG CHILDREN

MARY E. TUSING, DENISE E. MARICLE, AND LAURIE FORD

9

ASSESSMENT OF GIFTED CHILDREN WITH THE WOODCOCK–JOHNSON III

BETTY E. GRIDLEY, KIMBERLY A. NORMAN, MARY G. RIZZA, AND SCOTT L. DECKER

10

USING THE *WOODCOCK–JOHNSON III* TESTS OF *COGNITIVE ABILITIES* WITH STUDENTS WITH ATTENTION DEFICIT/HYPERACTIVITY DISORDER

LAURIE FORD, TIMOTHY Z. KEITH, RANDY GRANVILLE FLOYD, CHERYL FIELDS, AND FREDRICK A. SCHRANK

11

A COGNITIVE NEUROPSYCHOLOGY ASSESSMENT SYSTEM

RAYMOND S. DEAN, RICHARD W. WOODCOCK, SCOTT L. DECKER, AND FREDRICK A. SCHRANK

12

THE *WOODCOCK–JOHNSON III* TESTS OF *COGNITIVE*
ABILITIES IN COGNITIVE ASSESSMENT COURSES

JEFFERY P. BRADEN AND VINCENT C. ALFONSO

PREFACE

The Woodcock–Johnson III (WJ III) is an extensive revision of its predecessor, expanded in depth, breadth, and complexity. It is widely used for assessing the cognitive abilities, oral language capabilities, and academic achievement levels of children, adolescents, and adults. The WJ III includes extensive examiner and technical manuals, and several interpretive texts are available. Although much is already written about how to interpret the WJ III, a need exists for documenting its clinical utility, particularly from a scientist–practitioner perspective. To address this need, *WJ III Clinical Use and Interpretation* presents a wide variety of exemplary clinical applications of the WJ III from its leading experts.

In the introductory chapter of this volume (Chapter 1), Floyd, Shaver, and McGrew summarize the scientific evidence that can be used as a basis for interpretation of the WJ III, particularly as it applies to the *Tests of Cognitive Abilities* (WJ III COG). The authors provide data that support interpretation of the WJ III Cattell-Horn-Carroll factor clusters. The evidence suggests that the WJ III can provide insight into cognitive ability deficits associated with a number of clinical conditions. Next, Read and Schrank (Chapter 2) articulate an analytic method for deriving qualitative information from observable attributes of an individual's performance on the WJ III. Mather and Wendling (Chapter 3) explain how patterns of WJ III cluster and test scores can be used to inform instruction when gathered as part of an intensive diagnostic study of an individual. Although the focus of their chapter is on the WJ III *Tests of Achievement* (WJ III ACH), they describe how patterns of both the WJ III COG and WJ III ACH cluster and test scores can assist with interpretation and formulation of diagnostic hypotheses.

Traditionally, the Woodcock–Johnson has been used for assessment of children, adolescents, and adults with suspected or known learning disabilities.

Four chapters in this volume reflect the utility—and diversity—of clinical applications of the WJ III for learning disabilities identification and diagnosis. Gregg, Coleman, and Knight (Chapter 4) review three models for learning disabilities determination, and advocate for use of a clinical model that integrates quantitative data, qualitative data, self-report background information, and the clinical judgments of a multidisciplinary team. These authors integrate extant scientific and clinical knowledge of learning disabilities in a case study approach that illustrates the usefulness of the WJ III in diagnosing reading, mathematics, and written language disabilities. Mather and Schrank (Chapter 5) describe how to use the various WJ III discrepancy procedures for learning disability identification and diagnosis, emphasizing the benefits of the intra-ability discrepancy procedures for determining profiles of educationally-relevant strengths and weaknesses. Flanagan (Chapter 6) demonstrates the use of the WJ III within the context of an operational definition of learning disabilities that includes a "below-average aptitude-achievement consistency analysis" for the identification and diagnosis of learning disabilities. Phelps and McGrew (Chapter 7) provide a rationale and step-by-step procedure for using correction for regression when comparing the *Wechsler Intelligence Scale for Children-III* (WISC-III) and the *Wechsler Adult Intelligence Scale-III* (WAIS-III) to the WJ III ACH for determining the presence and severity of ability/achievement discrepancies.

Increasingly, the WJ III is being used with populations other than individuals suspected of having specific learning disabilities. Therefore, several chapters in this volume illustrate the principle of selective testing to address the specific assessment needs of gifted children and adolescents, young children (including preschool children), and children with Attention Deficit/Hyperactivity Disorder (ADHD). Tusing, Maricle, and Ford (Chapter 8) review the developmental nature of cognitive abilities in preschool children that provides guidance for selecting WJ III tests and clusters that best represent the cognitive capabilities of young children. Gridley, Norman, Rizza, and Decker (Chapter 9) highlight the value of the WJ III in identification of gifted children and adolescents, particularly for documentation of superior performance in general intellectual ability and/or a specific intellectual ability. Additionally, the authors compared overall scores from the WISC-III and WJ III COG using a combined sample and developed a regression model to determine the equivalence of cut-off scores for identification purposes. Ford, Keith, Floyd, Fields, and Schrank (Chapter 10) present the results of a study using the WJ III Executive Processes, Broad Attention, and Working Memory tests and selected checklists from the *Report Writer for the WJ III* for diagnosis of ADHD. Based on their study, and a review of previous research, they recommend a set of WJ III tests, clusters, and checklists that may be useful in the identification of ADHD.

More than ever before, the WJ III is being utilized in the fields of neuropsychology and school psychology and this has resulted in an increased need for training models. For example, graduate training programs in school and applied psychology are embracing contemporary models of intellectual ability assessment, and the WJ III COG is now used as a primary theoretical and applied training tool in more than one-third of all school psychology training programs. Dean, Woodcock, Decker, and Schrank (Chapter 11) describe a cognitive neuropsychological model for interpreting an individual's performance on the WJ III. They articulate a method for determining an individual's functional levels in a broad array of cognitive, academic, and sensory-motor functions and present two case studies that demonstrate use of the functional levels. Braden and Alfonso (Chapter 12) review historical surveys of cognitive ability assessment courses and propose a paradigm shift whereby intellectual ability assessment courses are taught by providing innovative ways of integrating the WJ III COG into existing course content.

As editors, we thank all those who contributed to this volume for their expertise, time, and adherence to the scientist–practitioner model. In addition to the chapter authors, we are indebted to a stellar team of professionals who edited text, designed figures, and produced the finished volume, including Carissa Kowalski, Kaaren Watson-Winkler, Kristi Anderson, Barbara Makinster, and Nikki Levy.

Fredrick A. Schrank
Dawn P. Flanagan

Contributors

Vincent C. Alfonso (377)   Graduate School of Education, Fordham University, New York, New York 10023.

Jeffery P. Braden (377)   School Psychology Program, Department of Educational Psychology, University of Wisconsin—Madison, Madison, Wisconsin 53706.

Christopher Coleman (125)   University of Georgia, Athens, Georgia 30602.

Raymond S. Dean (345)   Neuropsychology Laboratory, Ball State University, Muncie, Indiana 47306.

Scott L. Decker (285, 345)   Riverside Publishing Company, Itasca, Illinois 60143.

Cheryl Fields (319)   Department of Psychology, University of South Carolina, Columbia, South Carolina 29208.

Dawn P. Flanagan (199)   Department of Psychology, St. John's University, Jamaica, New York 11439.

Randy Granville Floyd (1, 319)   The University of Memphis, Memphis, Tennessee 38152.

Laurie Ford (243, 319)   Department of Educational and Counseling Psychology and Special Education, University of British Columbia, Vancouver, British Columbia, Canada V6T 1Z4.

Noël Gregg (125)   University of Georgia, Athens, Georgia 30602.

Betty E. Gridley (285)   Department of Educational Psychology, Ball State University, Muncie, Indiana 47306.

Timothy Z. Keith (319)   Department of Educational Psychology, The University of Texas at Austin, Austin, Texas 78712.

Deborah Knight (125)   School of Education, University of Delaware, Newark, Delaware 19716.

Denise E. Maricle (243)   Department of Education, School Counseling, School Psychology, University of Wisconsin—Stout, Menomonie, Wisconsin 54751.

Nancy Mather (93, 175)   The University of Arizona, Tucson, Arizona 85721.

Kevin S. McGrew (1, 229)   The University of Minnesota, Minneapolis, Minnesota 55455.

Kimberly A. Norman (285)   Department of Educational Psychology, Ball State University, Muncie, Indiana 47306.

LeAdelle Phelps (229)   State University of New York at Buffalo, Buffalo, New York 14260.

Barbara G. Read (47)   Educational Diagnostic and Consultant Service, Inc., Woodstock, Vermont 05091.

Mary G. Rizza (285)   Educational Foundations and Inquiry, Bowling Green State University, Bowling Green, Ohio 43403.

Fredrick A. Schrank (47, 175, 319, 345)   The Woodcock - Muñoz Foundation, Olympia, Washington 98501.

Renee B. Shaver (1)   The University of Memphis, Memphis, Tennessee 38152.

Mary E. Tusing (243)   Eau Claire Area School District, Eau Claire, Wisconsin 54701.

Barbara J. Wendling (93)   BJ Consulting, Dallas, Texas 75248.

Richard W. Woodcock (345)   Vanderbilt University, Nashville, Tennessee 37235.

1

INTERPRETATION OF THE WOODCOCK–JOHNSON III TESTS OF COGNITIVE ABILITIES

ACTING ON EVIDENCE

RANDY GRANVILLE FLOYD AND RENEE B. SHAVER

The University of Memphis, Memphis, Tennessee 38152

KEVIN S. MCGREW

The University of Minnesota, Minneapolis, Minnesota 55455

"The process of validation involves accumulating evidence to provide a sound scientific basis for the proposed score interpretations." (American Educational Research Association [AERA], American Psychological Association [APA], & National Council on Measurement in Education [NCME], 1999, p. 9)

The *Woodcock–Johnson III Tests of Cognitive Abilities* (WJ III COG) (Woodcock, McGrew, & Mather, 2001) represents the culmination of nearly four decades of systematic psychometric test development by Dr. Richard Woodcock and his colleagues. The WJ III COG was developed to provide reliable and valid measures of a number of important cognitive abilities for individuals ranging from preschool-age children to persons in late adulthood. Its strong theoretical and empirical underpinnings, its adept construction, and

1

its large and nationally representative standardization and co-norming with the *WJ III Tests of Achievement* (ACH; Woodcock et al., 2001) make the WJ III COG an assessment battery that should receive serious attention by assessment professionals.

The most recent revision of the *Standards for Educational and Psychological Testing* (AERA, APA, & NCME, 1999) also represents the culmination of decades of effort to provide guidance and accountability regarding the development and use of psychological and educational tests like the WJ III COG (Kane, 2001). The most recent revision of *Standards* continues to increase the accountability and sophistication demanded of test authors, publishers, and users. *Standards* covers the three broad areas of (a) test construction, evaluation, and documentation; (b) fairness in testing; and (c) testing applications. The first broad area includes evaluation of core psychometric characteristics such as test development and revision, reliability, and validity. In order for assessment professionals to incorporate the WJ III COG into their practice appropriately, they must "know thy instrument" within the context of *Standards*. Of the core psychometric characteristics, validity is "the most fundamental consideration in developing and evaluating tests" (p. 9). It is important to recognize that the validity framework for *Standards* differs in a number of ways from traditional notions of validity held by many professionals in psychology, education, and related fields. Consistent with contemporary conceptualizations of validity (viz., Benson, 1998; Cronbach & Meehl, 1955; Loevinger, 1957; Messick, 1989, 1995; Nunnally & Bernstein, 1994), *Standards* specifies that validity investigations should focus on the *uses and interpretations* of measures and the constructs they are intended to represent. Thus, uses and interpretations of scores from tests and *not the tests themselves* must demonstrate validity. Furthermore, *Standards* conceptualizes validity as a unitary and multidimensional concept (Messick, 1989, 1995). Many assessment professionals may have learned the traditional tripartite model of validity that treated content, construct, and criterion-related validity as relatively separate and equal forms of validity. *Standards* advocates against the notion of distinct types of validity that are either present or absent.

In accordance with *Standards* (AERA, APA, & NCME, 1999), the WJ III COG authors have woven together multiple strands of evidence to construct a network of validity evidence supporting the uses and interpretation of scores from their instrument (McGrew & Woodcock, 2001). This chapter synthesizes the network of validity evidence available for the WJ III COG.[1] Understanding the WJ III COG in the context of *Standards* and how this knowledge bears on its use and interpretation is the focal point of this chapter.

---

[1]Space limitations require a singular focus on validity. The reader should consult the *WJ III Technical Manual* (McGrew & Woodcock, 2001) in order to evaluate the WJ III COG as per adherence to the other standards (e.g., reliability and scale development).

REVIEW OF WJ III COG VALIDITY EVIDENCE

LITERATURE REVIEW

In order to collect sources contributing to the network of validity evidence for the WJ III COG, three strategies were employed. First, the technical manuals for the three editions of the *Woodcock–Johnson Tests of Cognitive Abilities*[2] were reviewed (McGrew, Werder, & Woodcock, 1991; McGrew & Woodcock, 2001; Woodcock, 1978). Second, an electronic bibliographic search of journal articles, books, and book chapters published between January 1977 and March 2002 was conducted using PsychInfo, PsychFirst, and ERIC. Search terms included "Woodcock," "WJ," and "Tests of Cognitive Ability." Third, the reference sections of sources obtained during the initial stages of the search were reviewed. References that included tests from any of the three editions of the *Woodcock–Johnson Tests of Cognitive Abilities* and that provided direct validity evidence supporting interpretation of its tests and clusters were reviewed. Sources that focused solely on the *Woodcock–Johnson Tests of Achievement* were excluded. Appendix A at the end of this book provides a list of the references included in this review and presents the results of the classification of these references according to the areas of validity evidence they represent and other study characteristics. In order to prevent overinterpretation of scores from single tests of ability (e.g., subtests), and consistent with the recommendation of the WJ III COG authors, the review and synthesis are limited to interpretations of the WJ III COG clusters and composites.

ORGANIZATION OF REVIEW

Rather than presenting a "minitechnical manual" replete with tables upon tables of numbers, a conceptual, "big picture" approach was chosen to display the validity evidence for the WJ III COG. First, validity evidence for the seven Cattell–Horn–Carroll (CHC) factor clusters and the global ability composites (e.g., General Intellectual Ability, Brief Intellectual Ability, and Predicted Achievement) is presented. This evidence is supported by visual-schematic figures that summarize and illustrate the relationships among the different forms of validity evidence (see Figures 1-1 through 1-7 and Figure 1-9). Each figure is intended to synthesize, on one page, the preponderance of validity evidence for selected measures. Each figure contains references to the relevant sources listed in Appendix A. The validity evidence supporting interpretation of the WJ III Cognitive Performance Model clusters and the WJ III clinical clusters is also reviewed in this chapter. Consistent with the focus of this chapter, examples are provided that illustrate how to draw upon this validity evidence during the

[2]The previous name for WJ III COG was "Tests of Cognitive Ability." To increase readability, the most current name, "Tests of Cognitive Abilities," was used in this chapter when referring to all three editions of the battery.

practice of psychoeducational assessment. Finally, the chapter ends with a brief discussion of consequential validity evidence and its application to the WJ III COG.

WJ III COG VALIDITY EVIDENCE

CHC FACTOR CLUSTERS

Figures 1-1 through 1-7 present validity evidence for seven CHC factor clusters. The left side of each figure introduces evidence that focuses on determining if the Theoretical Domain and Measurement Domain have been adequately developed. Evidence supporting the substantive base of test development and the validity of test content is presented in the Theoretical Domain section. Although not included explicitly in *Standards*, recent conceptualizations of validity have focused on the requirement that test development and test interpretation should build upon a conceptual map based on accumulated knowledge about the phenomenon under study (Benson, 1998; Messick, 1989, 1995). Thus, sound theory and research findings should guide item and scale development and should support and enhance users' interpretations. Figures 1-1 through 1-7 present the theoretical framework underlying each cluster. For example, Figure 1-1 indicates that the Short-Term Memory (*Gsm*) CHC factor cluster was designed to represent the respective CHC broad cognitive ability (Carroll, 1993, 1997; Horn, 1991; Horn & Noll, 1997). In order to represent this broad cognitive ability, the *Gsm* cluster includes measurement of two CHC narrow cognitive abilities, Working Memory and Memory Span (Carroll, 1993; Flanagan, McGrew, & Ortiz, 2000). Near the top center of Figures 1-1 through 1-7, the large, darkened ovals represent broad cognitive abilities, and small white ovals within these larger, shaded ovals represent the narrow cognitive abilities likely measured by each test composing the CHC factor clusters. At the bottom of the Theoretical Domain section, there is a summary of validity evidence based on test content and supporting references (corresponding to those in Appendix A). Evidence based on test content reflects whether the items and components of a test represent the construct under study in a complete, accurate, and unbiased manner.

The Measurement Domain section of Figures 1-1 through 1-7 provides (a) evidence of the response processes required by tests that compose the CHC factor clusters and (b) evidence of the internal structure of the battery. The measurement domain represents the complete array of possible measures and procedures that a test author could select to operationally measure constructs in the theoretical domain. Test authors must select from a wide variety of available procedures, item and response formats, and scoring procedures when designing tests that are intended to measure an aspect of the theoretical construct domain.

Research examining response processes focuses on the overt or covert steps that examinees follow to complete test items. For example, the nature of test

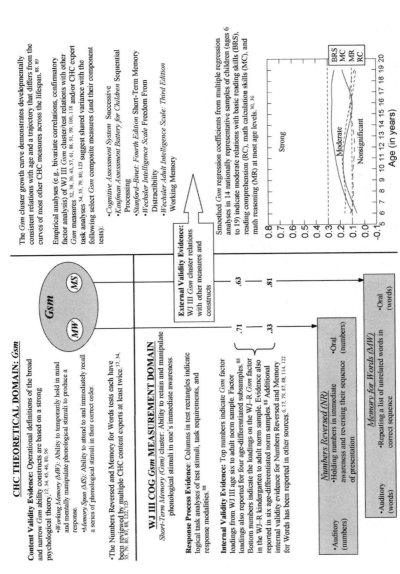

CHC THEORETICAL DOMAIN: *Gsm*

Content Validity Evidence: Operational definitions of the broad and narrow *Gsm* ability constructs are based on a strong psychological theory.[17, 34, 45, 46, 80, 96]

- *Working Memory (MW):* Ability to temporarily hold in mind and mentally manipulate phonological stimuli to produce a response.
- *Memory Span (MS):* Ability to attend to and immediately recall a series of phonological stimuli in their correct order.

- The Numbers Reversed and Memory for Words tests each have been reviewed by multiple CHC content experts at least twice.[17, 34, 35, 79, 80, 97, 88, 122, 123]

The *Gsm* cluster growth curve demonstrates developmentally consistent relations with age and a trajectory that differs from the curves of most other CHC measures across the lifespan.[88, 89]

Empirical analyses (e.g. bivariate correlations, confirmatory factor analysis) of WJ III *Gsm* cluster/test relations with other *Gsm* measures[32, 38, 39, 43, 57, 61, 88, 91, 99, 100, 118] and/or CHC expert task analyses[34, 35, 79, 80, 123] suggest shared variance with the following select *Gsm* composite measures (and their component tests):

- *Cognitive Assessment System* Successive
- *Kaufman Assessment Battery for Children* Sequential Processing
- *Stanford–Binet: Fourth Edition* Short-Term Memory
- *Wechsler Intelligence Scale* Freedom From Distractibility
- *Wechsler Adult Intelligence Scale: Third Edition* Working Memory

WJ III COG *Gsm* MEASUREMENT DOMAIN

Short-Term Memory (Gsm) cluster: Ability to retain and manipulate phonological stimuli in one's immediate awareness.

Response Process Evidence: Columns in test rectangles indicate logical task analyses of test stimuli, task requirements, and response modalities.[88]

Internal Validity Evidence: Top numbers indicate *Gsm* factor loadings from WJ III age six to adult norm sample. Factor loadings also reported for four age-differentiated subsamples.[88] Bottom numbers indicate the loadings on the WJ–R *Gsm* factor in the WJ–R kindergarten to adult norm sample. Evidence also reported in six age-differentiated norm samples.[88] Additional internal validity evidence for Numbers Reversed and Memory for Words has been reported in other sources.[6, 17, 79, 87, 88, 114, 122]

External Validity Evidence: WJ III *Gsm* cluster relations with other measures and constructs

Smoothed *Gsm* regression coefficients from multiple regression analyses in 14 nationally representative samples of children (ages 6 to 19) indicate moderate relations with basic reading skills (BRS), reading comprehension (RC), math calculation skills (MC), and math reasoning (MR) at most age levels.[30, 36]

Gsm
MW
MS

.71
.33
.63
.81

Numbers Reversed (NR)
- Holding numbers in immediate awareness and reversing their sequence of presentation
- Oral (numbers)

Memory for Words (MW)
- Repeating a list of unrelated words in correct sequence
- Oral (words)

- Auditory (numbers)
- Auditory (words)

Strong
Moderate
Nonsignificant

0.8
0.7
0.6
0.5
0.4
0.3
0.2
0.1
0.0
-0.1

5 6 7 8 9 10 11 12 13 14 15 16 17 18 19 20
Age (in years)

BRS
MC
MR
RC

FIGURE 1-1   Summary of validity evidence for the Short-Term Memory (*Gsm*) Cattell–Horn–Carroll (CHC) factor cluster. Superscript numbers refer to sources in Appendix A. By permission of the Institute for Applied Psychometrics, LLC.

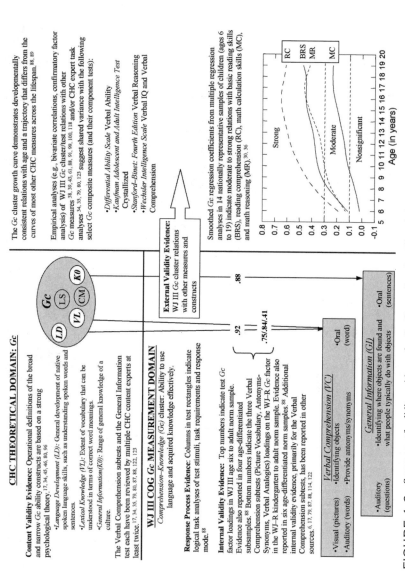

CHC THEORETICAL DOMAIN: *Gc*

Content Validity Evidence: Operational definitions of the broad and narrow *Gc* ability constructs are based on a strong psychological theory.[17, 34, 45, 46, 80, 96]

- *Language Development (LD):* General development of native spoken language skills, such as understanding spoken words and sentences.
- *Lexical Knowledge (VL):* Extent of vocabulary that can be understood in terms of correct word meanings.
- *General Information(K0):* Range of general knowledge of a culture.

The Verbal Comprehension subtests and the General Information test each have been reviewed by multiple CHC content experts at least twice.[17, 34, 35, 79, 80, 87, 88, 122, 123]

WJ III COG *Gc* MEASUREMENT DOMAIN
Comprehension–Knowledge (Gc) cluster: Ability to use language and acquired knowledge effectively.[88]

Response Process Evidence: Columns in test rectangles indicate logical task analyses of test stimuli, task requirements and response mode.[88]

Internal Validity Evidence: Top numbers indicate test *Gc* factor loadings in WJ III age six to adult norm sample. Evidence also reported in four age-differentiated subsamples.[88] Bottom numbers indicate the three Verbal Comprehension subtests (Picture Vocabulary, Antonyms-Synonyms, Verbal Analogies) loadings on the WJ–R *Gc* factor in the WJ–R kindergarten to adult norm sample. Evidence also reported in six age-differentiated norm samples.[88] Additional internal validity evidence, primarily for the Verbal Comprehension subtests, has been reported in other sources.[6, 17, 79, 87, 88, 114, 122]

The *Gc* cluster growth curve demonstrates developmentally consistent relations with age and a trajectory that differs from the curves of most other CHC measures across the lifespan.[88, 89]

Empirical analyses (e.g., bivariate correlations, confirmatory factor analysis) of WJ III *Gc* cluster/test relations with other *Gc* measures[38, 39, 43, 61, 88, 91, 99, 100, 118] and/or CHC expert task analyses[34, 35, 79, 80, 123] suggest shared variance with the following select *Gc* composite measures (and their component tests):

- *Differential Ability Scale Verbal Ability*
- *Kaufman Adolescent and Adult Intelligence Test Crystallized*
- *Stanford–Binet: Fourth Edition Verbal Reasoning*
- *Wechsler Intelligence Scale Verbal IQ and Verbal Comprehension*

External Validity Evidence: WJ III *Gc* cluster relations with other measures and constructs

Smoothed *Gc* regression coefficients from multiple regression analyses in 14 nationally representative samples of children (ages 6 to 19) indicate moderate to strong relations with basic reading skills (BRS), reading comprehension (RC), math calculation skills (MC), and math reasoning (MR).[30, 36]

Verbal Comprehension (VC)
- Visual (pictures) • Identifying objects
- Auditory (words) • Provide antonyms/synonyms
- Oral (word)

General Information (GI)
- Identifying where objects are found and what people typically do with objects
- Auditory (questions)
- Oral (sentences)

FIGURE 1-2 Summary of validity evidence for the Comprehension–Knowledge (*Gc*) Cattell–Horn–Carroll (CHC) factor cluster. Superscript numbers refer to sources in Appendix A. By permission of the Institute for Applied Psychometrics, LLC.

CHC THEORETICAL DOMAIN: Gv

Content Validity Evidence: Operational definitions of the broad and narrow Gv ability constructs are based on a strong psychological theory.[17, 34, 45, 46, 80, 96]

- *Spatial Relations (SR):* Ability to rapidly construct specified visual patterns or to understand how visual stimuli relate to each other.
- *Visualization (Vz):* Ability to hold visual stimuli and spatial forms in mind and to alter them in some way.
- *Visual Memory (MV):* Ability to retain representations of visual stimuli in mind and to recognize or recall them soon afterward.

• The Spatial Relations and Picture Recognition tests each have been reviewed by multiple CHC content experts at least twice.[17, 34, 35, 79, 80, 87, 88, 122, 123]

WJ III COG Gv MEASUREMENT DOMAIN

Visual–Spatial Thinking (Gv) cluster: Ability to identify spatial relationships and to hold and manipulate mental representations of visual stimuli in mind.

Response Process Evidence: Columns in test rectangles indicate logical task analyses of test stimuli, task requirements, and response modalities.[88]

Internal Validity Evidence: Top numbers indicate Gv factor loadings from WJ III age six to adult norm sample. Factor loadings also reported for four age-differentiated subsamples.[88] Bottom numbers indicate the loadings on the WJ–R Gv factor in the WJ–R kindergarten to adult norm sample. Evidence also reported in six age-differentiated norm samples.[88] Additional internal validity evidence for Spatial Relations and Picture Recognition has been reported in other sources.[6, 17, 79, 87, 88, 114, 122]

The Gv cluster growth curve demonstrates developmentally consistent relations with age and a trajectory that differs from the curves of most other CHC measures across the lifespan.[88, 89]

Empirical analyses (e.g., bivariate correlations, confirmatory factor analysis) of WJ III Gv cluster/test relations with other Gv measures[38, 39, 43, 61, 88, 91, 96, 99, 100, 118] and/or CHC expert task analyses[34, 35, 79, 80, 123] suggest shared variance with the following select Gv composite measures (and their component tests):

- *Differential Ability Scale* Spatial Ability
- *Kaufman Assessment Battery for Children* Simultaneous Processing
- *Stanford–Binet: Fourth Edition* Abstrac/Visual Reasoning
- *Wechsler Intelligence Scale* Performance IQ and Perceptual Organization

External Validity Evidence: WJ III Gv cluster relations with other measures and constructs

Smoothed Gv regression coefficients from multiple regression analyses in 14 nationally representative samples of children (ages 6 to 19) indicate generally nonsignificant relations with basic reading skills (BRS), reading comprehension (RC), math calculation skills (MC), and math reasoning (MR).[30, 36]

Spatial Relations (SR)
- •Visual (drawings): •Identifying the subset of pieces needed to form a complete shape
- •Oral (letters)
- •Motoric (pointing)

Picture Recognition (PR)
- •Visual (pictures): •Identifying a subset of previously presented pictures within a field of distracting pictures
- •Oral (words)
- •Motoric (pointing)

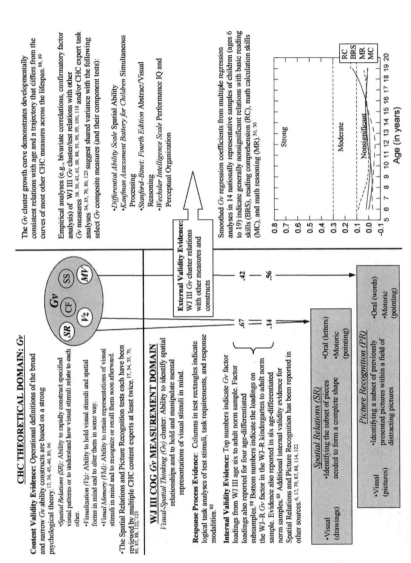

FIGURE 1-3   Summary of validity evidence for the Visual–Spatial Thinking (Gv) Cattell–Horn–Carroll (CHC) factor cluster. Superscript numbers refer to sources in Appendix A. By permission of the Institute for Applied Psychometrics, LLC.

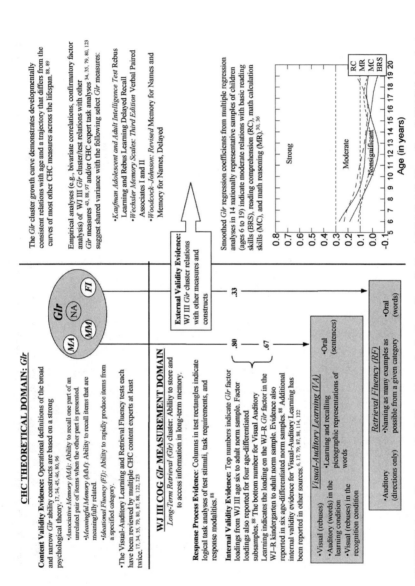

FIGURE 1-4 Summary of validity evidence for the Long-Term Retrieval (*Glr*) Cattell–Horn–Carroll (CHC) factor cluster. Superscript numbers refer to sources in Appendix A. By permission of the Institute for Applied Psychometrics, LLC.

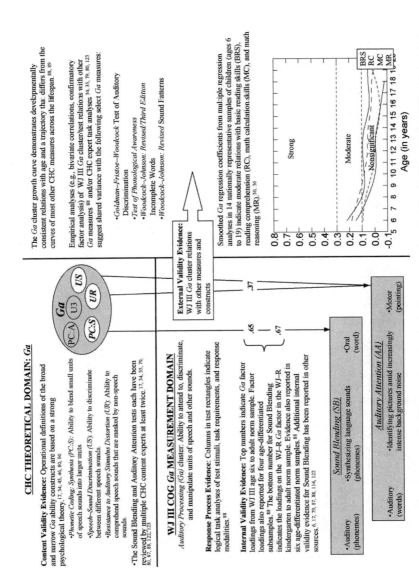

CHC THEORETICAL DOMAIN: *Ga*

Content Validity Evidence: Operational definitions of the broad and narrow *Ga* ability constructs are based on a strong psychological theory.[17, 34, 45, 46, 80, 96]

- *Phonetic Coding: Synthesis (PC:S)*: Ability to blend small units of speech sounds into larger units.
- *Speech–Sound Discrimination (US)*: Ability to discriminate between different speech sounds.
- *Resistance to Auditory Stimulus Distortion (UR)*: Ability to comprehend speech sounds that are masked by non-speech sounds.

- The Sound Blending and Auditory Attention tests each have been reviewed by multiple CHC content experts at least twice.[17, 34, 35, 79, 80, 87, 88, 122, 123]

WJ III COG *Ga* MEASUREMENT DOMAIN

Auditory Processing (Ga) cluster: Ability to attend to, discriminate, and manipulate units of speech and other sounds.

Response Process Evidence: Columns in test rectangles indicate logical task analyses of test stimuli, task requirements, and response modalities.[88]

Internal Validity Evidence: Top numbers indicate *Ga* factor loadings from WJ III age six to adult norm sample. Factor loadings also reported for four age-differentiated subsamples.[83] The bottom number for Sound Blending indicates the loadings on the WJ–R *Ga* factor in the WJ–R kindergarten to adult norm sample. Evidence also reported in six age-differentiated norm samples.[88] Additional internal validity evidence for Sound Blending has been reported in other sources.[6, 17, 79, 87, 88, 114, 122]

The *Ga* cluster growth curve demonstrates developmentally consistent relations with age and a trajectory that differs from the curves of most other CHC measures across the lifespan.[88, 89]

Empirical analyses (e.g., bivariate correlations, confirmatory factor analysis) of WJ III *Ga* cluster/test relations with other *Ga* measures[88] and/or CHC expert task analyses[34, 35, 79, 80, 123] suggest shared variance with the following select *Ga* measures:

- *Goldman–Fristoe–Woodcock* Test of Auditory Discrimination
- *Test of Phonological Awareness*
- *Woodcock–Johnson: Revised/Third Edition* Incomplete Words
- *Woodcock–Johnson: Revised* Sound Patterns

External Validity Evidence: WJ III *Ga* cluster relations with other measures and constructs

Smoothed *Ga* regression coefficients from multiple regression analyses in 14 nationally representative samples of children (ages 6 to 19) indicate moderate relations with basic reading skills (BRS), reading comprehension (RC), math calculation skills (MC), and math reasoning (MR).[30, 96]

Sound Blending (SB)
- **Auditory (phonemes)**: Synthesizing language sounds (phonemes)
- **Oral (word)**

Auditory Attention (AA)
- **Auditory (words)**: Identifying pictures amid increasingly intense background noise
- **Motor (pointing)**

.65

.67

.37

FIGURE 1-5 Summary of validity evidence for the Auditory Processing *(Ga)* Cattell–Horn–Carroll (CHC) factor cluster. Superscript numbers refer to sources in Appendix A. By permission of the Institute for Applied Psychometrics, LLC.

9

CHC THEORETICAL DOMAIN: *Gf*

Content Validity Evidence: Operational definitions of the broad and narrow *Gf* ability constructs are based on a strong psychological theory.[17, 34, 45, 46, 80, 96]

- *Induction (I):* Ability to identify the concept or rule that underlies a problem or set of stimuli.
- *General Sequential Reasoning (RG):* Ability to start with stated rules and engage in steps to reach a solution to a novel problem.

- The Concept Formation and Analysis-Synthesis tests each have been reviewed by multiple CHC content experts at least twice.[17, 34, 35, 79, 80, 87, 88, 122, 123]

WJ III COG *Gf* MEASUREMENT DOMAIN

Fluid Reasoning (Gf) cluster: Ability to perceive logical relationships and to solve problems using unfamiliar stimuli.

Response Process Evidence: Columns in test rectangles indicate logical task analyses of test stimuli, task requirements, and response modalities.[88]

Internal Validity Evidence: Top numbers indicate *Gf* factor loadings from WJ III age six to adult norm sample. Factor loadings also reported for four age-differentiated subsamples.[88] Bottom numbers indicate the loadings on the identical WJ-R *Gf* factor in the WJ-R kindergarten to adult norm sample. Evidence also reported in six age-differentiated norm samples.[88] Additional internal validity evidence for Concept Formation and Analysis-Synthesis has been reported in other sources.[6, 17, 79, 87, 88, 114, 122]

The *Gf* cluster growth curve demonstrates developmentally consistent relations with age and a trajectory that differs from the curves of most other CHC measures across the lifespan.[88, 89]

Empirical analyses (e.g., bivariate correlations, confirmatory factor analysis) of the WJ III *Gf* cluster/test with other *Gf* measures[32, 39, 39, 43, 57, 61, 70, 88, 91, 97, 118] and/or CHC expert task analyses[34, 35, 79, 80, 123] suggest shared variance with the following select *Gf* composite measures (and their component tests):

- *Cognitive Assessment System Simultaneous Processing*
- *Differential Ability Scale* Nonverbal Reasoning Ability and Nonverbal Ability
- *Kaufman Adolescent and Adult Intelligence Test Scale* Fluid
- *Wechsler Adult Intelligence Scale: Third Edition* Perceptual Organization

External Validity Evidence: WJ III *Gf* cluster relations with other measures and constructs

Gf (RP, RQ, I, RE, RG)

.76
.67

.73
.65

Concept Formation (CF)
- Identifying, categorizing, and determining rules
- Oral (words)
- Visual (images of shapes)

Analysis-Synthesis (AS)
- Analyzing puzzles (using symbolic formulations) to determine missing components
- Oral (words)
- Visual (drawings)

Smoothed *Gf* regression coefficients from multiple regression analyses in 14 nationally representative samples of children (ages 6 to 19) indicate moderate relations with math reasoning (MR) and math calculation (MC) and nonsignificant relations with reading comprehension (RC) and basic reading skills (BRS).[30, 36]

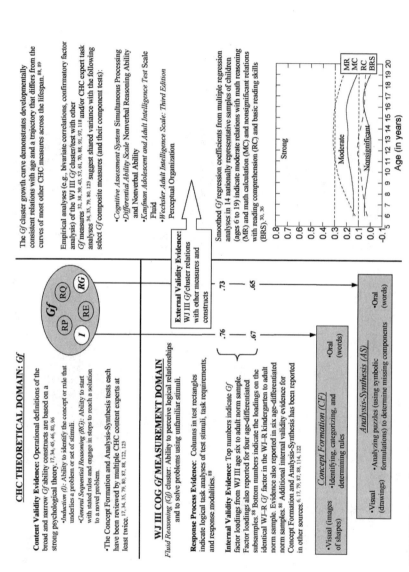

FIGURE 1-6   Summary of validity evidence for the Fluid Reasoning (*Gf*) Cattell–Horn–Carroll (CHC) factor cluster. Superscript numbers refer to sources in Appendix A. By permission of the Institute for Applied Psychometrics, LLC.

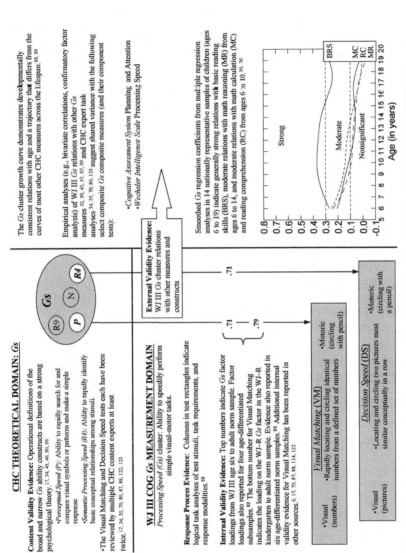

CHC THEORETICAL DOMAIN: Gs

Content Validity Evidence: Operational definitions of the broad and narrow Gs ability constructs are based on a strong psychological theory. [7, 34, 45, 46, 80, 96]

•*Perceptual Speed (P):* Ability to rapidly search for and compare visual symbols or patterns and make a simple response.

•*Semantic Processing Speed (R4):* Ability to rapidly identify basic conceptual relationships among stimuli.

•The Visual Matching and Decision Speed tests each have been reviewed by multiple CHC content experts at least twice. [17, 34, 35, 79, 80, 87, 88, 122, 123]

The Gs cluster growth curve demonstrates developmentally consistent relations with age and a trajectory that differs from the curves of most other CHC measures across the Lifespan. [88, 89]

Empirical analyses (e.g., bivariate correlations, confirmatory factor analysis) of WJ III Gs relations with other Gs measures [32, 39, 43, 57, 97, 99] and CHC expert task analyses [34, 35, 79, 80, 123] suggest shared variance with the following select composite Gs composite measures (and their component tests):

•*Cognitive Assessment System Planning and Attention*
•*Wechsler Intelligence Scale Processing Speed*

WJ III COG Gs MEASUREMENT DOMAIN

Processing Speed (Gs) cluster: Ability to speedily perform simple visual-motor tasks.

Response Process Evidence: Columns in test rectangles indicate logical task analyses of test stimuli, task requirements, and response modalities. [88]

Internal Validity Evidence: Top numbers indicate Gs factor loadings from WJ III age six to adult norm sample. Factor loadings also reported for four age-differentiated subsamples. [88] The bottom number for Visual Matching indicates the loading on the WJ-R Gs factor in the WJ-R kindergarten to adult norm sample. Evidence also reported in six age-differentiated norm samples. [88] Additional internal validity evidence for Visual Matching has been reported in other sources. [6, 17, 79, 87, 88, 114, 122]

External Validity Evidence: WJ III Gs cluster relations with other measures and constructs

Smoothed Gs regression coefficients from multiple regression analyses in 14 nationally representative samples of children (ages 6 to 19) indicate generally strong relations with basic reading skills (BRS), moderate relations with math reasoning (MR) from ages 6 to 14, and moderate relations with math calculation (MC) and reading comprehension (RC) from ages 6 to 10. [30, 36]

Visual Matching (VM)
•Rapidly locating and circling identical numbers from a defined set of numbers

•Visual (numbers)
•Motoric (circling with pencil)

Decision Speed (DS)
•Locating and circling two pictures most similar conceptually in a row

•Visual (pictures)
•Motoric (circling with a pencil)

.71   .71   .79

FIGURE 1-7   Summary of validity evidence for the Processing Speed (Gs) Cattell–Horn–Carroll (CHC) factor cluster. Superscript numbers refer to sources in Appendix A. By permission of the Institute for Applied Psychometrics, LLC.

stimuli (e.g., pictures, oral presentation, written words) and the types of responses required by the examinee (e.g., oral, written, motoric) can be evaluated to conclude if a test characteristic generates influences that are *not* directly associated with the ability targeted by the test (i.e., construct-irrelevant influences). Thus, attention to response processes is particularly relevant when testing individuals with sensory, communication, and motor impairments; individuals who are English-language learners; and young children, because characteristics of these individuals that are not associated with the ability measured by the test may systematically influence how they perform (Pitoniak & Royer, 2001). For instance, in Figure 1-1, verbalized words (i.e., the names of numbers presented orally by the examiner or by tape) are the primary test stimuli for Numbers Reversed. The examinee is required to hold numbers in immediate awareness, to reverse their sequence of presentation, and to respond by repeating the correct sequence of numbers orally. Based on this information, it would be possible for an examiner to evaluate (a) whether the performance of an examinee who had mild hearing deficits was negatively affected because of the nature of the test stimuli or (b) whether the performance of an examinee with severe articulation problems was negatively affected because of the test's response format.

Research providing evidence of the internal structure of test batteries focuses on determining if the tests within a single battery covary in a manner consistent with the theoretical constructs they were designed to measure. To evaluate evidence of internal structure, item scaling procedures, analyses of the differential performance of specified groups of individuals on items, and structural analyses such as exploratory factor analysis, confirmatory factor analysis, and cluster analysis may be conducted. Figures 1-1 through 1-7 focus on evidence of internal structure based on confirmatory factor analyses using data from the WJ III standardization sample. In addition, these figures present evidence of internal structure from similar confirmatory factor analyses using the Woodcock–Johnson Psycho-Educational Battery—Revised (WJ-R) standardization sample (McGrew et al., 1991; Woodcock & Johnson, 1989). Factor loadings, which represent the empirical relations between tests and the statistically derived factors measured by the tests, are reported for each test composing the CHC factor clusters. For example, in Figure 1-1, Numbers Reversed demonstrated a factor loading of .71 with the Gsm factor in the WJ III analysis, and its factor loading was .33 with the Gsm factor in the WJ-R analysis.3

The right sides of Figures 1-1 through 1-7 introduce External Validity Evidence. This section of each figure presents evidence of the relations between test scores and variables from *outside* of the test battery. Thus, this strand of validity evidence encompasses the traditional psychometric properties of convergent validity and discriminant validity as well as criterion-related validity

---

[3]The difference in the magnitude of the factor loadings of Numbers Reversed is most likely due to the fact that the WJ-R and WJ III Short-Term Memory (*Gsm*) factors are defined differently. The WJ III *Gsm* factor was defined by a greater breadth of abilities than that in the WJ-R.

(i.e., concurrent and predictive validity). It may also include discriminative validity, in which the scores of groups that differ on certain characteristics (e.g., developmental level or diagnostic category) are compared using techniques such as growth curve analysis, profile analysis, and discriminant function analysis. Figure 1-1 presents selected external validity evidence for the Short-Term Memory (*Gsm*) CHC factor cluster. This evidence includes the results of growth curve analyses, studies of the relations between the *Gsm* cluster and related measures of cognitive abilities, and examinations of the relations between this cluster and achievement domains. The following discussions build on this introduction to the visual-schematic figures and the information provided within them and offer additional validity evidence for the CHC factor clusters.

Evidence Based on Test Content

A review of Figure 1-8 indicates that the WJ III COG has benefited from two different rounds of test design grounded in the CHC theory of cognitive abilities.

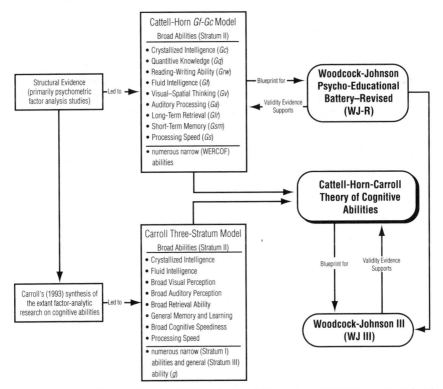

FIGURE 1-8   Relationship of the WJ III to the Cattell–Horn–Carroll (CHC) theory. Reproduced with permission of the publisher, from Figure 2-1 of the *Woodcock–Johnson III Technical Manual* (2001) by Kevin S. McGrew and Richard W. Woodcock. All rights reserved. The Riverside Publishing Company, Itasca, Illinois.

This theory was established based on synthesis of the Cattell–Horn *Gf–Gc* theory (Horn, 1991; Horn & Noll, 1997) and the Carroll three-stratum theory of cognitive abilities (Carroll, 1993, 1997). CHC theory is grounded in more than half a century of empirical evidence derived from structural analyses (e.g., factor analysis). Furthermore, developmental studies, genetic and heritability research, and neurocognitive analyses provide additional empirical support for this theory (Flanagan et al., 2000; Horn & Noll, 1997).

As summarized in Figures 1-1 through 1-7, the content validity of the WJ III tests is supported by (a) the development of theory-based operational definitions of constructs (i.e., abilities) to be measured, (b) revision of existing items and the generation of new items as per the specified constructs, and (c) expert review to evaluate the adequacy of the construct definitions and the correspondence of test items to these definitions. Most notably, the test authors met periodically with John Horn and John Carroll over a period of approximately 15 years to establish and refine operational definitions of the cognitive ability constructs and to discuss WJ-R and WJ III COG items and test formats. One would be hard pressed to find two more qualified experts with whom to consult during test development than Horn and Carroll. The professional fingerprints of these researchers are clearly evident in the test content of the WJ III COG.

Numerous other content experts, psychologists, special educators, and academics have reviewed the items across all three versions of the Woodcock–Johnson Tests of Cognitive Abilities. In fact, the *WJ III Technical Manual* (McGrew & Woodcock, 2001) acknowledged approximately 30 different individuals with training and experiences in special education and psychology who participated in the collection of special study data and who provided routine feedback and critiques of the items during early stages of test standardization. Based on this process, items from 12 WJ III COG tests have benefited from item development, review, try-outs, and statistical analyses across two or three generations of the battery (McGrew & Woodcock, 2001).[4] Although not represented in Figures 1-1 through 1-7, empirical item analyses of the WJ III tests using the Rasch single-parameter logistic model also have been conducted (Rasch, 1960; Woodcock, 1999; Wright & Stone, 1979). In addition, all of the WJ III COG tests have benefited from at least one round of expert-consensus reviews. For example, the initial expert-consensus process described by McGrew (1997) and its extension by McGrew and Flanagan (1998) classified 12 of the WJ III COG tests (in their WJ-R form) as per CHC narrow cognitive abilities. Furthermore, Flanagan and Ortiz (2001) offered a postpublication review of the content of the WJ III COG tests.

---

[4]The WJ III COG tests that have been included in either two or three rounds of item analyses include Verbal Comprehension (which includes four subtests: Picture Vocabulary, Oral Vocabulary: Synonyms, Oral Vocabulary: Antonyms, Verbal Analogies), Sound Blending, Incomplete Words, Spatial Relations, Picture Recognition, Visual–Auditory Learning, Numbers Reversed, Memory for Words, Visual Matching, Concept Formation, Analysis–Synthesis, and Visual Matching.

Evidence Based on Response Processes

As noted previously, the boxes at the top of the Measurement Domain section in Figures 1-1 through 1-7 include the test authors' logical, task-analytic summaries of the test stimuli, test requirements, and response modalities of 14 WJ III COG tests (see also McGrew & Woodcock, 2001 and Schrank, Flanagan, Woodcock, & Mascolo, 2002). These summaries reflect one acceptable method for presenting evidence of response processes. Also relevant to evidence based on response processes is the fact that the WJ III authors have constructed the COG tests to remove many construct-irrelevant influences on performance. For example, although a number of tests contributing to the CHC factor clusters require motoric responses, no test items require the use of manipulatives (e.g., blocks or puzzles pieces) because they may increase the likelihood of construct-irrelevant influences (viz., fine motor skill deficits) affecting performance on the cognitive ability tests. In addition, during test development, a section of Visual Matching (see Figure 1-7) was added for young children and low-functioning persons in order to eliminate pencil use while measuring Processing Speed (*Gs*). Thus, during the 2-minute administration of this section of Visual Matching (called Visual Matching 1), examinees must point to matching shapes within rows presented on the easel page. Based on knowledge about response processes, the authors of the WJ III COG provide a list of possible accommodations intended to reduce the effects of sensory or motor deficits during test administration (Mather & Woodcock, 2001).

Despite the authors' logical task analysis of response processes, the test development practices designed to remove construct-irrelevant influences, and the listing of useful testing accommodations for individuals with sensory or motor deficits, no empirical evidence (e.g., componential analyses and experimental analyses; Carroll, 1993; Messick, 1995) has been presented, to date, that supports the WJ III authors' characterizations of the response processes of the WJ III COG tests (or their previous editions). Furthermore, no studies have been conducted that provide evidence that the *thought processes* used during test performance are consistent with the theoretical constructs they were designed to measure.

Evidence Based on Internal Structure

The *WJ III Technical Manual* (McGrew & Woodcock, 2001) presented the results from a variety of bivariate and multivariate statistical analyses (e.g., confirmatory factor analysis) used to examine the relations among the WJ III tests. Select evidence of internal structure supporting the CHC factor clusters is presented in Figures 1-1 through 1-7, and the extant studies examining internal structure are presented in Appendix A.

Building on an accumulating body of evidence based on internal structure stemming from analyses of data from the standardization samples of the *Woodcock–Johnson Tests of Cognitive Abilities* and other samples, confirmatory factor analyses were used to examine the internal structure of the WJ III (McGrew & Woodcock, 2001). Initial analysis included all 20 WJ III COG tests, 22 WJ III ACH tests, and 8 research tests (see p. 61 in McGrew & Woodcock, 2001, for a review of research tests). When compared to alternative models representing factor structures of other intelligence test batteries and a model specifying only a single general intelligence factor, the CHC model that included a general intelligence factor and the CHC broad ability factors was found to most completely represent the intercorrelations among the tests. These analyses provide evidence that the CHC model is likely the most plausible structure for the WJ III COG. However, it is important to note that models that were not tested may also be plausible and that exploratory factor analyses of the WJ III standardization data have not been reported to date. Although a convergence of findings from confirmatory factor analysis and exploratory factor analysis is ideal, there recently has been increasing concern that exploratory factor analysis may not be best suited for testing hierarchical models of intelligence such as CHC theory. For example, Gustaffson (1999) asserted that the results of exploratory factor analysis are muddled by disagreement about the number of factors to extract, how best to estimate the correlations between tests and factors (i.e., factor loadings), and which statistical techniques to use to estimate the relations among the factors. Drawing upon existing research examining the human cognitive abilities and CHC theory, the authors of the WJ III COG chose confirmatory factor analysis to represent the hierarchical organization of these abilities and to provide the most well-informed structural validity evidence. Furthermore, a priori specification of a detailed test design blueprint based on CHC theory and a large body of research focusing on human cognitive abilities required a confirmatory approach to validation (see Figure 1-8).

Evidence Based on External Relations

One type of external validity evidence supporting the interpretation of the CHC factor clusters is provided vis-à-vis differential cross-sectional growth curves derived from the WJ III standardization sample (McGrew & Woodcock, 2001). As summarized in the External Validity Evidence section of Figures 1-1 through 1-7, Short-Term Memory (*Gsm*), Fluid Reasoning (*Gf*), and Processing Speed (*Gs*) demonstrated rapid increases during childhood and systematic declines after approximately age 25. Comprehension–Knowledge (*Gc*) also demonstrated rapid increases during childhood, which is consistent with abilities that are influenced by formal learning situations (viz., schooling). However, the Comprehension–Knowledge trajectory was stable after adolescence and did not decline until the latest ages of development (i.e., 65 and older). In contrast, Visual-Spatial Thinking (*Gv*), Long-Term Retrieval (*Glr*), and Auditory Processing (*Ga*) displayed the least amount of age-related changes, which is consistent with cognitive abilities that develop more through informal and indirect learning. Thus, the developmental patterns of growth and decline displayed by the CHC factor clusters is in concordance with what is known about human cognitive development and aging (Horn & Noll, 1997; McArdle, Ferrer-Caja, Hamagami, & Woodcock, 2002; Noll & Horn, 1998).

Empirical and logical relations between the CHC factor clusters and similarly defined measures from other intelligence test batteries (and the absence of these relations between these clusters and dissimilar measures) also provide external validity evidence (McGrew & Woodcock, 2001). For example, evidence of convergent validity is provided by high correlations between tests purported to measure the same theoretical construct (see Figures 1-1 through 1-7), whereas evidence of discriminant validity is provided by low correlations between tests purported to measure different constructs. The Comprehension–Knowledge (*Gc*), Visual–Spatial Thinking (*Gv*), Fluid Reasoning (*Gf*), Processing Speed (*Gs*), and Short-Term Memory (*Gsm*) clusters demonstrated consistent evidence of convergent and discriminant validity. Establishing these patterns of evidence for the Long-Term Retrieval (*Glr*) and Auditory Processing (*Ga*) clusters is hindered by a lack of measures of these constructs in other intelligence test batteries (Flanagan et al., 2000; McGrew & Flanagan, 1998). However, the statistical relations between the CHC factor clusters and other WJ III measures and classification of measures from special-purpose test batteries based on expert consensus provide evidence of their convergent validity (see Figures 1-4 and 1-5). For example, Figure 1-4 indicates that, based on empirical analyses of similar measures and expert consensus, the Long-Term Retrieval (*Glr*) cluster likely measures the same abilities as the Rebus Learning and Rebus Learning Delayed Recall subtests from the *Kaufman Adolescent and Adult Intelligence Test* (KAIT) (Kaufman & Kaufman, 1993) and the Verbal Paired Associates I and II subtests from the *Wechsler Memory Scale—Third Edition* (Wechsler, 1997b). Although the patterns of correlations between the CHC factor clusters and related measures provide evidence of the external relations of these clusters, in practice, the magnitude of the correlations should not lead test users to expect identical scores from similar measures. For example, a significant and high concurrent correlation of .70 between two measures of "verbal abilities" (such as the WJ III Comprehension–Knowledge [*Gc*] cluster and the Verbal Comprehension factor index from the *Wechsler Intelligence Scale for Children—Third Edition* [WISC-III]; Wechsler, 1991) translates to approximately 50% shared variance. Although statistically significant, such a value indicates that the two reliable measures also measure unique abilities.

Another type of evidence based on external relations that supports the interpretation of the CHC factor clusters is their relations with concurrent measures of academic achievement in samples of preschool-, school-, and college-age individuals. For example, correlational analyses of the CHC factor clusters and WJ III ACH clusters showed expected levels of convergence using data from the WJ III standardization sample and validity study samples (McGrew & Woodcock, 2001). In addition, Figures 1-1 through 1-7 present the results of two regression-based studies using the WJ III standardization sample that examined the relative contribution of the CHC factor clusters to the prediction of reading and mathematics clusters from the WJ III ACH (Evans, Floyd, McGrew, & Leforgee, 2002; Floyd, Evans, & McGrew, in press). In summary, the WJ III Comprehension–Knowledge (*Gc*) cluster demonstrated moderate to strong relations with measures of basic reading skills, reading comprehension, math calculation skills, and mathematics reasoning as well as moderate to strong relations with basic writing skills and written expression (Evans et al., 2002; Floyd et al., in press; Floyd, Flanagan, Evans, & McGrew, 2002). These findings are supported by similar findings from studies using the WJ-R Comprehension–Knowledge (*Gc*) cluster (McGrew, 1993; McGrew & Hessler, 1995; McGrew & Knopik, 1993). The WJ III Short-Term Memory (*Gsm*) cluster also exhibited moderate relations with each of the components of reading, mathematics, and writing achievement. The WJ III Processing Speed (*Gs*) cluster displayed strong to moderate relations with math calculation skills and basic writing skills and moderate relations with math reasoning and written expression; however, it displayed moderate relations with the components of reading achievement only during the early elementary school years.

Several CHC factor clusters (e.g., Long-Term Retrieval [*Glr*]) also demonstrated significant relations with the domains of academic achievement only during the elementary school years. In addition, some clusters showed differential predictive power for various achievement domains. The WJ III Auditory Processing (*Ga*) cluster exhibited moderate relations with basic reading skills, reading comprehension, math calculation skills, and written expression during the elementary school-age years; however, it exhibited weak relations with mathematics reasoning and basic writing skills during the same period. Across a number of studies incorporating the Fluid Reasoning (*Gf*) cluster from the WJ-R and WJ III, the *Gf* cluster demonstrated strong to moderate relations with mathematics skills but weak relations with basic reading skills, basic writing skills, and written expression. The WJ III Visual-Spatial Thinking (*Gv*) cluster demonstrated the weakest relations with the components of reading, mathematics, and writing across the periods of analysis.

Evidence based on external relations may also support the ability of measures to accurately discriminate between individuals with educational or diagnostic classifications and those without such classifications. Across the three editions of the *Woodcock–Johnson Tests of Cognitive Abilities*, a number of studies have examined the ability of the measures to discriminate between groups based on educational or diagnostic classifications, such as learning disabilities, mental retardation, giftedness, and Attention Deficit/Hyperactivity Disorder (see Appendix A and other chapters in this book). However, no consistent and clear picture has emerged from this research that indicates which CHC factor cluster or combination of clusters provides the most valuable discriminative validity evidence for these clinical groups. This lack of clarity has likely occurred due to imprecise and inconsistent selection criteria for inclusion of participants from special groups, frequent inclusion of achievement tests and other cognitive ability measures in discriminant function analysis, and other design limitations that reduce the confidence that can be placed on group comparisons and classification rates.

Acting on Evidence

A number of interpretations of the scores from the CHC factor clusters have demonstrated a well-developed network of validity evidence.[5] First, test users can feel confident that their interpretations are well grounded in what is perhaps the most empirically supported theory of cognitive abilities—CHC theory. When making decisions about an examinee's cognitive abilities represented by the CHC factor clusters, test users can trust that they have valid measures of these abilities. The attributes of these cognitive abilities that have been demonstrated across thousands of studies of human cognitive abilities likely generalize to the CHC factor clusters. For example, research has indicated that Fluid Reasoning (*Gf*) abilities are strongly related to mathematics achievement, occupational outcomes in science and mathematics, and personality traits such as *openness to experience* (see McGrew & Flanagan, 1998, for a review). Consequentially, based on this body of research, test users can be certain that scores from the *Gf* CHC factor cluster and other CHC factor clusters are also associated with such outcomes.

Second, test users should feel assured that the test content contributing to these clusters has been reviewed for bias and for construct representation and that it has been found to meet the highest standards of test item development. Similarly, evidence based on content, response processes, and internal structure indicates that interpretations based on the CHC factor clusters are not typically contaminated by construct-irrelevant influences. Third, there is evidence that the CHC factor clusters demonstrate strong and significant relations with other cognitive ability measures, such as those from the WISC-III (Wechsler, 1991). Fourth, test users have evidence that a number of CHC factors can be interpreted as strong predictors of concurrent levels of achievement in reading, math, and writing skills across the school-age years. For example, when assessing reading decoding abilities during the early school-age years, test users may choose to administer the tests composing the Comprehension–Knowledge (*Gc*), Short-Term Memory (*Gsm*), Processing Speed (*Gs*), Long-Term Retrieval (*Glr*), and Auditory Processing (*Ga*) CHC factor clusters because they are aptitudes for basic reading skills.

Finally, it is likely that interpretation of the CHC factor clusters can provide insight into the cognitive ability deficits that lead to a number of diagnostic conditions. At minimum, these clusters can be used in concert with other sources of assessment information to develop and test hypotheses (for details about hypothesis testing, see Flanagan et al., 2000; Flanagan, Ortiz, Alfonso, & Mascolo, 2002; and Kamphaus, 2001). Although information about specific

---

[5]The vast majority of validity evidence for the CHC factor clusters is based on studies that primarily include school-age children (i.e., ages 5 to 18). Review of Appendix A indicates that five studies were conducted using only preschool-age participants, seven included only college-age participants, and a single study included only older adults.

cognitive abilities can contribute to diagnostic decision making, at present it is probably ideal that assessment professionals rely first upon well-developed and validated classification systems (e.g., the *Diagnostic and Statistical Manual of Mental Disorders*; American Psychiatric Association, 1994, 2000) and additional sources of assessment information about the focal characteristics of the diagnostic conditions in the settings in which they occur (e.g., academic impairment in school settings or hyperactivity in the home and classroom) for diagnostic or classification purposes.

MEASURES OF GENERAL INTELLIGENCE

Figure 1-9 presents validity evidence for the three measures of general intelligence from the WJ III COG: General Intellectual Ability—Extended (GIA—Ext), General Intellectual Ability—Standard (GIA—Std), and Brief Intellectual Ability (BIA). In a format similar to that in Figures 1-1 through 1-7, the left side of Figure 1-9 introduces evidence that focuses on determining if the Theoretical Domain and Measurement Domain of interest have been adequately developed. The right side of Figure 1-9 also introduces External Validity Evidence.

Evidence Based on Test Content

As noted in the Theoretical Domain section of Figure 1-9, a large body of research has indicated that general intelligence (or psychometric *g*) invariably surfaces from appropriate statistical analysis of measures of human cognitive abilities. As a result, general intelligence is represented at the peak of the hierarchical framework of CHC theory (Carroll, 1993; Jensen, 1998; Mather & Woodcock, 2001). This body of research has indicated that measuring general intelligence is important because it is perhaps the single best predictor of a number of indices of career success and academic competency, such as the number of school years completed, school grades, and performance on standardized achievement tests (Jensen, 1998; Neisser et al., 1996; Ree & Earles, 1991; Ree, Earles, & Teachout, 1994). This research also suggests that some broad cognitive abilities have stronger relations with *g* than others (e.g., Comprehension–Knowledge [*Gc*] demonstrates stronger relations with *g* than Processing Speed [*Gs*]). In the design of the WJ III COG, these research findings of differential relations of broad cognitive abilities with general intelligence were incorporated via the differential weighting of tests contributing to the GIA—Ext and GIA—Std scores.

Evidence Based on Internal Structure

The WJ III COG is the only standardized cognitive ability test battery that provides a measure of general intelligence based on the differential weighting of tests according to their loadings on the first principal component. This first principal component surfaces from principal component analysis, a type of structural analysis similar to factor analysis. The construct of general intelligence was founded on such statistical analyses, and it continues to be one of the most

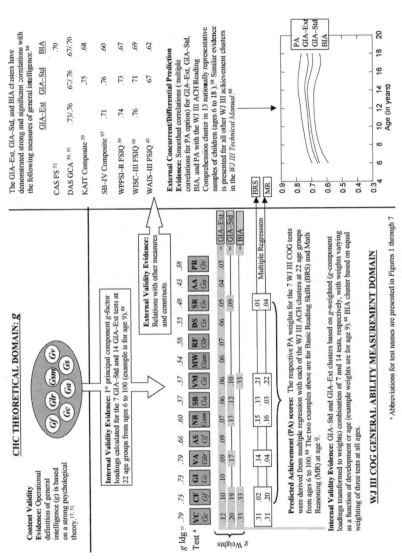

FIGURE 1-9 Summary of validity evidence for the global ability clusters. Superscript numbers refer to sources in Appendix A. By permission of the Institute for Applied Psychometrics, LLC.

frequent ways of obtaining estimates of general intelligence (Jensen, 1998; Jensen & Weng, 1994). However, most intelligence tests (e.g., the WISC–III [Wechsler, 1991] and the KAIT [Kaufman & Kaufman, 1993]) provide a general intelligence score derived from an aggregation of subtest scores that each contributes equally to this score (Jensen, 1998; Schrank et al., 2002). In contrast, as outlined in the Measurement Domain section of Figure 1-9, GIA—Std is formed by a differential weighting of the first 7 tests from the WJ III COG, and GIA—Ext is formed by a differential weighting of 14 tests from the battery (i.e., Tests 1 through 7 and Tests 11 through 17). To obtain the test weights for these scores, principal component analyses were conducted for 25 age groups and the loadings of each test on the first principal component were plotted by age and smoothed across ages to provide the best fit to the data. Component weights were then specified based on these values from the smoothed curves, and these weights were used to derive the GIA scores for all participants in the norm group (see Appendix C in McGrew & Woodcock, 2001 for specific test weights). Comprehension–Knowledge (Gc) and Fluid Reasoning (Gf) generally demonstrated the highest component loadings with general intelligence, a finding that is largely consistent with the extant factor analytic evidence (Carroll, 1993; Jensen, 1998). Because of this weighting procedure, the WJ III GIA—Ext and GIA—Std can be seen as distillates or concentrates because they represent the primary shared characteristic across all contributing tests (i.e., general intelligence)—without the unique abilities (i.e., test specificity) measured by these tests (Schrank et al., 2002). Because of the sound construction of GIA—Ext and GIA—Std, which adhered to one of the standard techniques for extracting psychometric g, test users can interpret these scores as accurately representing the statistically derived construct of general intelligence (Jensen, 1998; Jensen & Weng, 1994).

In addition to the GIA scores, the WJ III provides a brief measure of general intelligence, the BIA score. This measure was developed to be used for screening or research purposes (Mather & Woodcock, 2001). As evident in the Measurement Domain section of Figure 1-9, the BIA is formed from three tests—Concept Formation, Verbal Comprehension, and Visual Matching—that each contribute equal weight to the composite. Because a body of content and internal validity evidence indicates that these three tests measure distinct cognitive abilities, test users can interpret the BIA more confidently as a rough estimate of general intelligence as compared to those scores from brief intelligence tests that measure only one ability (Kline, 2001). Thus, validity evidence based on internal structure indicates that the BIA score has broad construct representation. However, because the three tests contribute equally to the BIA score, variance in the BIA score can likely be attributed to specific abilities (e.g., Processing Speed [Gs]) in a manner not observed with the GIA scores.

Evidence Based on External Relations

The right side of Figure 1-9 summarizes the results from studies providing support for the external validity of the GIA and BIA scores as measures of general intelligence. Most notably, across a variety of samples, GIA—Std and GIA—Ext demonstrated correlations ranging from .67 to .76 with composite scores from a variety of standardized intelligence test batteries.[6] These batteries include the *Wechsler Preschool and Primary Scale of Intelligence—Revised* (WPPSI-R) (Wechsler, 1989), the WISC-III (Wechsler, 1991), the *Wechsler Adult Intelligence Scale—Third Edition* (WAIS-III) (Wechsler, 1997a), the *Differential Ability Scales* (DAS) (Elliott, 1990), the *Stanford–Binet Intelligence Scale— Fourth Edition* (SB-IV) (Thorndike, Hagen, & Sattler, 1986), the KAIT (Kaufman & Kaufman, 1993), and the *Cognitive Assessment System* (CAS) (Naglieri & Das, 1997). These correlations are comparable to those reported between composite scores from other major intelligence test batteries. Figure 1-9 also summarizes correlations between the BIA and other measures of general intelligence, which range from .62 to .70. When considered within the context of other validity evidence, these sizeable correlations support the use of the BIA score as a screening measure or proxy for general intelligence.

Across all age ranges, the GIA—Std and GIA—Ext scores have consistently demonstrated strong relations with measures of reading, mathematics, written language, and academic knowledge (McGrew & Woodcock, 2001). Correlations between the GIA scores and concurrently administered WJ III ACH clusters ranged from .66 to .86 in five subsamples of the standardization sample. For demonstration purposes, the graph at the bottom right corner of Figure 1-9 presents the smoothed correlations between GIA—Std, GIA—Ext, and BIA scores and the Reading Comprehension cluster from the WJ III ACH. This graph indicates that the degree of association with reading comprehension is a function of the breadth of the respective general intelligence composites.

Acting on Evidence

A number of interpretations based on the WJ III COG general intelligence measures have demonstrated a large network of validity evidence. First, test users can feel confident that their interpretations of these measures are grounded in almost a century of study of general intelligence. In fact, due to the breadth of ability coverage and the empirical weighting of the tests that contribute to GIA scores, these scores can be interpreted as strong, valid measures of this construct. When using the GIA scores, test users should feel confident that they are drawing valid inferences about test performance when assessing conditions of exceptionality that place general intelligence at or near the core of their definitions (e.g., mental retardation and giftedness). Thus, the attributes associated with general intelligence found in previous research can logically be applied to interpretation of the GIA scores.

Second, test users should feel confident that the general intelligence measures demonstrate strong and statistically significant relations with other measures that

---

[6]As reported by McGrew and Woodcock (2001), the samples from which these correlations were calculated showed mild to moderate restriction of range of ability. The reported correlations must therefore be considered underestimates of the true population correlations.

were designed to be estimates of general intelligence. Although their patterns of correlations with other measures of general intelligence provide solid validity evidence for the WJ III GIA and BIA scores, the magnitude of these correlations should not lead test users to expect *identical* scores or even scores that converge within the recommended confidence intervals across measures of general intelligence. Although the correlations between the WJ III general intelligence score and related measures are statistically significant, these correlations indicate that the scores are not interchangeable in samples of children and adults without learning or behavioral problems. Thus, it is likely that that scores may occasionally be markedly different because of the different specific cognitive abilities measured by each battery, different methods of computing the measures of general intelligence, different compositions of norming samples, and different technical characteristics of tests and subtests (see Bracken, 1987; Flanagan et al., 2000; Flanagan & Ortiz, 2001; McGrew & Flanagan, 1998). Furthermore, it is likely that scores from clinical samples of children and adults with identified learning difficulties would produce scores that are more discrepant than indicated using samples of nonimpaired individuals (Flanagan et al., 2002).

PREDICTED ACHIEVEMENT SCORES

In a manner similar to the validity evidence presented for the measures of general intelligence, Figure 1-9 presents a variety of evidence supporting the interpretation of the Predicted Achievement scores. In order to provide a pragmatic measure for predicting *near-term* levels of academic achievement (Mather & Schrank, 2001), the Predicted Achievement scores were developed based on multiple regression analyses (see Measurement Domain section in Figure 1-9). In separate analyses of 25 age groups, the first seven WJ III COG tests were used to predict performance on the reading, mathematics, writing, and academic knowledge clusters from the WJ III ACH. These clusters include Broad Reading, Broad Math, Broad Written Expression, Basic Reading Skills, Math Calculation Skills, Math Reasoning, Basic Writing Skills, Written Expression, and Academic Knowledge. The graph on the bottom right of Figure 1-9 presents the smoothed multiple correlations between the Predicted Achievement score and the WJ III ACH Reading Comprehension cluster. Across all developmental levels, the Predicted Achievement score consistently served as the strongest predictor of Reading Comprehension when compared to the three WJ III general intelligence measures. As expected, this pattern held true for all other relevant achievement clusters. For example, across the normative analyses, correlations between the Predicted Achievement score and academic clusters ranged from .75 to .88 for reading clusters, from .71 to .83 for mathematics clusters, and from .71 to .85 for writing clusters.

The Predicted Achievement scores differ in two notable ways from the WJ-R Scholastic Aptitude clusters (Woodcock & Mather, 1989), which were composed of four tests that contributed equally to the prediction of the achievement domain. First, the contributions of the first seven WJ III COG tests to the prediction of the achievement domains vary across achievement cluster and across age groups. For example, Sound Blending is weighted more heavily in predicting Basic Reading Skills during the early elementary school years, and the relative weight of Verbal Comprehension becomes greater with age. In addition, as presented in the example in Figure 1-9, Verbal Comprehension contributes equal weight (i.e., .31) to the prediction of Basic Reading Skills and Math Reasoning; Concept Formation contributes much greater weight to the prediction of Math Reasoning (i.e., .20) than to Basic Reading Skills (i.e., .02). Second, the Predicted Achievement scores are not presented as distinct cluster scores that appear prominently in hand-calculated or computer-generated score reports in the same manner as the WJ-R Scholastic Aptitude clusters (Woodcock & Mather, 1989). The Predicted Achievement scores appear in the WJ III *Compuscore and Profiles Program* score report only when the Predicted Achievement button is marked under Ability–Achievement Discrepancy Basis in the Score Report Options window (Schrank & Woodcock, 2001). The Predicted Achievement scores appear as standard scores in the Predicted column of the Predicted Achievement–Achievement Discrepancies section of the score report.

Acting on Evidence

Validity evidence suggests that test users should feel confident that they are making valid statements regarding near-term expected achievement for individuals at specific developmental levels and within a specific academic domain when using the Predicted Achievement scores. For example, *consistency* between a Reading Comprehension standard score of 81 and its associated Predicted Achievement score indicates that the examinee likely displays reading comprehension skills at the expected level based on performance on Tests 1 through 7 on the WJ III COG. In contrast, a large and statistically rare *discrepancy* between a Reading Comprehension standard score of 81 and the Predicted Achievement score of 114 indicates that the abilities represented in Tests 1 through 7 are not the primary factors leading to poor performance in Reading Comprehension. Thus, factors extrinsic to the individual, such as weak instruction or excessive school absences, or other cognitive abilities not represented in the Predicted Achievement score are more likely contributing to poor performance in reading comprehension (Flanagan et al., 2000; Flanagan et al., 2002; Schrank et al., 2002).

CLINICAL CLUSTERS

CHC theory is the cornerstone for the organization of the WJ III COG, but the development of the WJ III COG clinical clusters also drew from recent research examining the cognitive predictors of reading and reading disabilities, as well as from research and theory in the fields of cognitive psychology and neuropsychology. Based on these bodies of information, the WJ III authors developed the clinical clusters Phonemic Awareness, Working Memory, Broad Attention, Cognitive Fluency, and Executive Processes (see Table 1-1 for descriptions of these clusters and the tests they comprise). For example, contemporary reading

TABLE 1-1   Descriptions of WJ III Clinical Clusters

Cluster	Description of cluster	Tests composing cluster
Phonemic Awareness	Ability to perceive separate units of speech sounds in order to analyze and synthesize those units	Sound Blending Incomplete Words
Working Memory	Ability to temporarily store and mentally manipulate information held in immediate memory	Numbers Reversed Auditory Working Memory
Broad Attention	General ability to utilize attention capacity and to maintain divided attention, selective attention, and sustained attention	Numbers Reversed Auditory Working Memory Auditory Attention Pair Cancellation
Cognitive Fluency	Ability to perform simple and complex cognitive tasks quickly and fluently	Retrieval Fluency Decision Speed Rapid Picture Naming
Executive Processes	General ability to use strategic planning, to resist distractions, and to shift mental set	Concept Formation Planning Pair Cancellation

research has indicated that specific auditory abilities (viz., phonological or phonemic awareness and speech perception) and speed of lexical access (often referred to as rapid automatic naming, or RAN) contribute to early reading skill development and reading failure (Blachman, 2000; McBride-Chang, 1996; Morris et al., 1998; Stanovich, Siegel, & Gottardo, 1997; Torgesen et al., 1997). Because of the importance of specific auditory abilities and RAN abilities to reading, the WJ III COG provides a cluster measuring specific phonological or phonemic awareness abilities (i.e., Phonemic Awareness) and two tests (Rapid Picture Naming and Retrieval Fluency) tapping aspects of speed of lexical access. Borrowing from information processing theory and research, the WJ III COG also includes tests designed to operationalize components of the memory management system called working memory (Adams & Gathercole, 1996; Baddeley, 1986, 2001; Baddeley & Hitch, 1994; Gathercole, 1994; Goldman-Rakic, 1995). In addition, information processing and neuropsychological theories and empirical research led to the development of tests focusing on executive processes and attention (Anderson, 1998; Barkley, 1996; Cooley & Morris, 1990; Lezak, 1995; Lyon & Krasnegor, 1996; Mirsky, 1996; Pennington & Ozonoff, 1996; Riccio, Reynolds, & Lowe, 2001). The validity evidence for these clinical clusters is described in the following discussion.

Phonemic Awareness

The Phonemic Awareness cluster operationalizes the CHC narrow cognitive ability of Phonetic Coding, which is subsumed by Auditory Processing (*Ga*)

(Carroll, 1993; McGrew, 1997). The content of earlier versions of Sound Blending and Incomplete Words, the two tests that form the Phonemic Awareness cluster, has been reviewed multiple times and classified according to the CHC framework (Flanagan et al., 2000; Flanagan & Ortiz, 2001; McGrew, 1997; McGrew & Flanagan, 1998). This content validity evidence supports the link between their theoretical underpinnings and operationalization in the WJ III COG. In addition, both tests that compose the Phonemic Awareness cluster appear to require related response processes (McGrew & Woodcock, 2001).

Exploratory and confirmatory factor analyses of the WJ-R standardization data (McGrew et al., 1991) and analyses provided by McGrew and Woodcock (2001) offered structural evidence that supports the grouping of Sound Blending and Incomplete Words into the Phonemic Awareness cluster. Through a process of model generation drawing upon CHC theory and previous confirmatory factor analyses using the WJ-R and WJ III standardization data, McGrew and Floyd (2001) developed a structural model using confirmatory factor analysis that included general intelligence and the CHC broad and narrow cognitive abilities. Using the WJ III standardization data for children ages 9 to 13, an admissible narrow factor representing Phonetic Coding was formed from the WJ III COG Sound Blending and Incomplete Words tests and the WJ III ACH Sound Awareness test. The findings from these analyses provide empirical evidence for grouping these tests in a cluster measuring a CHC *narrow* cognitive ability.

External validity evidence also supports the interpretation of the Phonemic Awareness cluster as an aptitude for achievement in several academic domains (see Appendix A).[7] Correlational studies using the WJ III standardization sample and samples of preschool- and school-age children and college students indicate that this cluster is significantly related to measured achievement. When included with other CHC cognitive abilities in regression models to predict reading achievement, the Phonemic Awareness cluster has demonstrated moderate relations with basic reading skills (a) throughout the school-age years and early adulthood (McGrew, 1993) and (b) during the early elementary school years (Evans et al., 2002). Furthermore, data analyses reported by McGrew, Woodcock, and Ford (2002) indicated that it is an important variable in discriminating between college students with and without learning disabilities. However, at present, no growth curve analysis for the Phonemic Awareness cluster has been provided.

Working Memory

The Working Memory cluster was designed to operationalize the CHC narrow cognitive ability of Working Memory, which is subsumed by Short-Term Memory (*Gsm*) (Flanagan et al., 2000; McGrew & Woodcock, 2001). The content of earlier versions of Numbers Reversed, which contributes to the Working Memory cluster, was reviewed multiple times and classified according to the CHC framework

---

[7]Because the WJ III Phonemic Awareness cluster includes the same tests as the WJ-R Auditory Processing (*Ga*) cluster, evidence from the WJ-R also contributes to its validity.

(Flanagan et al., 2000; Flanagan & Ortiz, 2001; McGrew, 1997; McGrew & Flanagan, 1998). Experts also reviewed the content of Auditory Working Memory during the development of the WJ III. This content validity evidence supports the link between their theoretical underpinnings and operationalization. In addition, both tests that compose the Working Memory cluster appear to require response processes that are consistent with the construct they represent (McGrew & Woodcock, 2001).

Confirmatory factor analyses presented by McGrew and Woodcock (2001) and the unpublished analyses offered by McGrew and Floyd (2001) provide structural evidence that supports the groupings of tests into the Working Memory cluster. In these analyses, two admissible factors representing Short-Term Memory (*Gsm*) narrow cognitive abilities were formed: one represented the Working Memory cluster and another represented a passive short-term memory factor represented by the CHC narrow cognitive ability Memory Span (Carroll, 1993; Flanagan et al., 2000; McGrew, 1997). These findings provide empirical evidence for the grouping of these tests in a cluster measuring a well-specified CHC narrow cognitive ability.

External validity evidence for the interpretation of the Working Memory cluster is provided by its correlations with measures of related cognitive abilities from other batteries (e.g., the Working Memory index of the WAIS-III [Wechsler, 1997a] and the Digit Span subtest of the WISC-III [Wechsler, 1991]). In addition, its correlations with achievement measures from the WJ III ACH indicate that it is strongly related to the academic achievement of children and adults (McGrew & Woodcock, 2001). Furthermore, recent regression analyses including the Working Memory cluster reveal that it displays consistent moderate relations with the components of reading, mathematics, and writing achievement across childhood and adolescence (Evans et al., 2002; Floyd et al., in press; Floyd et al., 2002).

Cognitive Fluency

The Cognitive Fluency cluster was developed to operationalize the construct of *automaticity*, which is the ability to develop or utilize skills in a speedy manner so that they become routine and do not require effortful processing. The Rapid Picture Naming, Retrieval Fluency, and Decision Speed tests contribute to this cluster. The design of the Cognitive Fluency cluster is consistent with Carroll's (1993) distinction between factors representing *level* and those representing *rate*. Tests of level, which are thought to measure ability, per se, are most frequently scaled so that items become more difficult as examinees progress through them. However, tests of rate, which focus on speed of performance, are constructed so that most examinees could complete all items correctly or receive the maximum score if provided enough time. Review of the response processes associated with the tests composing the Cognitive Fluency cluster indicates that speed of naming pictures, verbalizing words, and marking images are key components of performance. Thus, in a manner similar to the Processing Speed (*Gs*) CHC factor cluster, this cluster measures the speed with which an individual performs simple cognitive tasks. The Cognitive Fluency cluster, however, appears to place greater importance on speed in completing complex cognitive tasks than does the Processing Speed (*Gs*) CHC factor cluster.

The internal validity of the Cognitive Fluency cluster is supported by the aforementioned confirmatory factor analyses by McGrew and Woodcock (2001) and McGrew and Floyd (2001), which yielded admissible factors that were formed by the three tests that contribute to the Cognitive Fluency cluster. It is possible that this factor embodies those abilities associated with speed of lexical access or RAN. Correlational analyses examining the relations between the Cognitive Fluency cluster, achievement measures, and other cognitive ability measures using the WJ III standardization sample and samples of preschool- and school-age children and college students indicate that this cluster is significantly related to these measures in a manner similar to the Processing Speed (*Gs*) and Long-Term Retrieval (*Glr*) clusters (McGrew & Woodcock, 2001). However, at present, no growth curve analyses have been provided for the Cognitive Fluency cluster.

Broad Attention and Executive Processes

During the past two decades, research from the field of neuropsychology has led to a heightened interest in the cognitive operations known as executive functions (see Lyon & Krasnegor, 1996, for a review). Executive functions have been conceptualized as the mental operations that promote the organization of thought and behavior. These operations include attention regulation, mental flexibility, planning, problem solving, volition, and emotional control (Lezak, 1995). The WJ III COG includes two clusters designed primarily to assess types of executive functions. The Broad Attention cluster was designed to be a global measure of attention that demonstrates broad construct representation by measuring qualitatively different aspects of attention. Based on integration of components of recent models of attention and other sources (Carroll, 1993; Lezak, 1995; Mirsky, 1996; Mirsky et al., 1991), the four tests composing this cluster likely measure four types of attention: *attentional capacity*, *divided attention*, *selective attention*, and *sustained attention* (Schrank et al., 2002; see Table 1-2). The Executive Processes cluster was designed to measure the core cognitive processes associated with executive functions such as response inhibition, cognitive flexibility, and planning.

Table 1-2 presents the proposed response processes used during completion of tests contributing to these clusters (McGrew & Woodcock, 2001; Schrank et al., 2002). In addition, a variety of external validity evidence (e.g., correlations with achievement scores and correlations with measures of general intelligence) has been provided for the tests that form the Broad Attention and Executive Processes clusters. This evidence includes relations with other measures of abilities associated with attention and other executive functions. For example, according to McGrew and Woodcock (2001), Vesley found that Concept Formation was significantly correlated with a composite measure derived from a continuous performance test, which is purported to provide indices of sustained attention and

TABLE 1-2 Executive Functions and Processing Characteristics of the Tests Forming the Broad Attention and Executive Processes Clusters

WJ III test	Executive function	Response processes	
Broad Attention			
Numbers Reversed	Working Memory, Attentional Capacity	Verbal/Auditory	Transformation	Verbal/Oral
Auditory Working Memory	Working Memory, Divided Attention	Verbal/Auditory	Reorganization, Sorting	Verbal/Oral
Auditory Attention	Selective Attention	Verbal/Auditory, Nonverbal/Visual	Sequencing Discrimination	Nonverbal/Motor
Pair Cancellation	Sustained Attention	Nonverbal/Visual	Recognition, Monitoring	Nonverbal/Motor
Executive Processes			
Concept Formation	Concept Shifting	Nonverbal/Visual	Categorization	Verbal/Oral
Planning	Planning	Nonverbal/Visual	Forethought	Nonverbal/Motor
Pair Cancellation	Sustained Attention	Nonverbal/Visual	Recognition, Monitoring	Nonverbal/Motor

Note: Adapted from Schrank et al. (2002), *Essentials of WJ III Cognitive Abilities Assessment* (This material is used by permission of John Wiley & Sons, Inc.).

impulsive responding (Barkley, 1996; Mirsky, 1996; Riccio et al., 2001). Furthermore, Concept Formation, Decision Speed, and Auditory Working Memory were found to be significantly correlated with a composite from the *Behavior Assessment System for Children Teacher Rating Scale* (BASC) (Reynolds & Kamphaus, 1992) that subsumes the Attention Problems and Learning Problems subscales. Although this supports the use of these tests as measures of attention and other executive functions, this type of evidence has been lacking for the Broad Attention and Executive Processes clusters. McGrew and Woodcock (2001) reported correlations between these clusters and other measures from the WJ III COG and WJ III ACH, but no developmental evidence was provided. However, promising discriminative validity evidence and evidence of relations between these clusters and caregiver ratings of disinhibited behaviors and executive functions are reported in this book (see Chapter 10, this volume).

Acting on Evidence

The Phonemic Awareness and Working Memory clusters have demonstrated a sizeable body of validity evidence, and the Cognitive Fluency cluster has demonstrated initial content validity evidence, emerging internal validity evidence, and evidence of relations with external variables. However, at present, evidence informing the interpretation of the Broad Attention and Executive Processes clusters is beginning to emerge (see Chapter 10, this volume). Although the authors of the WJ III COG provide evidence for the construct representation of the Broad Attention and Executive Processes clusters and outline the presumed response processes associated with performance on these clusters, it is likely that these tests also measure constructs not directly associated with any executive function (Barkley, 1996). In fact, four of the six tests (Numbers Reversed, Auditory Working Memory, Auditory Attention, and Concept Formation) contributing to these clusters were designed to be strong and valid measures of CHC broad and narrow cognitive abilities. Consequentially, the measurement of construct-irrelevant influences (i.e., CHC cognitive abilities when measuring attention or executive processes) may cloud the interpretation of these clinical cluster scores unless a test user is aware of the intended purposes of these clusters. Simply stated, the tests included in the Broad Attention and Executive Processes clusters are likely most sensitive to the types of observable behaviors that are often associated with problems with executive functions. Thus, they provide the clinician with the greatest opportunity to observe behaviors suggestive of hypothesized problems in various aspects of executive functioning.

Because the purpose of grouping tests into the Broad Attention and Executive Processes clusters was to encourage test users to evaluate test performance at a qualitative level, test users should be vigilant for examinees' overt behaviors indicating lack of focus, distractibility, low frustration tolerance, and other executive functioning deficits that may be evident during these tests. Because tests users are also provided scores (i.e., quantitative indexes) representing performance on these clusters, these scores can be used in combination with observations of test session behavior to evaluate the degree to which executive functioning deficits contribute to lower-than-expected test performance during other WJ III COG tests (i.e., those not included in these clusters). Thus, it is logical that the Short-Term Memory (*Gsm*), Auditory Processing (*Ga*), and Fluid Reasoning (*Gf*) clusters would be the most influenced by executive functioning deficits, because these clusters include tests included in the Broad Attention and Executive Processes clusters.

COGNITIVE PERFORMANCE MODEL CLUSTERS

In a series of articles, chapters, and other publications during the past decade, Woodcock and colleagues have presented a Cognitive Performance Model (CPM) that integrates the broad cognitive abilities from CHC theory, the components of human information processing, and neuropsychological functions (Dean & Woodcock, 1999; Mather & Woodcock, 2001; Woodcock, 1993, 1998). In recent revisions of this model, three broad categories of cognitive abilities are specified: *stores of acquired knowledge, thinking abilities,* and *cognitive efficiency.* Stores of acquired knowledge represent declarative and procedural knowledge that is contained in long-term memory. This category includes the CHC broad cognitive abilities of Comprehension–Knowledge (*Gc*), Reading and Writing (*Grw*), and Quantitative Knowledge (*Gq*). Thinking abilities represent abilities that require effortful or controlled cognitive processing, such as Visual-Spatial Thinking (*Gv*), Auditory Processing (*Ga*), Long-Term Retrieval (*Glr*), and Fluid Reasoning (*Gf*). Cognitive efficiency represents relatively automatic cognitive operations such as Short-Term Memory (*Gsm*) and Processing Speed (*Gs*). These three categories are operationalized by the WJ III COG via the CPM clusters Verbal Abilities, Thinking Abilities, and Cognitive Efficiency. These clusters may be formed by tests from only the WJ III COG Standard Battery (i.e., Tests 1 through 7) or by tests from both the Standard and Extended Batteries (i.e., Tests 1 through 7 and Tests 11 through 17). Table 1-3 presents a description of the CPM clusters and lists the tests that compose them.

Building further on the categorization of abilities according to the CPM, Woodcock and colleagues also developed an information processing model that outlines the organization of and interactions among the broad cognitive abilities specified in CHC theory and the external and internal influences on cognitive and academic performance called *facilitators–inhibitors* (Dean & Woodcock, 1999; Mather & Woodcock, 2001; Woodcock, 1993, 1998). This model serves as the basis for the WJ III Information Processing Model and the WJ III Diagnostic Worksheet (see Mather & Woodcock, 2001; Schrank & Woodcock, 2002). The latest incarnation of this model and worksheet focuses on the interactions among the CHC factor clusters, clinical clusters (from the WJ III COG), and achievement clusters (from the WJ III ACH). Thus, the CPM cluster scores are not incorporated into this model or its accompanying diagnostic worksheet.

TABLE 1-3   Descriptions of WJ III Cognitive Performance Model Clusters

Cluster	Description of cluster	Tests composing cluster
Verbal Ability—Standard	Ability to use language and acquired knowledge effectively. Synonymous with Comprehension–Knowledge	Verbal Comprehension
Verbal Ability—Extended	Ability to use language and acquired knowledge effectively. Synonymous with Comprehension–Knowledge	Verbal Comprehension General Information
Thinking Abilities—Standard	General ability to use abilities that require effortful cognitive processing, such as Long-Term Retrieval, Visual–Spatial Thinking, Auditory Processing, and Fluid Reasoning	Visual–Auditory Learning Spatial Relations Sound Blending Concept Formation
Thinking Abilities—Extended	General ability to use abilities that require effortful cognitive processing, such as Long-Term Retrieval, Visual–Spatial Thinking, Auditory Processing, and Fluid Reasoning	Visual–Auditory Learning Retrieval Fluency Spatial Relations Picture Recognition Sound Blending Auditory Attention Concept Formation Analysis–Synthesis
Cognitive Efficiency—Standard	General ability to use abilities that require automatic cognitive processing, such as Processing Speed and Short-Term Memory	Visual Matching Numbers Reversed
Cognitive Efficiency—Extended	General ability to use abilities that require automatic cognitive processing, such as Processing Speed and Short-Term Memory	Visual Matching Decision Speed Numbers Reversed Memory for Words

Evidence Based on Test Content

The CPM and the associated Information Processing Model are based on a thoughtful and logical integration of research, and they provide potentially valuable organizing heuristics for test interpretation. However, Mather and Woodcock (2001) and McGrew et al. (2002) noted that the CPM is based on logical—and not empirical—classifications of abilities into these categories. At present, there have been no independent analyses of the match between the CPM and WJ III COG test content.

Evidence Based on Response Processes

McGrew and Woodcock (2001) present logical, task-analytic summaries of the test stimuli, test requirements, and the response modalities of each of the 14 tests that contribute to the CPM clusters. However, neither the test authors nor independent evaluators have provided formal, detailed descriptions of the links between these response processes and the CPM groupings.

Evidence Based on Internal Structure

Research investigating the internal validity of the CPM clusters has recently appeared. For instance, Keith (1997) demonstrated that an earlier version of the CPM showed a good fit to the WJ-R standardization data. Keith's model comparisons using confirmatory factor analysis indicate that the CPM may provide a plausible organizational framework for the human cognitive abilities measured by the WJ III. More recently, McGrew (2002) presented a preliminary multidimensional scaling analysis of a portion of the WJ III standardization sample that supports the primary components of the CPM. However, more evidence is needed to corroborate and extend the findings from these two studies.

Evidence Based on External Relations

At present, no growth curve analyses have been presented for the CPM clusters (McGrew & Woodcock, 2001; McGrew et al., 2002). However, growth curve analyses of the CHC factor clusters that compose the typically more global CPM clusters indicate that Visual Processing (Gv), Long-Term Retrieval (Glr), and Auditory Processing (Ga)—all Thinking Abilities in the CPM—demonstrate growth curves of similar shape throughout development. However, the Fluid Reasoning (Gf) cluster, which is also considered a Thinking Ability, appears to show (a) much greater developmental change between ages 5 and 25 and (b) much greater decline after age 25 than the three aforementioned abilities. Thus, the divergent growth curve for Gf does not support the inclusion of Gf abilities with the other three abilities in the Thinking Abilities clusters. Within the Cognitive Efficiency clusters, both Short-Term Memory (Gsm) and Processing Speed (Gs) display substantial growth during childhood and adolescence and decline steadily after this period. However, the growth curve for Gs displays much more growth during childhood and adolescence and much more decline throughout late adulthood than does Gsm. In fact, Gsm displays a growth curve that is almost identical in form to that of Fluid Reasoning (Gf) at all ages. The growth curve for the Comprehension–Knowledge (Gc) CHC factor cluster, which is identical to the Verbal Abilities—Extended cluster, appears to be consistent with other abilities that stem largely from formal instruction (i.e., stores of acquired knowledge) that were included in the WJ III ACH (e.g., reading comprehension, spelling, and editing abilities).

Consistent patterns of external validity evidence have been demonstrated for the Verbal Ability—Extended and Verbal Ability—Standard clusters across a number of samples (McGrew & Woodcock, 2001). Convergent validity evidence is provided by high correlations between the Verbal Ability clusters and the WISC-III (Wechsler, 1991) Verbal IQ and Verbal Comprehension index ($r = .71$ to $.79$), the WAIS-III (Wechsler, 1997a) Verbal IQ ($r = .71$) and Verbal Comprehension index ($r = .65$), the WPPSI-R (Wechsler, 1989) Verbal IQ ($r = .57$ to $.70$), KAIT (Kaufman & Kaufman, 1993) Crystallized Intelligence ($r = .66$), and SB-IV (Thorndike et al., 1986) Verbal

35

Reasoning ($r = .60$ to $.65$). Discriminant validity is evidenced by the lower correlations ($r = .39$ to $.55$) between the Verbal Ability clusters and the Performance IQ and Perceptual Organization index from the WISC-III and WAIS-III, respectively.

Because measures of multiple abilities form the Thinking Ability—Standard and Thinking Ability—Extended clusters, convergent validity is evidenced by high correlations between these clusters and the WISC-III (Wechsler, 1991) Full Scale IQ ($r = .57$ and $.58$, respectively), the WPPSI-R (Wechsler, 1989) Full Scale IQ ($r = .68$ and $.64$, respectively), the WAIS-III (Wechsler, 1997a) Full Scale IQ ($r = .59$ and $.57$, respectively), the KAIT (Kaufman & Kaufman, 1993) Composite Intelligence Scale ($r = .64$ and $.67$, respectively), the DAS (Elliott, 1990) General Conceptual Ability ($r = .63$ to $.69$, respectively), and the SB-IV (Thorndike et al., 1986) Test Composite ($r = .73$ and $.69$, respectively). In addition, the Cognitive Efficiency—Standard and Cognitive Efficiency—Extended clusters also display consistent patterns of convergent and discriminant validity with measures from other batteries. For example, the Cognitive Efficiency—Standard and Cognitive Efficiency—Extended clusters demonstrated high correlations with the WISC-III Processing Speed and Freedom from Distractibility index scores ($r = .48$ to $.62$). Correlational studies examining the relations between the CPM clusters and performance on measures from the WJ III ACH indicate that the CPM clusters are significantly related to measured achievement in a manner similar to the CHC factor clusters that compose them. These results were consistent across analyses using data from the WJ III standardization sample and samples of preschool- and school-age children and college students (see pp. 90–93 in McGrew & Woodcock, 2001).

Acting on Evidence

Despite the significant relations among the CPM clusters, the significant relations with other cognitive ability measures, and the significant relations with WJ III ACH tests, additional evidence based on test content, response processes, and internal structure is needed to provide a strong network of validity evidence supporting these scores and their interpretation. Although the WJ III Information Processing Model and the WJ III Diagnostic Worksheet describe a very plausible organization of the interactions among the WJ III cognitive and achievement clusters and other influences (i.e., facilitator–inhibitors), test users should be aware that the CPM cluster *scores* stem primarily from theoretically and logically derived groupings of tests and not from empirical relations. However, test users may find that Woodcock's models provide a useful clinical framework to conceptualize test performance. The value of these models and their associated scores will be determined with additional research.

CONSEQUENTIAL VALIDITY

Another type of validity evidence, which has not been addressed in this review thus far, focuses on the intended and unintended consequences of testing. Assessment professionals often choose tests following the premise that positive gains will result from the time, effort, and expenses devoted to administering, scoring, and interpreting these tests. According to *Standards*, "a fundamental purpose of validation is to indicate whether these specific benefits are likely to be realized" (AERA, APA, & NCME, 1999, p. 16). In a manner consistent with most professional ethics codes that emphasize beneficence to clients, the results of testing should help prevent problems, help remedy or remediate problems, or help others provide interventions that accommodate problems. Although scholars are debating whether evidence in this area should be included under the concept of *validity* (Kane, 2001; Mehrens, 1997; Popham, 1997; Shepard, 1997), psychological and educational assessment techniques are increasingly being called upon to contribute to tangible positive outcomes. Discussions have focused on evidence of consequential validity stemming from links between test results and psychosocial interventions and have used the terms *test utility* and *treatment validity* to refer to these characteristics (Braden & Kratochwill, 1997; Fuchs & Fuchs, 1998; Hayes, Nelson, & Jarrett, 1987; Haynes, 2001). Several researchers have drawn attention to the general lack of evidence that scores from cognitive ability or intelligence tests provide valuable information for the development of interventions (Good et al., 1993; Reschly, 1990, 1997a,b).

Because the WJ III COG operationalizes many of the specific cognitive abilities that appear to be important predictors of a number of achievement domains, this battery offers the promise of yielding positive outcomes from its use with preschool- and early school-age children. For instance, a number of studies have focused on the specific cognitive aptitudes that predict reading development during this period. Phonemic awareness, vocabulary development, and RAN have consistently been shown to be predictive of early reading skills (Meyer, Wood, Hart, & Felton, 1998; Vellutino, Scanlon, & Lyon, 2000; Wolfe, Bowers, & Biddle, 2000). In addition, Vellutino et al. (1996) found that young children with weaknesses on tests that measure phonemic awareness, associative memory, speeded naming, and processing speed were *least likely* to benefit from empirically validated reading interventions. It is notable that the WJ III COG provides measures of these abilities that are appropriate to administer to children of this age group.

Although the WJ III COG offers the promise of providing links to intervention, no studies have been published in peer-reviewed journals or presented in the *WJ III Technical Manual* that examine the links between interpretation of its scores and educational or psychosocial interventions. Although a study of the treatment utility of a number of assessment techniques, including the WJ III, is underway (J. Braden, personal communication, November 27, 2001), and one of the authors of the WJ III and her colleagues have provided a wealth of logical links between assessment results from the WJ III COG (and its previous editions) and academic domains (Goldstein & Mather, 1998; Mather, 1991; Mather & Goldstein, 2001; Mather & Jaffe, 1993, 2002), much additional research is needed. This information, which is absent from almost all contemporary cognitive ability or intelligence test batteries, is clearly needed in order for the practitioner to "act on evidence."

SUMMARY

When the accumulated evidence for the validity of the WJ III COG is evaluated within the context of the *Standards for Educational and Psychological Testing* (AERA, APA, & NCME, 1999), it is clear that the WJ III COG has "raised the bar" with regard to state-of-the-art assessment of human cognitive abilities. Because test validation is considered an ongoing process, further research by the test authors and by independent researchers should reveal additional valid uses and interpretations of the battery and, most likely, uses and interpretations that should not be undertaken because little or no validity evidence supports them. Psychologists, educators, and other assessment specialists should continue to seek evidence supporting their interpretations and, when possible, act upon that evidence. This chapter provides the basis on which these professionals may accomplish these goals.

REFERENCES

Adams, A. M., & Gathercole, S. E. (1996). Phonological working memory and spoken language development in young children. *Quarterly Journal of Experimental Psychology, 49*, 216–233.

Algozzine, B., & Ysseldyke, J. E. (1981). An analysis of difference score reliabilities on three measures with a sample of low-achieving youngsters. *Psychology in the Schools, 18*, 133–138.

Algozzine, B., Ysseldyke, J. E., & Shinn, M. (1982). Identifying children with learning disabilities: When is a discrepancy severe? *Journal of School Psychology, 20*, 299–305.

American Educational Research Association, American Psychological Association, & National Council on Measurement in Education (1999). *Standards for educational and psychological testing.* Washington, DC: American Educational Research Association.

American Psychiatric Association. (1994). *Diagnostic and statistical manual of mental disorders* (4th ed.). Washington, DC: Author.

American Psychiatric Association. (2000). *Diagnostic and statistical manual of mental disorders* (4th ed., text revision). Washington, DC: Author.

Anderson, V. (1998). Assessing executive functions in children: Biological, psychological, and developmental considerations. *Neuropsychology Rehabilitation, 8,* 319–349.

Aram, D. M., & Ekelman, B. L. (1988). Scholastic aptitude and achievement among children with unilateral brain lesions. *Neuropsychologia, 26,* 903–916.

Arffa, S., Rider, L., & Cummings, J. A. (1984). Validity study of the Woodcock–Johnson Psycho-Educational Battery and the Stanford–Binet with black preschool children. *Journal of Psychoeducational Assessment, 2,* 73–77.

Baddeley, A. (1986). *Working memory.* New York: Oxford University Press.

Baddeley, A. (2001). Is working memory still working? *American Psychologist, 56,* 851–864.

Baddeley, A. D., & Hitch, G. J. (1994). Development in the concept of working memory. *Neuropsychology, 8,* 485–493.

Barkley, R. A. (1996). Critical issues in research on attention. In G. R. Lyon & N. A. Krasnegor (Eds.), *Attention, memory, and executive function* (pp. 45–56). Baltimore: Paul H. Brookes.

Beden, I., Rohr, L., & Ellsworth, R. (1987). A public school validation study of the achievement sections of the *Woodcock–Johnson Psycho-Educational Battery* with learning disabled students. *Educational and Psychological Measurement, 47,* 711–717.

Benson, J. (1998). Developing a strong program of construct validation: A test anxiety example. *Educational Measurement: Issues and Practice, 17,* 10–22.

Bickley, P. G., Keith, T. Z., & Wolfle, L. M. (1995). The three-stratum theory of cognitive abilities: Tests of the structure of intelligence across the lifespan. *Intelligence 20*, 309–328.

Binks, S. W., & Gold, J. M. (1998). Differential cognitive deficits in the neuropsychology of schizophrenia. *The Clinical Neuropsychologist, 12*, 8–20.

Blachman, B. A. (2000). Phonological awareness. In M. L. Kamil, P. B. Mosenthal, P. D. Pearson, & R. Barr (Eds.), *Handbook of reading research* (Vol. III, pp. 483–502). Mahwah, NJ: Erlbaum.

Bohline, D. S. (1985). Intellectual and affective characteristics of attention deficit disordered children. *Journal of Learning Disabilities, 18*, 604–608.

Bolen, L. M., Kimball, D. J., Hall, C. W., & Webster, R. E. (1997). A comparison of visual and auditory tests on the Woodcock–Johnson Tests of Cognitive Ability, Revised in the Learning Efficiency Test—II. *Psychology in the Schools, 34*, 321–328.

Bracken, B. A. (1987). Ten psychometric reasons why similar tests produce dissimilar results. *Journal of School Psychology, 26*, 155–166.

Bracken, B., Prasse, D., & Breen, M. (1984). Concurrent validity of the Woodcock–Johnson Psycho-Educational Battery with regular and learning disabled children. *Journal of School Psychology, 22*, 185–192.

Braden, J. P., & Kratochwill, T. R. (1997). Treatment utility of assessment: Myths and realities. *School Psychology Review, 26*, 467–474.

Breen, M. J. (1984). The temporal stability of the Woodcock–Johnson Tests of Cognitive Ability for elementary-aged learning-disabled children. *Journal of Psychoeducational Assessment, 2*, 257–261.

Breen, M. J. (1985). The Woodcock–Johnson Tests of Cognitive Ability: A comparison of two methods of cluster scale analysis for three learning disability subtypes. *Journal of Psychoeducational Assessment, 3*, 167–174.

Breen, M. J. (1986). Cognitive patterns of learning disability subtypes as measured by the Woodcock–Johnson Psycho-Educational Battery. *Journal of Learning Disabilities, 19*, 86–90.

Buchanan, M., & Wolf, J. S. (1986). A comprehensive study of learning disabled adults. *Journal of Learning Disabilities, 19*, 34–38.

Buckhalt, J. A., McGhee, R. L., & Ehrler, D. J. (2001). An investigation of Gf–Gc theory in the older adult population: Joint factor analysis of the Woodcock–Johnson—Revised and the Detroit Test of Learning Aptitude—Adult. *Psychological Reports, 88*, 1161–1170.

Burns, N. R., Nettelbeck, T., & Cooper, C. J. (2000). Event-related potential correlates of some human cognitive ability constructs. *Personality and Individual Differences, 29*, 157–168.

Carroll, J. B. (1993). *Human cognitive abilities: A survey of factor analytic studies*. New York: Cambridge University Press.

Carroll, J. B. (1997). The three-stratum theory of cognitive abilities. In D. P. Flanagan, J. L. Genshaft, & P. L. Harrison (Eds.), *Contemporary intellectual assessment: Theories, tests, and issues* (pp. 122–130). New York: Guilford.

Carroll, J. B. (in press). The higher stratum structure of cognitive abilities: Current evidence supports *g* and about ten broad factors. In H. Nyborg (Ed.), *The scientific study of general intelligence: Tribute to Arthur R. Jensen*. New York: Pergamon.

Casey, M. B., Cohen, M., Schuerholz, L. J., Singer, H. S., & Denckla, M. B. (2000). Language-based cognitive functioning in parents of offspring with ADHD comorbid for Tourette syndrome or learning disabilities. *Developmental Neuropsychology, 17*, 85–110.

Coleman, M. C., & Harmer, W. R. (1985). The WISC-R and Woodcock–Johnson Tests of Cognitive Ability: A comparative study. *Psychology in the Schools, 22*, 127–132.

Cooley, E. L., & Morris, R. D. (1990). Attention in children: A neuropsychologically based model for assessment. *Developmental Neuropsychology, 6*, 239–274.

Cronbach, L. J., & Meehl, P. E. (1955). Construct validity in psychological tests. *Psychological Bulletin, 52*, 281–302.

Cuenin, L. H. (1990). Use of the Woodcock–Johnson Psycho-Educational battery with learning disabled adults. *Learning Disability Focus, 5*, 119–123.

Cummings, J. A. (1982). Interpreting functioning levels: Woodcock–Johnson Psycho-Educational Battery. *Psychological Reports, 50*, 1167–1171.

Cummings, J., & Sanville, D. (1983). Concurrent validity of the Woodcock–Johnson Tests of Cognitive Ability with the WISC-R: EMR children. *Psychology in the Schools, 20*, 298–303.

Daleiden, E., Drabman, R. S., & Benton, J. (2002). The Guide to the Assessment of Test Session Behavior: Validity in relation to cognitive testing and parent-reported behavior problems in a clinical sample. *Journal of Clinical Child Psychology, 31*, 263–271.

Dalke, C. (1988). Woodcock–Johnson Psycho-Educational Test Battery profiles: A comparative study of college freshmen with and without learning disabilities. *Journal of Learning Disabilities, 9*, 567–570.

Dean, R. S., & Woodcock, R. W. (1999). *The WJ-R and Bateria-R in neuropsychological assessment* (Research Report No. 3). Itasca, IL: Riverside Publishing.

Dumont, R., Willis, J. O., Farr, L. P., McCarthy, T., & Price, L. (2000). The relationship between the Differential Ability Scales (DAS) and the Woodcock–Johnson Tests of Cognitive Ability—Revised (WJ-R COG) for students referred for special education evaluations. *Journal of Psychoeducational Assessment, 18*, 27–38.

Elliot, C. D. (1990). *Differential Ability Scales.* San Antonio, TX: Psychological Corporation.

Estabrook, G. E. (1984). A canonical correlation analysis of the Wechsler Intelligence Scale for Children—Revised and the *Woodcock–Johnson Tests of Cognitive Ability* in a sample referred for suspected learning disabilities. *Journal of Educational Psychology, 76*, 1170–1177.

Evans, J. H., Carlsen, R. N., & McGrew, K. S. (1993). Classification of exceptional students with the Woodcock–Johnson Psycho-Educational Battery—Revised. *Journal of Psychoeducational Assessment, Monograph Series: Woodcock–Johnson Psycho-Educational Assessment Battery—Revised*, 6–19.

Evans, J. J., Floyd, R. G., McGrew, K. S., & Leforgee, M. H. (2002). The relations between measures of Cattell–Horn–Carroll (CHC) cognitive abilities and reading achievement during childhood and adolescence. *School Psychology Review, 31*, 246–262.

Flanagan, D. P. (2000). Wechsler-based CHC cross-battery assessment and reading achievement: Strengthening the validity of interpretations drawn from Wechsler test scores. *School Psychology Quarterly, 15*, 295–329.

Flanagan, D. P., & McGrew, K. S. (1998). Interpreting intelligence tests from a contemporary *Gf–Gc* theory: Joint confirmatory factor analysis of the WJ-R and KAIT in a non-white sample. *Journal of School Psychology, 36*, 151–182.

Flanagan, D. P., McGrew, K. S., & Ortiz, S. (2000). *The Wechsler intelligence scales and* Gf–Gc *theory: A contemporary approach to interpretation.* Needham Heights, MA: Allyn and Bacon.

Flanagan, D. P., & Ortiz, S. (2001). *Essentials of cross-battery assessment.* New York: Wiley.

Flanagan, D. P., Ortiz, S. O., Alfonso, V. C., & Mascolo, J. T. (2002). *The achievement test desk reference (ATDR): A comprehensive framework for LD determination.* Boston: Allyn & Bacon.

Floyd, R. G., Evans, J. J., & McGrew, K. S. (in press). Relations between Cattell–Horn–Carroll (CHC) cognitive abilities and mathematics achievement across the school-age years. *Psychology in the Schools.*

Floyd, R. G., Flanagan, D. P., Evans, J. J., & McGrew, K. S. (2002). The relations between measures of Cattell–Horn–Carroll (CHC) cognitive abilities and writing achievement during childhood and adolescence. Manuscript in preparation.

Frattali, C. M., Liow, K., Craig, G. H., Korenman, L. M., Makhlouf, F., Sato, S., Biesecker, L. G., & Theodore, W. H. (2001). Cognitive deficits in children with gelastic seizures and hypothalamic hamartoma. *Neurology, 57*, 43–46.

Fuchs, L. S., & Fuchs, D. (1998). Treatment validity: A unifying concept for reconceptualizing the identification of learning disabilities. *Learning Disabilities Research and Practice, 13*, 204–219.

Garcia, G. M., & Stafford, M. E. (2000). Prediction of reading by *Ga* and *Gc* specific cognitive abilities for low-SES White and Hispanic English-speaking children. *Psychology in the Schools, 37*, 227–235.

Gathercole, S. E. (1994). Neuropsychology and working memory: A review. *Neuropsychology, 8,* 494–505.

Goldman-Rakic, P. S. (1995). Architecture of the prefrontal cortex and central executive. In J. Grafman, K. J. Holyoak, & F. Boller (Eds.), *Structure and Functions of the Human Prefrontal Cortex* (pp. 71–84). New York: New York Academy of Sciences.

Goldstein, S., & Mather, N. (1998). *Overcoming underachieving: An action guide to helping your child succeed in school.* New York: Wiley.

Good, R. H., Vollmer, M. C., Roy, J., Katz, L. I., & Chowdhi, S. (1993). Treatment utility of the *Kaufman Assessment Battery for Children*: Effects of matching instruction and student processing strength. *School Psychology Review, 22,* 8–26.

Gregg, N., & Hoy, C. (1985). A comparison of the WAIS-R and the Woodcock–Johnson Tests of Cognitive Ability with learning-disabled college students. *Journal of Psychoeducational Assessment, 3,* 267–274.

Gustaffson, J. E. (1999). Measuring and understanding *g*: Experimental and correlational approaches. In P. L. Ackerman, P. C. Kyllogen, & R. D. Roberts (Eds.), *Learning and individual differences: Process, trait, and content determinants* (pp. 275–291). Atlanta, GA: Georgia Institute of Technology.

Harrington, R. G., Kimbrell, J., & Dai, X. (1992). The relationship between the Woodcock–Johnson Psycho-Educational Battery—Revised (Early Development) and the Wechsler Preschool and Primary Scale of Intelligence—Revised. *Psychology in the Schools, 29,* 116–125.

Hayes, S. C., Nelson, R. O., & Jarrett, R. B. (1987). The treatment utility of assessment: A functional approach to evaluating assessment quality. *American Psychologist, 42(11),* 963–974.

Haynes, S. N. (2001). Clinical applications of analogue behavioral observation: Dimensions of psychometric evaluation. *Psychological Assessment, 11,* 73–85.

Horn, J. L. (1991). Measurement of intellectual capabilities: A review of theory. In K. S. McGrew, J. K. Werder, & R. W. Woodcock, *WJ-R technical manual* (pp. 197–232). Itasca, IL: Riverside Publishing.

Horn, J. L., & Noll, J. (1997). Human cognitive capabilities: *Gf–Gc* theory. In D. P. Flanagan, J. L. Genshaft, & P. L. Harrison (Eds.), *Contemporary intellectual assessment: Theories, tests, and issues* (pp. 53–93). New York: Guilford.

Hoy, C., & Gregg, N. (1986). The usefulness of the Woodcock–Johnson Psycho-Educational Battery Cognitive cluster scores for learning disabled college students. *Journal of Learning Disabilities, 8,* 489–491.

Hoy, C., Gregg, N., Jagota, M., King, M., Moreland, C., & Manglitz, E. (1993). Relationship between the *Wechsler Adult Intelligence Scale—Revised* and the *Woodcock–Johnson Test of Cognitive Ability—Revised* among adults with learning disabilities in university and rehabilitation settings. *Journal of Psychoeducational Assessment, Monograph Series: Woodcock–Johnson Psycho-Educational Battery—Revised Monograph,* 54–63. Cordova, TN: Psychoeducational Corporation.

Ingram, G. F., & Hakari, L. J. (1985). Validity of the Woodcock–Johnson Tests of Cognitive Ability for gifted children: A comparison study with the WISC-R. *Journal for the Education of the Gifted, 9,* 11–23.

Ipsen, S. M., McMillan, J. H., & Fallen, N. H. (1983). An investigation of the reported discrepancy between the *Woodcock–Johnson Tests of Cognitive Ability* and the *Wechsler Intelligence Scale for Children—Revised. Diagnostique, 9,* 32–44.

Jensen, A. R. (1998). *The g factor.* Westport, CT: Preager.

Jensen, A. R., & Weng, L-J. (1994). What is good *g*? *Intelligence, 18,* 231–258.

Kamphaus, R. W. (2001). *Clinical assessment of child and adolescent intelligence* (2nd ed.). Boston: Allyn & Bacon.

Kane, M. T. (2001). Current concerns in validity theory. *Journal of Educational Measurement, 38,* 319–342.

Kaufman, A. S., & Kaufman, N. L. (1993). *The Kaufman Adolescent and Adult Intelligence Test.* Circle Pines, MN: American Guidance Service.

Kaufman, A. S., & O'Neal, M. R. (1988a). Analysis of the cognitive, achievement, and general factors underlying the *Woodcock–Johnson Psycho-Educational Battery. Journal of Clinical Child Psychology, 17,* 143–151.

41

Kaufman, A. S., & O'Neal, M. (1988b). Factor structure of the Woodcock–Johnson cognitive subtests from preschool to adulthood. *Journal of Psychoeducational Assessment, 6,* 35–48.

Kaufman, F. R., Horton, E. J., Gott, P., Wolff, J. A., Nelson, M. D., Jr., Azen, C., & Manis, F. R. (1995). Abnormal somatosensory evoked potentials in patients with classic galactosemia: Correlation with neurologic outcome. *Journal of Child Neurology, 10,* 32–36.

Keating, D. P., List, J. A., & Merriman, W. E. (1985). Cognitive processing and cognitive ability: A multivariate validity investigation. *Intelligence, 9,* 149–170.

Keith, T. Z. (1997). Using confirmatory factor analysis to aid in understanding the constructs measured by intelligence tests. In D. P. Flanagan, J. L. Genshaft, & P. L. Harrison (Eds.), *Contemporary intellectual assessment: Theories, tests, and issues* (pp. 373–402). New York: Guilford.

Keith, T. Z. (1999). Effects of general and specific abilities on student achievement: Similarities and differences across ethnic groups. *School Psychology Quarterly, 14,* 239–262.

Keith, T. Z., Kranzler, J. H., & Flanagan, D. P. (2001). What does the Cognitive Assessment System (CAS) measure? Joint confirmatory factor analysis of the CAS and the Woodcock–Johnson Tests of Cognitive Ability (3rd. edition). *School Psychology Review, 30,* 89–119.

Kline, R. B. (2001). Brief cognitive assessments of children: Review of instruments and recommendations for best practice. In J. J. W. Andrews, D. H. Saklofske, & H. L. Janzen (Eds.), *Handbook of psychoeducational assessment: Ability, achievement, and behavior in children* (pp. 103–132). San Diego, CA: Academic Press.

Konold, T. R., Glutting, J. J., & McDermott, P. A. (1997). The development and applied utility of a normative aptitude–achievement taxonomy for the Woodcock–Johnson Psycho-Educational Battery—Revised. *The Journal of Special Education, 31,* 212–232.

Laughon, P., & Torgesen, J. K. (1985). Effects of alternate testing procedures on two subtests of the Woodcock–Johnson Psycho-Educational Battery. *Psychology in the Schools, 22,* 160–163.

Laurent, J. (1997). Characteristics of the standard and supplemental batteries of the Woodcock–Johnson Tests of Cognitive Ability—Revised with a college sample. *Journal of School Psychology, 35,* 403–416.

Lezak, M. (1995). *Neuropsychological assessment* (3rd ed.). New York: Oxford University Press.

List, J. A., Keating, D. P., & Merriman, W. E. (1985). Differences in memory retrieval: A construct validity investigation. *Child Development, 56,* 138–151.

Loevinger, J. (1957). Objective tests as instruments of psychological theory. *Psychological Reports, 3,* 635–694.

Lyon, G. R., & Krasnegor, N. A. (Eds.) (1996). *Attention, memory, and executive function.* Baltimore: Paul H. Brooks.

Manis, F. R., Cohn, L. B., McBride-Chang, C., Wolff, J. A., & Kaufman, F. R. (1997). A longitudinal study of cognitive functioning in patients with classical galactosaemia, including a cohort treated with oral uridine. *Journal of Inherited Metabolic Disease, 20,* 549–555.

Marston, D., & Ysseldyke, J. (1984). Concerns in interpreting subtest scatter on the Tests of Cognitive Ability from the Woodcock–Johnson Psycho-Educational Battery. *Journal of Learning Disabilities, 17,* 588–591.

Masterson, J. J. (1993). The performance of children with language-learning disabilities on two types of cognitive tasks. *Journal of Speech and Hearing Research, 36,* 1026–1036.

Mather, N. (1991). *An instructional guide to the Woodcock–Johnson Psycho-Educational Battery—Revised.* New York: Wiley.

Mather, N., & Bos, C. (1984). Performance of gifted and talented subjects on the Woodcock–Johnson Tests of Cognitive Ability and the WISC-R. *Diagnostique, 9,* 135–141.

Mather, N., & Burch, M. (1986). An examination of Woodcock–Johnson suppressor effects with learning-disabled and gifted students. *Journal of Psychoeducational Assessment, 4,* 45–51.

Mather, N., & Goldstein, S. (2001). *Learning disabilities and challenging behaviors: A guide to intervention and classroom management.* Baltimore: Brookes.

Mather, N., & Jaffe, L. (1993). *Woodcock–Johnson Psycho-Educational Battery—Revised: Recommendations and reports.* New York: Wiley.

Mather, N., & Jaffe, L. (2002). *Woodcock–Johnson III: Recommendations and reports.* New York: Wiley.

Mather, N., & Schrank, F. A. (2001). Use of the WJ III discrepancy procedures for learning disabilities identification and diagnosis. *Assessment Service Bulletin No. 3*. Itasca, IL: Riverside Publishing.

Mather, N., & Udall, A. J. (1985). The identification of gifted underachievers using the *Woodcock–Johnson Psycho-Educational Battery*. *Roeper Review, 8(1)*, 54–56.

Mather, N., & Woodcock, R. W. (2001). Examiner's Manual. *Woodcock–Johnson III Tests of Cognitive Abilities*. Itasca, IL: Riverside Publishing.

McArdle, J. J., Ferrer-Caja, E., Hamagami, F., & Woodcock, R. W. (2002). Comparative longitudinal structural analyses of the growth and decline of multiple intellectual abilities over the life span. *Developmental Psychology, 38*, 115–142.

McBride-Chang, C. (1996). Models of speech perception and phonological processing in reading. *Child Development, 67*, 1836–1856.

McGhee, R. (1993). Fluid and crystallized intelligence: Confirmatory factor analysis of the *Differential Abilities Scale, Detroit Tests of Learning Aptitude—3*, and Woodcock–Johnson Psycho-Educational Battery—Revised. *Journal of Psychoeducational Assessment Monograph Series: Woodcock–Johnson Psycho-Educational Assessment Battery—Revised, 20–38*. Cordova, TN: Psychoeducational Corporation.

McGhee, R., & Liberman, L. (1994). *Gf–Gc* theory of human cognition: Differentiation of short-term auditory and visual memory factors. *Psychology in the Schools, 31*, 297–304.

McGrew, K. S. (1983). Comparison of the WISC-R and Woodcock–Johnson Tests of Cognitive Ability. *Journal of School Psychology, 21*, 271–276.

McGrew, K. S. (1984). Normative-based guidelines for subtest profile interpretation of the Woodcock–Johnson Tests of Cognitive Ability. *Journal of Psychoeducational Assessment, 2*, 141–148.

McGrew, K. S. (1985). Investigation of the verbal/nonverbal structure of the Woodcock–Johnson: Implications for subtest interpretation and comparisons with the Wechsler Scale. *Journal of Psychoeducational Assessment, 3*, 65–71.

McGrew, K. S. (1987a). A multivariate analysis of the Wechsler/Woodcock–Johnson discrepancy controversy. *Journal of Psychoeducational Assessment, 5*, 49–60.

McGrew, K. S. (1987b). Exploratory factor analysis of the Woodcock–Johnson Tests of Cognitive Ability. *Journal of Psychoeducational Assessment, 5*, 200–216.

McGrew, K. S. (1993). The relationship between the *Woodcock–Johnson Psycho-Educational Assessment Battery—Revised Gf–Gc* cognitive clusters and reading achievement across the life-span. *Journal of Psychoeducational Assessment Monograph Series: Woodcock–Johnson Psycho-Educational Assessment Battery—Revised, 39–53*. Cordova, TN: Psychoeducational Corporation.

McGrew, K. S. (1997). Analysis of the major intelligence batteries according to a proposed comprehensive *Gf–Gc* framework. In D. P. Flanagan, J. L. Genshaft, & P. L. Harrison (Eds.), *Contemporary intellectual assessment: Theories, tests, and issues* (pp. 131–150). New York: Guilford.

McGrew, K. S. (2000, February). Advanced interpretation of the Woodcock–Johnson III. Presented at the meeting of the National Association of School Psychologists, Chicago, IL.

McGrew, K. S., & Flanagan, D. P. (1998). *The intelligence test desk reference (ITDR)*: Gf–Gc cross-battery assessment. Boston: Allyn & Bacon.

McGrew, K. S., Flanagan, D. P., Keith, T. Z., & Vanderwood, M. (1997). Beyond g: The impact of *Gf–Gc* specific cognitive abilities research on the future use and interpretation of intelligence tests in the schools. *School Psychology Review, 26*, 189–210.

McGrew, K. S., & Floyd, R. G. (2001). [Narrow ability structural analysis of the Woodcock–Johnson III standardization sample for ages 9 to 13]. Unpublished data analysis.

McGrew, K. S., & Hessler, G. L. (1995). The relationship between the WJ-R *Gf–Gc* cognitive clusters and mathematics achievement across the life-span. *Journal of Psychoeducational Assessment, 13*, 21–38.

McGrew, K. S., & Knopik, S. N. (1993). The relationship between the WJ-R *Gf–Gc* cognitive clusters and writing achievement across the life-span. *School Psychology Review, 22*, 687–695.

McGrew, K. S., & Knopik, S. N. (1996). The relationship between intra-cognitive scatter on the Woodcock–Johnson Psycho-Educational Battery—Revised and school achievement. *Journal of School Psychology, 34,* 351–364.

McGrew, K. S., & Murphy, S. R. (1995). Uniqueness and general factor characteristics of the Woodcock–Johnson Tests of Cognitive Ability—Revised. *Journal of School Psychology, 33,* 235–245.

McGrew, K. S., & Pehl, J. (1988). Prediction of future achievement by the *Woodcock–Johnson Psychoeducational Battery* and the WISC-R. *Journal of School Psychology, 26,* 275–281.

McGrew, K. S., Werder, J. K., & Woodcock, R. W. (1991). *WJ-R Technical Manual.* Itasca, IL: Riverside Publishing.

McGrew, K. S., & Woodcock, R. W. (2001). Technical manual. *Woodcock–Johnson III.* Itasca, IL: Riverside Publishing.

McGrew, K. S., Woodcock, R. W., & Ford, L. A. (2002). The Woodcock Johnson Battery—Third Edition (WJ III). In A. S. Kaufman & E. O. Lichtenberger (Eds.), *Assessing adolescent and adult intelligence* (2nd ed., pp. 561–628). Needham Heights, MA: Allyn & Bacon.

McGue, M., Shinn, M., & Ysseldyke, J. (1982). Use of the cluster scores on the *Woodcock–Johnson Psycho-Educational Battery* with learning disabled students. *Learning Disability Quarterly, 5,* 274–287.

Mehrens, W. A. (1997). The consequences of consequential validity. *Educational Measurement: Issues and Practice, 16*(2), 16–18.

Meinhardt, M., Hibbett, C., Koller, J., & Busch, R. (1993). Comparison of the *Woodcock–Johnson Psycho-Educational Battery—Revised* and the *Wechsler Intelligence Scale for Children—Revised* with incarcerated adolescents. *Journal of Psychoeducational Assessment, Monograph Series: WJ-R Monograph,* 64–70.

Merrell, K. W. (1990). Differentiating low achieving students and students with learning disabilities: An examination of performances on the *Woodcock–Johnson Psycho-Educational Battery. Journal of Special Education, 24,* 296–305.

Merrell, K. W., & Shinn, M. R. (1990). Critical variables in the learning disabilities identification process. *School Psychology Review, 19,* 74–82.

Merriman, W. E., Keating, D. P., & List, J. A. (1985). Mental rotation of facial profiles: Age-, sex-, and ability-related differences. *Developmental Psychology, 21,* 888–900.

Messick, S. (1989). Validity. In R. Linn (Ed.), *Educational Measurement* (3rd ed., pp. 13–103). Washington, DC: American Council on Education.

Messick, S. (1995). Validity of psychological assessment: Validity of inferences from persons' responses and performances as scientific inquiry into score meaning. *American Psychologist, 50,* 741–749.

Meyer, M. S., Wood, F. B., Hart, L. A., & Felton, R. H. (1998). Selective predictive value in rapid automatic naming in poor readers. *Journal of Learning Disabilities, 31,* 106–117.

Mirsky, A. F. (1996). Disorders of attention: A neurological perspective. In G. R. Lyon & N. A. Krasnegor (Eds.), *Attention, memory, and executive function* (pp. 71–95). Baltimore: Paul H. Brookes Publishing Co.

Mirsky, A. F., Anthony, B. J., Duncan, C. C., Ahearn, M. B., & Kellam, S. G. (1991). Analysis of the elements of attention: A neuropsychological approach. *Neuropsychology Review, 2,* 109–145.

Morris, R. D., Shaywitz, S. E., Shankweiler, D. P., Katz, L., Steubing, K. K., Fletcher, J. M., Lyon, G. R., Francis, D. J., & Shaywitz, B. A. (1998). Subtypes of reading disability: Variability around a phonological core. *Journal of Educational Psychology, 90,* 347–373.

Naglieri, J. A., & Das, J. P. (1997). *Cognitive Assessment System.* Itasca, IL: Riverside Publishing.

Neisser, U., Boodoo, G., Bouchard, T. J., Boykin, A. W., Brody, N., Ceci, S. J., Halpern, D. F., Loehlin, J. C., Perloff, R., Sternberg, R. J., & Urbani, S. (1996). Intelligence: Knowns and unknowns. *American Psychologist, 51,* 77–101.

Noll, J. G., & Horn, J. L. (1998). Age differences in processes of fluid and crystallized intelligence. In J. J. McArdle & R. W. Woodcock (Eds.), *Human cognitive abilities in theory and practice* (pp. 263–281). Mahwah, NJ: Erlbaum.

Nunnally, J. C., & Bernstein, I. H. (1994). *Psychometric theory* (3rd ed.). New York: McGraw-Hill.

Patel, B. N., Seltzer, G. B., Wu, H. S., & Schupf, N. (2001). Effect of menopause on cognitive performance in women with Down syndrome. *NeuroReport, 12*, 2659–2662.

Pennington, B. F., & Ozonoff, S. (1996). Executive functions and developmental psychopathology. *Journal of Child Psychology and Psychiatry, 37*, 51–87.

Phelps, L., & Rosso, M. (1985). Validity assessment of the Woodcock–Johnson Broad Cognitive Ability and Scholastic Aptitude Cluster scores for behavior-disordered adolescents. *Psychology in the Schools, 22*, 398–403.

Phelps, L., Rosso, M., & Falasco, S. L. (1984). Correlations between the Woodcock–Johnson and the WISC-R for a behavior disordered population. *Psychology in the Schools, 21*, 442–446.

Phelps, L., Rosso, M., & Falasco, S. L. (1985). Multiple regression data using the WISC-R and the Woodcock–Johnson Tests of Cognitive Ability. *Psychology in the Schools, 22*, 46–49.

Pitoniak, M. J., & Royer, J. M. (2001). Testing accommodations for examinees with disabilities: A review of psychometric, legal, and social policy issues. *Review of Educational Research, 71*, 53–104.

Popham, W. J. (1997). Consequential validity: Right concern-wrong concept. *Educational Measurement: Issues and Practice, 16*(2), 9–13.

Rasch, G. (1960). *Probabilistic models for some intelligence and attainment tests*. Copenhagen, Denmark: Danish Institute for Educational Research.

Ree, M. J., & Earles, J. A. (1991). Predicting training success: Not much more than *g. Intelligence, 15*, 271–278.

Ree, M. J., Earles, J. A., & Teachout, M. S. (1994). Predicting job performance: Not much more than *g. Journal of Applied Psychology, 79*, 518–524.

Reed, M. T., & McCallum, S. (1995). Construct validity of the *Universal Nonverbal Intelligence Test* (UNIT). *Psychology in the Schools, 32*, 277–290.

Reeve, R. E., Hall, R. J., & Zakreski, R. S. (1979). The *Woodcock–Johnson Tests of Cognitive Ability*: Concurrent validity with the WISC-R. *Learning Disability Quarterly, 2*, 63–69.

Reilly, T. P., Drudge, O. W., Rosen, J. C., Loew, D. E., & Fischer, M. (1985). Concurrent and predictive validity of the WISC-R, McCarthy Scales, Woodcock–Johnson, and academic achievement. *Psychology in the Schools, 22*, 380–382.

Reschly, D. J. (1990). Found: Our intelligence*s*: What do they mean? *Journal of Psychoeducational Assessment, 8*, 259–267.

Reschly, D. J. (1997a). Diagnostic and treatment utility in intelligence tests. In D. P. Flanagan, J. L. Genshaft, & P. L. Harrison (Eds.), *Contemporary intellectual assessment: Theories, tests, and issues* (pp. 437–456). New York: Guilford.

Reschly, D. J. (1997b). Utility of individual ability measures and public policy choices for the 21st century. *School Psychology Review, 26*, 234–241.

Reynolds, C. R., & Kamphaus, R.W. (1992). *Behavior Assessment System for Children*. Circle Pines, MN: American Guidance.

Riccio, C. A., Reynolds, C. R., & Lowe, P. A. (2001). *Clinical applications of continuous performance tests: Measuring attention and impulsive responding in children and adolescents*. New York: Wiley.

Rizza, M. G., McIntosh, D. E., & McCunn, A. (2001). Profile analysis of the *Woodcock–Johnson III Tests of Cognitive Abilities* with gifted students. *Psychology in the Schools, 38*, 447–455.

Rosso, M., & Phelps, L. (1988). Factor analysis of the Woodcock–Johnson with conduct disordered adolescents. *Psychology in the Schools, 25*, 105–110.

Salthouse, T. A. (1998). Independence of age-related influences on cognitive abilities across the life span. *Developmental Psychology, 34*, 851–864.

Santos, O. B. (1989). Language skills and cognitive processes related to poor reading comprehension performance. *Journal of Learning Disabilities, 22*, 131–133.

Schrank, F. A., Flanagan, D. P., Woodcock, R. W., & Mascolo, J. T. (2002*). Essentials of WJ III cognitive abilities assessment*. New York: Wiley.

Schrank, F. A., & Woodcock, R. W. (2001). *WJ III Compuscore and Profiles Program* [Computer software]. Itasca, IL: Riverside Publishing.

Schrank, F. A., & Woodcock, R. W. (2002). *Report Writer for the WJ III Compuscore and Profiles Program* [Computer software]. Itasca, IL: Riverside Publishing.

Shepard, L. A. (1997). The centrality of test use and consequences for test validity. *Educational Measurement: Issues and Practice, 16*(2), 5–8, 13, 24.

Shinn, M., Algozzine, B., Martson, D., & Ysseldyke, J. (1982). A theoretical analysis of the performance of learning disabled students on the *Woodcock–Johnson Psycho-Educational Battery. Journal of Learning Disabilities, 15*, 221–226.

Stanovich, K. E., Siegel, L. S., & Gottardo, A. (1997). Converging evidence for phonological and surface subtypes of reading disability. *Journal of Educational Psychology, 89*, 114–127.

Stormont-Spurgin, M., & Zentall, S. S. (1995). Contributing factors in the manifestation of aggression in preschoolers with hyperactivity. *Journal of Child Psychology and Psychiatry, 36*, 491–509.

Strein, W. (1990). Theoretical analysis of the Woodcock–Johnson Tests of Cognitive Ability: A second look. *Journal of School Psychology, 28*, 21–25.

Teeter, P. A., & Smith, P. L. (1993). WISC-III and WJ-R: Predictive and discriminant validity for students with severe emotional disturbance. In B. A. Bracken & R. S. McCallum (Eds.), *Wechsler Intelligence Scale for Children: Third Edition. Journal of Psychoeducational Assessment. Advances in psychoeducational assessment* (pp. 114–124). Brandon, VT: Clinical Psychology Publishing.

Telzrow, C. F., & Harr, G. A. (1987). Common variance among three measures of nonverbal cognitive ability: WISC-R Performance Scale, WJPB-TCA Reasoning Cluster, and Halstead Category Test. *Journal of School Psychology, 25*, 93–95.

Thompson, P. L., & Brassard, M. R. (1984). Validity of the Woodcock–Johnson Tests of Cognitive Ability: A comparison with the WISC-R in LD and normal elementary students. *Journal of School Psychology, 22*, 201–208.

Thorndike, R. L., Hagen, E. P., & Sattler, J. M. (1986). *Stanford–Binet Intelligence Scale: Guide for administering and scoring the Fourth Edition.* Itasca, IL: Riverside Publishing.

Torgesen, J. K., Wagner, R. K., Rashotte, C. A., Burgess, S., & Hecht, S. (1997). Contributions of phonological awareness and rapid automatic naming ability to the growth of word-reading skills in second- to fifth-grade children. *Scientific Studies of Reading, 1*, 161–185.

Tupper, D. E. (1990). Some observations on the use of the Woodcock–Johnson Tests of Cognitive Abilities in adults with head injury. *Journal of Learning Abilities, 23*, 306–310.

Vellutino, F. R., Scanlan, D. M., & Lyon, R. G. (2000). Differentiating between difficult-to-remediate and readily remediated poor readers: More evidence against the IQ–achievement discrepancy definition of reading disability. *Journal of Learning Disabilities, 33*, 223–238.

Vellutino, F. R., Scanlon, D. M., Sipay, E. R., Small, S. G., Pratt, A., Chen, R., & Denckla, M. B. (1996). Cognitive profiles of difficult-to-remediate and readily remediated poor readers: Early intervention as a vehicle for distinguishing between cognitive and experimental deficits as basic causes of specific reading disability. *Journal of Educational Psychology, 88*, 601–638.

Walsh, P. C., Lowenthal, B., & Thompson, G. (1989). Cluster score performance of learning disabled students on the *Woodcock–Johnson Psycho-Educational Battery. Psychology in the Schools, 26*, 19–26.

Waschbusch, D. A., Daleiden, E., & Drabman, R. S. (2000). Are parents accurate reporters of their child's cognitive abilities? *Journal of Psychopathology and Behavioral Assessment, 22*, 61–77.

Wechsler, D. (1989). *Wechsler Preschool and Primary Scale of Intelligence—Revised.* San Antonio, TX: Psychological Corporation.

Wechsler, D. (1991). *The Wechsler Intelligence Scale for Children—Third Edition.* San Antonio, TX: Psychological Corporation.

Wechsler, D. (1997a). *Wechsler Adult Intelligence Scale—Third Edition.* San Antonio, TX: Psychological Corporation.

Wechsler, D. (1997b). *Wechsler Memory Scale—Third Edition.* San Antonio, TX: Psychological Corporation.

Williams, P. C., McCallum, R. S., & Reed, M. T. (1996). Predictive validity of the Cattell–Horn *Gf–Gc* constructs to achievement. *Journal of Psychoeducational Assessment, 3,* 43–51.

Wolfe, M., Bowers, P. G., & Biddle, K. (2000). Naming-speed processes, timing, and reading: A conceptual review. *Journal of Learning Disabilities, 33,* 387–407.

Woodcock, R. W. (1978). *Development and standardization of the Woodcock–Johnson Psycho-Educational Battery.* Allen, TX: DLM Teaching Resources.

Woodcock, R. W. (1990). The theoretical foundations of the WJ-R measures of cognitive ability. *Journal of Psychoeducational Assessment, 8,* 231–258.

Woodcock, R. W. (1993). An information processing view of the *Gf–Gc* theory. *Journal of Psychoeducational Assessment Monograph Series: Woodcock–Johnson Psycho-Educational Assessment Battery—Revised, 80*–102. Cordova, TN: Psychoeducational Corporation.

Woodcock, R. W. (1998). Extending *Gf–Gc* theory into practice. In J. J. McArdle & R. W. Woodcock (Eds.), *Human cognitive abilities in theory and practice* (pp. 137–156). Mahwah, NJ: Erlbaum.

Woodcock, R. W. (1999). What can Rasch-based scores convey about a person's test performance? In S. E. Embretson & S. L. Hershberger (Eds.), *The new rules of measurement: What every psychologist and educator should know* (pp. 105–128). Mahwah, NJ: Erlbaum.

Woodcock, R. W., & Johnson, M. B. (1989). *Woodcock–Johnson Psycho-Educational Battery—Revised.* Allen, TX: DLM Teaching Resources.

Woodcock, R. W., & Mather, N. (1989). Woodcock–Johnson Tests of Cognitive Ability—Standard and Supplementary Batteries: Examiner's manual. In R. W. Woodcock & M. B. Johnson, *Woodcock–Johnson Psycho-Educational Battery* (rev. ed.). Chicago: Riverside Publishing.

Woodcock, R. W., McGrew, K. S., & Mather, N. (2001). *Woodcock–Johnson III Tests of Cognitive Abilities.* Itasca, IL: Riverside Publishing.

Wright, B. D., & Stone, M. H. (1979). *Best test design.* Chicago: MESA Press.

Ysseldyke, J. E., Algozzine, B., & Shinn, M. (1981). Validity of the *Woodcock–Johnson Psycho-Educational Battery* for learning disabled youngsters. *Learning Disability Quarterly, 4,* 244–249.

Ysseldyke, J. E., Algozzine, B., Shinn, M. R., & McGue, M. (1982). Similarities and differences between low achievers and students classified learning disabled. *The Journal of Special Education, 16,* 73–85.

Ysseldyke, J. E., Shinn, M. R., & Epps, S. (1981). A comparison of the WISC-R and the Woodcock–Johnson Tests of Cognitive Ability. *Psychology in the Schools,18,* 15–19.

2

QUALITATIVE ANALYSIS OF WOODCOCK–JOHNSON III TEST PERFORMANCE

BARBARA G. READ

Educational Diagnostic and Consultant Service, Inc.,
Woodstock, Vermont 05091

FREDRICK A. SCHRANK

The Woodcock–Muñoz Foundation,
Olympia, Washington 98501

The Woodcock–Johnson III (WJ III) affords the skilled professional with unique opportunities to observe and analyze behaviors that may be reflective of individual differences in information processing and learning style. The WJ III is especially useful for this purpose because of the breadth and depth of cognitive abilities and academic skills measured and because of the varied task requirements and response formats of the tests.

Clinical observations of test performance are useful for gathering information on the characteristics that may facilitate or inhibit an individual's cognitive and academic performance in other settings. For example, assessment occurs in an environment that has high demand requirements for performance. Because the WJ III tasks increase in level of difficulty, and the individual must fail a defined sequence of items in order to reach a ceiling on each test, the individual is presented with tasks that are at first within, and then beyond, his or her developmental zone. An individual's responses to tasks that are difficult can be useful in interpreting performance. Some individuals persist with tasks that are very difficult. This characteristic is associated with a high need for achievement (Klonsky, 1989). However, test performance is sometimes accompanied by feelings that performance below expectations is a negative reflection on the self. A combination of these factors can result in a stress-ful or anxious situation. High test anxiety is associated with poor test performance (Carver & Scheier, 1989), especially on tasks that are difficult for the individual. Anxiety has also been shown to affect long-term storage and retrieval. Eysenck and Eysenck (1985) demonstrated that test-anxious subjects demonstrated poorer reten-tion over time. Poor attention and concentration, increased distractibility, reduced overall cognitive efficiency, and problems with working memory have been associ-ated with test anxiety (Zeidner, 1995; Mueller, 1980).

Certain temperament characteristics (e.g., extraversion, emotionality, or reac-tivity) can be observed during test performance (Strelau, 1995; Strelau, Zawadzki, & Piotrowska, 2001). Eysenck and Eysenck (1985) found that introverts and extroverts respond differently to certain types of tasks: "Extroverts perform faster than introverts under relatively arousing conditions, whereas introverts respond faster than extraverts when long and monotonous tasks are used" (p. 274). Cattell (1987) suggested that several of the broad cognitive ability constructs could be accounted for (at least in part) by personality variables. Motivation and attention variables are individual characteristics that influence attention and concentration (Hidi, 1990; Snow, 1989). These attributes are often task specific, but may vary for a given task. Significant motivation/attention variables include attention deficits, anxiety, interests, and the need for achievement. These variables represent the longer term, often modifiable, characteristics of an individual that may be observed in an individual's test-taking strategies and problem-solving behaviors. One example is *reflection–impulsivity*, or an individual's tendency to respond either carefully and accurately or rapidly but less accurately.

Finally, an examiner with an astute observational eye and honed skills in response process analysis can use *observable attributes* to validate his or her inter-pretation of an individual's test performance (Kane, 2001). That is, a valid inter-pretation of the *theoretical constructs* measured by the WJ III can be accomplished, in part, through analysis and documentation of relevant observable attributes.

Unfortunately, clinical observation procedures and process-based analysis methods for the WJ III tests have not been sufficiently emphasized in many train-ing programs. Consequently, the focus in this chapter is on providing a means for the professional and professional-in-training to learn a process of clinical data gathering and analysis for the *Woodcock–Johnson III Tests of Cognitive Abilities* and *Tests of Achievement* (WJ III COG and ACH). Included are several sugges-tions for gathering clinical observations and analyzing test-taking behaviors during administration of the WJ III.

INTERPRETATION OF THE WJ III

The interpretive plan for the WJ III includes four levels of information. Each level of information has a purpose. Level 1, the qualitative level, provides information

about information-processing characteristics that can be used to support understanding of an individual's test scores or to develop clinical hypotheses. Level 2 information describes an individual's level of development, such as age or grade equivalents.
Level 3 information indicates the quality of a person's performance on criterion tasks
of a given difficulty level. Level 4 information provides peer comparison data
(e.g., percentile rank and standard scores). Table 2-1 presents the range of interpretive information available from the WJ III at these four levels.

   Level 1 methods include clinical observations of test performance, analysis of
individual responses to test items, and integration of background and contextual information. Qualitative procedures for gathering this type of information are grounded in
broad psychological and epistemological constructs (Polkingborne & Gribbons,
1999) that are consistent with expert practice. That is, the outcomes achieved by
qualitative assessment procedures are similar in form to the experiential and practical
knowledge possessed by experienced practitioners (Lave & Wenger, 1991). For
example, as professionals gain more experience in their areas of interest and expertise,
they rely less and less on formulaic procedures learned in training and rely more
heavily on qualitative methods (Skovholt & Ronnestad, 1992).

   Scores or information from one level are not inherently better or worse than
scores or information from another level. Additionally, scores or information

TABLE 2-1   Levels, Purposes, and Examples of Interpretive Information Available
from the WJ III

Level	Type of information	Purpose	Examples
One	Qualitative	Clinical description and interpretation of contextual or situational variables that affect cognitive or academic performance	• Test Session Observations • Response Analysis • Parent, Teacher, and Self-Reports
Two	Developmental	Level of task accuracy (age- or grade-level in norming sample at which the average score is the same as the individual's score)	• Age-equivalent • Grade-equivalent
Three	Proficiency	Criterion-referenced interpretation of test performance (description of proficiency with tasks of average difficulty for peers)	• Proficiency Level • Impairment Level • Developmental Delay • Relative Proficiency Index • Developmental Zone • Instructional Zone • CALP Level
Four	Peer comparison	Communication of relative standing among peers	• Standard Score • Percentile Rank • Discrepancy Scores

from one level cannot be used interchangeably with information from another. Instead, using different levels of information adds greater depth to the interpretation of test results and avoids any tendency toward overfocusing on only one perspective. For example, one could consider the test participant's performance on the abstract Fluid Reasoning tests using a Level 4 score (e.g., Percentile Rank) that would reveal normative information about the participant's statistical rank relative to his or her peers—information that might be useful or necessary for procedural discussions in special education eligibility. Carrying the example further, utilizing a Level 3 score such as a Relative Proficiency Index (RPI) for this cluster would describe the proficiency with which the participant is able to carry out abstract thinking and problem-solving tasks. A Level 2 score, such as an age equivalent, would provide information about the developmental level with which the individual can accurately perform the tasks. All of this information could be important for educational programming and instructional intervention. Although scores from Levels 2 through 4 are useful for making decisions about an individual, they all retain the limitations inherent in probability correlations using aggregate groups. That is, all derived scores are based on how a previously examined group of individuals responded to the test items.

At best, any one type of score represents only one part of a comprehensive psychological study of an individual. Level 1 information enhances the information provided in Levels 2 through 4 by providing a broader understanding of the individual. Sometimes the results from a Level 1 assessment can bring about a complete change in a professional's understanding of an individual or of the quantitative test scores obtained from testing. Consequently, Level 1 information should be gathered and carefully considered, especially when making high-stakes decisions that warrant an individual psychoeducational assessment. Far too frequently, qualitative assessment procedures are overlooked or even dismissed as overly subjective by some professionals. However, as Simon (2001) enjoined, "Don't be so easy to agree with those who are dismissive of clinical judgment in order to avoid arguments. Clinical decision-making is what separates the trained professional from a clerk or computer. If the only information of value were scores, there would be no need for trained professionals" (p. 11).

TEST PERFORMANCE ANALYSIS GUIDELINES

It is important to integrate test session observations with an understanding of the specific task demands, especially as they change across the range of items within a test. For example, an examiner may notice what appears to be some erratic incorrect responses scattered throughout COG Test 3: Spatial Relations. Closer scrutiny and task analysis of the incorrect items may reveal a more helpful explanation or hypothesis. The pattern of incorrect responses may not have been truly erratic, but rather may have corresponded only to those items that required mental rotation of puzzle pieces.

The following guidelines are intended to serve as a catalyst for the process of qualitative analysis. They are not intended to represent an exhaustive list of behavioral observations or task demands. When used in conjunction with knowledge about the theoretical constructs measured by each test and cluster, these guidelines may promote a better understanding of the process of clinical interpretation of test performance. The test performance analysis guidelines are grouped according to the broad WJ III clusters. General considerations are outlined. These are the conditions that can influence test performance across all measures of the factor. Interpretation guidelines for each WJ III test within the cluster or academic area are also provided.

Examiners should pay particular attention to the description of task demands across test or subtest items. It is important to consider the multidimensional nature of the task requirements. For example, a cancellation task, such as COG Test 20: Pair Cancellation, involves or requires several abilities and processes, including sustained attention, processing, motoric speed, and executive functioning. To help the examiner develop clinical hypotheses, several possible implications of performance are included. Clinical hypotheses generated should be substantiated with information about the individual's proficiency with the task (as determined by the Relative Proficiency Index), and developmental level (as determined by the individual's age- or grade-equivalent score).

COMPREHENSION–KNOWLEDGE

Comprehension–Knowledge (*Gc*) is one's breadth and depth of declarative (factual) and procedural knowledge and its effective application (verbal reasoning), including language comprehension. There are many factors or conditions that can influence individual performance on Comprehension–Knowledge tests, including the following factors:

• Consistency of responses, and the ease or difficulty of obtaining a basal or ceiling response. Response consistency or inconsistency may suggest the need to consider the individual's level of acculturation. The individual's access to experiences outside the immediate home, school, or community environment can influence the depth, breadth consistency, and precision of his or her knowledge base.

• Response time on administered items. Consider whether difficulties with recall/retrieval or speed of recall may be influencing expressive performance. Look at other tests that require recall fluency to determine if there are weaknesses. Also look at the individual's performance on general measures of automatic processing speed. Evaluate whether the individual has an adequate fund of *receptive* knowledge.

• Vague responses and/or the need for frequent queries. Examine whether queried responses are able to be upgraded to correct responses. This may suggest that providing additional time and/or a probing question or prompt can improve the individual's performance. Determine that the individual has an adequate fund of *receptive* knowledge.

COG TEST 1: VERBAL COMPREHENSION

The Verbal Comprehension test includes four subtests: Picture Vocabulary, Synonyms, Antonyms, and Verbal Analogies. The Picture Vocabulary subtest requires the subject to recognize and name pictured objects. The Synonyms and Antonyms subtests require the subject to state words having the same meaning (Synonyms) and words having the opposite meaning (Antonyms) when orally presented with a stimulus word. The Verbal Analogies subtest measures depth of word knowledge and the ability to infer relationships and reason with verbal concepts by stating words that complete orally presented analogies. It is a verbal task using relatively simple vocabulary with increasingly complex relationships among words.

Subtest 1A Picture Vocabulary

Consider the subtest's task demands across items. Some lower level items require receptive identification through a pointing process. Expressive language requirements begin with Item 3.

Observe the individual's response patterns. Note if the individual

• Displays automaticity or delays in response time. If present, is it general or specific to certain items?
• Demonstrates precision or imprecision in his or her vocabulary. Does he or she provide vague associations, description by functions, and circumlocutions or is he or she verbally precise?

Subtest 1B and 1C: Synonyms and Antonyms

Consider the task demands across items. Note the depth of word knowledge and comprehension of words that mean the same thing (synonyms) or words that mean the opposite (antonyms) of the stimulus words.

Observe the individual's response patterns. Note if the individual

• Has a quick response time per item with good accuracy.
• Demonstrates good precision in responses and/or multiple correct responses per item.
• Makes errors during the training of the task within the sample items, and/or demonstrates difficulty in establishing a basal.
• Responds with answers that are close in meaning but incorrect in terms of the part of speech.

- Provides vague association or limited knowledge about the stimulus words without an appropriate synonym or antonym.

Subtest 1D: Verbal Analogies

Consider the task demands across items. Note verbal reasoning by stating words that complete oral analogies. Remember that the analogy format for Items 1 through 8 begins as A:B :: C:D. Word relationships begin at a fairly concrete level (same/different) but become increasingly complex (e.g., related by function, classification order, or degree of difference). Analogy order changes to an A:C :: B:D format for some items beginning with Item 9. This level of the test requires the individual to make a fluid shift in his or her verbal reasoning and logic, and then identify the salient relationships between the appropriate vocabulary terms.

Observe the individual's response patterns. Note if the individual

- Exhibits ease or difficulty in learning the nature of the task within the sample items. (It may be developmentally appropriate for young subjects to have difficulty understanding or learning the Analogies activity. Consider whether any observed difficulty is unusual for the individual's age or grade level.)
- Displays relative efficiency or inefficiency in making a conceptual shift when the order of the analogy format changes. Consider whether any observed difficulties may be developmentally appropriate.

COG TEST 11: GENERAL INFORMATION

The General Information test consists of two subtests: Where and What. The Where portion presents question formats such as "Where would you find… (object)?" and the What portion involves questions such as "What would you do with… (object)?"; the General Information test measures the narrow ability of General Knowledge.

Consider the task demands across items for subtests 11A—Where and 11B—What. Each subtest consists of verbal questions from the examiner requiring verbal responses from the examinee. There are no visual stimuli for the examinee. The items in the stimulus questions initially involve objects that are commonly found within the environment. The difficulty of items increases to objects that are more unusual and require a greater depth of knowledge and experience.

Observe the individual's response patterns. Note if the individual

- Demonstrates precision or imprecision in his or her explanations or knowledge of the stimulus items.
- Shows consistency or inconsistency in his or her knowledge of the stimulus items.

- Responds in a way that suggests confusion between "what" and "where" questions.

POSSIBLE PERFORMANCE IMPLICATIONS FOR COMPREHENSION–KNOWLEDGE

- Effective recall of declarative information and how well a person can answer factual questions orally and on tests.
- Ability to comprehend verbal and written directions and general proficiency in verbal ability.
- Reading comprehension and written expression tasks for which prior background knowledge and comprehension of concepts and relationships is important.
- Efficiency for learning and retaining new information and vocabulary and/or the ability to apply one's knowledge within content subjects.
- Ability to understand relationships of words and concepts in mathematics.

LONG-TERM RETRIEVAL

Long-Term Retrieval (*Glr*) is defined as a thinking ability for learning new information and effectively storing and retrieving that information through association over a period of extended time. The individual's general comfort level for or nervousness with on-demand recall tasks can play an important role in his or her performance within these tests. In addition, the individual's receptivity to novel tasks and/or feedback may also play an influential role in his or her test performance.

COG TEST 2: VISUAL–AUDITORY LEARNING

The Visual–Auditory Learning test requires the subject to learn and retrieve rebuses (pictures/symbols representing words) that are paired with familiar words. These symbols are then strung together into passages of several sentences that the individual is required to read orally. This test utilizes a controlled-learning format in which the individual is instructed how to do the task and then provided with immediate corrective feedback for incorrect responses.

Consider the test's task demands across items. This test requires the cumulative learning and recall of increasing amounts of new symbol-to-word associations. The rebus stories start out short, but increase in length across the span of the test. The controlled-learning instructional format can be viewed as a simple miniature learning-to-read activity.

Observe the individual's response patterns. Note if the individual

- Requires little correction throughout the test. Does he or she show efficient learning?

- "Reads" the symbol sentences with relative fluency or dysfluency.
- Pauses on a symbol, then quickly (in under 5 seconds) looks ahead at the next several symbols. (This may be a context strategy for retrieval).
- Exhibits ease or difficulty in learning some symbols versus others (e.g., learning more concrete or meaningful symbols such as "cowboy," "dog," "horse," versus confusion with positional symbols such as "on," "under," and "by").
- Needs discretionary pointing to cues by the examiner beyond the first story.
- Seems sensitive to the amount of visual-graphic information on a page (i.e., the examiner needs to uncover one line at a time).
- Appears to become frustrated with or negatively inclined toward the correction–feedback.
- Appears receptive to the correction–feedback structure (i.e., anticipates the examiner's help when he or she is uncertain about a symbol).

COG TEST 12: RETRIEVAL FLUENCY

The Retrieval Fluency test measures the ability to retrieve fluently information from one's stored knowledge. This test requires the individual to name as many examples as possible from three specific categories (things to eat or drink, names of people, and animals). The individual has 1 minute for each category.

Observe the individual's response patterns. Note if the individual

- Employs strategies to facilitate recall, such as grouping objects by super ordinate categories, or appears to use visualization techniques. (Some strategies are not readily apparent to examiners. It is sometimes necessary or helpful to ask the examinee how he or she did the task in order to gain insight into his or her strategies.)
- Seems enthusiastic, relaxed, or agitated with the task.
- Displays a particular response rate and style (i.e., steady, long pauses between responses right from the outset, initial flow of responses with a slowing in response rate after 20 or 30 seconds, sporadic and random responses seemingly unrelated by categorical groupings, or a tendency to digress or become distracted within the task).
- Gives up or cannot sustain for the full minute per topic area.

COG TEST 10: VISUAL–AUDITORY LEARNING—DELAYED

Visual–Auditory Learning—Delayed measures the individual's ability to recall previously learned word-to-symbol associations that were presented within COG Test 2: Visual–Auditory Learning. The score for this delayed-recall measure is calculated by comparing the individual's obtained performance on the delayed-recall test to the individual's original performance on Visual–Auditory Learning. Specific consideration is given for the interval of delay between the two tests.

This test can be administered only if the subject was able to complete Visual–Auditory Learning in its entirety.

Consider the test's task demands across items. The symbols are presented in the form of rebus phrases or short rebus sentences that are different from the original phrases and sentences that were presented in Visual–Auditory Learning. Note that the rebus phrases begin as very simple two-symbol combinations and progress to lengthier phrases, and then finally to full rebus sentences. This test also has a feedback component whereby any misread or unknown symbols are retaught. Therefore, this test is not only measuring how much someone is able to retain over a period of time, but also how efficiently the subject is able to relearn information.

Observe the individual's response patterns. Note if the individual

- Exhibits ease or discomfort with the task through comments that may indicate nervousness, reluctance, or eager recognition of the activity. Some individuals may find it disconcerting to confront this format of task again, whereas others may find it familiar and therefore feel more favorable to the task.
- Reacts in a certain way to feedback. Does the individual react similarly or differently than he or she did in Test 2 to the instruction and correction procedure?
- Displays relative efficiency or inefficiency in responses. Does the individual show ease or difficulty in recalling and/or relearning the rebus symbols? Does the individual appear to benefit from the reteaching of the symbols?
- Reveals a particular pattern of errors between Visual–Auditory Learning and Visual–Auditory Learning—Delayed. Does the individual show difficulties with learning and recalling the same rebuses across both tests?

COG TEST 18: RAPID PICTURE NAMING

Rapid Picture Naming is a measure of speeded retrieval that relates to elements of cognitive fluency. It requires the subject to quickly name pictures of common objects across a row of five objects. The individual needs to name as many as he or she can in 2 minutes. Consider the test's task demands across items. The naming facility that is measured by this test involves the individual's speed of direct recall for verbal/picture associations; the information that is to be retrieved comes from the individual's fund of knowledge. This test involves elements of both automatic processing speed and long-term retrieval.

Observe the individual's response patterns. Note if the individual

- Is relatively accurate or inaccurate in naming the depicted objects.
- Shows a certain pace/response rate or consistency in rate (i.e., slowing up in his or her rate of responses over the span of the 2 minutes).

- Exhibits ease or difficulty in maintaining the visual tracking of the information across the rows on the page (e.g., using a finger as a tracking prompt across the rows).
- Reacts or comments in a way that may suggest nervousness or anxiety.

POSSIBLE PERFORMANCE IMPLICATIONS FOR LONG-TERM RETRIEVAL

- Learning efficiency and sustaining cumulative new learning (COG Test 2: Visual–Auditory Learning).
- Receptivity to novelty and/or correction feedback in an instructional activity (COG Test 2: Visual–Auditory Learning).
- Durability of retention of newly learned information over time (COG Test 10: Visual–Auditory Learning—Delayed). This may imply the need to consider the quantity of information to be learned at a given time, mastery criteria for newly learned information, study strategies, and mnemonic techniques.
- Comfort or anxiety for speeded tasks or those that require on-demand recall of information.
- Encoding and recall of knowledge and vocabulary.
- Learning and recalling phoneme/grapheme associations for basic reading and spelling skills.
- Learning and recalling math facts and procedures.
- Developing strategies for on-demand recall in note-taking and test-taking.
- Organizing and recalling information for oral and written expression.

VISUAL–SPATIAL THINKING

Visual–Spatial Thinking (*Gv*) is an ability required for the perception of nonlinguistic visual patterns, spatial configurations, visual details, and visual memory. When observing performance on tasks involving Visual–Spatial Thinking, it is important to rule out concerns or questions about the individual's visual acuity. Attention and concentration may also play a role in performance— particularly within the format of COG Test 13: Picture Recognition.

COG TEST 3: SPATIAL RELATIONS

The Spatial Relations test requires the visualization of spatial configurations. The individual is presented a series of shapes, some of which form a target shape (also shown). The individual is required to select the correct parts to make the whole. The items increase in difficulty as the designs become more complex.

Consider the test's task demands across items. Puzzles begin at preschool level. Puzzles are familiar, simple geometric forms (e.g., circles, rectangles) and there are distinctive differences between correct and incorrect response choices. Puzzles increase in difficulty in the following ways: (a) the shapes of the puzzle forms and pieces become more irregular and complex; (b) the puzzle constructions require more mental manipulation (i.e., rotations) of some of the pieces, and (c) the visual differences among the response choices become less obvious; the distinctions of size, shape, and overall form/configuration in the options become more subtle.

Observe the individual's response patterns. Note if the individual

- Displays relative efficiency or inefficiency in learning the task as noted within the sample items.
- Reveals a particular pattern of response time across items (i.e., slow and tentative even from the easiest items, or quick and accurate at the outset until the task progresses into the more difficult items).
- Demonstrates a careful and reflective work habit across items.
- Displays differentially better or poorer performance on some items over others (e.g., items that require perception or judgment of size or shape, difficulties with items requiring mental rotation, or gauging configuration or size while having to mentally rotate a piece).
- Exhibits ease or difficulty with the response format. Does the individual identify the pieces by letters or by pointing to the pieces because of uncertainty with letter identification?

POSSIBLE EDUCATIONAL IMPLICATIONS FOR SPATIAL RELATIONS

- If an individual above first-grade level needs to point to rather than name the letters of items, consider whether there is mastery of letter identification skills.
- Difficulties with negotiating visual-spatial materials such as maps, charts, graphs.
- Difficulties with the spatial demands of mathematics concepts and procedures, including place value, sequence and direction of steps in long division, translating the language of word concepts to visual/graphic numerical algorithms, and fractions and geometry.
- Difficulties with organization and sequencing.
- Difficulties with lateral comprehension (left/right confusion).
- Confusion with language concepts that are predicated on spatial ability, such as ordinals and degree of difference (farthest/closest, under/over, in front of/behind, etc.).
- Emotional discomfort with unanticipated changes in routines or daily activities.
- Difficulty, delay, or inflexibility in establishing a left-to-right work habit for reading and writing, in shifting to a right-to-left work habit for arithmetic.

COG TEST 13: PICTURE RECOGNITION

The Picture Recognition test requires the individual to identify one or more pictures in a field of distracting pictures. The individual is shown a set of objects for 5 seconds and is then shown another page with some of the stimulus items as well as distractors. The same type of object is used for both the stimuli and distractors (e.g., several types of hats) to minimize the ability to use verbal mediation as a recognition strategy.

Consider the test's task demands across items. At the early levels in this test the stimulus pages have only two or three pictures, with responses requiring the recognition of only one or two items. The items increase in difficulty with an increase in the number of stimulus items per page and in the number of distractors on the response page.

Observe the individual's response patterns. Note if the individual

- Shows erratic responses even from the easiest items.
- Shows consistent performance to the point of ceiling.
- Attempts to describe the pictures as a way of attempting to remember them better.
- Makes comments or displays behaviors that indicate enjoyment or frustration as the tasks increase in difficulty.
- Looks carefully over all the stimulus items for the entire allotted 5 seconds or gives only a cursory glance to the stimulus page and indicates readiness after only a second or two.

COG TEST 19: PLANNING

The Planning test is a complex thinking task that draws upon elements of both visual-spatial scanning and abstract fluid reasoning. It also can measure elements of executive processes relating to the ability to use mental control and forward thinking. This test can provide additional information about the individual's Visual-Spatial Thinking and Fluid Reasoning abilities but it does not contribute to either cluster score.

Consider the test's task demands across items. This test does not have a conventional basal/ceiling format; the individual is presented with blocks of items with visual designs. The individual is required to trace over each of the designs without lifting the pencil from the paper. The individual is taught that he or she is permitted to cross over/intersect a line that is already drawn but he or she is not permitted to retrace any lines that have already been drawn. The designs increase in difficulty within each block of items and across blocks of items, from relatively simple patterns to more intricate forms that require greater planning.

Variations in personal style are often noticeable in this test. The individual may be observed to make several tracing attempts with his or her finger before starting. He or she may study a design carefully before starting, or may begin straight off without any noticeable review or study of the design. The various stylistic approaches may or may not influence the individual's performance efficiency or reveal his or her strategy. For example, simply spending time carefully studying a design does not necessarily ensure good accuracy if the individual lacks the ability to scan and analyze the forms effectively. Similarly, a quick and unstudied approach may not result in poor performance or indicate inefficiency. Rather, the individual may be very automatic and proficient in the abilities that underlie this task, and may not require any observable study time in order to visualize and plan his or her responses.

Observe the individual's response patterns. Note if the individual

- Notices when his or her drawing plan is not going to complete the form correctly but goes as far as he or she can without retracing any lines.
- Does not appear to preplan his or her responses. Does he or she appear to start impulsively and work inefficiently?
- Needs reminders not to lift pencil.
- Appears to become frustrated with his or her inability to complete the form and/or resists examiner instructions to move on to next items.
- Makes comments or behaves in a way that may indicate his or her positive or negative inclination for the tasks.

POSSIBLE PERFORMANCE IMPLICATIONS FOR VISUAL–SPATIAL THINKING

- Consider the general inefficiency with memory-level processes (COG Test 13: Picture Recognition). Consider the individual's performance on COG Test 13: Picture Recognition relative to other measures of associative memory and short-term memory.
- General inefficiency with consistent attention and concentration. Consider performance relative to other tasks that require attention and concentration across tasks, materials, and settings.
- Awareness of and efficiency with negotiating visually based materials in curriculum and classroom environments, and for vocational materials and tasks.
- Functional awareness of one's visual environment for adaptive skill development.
- Visual recognition/memory for material in pictures, charts, etc.
- Designing, building, and other types of "hands-on" activities.
- Working with visual patterns in geometry, maps, and blueprints.
- General spatial awareness and orientation to one's physical environment—sensing physical boundaries, comfort with making physical transitions or negotiating unfamiliar spaces/places.

AUDITORY PROCESSING

Auditory Processing (*Ga*) is defined as a thinking ability relating to the perception and processing of auditory information. Included in this factor is the ability to analyze and synthesize sounds within words, and to discern spoken language in the presence of distortions or competing noise. Assessment of Auditory Processing requires the integrity of the individual's hearing acuity. It is necessary to either confirm or rule out whether problems exist or are suspected. General attention and concentration can also impact the efficiency and consistency for working with auditory presentations. Because all Auditory Processing tests are presented through an audio format, it is important to note whether the subject is able to adapt to the cueing system and taped presentation or whether he or she ignore the cueing prompts. Consider whether the individual becomes more physically restless (e.g., shifting around in chair) on auditory presentations.

COG TEST 4: SOUND BLENDING

The Sound Blending test requires the subject to listen to parts of a word (syllables and/or phonemes) that are presented orally and then integrate the parts and say the whole word.

Consider the task demands across items. Items begin with two-syllable words (e.g., flow-er) and simple onset-rime (k-at) and progress to more difficult phonemic breaks wherein words are a stream of individual sounds (e.g., f-oo-d, i-l-e-k-t-r-i-k).

Observe the individual's response patterns. Note if the individual

- Displays any difficulty in learning the nature of the task.
- Is accurate in his or her responses. Does the individual show consistent performance to the point of ceiling or does he or she display erratic response patterns? Does the individual begin to experience difficulty when items exceed two syllables or is he or she efficient all the way through to items that exceed four phonemic pieces?
- Substitutes nasals, vowels, or unvoiced consonants (e.g., says "neat" instead of "meat," says "collar" instead of "color").
- Needs to have the tape paused frequently, even for items that should be easily performed by the subject's age or grade.

COG TEST 14: AUDITORY ATTENTION

The Auditory Attention test measures the ability to discriminate speech sounds in the presence of competing noise. It requires the individual to detect differences among similar-sounding words as background noise increases. There is no cueing system of "beeps" in this test, and pausing the tape between items is not permitted. The individual is shown four pictures while listening to a tape that presents a word. The individual must point to the picture that goes with the word.

Consider the test's task demands across items. Sample Items 1 through 57 (presented to all examinees) permit the examiner to rule out lack of knowledge for the depicted words as a primary issue accounting for low performance. Two trials per item are provided (if necessary) to train the examinee in the knowledge of any pictures with which he or she is not familiar. In the norming sample this section of the task (i.e., training trials) was readily accomplished by individuals who were functioning within the preschool age range. Sample Items A, B, and C train the examinee to point to one picture per horizontal row. Beginning with Item 1 in the actual test, the examinee is shown four pictures in a horizontal row while listening to a tape that presents a word. The examinee must point to the picture that goes with the word. There is a bed of background noise underneath the voice that is presenting the stimulus word. The background noise is cafeteria noise, recorded backwards so that the subject does not pick up on any real words or conversations within the bed of background sound. The task becomes increasingly difficult in two ways: the level of background noise increases while the announcer's voice maintains a stable decibel level, and the differences in sound discriminations become more subtle.

Observe the individual's response patterns. Note if the individual

- Exhibits ease or difficulty with the training items.
- Shows a consistent pattern of correct responses until the point of a ceiling, or if he or she displays a more an erratic response pattern across test items.
- Shows difficulties with some types of speech sound versus others (e.g., difficulty in perceiving nasals or unvoiced consonants).
- Demonstrates a negative reaction to the task or the taped presentation.
- Is nonresponsive or unable to respond in the allotted time.

COG TEST 8: INCOMPLETE WORDS

The Incomplete Words test is a supplemental test of auditory processing. It consists of a taped presentation during which portions of a word are presented. The individual must demonstrate recognition of the word by responding with the complete word (auditory closure).

Consider the test's task demands across items. Words are presented only once from the taped presentation. The items begin with simple words with only one sound missing. Word knowledge for low-level items is likely to be within the repertoire of receptive vocabulary and experience for preschool examinees (e.g., "koo_e" for "cookie"). Stimulus words gradually increase in difficulty to multisyllable words with more two to four phonemic omissions.

Observe the individual's response patterns. Note if the individual

- Initially "jumps the gun" on the easier items, but self-adjusts his or her behavior to the cueing system as items increase in difficulty.
- Shows consistency or inconsistency in his or her response accuracy across items.
- Shows automaticity in his or her responses.
- Needs to have the tape paused frequently.
- Shows difficulty with perceiving/analyzing the number of missing sounds and/or the position of missing sounds.

- Responds with words that are not real words (e.g., says "paracoo" for "parachute") and/or simply repeats the fragments that were presented.

ACH TEST 21: SOUND AWARENESS

The Sound Awareness test consists of four subtests of phonological awareness: Rhyming, Deletion, Substitution, and Reversal. Consider each subtest task demands across items. Rhyming progresses in difficulty from receptive demonstration of rhyming awareness (pointing to pictures), to expressive demonstration of rhyming awareness with simple rhyme phrases and then the rhyming of single words. Deletion requires the examinee to listen to a word, mentally delete a specified portion of the word (syllable or sound), and then recode and pronounce the new word (e.g., say "make" without the "/m/" sound). Subtest items progress from easy to more difficult by beginning with compound words and progressing to syllables, initial sounds, ending sounds, and then phonemic segments for blends. Substitution requires the examinee to listen to a word, mentally substitute a specified portion of the word, and then recode and pronounce the final word. Test items increase in difficulty from compound words to single phonemic substitutions. On the Reversal subtest, the individual listens to a word and then mentally reverses the sounds and pronounces the new word. Test items increase in difficulty from compound words to single words.

Observe the individual's response patterns. Note if the individual

- Has difficulty learning the nature of the tasks.
- Performs all four tasks in a relatively even manner, or if he or she is differentially stronger on some types of tasks versus others. It is developmentally appropriate for younger children (i.e., under 7 years of age) to show qualitatively stronger performance on Rhyming than on Deletion, Substitution, and Reversal.
- Is consistent across all four subtests. Does the individual appear to have greater difficulties with tasks that involve more sophisticated mental manipulation (e.g., sound reversal)?
- Has any limitations in working memory that may be playing a role in this test.

POSSIBLE PERFORMANCE IMPLICATIONS FOR AUDITORY PROCESSING

- General perceptual efficiency in auditory processing and competence in general language development and listening comprehension (particularly for the COG Test 14: Auditory Attention).
- Phonemic Awareness: understanding the sound structure of spoken words in order to learn how speech maps to print for decoding and spelling.
- Consider whether the individual's phonemic awareness is being undercut by difficulties with Short-Term Memory and Working Memory.

- Learning foreign languages and musical ability.
- Ability to sustain concentration with minimal visual cues.
- Needing to pause the tape frequently may suggest processing speed concerns for auditory information.

FLUID REASONING

Fluid Reasoning (*Gf*) is a thinking ability for reasoning, forming concepts, and solving problems that include unfamiliar information or novel situations. A number of general observations can be made across both tests within this factor. The subject may show difficulty or ease with the controlled-learning formats of these tests. Such formats present a structured teaching/learning procedure with instructional feedback provided for both correct and incorrect responses. These tests also both require a considerable investment of sustained concentration for cumulative learning and receptivity to novel/unfamiliar tasks at an abstract level.

COG TEST 5: CONCEPT FORMATION

Concept Formation requires the individual to learn and apply concepts by determining (inferring) the "rules" for solving visual puzzles that are presented in increasing levels of difficulty.

Consider the test's task demands across items. For Preschool Level Items 1 through 3, the examinee is being tested on his or her receptive understanding of the concept of same/different. The individual simply has to point to a shape that is different. For Preschool Level Items 4 through 5, the examinee must demonstrate receptive understanding of same/different with a slight increase in concept difficulty. On these items, the individual has to identify a shape that is "most different." On Sample Item C through Item 11, the examinee needs to demonstrate (expressively) what constitutes the key difference or the "rule" for puzzle solutions. The rule statements involve a one-to-one comparison for these items. On Sample Item F through Item 20, the examinee is asked to consider sets of drawings. The "rule" statements now require the individual to identify common differences among a set of items. For Sample H through Item 23, the items require the understanding of the concept of "and" as it infers partial inclusion among a set of attributes (i.e., solutions have to have some of this, and some of that). Sample I through Item 29 require the examinee to demonstrate an understanding of the concept of "or" as an exclusionary concept (i.e., in order for the puzzle rule to be "this or that" implies that neither of those features exist outside the boxes). Items 30 through 40 require fluid transformations and cognitive shifting between all the different types of concept puzzles that the individual has worked with previously.

Observe the individual's response patterns. Note if the individual

- Readily responds correctly to sample items and performs consistently from the outset, requiring little or no correction. The individual makes smooth transitions through the various sample item junctions and makes conceptual shifts easily.

- Shows the need for some corrective feedback at times, but is able to utilize the instruction and feedback effectively to learn the tasks and improve performance.
- Appears confused and uncertain about the nature of the puzzles from the beginning and/or shows only limited ability to benefit from correction and instruction.
- Never progresses effectively beyond the one-to-one comparisons (i.e., beyond Item 11). It is developmentally appropriate for young elementary school children (7 years or younger) to *not* progress beyond Item 20.
- Confuses the "and/or" statements in the final section of mixed items (i.e., Items 30 through 40).
- Shows by comments or behaviors that he or she has reached a frustration ceiling even before his or her performance indicates a cut-off or discontinuation.
- Seems confused, distracted, or overwhelmed by multiple puzzles on a page—the examiner needs to uncover only one puzzle at a time in order for the examinee to work effectively.

COG TEST 15: ANALYSIS–SYNTHESIS

The Analysis–Synthesis test requires the individual to learn and orally state the solutions to incomplete logic puzzles that mimic a miniature mathematics system. The puzzles progress from simple to more complex abstract reasoning and logic requirements.

Consider the test's task demands across items. The individual is presented with the "key"—a set of logic rules that is used to solve picture puzzles. The rules are equation statements that are constructed of colored squares. The key is always at the top of each puzzle page and is available for the subject to use throughout the test. The examinee is taught to use the key to determine the missing colors within each of the puzzles. Puzzles begin at a very simple level with only one missing color (blank square). The spatial position of the blank square changes, requiring the subject to shift his or her strategy. At Item 8, more colors are added to the key but the level of difficulty of the puzzles does not increase. At Sample Item C, the puzzles increase in difficulty. The examinee is presented with puzzles that require two or more sequential mental manipulations of the key in order to derive a final solution. Items 26 and above involve a more complex mixture of puzzles that require fluid shifts in deduction, logic, and inference. The individual is provided with positive feedback for correct answers, and correction feedback for wrong answers up until Item 28. No positive or corrective feedback is provided from Item 29 through the end of the test at Item 35.

Observe the individual's response patterns. It is sometimes helpful (when the testing is completed) to ask an individual if he or she is able to reveal some of the "silent" strategies he or she may have used. During testing, note if the individual

- Exhibits ease or difficulty in learning and using the key.
- Demonstrates an audible verbal strategy (e.g., murmurs or talks through the puzzles while working).
- Uses a finger on the easel page to physically hold or hang onto the middle steps in the sequential puzzles above Sample C. (Consider whether this is simply a stylistic tendency or whether it may indicate a sensitivity to the mental manipulation requirement of the more complex puzzles.)
- Exhibits ease or difficulty in working effectively with higher levels of sequential problem solving.

POSSIBLE PERFORMANCE IMPLICATIONS FOR FLUID REASONING

- Performance in quantitative concepts, procedural mathematics, and mathematics reasoning.
- Comprehension of conceptual language and listening comprehension (e.g., understanding word relationships, syntax, and word order as it affects meaning).
- Reading comprehension: inferential meaning, generalizations from specifics, reading between the lines, author's intent/voice, etc.
- Cognitive-level basic reading skills (e.g., understanding root words, prefixes, suffixes).
- Written expression: organizing and connecting ideas and concepts, choice and variety of vocabulary, construction of complex sentences and paragraphs.
- Comprehension of abstract material in content area subjects.
- Solving abstract problems.
- Receptivity to novelty.
- The ability to transfer and generalize information, learning, and strategies.
- The ability to work with cognitive flexibility in abstract tasks.

PROCESSING SPEED

Processing Speed (*Gs*) is the ability to maintain speed and accuracy on activities requiring sustained attention for a period of time. It is also described as the fluency and speed with which one can "cycle" or integrate all types of information. This is an area that is related to cognitive fluency and is considered to be an important automatic process for cognitive efficiency and academic fluency. All Processing Speed tests require sustained attention, concentration, and effort for specific spans of time. Because speeded processing tests require the scanning of visual stimuli, it is important to consider the integrity of the individual's visual acuity as it affects his or her performance. Both measures of Processing Speed have untimed practice items to ensure that the subject understands the tasks.

COG TEST 6: VISUAL MATCHING

The Visual Matching test has two different levels/versions. Version 1 is designed for individuals whose age or ability is estimated to be at the preschool level. Version 2 is designed for individuals whose ability level is estimated to be school-age or above. The task demands for this test vary between versions. Version 1 of the test is done within the test easel. The child is required to point to two matching shapes in a row of four or five shapes. This version has a 2-minute time limit. Version 2 requires the subject to circle two identical numbers from a horizontal row of six numbers. The test progresses in difficulty only slightly, from rows with single digits to rows with double- and triple-digit numbers. This version lasts for 3 minutes.

Observe the individual's response patterns. Note if the individual

- Exhibits ease or difficulty in learning the task through the untimed samples.
- Works slowly but with accuracy.
- Appears to sacrifice accuracy in favor of speed.
- Appears overwhelmed or distracted by the amount of visual-graphic information on the page (e.g., tries to cover up items with uninvolved hand).
- On Version 2, initially learns the task but then loses track of the task demands after timing starts. This may mean the individual begins to track vertically instead of horizontally (as he or she had practiced) or the individual may circle identical numbers within different rows, rather than scanning and finding two numbers that are alike in the same row (as he or she had practiced).
- On Version 2, erases incorrect answers rather than crossing out as instructions had indicated.
- Comments or behaves in a way that indicates stress in working under timed constraints.
- Shows perfectionistic behaviors (e.g., checking over each row before moving on to the next) that may reduce rate of work.

COG TEST 16: DECISION SPEED

The Decision Speed test measures the ability to make simple decisions quickly. It is a measure of cognitive efficiency that requires the examinee to locate two pictures in a row that are most conceptually similar. This test has a 3-minute time limit. The task demands across items are the same. The examinee needs to find two pictures out of a row of seven, identifying objects that are categorically similar or have a functional relationship or semantic association (e.g., two cats, but not identical cats; two pieces of furniture; pen and paper).

Observe the individual's response pattern. Note if the individual

- Exhibits ease or difficulty in learning the task through the untimed samples.
- Demonstrates automaticity for identifying the most salient associations among the target pictures.
- Often focuses on less relevant relationships between the stimulus pictures.
- Works with consistent accuracy or skips over items.

COG TEST 20: PAIR CANCELLATION

The Pair Cancellation test is a complex measure. It involves the ability to use one's cognitive speed, sustained attention, and elements of executive processes proactively for interference control.

Consider the task demands of this test. The examinee needs to scan a page of items heavily laden with little pictures (soccer balls, dogs, tea cups) and is required to locate and mark a repeating pattern (ball followed by a dog) in rows of pictures that are purposely designed to be visually "busy." This test has a 3 minute time limit.

Observe the individual's response patterns. After the testing is completed, it may be helpful to query the individual about any strategy that he or she may have used. Because this is an independent nonverbal test, the individual's strategy may not be readily apparent to the examiner. Consider whether the examinee's response style is fast and accurate, slow and accurate, fast but inaccurate, or slow and inaccurate. Note if the individual

- Uses verbal mediation to focus on the repeating pattern.
- Focuses on either the soccer ball or the dog and then looks to see if the other picture is to the right or left, respectively.
- Scans fluently left-to-right, and then back again on the next row.
- Is undaunted by the timed feature and the sustained concentration that is required.

POSSIBLE PERFORMANCE IMPLICATIONS FOR PROCESSING SPEED

- Perceptual fluency and accuracy even under untimed conditions.
- Rapid processing and recall of information.
- Automaticity for reading decoding, rapid single-word reading, and text fluency.
- Integration of subskills for written expression, spelling, and handwriting.
- Fluency in mathematics operations.
- General automaticity in all academic subject areas.
- Ability to function under explicit or implicit timed constraints.
- Work speed and production rate in occupational settings.

SHORT-TERM MEMORY

Short-Term Memory (*Gsm*) involves the ability to retain information and use that information within a very short period of time. This skill is considered to be an important automatic process necessary for general cognitive efficiency. Considerations of attention and concentration are important. These tests are presented through an audio tape, so observations regarding the examinee's response to the cueing system and/or the need to pause the tape are important.

COG TEST 7: NUMBERS REVERSED

The Numbers Reversed test requires the examinee to hold a series of random numbers in immediate memory, reverse the sequence, and then repeat the numbers in the reversed order. Item difficulty increases as more numbers are added to the sequences.

Consider the test's task demands across items. Items are grouped by the quantity of numerals in a series (i.e., Items 1 through 5 all contain two-digit sequences; Items 6 through 10 all contain three-digit sequences). The difficulty level of the items increases from group to group.

Observe the individual's response patterns. After the testing is completed, it may be helpful to query the individual about any strategy that he or she may have used. The individual's strategy may not be readily apparent to the examiner. During testing, note if the individual

- Exhibits ease or difficulty in learning or sustaining his or her understanding of the task as evidenced by performance within sample items.
- Exhibits ease or difficulty in his or her ability to hold and reverse sequences (e.g., responds correctly without hesitation, appears to work with greater deliberateness or effort across items that should be developmentally appropriate for age/grade).
- Articulates or appears to demonstrate strategies in response to increase in difficulty, such as rehearsing forward several times before presenting reversed sequence, "chunking" or grouping items within series, visualizing numbers and presenting the series back as a single whole number (e.g., takes the forward presentation of "6-3-7" and verbalizes it back as "seven hundred thirty-six").
- Shows consistency and accuracy across items to the point of ceiling.
- Reorders sequence but hangs onto all the numbers.
- Omits some of the numbers.
- Seems unable to devise or maintain a strategy as items become more difficult.
- Becomes more restless or inattentive with increase in difficulty of items.

COG TEST 17: MEMORY FOR WORDS

The Memory for Words test requires the individual to orally repeat lists of unrelated words in the correct sequence.

Consider the test's task demands across items. As the number of words in a list increases, so does the level of difficulty. Items are grouped by number of words in the series (e.g., Items 10 through 12 are items with a three-word series, Items 13 through 15 are four-word series). Difficulty increases across groups, rather than within groups.

Observe the individual's response patterns. Note if the individual

- Responds with a phonetically similar or rhyming word in the proper sequence. The item is scored as correct but the behavior may be noteworthy relative to auditory processing (discrimination, phonemic confusion).
- Reorders words or omits words within the sequence.
- Becomes more restless or inattentive as difficulty level increases.

COG TEST 9: AUDITORY WORKING MEMORY

Auditory Working Memory is a test of working memory and divided attention. The examinee is required to listen to a mixed series of numbers and objects (e.g., dog, 1, shoe, 8,) and then repeat the objects in the correct order, followed by the numbers in the correct order (e.g., dog, shoe, 1, 8). The test starts off with one number and one object and progresses in difficulty to more objects and numbers. Consider task demands across items, such as the need to mentally "divide and conquer"—sorting mixed information into two different mental categories before verbally presenting information within each category in the proper order. The task essentially requires that the examinee hold information in short-term memory, divide the information into two groups, and then shift attentional resources to the two new groups in order to present the new sequences.

Observe the individual's response patterns. After the testing is completed, it may be helpful to query the individual about any strategy that he or she may have used. The individual's strategy may not be readily apparent to the examiner. During testing, note if the individual

- Exhibits ease or difficulty in learning the nature of the task (as evidenced in the sample items) and/or demonstrates consistency/accuracy or inconsistency in responses to the point of the ceiling.
- Tends to sacrifice one category over another (e.g., seems to remember the objects but not the numbers or vice versa) or shows a tendency to reorder information within a category.

POSSIBLE PERFORMANCE IMPLICATIONS OF
SHORT-TERM MEMORY

- Integrity in all cognitive and academic tasks.
- Listening Comprehension and organized Oral Expression (consider performance on the Listening Comprehension tests of ACH Test 4: Understanding Directions and ACH Test 15: Oral Comprehension, and the Oral Expression test of ACH Test 3: Story Recall). Following directions in a classroom or occupational setting.
- General efficiency for encoding, processing, and recall of information.

- Phonemic Awareness: consider whether working memory impairs the individual's ability to respond to more manipulative phonemic awareness activities such as deletion, multisyllabic blending, or identifying positions of sounds in words. Consider performance on several subtests of ACH Test 21: Sound Awareness, specifically the subtests of Sound Deletion, Sound Substitution, and Sound Reversal.
- Development of basic reading and spelling skills.
- Information and language sequencing within Reading Comprehension tasks.
- Organization and sequencing in Written Expression for construction of sentences, paragraphs, and composition.
- Note-taking skills and information processing in extended lecture formats.
- Sequential mathematics calculations and organizing and solving math word problems.

READING

Interpretation of the individual's performance on tests of reading should always include consideration for a variety of factors. Dynamics that are intrinsic to the individual (i.e., cognitive processes) and external conditions (i.e., methods of instruction) interact uniquely for different individuals. The following elements related to the development of basic skills and reading fluency should be considered:

- Performance on the cognitive tests/clusters of Phonemic Awareness (specifically COG Test 4: Sound Blending), Short-Term Memory and Working Memory (specifically COG Test 7: Numbers Reversed), Processing Speed (specifically COG Test 6: Visual Matching) and Cognitive Fluency (specifically COG Test 18: Rapid Picture Naming and COG Test 12: Retrieval Fluency), Long-Term Retrieval (specifically COG Test 2: Visual–Auditory Learning), and Comprehension–Knowledge (specifically COG Test 1: Verbal Comprehension).
- Curriculum and instructional orientation (i.e., explicit code-emphasis/ phonics, literature-based instruction).
- Instructional history and consistency (i.e., frequent changes of schools in early elementary school).
- The quality and consistency of the individual's attention and concentration, emotional/behavioral status, and general health integrity. These factors are implied facilitators to all learning efficiency in that they speak to the individual's "availability" to instruction.

The following elements related to the development of reading comprehension skills should be considered:

- Automaticity and fluency in basic reading skills.

- Performance on the cognitive clusters/tests of Comprehension–Knowledge, Fluid Reasoning (specifically Concept Formation), Short-Term Memory, and Processing Speed (specifically COG Test 6: Visual Matching).
- General proficiency in oral language comprehension and verbal reasoning.
- Curriculum emphasis and instructional history.
- Motivation and interest in pleasure reading outside of school-assigned material.

Interpretation of the WJ III reading tests and clusters can be further informed through criterion-referenced or curriculum-based assessments and the utilization of diagnostic teaching reports. It may also be important or helpful to consider the individual's performance on other formal or informal measures of reading rate and accuracy for single words and more extended amounts of text.

ACH TEST 1: LETTER–WORD IDENTIFICATION

The Letter–Word Identification test requires the examinee to orally identify letters and words presented in lists. The examinee may not have had prior experience with the items presented. The task items involve both identification and recognition.

Consider the test's task demands across items. Items 1 through 15 involve print awareness for letters, receptive knowledge of upper and lower case letters, print awareness for words, and verbal identification of upper and lower case letters. Items 16 through 76 require the reading of single words. Each page contains a single vertical list with eight words per page. The individual is required to respond with a fluent pronunciation of the words.

Observe the individual's response patterns. Note if the individual

- Displays ease or difficulty in obtaining basals and ceilings.
- Reads words accurately and effortlessly with a second or less response time per item until the point of ceiling.
- Is able to apply efficient decoding strategies to identify words that are not readily recognized.
- Responds in a way that suggests that he or she is unable to employ systematic decoding strategies (e.g., looks only at the first letter and then guesses, or declines to attempt decoding).
- Responds in a way that suggests perceptual/orthographic inaccuracies (i.e., responds with a word that has a similar visual configuration: while/ whale, become/because, etc.)
- Omits or inserts syllables, sounds, endings (e.g., unusual/usually, sufficiently/sufficient).
- Appears to demonstrate a slow rate of word reading, frequently requiring maximum response time per item.

ACH TEST 13: WORD ATTACK

The Word Attack test requires the examinee to orally read nonsense words. The ability to apply phonetic and structural analysis skills to both linguistically regular and irregular letter combinations is required.

Consider the task demands across items. Item 1 requires receptive knowledge of letter sound. Items 2 and 3 require expressive knowledge of letter sounds. Sample Item A through Item 32 require expressive responses that indicate decoding and fluent pronunciation for pseudowords with both regular and irregular phonetic and orthographic patterns.

Observe the individual's response patterns. Note if the individual

- Shows efficiency and consistency in his or her responses across items to the point of ceiling.
- Demonstrates limited overall mastery of letter-sound (phoneme/grapheme) knowledge.
- Exhibits erratic or inconsistent patterns of phoneme/grapheme knowledge related to curriculum.
- Has a tendency to reorder, omit, or insert sounds when decoding words.
- Displays accurate but slow decoding.

ACH TEST 2: READING FLUENCY

The Reading Fluency measures the ability to silently read simple sentences and decide if the statement is true or false. It has a 3-minute time limit. Because this test measures reading speed, it may not be appropriate below age six because children younger than age 6 or 7 are typically not expected to have developed enough reading to demonstrate coordinated independent reading skills.

Consider the task demands of the test. The test begins with untimed models and practice items. The individual reads simple sentences and is required to circle "Y" if the statement is true and "N" if the statement is not true. The meaning of each of the statements is very concrete and straightforward. The statements are not intended to challenge reading comprehension (e.g., "A bus has wings." "A door may have a lock."). The readability and vocabulary levels and the decoding demands do not increase incrementally across raw score items.

Observe the individual's response patterns. Note if the individual

- Is quick and accurate. Is the individual's response time and accuracy within or ahead of expectations for age and/or grade?
- Works slowly but accurately. Does the individual accomplish fewer items than is typical for age or grade, but works without errors?
- Is fast but inaccurate. Does the individual try to work quickly but still makes mistakes?
- Exhibits inconsistency. Does the individual skip several items as he or she is doing the task? (Although these items are not counted as errors, skipping

behavior results in a raw score that is based upon fewer items. Skipping behavior may be related to inconsistencies in decoding accuracy and/or general inefficiency in text fluency.)
- Appears relaxed/undaunted or nervous/uncomfortable under timed pressure.
- Is unable to learn the task in the practice items or sustain his or her performance for the span of 3 minutes.
- Becomes distracted by elements within the statements or by sentence content. The individual may also show puzzlement about whether the intended meaning of the sentence could be both true and false. This may prompt the individual to digress or focus on irrelevant features of sentence meaning.
- Makes concrete, personal associations to specific statements rather than interpreting the broader and more basic sense of the meaning. For example, a child whose only association to milk is through his or her own personal experience of drinking milk with strawberry flavoring, may answer "Y" to the statement "The color of milk is pink." Even though the statement may be "true" for that child, the answer is not scored as correct. Response patterns such as those may be more clinically important if the child's age/grade suggests the expectation of broader knowledge and awareness.

POSSIBLE PERFORMANCE IMPLICATIONS FOR BASIC READING SKILLS AND READING FLUENCY

- Response patterns that indicate limited or inconsistent development of skills suggests the need to more discretely examine the incremental skills that the individual may or may not have mastered. Limitations in the individual's automaticity and mastery for phoneme/grapheme knowledge, and/or faulty word analysis strategies should also prompt the examiner to consider:
    The individual's instructional history.
    The individual's cognitive profile of strengths and weaknesses in the constituent processes related to the development of basic reading skills (e.g., phonemic awareness, working memory, associative memory, cognitive speed and rapid naming, lexical knowledge).
    The individual's need for explicit code-based instruction in phonics skills (synthetic and analytic).
- Limitations in Basic Reading Skills can result in compromised efficiency in reading comprehension within more extended reading assignments and activities.
- Efficiency or inefficiency in Basic Reading Skills can influence general functional literacy in all academic areas and in life-skills-based reading.

ACH TEST 9: PASSAGE COMPREHENSION

The Passage Comprehension test requires the subject to silently read short passages and then provide an appropriate response for a word that is missing from the passage. This test is a cloze procedure that requires a variety of comprehension and vocabulary skills. By design this test measures whether the subject understands what he or she is reading *while* reading. The quantity of reading is intentionally abridged (as compared with school-type reading assignments) to reduce the impact of decoding and fluency on the measurement of reading comprehension.

Consider the test's task demands across items. Items 1 through 4 measure receptive understanding of representational learning (i.e., the idea that symbols can represent objects). Examinees must point to a rebus symbol that represents a depicted object. Items 5 through 10 measure reading comprehension for simple phrases. Examinees must read two- or three-word phrases and point to a picture that exemplifies the meaning of the phrase. Sample Item B through Item 47 require the individual to read items in which a word is missing in one of the sentences. The subject must verbalize a single word that effectively fills in the blank. Items 11 through 18 involve the reading of only a single sentence. Some of these items include picture cues, and/or the cloze format is at a concrete level (i.e., the missing word is the last word in the sentence). A few of these items do not have picture cues and/or the cloze format is slightly more difficult (i.e., the missing word is in the middle of the sentence). Items 19 through 47 contain two or three sentences. The missing word is situated in various positions, requiring more sophisticated comprehension and cloze ability. Trying to determine the missing word by using simple prediction through context is not likely to be successful. Accurate comprehension of these items presumes more sophisticated comprehension of syntax, concepts, and vocabulary.

Observe the individual's response patterns. It may not always be possible to observe strategies or behaviors if the individual is reading silently. It may be helpful to talk with the individual about his or her strategies after the testing is completed. During testing, note if the individual

- Exhibits ease or difficulty in establishing a basal and ceiling.
- Displays relative efficiency for the general response time per item. Is it often necessary to encourage the subject to respond or move on?
- Uses a silent reading system or reads aloud or murmurs while reading.
- Is quick to say "I don't know" or to decline to attempt an item because of difficulties with the decoding of words. (This may not be readily apparent if the student is reading silently. It may be necessary for the examiner to track response patterns through extension testing and/or informal assessment.)
- Responds with a term that is correct in terms of the part of speech, but inappropriate to the content of the passage.
- Has the ability to upgrade his or her responses when queried (as indicated by test easels).

ACH TEST 17: READING VOCABULARY

The Reading Vocabulary test consists of three subtests: Synonyms, Antonyms, and Analogies. On the Synonyms and Antonyms subtests, the individual reads stimulus words aloud and provides words having the same meaning (Synonyms) or opposite meaning (Antonyms). The Analogies subtest requires the individual to silently read three words of an analogy and then provide a fourth word to complete the analogy.

Consider the test's task demands across items. Items begin at easy, concrete levels. Difficulty increases incrementally across items on all three subtests. The individual needs to be able to make conceptual shifts from one subtest to another. Analogies also require the individual to make conceptual shifts across items as he or she determines salient relationships among words and concepts.

Observe the individual's response patterns. Note if the individual

- Exhibits ease or difficulty in learning the nature of the task. Is it difficult for the individual to understand the activity despite the sample items?
- Reads the stimulus word incorrectly but attempts to provide an appropriate Synonym or Antonym to the misread word (e.g., reading "small" as "smell" and stating "sniff" as the response).
- Reads the stimulus word correctly but is unable to demonstrate appropriate comprehension or vocabulary knowledge for the item (e.g., reading "ill" correctly but responds with "spill" or other rhyming word rather than a synonym).
- Shows generally efficient performance in both the reading and the content of his or her responses.

POSSIBLE PERFORMANCE IMPLICATIONS FOR READING COMPREHENSION

- Consider response patterns that indicate limited or inconsistent development of comprehension skills. It may be important to conduct a more in-depth assessment of incremental comprehension skills that are developmentally appropriate for a student's age/grade.
- Consider the individual's performance on the cognitive processes related to reading comprehension. Specific attention should be given to measures of Verbal Comprehension and Comprehension–Knowledge, general oral language ability, abstract Fluid Reasoning (specifically Concept Formation), measures of Processing Speed, and measures of Short-Term Memory and Working Memory.
- Consider the influence that limited basic reading skills may exert on the consistency of comprehension in more extended amounts of reading (i.e., lengthier school assignments or other materials that the student needs to read on a daily basis).
- Reading Comprehension is implicated in all academic applications and content subjects. Consider the need to address comprehension difficulties through enhanced instruction for specific comprehension strategies, modification of reading assignments for quantity or level, pretraining of key vocabulary, and/or use of assistive technology (i.e., books on tape, computer programs).

WRITTEN LANGUAGE

When reviewing the individual's test performance in written language skills, it is important to consider the individual's general level of competence with a variety of foundational skills. When embarking upon the qualitative and quantitative interpretation of written expression, an examiner needs to understand the proficiency or limitations that the individual experiences in his or her oral language and Comprehension–Knowledge abilities (listening comprehension, vocabulary development, expressive organization, general information). It is also important to consider the individual's writing skills in conjunction with an understanding of other cognitive strengths and weaknesses that he or she may demonstrate. Cognitive processes such as short-term memory and working memory, long-term retrieval, phonological processing (auditory processing), and processing speed can all influence one's proficiency in various elements of written language development. Attentional stamina and fine-motor skills should also be considered. Aside from the cognitive foundational skills, the individual's overall competence and automaticity with reading skills and his or her instructional experiences are also important factors that inform the interpretation of writing test performance.

ACH TEST 8: WRITING FLUENCY

The Writing Fluency test requires the individual to formulate and write simple sentences quickly. Each sentence must use a set of three stimulus words. On this test there is generally no penalty for responses that contain basic writing skills errors.

Consider the test's task demands across items. Sample items are presented untimed—if the individual is unable to perform on the sample items, the test is assigned a raw score of zero. Each item has a set of three stimulus words next to a picture. The individual must use the three stimulus words (along with any other that he or she needs) to construct a sentence that tells about the picture. The individual is not permitted to change the stimulus words in any way. This test has a 7-minute time limit or a 2-minute discontinuation rule for individuals who complete three or fewer items correctly within the first 2 minutes of the test. Readability level of the stimulus words remains low throughout all the items. Basic skills or handwriting are not considered in the scoring of an item unless it renders an item to be illegible.

Observe the individual's response patterns. Note if the individual

- Exhibits ease or difficulty in learning the task within the sample items.
- Is able to work with sustained effort for the full 7 minutes.
- Writes well-constructed sentences or sentences that are poorly organized or incomplete.
- Demonstrates good quality of spelling accuracy and handwriting legibility for age/grade (even though they are not counted in the scoring of items).

- Shows behaviors suggesting significant fine-motor fatigue (pausing to rub wrist or hand, shaking out hand).
- Works slowly but consistently and accurately across the span of the test.
- Needs to skip items. This may suggest inconsistency in the organizational fluency for formulating and producing writing.
- Writes phrases rather than sentences despite having been trained during the sample items.

ACH TEST 11: WRITING SAMPLES

The Writing Samples test measures the individual's ability to write responses to a variety of writing demands (prompts). Responses are evaluated with respect to the quality and clarity of expressive communication. In general, responses are not penalized with respect to basic skills errors (i.e., spelling, punctuation, handwriting) unless these issues render a response illegible.

Consider the test's task demands across items. Items begin at level appropriate for early first grade (writing of name and single-word and two-word descriptions of pictures for phonetically regular, high-frequency words). Items progress in difficulty across the test. Item prompts are intended to elicit constructions such as writing simple concrete descriptive sentences, connecting ideas to form simple to more complex paragraphs, embedding clauses, or writing compare/contrast sentences, cause/effect statements, and topic sentences.

Observe the individual's response patterns. Note if the individual

- Views writing activities favorably and is cooperative and well invested across items.
- Balks at the requirement to produce even minimal amounts of writing.
- Is careful and reflective in response style, but not overly slow in rate of response.
- Produces very sparse content—only the bare minimum needed to respond to the task requirements.
- Is able to respond to a variety of prompts, making good shifts with change in item demands.
- Misconstrues or misinterprets the conceptual requirements of task demands (e.g., writes "The bird is pretty" when asked to write a sentence that tells what the bird is doing).
- Spontaneously embellishes items or attempts to bring creativity and imagination to item demands.
- Is unable to respond to a block of items typically appropriate for his or her age/grade (e.g., examiner needs to give a very low-level block of items to a high school student).
- Misinterprets a picture (use guidelines in WJ III Examiner's Manuals for determining how to score such items).
- Shows diminished quality in penmanship across the block of administered items.

POSSIBLE PERFORMANCE IMPLICATIONS FOR
WRITTEN EXPRESSION

- It is important for the examiner to integrate all formal test scores and qualitative observations of the individual's writing skills both within test conditions, and in the context of more extended academic formats. Consider the individual's ability to generalize, transfer, and sustain his or her skills for lengthier writing demands in general daily educational settings.
- Teach organizational writing skills sequentially and systematically— progressing from concrete/descriptive levels to abstract/imaginative. Provide direct instruction in the construction of various types of paragraphing forms and syntax.
- Consider the amount of writing that the student is required to demonstrate in specific classes and determine whether it is necessary to provide accommodations and/or modifications for his or her work.
- Consider if the student is positively inclined toward writing tasks and is efficient and creative for various types of writing demands. Provide embellished instruction for talented writers.
- For students with significant limitations in writing skills, consider alternative methods of assessing the student's knowledge of content until his or her writing skills become more proficient.
- Provide explicit instruction and practice in proofing, editing, outlining, and note-taking.
- Assist subjects with organizational writing problems by providing outlines and/or graphic organizers.
- For individuals who show sparse content and/or limited motivation for writing, consider his or her performance on measures of knowledge and vocabulary, and his or her personal interests. Whenever possible, enhance knowledge, vocabulary, and positive affect through activities that orient to an individual's own interests.

ACH TEST 7: SPELLING

The Spelling test measures the ability to correctly spell orally presented words. Lower level items begin at a prewriting level (drawing, tracing, and writing of single letters) and items progress in difficulty across the span of the test. The individual is required to spell words with both regular and irregular patterns.

Consider the test's task demands across items. Items are presented in a direct, dictation-style spelling test format. Items 1 through 4 involve prewriting with demonstration/modeling. Items 5 and 6 involve tracing with demonstration/ modeling. Items 7 through 13 require copying and printing letters. Items 14 through 59 require spelling words.

Observe the individual's response patterns. Note if the individual

- Exhibits ease or difficulty in establishing a basal and ceiling.

- Is consistent and accurate to the point of ceiling, or if his or her performance is erratic and inaccurate across items.
- Displays accurate spelling. Is the individual confused with copying and independently producing letter formations? Is he or she aware of the sound structures in phonetically regular words (e.g., "rlee" for "early"; "tabul" for "table")? Does he or she have an awareness of a word and an ability to represent words with irregular structures (e.g., shows knowledge of "ough" in "cough" or can spell words such as "saucer," choosing the proper structures to represent sounds within each syllable)? Does he or she display the tendency to reorder sounds or orthographic structures within words?
- Is ultimately accurate, but requires a long response time per item, making multiple attempts and erasures for each item before finally arriving at the correct spelling.
- Demonstrates consistency with other indicators of spelling competence across materials and settings. Utilize error analysis and daily work samples to determine the stage of the individual's spelling development (i.e., prephonetic, semiphonetic, phonetic, transitional, or correct).

ACH TEST 16: EDITING

The Editing test measures the ability to identify and correct errors within a written passage. Errors may involve spelling, punctuation, capitalization, or word usage.

Consider the test's task demands across items. The individual is required to read sentences with mistakes and identify and correct the errors in order to receive credit for an item. Each item generally contains two sentences but with only one error present. The subject must both identify the mistake within typewritten sentences and indicate how it should be corrected. The examiner is permitted to provide help with reading an occasional word, but is not permitted to read the sentences to the student.

Observe the individual's response patterns. Note if the individual

- Exhibits ease or difficulty in establishing a basal and ceiling.
- Is unable to read items with sufficient accuracy to support this type of skill.
- Shows limited knowledge of conventions of grammar and basic skills despite what appears to be adequate reading skill (e.g., appears to supply only one type of error identification to all items, such as "Comma is missing").

ACH TEST 20: SPELLING OF SOUNDS

The Spelling of Sounds test is a diagnostic measure of spelling that evaluates the individual's knowledge of phoneme/grapheme correspondence for the spelling of words. This is a measure of encoding. Items elicit the individual's knowledge of phonetic and orthographic principles. The subject is required to listen to an audio recording that presents pseudowords (nonwords or nonsense words). He or she must then write representations of those words.

Consider the test's task demands across items. The words progress from single letters to words that include both regular and irregular patterns of English spelling.

Observe the individual's response patterns. Note if the individual

- Exhibits ease or difficulty in obtaining a basal or ceiling or difficulty in training the task within sample items.
- Demonstrates accuracy and consistency across items. If the subject is inaccurate, attempt to ascertain for which structures he or she shows limited mastery. Consider performance in conjunction with ACH Test 13: Word Attack to determine consistency in phoneme/grapheme knowledge for decoding.
- Works very slowly and tentatively. Examiner needs to pause the tape frequently.
- Asks for items to be repeated (this is permitted).

ACH TEST 22: PUNCTUATION AND CAPITALIZATION

The Punctuation and Capitalization test requires the subject to demonstrate his or her knowledge of conventional formatting for written English.

Consider the test's task demands across items. The items begin with knowledge of upper and lower case letters and progress through a range of items requiring expressive/written demonstration of knowledge of conventions. Each item requires the individual to write specific words or phrases using correct forms of capitalization or punctuation.

Observe the individual's response patterns. Note if the individual

- Shows consistency and accuracy of performance across items.
- Hesitates or is more confident with demonstrating his or her skills.

POSSIBLE PERFORMANCE IMPLICATIONS FOR
BASIC WRITING SKILLS

- Consider the instructional programs being used for spelling skills, the frequency of practice and instruction, and directly guided opportunities for generalization. Provide instructional support using methods/interventions appropriate for the particular stage of spelling development for the individual.
- Provide explicit instruction and practice in proofing, editing, outlining, and note-taking.
- For individuals who show diminished legibility in handwriting across items, consider the general integrity of his or her fine-motor skills. Use a handwriting evaluation to document support for these concerns. Seek the input of an occupational therapist if necessary, and provide accommodations

such as reducing the quantity of writing and copying and encouraging development of keyboarding and computer-based word-processing skills, voice-activated word processing, and other assistive technology.

QUANTITATIVE KNOWLEDGE

Quantitative Knowledge (*Gq*) is defined as representing an individual's store of acquired knowledge (declarative and procedural) for quantitative information. This broad ability is typically assessed through measures of math achievement and math problem solving. In the development of mathematics calculation skills and mathematics fluency, it is important to understand the individual's performance on cognitive measures of abstract fluid reasoning (COG Test 5a: Concept Formation and COG Test 15: Analysis–Synthesis), verbal knowledge and oral language proficiency (Comprehension–Knowledge and Oral Language clusters), Short-Term Memory and Working Memory, Visual-Spatial Thinking (specifically COG Test 3: Spatial Relations), and ability to demonstrate on-demand recall of information (see Long-Term Retrieval cluster). The individual's instructional experiences also play a role in the integrity of developing math skills (e.g., curriculum emphasis, opportunities for practice). In addition, the individual's motivation and interest in math and the consistency in his or her attention and concentration can also impact the performance efficiency on math tests.

ACH TEST 5: CALCULATION

The Calculation test requires the individual to accurately do computations. Items are presented in a traditional format and range in difficulty from basic arithmetic operations to higher level mathematics. This test is a paper-and-pencil task.

Consider the test's task demands across items. The sample items require the writing of simple numerals. These items are primarily at the preschool or kindergarten level. Test items begin with simple addition and subtraction of single digit numbers; the test moves from horizontal to vertical formats. Operations progress in difficulty across items, sampling a variety of procedural calculation skills. The individual performs the actual calculations within the Subject Response Booklet and is permitted additional scrap paper if necessary (asks for or appears to need it). The individual is told to skip any items he or she does not know how to do.

Observe the individual's response patterns. Note if the individual

- Exhibits ease or difficulty in establishing a basal.
- Works with good efficiency and accuracy to the point of ceiling, or if his or her performance suggests omitted skills or inconsistent mastery.
- Responds automatically for each item (i.e., he or she does not stall or show undue difficulty with any particular type of algorithm or operation) or if he or she works with tentative skill and a slow rate.

- Attends to shifts with the changes in the operational signs and perceptual details of items.
- Commits errors that are related to lack of knowledge of procedures, basic facts, difficulties in sequencing multiple-step operations, conceptual understanding of concepts that undergird more complex procedures (i.e., comprehension of concepts for place value, percents, decimals, fractions).

ACH TEST 6: MATH FLUENCY

The Math Fluency test measures the ability to solve simple arithmetic facts quickly. This test has a 3-minute time limit. It may be developmentally appropriate for children at the early kindergarten grade placement level, or younger to not be able to engage with or perform on this test. Children from middle kindergarten and upward in the norm sample are able to understand and perform on this test, accomplishing between 5 and 10 correct responses within the 3 minutes.

Consider the test's task demands across items. The individual is presented with the Subject Response Booklet, which has two pages of math facts. Each page has eight rows with 10 facts of mixed operations in each row. The first six rows include only addition and subtraction facts. Simple multiplication facts begin on the seventh row.

Observe the individual's response patterns. Note if the individual

- Is able to understand the nature of the task and to sustain work for the duration of the test.
- Shifts flexibly with the changes in operational signs.
- Appears nervous or daunted by the timing feature of the task.
- Is quick or slow, accurate or inaccurate.
- Appears to use fingers as a counting strategy for some facts.

POSSIBLE PERFORMANCE IMPLICATIONS FOR BASIC MATH SKILLS

- Efficient performance on tests may suggest that the individual has a personal academic strength in mathematics.
- Consider the individual's ability to work flexibly with mixed formats and operations.
- Review qualitative analysis of math with regards to the individual's current instructional opportunities.
- Consider the need to provide frequent practice and mastery reviews of skills and facts.
- Use multisensory techniques for teaching sequential operations (e.g., verbal talk-through strategies).
- Provide accommodations and adapted materials as necessary (calculators, math fact charts) and modifications as necessary (untimed tests).

ACH TEST 10: APPLIED PROBLEMS

The Applied Problems test requires the individual to understand and solve practical mathematics problems that are presented orally. These problems require the individual to determine the appropriate operation and to differentiate essential from nonessential information. The individual may choose or be encouraged to use paper and pencil as an aid to completing the task.

Consider the test's task demands across items. Items begin at a young preschool level with concrete-level, "show-me" items. Early items (preschool through early elementary levels) utilize depicted information and verbal queries from the examiner. The examinee is not required to read any of the problems. Early items assess the application of essential foundational concepts (more than/less than, multiple language cues that denote specific quantitative concepts and operations, and the ability to differentiate essential from nonessential information at a basic, concrete level). Early elementary items include problems related to coin recognition and values, and time concepts. Word problems progress in difficulty across raw scores, moving from single-step problems that require the individual to discern essential from nonessential information, to sequential problems that involve the organization and application of multiple concepts and operations.

Observe the individual's response patterns. Note if the individual

- Shows ease or difficulty in cueing into the concepts and language of the word problems.
- Shows diligence and consistency, or limited effort and inconsistency in his or her performance.
- Shows creative or flexible strategies and is able to articulate how he or she solved the problem if queried during extension testing.
- Gives responses suggesting an inability to discern essential from nonessential information, has difficulty with visualizing and organizing the setup of the problem, and/or demonstrates difficulty with carrying the problem out independently.
- Becomes confused by the vocabulary and syntax of the word problems.

ACH TEST 18: QUANTITATIVE CONCEPTS

The Quantitative Concepts test measures knowledge of math concepts, symbols, vocabulary, and numeration skills. It contains the subtests of Concepts and Number Series. Neither of these subtests requires any significant degree of pencil-and-paper computations, although pencil and paper are offered beginning with Sample Item B of the Number Series subtest.

Consider task demands across items. For the Concepts subtest, the individual is required to answer questions that show knowledge of basic foundational concepts. Items begin at preschool level and move through concepts involving higher mathematics. Items begin at a receptive level ("Show me ...") and progress to expressive knowledge of math symbols, abbreviations, and other representations of essential concepts.

For the Number Series Subtest, the subject is required to verbally provide a number that is missing from a pattern (e.g., 3, 2, 1, _). Items begin with simple, basic numeration patterns and progress to more complex items that may involve the use of pencil and paper in order to determine the numerical relationships and solve the patterns.

Observe individual's response patterns. Note if the individual

- Shows consistency/inconsistency in quantitative concepts through a review of the basal and the performance across items.
- Employs the use of pencil and paper effectively when necessary or shows efficiency without the aid of pencil and paper.
- Attempts to solve problems without using pencil and paper but is inaccurate.

POSSIBLE PERFORMANCE IMPLICATIONS FOR MATH REASONING

- Consider the individual's performance relative to his or her instructional history in math, current curriculum, and his or her cognitive strengths and weaknesses.
- If the individual demonstrates difficulties with reading, ensure that his or her math performance is not predicated on the accuracy of his or her basic reading skills.
- Develop instruction in math reasoning with an awareness of the individual's general levels in oral language, reasoning and abstract thinking, and memory skills.
- Provide organizational strategies to assist the individual with visualizing, setting up, and carrying out multiple-step problems.

ORAL LANGUAGE

Oral Language includes Listening Comprehension and Oral Expression. For Listening Comprehension, it is important to consider the general integrity of the individual's auditory processing and his or her consistency in attention and concentration. Also consider the integrity of the individual's cognitive efficiency (short-term memory, working memory, and processing speed), his or her capability with abstract thinking and Fluid Reasoning (specifically consider COG Test 5: Concept Formation), and his or her cultural orientation as it pertains to experiential access and bilingual or multilingual environments.

The area of Oral Expression also presumes a number of common considerations across tasks. When evaluating responses on measures of Oral Expression, consider the individual's integrity of listening comprehension skills and his or her interpersonal comfort or discomfort for engaging in conversational exchanges or verbal responses.

ACH TEST 3: STORY RECALL

The Story Recall test measures aspects of language development and meaningful memory. It requires the individual to listen to audio recordings of stories (ranging from very short and simple to more complex). After each story the individual is asked to recall as many details from the story as he or she can remember.

Consider the test's task demands across items. Stories begin at a preschool level with simple two- and three-sentence stories. Each story is broken up into smaller, ideational segments. Individual responses are scored with regard to whether he or she is able to recall and paraphrase segments, retaining the basic concepts or ideas of each segment. Some segments contain specific "detail" words shown in bold typeface in the Test Record Booklet. If a segment contains a "detail" word, that word needs to be specifically recalled/included in the retelling in order for that segment to be considered correct. Longer stories contain increasing amounts of "detail words." The individual does not need to provide the paraphrase of segments in sequential order.

Observe the individual's response patterns. Note if the individual

- Attends well to all stories that are considered as appropriate for the individual's age/grade or if his or her attention is inefficient.
- Follows the sequence of the story segments or verbally lists information in random order.
- Retells stories for creative or personalized interpretations, associations, and embellishments that lend solidity to the recall of the content and details.
- Uses language that is more efficient or with higher level language structure and vocabulary than the original story (i.e., efficiently combining two segments while retaining the critical ideas and detail words).
- Is undaunted or becomes nervous by the increase in difficulty across stories.
- Holds onto the general ideas of some of the segments but misses the "detail" words.
- Retains segments only at the beginning (or the end) of the story.
- Recounts information in a disorganized manner and is inconsistent in his or her accuracy for details and sequence.
- Appears to become nervous or anxious at the thought of having to recall, on demand, verbally presented information.

ACH TEST 12: STORY RECALL—DELAYED

The Story Recall—Delayed test assesses how much information from the original stories the individual is able to remember after a period of time. Administration options range from 30 min to up to 8 days after the original administration of ACH Test 3: Story Recall.

Consider the test's task demands across items. The individual is given a started sentence for each previously administered story. The individual is asked to verbalize as many ideas and details that he or she can remember.

Observe the individual's response patterns. Note if the individual

- Appears at ease with the task and does his or her best to recall and relate as much information as possible.
- Appears to be uncomfortable or anxious with the notion that he or she is being "tested again" on material he or she had already worked with.
- Is slow to recall segments of the story, but eventually retrieves some of the information.

ACH TEST 14: PICTURE VOCABULARY

The Picture Vocabulary test requires the subject to recognize and name pictured objects. It is a measure of precise expressive vocabulary at the single-word level.

Consider the test's task demands across items. Some lower level items require receptive identification through a pointing response. Expressive language requirements begin with Item 3.

Observe the individual's response patterns. Note if the individual

- Shows any delays in response time. If delays are observed, are they general or specific to certain items?
- Demonstrates precision or imprecision in his or her vocabulary. For example, does the individual provide vague associations, description by functions, or circumlocutions, or is he or she verbally precise?

POSSIBLE PERFORMANCE IMPLICATIONS FOR
ORAL EXPRESSION

- Efficiency in recalling and relating meaningful information for essential elements and ideas.
- Individuals who show a matter-of-fact listing approach to the elements of the stories may be suggesting a pragmatic stylistic preference in their approach to comprehension and recall. Some specific educational techniques may be more interesting/palatable over others. For example, techniques that present and prompt the organization of information in practical, logical lists with key word associations may be compatible. Note-taking strategies that emphasize "Key Word" formats may be appropriate.
- Precision in response formulation and/or those who show personalized associations/embellishments to their responses may show comfort with academic opportunities that allow them to demonstrate their verbal competence. Prepared oral presentations, recitations, drama, and performance may be motivating formats for this type of individual. Review the individual's

skills with creative written expression. Enhance development of written expression through the individual's foundation with oral expression.

- Implications for acquiring and demonstrating general knowledge and information.
- Provide visual outlines or other visual cues to prompt more efficiency in listening comprehension. Accommodations and modifications for oral presentations in a classroom setting should be considered.
- Difficulties with generalized retention and recall of information. Consider performance on Story Recall—Delayed and other measures of Long-Term Retrieval. Instructional considerations may include frequency of practice, criteria for mastery, and frequency of review for previously "learned" information.
- Provide multisensory materials and prompts when presenting orally based activities; consider reducing the quantity of information and increasing the frequency of exposure and practice to enhance the retention and recall of orally presented information.

ACH TEST 4: UNDERSTANDING DIRECTIONS

The Understanding Directions test requires the subject to point to various objects in a picture after listening to a sequence of recorded instructions. The task increases in linguistic complexity in terms of the number of items to be remembered and the syntax of the directions.

Consider the test's task demands across items. The individual is shown pictures of different scenes (Pastoral, Jungle, City Park, Mountain, Living Room, etc.) and is given several seconds to look over the pictures. Then, with the picture available, the individual listens to a sequence of recorded instructions and is asked to point to various objects in the picture. The task increases in linguistic complexity in terms of the number of items to be remembered and the syntax of the directions. Items assess not only the ability to follow multiple-step directions in sequence, but also to discern implied order through the understanding of conditional statements (e.g., "If there is a cat on the couch, point to ____, and ____. If not, point to ____, and ____").

Observe the individual's response patterns. Note if the individual

- Adjusts to the double-cueing system or whether he or she responds too quickly.
- Requires the tape to be paused to allow more time.
- Carries out the directions with accuracy or inefficiency.
- Displays relatively efficient or inefficient comprehension or strategies when he or she needs to process more complex language with embedded clauses, spatial/directional concepts, or within conditional syntax.
- Is able to respond to single or simple two-step instructions, but begins to falter when instructions require the sequencing of more information.

- Shows inconsistent attention and concentration as items increase in difficulty.
- Finds it difficult to negotiate the visual detail of the pictures. Does the individual need the tape paused after the instruction is presented in order to have additional time to scan the picture for the objects he or she is looking for?

ACH TEST 15: ORAL COMPREHENSION

The Oral Comprehension test requires the individual to listen to passages and then orally provide a one-word response to fill in a missing last word. This test requires accurate comprehension of vocabulary and syntax.

Consider task demands across items. The individual is essentially required to demonstrate the ability to understand what he or she is listening to, while he or she is listening to it. Items begin at preschool level and difficulty increases. The task requires comprehension of vocabulary and syntax. Although statements have meaning and context, the specific information may not be meaningful to a given individual.

Observe the individual's response patterns. Note if the individual

- Exhibits ease or difficulty in obtaining a basal.
- Shows consistency in performance to the point of ceiling.
- Needs the tape paused multiple times.
- Shows inconsistency in his or her attention across items.
- Is stymied by some types of items but not others—errors may be related to lack of knowledge of vocabulary, or to the sophistication of the syntax that is involved.

POSSIBLE PERFORMANCE IMPLICATIONS FOR LISTENING COMPREHENSION

- Integrity of listening comprehension can impact all academic skills.
- Consider corroborative information from other measures of oral language and listening comprehension.
- Consider cross-instrument comparisons. For example, if ACH Test 9: Passage Comprehension is weaker than ACH Test 15: Oral Comprehension, this may illustrate a difficulty with basic reading skills, because it negatively affects comprehension.
- Consider the impact of automatic processing speed on the efficiency of listening comprehension if there was a frequent need to pause the tape.
- Compare the individual's attentional consistency to other measures that require listening, auditory presentations, and the general processing of language.
- Consider the individual's performance in conjunction with other measures of Comprehension–Knowledge to determine the degree that knowledge inconsistency may be adversely affecting listening ability.

CONCLUSION

Qualitative analysis of test performance is paradoxically as old as the field of psychology and as current as the WJ III. Henry A. Murray, an early director of the Psychological Clinic at Harvard, emphasized the analysis of the organic, or whole, character of human behavior. In his book, *Explorations in Personality*, Murray (1938) advocated the position that an adequate understanding of an individual can come only from a comprehensive and multifaceted study. He suggested that group norms are important only when accompanied by and interpreted in the context of a careful inquiry into the ways in which an individual represents an exception to the norm. That is, a skilled professional should study the ways an individual differs from the norm.

If an individual's test scores are viewed as a foundational skeletal frame of data from which clinical hypotheses can be generated, then qualitative analysis of the subject's responses may be metaphorically thought of as the "connective and soft tissue" that holds that numerical structure together. Understanding *how* a person responded is often more informative and clinically useful than the scores that are used to generate developmental level or normative standing. This type of analysis allows the practitioner to consider the unique characteristics of an individual's style of performance and to postulate the implications of that performance.

Because of the wide array of cognitive and academic abilities measured, the WJ III tests can provide data on the information-processing characteristics required to complete the tasks. These processes occur within individuals, and interpretive information can be informed by careful observation and qualitative analysis of the individual's differential responses to task requirements. This information is useful for informing the significance of scores obtained for the WJ III tests and clusters and validating the clinician's interpretation of the WJ III.

REFERENCES

Carver, C. F., & Scheier, M. F. (1989). Expectancies and coping: From test anxiety to pessimism. In R. Schwarzer, H. M. Van der Pleog, & C. D. Spielberger (Eds.), *Advances in test anxiety research* (Vol. 6, pp. 3–11). Lisse, Netherlands: Swets and Zeitlinger.

Cattell, R. R. (1987). *Intelligence: Its structure, growth and action.* New York: North-Holland.

Eysenck, H. J., & Eysenck, M. W. (1985). *Personality and individual differences: A natural science approach.* New York: Plenum.

Hidi, S. (1990). Interest and its contribution as a mental resource for learning. *Review of Educational Research, 60,* 549–571.

Kane, M. T. (2001). Current concerns in validity theory. *Journal of Educational Measurement, 38*(4), 319–342.

Klonsky, B. G. (1989). Development of achievement orientation. In J. Husen & T. N. Postlethwaite (Eds.), *The international encyclopedia of education: Research and studies* (Vol. 1, pp. 1–5). New York: Pergamon.

Lave, J., & Wenger, E. (1991). *Situated learning: Legitimate peripheral participation.* Cambridge, UK: Cambridge University Press.

Mueller, J. H. (1980). Test anxiety and the encoding and retrieval of information. In I. Sarason (Ed.), *Test anxiety: Theory, research, and applications* (pp. 63–86). Hillsdale, NJ: Erlbaum.

Murray, H. A. (1938). *Explorations in personality: A clinical and experimental study of fifty men of college age.* New York: Oxford University Press.

Polkingborne, D. E., & Gribbons, B. C. (1999). Applications of qualitative research strategies to school psychology research problems. In C. R. Reynolds & T. B. Gutkin (Eds.), *The handbook of school psychology* (pp. 108–136). New York: John Wiley and Sons.

Simon, J. (2001). Bartlett v. New York State Board of Law Examiners: Lessons to be learned. *LDA Newsbriefs, 36*(6), 6–8, 11.

Skovholt, T. M., & Ronnestad, M. H. (1992). *The evolving professional self: Stages and themes in therapist and counselor development.* New York: Wiley.

Snow, R. E. (1989). Cognitive-conative aptitude interactions in learning. In R. Kanfer, P. L. Ackerman, & R. Cudeck (Eds.), *Abilities, motivation, methodology: The Minnesota Symposium on Learning and Individual Differences* (pp. 435–474). Hillsdale, NJ: Erlbaum.

Strelau, J. (1995). Temperament and stress: Temperament as a moderator of stressors, emotional states, coping, and costs. In C. D. Spielberger & I. G. Sarason (Eds.), *Stress and emotion: Anxiety, anger, and curiosity.* (Vol. 15, pp. 215–254). Washington, DC: Taylor and Francis.

Strelau, J., Zawadzki, B., & Piotrowska, A. (2001). Temperament and intelligence: A psychometric approach to the links between both phenomena. In J. M. Collis & S. Messick (Eds.), *Intelligence and personality: Bridging the gap in theory and measurement* (pp. 61–78). Mahwah, NJ: Erlbaum.

Zeidner, M. (1995). Personality trait correlates of intelligence. In D. H. Saklofske & Zeidner, M. (Eds.), *International handbook of personality and intelligence* (pp. 299–320). New York: Plenum.

3

Instructional Implications from the Woodcock– Johnson III

Nancy Mather

The University of Arizona, Tuscon, Arizona 85721

Barbara J. Wendling

BJ Consulting, Dallas, Texas 75248

"Evaluation should go hand-in-hand with instruction."
(Kirk, Kleibhan, & Lerner, 1978, p. 155).

The central purposes of a student evaluation are to address and answer a referral question or questions in order to create positive changes in the student's instructional environment. Unfortunately, the emphasis on scores and eligibility criteria have led some practitioners away from using tests as tools for instructional planning or even from taking the time to conduct a careful analysis of patterns and errors. The central purpose of diagnosing learning disabilities is for treatment, not classification (Kirk, 1975). Standardized tests, such as the Woodcock–Johnson III (WJ III), should be the beginning, not the end, of the diagnostic process (Mather, 1993). Once areas of instructional need are clearly identified, a more in-depth assessment is often needed, including criterion-referenced testing, curriculum-based measurements, and informal analyses of work samples. The purpose of this chapter is to explore instructional implications from the WJ III.

Although the focus of this chapter is on the *WJ III Tests of Achievement* (WJ III ACH), it incorporates some information from the *WJ III Tests of Cognitive Abilities* (WJ III COG) that can assist with interpretation and formulation of diagnostic hypotheses. This chapter begins with a review of the importance of both quantitative and qualitative observations in conjunction with considering a student's present instructional levels. Next, there is an illustration of how patterns of cluster and test scores and a comparison of oral language abilities to various areas of achievement can help inform instruction. Then, the relationship between various cognitive factors and academic performance is discussed. Finally, performance and instructional implications are addressed within three broad areas: academic skills; academic fluency; and oral language, knowledge, and academic applications. A case study is presented to illustrate how these clusters can help identify a student's instructional needs.

GENERAL CONSIDERATIONS

A skilled clinician can obtain a variety of instructional implications by evaluating an individual's performance on the WJ III. Understanding the instructional implications from the WJ III requires interpreting the obtained scores within the context of information gathered through a review of records, interviews, and observations.

QUANTITATIVE AND QUALITATIVE OBSERVATIONS

Clinical evaluations involve information obtained from interviews and direct observations as well as test scores. The manner in which an individual attempts a task is as important as the resultant score. Two individuals can obtain identical scores, but one individual's performance may be indicative of a problem, whereas the other's may not. All test scores have to be woven into a web that integrates linguistic factors, cultural factors, educational history and opportunities, genetic factors, family supports, prior interventions, social economic status, and emotional and affective factors. Test scores are an aid to interpretation but they cannot replace clinical judgment or the inferences obtained through error analysis and careful observation. Further, normative scores provide only part of the performance picture. Important information is available from two criterion-referenced features available in the WJ III: the Relative Proficiency Index and the Instructional Zone.

Relative Proficiency Index

The Relative Proficiency Index (RPI) provides a criterion-referenced statement about the individual's functionality, or quality of performance, on a task. An index ranging from 0/90 to 100/90, the RPI compares the individual's performance to average age- or grade-mates who demonstrate 90% proficiency on the task. For individuals with below-average proficiency on a task, the RPI describes the level of impairment. For example, if a student has an RPI of 45/90 on spelling, it would indicate that the student is about half as proficient on this task as average age- or grade-mates. In addition to describing the individual's performance on the task, the RPI is predictive of how the individual will perform on tasks similar to the test item tasks.

The RPI can document a performance deficit that may not be apparent in the normative scores. Normative scores (standard scores, percentile ranks) describe an individual's relative standing compared to age- or grade-mates. The RPI describes functionality or quality of performance on a task. When there appears to be a contradiction between the standard score and the RPI—for example, a standard score of 92 (average) and an RPI of 39/90 (limited)—the evaluator must remember that these scores are communicating different information and they are not interchangeable. The standard score (SS) reflects an individual's relative standing within a distribution of age- or grade-mates. The RPI is based on the number of W points the person's score falls above or below the average W for his or her age or grade. This means that the RPI will be influenced by the characteristics of the underlying ability or trait being measured. When the ability is in a period of rapid growth or development, the RPI may appear deficient even when the SS is average. Periods of rapid growth will cover a wide range of W scores, so distance from the mean W for an age or grade can be dramatic. When the ability is in a period of slow growth, the SS may appear deficient but the RPI is average because the range in W scores is limited.

The RPI is analogous to the familiar Snellen Index used to describe the quality of an individual's visual acuity (Woodcock, 1999). An individual with 20/20 vision is predicted to see an object at a distance of 20 feet as well as a person with normal vision. However, if the person's vision is 20/80, that person needs to be within 20 feet of an object to see it as well as a person with normal vision sees the object from 80 feet. The quality of the individual's visual acuity is described with a criterion-referenced statement. Needed support or services are determined based on this criterion-referenced statement, rather than on a norm-based score. In determining the need for corrective lenses, it is more important to consider the individual's quality of vision than his or her relative standing compared to age- or grade-mates. If vision is impaired, the individual will benefit from corrective lenses regardless of relative standing with peers. Like the Snellen Index, the RPI provides a criterion-referenced statement of an individual's performance. An RPI of 75/90 or lower indicates the individual will find the task difficult, whereas an RPI of 96/90 or greater indicates the individual will find the task easy. An RPI of 75/90 means that when average age- or grade-mates would experience 90% success, this individual would have only 75% success on similar tasks. Table 3-1 provides information about the performance implications of the RPI.

Instructional Zone

The Relative Proficiency Index is used to establish the instructional zone. An RPI of 96/90 represents the easy, or independent, level and an RPI of 75/90 represents the difficult, or frustration, level. A critical factor for effective instruction is to ensure that students have the appropriate level of instructional materials. For example, when a student is asked to read a book without assistance, the assigned book should be at the independent level. The Instructional Zone on the WJ III ACH (the Developmental Zone in the WJ III COG) is designed to estimate

TABLE 3-1   Relative Proficiency Index (RPI) Performance Implications

RPI range	Skill with age- or grade-level tasks	Age/grade-level tasks will be
98/90 to 100/90	Advanced	Very easy
96/90 to 97/90	Age/grade appropriate to advanced	Easy
82/90 to 95/90	Age/grade appropriate	Manageable
68/90 to 81/90	Limited to age/grade appropriate	Difficult
34/90 to 67/90	Limited	Very difficult
19/90 to 33/90	Limited to very limited	Very difficult to extremely difficult
5/90 to 18/90	Very limited	Extremely difficult
0/90 to 4/90	Very limited to negligible	Extremely difficult to impossible

the instructional level ranging from easy to difficult. The interpretation of this zone is similar to the criteria used in informal reading inventories. Betts (1946) described three levels of reading performance: the independent level, the instructional level, and the frustration level. When an individual's Instructional Zone is far below that of classmates, adaptations and accommodations need to be made. Examples of program modifications include altering the difficulty level of the material or increasing the level of assistance.

PATTERNS OF CLUSTER AND TEST SCORES

Often times, the patterns obtained on the cluster and test scores can help reveal the strengths and weaknesses among a person's abilities. Analysis and understanding of a person's present performance levels lead to the development of appropriate instructional recommendations. When basic skills, fluency, and application tasks are compared, a variety of patterns can exist. Examples include: (a) low-level basic skills with adequate performance on fluency and application tests, (b) low-level performance on fluency with adequate performance on skills and application tests, (c) low-level performance on application tests with adequate performance on skills and fluency tests, (d) variability among areas of performance (e.g., math performance level lower than reading level), and (e) generalized low or high performance levels.

The cross-academic clusters in the WJ III ACH (Academic Skills, Academic Fluency, and Academic Applications) can be useful in documenting the need for an accommodation. Each cross-academic cluster includes three tests—one from each of the three main academic domains: reading, written language, and mathematics. Considering an individual's performance in terms of the cross-academic clusters has implications for either the Individual Education Plan (IEP) or Section 504 (from the Rehabilitation Act of 1973) accommodation plans. Some students perform poorly on application tasks because of limited knowledge, poor reasoning, poor language skills, or limited exposure to cultural or educational experiences but have average performance on measures of basic skills. Their profiles tend to yield higher scores on lower order basic skills tests, and lower scores on tests involving language and reasoning. For these students, intervention is directed to building background knowledge, increasing use of strategies, and developing problem-solving abilities. Other students exhibit limited variability among test scores and have generalized high or low performance on the majority of academic tasks. These students will tend to require adjustments in the curricular demands (e.g., enrichment and/or adjustment of the instructional level of the materials). Table 3-2 indicates possible program accommodations and instructional implications for weaknesses in skills, fluency, or applications.

Clearly, all students with academic disabilities will not exhibit these exact profiles. As a general observation, students with "specific" academic disabilities tend to perform lower on measures of basic skills and speed, and higher on measures of application and oral language. The following discussions address three patterns of specific learning disabilities: reading, writing, and math. These patterns reflect the general findings in the literature and are not based on specific WJ III research.

Reading Disability

Because the most common referral for educational testing is difficulty in learning to read, a major focus of this chapter is on reading disabilities. Analysis of test scores can help the evaluator determine if the individual has dyslexia (an impairment in phoneme/grapheme knowledge and rapid word recognition) or if the reading difficulties are best explained by other factors (e.g., limited instruction or low level of oral language abilities). A common profile for students with dyslexia shows higher performance on reading tasks that involve more context (e.g., Passage Comprehension) than on tasks relying on the application of phoneme/ grapheme correspondences (e.g., Word Attack). Clark and Uhry (1995) indicate that older students with reading disabilities who have had remediation often exhibit the following pattern of scores: listening comprehension > reading

TABLE 3-2 Possible Accommodations and Instructional Implications Based on Academic Cluster Results

Academic cluster results	Accommodation	Instructional implication
Skills lower than Fluency and Applications	No penalty for poor skills (e.g., poor spelling)	Provide direct instruction in deficient skills
Fluency lower than Skills and Applications	Extend time or shorten assignments	Provide activities to promote automaticity (e.g., speed drills)
Applications lower than Skills and Fluency	Modify instructional level	Provide instruction to build acquired knowledge; teach use of strategies

comprehension > decoding words in text > decoding words in isolation > spelling/reading nonsense words. Using WJ III ACH tests, this pattern would translate as Oral Comprehension > Passage Comprehension > Reading Fluency > Letter–Word Identification > Spelling of Sounds and Word Attack. Similarly, Goldsmith-Phillips (1994) illustrates that individuals with phonological dyslexia "will have the greatest difficulty with reading nonwords and the most success with passage comprehension, which is a more cognitively loaded task. The task of word identification will be at an intermediate level because the words may have been learned by Gestalt" (p. 97).

Writing Disability

For students with specific writing disabilities, a similar pattern is often apparent. They obtain their highest score on Writing Samples, which requires expression of ideas, and have lower scores on Writing Fluency, Editing, and Spelling; their lowest score is on spelling nonwords on the Spelling of Sounds test. Some individuals with writing disabilities have coexisting reading difficulties. However, some individuals with writing difficulties learn to read easily.

Math Disability

In math performance, individuals are likely to have higher scores on the Applied Problems test, a measure of mathematical reasoning, and lower scores on measures of fluency and basic skills. These individuals understand concepts, but have trouble memorizing facts and the steps in various algorithms.

COMPARISON OF ORAL LANGUAGE TO ACADEMIC PERFORMANCE

Insights can be gained about instructional needs by examining the relationships among oral language and achievement, as well as among achievement areas. The WJ III ACH provides an ability–achievement discrepancy in which oral language performance can be used to predict academic performance. This discrepancy procedure is described in detail in *Essentials of WJ III Tests of Achievement Assessment* (Mather, Wendling, & Woodcock, 2001). This type of comparison is particularly relevant for deciding if the instructional focus needs to be directed to general language proficiency or to specific academic skills. Comparing listening comprehension measures to reading and writing performance can help determine the source of the weakness (Johnson, 1998). A key element for establishing a reading disability is determining that oral comprehension is significantly higher than reading performance (Clark & Uhry, 1995; Goldsmith-Phillips, 1994). Essentially, what distinguishes an individual with a reading disability from other poor readers is that their listening comprehension ability is higher than their ability to decode words (Rack, Snowling, & Olson, 1992). For these students, intervention is directed toward improving basic reading and writing skills rather than overall language development; if all language skills are low level, the intervention is directed toward all aspects of language development. Many examples of recommendations and possible interventions are available in *Woodcock–Johnson III: Reports, Recommendations, and Strategies* (Mather & Jaffe, 2002).

PERFORMANCE IMPLICATIONS OF THE
CATTELL–HORN–CARROLL COGNITIVE FACTORS

Analyzing performance on the seven cognitive abilities in the WJ III COG can help explain why the student is struggling in certain aspects of school. For example, low Comprehension–Knowledge (*Gc*) may influence reading comprehension, whereas low Auditory Processing (*Ga*) may influence decoding abilities. Table 3-3 presents the seven cognitive abilities measured in the WJ III COG,

TABLE 3-3 Performance Implications of the Seven CHC Cognitive Factors

CHC cognitive factor	Descriptors	Achievement area	Recommendations
Comprehension–Knowledge (*Gc*)	Acquired knowledge Vocabulary Information	Language-related learning Reading Written language Mathematics	Specific instruction in vocabulary Relate new learning to prior knowledge
Fluid Reasoning (*Gf*)	Inductive and deductive reasoning Problem-solving	Mathematics Reading[a] Written language	Teach problem-solving techniques and strategies Use concrete vs. abstract
Long-Term Retrieval (*Glr*)	Memorization Fluency of retrieval Association and retrieval	Reading Written language Mathematics	Provide overlearning, review, and repetition Teach memory aids
Auditory Processing (*Ga*)	Phonological awareness Auditory discrimination	Reading Written language	Provide specific training in sound discrimination, blending, segmentation
Visual-Spatial Thinking (*Gv*)	Spatial relations Visual imagery Visual memory	Mathematics Reading[a]	Verbally describe graphics Use manipulatives
Processing Speed (*Gs*)	Automaticity Visual scanning Perceptual speed	Reading Mathematics Written language	Limit amount of work Provide rate-building activities
Short-Term Memory (*Gsm*)	Sequential memory Immediate awareness Limited capacity	Reading Mathematics Written language	Keep directions short Provide compensatory aids Teach memory strategies

[a]Indicates conflicting research on the relationship between the cognitive ability and achievement area.

gives descriptors of those abilities, lists the achievement areas that are most significantly related to the seven Cattell–Horn–Carroll (CHC) cognitive abilities (Evans et al., 2001; McGrew & Flanagan, 1998; McGrew & Hessler, 1995; McGrew & Knopik, 1993), and provides instructional recommendations. One caution to keep in mind is that the relationship of cognitive factors to academic performance changes with age and stage of development. For example, McGrew and Hessler (1995) found that fluid reasoning (*Gf*), acquired knowledge (*Gc*), and processing speed (*Gs*) abilities were correlated consistently and significantly with math achievement, but the *Gc* relationship increased with age, whereas the *Gs* relationship decreased with age. *Gf* was related consistently and significantly across all ages.

Another note of caution is applicable to the conflicting results reported in studies that explore the significance of the relationship between specific cognitive abilities and academic performance. One reason for contradictions may be due to specification error or the inclusion of a limited number of important variables. For example, phonemic awareness and rapid automatized naming (RAN) tasks have been described as the "double-deficit hypothesis" or the two most important correlates of reading failure (e.g., Wolf & Bowers, 1999). Conceivably, the importance of these abilities may diminish when other possible correlates (e.g., working memory, processing speed) are included in the design. Although considerable progress has been made in our understanding of how cognitive abilities relate to academic performance, continued research is needed to document and further clarify the relationships among a broad range of cognitive abilities and achievement.

ACADEMIC SKILLS

Academic basic skills are lower order tasks that become automatic with repeated practice, such as knowing the multiplication facts or spelling words with ease. These abilities involve both perceptual and motoric processes that are critical for school success. When these low-level processes become routine and automatic, they require minimal attentional resources (Schneider & Shiffrin, 1977). In analyzing a student's performance on basic skills, the evaluator should consider what strategies the student employs and how quickly the student responds. In addition, the evaluator should attempt to discern if patterns exist among the incorrect responses. Table 3-4 identifies the achievement and cognitive clusters that may provide relevant information when interpreting performance on the basic skills clusters.

PHONOLOGICAL AWARENESS

Although phonological awareness is an aspect of oral language, it may be placed under the category of basic skills because a substantial body of research supports the link between phonological processing abilities and the subsequent

TABLE 3-4   Clusters to Consider When Interpreting Performance in Academic Skills

Achievement cluster/tests	Relevant achievement clusters	Relevant cognitive clusters
Academic Skills 　Letter–Word Identification 　Calculation 　Spelling	Academic Fluency Academic Applications Basic Reading Skills Math Calculation Skills Basic Writing Skills	Comprehension–Knowledge Long-Term Retrieval Processing Speed Short-Term Memory
Basic Reading Skills 　Letter–Word Identification 　Word Attack	Phoneme/Grapheme Knowledge Reading Comprehension	Auditory Processing Comprehension–Knowledge Long-Term Retrieval Processing Speed Short-Term Memory Working Memory Phonemic Awareness
Math Calculation Skills 　Calculation 　Math Fluency	Math Reasoning	Comprehension–Knowledge Fluid Reasoning Long-Term Retrieval Processing Speed Short-Term Memory Visual-Spatial Thinking Working Memory
Basic Writing Skills 　Spelling 　Editing	Phoneme/Grapheme Knowledge Written Expression	Auditory Processing Comprehension–Knowledge Long-Term Retrieval Processing Speed Short-Term Memory Working Memory Phonemic Awareness

development of reading and spelling skills (e.g., Lyon, 1995; Perfetti, 1992; Torgesen, 1992, 1993; Wagner & Torgesen, 1987). Deficits in phonological skill have been identified as the major cause of severe reading problems (Ehri, 1998; Morris et al., 1998; Wagner et al., 1993). Results from longitudinal studies suggest that 75% of the children who struggle with reading in third grade, particularly with the development of phonological awareness, will still be poor readers by the end of high school (Francis et al., 1996; Lyon, 1998).

The WJ III COG includes two measures of phonological awareness. The Sound Blending test requires the subject to synthesize speech sounds to form a word; the Incomplete Words test requires the subject to analyze a word with missing phonemes and then identify the complete word. If a more in-depth analysis of abilities is needed, the Sound Awareness test on the WJ III ACH may also be administered to provide additional measures of phonological awareness involving rhyming words and manipulating phonemes.

Phonological awareness is an important underlying linguistic ability for both reading and spelling unfamiliar words. Phonetic coding, an aspect of auditory processing (*Ga*), is especially important in kindergarten through third grade (McGrew & Flanagan, 1998). Reading unfamiliar words requires blending skill and is required to arrive at a unified pronunciation of the parts; spelling unfamiliar words requires segmentation skill to pull apart the phonemes so that the graphemes can be selected (Ehri, 2000).

NONWORD READING AND SPELLING

A substantial body of research has confirmed that poor readers have more difficulty reading pseudowords (Rack, Snowling, & Olson, 1992) and spelling pseudowords (Siegel & Ryan, 1988) than do normally developing readers. The WJ III ACH has two tests that measure the ability to read and spell nonwords— Word Attack and Spelling of Sounds. These two tests are particularly helpful for determining a student's knowledge of phoneme/grapheme correspondences (knowledge of spoken and written symbols). When combined, the tests form the Phoneme/Grapheme Knowledge cluster.

Phonological dyslexia is often described as an impairment in nonword reading (Coltheart, 1996). Although the reading of nonwords is sometimes described as a phonological coding test, both phonology and orthography are required (Johnson, 1998). The ability to pronounce and spell nonwords requires both knowledge of phonology (the sound system) and orthography (the spelling system). Orthographic coding, the ability to recall letters and letter strings, is important to both reading and spelling success (Berninger, 1996). The English language is described as a "deep orthography" because of the inconsistencies and complexities of the match between the phonemes (speech sounds) and the graphemes (a letter or letter group that represents a phoneme).

Several abilities are required to pronounce a nonword that has regular grapheme/ phoneme correspondence and corresponds to English spelling rules. For example, consider the skills that are needed to pronounce the nonword "tramble," a nonword similar to a multisyllabic nonword on the WJ III Word Attack test. Coltheart (1996) states that nonword reading involves the following three stages: (a) grapheme parsing, which requires converting a letter or letter group into a grapheme string; (b) phoneme assignment, which requires determining what phoneme corresponds to each of the graphemes; and (c) phoneme blending, which requires converting phonemes into a single, unified form. The first two processes involve orthography, whereas the third stage involves phoneme manipulation. Therefore, difficulty in nonword reading can occur for reasons other than poor phonological awareness.

Although it is well established that poor phonological awareness impacts nonword reading, the orthographic influences on nonword reading, reading accuracy, and reading rate are not as well understood. By administering the Sound Blending test from the WJ III COG and the Sound Awareness test from the WJ III ACH, the evaluator can determine if the individual has difficulties on a variety of phonological tasks. The evaluator can also determine if nonword reading is lower than word reading on the Letter–Word Identification test. This would indicate that the individual recognizes some real words because of prior experience and exposure to print, but has not yet fully mastered phoneme/grapheme relationships. In analyzing spellings on the Spelling of Sounds tests, the evaluator should note whether the writer records a plausible grapheme for each phoneme in the word. For example, an individual that writes "lich" for the target word "litch," demonstrates good sound knowledge (phonology), but limited knowledge of English spelling patterns (orthography). If the individual does not have difficulty with tasks involving phonemic blending, low performance on Word Attack and Spelling of Sounds may be more indicative of limited exposure to printed material or a weakness in orthography.

Some students can obtain scores that fall within the average range on nonword reading tests but their performance is still compromised by their speed of word recognition. Younger students who are slow to develop decoding skills may eventually read nonwords accurately, but they will still read slowly (Holopainen, Ahonen, & Lyytinen, 2001). Older students who have had intensive reading intervention are likely to obtain average nonword reading scores, but their speed of word perception is compromised. In describing the reading performance of college students with dyslexia, Bruck (1998) reported that for college students with dyslexia, the average latency to pronounce a nonword was 2019 msec, whereas the average latency for age-matched controls and reading-matched controls was 882 and 839 msec, respectively. Similarly, Wilson and Lesaux (2001) found that although college students with dyslexia had age-appropriate performance on standardized measures of reading and spelling, their performance was still compromised on phonological processing measures and measures involving speed. For example, a student may have an average standard score on the Letter–Word Identification test because this score is based on the number of words read correctly, which does not take into account the manner in which the student approached the task. An individual may eventually pronounce a word correctly after several attempts and repeated self-corrections. In considering the older student with a history of reading impairment, average reading test scores do not rule out the need for services, including appropriate accommodations, nor should services be denied on the basis of a lack of an ability–achievement discrepancy (Wilson & Lesaux, 2001). With older readers, college students, and adults, the speed of decoding is often more impaired than the accuracy of word reading.

BASIC WRITING SKILLS

Handwriting, spelling, and knowledge of the rules of written language underlie performance in basic writing skills. Writing speed (automaticity of handwriting) has been found to be a good predictor of performance on more complex written language tasks (Berninger, 1996). Automatic letter formation permits the writer to focus on the ideas and organization needed in the writing process.

Spelling difficulties appear to result from weaknesses in phonology and orthography. Individuals with spelling difficulties often have trouble analyzing and memorizing the sounds, syllables, and meaningful parts of words. Poor spellers may experience difficulty learning math facts and math operation signs, further reflecting difficulty in learning and memorizing symbolic codes (Moats, 1995).

BASIC MATH SKILLS

Mathematics is a complex area, affected by many variables, and is not as well researched as reading. Some students seem to have trouble primarily with computational skills, such as adding, subtracting, and multiplying. One common characteristic for individuals with limited basic math skills is difficulty memorizing and recalling math facts. Many individuals with learning disabilities have persistent trouble memorizing basic number facts in all four operations despite great effort and adequate understanding (Fleischner, Garnett, & Shepherd, 1982). Novick and Arnold (1988) found that there were individuals who demonstrated deficits in fundamental arithmetic operations, even though they evidenced adequate reasoning, language, and visual-spatial skills.

INSTRUCTIONAL IMPLICATIONS FOR
ACADEMIC SKILLS

Students with weaknesses in basic skills often need specific accommodations in the classroom. Some students will require shortened assignments or assignments for which materials are matched to their instructional level. Others will need to use technology to help reduce the impact of deficiencies in basic skills.

Phonological Awareness

Students with low-level performance on measures of phonological awareness should engage in a variety of tasks that will increase skill acquisition. Tasks should be ordered by the difficulty level: rhyme, alliteration, blending, segmentation, and manipulation (Ball, 1993; Chafouleas, Lewandowski, Smith, & Blachman, 1997). Table 3-5 provides definitions and examples of these five phonological awareness tasks. Chafouleas et al. found that 90% of children are able to perform most of these tasks by the age of 7. The most important abilities for reading and spelling performance, however, are the abilities to blend and segment sounds.

Phoneme/Grapheme Knowledge

Students with weaknesses in phoneme/grapheme knowledge will require specific instruction in the alphabetic system. For students with weaknesses in phonology, explicit instruction in phonemic awareness should be coupled with instruction in letter–sound relationships (Calfee, 1998). By the end of kindergarten, children should be able to blend and segment sounds and use sounds to spell simple words (Chard & Dickson, 1999).

TABLE 3-5   Definitions and Examples of Five Types of Phonological Awareness Tasks

Task	Definition	WJ III test	Example
Rhyming Identification	Identifies words that end alike, or rhyme	Sound Awareness	Which two words end alike or rhyme? (Rat, horse, cat)
Production	Produces word that rhymes with a target word	Sound Awareness	Tell me a word that rhymes with "big"
Alliteration	Identifies words that have the same sound (beginning, middle, or ending sounds)	—	Which two words begin with the same sound? (Boy, baby, car)
Blending	Combines individual syllables or sounds into a whole word; pushes sounds together	Sound Blending Incomplete Words	Tell me the word I'm trying to say (/t/../a/../b/../l/)
Segmentation	Identifies the number of words in a sentence, syllables in a word, or phonemes in a word; pulls sounds apart	—	How many words are in this sentence? (The boy threw the ball) How many syllables are in "raincoat"? How many sounds do you hear in the word "dog"?
Manipulation	Deletes, substitutes, or reverses sounds in a word	Sound Awareness	Change the /n/ in "can" to /t/ Say "hat" without the /h/ Say the sounds in the word "pot" backward

As a first step for increasing phoneme/grapheme knowledge, students must grasp the alphabetic principle. This principle has been defined simply as the understanding that the discrete letters of the alphabet represent the discrete sounds of speech (Liberman, Shankweiler, & Liberman, 1989). In other words, the beginning reader must discover that words have an internal phonemic structure that is represented by letters. They then must be able to use and apply this knowledge. Students with word recognition and spelling problems require explicit instruction and practice in reading and spelling single words (Berninger et al., 2000), which can often be accomplished by using a synthetic phonics approach.

With synthetic phonics instruction, the student is explicitly taught the relationship between letters and sounds. After sounds are taught in isolation, the student is then taught how to blend the letter sounds together to pronounce words.

Once the student can blend single phonemes, additional graphemes are introduced and emphasis is placed on learning to chunk or break words into their basic parts. The goal of this instruction is to help children understand, as much as possible, why English words are pronounced and spelled the way that they are. Because learning to read and learning to spell are closely related and rely on the same knowledge sources, instruction should be designed so that "their acquisition is mutually facilitative and reciprocal" (Ehri, 2000, p. 34). In addition, individuals with reading difficulties need extensive practice applying their knowledge of letter–sound relationships to the task of reading (Grossen, 1997).

Initial instruction is done with decodable text that consists primarily of words with regular sound–symbol relationships and a few sight words that are taught systematically. This type of text allows beginning readers to integrate their knowledge within the context of connected reading and to practice and apply their developing knowledge of letter–sound correspondences to text. As grapheme/phoneme knowledge increases, attention is directed to building reading speed and recalling common English spelling patterns. Even with adequate instruction, older students with a history of reading and spelling difficulties will often require the accommodation of extended time on tasks that require lengthy reading or writing.

Basic Math Skills

For instruction in basic math skills, the evaluator should first determine the reasons for poor performance. Is low performance a result of not knowing the meaning of the signs, not following the steps in the algorithm, or something as basic as a lack of one-to-one correspondence or counting skills? Success in math, more than any other academic area, is predicated on acquiring the prerequisite skills and knowledge. Prerequisites include concepts such as shape and form, size and length, one-to-one correspondence, and counting. If students do not understand early mathematical concepts, they will have difficulty acquiring concepts that are taught later in the developmental sequence. For example, an understanding of one-to-one relationships is necessary for meaningful counting. Any gaps in the student's mastery of the developmental sequence of mathematical concepts or skills must be addressed. In general, remediation should include concrete materials that can be manipulated, structured presentations using very minute steps, and specific verbalization of instructions followed by conversion into mathematical symbols. A variety of aids have proved useful in remediation, including number lines and Cuisenaire Rods (Harrison & Harrison, 1986; Herbert, 1985; Suydam, 1984).

The language of mathematics is a critical element affecting performance. Students should not be expected to use symbols until they understand their meaning. The signs in mathematics indicate the relationship between the numbers and how they should be manipulated. If the student does not pay attention to or understand the meaning of the sign, he or she will be unsuccessful in solving the problem. For some students, color coding math signs can draw attention to the operation.

The visual-spatial aspects of an arithmetic problem can also impact performance. To solve math problems, the student must understand that the numbers go left to right, top to bottom, and that solutions often go right to left. Careful explanation must be given each time a new process is introduced. No assumptions can be made about what the student does and does not know. Both memory span and working memory can also interfere with calculation if the student has difficulty memorizing math facts and retaining the sequence of steps necessary for solving the problem. Verbalizing each step can be helpful, as can using visual cues to indicate the starting point and direction in which to work the problem. The Short-Term Memory (*Gsm*), Long Term Retrieval (*Glr*), and Working Memory clusters in the WJ III COG may provide valuable information for determining the aspects of memory that are impacting performance in basic math skills.

ACADEMIC FLUENCY

The WJ III ACH fluency measures are all timed tests that relate to automaticity and speed of processing. In interpreting performance on the fluency tests, the evaluator should first determine if scores are low in all academic domains or only in one or two academic domains. The student's performance on the Cognitive Fluency cluster can be compared to the Academic Fluency cluster to determine if the lack of automaticity generalizes to most types of speeded tasks, or applies only to tasks involving a type of academic content. If a student has a low score on one or more measures of fluency, consider if the problem is related to low-level performance in basic skills, delayed automaticity, or a generalized slow response style that is pervasive across timed tasks.

One caution is in order for interpreting performance on the Academic Fluency tests. The academic demands of the WJ III ACH Reading, Math, and Writing Fluency tests are controlled for difficulty level so that they measure automaticity in performance. As the difficulty level of materials increases, a student who was fluent on easy materials may become dysfluent when the vocabulary and conceptual demands increase. In other words, a student may perform automatically on simple tasks, such as solving single-digit addition and subtraction problems on the Math Fluency test, but not on tasks of greater complexity, such as solving a problem involving long division. Automaticity occurs when a known procedure is practiced enough times that it is completed with little cognitive effort. Thus, in considering fluency, the difficulty level of the material for the student is a factor. For example, a college student with a reading disability may appear quite fluent on text at the third-grade instructional level, but very dysfluent when reading college-level textbooks, whereas the typical college student decodes both texts with ease. Table 3-6 lists clusters that should be considered when interpreting performance on academic fluency tasks.

TABLE 3-6 Clusters to Consider When Interpreting Performance in Academic Fluency

Achievement cluster/test	Relevant achievement clusters	Relevant cognitive clusters
Academic Fluency Reading Fluency Math Fluency Writing Fluency	Basic Skills Oral Language	Cognitive Fluency Comprehension–Knowledge Fluid Reasoning Processing Speed Short-Term Memory
Reading Fluency	Basic Reading Skills Reading Comprehension Oral Language	Auditory Processing Comprehension–Knowledge Fluid Reasoning Processing Speed Short-Term Memory
Math Fluency	Basic Math Calculation Skills Oral Language	Comprehension–Knowledge Fluid Reasoning Processing Speed Short-Term Memory Visual-Spatial Thinking
Writing Fluency	Basic Writing Skills Written Expression Oral Language	Auditory Processing Comprehension–Knowledge Fluid Reasoning Processing Speed

READING FLUENCY

Reading fluency encompasses the speed or rate of reading, as well as the ability to read materials with expression. Meyer and Felton (1999) define fluency as "the ability to read connected text rapidly, smoothly, effortlessly, and automatically with little conscious attention to the mechanics of reading, such as decoding" (p. 284). Children are successful with decoding when the process used to identify words is fast and nearly effortless or automatic. As noted, the concept of automaticity refers to a student's ability to recognize words rapidly with little attention required to the word's appearance. Lack of automaticity causes the attentional system to be overloaded and places heavy demands on memory. In addition, slow word identification adversely affects comprehension (Stanovich, 1982). The key to skilled reading, therefore, is the ability to read words automatically by sight (Ehri, 1998).

Some individuals may have developed accurate word pronunciation and spelling skills, as measured on the Letter–Word Identification and Spelling tests, but read or write slowly. For slow readers, decoding is not automatic or fluent and their limited fluency can affect performance in the following ways: (a) they read less text than peers and have less time to remember, review, or comprehend the text; (b) they expend more cognitive energy than peers trying to identify individual words; and (c) they may be less able to retain text in their memories and less likely to integrate those segments with other parts of the text (Mastropieri, Leinart, & Scruggs, 1999).

A major problem for poor readers is rapid identification of individual words (Torgesen, Rashotte, & Alexander, 2001). Individuals with dyslexia often display a disruption in word-reading automaticity (Goldsmith-Phillips, 1994) and obtain low scores on measures of processing speed, particularly the WJ III COG Visual Matching test (Johnson, 1998). In addition to processing speed measures, a variety of factors can affect reading fluency and rate. Torgesen et al. (2001) explain that the following components can underlie individual differences in rate and accuracy in oral reading: (a) the number of words recognized by sight, (b) the speed with which sight words are processed, (c) the speed of processes used to pronounce unfamiliar words, (d) the use of context to facilitate speed of word identification, and (e) the rate that word meanings can be accessed.

WRITING FLUENCY

As with reading, fluent and automatic basic skills are fundamental to the expression of more complex meaningful writing (Gerber & Hall, 1987). A number of factors, in addition to automaticity with basic skills, can influence writing fluency: visual–motor abilities, handwriting speed, facility with syntax, and reading ability. In some instances, handwriting speed is the reason for a low score on the Writing Fluency test. Levine (1987) described several stages of hand-writing proficiency: (a) imitation, whereby young children pretend to write by copying others; (b) graphic presentation, during first and second grade, when children learn how to form letters and to write on a line with proper spacing and fine-motor skills become better developed; (c) progressive incorporation, from late second to fourth grade, when letters are produced with less effort; and (d) automatization, in fourth through seventh grade, when children write rapidly and efficiently. In the final stages, children develop personalized styles and increase writing proficiency. If a student has a low score on the Writing Fluency test, examine the individual's performance in handwriting, the WJ III COG Processing Speed (*Gs*) cluster, and the WJ III ACH Oral Language cluster. Difficulties may be caused by poor motor control or slow handwriting speed, generalized slow processing speed, or difficulty formulating sentences quickly. If oral language abilities are low, then the low Writing Fluency score may be due to difficulties manipulating syntax, resulting in slow sentence formulation.

MATH FLUENCY

As with reading and writing performance, fluency with basic skills is fundamental to success with more complex math (Cawley, 1985; Hasselbring, Goin, & Bransford, 1987; Kirby & Becker, 1988). A lack of automaticity with basic math facts interferes with performance on higher level skills and is an important predictor of math performance (Meltzer, 1994). Acquisition of basic math skills may be affected by problems similar to those that affect decoding and encoding. A student who has trouble memorizing basic math facts and developing numerical facility often has trouble solving mathematical problems. More advanced levels of mathematics require rapid and accurate handling of numerical quantities (Carroll, 1993). Carroll defines numerical facility and explains the importance of this ability to mathematical thinking:

> ... the degree to which the individual has developed skills in dealing with numbers, from the most elementary skills of counting objects and recognizing written numbers and their order, to the more advanced skills of correctly adding, subtracting, multiplying, and dividing numbers with an increasing number of digits, or with fractions and decimals. These are skills that are learned through experiences in the home, school, or even in the workplace. In the early years, skills deal with simple numbers and operations, and the important object is to be able to deal with number problems correctly, at whatever speed. In later years, practice is aimed at handling computations with greater speed as well as accuracy. More complex problems can be dealt with effectively and efficiently only if skills with simple problems are increasingly automatized (p. 469).

Just as with reading and writing fluency, the lower level skills involved in rapid calculation must become increasingly automatized so that full attention can be devoted to problem solving.

INSTRUCTIONAL IMPLICATIONS FOR ACADEMIC FLUENCY

The main accommodation typically needed for students with delayed automaticity is extended time. These students are not able to complete work at the rate of many of their classmates. On some occasions, assignments can be shortened or targeted for a certain amount of time, rather than a certain number of pages. For example, the teacher may ask students to read for 20 minutes, regardless of the number of pages that are completed in that time period. Students with low fluency levels can often benefit from technology, such as using taped books to complete reading assignments.

The goal of fluency intervention is to establish automaticity: rapid and easy recognition of words, rapid recall of math facts, and rapid and easy production of letter forms. In general, limited fluency and rate in reading, writing, and/or math are addressed through various rate-building and timed activities. A variety of speed drills can be used in which the student is asked to read, or write, or calculate math facts as rapidly as possible over a 1-minute period. For reading lists of words as a 1-minute speed drill, Fischer (1999) suggests using the following general guidelines: 30 correct words per minute (wpm) for first- and second-grade children, 40 correct wpm for third-grade children, 60 correct wpm for mid-third-grade children, and 80 correct wpm for students in fourth grade and above.

Reading Fluency

Another well-known procedure for students who read slowly despite adequate word recognition is the repeated reading technique (Samuels, 1979). For this procedure, the individual reads the same passage aloud over and over again.

The time and number of errors are recorded until a predetermined goal is reached or the student is able to read the passage fluently with few mistakes.

Research on repeated readings suggests that fluency can be improved as long as students are provided with specific instructions, and procedures are used to monitor their progress (Mastropieri, Leinart, & Scruggs, 1999; Meyer & Felton, 1999). Repeated readings have also been used as a component of classwide peer tutoring (Mathes & Fuchs, 1993). In one study of this intervention, pairs of students in one group read continuously over a 10-minute period while pairs of students in another group read a passage together three times before going on to the next passage. Although both experimental conditions produced higher results than the typical reading instruction, no difference existed between the procedures, suggesting that the main benefit of the intervention is the student reading involvement and the increased time spent in reading (Mastropieri et al., 1999).

In a review of methods that are effective for building fluency, Meyer and Felton (1999) provided the following recommendations for helping students to improve fluency: (a) have students engage in multiple readings (three to four times); (b) use instructional-level text; (c) use decodable text with struggling readers; (d) provide short, frequent periods of fluency practice; and (e) provide concrete measures of progress. For students with poor reading skills, modeling and practicing words between readings will improve student performance and reduce frustration. Additional procedures that can be used to increase rate include rapid word recognition charts (Carreker, 1999), taped books (Carbo, 1989), and *Great Leaps Reading* (Campbell, 1996).

Writing Fluency

As with reading speed, one goal for writing instruction is to establish automaticity or rapid and easy production of letter forms. Practice contributes to automaticity as the motor patterns needed for legible writing become more firmly established. One technique that may be used to improve writing rate and fluency and to encourage reluctant writers to increase their productivity is daily timed writings (Alvarez, 1983; Douglass, 1984; Houten, Morrison, Jarvis, & MacDonald, 1974). For this procedure, students write about a topic for 5 to 10 minutes, trying to write more words than they did on the previous day. At the end of the time period, students count the number of words and record the word count on the top of the paper. Individual reinforcements can be provided contingent upon performance, such as points for an assigned number of letters, words, or sentences.

Math Fluency

For automaticity with math facts, daily speed drills may increase the speed and accuracy of recall. One way to help students become more automatic with math facts is to practice with flashcards. First, identify the facts that the student does not know. Then, practice three unknown facts at a time. Present the card and ask the student to respond. If the response takes longer than 2 seconds, tell the student the answer and move on to the next card. Once the student has mastered these three facts, place them in a pile for review the next day.

Using a pocket-size facts chart is another helpful technique. Once the student demonstrates speed and accuracy with a fact, it can be removed or blocked out from his or her personal chart. This approach motivates the student to learn another fact and discourages overreliance on the chart. In addition to providing support and instruction, this type of approach builds in a self-monitoring feature.

Another method for increasing speed with math facts is using verbal reasoning strategies to make the task more meaningful. For example, one might demonstrate the strategy of verbalizing the relationship between a known fact and a new fact: "Since 5 + 5 is 10, 5 + 6 is 11." Helping the student see relationships between facts or building knowledge of fact "families" can ease the burden on memory.

When working with students who have slow rates and limited automaticity with reading or writing words, or math facts, more repetition and practice are required for mastery, and timed activities that require rapid responses seem most effective. Fluency-building activities should use content on which the student has demonstrated accuracy so that the student does not make errors. In addition, short, frequent periods of practice are better than one long session. Finally, concrete measures of progress, such as charts and graphs, are effective for displaying gains.

ORAL LANGUAGE, KNOWLEDGE, AND ACADEMIC APPLICATIONS

Oral language abilities, acquired knowledge, and reasoning abilities provide the foundation for success in tasks involving comprehension, problem solving, and self-monitoring. Oral language is positively related to success in reading, math, and written language (Gregg, 2001; Stanovich, 1986; Wiig & Semel, 1984). The WJ III ACH measures an individual's receptive and expressive oral language abilities, as well as his or her knowledge of curricular areas. Receptive oral language abilities refer to an individual's ability to understand what is being said to them or to listen with understanding. Expressive oral language relates to the ability to retrieve ideas and vocabulary and express thoughts in an appropriate manner through speaking. Low-level expressive language in preschool children often predicts subsequent academic difficulties (Bishop & Adams, 1990; Tallal, Curtiss, & Kaplan, 1989).

Some students have adequate receptive language but poor expressive language; they understand what is said to them but have trouble responding orally. These students tend to have higher scores on measures that involve pointing (such as the Understanding Directions test) and lower scores on measures involving speaking (such as the Story Recall test). Other students have poor receptive language and expressive language and have difficulties with many linguistic tasks. Language difficulties can affect performance in many domains. Masterson (1993) explained that students with language impairments have particular difficulty with tasks that require increasing amounts of information to solve a problem successfully. She found that students with language disorders had more difficulty on the

Woodcock–Johnson—Revised (WJ-R) Concept Formation test than on the Analysis Synthesis test, both of which are measures of fluid reasoning (*Gf*).

A critical factor that influences oral expression, reading comprehension, written expression, and math problem solving is background knowledge. The attainment of knowledge is an important aim of education and may be the dominant correlate of school success (Rolfhus & Ackerman, 1999). The Knowledge cluster is obtained by combining the WJ III COG General Information test and the WJ III ACH Academic Knowledge test. This cluster represents an estimate of lexical knowledge as well as the knowledge obtained from educational and general life experiences. If a student obtains low scores on measures of oral language and knowledge, the evaluator should consider if the difficulties are related to (a) poor word retrieval, (b) limited lexical knowledge, (c) lack of exposure and experience, (d) poor memory, (e) limited English proficiency, or (f) a specific language impairment. Several tests from the WJ III COG can also help an evaluator determine the nature and extent of the linguistic difficulties. For example, performance on the Retrieval Fluency and Rapid Picture Naming tests can be used to estimate word retrieval abilities and speed of lexical access, whereas the Verbal Comprehension and General Information tests provide an estimate of lexical knowledge.

The WJ III ACH measures of academic applications involve conceptual processes that require the use of procedural knowledge and strategies. These types of tasks are of a higher order in that they involve linguistic and reasoning abilities that are required for writing an idea, solving a verbal math problem, or defining words. If a student has low-level performance on application tasks, the first step is to determine which of the following factors are most related to the poor performance: (a) low-level performance in basic skills, (b) limited oral language proficiency, (c) limited background or procedural knowledge, (d) ineffective or limited instruction, or (e) limited knowledge of or failure to apply strategies. Some individuals with learning disabilities appear to be inflexible and inefficient in applying problem-solving strategies that are required for tasks such as reading comprehension. Successful completion of application tasks requires integration of language, procedural (how to), and declarative (factual) knowledge; reasoning abilities; self-monitoring; and self-evaluation. Weaknesses in metacognition, or the ability to think about one's own thinking, appear to adversely affect the development and use of strategies and impede progress in academic tasks (Montague, 1997).

Several of the WJ III COG factors appear related to the ability to perform academic applications. McGrew and Flanagan (1998) report that both acquired knowledge (*Gc*) and Short-Term Memory (*Gsm*) have a consistent, significant relationship with reading achievement. The significance of Comprehension–Knowledge (*Gc*) with respect to reading and writing achievement increases with age. In addition, memory span (the ability to attend to and immediately recall temporally ordered items) appears to influence comprehension. Naming facility, an aspect of Long-Term Retrieval (*Glr*), appears to be related to word-retrieval abilities. Fluid Reasoning (*Gf*) is also important to comprehension but not to decoding. In contrast, Visual-Spatial Thinking abilities (*Gv*) have little significance in explaining or predicting reading achievement.

Visual-Spatial thinking abilities (*Gv*) appear, however, to be related to math tasks that require higher level skills and thinking but not to basic math skills (McGrew & Flanagan, 1998). Some students have trouble with the conceptual component of math, such as the abilities involved in learning mathematical concepts and solving story problems. For students with weaknesses in math problem solving, it is important to determine whether language or reading problems are contributing to a mathematics problem, or if the difficulty results from weaknesses in quantitative knowledge and thinking. Table 3-7 indicates which achievement

TABLE 3-7   Clusters to Consider When Interpreting Performance in Academic Applications

Academic applications cluster/test	Relevant achievement clusters	Relevant cognitive clusters
Oral Language/Knowledge Story Recall Understanding Directions Picture Vocabulary Oral Comprehension Academic Knowledge	Oral Language—Extended Academic Knowledge	Auditory Processing Comprehension– Knowledge Fluid Reasoning Long-Term Retrieval Short-Term Memory
Oral Expression Story Recall Picture Vocabulary	Reading Comprehension	Auditory Processing Comprehension– Knowledge Long-Term Retrieval
Listening Comprehension Understanding Directions Oral Comprehension	Reading Comprehension	Auditory Processing Comprehension– Knowledge Fluid Reasoning Short-Term Memory
Reading Comprehension Passage Comprehension Reading Vocabulary	Basic Reading Skills Oral Language	Comprehension– Knowledge Fluid Reasoning Short-Term Memory
Written Expression Writing Fluency Writing Samples	Basic Writing Skills Oral Language Reading Comprehension	Comprehension– Knowledge Fluid Reasoning Processing Speed Short-Term Memory
Math Reasoning Applied Problems Quantitative Concepts	Math Calculation Skills Oral Language	Comprehension– Knowledge Fluid Reasoning Processing Speed Short-Term Memory Visual-Spatial Thinking

and cognitive clusters should be considered when interpreting the academic application clusters.

INSTRUCTIONAL IMPLICATIONS FOR
ACADEMIC APPLICATIONS

Students with weaknesses in language, knowledge, and/or application tasks often require an adjustment in the level of the instructional materials to be successful. Rather than providing more time to complete assignments, the content of the assignments needs to be matched to the student's level of linguistic competence.

Most students can be successful in school if they learn how to be organized, reflective, and strategic. Regardless of whether a strategy is designed primarily to enhance oral language, knowledge, reading comprehension, written expression, or math problem-solving ability, several general principles apply (Meltzer, Roditi, & Stein, 1998): (a) teach strategies in the context of the curriculum, (b) teach different strategies so students can choose among strategies, (c) provide a balance between instruction in strategies and skills, (d) encourage students to understand their own learning styles, and (e) show students how to adapt strategies as needed.

Oral Language, Reading Comprehension, Written Expression

One goal of instruction for students with weaknesses in language and academic applications is to increase background knowledge. A simple strategy for helping students increase their knowledge is called the K-W-L strategy (Ogle, 1986). Three columns are written across the top of a paper: What I Know, What I Want to Learn, and What I Learned. The K-W-L procedure provides an opportunity for the student to organize what is known, record new information, and then review and rehearse what has been learned.

Another goal for instruction is to increase vocabulary and knowledge of word meanings. As students progress through school, the vocabulary in classes becomes increasingly more specialized. Some students benefit from direct instruction on the use of common prefixes and suffixes and the study of word origins. Students can also study the various derivations of words to increase their understanding of how common morphemes, as well as prefixes and suffixes, alter word meaning. As a cautionary note, if oral language abilities are the primary area of concern, a more comprehensive evaluation by a speech and language therapist is often needed to pinpoint the linguistic difficulties and plan a therapeutic program.

Math Reasoning

Students who have difficulty with math problem solving require instruction that focuses on meaning and establishing prerequisite skills and concepts. Because students progress through different stages of learning at different rates, the teacher needs to identify the stage of learning the student has reached and adjust intervention accordingly. Smith and Rivera (1998) identify the following stages: In the first stage, the emphasis is on the student *acquiring the skill*: learning how to perform the skill, practicing the skill, and becoming increasingly accurate in using the skill. During the second stage, the student becomes *proficient with the skill*—in other words, develops the ability to respond more easily while maintaining accuracy. In the third stage, maintenance, the student extends his or her ability to continue to *maintain, or use, the skill* once mastery is achieved. Some students find this particularly difficult without ongoing practice and review. For these students, it is necessary to provide periodic assessment to determine that the skill is still maintained. *Generalization*, the fourth stage, is the ability to use the skill in different situations. Generalization should occur throughout all stages of learning mathematics and should be presented conscientiously throughout instruction. Demonstrate and model for students the times, places, and situations that the skill can be used. In the final stage, students learn *adaptation*, or ways to extend their knowledge and skills through problem solving.

General interventions that assist in teaching mathematics include modeling (particularly useful during the first two stages of instruction), shaping (using reinforcement as the student works toward successive approximations of the skill), drills, rewards for accuracy, feedback, and strategy instruction. Guided practice as students engage in problem solving can be critical. Jones, Wilson, and Bhojwani (1997) found that many teachers move on to teach new math material even though students are answering only about 60% of the problems correctly.

Verbal explanations and discussions can also facilitate learning quantitative concepts. As with strategies for reading and writing, instructors should provide students with opportunities to discuss, clarify, and state what is being learned to help increase understanding. In addition, teachers should provide explicit instruction in the language of mathematics, including signs, symbols, and terms as well as the vocabulary used to express mathematical ideas. Students who have difficulty using language need to talk through possible answers to word problems to help identify and resolve incorrect assumptions (Tobias, 1993).

Students with weaknesses in language, knowledge, and/or reasoning abilities need to have teachers who will establish realistic expectations and set clear educational goals. The teacher must attempt to adjust explanations to the level of the student's understanding. This does not mean that the teacher has lowered expectations, but rather that the teacher formulates a program that is challenging yet possible for the student to learn and succeed. Good instruction is one step above a student's present performance level (Vygotsky, 1978).

SAMPLE CASE

Considering an individual's cognitive strengths and weaknesses in the context of academic performance provides a meaningful framework for discerning instructional implications. The following example illustrates some of the comparisons that can be made. The three cross-academic clusters—Academic Skills, Academic Fluency, and Academic Applications—are used as focal points.

EXAMPLE OF JEFF: AGE 17-3, GRADE 11.2

Jeff was referred for an evaluation by his high school English teacher, Ms. Moore. Ms. Moore expressed concerns about Jeff's ability to complete tasks in a timely manner and felt that he needed adjustments in his curriculum to be successful. She reported that he rarely finished assignments when time constraints were imposed. Classroom observations in Jeff's history class also supported that Jeff was slow to complete lengthy reading assignments. Furthermore, Jeff's mother noted that he often spent more than 4 hours a night trying to complete class readings. For this assessment, the evaluator selected the WJ III because it provides opportunities to analyze patterns of performance between and among cognitive and academic abilities. This process helps the evaluator document specific academic difficulties as well as the underlying cognitive abilities that may be impacting performance.

A review of Jeff's normative scores (Standard Score/Percentile Rank; SS/PR) for the three cross-academic clusters indicates average to low-average performance in Academic Skills and Academic Fluency, with average to above-average performance in Academic Applications (see Table 3-8). The criterion-referenced scores (RPIs) indicate that Jeff is functionally limited in his performance on tasks involving basic skills and timed tasks compared to average grade-mates. The Instructional Zones indicate that Jeff will struggle with skills and fluency tasks presented at a difficulty level commensurate with his current grade placement. The results of an informal reading inventory also indicate that Jeff has limited automaticity with word identification, which reduces his reading rate.

These findings suggest that Jeff may benefit from accommodations on tasks involving basic skills or rapid performance. In contrast, if no penalty exists for basic skills and sufficient time is allotted on tasks, Jeff will not need adjustments on tasks involving reasoning and problem solving. To further substantiate these conclusions, it is necessary to examine the tests within each cluster to determine whether the problems are generalized or domain specific.

In Academic Skills (see Table 3-9), math is not an area of concern. However, reading and writing levels are low from all perspectives—normative, criterion

TABLE 3-8 Jeff's Cross-Academic Cluster Scores[a]

Cross-academic cluster	GE	Instructional Zone		RPI	PR	SS
		Easy	Difficult			
Academic Skills	7.7	6.0	10.3	69/90	19	87 (84–90)
Academic Fluency	9.1	7.5	10.8	71/90	30	92 (90–94)
Academic Applications	14.2	10.6	>18.0	96/90	74	110 (106–113)

[a]Abbreviations: GE, Grade Equivalent; RPI, Relative Proficiency Index; PR, Percentile Rank; SS, Standard Score.

TABLE 3-9   Jeff's Academic Skills Cluster and Test Scores[a]

| | | Instructional zone | | | | |
Cluster/Test	GE	Easy	Difficult	RPI	PR	SS
Academic Skills	7.7	6.0	10.3	69/90	19	87 (84–90)
Letter–Word Identification	7.1	5.7	8.8	51/90	20	87 (84–91)
Calculation	12.9	9.6	>18.0	94/90	60	104 (100–108)
Spelling	5.4	4.2	7.0	40/90	9	80 (75–84)

[a]See Table 3-8 for abbreviations.

referenced, and instructional. In Academic Fluency (see Table 3-10), reading and writing are both problematic, whereas math is not. This example also illustrates the importance of considering the RPI in addition to the Standard Score. On Reading Fluency the SS of 92 falls within the average range. However, the RPI of 39/90 indicates "limited" proficiency or mastery on this task compared to average grade-mates. The tests within the Academic Applications cluster (see Table 3-11) indicate performance in the average to high-average range in reading comprehension and math problem solving and in the average range for written expression.

Next, Jeff's cognitive abilities were examined to determine if any factors would help explain his academic strengths and weaknesses and would assist in planning an appropriate instructional program. On the intracognitive discrepancies, Jeff demonstrates significant strengths in Comprehension–Knowledge (*Gc*) and Fluid Reasoning (*Gf*) and significant weaknesses in Auditory Processing (*Ga*), Processing Speed (*Gs*), and Short-Term Memory (*Gsm*).

Jeff's cognitive strengths help explain his strengths in Academic Applications (see Table 3-12). His strong knowledge base and reasoning skills facilitate his ability to comprehend, organize his thoughts for writing, and solve math problems. In contrast, Jeff's cognitive weaknesses help explain his difficulties in the

TABLE 3-10   Jeff's Academic Fluency Cluster and Test Scores[a]

| | | Instructional zone | | | | |
Cluster/Test	GE	Easy	Difficult	RPI	PR	SS
Academic Fluency	9.1	7.5	10.8	71/90	30	92 (90–94)
Reading Fluency	9.2	8.3	10.0	39/90	30	92 (91–94)
Math Fluency	15.3	9.9	>18.0	95/90	74	110 (107–112)
Writing Fluency	6.6	5.2	8.5	53/90	18	86 (82–90)

[a]See Table 3-8 for abbreviations.

TABLE 3-11   Jeff's Academic Application Cluster and Test Scores[a]

Cluster	GE	Instructional zone		RPI	PR	SS
		Easy	Difficult			
Academic Applications	14.2	10.6	>18.0	96/90	74	110 (106–113)
Passage Comprehension	>18.0	11.0	>18.0	96/90	77	111 (105–117)
Applied Problems	>18.0	13.0	>18.0	98/90	75	110 (107–113)
Writing Samples	10.0	4.1	>18.0	89/90	42	97 (88–106)

[a]See Table 3-8 for abbreviations.

reading and writing areas within Academic Skills and Academic Fluency (see Table 3-13). All three cognitive abilities—Auditory Processing, Processing Speed, and Short-Term Memory—have documented relationships to reading and writing, especially in the area of basic skills. A review of other achievement results indicates that his oral language scores are in the superior range (SS ±1 SEM: 119–129), a significant strength for Jeff. This information helps document that he has domain-specific problems in reading and writing. In addition, his strong oral language performance provides supporting evidence for his strength in Comprehension–Knowledge.

When Oral Language is used as a predictor in the ability/achievement discrepancy procedure, Jeff demonstrates significant discrepancies in Broad Reading, Basic Reading Skills, Broad Written Language, Basic Writing Skills, and Written Expression (see Table 3-14). This information provides additional support for documenting Jeff's domain-specific problems in reading and writing.

Based on the results of his evaluation as well as qualitative information from teachers and classroom observations, Jeff was determined to be eligible for learning disabilities services. A 504 Accommodation Plan was completed for Jeff in the areas of reading and written language to address his difficulties on timed tasks involving basic skills. The primary accommodations included no penalty for spelling errors, extended time on tests as needed, and/or shortened assignments. No accommodations were necessary for higher level tasks involving reasoning and problem solving as long as sufficient time was allotted.

TABLE 3-12   Jeff's Intracognitive Strengths[a]

Strengths	PR	SS
Comprehension–Knowledge (Gc)	88	117 (113–121)
Fluid Reasoning (Gf)	79	112 (107–117)

[a]PR, Percentile Rank; SS, Standard Score.

TABLE 3-13   Jeff's Intracognitive Weaknesses[a]

Weaknesses	PR	SS
Auditory Process (Ga)	7	77 (72–83)
Processing Speed (Gs)	4	73 (70–77)
Short-Term Memory (Gsm)	8	79 (75–83)

[a]PR, Percentile Rank; SS, Standard Score.

CONCLUSION

As stated by Johnson and Myklebust (1967), "The single most important factor in planning for a child with a learning disability is an intensive diagnostic study. Without a comprehensive evaluation of his deficits and assets, the educational program may be too general, or even inappropriate" (p. 50). The WJ III is a sophisticated diagnostic instrument that serves as a valuable tool when in the hands of a skilled clinician. An evaluator can determine if the problem is related to generalized low-level performance or to performance on certain types of tasks across the academic domains (skills, fluency, and/or applications), or if the difficulties are circumscribed to one area of functioning. Once the factors that both facilitate and inhibit academic performance have been identified, a specific instructional plan can be developed that will contribute to more successful outcomes for the individual.

TABLE 3-14   Jeff's Oral Language/Achievement Discrepancy Scores

	Standard Scores			Discrepancy		
Discrepancy	Actual	Predicted	Difference	PR	SD	Significant at ±1.50 SD (SEE)
Broad Reading	93	112	−19	5	−1.66	Yes
Basic Reading Skills	74	113	−39	0.1	−3.06	Yes
Broad Math	110	114	−4	38	−0.32	No
Math Calculation Skills	107	110	−3	41	−0.23	No
Broad Written Language	83	113	−30	1	−2.38	Yes
Basic Writing Skills	88	111	−23	4	−1.79	Yes
Written Expression	88	111	−23	4	−1.79	Yes

Note: These discrepancies are based on Oral Language (Ext) with ACH Broad, Basic, and Applied clusters.

REFERENCES

Alvarez, M. C. (1983). Sustained timed writing as an aid to fluency and creativity. *Teaching Exceptional Children, 15*, 160–162.

Ball, E. W. (1993). Assessing phoneme awareness. *Language, Speech, and Hearing Services in Schools, 24*, 130–139.

Berninger, V. W. (1990). Multiple orthographic codes: Key to alternative instructional methodologies for developing the orthographic–phonological connections underlying word identification. *School Psychology Review, 19*, 518–533.

Berninger, V. W. (1996). *Reading and writing acquisition: A developmental neuropsychological perspective*. Oxford: Westview Press.

Berninger, V. W. (1998). Assessment, prevention, and intervention for specific reading and writing disabilities in young children. In B. Wong (Ed.), *Learning about learning disabilities*, (2nd ed., pp. 529–555), New York: Academic Press.

Berninger, V. W., Vaughan, K., Abbott, R. D., Brooks, A., Begay, K., Curtin, G., Byrd, K., & Graham, S. (2000). Language-based spelling instruction: Teaching children to make multiple connections between spoken and written words. *Learning Disability Quarterly, 23*, 117–135.

Betts, E. A. (1946). *Foundations of reading instruction*. New York: American Book.

Bishop, D. V. M., & Adams, C. (1990). A prospective study of the relationship between specific language impairment, phonological disorders and reading retardation. *Journal of Child Psychology and Psychiatry, 31*, 1027–1050.

Bruck, M. (1998). Outcomes of adults with childhood histories of dyslexia. In C. Hulme & R. M. Joshi (Eds.), *Reading and spelling development and disorders* (pp. 179–200). Mahwah, NJ: Erlbaum.

Calfee, R. (1998). Phonics and phonemes: Learning to decode and spell in a literature-based program. In J. L. Metsala & L. C. Ehri (Eds.), *Word recognition in beginning literacy* (pp. 315–340). Mahwah, NJ: Erlbaum.

Campbell, K. U. (1996). *Great leaps reading program*. Micanopy, FL: Diarmuid.

Carbo, M. (1989). *How to record books for maximum reading gains*. New York: National Reading Styles Institute.

Carreker, S. (1999). Teaching reading: Accurate decoding and fluency. In J. R. Birsh (Ed.), *Multisensory teaching of basic language skills* (pp. 141–182). Baltimore: Paul H. Brookes Publishing.

Carroll, J. B. (1993). *Human cognitive abilities: A survey of factor-analytic studies*. New York: Cambridge University Press.

Cawley, J. F. (1985, February). *Arithmetical word problems and the learning disabled*. Paper presented at the Association for Children with Learning Disabilities, International Conference, San Francisco.

Chafouleas, S. M., Lewandowski, L. J., Smith, C. R., & Blachman, B. A. (1997). Phonological awareness skills in children: Examining performance across tasks and ages. *Journal of Psychoeducational Assessment, 15*, 331–347.

Chard, D. J., & Dickson, S. V. (1999). Phonological awareness: Instructional and assessment guidelines. *Intervention in School and Clinic, 34*, 261–270.

Clark, D. B., & Uhry, J. K. (1995). *Dyslexia: Theory and practice of remedial instruction* (2nd ed.). Baltimore: York Press.

Coltheart, M. (1996). Phonological dyslexia: Past and future. *Cognitive Neuropsychology, 13*, 749–762.

Douglass, B. (1984). Variation on a theme: Writing with the LD adolescent. *Academic Therapy, 19*, 361–363.

Ehri, L. C. (1998). Grapheme–phoneme knowledge is essential for learning to read words in English. In J. L. Metsala & L. C. Ehri (Eds.), *Word recognition in beginning literacy* (pp. 3–40). Mahwah, NJ: Erlbaum.

Ehri, L. C. (2000). Learning to read and learning to spell: Two sides of a coin. *Topics in Language Disorders, 20*(3), 19–36.

Evans, J. J., Floyd, R G., McGrew, K. S., & Leforgee, M. H. (2002). The relations between measures of Cattell-Horn-Carroll (CHC) cognitive abilities and reading achievement during childhood and adolescence. *School Psychology Review, 31*, 246–262.

Fischer, P. (1999). Getting up to speed. *Perspectives, The International Dyslexia Association, 25*(2), 12–13.

Fleischner, J. E., Garnett, K., & Shepherd, M. J. (1982). Proficiency in arithmetic basic fact computation of learning disabled and nondisabled children. *Focus on Learning Problems in Mathematics, 4*, 47–55.

Francis, D. J., Shaywitz, S. E., Stuebing, K. K., Shaywitz, B. A., & Fletcher, J. M. (1996). Developmental lag versus deficit models of reading disability: A longitudinal, individual growth curves study. *Journal of Educational Psychology, 88*, 3–17.

Gerber, M. M., & Hall, R. J. (1987). Information processing approaches to studying spelling deficiencies. *Journal of Learning Disabilities, 20*, 34–42.

Goldsmith-Phillips, J. (1994). Toward a research-based dyslexia assessment: Case study of a young adult. In N. C. Jordan & J. Goldsmith-Phillips (Eds.), *Learning disabilities: New directions for assessment and intervention* (pp. 85–100). Boston: Allyn and Bacon.

Gregg, N. (2001). Written expression disorders. In L. Bailet, A. Bain, & L. Moats (Eds.), *Written language disorders* (2nd ed., pp. 65–98). Austin, TX: Pro-Ed.

Grossen, B. (1997). *30 Years of research: What we now know about how children learn to read.* Santa Cruz, CA: The Center for the Future of Teaching & Learning.

Harrison, M., & Harrison, B. (1986). Developing numeration concepts and skills. *Arithmetic Teacher, 33*, 18–21.

Hasselbring, T. S., Goin, L. I., & Bransford, J. D. (1987). Developing automaticity. *Teaching Exceptional Children, 19* (3), 30–33.

Herbert, E. (1985). One point of view: Manipulatives are good mathematics. *Arithmetic Teacher, 32*, 4.

Holopainen, L., Ahonen, T., & Lyytinen, H. (2001). Predicting delay in reading achievement in a highly transparent language. *Journal of Learning Disabilities, 34*, 401–413.

Houten, R. V., Morrison, E., Jarvis, R., & MacDonald, M. (1974). The effects of explicit timing and feedback on compositional response rate in elementary school children. *Journal of Applied Behavior Analysis, 7*, 547–555.

Johnson, D. (1998). Dyslexia: The identification process. In B. K. Shapiro, P. J. Accardo, & A. J. Capute (Eds.), *Specific reading disability: A view of the spectrum* (pp. 137–154). Timonium, MD: York Press.

Johnson, D. J., & Myklebust, H. R. (1967). *Learning disabilities: Educational principles and practices.* New York: Grune & Stratton.

Jones, E. D., Wilson, R., & Bhojwani, S. (1997). Mathematics instruction for secondary students with learning disabilities. *Journal of Learning Disabilities, 30*(2), 151–163.

Kirby, J. R., & Becker, L. D. (1988). Cognitive components of learning problems in arithmetic. *Remedial and Special Education, 9*(5), 7–16.

Kirk, S. A. (1975). From labels to action. In S. A. Kirk & M. M. McCarthy (Eds.), *Learning disabilities: Selected ACLD papers* (pp. 39–45). Boston: Houghton Mifflin.

Kirk, S. A., Kleibhan, J. M., & Lerner, J. W. (1978). *Teaching reading to slow and disabled learners.* Boston: Houghton Mifflin.

Levine, M. (1987). *Developmental variations and learning disorders.* Cambridge, MA: Educators Publishing Service.

Liberman, I. Y., Shankweiler, D., & Liberman, A. M. (1989). The alphabetic principle and learning to read. In D. Shankweiler & I. Y. Liberman (Eds.), *Phonology and reading disability: Solving the reading puzzle* (pp. 1–33). Ann Arbor, MI: University of Michigan Press.

Lyon, G. R. (1995). Toward a definition of dyslexia. *Annals of Dyslexia, 45*, 3–27.

Lyon, G. R. (1998). Why reading is not natural. *Educational Leadership, 3*, 14–18.

Masterson, J. J. (1993). The performance of children with language-learning disabilities on two types of cognitive tasks. *Journal of Speech and Hearing Reseearch, 36,* 1026–1036.

Mastropieri, M. A., Leinart, A., & Scruggs, T. E. (1999). Strategies to increase reading fluency. *Intervention in School and Clinic, 34,* 278–283.

Mather, N. (1993). Critical issues in the assessment of learning disabilities addressed by the Woodcock–Johnson Psycho-Educational Battery—Revised. *Journal of Psychoeducational Assessment.* Monograph Series: Advances in psychoeducational assessment: Woodcock–Johnson Psycho-Educational Battery—Revised, 103–122.

Mather, N., & Jaffe, L. E. (2002). *Woodcock–Johnson III: Reports, recommendations, and strategies.* New York: John Wiley & Sons.

Mather, N., Wendling, B. J., & Woodcock, R. W. (2001). *Essentials of WJ III Tests of Achievement assessment.* New York: John Wiley & Sons.

Mathes, P. G., & Fuchs, L. S. (1993). Peer-mediated reading instruction in special education resource rooms. *Learning Disabilities Research & Practice, 8,* 233–243.

McGrew, K. S., & Flanagan, D. P. (1998). *The intelligence test desk reference (ITDR): Gf–Gc cross-battery assessment.* Boston: Allyn & Bacon.

McGrew, K. S., & Hessler, G. L. (1995). The relationship between the WJ-R *Gf–Gc* cognitive clusters and mathematics achievement across the life-span. *Journal of Psychoeducational Assessment, 13,* 21–38.

McGrew, K. S., & Knopik, S. N. (1993). Relationship between the WJ-R *Gf–Gc* cognitive clusters and writing achievement across the life-span. *School Psychology Review, 22,* 687–695.

Meltzer, L. J. (1994). Assessment of learning disabilities: The challenge of evaluating cognitive strategies and processes underlying learning. In G. R. Lyon (Ed.), *Frames of reference for the assessment of learning disabilities: New views on measurement issues* (pp. 571–606). Baltimore: Paul H. Brookes.

Meltzer, L., Roditi, B., & Stein, J. (1998). Strategy instruction: The heartbeat of successful inclusion. *Perspectives (The International Dyslexia Foundation), 24*(3), 10–13.

Meyer, M. S., & Felton, R. H. (1999). Repeated reading to enhance fluency: Old approaches and new directions. *Annals of Dyslexia, XLIX,* 283–306.

Moats, L. C. (1995). *Spelling: Development disability and instruction.* Baltimore: York Press.

Montague, M. (1997). Cognitive strategy instruction in mathematics for students with learning disabilities. *Journal of Learning Disabilities, 30,* 164–177.

Morris, R. D., Stuebing, K. K., Fletcher, J. M., Shaywitz, S., Lyon, G. R., Shankweiler, D. P., Katz, L., Francis, D. J., & Shaywitz, B. A. (1998). Subtypes of reading disability: Variability around a phonological core. *Journal of Educational Psychology, 90,* 347–373.

Novick, B. Z., & Arnold, M. M. (1988). *Fundamentals of clinical child neuropsychology.* Philadelphia: Grune & Stratton.

Ogle, D. M. (1986). K-W-L: A teaching model that develops active reading of expository text. *Reading Teacher, 39,* 564–570.

Perfetti, C. A. (1992). The representation problem in reading acquisition. In P. B. Gough, L. C. Ehri, & R. Treiman (Eds.), *Reading acquisition* (pp. 145–174). Hillsdale, NJ: Erlbaum.

Rack, J. P., Snowling, M., & Olson, R. (1992). The nonword reading deficit in developmental dyslexia: A review. *Reading Research Quarterly, 27,* 28–53.

Rolfhus, E. L., & Ackerman, P. L. (1999). Assessing individual differences in knowledge: Knowledge, intelligence, and related traits. *Journal of Educational Psychology, 91,* 511–526.

Samuels, S. J. (1979). The method of repeated readings. *Reading Teacher, 32,* 403–408.

Schneider, W., & Shiffrin, R. M. (1977). Controlled and automatic human information processing: Detection, search, and attention. *Psychological Review, 84,* 1–66.

Siegel, L. S., & Ryan, E. B. (1988). Development of grammatical sensitivity, phonological, and short-term memory in normally achieving and learning disabled children. *Developmental Psychology, 24,* 28–37.

Smith, D. D., & Rivera, D. P. (1998). Mathematics. In B. Wong (Ed.), *Learning about learning disabilities,* (2nd ed., pp. 346–374). San Diego, CA: Academic Press.

Stanovich, K. E. (1982). Individual differences in the cognitive processes of reading: I. Word decoding, *Journal of Learning Disabilities, 15*, 485–493.

Stanovich, K. E. (1986). Matthew effects in reading: Some consequences of individual differences in the acquisition of literacy. *Reading Research Quarterly, 21*, 360–406.

Suydam, M. N. (1984). Research report: Manipulative materials. *Arithmetic Teacher, 31*, 27.

Tallal, P., Curtiss, S., & Kaplan, R. (1989). *The San Diego longitudinal study: Evaluating the outcomes of preschool impairment in language development* (Final Report, NINCDS). Washington, DC.

Tobias, S. (1993). *Overcoming math anxiety.* New York: W.W.W. Norton & Co.

Torgesen, J. K. (1992). Learning disabilities: Historical and conceptual issues. In B. Y. L. Wong (Ed.), *Learning about learning disabilities* (pp. 3–38). San Diego, CA: Academic Press.

Torgesen, J. K. (1993). Variations on theory in learning disabilities. In G. R. Lyon, D. B. Gray, J. F. Kavanagh, & N. A. Krasnegor (Eds.), *Better understanding learning disabilities: New views from research and their implications for education and public policies* (pp. 153–170). Baltimore: Paul H. Brookes.

Torgesen, J. K., Rashotte, C. A., & Alexander, A. W. (2001). Principles of fluency instruction in reading: Relationships with established empirical outcomes. In M. Wolf (Ed.), *Dyslexia, fluency, and the brain* (pp. 333–355). Timonium, MD: York Press.

Vygotsky, L. S. (1978). *Mind in society.* Cambridge, MA: Harvard University Press.

Wagner, R. K., & Torgesen, J. K. (1987). The nature of phonological processing and its causal role in the acquisition of reading skills. *Psychological Bulletin, 101*, 192–212.

Wagner, R. K., Torgesen, J. K., Laughon, P., Simmons, K., & Rashotte, C. A. (1993). The development of young readers' phonological processing abilities. *Journal of Educational Psychology, 85*, 1–20.

Wiig, E., & Semel, E. (1984). *Language assessment and intervention for the learning disabled.* Columbus, OH: Charles E. Merrill.

Wilson, A. M., & Lesaux, N. K. (2001). Persistence of phonological processing deficits in college students with dyslexia who have age-appropriate reading skills. *Journal of Learning Disabilities, 34*, 394–400.

Wolf, M., & Bowers, P. G. (1999). The double-deficit hypothesis for the developmental dyslexias. *Journal of Educational Psychology, 91*, 415–438.

Woodcock, R. W. (1999). What can Rasch-based scores convey about a person's test performance? In S.E. Embretson & S. L. Hershberger (Eds.), *The new rules of measurement: What every psychologist and educator should know* (pp. 106–109). Mahwah, NJ: Erlbaum.

4

USE OF THE WOODCOCK–JOHNSON III IN THE DIAGNOSIS OF LEARNING DISABILITIES

NOËL GREGG AND CHRISTOPHER COLEMAN

University of Georgia
Athens, Georgia 30602

DEBORAH KNIGHT

University of Delaware, Newark, Delaware 19716

Over the years, many theories have contributed to current practice governing the diagnosis of learning disabilities—models such as perceptual-motor theory (Ayers, 1975; Barsch, 1967; Kephart, 1960), psycholinguistic theory (Kirk, McCarthy, & Kirk, 1968), psychoneurological theory (Johnson & Myklebust, 1967), neuropsychological theory (Gaddes, 1980), phonological and orthographic theories (Frith, 1985; Ehri, 1998), as well as the Cattell–Horn–Carroll theory upon which the Woodcock–Johnson III (WJ III) is based. Central to all these theories is the idea that specific cognitive and linguistic processes are used by individuals to collect, sort, store, and retrieve various types of information (e.g., verbal and nonverbal). These theories (and others) have led to the development of several competing definitions for the construct of learning disabilities (see Kavale & Forness, 2000, for a critical analysis of definitions of learning disabilities).

Controversy in the field of learning disabilities rests less with definition or theory than with the ability of professionals to operationalize definitions. An examination in the United States of the variability of policy and procedures across states and minority populations (Colarusso, Keel, & Dangel, 2001; Gregg & Scott, 2000) has led researchers to conclude that anywhere from 52 to 70% of school-identified students with learning disabilities would fail to meet standard aptitude/achievement eligibility criteria (MacMillan & Speece, 2000). However, as Bocian et al. (1999) cautioned, such "error rates" are validated by comparing the classification criteria used by schools for the purpose of services with criteria often more relevant for research purposes. As Keogh (1994) argued, there are three reasons to classify students with learning disabilities: advocacy, service, and scientific study. The WJ III provides professionals with different types of data useful in pursuing each of Keogh's classification purposes. However, as K. S. McGrew (personal communication, April 15, 2001) noted, the "clinician is the instrument." The need for professionals to see themselves as decision-makers, and not allow psychometric scores to override professional judgment, has been summarized by Myer et al. (2001):

> Although psychological tests can assist clinicians with case formulation and treatment recommendations, they are only tools. *Tests do not think for themselves*, nor do they directly communicate with patients. Like a stethoscope, a blood pressure gauge, or an MRI scan, a psychological test is a dumb tool, and the worth of the tool cannot be separated from the sophistication of the *clinician who draws inferences from it* and then communicates with patients and other professionals. (p. 153, emphasis added)

The profile of a student with learning disabilities is typically marked by significant scatter within and between cognitive, linguistic, and achievement abilities. In the diagnosis of learning disabilities, it is imperative that deficits in one or more processing abilities are shown to influence performance on specific tasks, such as tests of skills in reading, written expression, or mathematics. As noted by Lyon (1994), "the assessment of learning disabilities entails the measurement of skills and abilities in numerous complex domains (e.g., reading), which themselves are composed of specific and complex developmental abilities (e.g., phonological awareness and word recognition skills), all of which may co-occur with attention and social deficits" (p. 1).

The Woodcock–Johnson assessment instruments (1977, 1989, 2001) have been and continue to be one of the most comprehensive tools available for investigation of the cognitive, linguistic, and achievement constructs involved in learning. Psychometric and theoretical constructs underlying the WJ III provide a sophisticated tool to help clinicians faced with controversy over definition, diagnosis, and eligibility issues related to learning disabilities. The WJ III uses the Cattell–Horn–Carroll (CHC) theory as its framework. The CHC theory of cognitive abilities is based on correlation and factor analysis as well as other developmental, neurocognitive, heritability, and outcome-criterion validity evidence (Horn & Noll, 1997; Flanagan, McGrew, & Ortiz, 2000; McGrew, Ford, & Woodcock, in press).

ELIGIBILITY AND LEARNING DISABILITIES

The criteria used to discern whether an individual qualifies for services under the category of learning disabilities is most often determined by one of the following three models: underachievement cutoff scores, discrepancy formulas, and what has been labeled a "clinical model" (Gregg, 1994; Gregg & Scott, 2000). Each of these eligibility models (i.e., cutoff, discrepancy, clinical) has a different purpose. Professionals responsible for providing services to children and/or adults with learning disabilities should be cognizant that the kind of eligibility model used will determine the number and type of individuals identified and served by institutions (Hoy et al., 1996; Reynolds, 1984–1985; Torgesen, 1987). Under any model, the measurement tools used in selection criteria must be as reliable and accurate as are available to the field; the WJ III is exemplary in these areas.

CUTOFF MODELS

The cutoff model, as advocated by some researchers (Siegel, 1989), establishes an arbitrary (standard) score as the benchmark for defining "functional level." Quite often under such a model, achievement measures are the only instruments used to determine functional level. Advocates of this model frequently question the role of traditional intelligence tests in the identification of learning disabilities (Naglieri & Reardon, 1993; Siegel, 1989). Cutoff models tend to overidentify lower functioning individuals and underidentify bright, high-functioning persons with learning disabilities (Gregg & Scott, 2000; Gregg & Mather, 2002). This model relies heavily on the concept of the bell curve. Cutoff models treat ability and achievement as dichotomous benchmarks with no consideration of the influence of the interaction of learner abilities and item difficulty. For professionals using such a model, the WJ III provides percentile scores, relative proficiency scores, standard scores, and grade level scores—all of which can be used to determine eligibility status.

DISCREPANCY MODELS

The discrepancy models most often referred to are those in which a difference between broad ability and achievement is the critical focus. Ability/achievement discrepancy models have become the standard basis for identifying learning disabilities (LDA) (Gregg & Scott, 2000). Unfortunately, as Kavale (1987) warned, "discrepancy alone cannot diagnose learning disabilities; it can only indicate that a primary symptom is present. Discrepancy may be a necessary condition for LD but it is hardly sufficient" (p. 19). Examination of intracognitive and/or intraachievement discrepancies is also critical to the diagnosis of learning disabilities, particularly for individualizing instruction and accommodations. As Kavale (2001) warned, "within the context of LD indentification, discrepancy and the documentation of underachievement should represent only the initial step in the diagnosis" (p. 6).

Ability/achievement discrepancy models operate with estimated intelligence setting the upper limit of expected achievement. Discrepancy models are models of prediction, such that one measure (ability) predicts another (achievement). One drawback to such models is that they overidentify high-ability individuals, excluding the lower functioning population with learning disabilities (Gregg &

Scott, 2000). Despite this and other problems associated with discrepancy models, they are the most commonly used method of diagnosing children (Mercer et al., 1996) and adults (Gregg et al., 1999). The WJ III provides five main discrepancy procedures that can be used to support decision-making under a discrepancy eligibility model (i.e., predicted achievement/intellectual ability, oral language/achievement, intracognitive, intraachievement, and intraindividual). Observations and critiques of discrepancy and other WJ III procedures related to the diagnosis of learning disabilities are presented with the mathematics and reading disabilities case studies later in this chapter.

CLINICAL MODEL

The third type of eligibility model has been identified as the clinical model. Such a model integrates (a) quantitative data, (b) qualitative data, (c) self-reported background information, and (d) clinical judgment of a multidisciplinary team. The WJ III provides the framework and data to incorporate all four sources of information into the decision-making process. A clinical model of eligibility stresses the need to use both qualitative and quantitative information in making diagnostic decisions (Berninger & Abbott, 1994; Gregg, 1994; Gregg & Scott, 2000). The focus of a clinical model is the importance of weighing many different factors (e.g., cognitive, language, achievement, social/emotional, motivational, instructional, and historical data) that contribute to learning, not all of which have normative scores. Researchers have proposed selection criteria that would incorporate learning rate (Frances et al., 1994; Gresham, 2001) and response-to-intervention data (Berninger & Abbott, 1994; Gresham, 2001). Both learning rate and response-to-intervention eligibility models require the use of instruments based on interval scaling or item response theory, such as Rasch modeling, so that no bias by item difficulty is present (e.g., the WJ III). At the forefront of learning disabilities research pertaining to selection criteria is the proposal to consider individual growth curves "that seek to determine the underlying developmental function— that is, the mathematical function that best describes the ongoing learning process for a particular ability or skill" (Shaywitz & Shaywitz, 1994, p. 6). The WJ III will be a valuable tool for use with many of these proposed selection criteria.

CLINICAL CLUSTERS

The five new clinical clusters on the WJ III, consisting of tests from the *Woodcock–Johnson III Tests of Cognitive Abilities* (WJ III COG) and the *Woodcock–Johnson III Tests of Achievement* (WJ III ACH), may be valuable to diagnosticians concerned with the accurate identification of learning disabilities. Use of these clusters may have direct implications for the instruction and accommodation needs of individual students. The clusters are both psychometrically and theoretically sound, because they were constructed based on extensive exploratory and confirmatory factor analyses (McGrew & Woodcock, 2001). However, as Mather and Gregg (2001) cautioned, examiners must be careful to consider the multidimensional nature of any task and/or factor that is used to measure a cognitive processing area (e.g., cognitive fluency, working memory). For instance, poor performance on a phonemic awareness task might be the result of any one or combination of factors such as attention, auditory discrimination, working memory, and metalinguistics deficits. Examiners are encouraged to analyze intraability, intraachievement, and intraindividual patterns to investigate performance on any given factor.

PHONOLOGICAL AWARENESS AND PHONEME/GRAPHEME KNOWLEDGE

The relationship of phonological and orthographic processing to reading and spelling performance has been the focus of extensive literature (e.g., Frith, 1985; Ehri, 1998). Research has documented that the majority of children and adults with dyslexia have significant deficits in the area of phonology and/or orthography that impede reading and spelling competence (Bruck, 1993; Gregg et al., 2002; Landerl, Frith, & Wimmer, 1996; Wagner, Torgesen, & Rashotte, 1994). Therefore, it is vital that phonological and orthographic processing be measured in any assessment concerning a student's reading and/or writing skills.

The WJ III COG and WJ III ACH provide several measures of phonological processing but are somewhat limited in the assessment of orthographic processing. Phonological awareness measures on the WJ III ACH Sound Awareness test assess such constructs as rhyming, deletion, closure, and speech discrimination. In addition, the WJ III ACH Phoneme/Grapheme Knowledge cluster (Word Attack, Spelling of Sounds) measures an individual's skill at reading and spelling nonwords that conform to English phonological rules and spelling conventions. Children and/or adults with low scores on the WJ III COG Auditory Processing cluster (Sound Blending, Auditory Attention) and the Phonemic Awareness cluster (Sound Blending, Incomplete Words) might have significant difficulty with decoding and spelling. It is important that an examiner compare the auditory and phonological processes tapped by the WJ III COG (Auditory Processing, Phonemic Awareness) and the WJ III ACH (Phoneme/Grapheme cluster, Sound Awareness test). Each of these tests and/or clusters should then be compared to the examinee's reading and spelling performance on the WJ III ACH. Of course, just because an examinee scores within the normal range on these clusters does not mean that other phonological and/or orthographic processes not measured by the WJ III could not be impacting his/her decoding and/or spelling skills. One potential drawback to exclusive use of the WJ III in assessing phonological processing is that many pertinent cognitive tests (Sound Blending, Incomplete Words, and Auditory Attention, as well as Sound Awareness from the WJ III ACH) involve real words, all of which are familiar to adults and many of which are high-frequency lexical terms. College students demonstrating dyslexia—who often possess well-developed vocabularies, strong reasoning abilities, and at least some effective coping strategies—may be able to use these resources to perform well on a task such as Incomplete Words, thus masking underlying problems related to phonology. In many cases, these underlying problems are better revealed on tasks that feature pseudowords (for which examinees do not have established mental representations). Although the WJ III provides well-designed achievement tests that involve psuedowords (Word Attack and Spelling of Sounds), it does not provide parallel cognitive measures. Therefore, clinicians are advised to supplement their assessments with a measure such as Berninger's Phonological Segmentation task (as described in Gregg et al., 2002).

Deficient phonological processing has been firmly established by researchers as a cause of dyslexia (for a review of the literature, see Foorman [1994] or Roberts & Mather [1997]). However, researchers have also shown that reading and writing problems can stem from deficient orthographic processing (Bruck, 1993; Cunningham, Perry, & Stanovich, 2001; Foorman, 1994; Holmes & Castles, 2001; Roberts & Mather, 1997) or deficient naming speed (Wolf, Bowers, & Biddle, 2000; Wolf & Katzir-Cohen, 2001). The latter processing problem, which typically results in compromised reading fluency, can be identified through use of tests comprising the WJ III Cognitive Fluency cluster (this cluster will be discussed in the next section of this chapter). Orthographic dyslexia, on the other hand, may be more difficult for clinicians to recognize and distinguish from phonological dyslexia. As Foorman (1994) notes, "although orthographic and phonological processing can be dissociated statistically, they are conceptually intertwined" (p. 321). Orthographic coding has been described by Vellutino, Scanlon, and Taneman (1994) as "the ability to represent the unique array of letters that defines a printed word, as well as the general attributes of the writing system such as sequential dependencies, structural redundancies, and letter position frequencies" (p. 314). Individuals with poor orthographic processing struggle to encode and decode the visual symbols (i.e., printed letters, numbers, and letter clusters) used to represent spoken sounds and words. Clinicians using the WJ III are advised to consider the role of orthographic processing in tests such as Visual Matching, Letter–Word Identification, Word Attack, Spelling, and Spelling of Sounds. As noted in Roberts and Mather (1997), analysis of spelling errors on dictated and spontaneous writing tasks can help clinicians identify subtypes of dyslexia. For example, individuals with phonological dyslexia may produce "phonetically implausible" attempts, whereas those demonstrating orthographic dyslexia may accurately represent the sounds in target words but be unable to recall unusual or irregular sequences. Finally, clinicians are encouraged to supplement their assessment batteries with orthographic processing measures such as DeFries' Colorado Perceptual Speed Task (as described in Gregg et al., in press) or the computerized tasks developed by Holmes & Castles (2001).

Returning to the assessment of phonological processing, examiners are cautioned to carefully examine an individual's test scores within the WJ III COG Phonemic Awareness cluster for significant differences in performance across the Incomplete Words and Sound Blending tests. As a general rule, examiners should consider the standard deviation of test score distributions when interpreting any test or cluster score on the WJ III COG and WJ III ACH. Table A-1 of the *WJ III Technical Manual* (McGrew & Woodcock, 2001, pp. 109–130) includes this information. Based on the *WJ III Technical Manual*, one would not expect to see similar score distributions on tests with very different standard deviations. If a test has a very small standard deviation for a particular age group, the spread of ability within that population is so narrow that even small differences in performance can move an individual substantially away from the median. For example, Gregg, Stennett, & Coleman (2001) compared the performance of 202 college students (101 with learning disabilities and 101 with no disability) on Incomplete Words, Sound Blending, Word Attack, and the Phonemic Awareness cluster. The students with learning disabilities consistently scored slightly lower than their peers across all these measures. Although the differences were statistically significant, Gregg, Stennet, and Coleman (2001) found that the group differences were sometimes small in absolute value (mean differences in scaled scores ranged from 5.467 on Incomplete Words to 16.798 on Word Attack). Group differences in the correlations across these measures are also noteworthy; correlations for students with learning disabilities were substantially higher than for students without learning disorders.

For many purposes, the Relative Proficiency Index (RPI) may provide a better description of an individual's proficiency with the measured task than the standard score or percentile rank. Researchers have noted that the different standard deviations of the Incomplete Words and Sound Blending tests can have a significant impact on the Phonemic Awareness cluster for the college population (Gregg & Coleman, 2001). They reported that some college students with reading and spelling difficulties seemed to obtain unexpectedly high standard scores on the Incomplete Words test, thus increasing their Phonemic Awareness cluster standard score. Table 4-1 compares the standard score distributions for Sound

TABLE 4-1   WJ III Phonemic Awareness Cluster Comparison of Raw and Standard Scores Based on Age 21 Norms

WJ III Sound blending		WJ III Incomplete words	
# Correct (of 33 items)	SS[a]	# Correct (of 44 items)	SS[a]
16	83	22	93
20	92	26	102
24	100	30	118
26	105	32	127
28	110	34	139
30	117	36	151
32	128	40	178
33	136	44	218

[a]SS, Standard Score.

Blending and Incomplete Words for the college-age population, illustrating that it is possible for young adults to obtain extremely high standard scores on the latter test. In many cases, a sizable standard score difference between Sound Blending and Incomplete Words will also be reflected in the corresponding RPI ranges. Additional research is needed to explore the contribution of these two tests to the Phonemic Awareness cluster across the life span. As noted above, clinicians might want to take the approach of using the RPI to describe proficiency, because it is unaffected by a test's standard deviation. The RPI conveys how far away the individual is, in ability, from the reference group median.

COGNITIVE FLUENCY

The construct of fluency is currently being reconceptualized (Fuchs et al., 2001; Kame'enui & Simmons, 2001; Wolf & Katzir-Cohen, 2001). Certainly, researchers in the area of reading have demonstrated that fluency is developmental and necessary for competence across several lexical processes (Simmons et al., 2000). The critical role of fluency in reading was documented in the National Reading Panel Report (2000), in which the construct was shown to contribute to "high-speed word recognition" as well as "comprehension processes" (Chap. 3, p. 6). The WJ III COG Cognitive Fluency cluster measures several of the significant lexical processes that research has identified as important predictors of fluency in reading–decoding and spelling. Given the nature of the tests included in the Cognitive Fluency cluster (i.e., tasks requiring word recall, rapid picture naming, and semantic organization), one might predict that the cluster will have greater application to reading and written expression than to mathematics. For examiners presented with a reading and spelling referral, the examinee's Cognitive Fluency cluster performance should be compared with his/her performance on tests involving phonological awareness, alphabet understanding, and processing of connected text.

The WJ III has several clusters that measure fluency. Three specific cognitive aspects of fluency are measured by the Cognitive Fluency cluster: the Retrieval Fluency test measures *speed of retrieval of stored information*; the Decision Speed test measures *speed of forming simple categorical concepts*; and the Rapid Picture Naming test measures *speed of lexical (vocabulary) access*.

WORKING MEMORY

The construct of working memory grew out of the literature on short-term memory when researchers concerned with the comprehension and production of text began to find very little correlation between short-term memory tasks and understanding of discourse (Oakhill, Cain, & Yill, 1998). Thus, the construct of working memory began to evolve. Stolzfus, Hasher, and Zacks (1996) stated working memory was "conceptualized as a mental workspace consisting of activated memory representations that are available in a temporary buffer for manipulation during cognitive processing" (p. 66).

A variety of measures have been designed to investigate working memory and its relationship to learning performance (Baddeley & Hitch, 1974; Daneman & Carpenter, 1980; Wagner, Torgesen, & Rashotte, 1999). Clearly, the type of task used to measure working memory will influence the degree to which scores correlate with different academic areas (e.g., decoding, comprehension, spelling, written expression, calculation, math reasoning). Researchers have proposed that the core of working memory consists of information activated from long-term memory and/or the focus of attention (Richardson, 1996). Others have debated the importance of cognitive capacity and speed of processing to the construct of working memory (Engle & Cantor, 1992; Just & Carpenter, 1992; Perfetti, 1995). Therefore, an examiner using the WJ III should look across other WJ III COG clusters (e.g., Long-Term Retrieval, Processing Speed, Short-Term Memory, Cognitive Efficiency, Cognitive Fluency, Broad Attention) when interpreting results of the Working Memory cluster in order to account for the bidirectional influence of other cognitive processes on working memory.

The WJ III COG provides two tests (Numbers Reversed and Auditory Working Memory) that make up the Working Memory cluster. This cluster provides professionals with a means to measure an individual's ability to hold verbal information in immediate awareness while performing operations on it, a vital process for many academic tasks (i.e., reading, written language, and mathematics). Mather and Gregg (2001) note that it will be important for examiners to compare performance on the WJ III Working Memory cluster to other working memory measures, such as the *Wechsler Memory Scale—Third Edition* (WMS-III) Working Memory Index (Wechsler, 1997b) and/or the Phonological Memory Composite Score on the *Comprehensive Test of Phonological Processing* (CTOPP) (Wagner, Torgesen, & Rashotte, 1999). The demands of each of these working memory tasks are different and could prove difficult or quite manageable depending on the profile of the individual being tested. For instance, the WJ III COG Auditory Working Memory test requires a student to "chunk" and recall individual (real) words and numbers; on the WMS-III Letter–Number Sequencing task, groups of letters and numbers must be resequenced and recalled; on the CTOPP, nonwords and numbers are presented for manipulation and recall. Each of these tasks places different constraints on an examinee's cognitive and linguistic abilities. Therefore, an individual might perform within the average range on one measure but below average on another, depending on his/her strengths and weaknesses.

The WJ III Working Memory cluster appears to be a more factorially "pure" norm-based measure of the construct of working memory than other available measures. McGrew, Woodcock, and Ford (2002), using confirmatory factor analyses, found that the *Wechsler Adult Intelligence Scale—Third Edition* (WAIS-III) Working Memory Index contained a significant proportion of construct-irrelevant Mathematics (Gq) variance. This phenomenon is probably due to the presence of the Arithmetic test in this cluster. Examiners should be sensitive to such considerations when comparing scores across measures and/or attempting to select one instrument over another. In addition, Evans et al. (2002) found that the WJ III

COG Short-Term Memory and Working Memory clusters were both significantly related to the Basic Reading cluster across the life span, but were significantly related to the Reading Comprehension cluster only from ages 6 to 13. A partial explanation for this trend may involve the Auditory Working Memory test, the task demands of which appear to be related more to decoding than to comprehension. For examiners concerned that an examinee might have working memory problems impacting text comprehension and/or construction, it may be fruitful to look at that individual's performance on the WJ III ACH Understanding Directions test, because this measure also requires working memory.

EXECUTIVE PROCESSES

The term *executive functioning* has been used inconsistently and interchangeably with psychological, sociolinguistic, and anatomical definitions. Also, tests of executive functions have often had low test–retest reliability and uncertain validity. Rabbitt (1997) warned that many of the latent components used to define executive behavior (i.e., inhibition, planning, or monitoring) are in reality descriptors of task demands with very poor construct validity.

Researchers have now focused on the contribution of executive functions to several psychiatric conditions (e.g., autism, Gilles de la Tourette Syndrome, Attention Deficit/Hyperactivity Disorder (AD/HD), obsessive–compulsive disorder, learning disabilities). As a result, we are learning more about the influence of specific cognitive and linguistic processes on performance of tasks requiring executive functioning (Lyon & Krasnegor, 1996; Pennington et al., 1996; Barkley, 1996, 1997).

Different models have been proposed to describe the construct of executive functioning, emphasizing such cognitive and linguistic processes as inhibition (Barkley, 1997; Dempster, 1992, 1995), working memory (Kinberg & Farah, 1993), and self-regulation (Denckla, 1998; Denckla & Reader, 1993; Hayes, Gifford, & Ruckstuhl, 1996). Zelazo et al. (1997) offered an interesting perspective on executive functioning by presenting it in a problem-solving framework. In their model, executive functioning is a macroconstruct involving four phases of problem solving: representation, planning, execution, and evaluation. Therefore, executive functioning "is treated as a macroconstruct that captures the way in which subfactors of executive functioning work together to accomplish the higher order function of problem solution" (Zelazo et al., 1997, p. 4).

A problem-solving framework may be very useful to clinicians attempting to understand how behaviors observed in the assessment setting are related to the construct of executive functioning. In addition, the model provides a means to integrate research from sociolinguistics and cognitive psychology. The Executive Processes cluster on the WJ III COG includes tests that measure three critical aspects of executive functioning: strategic planning (Planning), proactive interference control (Pair Cancellation), and the ability to shift mental sets (Concept Formation). Examiners are also encouraged to use information from other WJ III COG clusters and tests, as well as qualitative information, to better understand the multidimensionality of executive functioning. The model developed by Zelazo et al. (1997) will be used to demonstrate how several WJ III COG and WJ III ACH clusters can provide documentation of performance on different phases of executive functioning from the perspective of a problem-solving framework.

Representation

According to Zelazo et al. (1997), executive functioning is called upon initially to construct a representation for a given problem. This aspect of executive functioning is very sensitive to age (Rock, Gopovik, & Hall, 1994) and selective attention abilities (Ewws & Cameron, 1987). Therefore, in addition to looking at a student's performance on the WJ III Executive Processes cluster, clinicians are encouraged to examine the Broad Attention cluster, particularly the Auditory Attention test, as well as data from the Executive Processes and Cognitive Fluency Checklist from the *Report Writer for the WJ III* (Schrank & Woodcock, 2002).

Planning

The second phase of the executive functioning framework of Zelazo et al. (1997) is the strategy referred to as planning. The Planning test of the WJ III was designed to minimize the influence of memory and speed and thus provide (as much as possible) a "pure" measure of response planning. However, response planning is a complex strategic task that varies across modalities. Thus, although Planning assesses planning within a well-defined clinical task, an examiner might want to know how an individual performs on other measures and in real-life situations in order to obtain a comprehensive assessment of planning. For instance, Zelazo et al. (1997) describe such planning strategies as logical search, route planning, planning to remember, and social planning. In addition, attention and working memory contribute significantly to the ability to plan (Baddeley, 1986). Consequently, cross-examination of an individual's performance on the Broad Attention and Working Memory clusters is advised for clinicians concerned about that person's ability to plan.

Execution

Zelazo et al. (1997) described the executive functioning strategy of execution as the "ability to keep a plan in mind and translate that plan into action" (p. 4). Within this construct are included intention and rule use (Zelazo & Jacques, 1997), both of which require the ability to sustain attention. Barkley (1996, 1997) proposed that executive functioning deficits are the result of impairment in inhibition or resistance to interference from automatic responses, an issue likely impacting the organizing and solving of problems. To explore execution performance, clinicians might want to analyze a student's performance across the WJ III COG Attention and Executive Processes clusters, giving special attention to the Pair Cancellation test. Examiners should also consider both the student's strategy choice (e.g., verbal mediation) and his/her execution of that strategy.

Rule use, or the ability to translate the solution of a problem into action, is critical to the execution strategy of problem solving. As Zelazo et al. (1997) point out, "one does not simply act; one acts when it is appropriate to do so" (p. 15). The Executive Processes cluster of the WJ III COG (which includes Concept Formation, Planning, and Pair Cancellation) provides an effective tool to measure rule use.

Evaluation

A significant component of executive functioning is the ability to recognize when goals have been obtained—or, alternately, when goals have not been reached. Children may exhibit particularly poor awareness of goals: "Children's tendencies to repeat a previously correct response without regard to its appropriateness for a new situation, especially in motorically complex tasks and other situations requiring effort, suggests a general difficulty in using an abstract goal to govern one's acting" (Zelazo et al., 1997, p. 21).

The concept of self-regulation is critical to the ability to evaluate a potential solution to a problem. Self-regulation, an ability missing from the Zelazo et al. framework, is at times subsumed (in the literature) by executive functioning; at other times, it is viewed as a separate rubric. Zimmerman (1989) discussed three subprocesses of self-regulation: self-monitoring, self-evaluation, and behavioral adjustment. Both executive functioning and self-regulation are important to metacognition (Barkley, 1997), and both of these metacognition strategies are mediated by language. Vygotsky (1962) clearly described the central role of language in the development of self-control, self-direction, problem-solving, and task performance. In addition, he discussed how language is acquired socially and becomes the tool for learning how to regulate one's behavior (Gregg & Jackson, 1989; Wertsch, 1998). Therefore, clinicians considering the impact of executive functioning on a student's performance should investigate the oral language abilities of that individual. On the WJ III COG and WJ III ACH, information from the Executive Processes, Broad Attention, Working Memory, and Oral Language clusters can provide insight into the executive functioning strategies students are using in solving problems (and where these strategies might be going wrong), especially when used in conjunction with clinical observation and task analysis of performance. Future research will need to address the question of which aspects of executive functioning (i.e., representation, planning, execution, and evaluation) might be lacking among specific types of learners (e.g., individuals with Attention Deficit/Hyperactivity Disorder or a learning disability).

BROAD ATTENTION CLUSTER

Attention is a multidimensional construct that is inclusive of learning, memory, and executive functioning. Four specific cognitive aspects of attention are included in the WJ III Broad Attention cluster: the Numbers Reversed test requires *attentional capacity*; the Auditory Working Memory test requires the ability to *divide attention* in short-term memory; the Auditory Attention test requires the ability to *attend to speech sounds* in the presence of competing noise; and the Pair Cancellation test requires the ability to *sustain attention* and maintain *interference control*. Low performance on the Broad Attention cluster may be indicative of different learning disorders (e.g., learning disabilities, AD/HD). Researchers have suggested that reading disorders are more closely associated with selective attention deficits, whereas AD/HD is characterized by sustained attention deficits (Douglas & Peters, 1979; Dykman, Ackerman, & Oglesby, 1979; Seidel & Joschko, 1990). In fact, van der Meere, van Baal, and Sergeant (1989) found that attentional problems demonstrated by students with learning disabilities involved the input processes of learning, whereas AD/HD appeared more closely related to response organization.

Parent and teacher checklists in the *Report Writer for the WJ III* (Schrank & Woodcock, 2002) should be used along with the Broad Attention, Working Memory, and Executive Processes clusters to determine the impact of attentional capacities on learning behavior (see Chapter 10, this volume). These checklists are useful for documenting behavioral manifestations of attention, inattention, distractibility, and/or hyperactivity. This information can be compared to or contrasted with an individual's Broad Attention score. In many cases, individuals who exhibit behavioral signs of inattention, distractibility, or hyperactivity do not show limitations or deficits on the Broad Attention cluster. This scenario would suggest that the individual exhibits behavior indicators of AD/HD, but his/her ability to focus, selectively attend, and/or divide attention is not the problem. That is, the clinician can be informed that symptoms reflect a behavioral management problem, not a cognitive inability to attend when required (F. A. Schrank, personal communication, September 2001). Given the high incidence of different types of attentional deficits co-occurring with learning disabilities, the parent and teacher checklists provide an excellent means of informant documentation. Other checklists in the *Report Writer* can be used to collect criterion-referenced behavioral information about an individual during testing. Information can also be systematically collected from teachers, other examiners, parents, and the individual being evaluated. The *Report Writer for the WJ III* includes critical items from the *Diagnostical and Statistical Manual of Psychological Disorders, Fourth Edition* (American Psychiatric Association, 1994) to help clinicians gather information that may be used as documentation for a diagnosis of AD/HD. Specific information from the Teacher's Checklist, the Parent's Checklist, the Adolescent/Adult Self-Report Checklist, and the Classroom Observation Form can be used to corroborate other data to support an AD/HD diagnosis (see Chapter 10).

ACADEMIC SKILLS, FLUENCY, AND APPLICATIONS

A unique and important contribution of the WJ III ACH battery is the inclusion of the Academic Skills, Academic Fluency, and Academic Applications clusters. A hallmark of many students with learning disabilities is discrepant performance among academic skills, fluency, and problem solving. For instance, students with dyslexia tend to be weak in the skills required for reading–decoding and reading fluency, but capable of understanding textual information (application) when decoding is deemphasized through either accommodations or contextual clues. Information obtained from WJ III ACH clusters provides strong documentation upon which to base specific instructional advice and accommodation decisions.

The Academic Fluency cluster represents an excellent means of documenting the impact of fluency deficits across academic areas (i.e., reading, written expression, and calculation). A clinician should compare an examinee's performance on the Academic Fluency cluster to his/her scores on the WJ III COG Cognitive Fluency and Cognitive Efficiency clusters. In a recent study of young adults with and without learning disabilities, the Academic Fluency cluster was the best predictor variable (across the entire WJ III) in differentiating between the two groups (McGrew, Ford, & Woodcock, 2002). Evaluators should also be cognizant that the tests contributing to the cluster (Reading Fluency, Writing Fluency, and Math Fluency) have markedly different standard deviations. As has already been discussed, this situation will influence the contribution of each of the academic fluency tests to the Academic Fluency cluster. The Reading Fluency test has a significantly larger standard deviation than either the Writing Fluency or Math Fluency tests; therefore, the cluster will correlate most highly with Reading Fluency. For example, a low-average Reading Fluency score can lead to a low-average Academic Fluency cluster score, despite average (or better) scores on Writing Fluency and Math Fluency. Again, careful examination of test scores within clusters (as well as RPI scores) is encouraged.

Clinicians are also encouraged to consider differences among the Academic Fluency, Academic Skills, and Academic Applications clusters. Recent research has indicated that among children and adults with learning disabilities, fluency is the academic area most resistant to remediation (McGrew, Ford, & Woodcock, 2002; Wolf & Katzir-Cohen, 2001). For example, intensive intervention may improve a dyslexic's decoding accuracy, but not his or her speed. Academic Skills and Applications performances—in conjunction with patterns from the WJ COG—provide examiners with information about the effectiveness of prior instruction and the potential efficacy of future remediation and accommodation strategies.

COGNITIVE PERFORMANCE CLUSTERS

The Cognitive Performance Model (CPM) (Woodcock, 1993, 1997) provides additional information pertinent to the diagnosis of learning disabilities. The CPM differentiates several components that influence cognitive or academic performance (Mather & Gregg, 2001). The functional components of this model are represented by the WJ III COG Verbal Abilities, Thinking Abilities, and

Cognitive Efficiency clusters. Woodcock's (1993, 1997) Facilitator–Inhibitor construct has not been fully operationalized on the WJ III, but many factors that may facilitate or inhibit an individual's performance can be identified when using the checklists on the *Report Writer for the WJ III*. Further research will be important in determining the effectiveness of the above clusters in the identification of learning disabilities.

The WJ III COG Cognitive Efficiency cluster, which includes measures of short-term memory and processing speed, appears to have significant relevance to the diagnosis of learning disabilities and AD/HD. Put simply, a student must be able to "work efficiently" with verbal and nonverbal information to perform optimally. Unlike the Cognitive Fluency cluster, which is strongly weighted to measure verbal fluency, the Cognitive Efficiency cluster combines both fluency and efficiency tasks across verbal and nonverbal modalities. Tests contributing to the Cognitive Efficiency cluster require less Long-Term Memory (*Glr*) than do fluency tests, but more in the way of Processing Speed (*Gs*), and Short-Term Memory (*Gsm*) abilities.

Research with adults diagnosed with learning disabilities has found that the Cognitive Efficiency cluster contributes significantly to performance on academic tasks (Gregg, Stennett, Coleman, Hoy, & Davis, 2001). In a study of young adults with and without learning disabilities, the Cognitive Efficiency cluster explained a significant amount of variance in the ability to decode and spell nonsense words (Gregg, Stennett, Coleman, Hoy, & Davis, 2001). Interestingly, among young adults with learning disabilities, the Cognitive Efficiency cluster was the strongest predictor of spelling of nonsense words; in contrast, the WJ III COG Verbal Comprehension cluster contributed the greatest variance to nonsense-word spelling for young adults with no disabilities. It appears that efficiency may be as important as crystallized knowledge in the academic performance of adults.

ORAL LANGUAGE CLUSTERS

Learning disabilities can be thought of as communication disorders affecting one's ability to process either verbal or nonverbal information. Oral language disorders are more prevalent than nonverbal communication deficits among the population with learning disabilities (Hoy & Gregg, 1994). Underlying language-based problems are at the core of reading, written language, and math underachievement for this population. The WJ III ACH provides examiners with an excellent tool for measuring language skills at the word (Picture Vocabulary), sentence (Oral Comprehension), and text (Story Recall) levels; it was a tool designed with the understanding that there is a bidirectional influence across these levels of language.

The contribution of oral language competence to other academic areas continues to be debated in the literature. In relationship to reading, Stricht and James (1984) cautioned that it is important to consider correlations across age levels because the correlation between language and reading comprehension tends to increase as students become more proficient at decoding. Therefore, after decoding skills are developed, listening comprehension is generally more highly correlated to reading comprehension. Some research has suggested that good readers (after the third grade) comprehend print at a higher level than they do oral language. The subprocesses involved in comprehending oral and written text appear to function very similarly. Vellutino, Scanlon, and Lyon (2000) suggested that the high correlation between verbal intelligence and reading comprehension might be an artifact of the shared variance of the underlying language processes implicit in both.

The precise relationships among global intelligence (General Intellectual Ability [GIA]), listening comprehension, decoding, working memory, and achievement have not been determined. Some researchers have advocated comparing oral language and achievement (rather than cognitive ability and achievement) in the diagnosis of children with dyslexia (Aaron & Joshi, 1992; Stanovich, 1991). Knight (2000) found that global verbal ability does influence adults' reading comprehension, but the effect is primarily indirect and mediated through listening comprehension and decoding—a finding that raises questions about the utility of the GIA in diagnosing dyslexia. In the case of a student with dyslexia who has underlying cognitive processing deficits in areas such as Auditory Processing (*Ga*) and Processing Speed (*Gs*), the GIA may not truly predict reading comprehension potential. In such circumstances, the WJ III ACH Oral Language discrepancy procedure is more likely appropriate. However, for many students with learning disabilities that involve significant reasoning and/or oral language difficulties, Oral Language tests would not provide the best estimate of overall ability. In such a case, the GIA would probably provide better, fairer predictor of ability.

Vocabulary, or word-level knowledge of language, is strongly correlated with academic success. Perfetti, Marron, and Foltz (1996) noted that words and concepts are the building blocks of text construction and comprehension. Vocabulary appears to explain a large degree of the variance in the comprehension of different types of text (Bell & Perfetti, 1994; Cunningham, Stanovich, & Wilson, 1990). A recent study of the expository writing of university students revealed that under standardized, timed conditions, subjects with learning disabilities produced (a) fewer words and (b) less sophisticated word choices (as gauged by syllable counts and frequency ranks) than did their nondisabled peers (Gregg, Coleman, & Davis, 2002). Students with learning disabilities often exhibit stunted expressive vocabularies, particularly in their written expression. Depending on the nature of a learning disability, however, receptive vocabulary may remain intact and age appropriate. Therefore, an examiner might want to compare an individual's WJ III ACH Listening Comprehension and Oral Expression clusters to one another, as well as to his/her performance on other achievement measures. In particular, specific attention should be given to the WJ III ACH Picture Vocabulary test.

The assessment of sentence- and text-level oral language is much more difficult to accomplish psychometrically. For students with deficits at these levels of language processing, the impact may be most evident on academic application tasks (e.g., reading comprehension, writing samples, applied problems). The Oral Comprehension test, a cloze task on the WJ III ACH, provides one means of identifying certain types of language disorders. For students with syntax disorders, determining the specific form of language required to make a sentence or text passage not only complete, but cohesive and grammatical as well, is very difficult. Students with word-finding problems may also have a great deal of trouble with cloze tasks—but for entirely different reasons.

Recall tasks such as the WJ III Story Recall test can serve as reliable measures of discourse comprehension, because examinees cannot rely on guessing as much as they can in the cloze format of the Oral Comprehension task. Story Recall requires an individual to attend carefully to and then recall the meaningful parts of orally presented narratives. In some cases, the individual must produce exact words or phrases in order to receive credit for particular details. No penalty is assessed for sequencing errors, however. Therefore, although a person's score might be within the average range on Story Recall—that is, he or she encoded and recalled an age-appropriate amount of meaningful material—the story might have been presented out of logical order. Such information is clinically important in making differential diagnoses and intervention recommendations.

In addition, Hildyard and Olson (1978) cautioned that the type of information remembered by listeners and readers may be different. They found that listeners remembered more of the gist of stories, while readers remembered more of the details and peripheral inferences. Based on this research, one could infer that normally achieving listeners and readers appear to remember different components of text. Danks and End (1987) suggested that differences in the types of information remembered across comprehension tasks (e.g., oral recall vs. reading recall) might be attributed to the different demands the tasks place on working memory. It is suggested, therefore, that examiners administer a reading recall task to compare with the WJ III ACH Story Recall task in order to examine a student's performance across modalities (Gregg & Mather, 2002).

Students with low scores on Oral Comprehension and/or Story Recall may often have low scores on Passage Comprehension, Writing Samples, and/or Applied Problems. The core explanation for low performance could be limited comprehension of language, attention/executive functioning, and/or experience with printed language. Thus, clinicians are encouraged to analyze score patterns thoroughly and in an open-minded fashion.

MATH CLUSTERS

Students with cognitive and linguistic deficits impacting the learning of low- and high-level mathematical skills have been underrepresented in the literature (Geary, 2000; Kulak, 1993; Padget, 1998; Rourke & Conway, 1998). However, it has been estimated that approximately 6% of students in the United States have some form of calculation disorder (Badian, 1983; Gross-Tsur, Manor, & Shalev, 1996). The incidence appears to be similar to that of students with reading disorders; however, the referral rate for math disabilities is usually much lower than that for reading and/or written expression disorders. Researchers have noted that dyslexia is comorbid with calculation disorders in roughly 40–50% of students with literacy problems (Badian, 1983; Gross-Tsur et al., 1996). Some authors have suggested that there is a common etiology when reading and math deficits coexist (Geary, 2000; Rourke, 1993), whereas others assert that many math deficits are secondary to problems with oral language or temporal processing (Davis, Bryson, & Hoy, 1992; Padget, 1998). Researchers are continuing to explore subtypes of mathematics disability in an attempt to better understand the cognitive and linguistic processes impacting the learning of arithmetic principles (Badian, 1983; Geary, 1993, 2000; Marolda & Davidson, 2000; Padget, 1998; Rourke, 1993).

Table 4-2 links specific areas of mathematics (i.e., calculation, concepts, and reasoning) to the WJ III COG and WJ III ACH clusters most directly related to performance in those areas. Some students will have difficulty with calculation problems due to trouble retrieving arithmetic facts; Geary (2000) noted that this problem often co-occurs with reading disabilities. In such a case, the examiner would want to compare scores on the WJ III COG Long-Term Retrieval, Short-Term Memory, and Working Memory clusters to the examinee's Calculation score.

TABLE 4-2   Cognitive–Achievement Connection: Mathematics

Area	WJ III COG clusters	WJ III ACH clusters
Calculation	Long-Term Retrieval Visual–Spatial Thinking Processing Speed Short-Term Memory Working Memory Broad Attention Cognitive Efficiency	Broad Math Math Calculation Broad Reading Academic Applications
Math concepts	Comprehension–Knowledge Fluid Reasoning Long-Term Retrieval Visual–Spatial Thinking Working Memory Broad Attention	Broad Math Math Reasoning Listening Comprehension Academic Knowledge Academic Applications
Math reasoning	Comprehension–Knowledge Fluid Reasoning Executive Processes Broad Attention	Broad Math Math Reasoning Oral Expression Listening Comprehension Reading Comprehension Academic Applications Academic Knowledge

In addition, a comparison should be made to determine if the issue might be one of recall and/or fluency; this would require examination of the Cognitive Fluency cluster score, the Cognitive Efficiency cluster score, and the Academic Fluency cluster score. It is important to note that the Math Fluency test has a significantly smaller standard deviation than does the Reading Fluency test, and thus a smaller contribution to the Academic Fluency cluster. Finally, it is always worthwhile to compare a student's WJ III ACH Broad Reading cluster score to his/her Broad Math and Math Calculation cluster scores. For some students, difficulty with calculation reflects visual-spatial deficits and may be characterized by problems such as misalignment of numerals; therefore, careful examination of the WJ III ACH Visual-Spatial Thinking tests is imperative.

The ability of a student to demonstrate mathematics knowledge (Quantitative Concepts) draws upon many cognitive and linguistic processes (as well as instructional factors). Geary (2000) discussed a subgroup of mathematics disorders characterized by procedural deficits. Individuals exhibiting such disorders would be likely to use immature procedures, make frequent errors in carrying out procedures, be delayed in learning math concepts, and demonstrate difficulty sequencing multistep procedures. However, other students could demonstrate deficits in verbal naming of mathematical terms and relations (Kosc, 1974; Sharma, 1986). Such individuals might not be able verbally to identify symbols for operations, although they could carry out the operations successfully. Difficulties with word finding could, however, influence their performance on a task such as Quantitative Concepts. Therefore, examiners should compare math scores to scores on the WJ III COG Comprehension–Knowledge, Long-Term Retrieval, and Listening Comprehension clusters to determine whether oral comprehension and/or expression difficulties might be impacting mathematics performance. Kosc (1974) described a subgroup of math disorders that he labeled "ideognostical dyscalculia," referring to difficulty understanding mathematical concepts and calculations. An individual with such problems may be unable to perform simple operations mentally, although he/she can read and write the necessary numbers. In addition, he/she might demonstrate difficulty understanding the quantitative relationships among numbers (e.g., 8 is 1 less than 9). Essentially, such abilities draw more on fluid reasoning than on crystallized intelligence; thus a clinician would want to examine the WJ III COG Fluid Reasoning cluster. Fluid reasoning problems would also impact a student's ability to perform adequately on the Applied Problems test.

Mathematical reasoning requires a combination of verbal and nonverbal abilities. Difficulties relative to oral language and reading could certainly affect a student's performance on the Applied Problems test. First, for students with poor reading skill, the task might require information to be held in immediate awareness because they cannot rely on reading problems accurately; thus an extra load would be placed on working memory. Careful examination of the WJ III ACH Oral Expression and Reading Comprehension clusters should be conducted when determining whether difficulty on Applied Problems stems from poor math reasoning or specific deficits in verbal task demands (or both). Particular attention should be given to the Understanding Directions test, because it provides an excellent means of observing a student's working memory for discourse—which might, particularly in the case of poor reading skill, be taxed on the Applied Problems test. When evaluating the nonverbal reasoning abilities influencing competence in applying math concepts, the examiner should consider a student's performance on the WJ III COG Fluid Reasoning, Executive Processing, and Broad Attention clusters.

Case Study A illustrates the usefulness of the WJ III COG and WJ III ACH in the diagnosis of students demonstrating poor math performance. The student is a 12-year-old male demonstrating learning disabilities and AD/HD. Throughout the case study, WJ III performances will be described in terms of Relative Performance Index scores. RPI scores, designed to resemble visual acuity indexes (e.g., 20/20), "are based on the distance along the W scale that a subject's score falls above or below the average score for the reference group" (Mather & Woodcock, 2001b, p. 70). An RPI indicates the relative ease or difficulty that similar age- or grade-level tasks will present (e.g., 90/90 = no particular difficulty; 20/90 = extreme difficulty).

CASE STUDY A: MATH DISORDER

Background Information

Eric, a 12-year-old student entering seventh grade, has been diagnosed with learning disabilities impacting mathematics. He was also diagnosed as exhibiting AD/HD. He currently attends a school located within a university; most of the students at the school have experienced academic or social difficulties in previous school settings. The director of the school referred Eric for a follow-up assessment.

Eric lives at home with his father and two brothers (ages 14 and 11). Eric's mother and father divorced when he was 5 years old. His contact with his mother is almost exclusively by phone, and these contacts are sporadic. Eric's father reported that Eric was delivered via cesarean section, but that no other complications occurred during the pregnancy or delivery. He also reported no delays in reaching developmental milestones. Eric's academic and attentional difficulties became evident in the fourth grade. At that time, he was diagnosed with AD/HD and math underachievement. Eric was placed on Adderall for his attention difficulties. Although his attention span increased significantly, he became belligerent and difficult to manage. Hence, the medication was discontinued.

Current Observations

Rapport was easily established during testing. During each session, Eric actively engaged the examiner in conversations about school, home life, and video games. He was responsive to questions asked and volunteered a great deal of information. He complained about having difficulty getting up for his appointments and about always feeling tired. When faced with challenging verbal questions or problems, Eric demonstrated adequate persistence. However, when faced with math problems or fluid reasoning tasks, his attention seemed to waver (e.g., he looked tired, yawned, and put his head down on the table). Although he was easily brought back to task, he did not appear to persist on mathematical and problem-solving tasks as well as he did on verbal tasks. In addition, his attention waned toward the end of the testing sessions, which lasted about 2 hours each (including breaks).

Summary—Cognitive, Language, and Achievement Measures

Figure 4-1 presents Eric's WJ III scores. His standard score for general intellectual ability (GIA RPI = 69/80; Standard Score [SS] = 82) is in the low-average range compared to same-age peers. Although attentional difficulties may have affected his GIA score, an examination of test scores in Broad Attention reveals that two of the four tests in this cluster were above his GIA RPI (Auditory Working Memory = 84/90 RPI and Auditory Attention = 87/90 RPI). By contrast, Eric's score on a visual task involving sustained attention and executive processing was 23/90 RPI (Pair Cancellation). It appears that many of Eric's attentional difficulties are specifically related to other areas of difficulty (e.g., executive processing and processing speed). His attention deficit disorder appeared to affect his success on tasks involving sustained and selective attention (e.g., Pair Cancellation and Visual Matching).

Eric obtained average to advanced RPI scores in the areas of Verbal Ability (87/90 RPI), memory (Long-Term Retrieval = 88/90 RPI), Auditory Skills (Auditory Processing = 91/90 RPI; Phonemic Awareness = 89/90 RPI), and Crystallized Knowledge (Comprehension–Knowledge = 87/90 RPI; Knowledge = 89/90 RPI). His scores in the achievement areas, strongly influenced by the above abilities, were also primarily within the average range and at or above his GIA RPI of 69/90: Oral Language (89/90 RPI); Oral Expression (83/90 RPI); Listening Comprehension (86/90 RPI); Broad Reading (90/90 RPI); Broad Written Language (72/90 RPI); and Academic Knowledge (87/90 RPI). Based on Eric's strengths in language skills and literacy achievement, one can conclude that his mathematics difficulties are not caused by a language-based problem. Eric's Broad Math cluster (39/90 RPI) consists of three tests: Math Calculation = 29/90 RPI; Math Fluency = 44/90 RPI; and Applied Problems = 46/90. His Math Calculation cluster score (36/90 RPI) was significantly discrepant from his GIA, and he obtained a Quantitative Concepts score of only 22/90 RPI. As previously mentioned in the discussion on math clusters, a number of cognitive factors can cause mathematics difficulties. In Eric's case, language and memory were relative strengths; therefore, they would not account for difficulty retrieving or manipulating math facts. It is quite possible that Eric's relatively stronger performance on Applied Problems reflects his stronger language skills. However, his Quantitative Concepts score of 22/90 RPI indicates difficulty with mathematics reasoning. Geary (2000) found that most children with mathematics disabilities do not experience visual-spatial deficits, and this is the case with Eric, whose Spatial Relations RPI was in the average range (83/90).

SCORE REPORT

Name: M, E
Date of Birth: 02/25/1989
Age: 12 years, 5 months   Grade: 4.9
Sex: Male   ID: Eric
Dates of Testing: 07/13/2001 (COG)   Examiner: Knight
        07/23/2001 (ACH)

TABLE OF SCORES: *Woodcock Johnson III Tests of Cognitive Abilities*
and *Tests of Achievement*
Norms based on age 12-5

CLUSTER/Test	RAW	AE	EASY to DIFF		RPI	PR	SS(90% BAND)
GIA (Ext)	-	9-4	7-10	11-7	69/90	11	82 (80-84)
VERBAL ABILITY (Ext)	-	11-9	9-10	14-2	87/90	42	97 (93-101)
THINKING ABILITY (Ext)	-	9-8	7-3	15-6	82/90	22	88 (85-91)
COG EFFICIENCY (Ext)	-	8-5	7-7	9-6	28/90	3	72 (69-76)
COMP-KNOWLEDGE (Gc)	-	11-9	9-10	14-2	87/90	42	97 (93-101)
L-T RETRIEVAL (Glr)	-	10-10	6-9	>22	88/90	36	95 (90-99)
VIS-SPATIAL THINK (Gv)	-	11-2	7-4	>25	88/90	42	97 (93-101)
AUDITORY PROCESS (Ga)	-	13-3	8-10	>25	91/90	56	102 (97-108)
FLUID REASONING (Gf)	-	7-9	6-11	9-3	46/90	8	79 (75-82)
PROCESS SPEED (Gs)	-	8-0	7-4	8-9	6/90	0.4	60 (57-63)
SHORT-TERM MEM (Gsm)	-	9-6	7-11	11-9	70/90	26	91 (86-96)
PHONEMIC AWARE	-	12-1	8-1	25	89/90	47	99 (93-105)
WORKING MEMORY	-	9-8	8-2	11-9	69/90	21	88 (84-92)
BROAD ATTENTION	-	9-2	7-8	11-2	64/90	7	78 (74-82)
COGNITIVE FLUENCY	-	9-0	7-7	10-10	59/90	10	81 (78-83)
EXEC PROCESSES	-	7-11	6-6	9-9	53/90	3	71 (68-74)
KNOWLEDGE	-	12-1	10-2	14-8	89/90	47	99 (95-102)
ORAL LANGUAGE (Ext)	-	11-2	8-10	14-7	85/90	33	94 (90-97)
ORAL EXPRESSION	-	10-8	8-1	14-3	83/90	30	92 (88-97)
LISTENING COMP	-	11-6	9-5	14-10	86/90	41	97 (93-100)
TOTAL ACHIEVEMENT	-	10-6	9-4	12-1	71/90	21	88 (86-90)
BROAD READING	-	12-5	11-1	13-11	90/90	50	100 (98-102)
BROAD MATH	-	9-2	8-3	10-4	39/90	7	78 (76-81)
BROAD WRITTEN LANG	-	9-10	8-8	12-0	72/90	21	88 (85-91)
BASIC READING SKILLS	-	12-11	11-2	15-0	92/90	57	103 (99-106)
READING COMP	-	12-5	10-1	15-7	90/90	50	100 (97-103)
MATH CALC SKILLS	-	8-7	7-7	9-9	36/90	2	68 (64-72)
MATH REASONING	-	9-3	8-5	10-2	33/90	11	82 (79-84)
BASIC WRITING SKILLS	-	11-10	10-1	13-11	87/90	45	98 (95-100)
WRITTEN EXPRESSION	-	9-3	8-0	11-0	60/90	9	80 (75-84)
ACADEMIC SKILLS	-	10-10	9-7	12-7	76/90	34	94 (92-96)
ACADEMIC FLUENCY	-	10-8	9-6	11-11	67/90	24	89 (87-91)
ACADEMIC APPS	-	10-0	8-8	11-10	69/90	21	88 (85-91)
ACADEMIC KNOWLEDGE	-	11-10	10-1	14-2	87/90	44	98 (93-102)
PHON/GRAPH KNOW	-	10-1	8-5	13-6	81/90	35	94 (91-97)
Verbal Comprehension	-	11-2	9-4	13-4	82/90	35	94 (90-99)
Visual-Auditory Learng	14-E	9-9	7-1	>19	84/90	31	92 (88-97)
Spatial Relations	62-D	9-1	6-5	19	83/90	30	92 (88-96)
Sound Blending	22	15-1	10-6	>26	94/90	63	105 (100-110)
Concept Formation	14-D	7-3	6-4	8-4	30/90	8	79 (75-82)
Visual Matching	30-2	8-3	7-9	8-10	3/90	0.4	60 (56-64)
Numbers Reversed	10	8-2	7-2	9-10	48/90	17	86 (80-91)
Incomplete Words	19	8-7	5-9	17-3	82/90	22	88 (81-96)
Auditory Work Memory	20	11-4	9-7	13-9	84/90	39	96 (92-100)
General Information	-	12-5	10-4	15-3	90/90	50	100 (95-105)
Retrieval Fluency	70	13-11	6-2	>30	91/90	62	104 (98-111)
Picture Recognition	50-D	14-3	8-7	>25	92/90	57	103 (97-108)

FIGURE 4-1 Woodcock–Johnson III Child Psychology Portfolio results for Eric. See text for discussion.

CLUSTER/Test	RAW	AE	EASY to DIFF	RPI	PR	SS(90% BAND)
Auditory Attention	37	10-8	7-1 >20	87/90	40	96 (90-102)
Analysis-Synthesis	20-D	8-6	7-4 10-10	64/90	19	87 (82-92)
Decision Speed	20	7-6	6-8 8-6	12/90	2	68 (64-72)
Memory for Words	17	11-4	9-2 15-4	86/90	44	98 (91-104)
Rapid Picture Naming	105	10-3	9-1 11-10	67/90	31	93 (91-95)
Planning	-	>28	5-5 >28	92/90	79	112 (100-125)
Pair Cancellation	39	8-0	7-0 9-1	23/90	3	72 (70-75)

Form A of the following achievement tests was administered:

Letter-Word ID	60	12-9	11-5 14-3	92/90	55	102 (98-106)
Reading Fluency	54	12-6	11-7 13-5	91/90	51	100 (98-102)
Story Recall	-	16-7	7-8 >21	92/90	66	106 (99-113)
Understanding Dirs	-	9-7	7-11 13-3	78/90	28	91 (87-95)
Calculation	14	9-0	8-3 9-11	29/90	6	76 (71-81)
Math Fluency	27	7-5	5-6 9-5	44/90	0.3	58 (55-61)
Spelling	37	11-10	9-6 14-6	88/90	46	99 (95-102)
Writing Fluency	15	10-0	8-11 11-2	54/90	14	84 (79-89)
Passage Comprehension	33	11-9	9-8 15-7	87/90	45	98 (94-102)
Applied Problems	33	10-1	9-3 11-1	46/90	21	88 (85-91)
Writing Samples	8-C	8-0	7-1 10-4	66/90	4	73 (65-81)
Word Attack	26	13-5	10-7 16-6	93/90	57	103 (98-107)
Picture Vocabulary	24	9-11	8-3 11-9	68/90	23	89 (84-94)
Oral Comprehension	23	12-11	10-10 16-6	92/90	55	102 (97-107)
Editing	17	11-10	10-6 13-6	85/90	43	97 (94-101)
Reading Vocabulary	-	12-11	10-7 15-6	92/90	56	102 (98-107)
Quantitative Concepts	-	8-4	7-8 9-3	22/90	5	75 (71-80)
Academic Knowledge	-	11-10	10-1 14-2	87/90	44	98 (93-102)
Spelling of Sounds	20	7-8	6-11 9-5	57/90	7	78 (73-83)
Punctuation & Capitals	10	7-1	6-7 7-8	5/90	<0.1	53 (44-61)

	STANDARD SCORES			DISCREPANCY		Significant at
DISCREPANCIES	Actual	Predicted	Difference	PR	SD	+ or - 1.50 SD
Intra-Individual						
COMP-KNOWLEDGE (Gc)	97	87	+10	87	+1.13	No
L-T RETRIEVAL (Glr)	95	90	+5	65	+0.37	No
VIS-SPATIAL THINK (Gv)	97	94	+3	59	+0.22	No
AUDITORY PROCESS (Ga)	102	92	+10	77	+0.74	No
FLUID REASONING (Gf)	79	91	-12	16	-0.99	No
PROCESS SPEED (Gs)	60	95	-35	1	-2.49	Yes
SHORT-TERM MEM (Gsm)	91	91	0	47	-0.07	No
PHONEMIC AWARE	99	92	+7	71	+0.55	No
WORKING MEMORY	88	91	-3	40	-0.25	No
BASIC READING SKILLS	103	88	+15	96	+1.73	Yes
READING COMP	100	89	+11	91	+1.33	No
MATH CALC SKILLS	68	93	-25	2	-2.09	Yes
MATH REASONING	82	90	-8	16	-0.98	No
BASIC WRITING SKILLS	98	89	+9	82	+0.92	No
WRITTEN EXPRESSION	80	91	-11	16	-1.00	No
ORAL EXPRESSION	92	90	+2	58	+0.21	No
LISTENING COMP	97	89	+8	77	+0.73	No
ACADEMIC KNOWLEDGE	98	89	+9	82	+0.93	No

	STANDARD SCORES			DISCREPANCY		Significant at
DISCREPANCIES	Actual	Predicted	Difference	PR	SD	+ or - 1.50 SD
Intellectual Ability/Achievement Discrepancies*						
BROAD READING	100	87	+13	89	+1.23	No
BASIC READING SKILLS	103	88	+15	89	+1.25	No
READING COMP	100	88	+12	89	+1.21	No
BROAD MATH	78	88	-10	17	-0.97	No
MATH CALC SKILLS	68	89	-21	6	-1.59	Yes
MATH REASONING	82	88	-6	26	-0.64	No
BROAD WRITTEN LANG	88	87	+1	52	+0.06	No
BASIC WRITING SKILLS	98	89	+9	79	+0.81	No
WRITTEN EXPRESSION	80	88	-8	25	-0.68	No
ORAL LANGUAGE (Ext)	94	85	+9	78	+0.76	No
ORAL EXPRESSION	92	87	+5	66	+0.42	No
LISTENING COMP	97	87	+10	82	+0.91	No
ACADEMIC KNOWLEDGE	98	87	+11	85	+1.02	No

*These discrepancies based on GIA (Ext) with ACH Broad, Basic, and Applied Clusters.

FIGURE 4-1 (Continued)

Eric did experience difficulty in the areas of cognitive processing most likely to affect math achievement (especially calculation and quantitative concepts): Cognitive Fluency (59/90 RPI), Processing Speed (6/90 RPI), Executive Processes (53/90 RPI), and Fluid Reasoning (49/90 RPI). Each of these areas and its possible impact on Eric's mathematics achievement is discussed below.

Eric's lowest score was on Math Fluency (44/90 RPI). Given this weakness, one might suspect a difficulty with academic and cognitive fluency. Further analysis, however, does not support this hypothesis. Fluency in reading was relatively strong. Eric's Reading Fluency score was 91/90 RPI. His Writing Fluency score (54/90 RPI) was quite likely an underestimate because he had to be brought back to task several times during the test, which requires 7 minutes of sustained attention. Eric's scores on the Cognitive Fluency cluster were mixed: Retrieval Fluency (91/90 RPI), Rapid Picture Naming (67/90 RPI), and Decision Speed (12/90 RPI). Retrieval Fluency and Rapid Picture Naming both involve retrieval of verbal stimuli, and these relatively strong scores were consistent with his other memory and retrieval scores. Thus, fluency itself appeared to be adequate. It is therefore likely that Eric's low score on Decision Speed reflects the fact that the test is primarily a measure of processing speed (*Gs* loading = 0.55 [McGrew & Woodcock, 2001, p. 197]). However, his weak fluid reasoning might also be a factor. In the WJ III standardization sample (ages 9 through 13), Decision Speed correlated .27 with Concept Formation (McGrew & Woodcock, 2001, p. 161), another test on which Eric struggled (30/90 RPI). Both processing areas are no doubt relevant to Eric's math disability.

Eric's scores on both of the Processing Speed cluster tests were quite low (Visual Matching = 3/90 RPI; Decision Speed = 12/90 RPI). These tests require the student to perform psychomotor tasks automatically with sustained and focused attention (Mather & Woodcock, 2001b). This ability was a consistent weakness in Eric's profile. In addition, these tasks require some degree of cognitive flexibility (e.g., set-shifting).

Difficulties with cognitive flexibility were also evident on tasks contributing to the Executive Processes and Fluid Reasoning clusters. Eric's two low scores on the Executive Processes cluster were Concept Formation (30/90 RPI) and Pair Cancellation (23/90 RPI). His difficulties with these tasks were most likely related to task demands such as the ability to repeatedly shift mental set and control interference (Mather & Woodcock, 2001b). Geary (2000) describes a procedural deficit in some cases of math disabilities that results in immature procedures and difficulty with multistep procedures. These skills are tapped by the fluid reasoning tasks, on which Eric had consistent difficulty (Concept Formation = 30/90 RPI; Analysis–Synthesis = 64/90 RPI). On the Analysis–Synthesis test, which approximates a rudimentary arithmetical system, Eric did understand the concept of combining the colors on the easier items. However, despite talking his way through the problems aloud, he was unable to transfer basic procedures to more complex items. On the Concept Formation test, his difficulties with shifting mental set were apparent early on. He never seemed to understand the task and answered most questions by simply describing all the features of each figure in a stimulus test. He became restless quickly, often looking around the room and at one point asking if he had reached the last page yet.

Discussion

Eric's most serious mathematical difficulties were in the area of calculation. It appears that he possesses adequate linguistic, retrieval, and memory skills to learn how to calculate. Indeed, he has learned most of his multiplication facts. However, Eric has not memorized addition and subtraction facts. Rather, he continues to use the immature counting principle to add—that is, he chooses the larger term and counts up from there. For example, when adding 7 + 3, he would say "7," and then count "8, 9, 10," to get the answer. Using the counting principle, Eric was able to add, including carrying. He was able to subtract providing he did not need to borrow. He was able to retrieve rote multiplication facts (e.g., $4 \times 3 = 12$). He was not able to perform the procedures of a multiplication problem that involved carrying (e.g., 15×3). On the Applied Problems test, Eric again employed an immature counting principle, solving several problems by placing tick marks on paper and counting them. Difficulty with more advanced counting principles and their flexible use was also evident in his performance on the Quantitative Concepts test. When asked to supply a missing number in a sequence, Eric was able to count by twos for numbers up to 10, but not thereafter. These mathematical difficulties are consistent with the procedural difficulties he encountered on the Analysis–Synthesis test—that is, he was able to deduce a basic procedure but was unable to apply it to complex examples or to apply it consistently. Clearly, his calculation weakness made it difficult for him to use math facts and procedures automatically to solve applied mathematics problems.

Eric's difficulties with mathematics can most likely be attributed to underlying deficits in attention, cognitive flexibility, and processing speed. Barrouillet et al. (1997, cited in Geary, 2000) found that seventh-grade students with learning disabilities had difficulty inhibiting irrelevant associations for simple multiplication problems. For example, the problem 7×4 might elicit a response of 21 (another multiple of 7). Geary (2000) confirmed the finding of difficulty with retrieval inhibition with first and second graders. In Eric's case, one of his lowest scores was on a task involving interference control (Pair Cancellation). In addition, his scores on tests of processing speed indicate that he struggles to make rapid decisions about relatively easy problems (e.g., circling two related objects on the Decision Speed test).

The cognitive flexibility, necessary to think categorically and abstractly, has direct implications for mathematical reasoning. Eric was simply unable to perform the categorical thinking necessary on fluid reasoning tasks. This difficulty was also evident on Part B of the Quantitative Concepts test, where Eric had difficulty completing even basic counting sequences. Eric's mathematical ability appears to be most seriously affected by his difficulties with calculation and quantitative concepts. These calculation difficulties, in turn, affect his ability to solve applied mathematical problems. In addition, his mathematical reasoning is most likely related to weaknesses in cognitive flexibility, processing speed, and possibly failure to inhibit retrieval of associated but inaccurate information.

During this case we have described test performance in terms of RPI scores, which predict how well a student will perform a certain task relative to his/her peers. For example, Eric's RPI for Broad Reading was 90/90. This score means that when other average students Eric's age demonstrate 90% success on their reading, Eric would also be expected to read with 90% success. In contrast, Eric's RPI of 6/90 on Processing Speed indicates that he would likely perform with 6% success on tasks involving processing speed when his average peers were performing with 90% proficiency. A glance at the RPI column of scores quickly reveals Eric's relative strengths and needs. By identifying Eric's proficiency relative to his peers, his teachers can more accurately plan instruction. For example, when examining the RPI scores for math achievement, a teacher can see that Eric's most pressing needs for remediation are in the areas of calculation (29/90) and quantitative concepts (22/90).

Points of Interest

Research into mathematics achievement and disability has increased in recent years (e.g., Geary, 2000; Hanich et al., in press). The cognitive profiles that researchers are uncovering involve problem areas that are measured on the WJ III (e.g., fluid reasoning, mental flexibility, working memory, spatial knowledge, long-term retrieval). As shown in the case of Eric, the WJ III offers a comprehensive means to compare performance across cognitive, language, and achievement tasks.

READING CLUSTERS

Evaluation of reading competence should include measures at the subword, word, sentence, and text levels. Table 4-3 links specific areas of reading (i.e., subword, word, sentence, and text) to the WJ III COG and WJ III ACH clusters most directly related to performance in those areas. The relationship of phonological and orthographic processing to the ability to decode appears to be dependent on a variety of subword processes, as well as on an individual's literacy experiences. A significant amount of research has demonstrated the predictive ability of phonological knowledge (i.e., phoneme segmentation, phoneme deletion, and phoneme blending) to reading achievement among children and adults (Gough & Tunmer, 1986; Gregg, Stennett, & Coleman, 2001; Wagner, Torgesen, & Rashotte, 1994). In addition, researchers have documented the bidirectional relationship of phonological and orthographic processing in the ability to read words (Andrews, 1982; Landerl et al., 1996; Seidenberg et al., 1984). Therefore, an examiner using the WJ III ACH and presented with a referral based on poor reading development would want to compare performance on the Sound

TABLE 4-3   Cognitive–Achievement Connection: Reading

Area	WJ III COG clusters	WJ III ACH clusters and subtests
Subword (phonology and orthography)	*Auditory Processing* *Phonemic Awareness* *Phonemic Awareness 3*	*Phoneme/Grapheme Knowledge* Sound Awareness Letter–Word Identification Word Attack Spelling of Sounds
Word (decoding)	*Comprehension–Knowledge* *Auditory Processing* *Processing Speed* *Long-Term Retrieval* *Short-Term Memory* *Phonemic Awareness* *Phonemic Awareness 3* *Broad Attention* *Cognitive Fluency* *Cognitive Efficiency* *Working Memory*	*Academic Fluency* *Phoneme/Grapheme Knowledge* *Broad Reading* *Reading Comprehension* *Basic Reading Skills* *Academic Knowledge* Reading Fluency Sound Awareness Word Attack Letter–Word Identification Picture Vocabulary Reading Vocabulary
Sentence (syntax)	*Comprehension–Knowledge* *Processing Speed* *Cognitive Fluency* *Cognitive Efficiency* *Working Memory Cluster* *Executive Processing* *Broad Attention*	*Academic Fluency* *Oral Language* *Listening Comprehension* *Oral Comprehension* *Academic Knowledge* *Broad Reading* *Broad Written Language* Understanding Directions Reading Vocabulary Picture Vocabulary
Text (discourse)	*Comprehension–Knowledge* *Processing Speed* *Cognitive Fluency* *Cognitive Efficiency* *Executive Processing* *Broad Attention*	*Academic Fluency* *Oral Language* *Oral Comprehension* *Listening Comprehension* *Oral Expression* *Academic Knowledge* *Broad Reading* *Understanding Directions* Reading Vocabulary Picture Vocabulary

Note: Italics indicate clusters.

Awareness test to performance on the Word Attack, Letter–Word Identification, Reading Fluency, and Passage Comprehension tests. Table 4-3 provides a list of the WJ III COG and WJ III ACH clusters that would be pertinent in determining whether underlying subword processes might be implicated. For example, the WJ III COG Auditory Processing, Phonemic Awareness, and Phonemic Awareness 3 clusters should be compared to the examinee's WJ III ACH Phoneme/Grapheme Knowledge cluster and Sound Awareness performance.

Verbal comprehension, vocabulary, and background knowledge are incidental correlates of reading comprehension. Some researchers have considered background knowledge as the trigger for other processes such as inference making and comprehension monitoring (Perfetti, Marron, & Foltz, 1996). The Comprehension–Knowledge (*Gc*) cluster on the WJ III COG consists of the Verbal Comprehension and General Information tests. Evans et al. (2002) found that among CHC clusters, the *Gc* cluster had the strongest and most consistent relationship to the Basic Reading and Reading Comprehension clusters. The significance of this relationship was seen to increase across the life span. Vocabulary knowledge is also strongly correlated with reading comprehension. According to Stothard and Hulme (1996), vocabulary may help to explain the relationship between verbal ability and reading comprehension, because it correlates strongly with both constructs. Therefore, it would be important (as described in Table 4-3) for an examiner to compare a student's WJ III COG Comprehension–Knowledge cluster and WJ III ACH Knowledge cluster with reading performance in order to consider the influence of background knowledge on reading competence. In addition, the WJ III ACH Reading Vocabulary test should be compared to its oral language equivalent (Picture Vocabulary), as well as to other reading-related measures. An examiner may want to consider, for example, whether a student can identify printed words at a level commensurate with his/her (oral) word knowledge.

Careful examination of a student's ability to decode both nonsense and real words is the next step an examiner will need to take in assessing reading problems. The reading of nonsense words (Word Attack) should always be compared to the reading of real words (Letter–Word Identification). For students with weak phonological processing skills as identified on the WJ III ACH Sound Awareness test, the task of reading nonsense words may prove very difficult. Some students who have received extensive phonological training and/or have strong orthographic skills may be able to perform better with nonsense words than real words. Gregg and Coleman (2001) noted that clinicians used to working with adults and administering the *Woodcock–Johnson Tests of Achievement—Revised* (WJ-R) (Woodcock & Johnson, 1989) version of Word Attack may think that the WJ III Word Attack-derived test scores seem lower (see Table 4-4 for an illustration of this phenomenon). Clinicians are encouraged to rely not just on test and cluster scores, but also on checklist responses and qualitative observations (e.g., automaticity, effort expended, and severity of errors). For example, a 21-year-old of superior overall ability who makes four errors on the 32-item WJ III Word Attack test (SS = 94 [81–100]; RPI = 76/90) may not have significant decoding problems, despite what the standard score might suggest. Examiners are advised to consider RPI scores, which describe a person's relative proficiency compared to his/her same-age peers, as well as other tests that yield insight into automaticity and accuracy of decoding (e.g., Letter–Word Identification, Reading Fluency, Passage Comprehension, and Editing).

TABLE 4-4   Comparison of WJ-R and WJ III Raw and Standard Scores
for Word Attack Based on Age 21 Norms

WJ-R Word Attack		WJ III Word Attack	
Errors (of 30 items)	SS	Errors (of 32 items)	SS
0	148	0	116
1	136	1	109
2	124	2	100
4	109	4	94
5	103	5	91
8	94	8	85
10	89	10	81
12	85	12	78

A typical consequence of weak phonological processing abilities (Sound
Awareness), in addition to poor performance on the reading of nonsense words,
is compromised fluency of reading. Therefore, an examiner will want to compare
a student's WJ III ACH Academic Fluency cluster with reading tests as well as
with the WJ III COG Cognitive Fluency and Cognitive Efficiency clusters (see
Table 3-4). Intervention in the area of reading fluency and/or accommodations
such as extended time will be supported by such information. Many times, students with poor phonological processing ability (and fluency) are stronger at discourse comprehension (understanding of language at the text level) than they are
at decoding single words. Students with dyslexia often have problems at the basic
skill level (i.e., decoding, fluency), but not in the application of language skills
(i.e., reading comprehension). For such students, the oral language/achievement
discrepancy procedure provides an excellent form of disability documentation.
It is also important that examiners recognize that the Processing Speed (Gs)
cluster has a significant relationship to the Basic Reading and Reading
Comprehension clusters only from ages 6 to 11 (Evans et al., 2002). Therefore,
using the Gs cluster score as an explanation for low reading rate is questionable.
In addition, the WJ III COG Auditory Processing cluster is significantly related
to the Basic Reading cluster only between the ages of 6 and 9 (Evans et al., 2002).
Clinicians should be aware that the processing abilities that contribute to reading
performance change during the course of the life span.

Reading comprehension has been found to be a multidimensional construct.
Deficits in comprehending at the sentence and/or discourse level can produce variable performance on reading comprehension measures. In addition, the format of
a reading comprehension measure can influence performance. Knight (2000),
using three different tests of reading comprehension (reading recall, multiple-
choice questions, and modified cloze), found that there was no significant

correlation among these tests because they were using fundamentally different formats. Table 4-3 provides the examiner with a list of WJ III COG and WJ III ACH clusters that should be compared when trying to determine what cognitive and/or linguistic processes may be impacting performance on the reading measures of the WJ III.

The WJ III ACH Passage Comprehension test measures reading via a cloze format (e.g., *Deserts are characterized by their _____ of water*). Fuchs, Fuchs, and Maxwell (1988) evaluated the concurrent validity of a variety of test formats measuring reading comprehension and found that all formats correlated most highly with their criterion measure with the exception of a cloze task, which correlated more highly with a test of word recognition. Sheen and Heerman (1985) found that a cloze format correlated more highly with the *Test of Standard Written English* than with the comprehension portion of the *Nelson Denny Reading Test*. McGrew and Woodcock (2001) state that in light of such findings, the authors of the WJ III paid special attention to content in ensuring that the omitted words on Passage Comprehension items could not be supplied solely on the basis of local context.

The WJ III ACH Passage Comprehension test helps examiners identify students with passage-level language comprehension problems. Students with specific types of syntax deficits and/or word-finding problems (as identified across oral language measures) may have difficulty appreciating grammatical constraints and supplying specific lexical items on reading (as well as oral) cloze tasks; therefore, their reading comprehension scores will be affected. The cloze format is not useful, however, in assessing reading recall from text passages. Therefore, an examiner should employ other types of reading comprehension formats (e.g., multiple choice, reading recall) in addition to that used on the WJ III ACH Passage Comprehension test.

Case Study B illustrates the utility of the WJ III COG and WJ III ACH in the evaluation of students demonstrating poor reading performance. The student is a 26-year-old graduate student seeking documentation to support accommodations at a university. The student has a previous diagnosis of learning disabilities. Throughout this case, WJ III standard score ranges will be described using the 90% confidence intervals. Following the case study, the text presents a brief critique of the WJ III COG and WJ III ACH with regard to dyslexia cases in general.

CASE STUDY B: READING DISORDER

Background Information

Bill, a 26-year-old graduate student working toward a Master's degree in Education, sought testing to update previous documentation of learning disabilities. He was first diagnosed with specific learning disabilities at age 7, after he had to repeat the first grade. As a high school senior he participated in a second evaluation, which confirmed the prior diagnosis and identified underachievement in written expression (including spelling), reading (decoding and rate), and math (calculation and reasoning). He has received support services (e.g., extra time on exams; use of notetakers, books on tape, and a word processor with spellchecker; proofreading help; and a reader for exams) throughout his undergraduate and graduate studies, but needs updated documentation of learning disabilities in order to receive accommodations on the Praxis II exam (a standardized test that prospective teachers must pass in order to become certified) and in future courses.

Bill reported no birth complications or delays in reaching developmental milestones. Recent screenings indicated normal hearing and vision. No attentional or emotional concerns were reported or identified. Bill was slow to learn the alphabet and develop basic spelling and reading skills; as a result, he was required to repeat the first grade. At the beginning of the second grade, he was diagnosed with learning disabilities (dyslexia) and placed in resource classes. Bill did not remain in resource classes because he felt they moved too slowly for him. He received accommodations throughout high school, where he was successful in both regular and advanced placement classes. He earned a B.S. in Biology at a competitive university and is currently nearing the end of a Master's program in Education. Current areas of academic difficulty include word-finding difficulties, written expression (he often "dumbs down" his writing because he cannot spell the words he wants to use), spelling "everyday words," reversing letters, and sounding out printed words. He noted that even though books on tape are helpful, he still finds reading to be a "labor-intensive process." He also described himself as "reliant" on computerized spellcheckers and dictation programs. Bill's hobbies include boating, listening to audiobooks, and making stained glass.

Summary—Cognitive and Language Measures

A multiple-battery approach was adopted in the evaluation of Bill's cognitive and linguistic abilities. He was administered the WJ III COG, the WAIS-III, the WMS-III, the Rey–Osterrieth Complex Figure Test (RCF), the Stroop Color and Word Test (Stroop), the University of Georgia's (UGA) Phonology and Orthography Battery, and neuropsychological measures of fine-motor speed and dexterity. Figure 4-2 summarizes Bill's scores on all standardized measures.

Because of the mix of abilities measured by each battery, the WJ III and WAIS-III yielded different estimates of overall ability (WJ III GIA—Ext SS = 100–108; WAIS-III FSIQ SS = 119–126). On both the WJ III COG and the WAIS-III, Bill's verbal abilities and crystallized knowledge fell in the high-average to superior Standard Score ranges (WJ III Comprehension–Knowledge RPI = 99/90, SS = 115–129; WAIS-III VIQ SS = 114–123; WAIS-III Verbal Comprehension Index SS = 123–133). Clearly, these verbal strengths have been critical to his success in academics. Additionally, Bill's fluid reasoning was average to advanced (WJ III Fluid Reasoning RPI = 97/90). His performance on the WAIS-III Matrix Reasoning test, another measure of *Gf*, was consistent with this estimate (Scale Score = 12).

Case Two: Bill, WJ III COG Score Summary

CLUSTER/Test	RAW	AE	EASY to DIFF		RPI	PR	SS (90% BAND)	z
CLUSTERS								
GIA (Ext)	-	>24	16-9	>24	93/90	60	104 (100-108)	0.27
VERBAL ABILITY (Ext)	-	>25	>25	>25	99/90	93	122 (115-129)	1.46
THINKING ABILITY (Ext)	-	>22	13-3	>22	93/90	69	107 (102-113)	0.48
COG EFFICIENCY (Ext)	-	14-9	12-4	18-11	77/90	35	94 (91-98)	-0.38
COMP-KNOWLEDGE (Gc)	-	>25	>25	>25	99/90	93	122 (115-129)	1.46
L-T RETRIEVAL (Glr)	-	>22	8-6	>22	91/90	55	102 (94-109)	0.11
VIS-SPATIAL THINK (Gv)	-	>25	10-5	>25	91/90	55	102 (94-110)	0.14
AUDITORY PROCESS (Ga)	-	>25	13-3	>25	93/90	64	105 (98-113)	0.35
FLUID REASONING (Gf)	-	>21	18-4	>21	97/90	77	111 (101-121)	0.73
PROCESS SPEED (Gs)	-	12-0	10-9	13-7	43/90	20	88 (84-91)	-0.82
SHORT-TERM MEM (Gsm)	-	>22	16-9	>22	94/90	59	103 (96-111)	0.22
PHONEMIC AWARENESS	-	>28	12-10	>28	91/90	53	101 (95-108)	0.08
PHONEMIC AWARENESS III	-	19	11-9	>26	88/90	46	98 (94-102)	-0.11
WORKING MEMORY	-	20	15-8	>22	92/90	54	102 (96-107)	0.11
BROAD ATTENTION	-	19	14-5	>21	92/90	59	103 (98-109)	0.23
COGNITIVE FLUENCY	-	9-6	7-11	11-5	25/90	5	75 (72-78)	-1.69
EXEC PROCESSES	-	>20	17-4	>20	97/90	87	117 (107-127)	1.13

TESTS								
Verbal Comprehension	-	>24	>24	>24	99/90	87	117 (108-125)	1.13
Visual-Auditory Learning	6-E	>19	10-0	>19	93/90	63	105 (97-113)	0.33
Spatial Relations	73-D	>25	10-7	>25	92/90	57	103 (96-110)	0.18
Sound Blending	25	>26	14-7	>26	92/90	54	102 (95-108)	0.10
Concept Formation	39-E	>21	>21	>21	99/90	89	118 (104-132)	1.21
Visual Matching	44-2	11-10	10-10	13-1	21/90	18	86 (82-91)	-0.91
Numbers Reversed	17	19	16-1	>22	90/90	50	100 (94-106)	-0.01
Incomplete Words	26	27	10-4	>33	90/90	51	100 (89-112)	0.02
Auditory Work Memory	30	>22	15-0	>22	93/90	61	104 (96-112)	0.27
Vis-Aud Learn--Delayed	3	-	-	-	-	-	-	0.96
General Information	-	>40	>40	>40	99/90	96	126 (115-136)	1.71
Retrieval Fluency	72	14-8	6-4	>30	87/90	32	93 (87-99)	-0.45
Picture Recognition	52-D	24	10-3	>25	90/90	50	100 (90-110)	0.00
Auditory Attention	43	>20	11-2	>20	95/90	78	112 (97-126)	0.78
Analysis-Synthesis	28-E	>20	14-0	>20	91/90	54	101 (90-113)	0.09
Decision Speed	32	12-4	10-8	14-6	69/90	28	91 (84-98)	-0.60
Memory for Words	19	>23	20	>23	96/90	66	106 (96-117)	0.41
Rapid Picture Naming	83	7-2	6-4	8-0	0/90	2	70 (68-72)	-1.97
Planning	-	>28	>28	>28	97/90	>99.9	151 (110-193)	3.42
Pair Cancellation	69	15-10	13-5	>19	91/90	53	101 (98-104)	0.07

Case Two: Bill, Cognitive/Linguistic Score Summary

INDEX/Test	SS	PR	SS (90% BAND)
WAIS-III			
VERBAL IQ	119	90	114-123
PERFORMANCE IQ	124	95	117-128
FULL SCALE IQ	123	94	119-126
VERBAL COMPREHENSION INDEX	129	97	123-133
PERCEPTUAL ORGANIZATION INDEX	133	99	125-137
WORKING MEMORY INDEX	97	42	91-103
PROCESSING SPEED INDEX	91	27	85-100
Vocabulary	17	99	
Similarities	15	95	
Arithmetic	10	50	
Digit Span	10	50	
Information	13	84	
Comprehension	14	91	
Letter-Number Sequencing	09	37	
Picture Completion	18	99	
Digit Symbol	07	16	
Block Design	15	95	
Matrix Reasoning	12	75	
Picture Arrangement	15	95	
Symbol Search	10	50	

FIGURE 4-2 Woodcock–Johnson COG, WAIS-III, WMS-III, RCF, Stroop Color and Word Test, and WJ III ACH results for Bill. See text for discussion.

WMS-III

AUDITORY IMMEDIATE	99	47	93-105
VISUAL IMMEDIATE	91	27	84-101
IMMEDIATE MEMORY	95	37	89-102
AUDITORY DELAYED	94	34	87-103
VISUAL DELAYED	100	50	92-108
AUDITORY RECOGNITION DELAYED	100	50	91-109
GENERAL MEMORY	96	39	90-103
WORKING MEMORY	91	27	84-100
Logical Memory I	10	50	
Faces I	05	05	
Verbal Paired Associates I	10	50	
Family Pictures I	13	84	
Spatial Span	08	25	
Logical Memory II	08	25	
Faces II	07	16	
Verbal Paired Associates II	10	50	
Family Pictures II	13	84	

RCF

Copy	NA	>16
Immediate Recall	T=57	76
Delayed Recall	T=57	76

Stroop Color & Word Test (percentiles only)
Word = 01   Color = 16   Color-Word = 05   Interference = 58

Case Two: Bill, WJ III ACH Score Summary

CLUSTER/Test	RAW	AE	EASY to DIFF		RPI	PR	SS (90% BAND)	z
ORAL LANGUAGE (Ext)	-	>24	17-3	>24	94/90	68	107 (101-113)	0.46
ORAL EXPRESSION	-	23	14-10	>59	89/90	48	99 (95-103)	-0.06
LISTENING COMP	-	>22	>22	>22	97/90	79	112 (104-121)	0.81
TOTAL ACHIEVEMENT	-	14-7	12-6	17-3	57/90	27	91 (89-92)	-0.63
BROAD READING	-	16-10	15-0	19	60/90	35	94 (92-96)	-0.39
BROAD MATH	-	12-10	11-2	15-3	50/90	16	85 (82-88)	-0.97
BROAD WRITTEN LANG	-	12-11	10-6	16-2	61/90	19	87 (82-91)	-0.90
BASIC READING SKILLS	-	16-1	13-9	19	75/90	38	95 (93-98)	-0.30
READING COMP	-	>34	>34	>34	98/90	86	117 (110-123)	1.10
MATH CALC SKILLS	-	11-8	10-0	14-0	49/90	10	81 (77-85)	-1.26
MATH REASONING	-	15-0	13-0	17-10	64/90	28	91 (88-95)	-0.58
BASIC WRITING SKILLS	-	10-8	9-4	12-6	17/90	10	80 (77-84)	-1.30
WRITTEN EXPRESSION	-	>21	13-11	>21	92/90	59	103 (95-112)	0.22
ACADEMIC SKILLS	-	12-8	11-0	14-9	36/90	18	86 (83-89)	-0.93
ACADEMIC FLUENCY	-	13-6	12-0	15-3	27/90	15	84 (82-87)	-1.04
ACADEMIC APPS	-	>27	16-10	>27	92/90	58	103 (97-109)	0.21
PHON/GRAPH KNOW	-	11-6	9-0	15-2	58/90	22	88 (85-92)	-0.78
TESTS								
Letter-Word Identification	70	19	16-6	>22	85/90	45	98 (94-102)	-0.13
Reading Fluency	57	13-2	12-3	14-1	1/90	17	86 (84-87)	-0.96
Story Recall	-	12-8	6-11	>21	87/90	36	95 (85-104)	-0.36
Understanding Directions	-	>21	16-2	>21	95/90	68	107 (96-118)	0.46
Calculation	21	11-9	10-5	13-8	50/90	17	86 (79-92)	-0.95
Math Fluency	75	11-6	9-2	14-6	49/90	6	76 (73-79)	-1.59
Spelling	29	8-7	8-1	9-3	3/90	5	76 (72-80)	-1.62
Writing Fluency	26	17-0	13-9	>20	90/90	50	100 (95-104)	-0.01
Passage Comprehension	45	>31	>31	>31	99/90	91	121 (109-132)	1.37
Applied Problems	46	14-10	13-1	17-8	51/90	27	91 (87-95)	-0.61
Writing Samples	17-E	>23	14-5	>23	94/90	76	111 (95-127)	0.71

FIGURE 4-2 (*Continued*)

Word Attack	25	12-6	10-0	15-6	62/90	27	91 (86-96)	-0.60
Picture Vocabulary	36	26	18-11	43	90/90	50	100 (92-108)	0.01
Oral Comprehension	31	>23	>23	>23	98/90	81	113 (103-123)	0.89
Editing	20	13-4	11-9	15-8	56/90	26	91 (86-95)	-0.63
Reading Vocabulary	-	>56	31	>56	97/90	70	108 (103-113)	0.54
Quantitative Concepts	-	15-1	12 10	18-0	75/90	34	94 (88-100)	-0.41
Spelling of Sounds	27	9-11	7-10	14-7	54/90	15	85 (79-90)	-1.03
Sound Awareness	41	14-7	10-6	>24	79/90	32	93 (85-101)	-0.45

Case Two: Bill, WJ III Discrepancy Summary

	STANDARD SCORES			DISCREPANCY		Significant at
DISCREPANCIES	Actual	Predicted	Difference	PR	SD	+ or - 1.50 SD
Intra-Individual						
COMP-KNOWLEDGE (Gc)	122	98	+24	99.7	+2.75	Yes
L-T RETRIEVAL (Glr)	102	100	+2	56	+0.15	No
VIS-SPATIAL THINK (Gv)	102	100	+2	56	+0.15	No
AUDITORY PROCESS (Ga)	105	100	+5	70	+0.51	No
FLUID REASONING (Gf)	111	99	+12	92	+1.42	No
PROCESS SPEED (Gs)	88	101	-13	12	-1.17	No
SHORT-TERM MEM (Gsm)	103	100	+3	62	+0.31	No
PHONEMIC AWARE	101	100	+1	56	+0.15	No
WORKING MEMORY	102	100	+2	56	+0.16	No
BROAD READING	94	101	-7	24	-0.71	No
BROAD MATH	85	102	-17	6	-1.54	Yes
BROAD WRITTEN LANG	87	102	-15	5	-1.68	Yes
ORAL LANGUAGE	104	100	+4	67	+0.44	No

	STANDARD SCORES			DISCREPANCY		Significant at
DISCREPANCIES	Actual	Predicted	Difference	PR	SD	+ or - 1.50 SD
*Intellectual Ability/Achievement Discrepancies**						
BROAD READING	94	103	-9	16	-0.98	No
BASIC READING SKILLS	95	103	-8	22	-0.76	No
READING COMP	117	103	+14	91	+1.33	No
BROAD MATH	85	103	-18	5	-1.64	Yes
MATH CALC SKILLS	81	103	-22	3	-1.85	Yes
MATH REASONING	91	103	-12	9	-1.32	No
BROAD WRITTEN LANG	87	103	-16	4	-1.77	Yes
BASIC WRITING SKILLS	80	103	-23	2	-2.17	Yes
WRITTEN EXPRESSION	103	103	0	52	+0.05	No
ORAL LANGUAGE (Ext)	107	103	+4	69	+0.50	No
ORAL EXPRESSION	99	103	-4	35	-0.38	No
LISTENING COMP	112	103	+9	83	+0.95	No

These discrepancies based on GIA (Ext) with ACH Broad, Basic, and Applied Clusters.

FIGURE 4-2 (*Continued*)

Bill demonstrated average proficiency on measures of long-term retrieval (WJ III Long-Term Retrieval RPI = 91/90), auditory processing (WJ III Auditory Processing RPI = 93/90), and short-term memory (WJ III Short-Term Memory RPI = 94/90). His average proficiency in these areas is also supported by his WMS-III General Memory (SS = 90–103), UGA Phonology tasks (within normal limits), WAIS-III Working Memory Index (SS = 91–103), and WMS-III Working Memory Index (SS = 84–100). His lowest performance among working memory tests came on the WMS-III Spatial Span test (Scale Score = 8), the only visual-modality test among Working Memory clusters/indexes. Although Bill's visual-spatial thinking ability, as measured by the WJ III, is average (WJ III Visual-Spatial Thinking RPI = 91/90), a similar index from the WAIS-III yielded a higher estimate of visual processing ability (WAIS-III Perceptual Organization Index SS = 125–137). Clinicians considered factors that might help to explain the differences in his performance across measures (e.g., time constraints; nature of visual stimuli [abstract versus tangible]) and found consistently higher scores on tests that included tactile activities (e.g., Block Design [Scale Score = 15]; Picture Arrangement [Scale Score = 15]). On a separate measure of visual-motor skill (the Rey Complex Figure Test), Bill produced an excellent copy of the abstract Rey Complex Figure. He subsequently demonstrated high average incidental learning and recall of its details (76th percentile). Given his generally strong performances on Visual-Spatial Thinking (*Gv*) measures, as well as his hobbies—which include sailing and making stained glass—clinicians hypothesized that spatial and/or tactile abilities may be relative strengths for Bill.

Bill's processing speed is limited (WJ III Processing Speed RPI = 43/90), although his WAIS-III Processing Speed Index did not reveal this (WAIS-III SS = 85–100). His proficiency with speeded processing of orthographic information was very limited (WJ III Visual Matching RPI 21/90); this is supported by his WAIS-III Digit Symbol Scale Score of 7. His speed of processing with other types of visual stimuli was limited to average (WJ III Decision Speed RPI = 69/90; this is supported by his WAIS-III Symbol Search Scale Score of 10. Additionally, his performance on UGA Orthographic tasks was well below average compared to others of his educational level. Bill had particular difficulty on the Colorado Perceptual Speed Test, which presented him with rows of letter clusters (with numbers sometimes mixed in) and asked him to circle the cluster in each row that matched the first one in that row (e.g., *zxc6: zcx6 zxc9 zxc6 zxc9*). He was administered three 1-minute trials, the third of which featured pseudoword clusters (e.g., *falp: falb flap flab falp*). He was markedly slow on all trials, and no faster with pseudoword clusters than with unpronounceable ones.

Bill's performance was negligible on tasks requiring him to rapidly name familiar (or overlearned) visual stimuli (WJ III Rapid Picture Naming RPI = 0/90; this is supported by his scores on the Stroop Word Naming (1st percentile) and Color Naming (16th percentile) tests. His overall cognitive fluency is limited (WJ III Cognitive Fluency RPI = 25/90). In short, Bill demonstrated deficient rapid naming abilities and processing of orthographic information (both of which are potential causes of dyslexia). His phonemic awareness, on the other hand, was average (WJ III Phonemic Awareness RPI = 91/90; Phonemic Awareness 3 RPI = 88/90).

Finally, Bill was administered brief tests of fine-motor speed and dexterity. His performance was within normal limits (which was consistent with his success on WAIS-III Perceptual Organization tasks), but his pattern of scores was abnormal in that he was faster and more dexterous with his left (nondominant) hand than with his right. In reporting and describing the performance of three dyslexic adults on a battery of neuropsychological measures, Bigler (1992) noted that "these three adults with residual reading/spelling learning disability displayed subtle motor findings wherein the dominant–nondominant-hand performance on finger oscillation and grip strength did not exhibit superiority of the dominant hand" (p. 500). In light of such findings, it is possible that Bill's performance pattern on motor tasks could reflect "a deficit in normal hemispheric specialization" (Bigler, 1992, p. 500) that is directly related to his long-standing difficulties with reading and spelling.

Summary—Achievement Measures

Bill's academic and oral language skills were assessed with the WJ III ACH (19 of 22 tests administered). He was also asked to write a spontaneous essay under timed conditions. Figure 4-2 shows the test and cluster scores for Bill. Bill's cluster scores for oral language ranged from average to advanced and indicated intact language comprehension skills (Oral Language [Ext] RPI = 94/90; Oral Expression RPI 89/90; Listening Comprehension RPI = 97/90). Advanced comprehension skills were also evident on measures of untimed reading comprehension (Reading Comprehension RPI = 98/90). However, Bill's proficiency on tests measuring other aspects of reading was limited (Broad Reading RPI = 60/90) or limited to average (Basic Reading Skills RPI = 75/90). Although his recognition of individual (printed) words was average (Letter–Word Identification RPI = 85/90), his skill at sounding out pseudowords was limited (Word Attack RPI = 62/90); this pattern is often seen in adult dyslexics. Bill's slow processing of familiar printed symbols (e.g., letters and words) was reflected in his negligible reading speed (Reading Fluency RPI = 1/90). Bill's automaticity and basic skills with reading, writing, and math tasks was limited (Academic Fluency RPI = 27/90; Academic Skills RPI = 36/90).

Bill's basic writing skills are very limited (Basic Writing Skills RPI = 17/90); his ability to spell familiar words was negligible (Spelling RPI = 3/90) and his ability to spell letter combinations that are regular patterns in English was limited (Spelling of Sounds RPI = 54/90). Qualitative analysis revealed that most of his incorrect attempts accurately represented the sound sequences in target words, but contained orthographic substitutions (e.g., *grane* for *grain*; *hedding* for *heading*). In other cases, letter transpositions rendered his attempts inaccurate (e.g., *brigde* for *bridge*; *edcuation* for *education*). On all tasks (standardized and otherwise) involving printed words, his sensitivity to spelling conventions, morphological cues, and the sequencing and identity of orthographic constituents was limited (WJ III Phoneme/Grapheme Knowledge RPI = 58/90). These difficulties did not affect his performance on tests that do not penalize for mistakes in spelling, or capitalization, where his proficiency was average (Writing Fluency RPI = 90/90; Writing Samples RPI = 94/90). Such mistakes were prominent, however, on those tests and in Bill's spontaneous expository essay (e.g., *These mezures would need to include incresing ful efichancy of Power plants and adomabils. Incintives need to be provided to bulders to construcct efient homes. Finly pepole need to lean to Recycle, drive less as well as tun of there lights.*). Of the 321 words in his essay, 59 were misspelled. Upon completion of his work, he noted, "I usually compose on the computer—with my spelling, it's hard not to." The contrast between the quality of ideas in Bill's essay and the state of his spelling skills was striking.

Bill's proficiency is limited across a broad range of mathematics tasks (Math Calculation Skills RPI = 49/90; Math Reasoning RPI = 64/90; Broad Math RPI = 50/90). He noted that he had not had a math class in several years and that his recall of geometry and algebra formulas was "abysmal." Error analysis revealed that in addition to these limiting factors, Bill misread arithmetical signs with alarming frequency, particularly under timed conditions (e.g., $3 + 5 = 15$). On the Math Fluency test (RPI = 49/90), he misread signs or numbers on approximately 1 of every 12 items attempted.

Discussion

When compared to others his age, estimates of Bill's overall intellectual ability range from average to superior. Bill performed well on measures of crystallized intelligence, verbal reasoning, listening comprehension, and visual-spatial abilities. Bill performed poorly across all tasks requiring him to rapidly scan or name visual stimuli; his slowness was exacerbated when such tasks featured orthographic information (printed letters, numbers, or words). His performance indicated (possibly related) deficits in rapid naming and orthographic processing. Deficiencies in these abilities (with or without accompanying phonological processing deficits) have recently been identified as causal agents in dyslexia (see Foorman, 1994; Gregg, Stennett, Coleman, Hoy, & Davis, 2001; Perfetti, Marron, & Foltz, 1996; Wolf et al., 2000).

Bill's academic scores indicated low-level difficulties stemming from the cognitive/linguistic processing deficits described above. Error analysis revealed that these difficulties may be severe. Bill's spelling and word-decoding skills were characterized by poor accuracy and automaticity; he transposed letters, misspelled many common words, and misread signs on basic math problems. Although his basic academic skills and fluency were limited and below expectations, his higher level skills—notably, reading comprehension and ideas in written expression—were consistent with expectations based on educational level. Bill's strengths and weaknesses were evident in the WJ III discrepancy analysis summarized in Figure 4-2. As noted earlier, his underachievement in math was attributable partly to noncognitive factors (e.g., lack of recent instruction/practice), but also to compromised processing of printed symbols.

Based on the evaluation results, clinicians determined that Bill continues to meet the criteria for a diagnosis of specific learning disability and that he should continue to receive appropriate accommodations (including extended time on exams, use of a word processor with spellchecker, access to books on tape, use of a calculator, and permission to use a notetaker).

Points of Interest

The preceding case demonstrates the value of using multiple assessment tools and procedures. Emphasis needs to be placed on the interaction among learner (e.g., abilities, history, and exposure to learning), task (e.g., complexity and difficulty), and psychometric characteristics of measures (e.g., indexes, clusters, or tests). In the case of Bill, for example, use of the WAIS-III, UGA Phonology and Orthography Battery, Stroop Color and Word Test, and Rey–Osterrieth Complex Figure Test allowed clinicians to identify strengths and weaknesses that were not evidenced on the WJ III. By the same token, the WJ III tapped abilities and skills that were not directly addressed by other measures. With regard to academic achievement, qualitative analysis of a spontaneous writing sample provided dramatic evidence demonstrating the impact of the word-level difficulties identified with the WJ III ACH.

Mather & Gregg (2001) indicated that "additional research is needed on the clinical efficacy of the special clinical clusters" introduced as part of the WJ III (p. 13). Of particular interest to researchers and clinicians concerned with non-phonologically based causes of dyslexia may be the Cognitive Fluency cluster, which the *WJ III COG Examiner's Manual* (Mather & Woodcock, 2001b) describes as measuring "the ease and speed by which an individual performs cognitive tasks" (p. 22). In Bill's case, this cluster served as a highly useful gauge of rapid naming abilities. It is recommended that the Cognitive Fluency cluster be thoroughly investigated by researchers interested in RAN tasks, the role of rapid naming in dyslexia, and the assessment of adults reporting reading and/or writing difficulties.

WRITTEN EXPRESSION CLUSTERS

The ability to compose text entails a nonlinear process drawing upon overlapping cognitive and linguistic processes at the subword, word, sentence, and discourse level (Englert & Raphael, 1988; Gregg, 1995; Gregg & Mather, 2002). Berninger (1996) encouraged professionals to focus on the various "constraints" influencing writing rather than seeking a single cause for underachievement. Understanding the multidimensional, bidirectional impact of constraints such as limited instruction, poor oral language abilities, specific cognitive processing deficits, limited cultural experiences, and poor motivation will aid professionals in the development of instruction and accommodations for students with learning disabilities. The WJ III COG and WJ III ACH provide professionals with a variety of tools to explore the cognitive and linguistic factors influencing writing performance. Again, as with reading and mathematics, the key is to understand the connections between cognitive processing and achievement profiles. Table 4-5 provides suggested WJ III COG clusters for examiners to compare to performance on WJ III ACH clusters when concerned about specific written expression disorders at various performance levels. An examiner should first compare a student's writing performance to scores on both oral language and reading measures to determine the impact of linguistic and cognitive strengths and weaknesses across academic areas.

A lack of automaticity at the subword (phonology and orthography) or word level (spelling) can inhibit the quality and fluency of written expression (Coleman, Gregg, & Davis, 2001). Children and adults with dyslexia may have

TABLE 4-5   Cognitive–Achievement Connection: Written Expression

Area	WJ III COG clusters	WJ III ACH clusters and tests
Subword (phonology and orthography)	*Auditory Processing* *Phonemic Awareness* *Phonemic Awareness 3*	*Phoneme/Grapheme Knowledge* Sound Awareness
Word (spelling)	*Auditory Processing* *Processing Speed* *Short-Term Memory* *Long-Term Retrieval* *Phonemic Awareness* *Broad Attention* *Cognitive Fluency* *Working Memory*	*Basic Written Language* *Basic Working Skills* *Broad Reading* *Basic Reading Skills* *Academic Skills* *Phoneme/Grapheme Knowledge* *Academic Fluency* *Academic Knowledge* Picture Vocabulary Spelling of Sounds Spelling Picture Vocabulary
Sentence (syntax)	*Comprehension–Knowledge* *Processing Speed* *Short-Term Memory* *Cognitive Fluency* *Cognitive Efficiency* *Working Memory* *Executive Processes*	*Listening Comprehension* *Broad Reading* *Broad Written Language* *Basic Writing Skills* *Written Expression* *Academic Fluency* *Academic Applications* *Academic Knowledge*
Text (discourse)	*Comprehension–Knowledge* *Processing Speed* *Cognitive Efficiency* *Thinking Ability* *Cognitive Fluency* *Executive Processes*	*Oral Expression* *Oral Language* *Listening Comprehension* *Broad Reading* *Reading Comprehension* *Broad Written Language* *Basic Writing Skills* *Written Expression* *Academic Fluency* *Academic Applications* *Academic Knowledge*

Note: Italics indicate clusters.

difficulty retrieving and spelling the words they wish to use; they may devote excessive amounts of time, attention, and working memory capacity to low-level tasks; they may make many more errors than their nondisabled peers. On timed essay tasks (such as the one administered to Bill—see Case Study B), students with dyslexia demonstrate the consequences of low-level problems, including limited vocabulary, damage to clarity and cohesion, restricted lexical and syntactic complexity, and lower grades (Coleman et al., 2001). When writers must concentrate on how to spell a word while composing, ideation and fluency are compromised (Graham et al., 1997). Although reading and spelling skills are based on shared linguistic and cognitive processes, the ability to recall and write words is a far more complex process than is word recognition. Several significant subword linguistic processes are required, including awareness and appreciation of phonological, orthographic, and morphological principles (Bruck, 1992). In addition, knowledge of word meanings plays a role in spelling accuracy, particularly in the spelling of homophones (e.g., *pair* and *pear*). Coleman et al. (2001) found that word complexity and sophistication made a significant contribution to impressionistic quality scores on expository writing samples and that college writers with learning disabilities were significantly below their peers in all areas measured, including fluency, lexical sophistication, overall quality, and spelling. In order to assess spelling, an examiner should begin by considering an individual's oral language competence on the WJ III ACH as well as his/her phonological, orthographic, and morphological awareness. Particular attention should be given to the student's WJ III COG Comprehension–Knowledge cluster and his/her WJ III ACH Oral Language cluster. The Picture Vocabulary test provides an excellent estimate of a student's receptive vocabulary knowledge, which can contrast with (or be obscured by) problems with spelling and fluency during the writing process (Coleman et al., 2001).

The WJ III COG Auditory Processing, Phonemic Awareness, and Phonemic Awareness 3 clusters, along with the WJ III ACH Phoneme/Grapheme cluster, should be administered to assess a writer's phonological and orthographic processing abilities. Phonological processing is the ability to analyze a word at the subword level (phonemes, morphemes, or syllables), whereas orthographic processing includes the ability to recall a whole word unit, a letter cluster, or a component letter (Berninger, 1996). A comprehensive body of literature documents that efficient phonological processing is needed to spell successfully (Felton & Wood, 1992; Rack, Snowling, & Olson, 1992; Uhry & Shepherd, 1993). When a child is first learning to spell, phonological processing skills are of critical importance (Moats, 1995). The ability to sequence and manipulate sounds accurately is the hallmark of good phonological processing abilities, and the WJ III ACH Sound Awareness test addresses such abilities by providing information about rhyming and phoneme manipulation. However, orthographic processing allows one to form complete word images (spellings) and to recall the exact visual sequence of individual letters needed to match the sounds in a word (Ehri, 1997; Moats, 1995). Research suggests that orthographic processing may be particularly important for speakers of English and other languages whose orthographic systems are "deep" (i.e., marked by frequent irregularities). Thus, an examiner should keep in mind that distinctly different cognitive and linguistic problems (singly or in combination) can lead to compromised writing skills. All potentially pertinent information should be used in decision-making about instructional intervention and accommodations.

An examiner might choose to begin by administering the WJ III ACH Spelling of Sounds test, which features a list of nonwords that conform to English phonological rules. Writers who understand that the conventional English spelling system works graphophonically can typically produce phonetically complete and graphemically plausible spellings for nonsense words (Ehri, 1998; Gregg & Mather, 2002). Students with dyslexia, however, often score very low on such tasks (Siegel & Ryan, 1988). Analysis of the errors a student makes on the Spelling of Sounds test is encouraged for two reasons: first, to identify possible patterns among incorrect attempts (e.g., vowel substitutions or voiced/voiceless alternations) and second, because the test's list of acceptable responses excludes some spellings that accurately represent target sounds, but do not do so in "orthographically optimal" fashion. In addition to nonsense words, administration of real spelling words (e.g., the WJ III ACH Spelling test) is important in any assessment of writing abilities. Some of the letters in the irregular and regular words presented on the Spelling test have direct grapheme–phoneme correspondences; observation of errors involving the letters that are silent or unpredictable should be noted. Students with problems in orthography (more than phonology) have particular problems forming the orthographic images for "spelling demons" and often spell nonwords (Spelling of Sounds) more plausibly than real words (Gregg & Mather, 2002; Roberts & Mather, 1997; Willows & Terepocki, 1993). In addition, students who have received direct training in phonological awareness have often mastered basic phonological processing skills well enough to perform in the average range on the WJ III Word Attack test. However, their scores on measures of fluency and spelling of real words will likely continue to be below the expected level. The WJ III provides several measures of *Ga* and phonological processing, but (as noted earlier) is weaker in identifying the cognitive and linguistic contributions to orthographic processing competence. Valuable supplementary information can be gained by administering spelling choice tasks, orthographic coding/segmentation measures, and instruments such as the Colorado Perceptual Speed Test (DeFries et al., 1981; Decker, 1989; described in Case Study B). Additionally, clinicians should look for performance patterns within *Gs* and rapid naming tasks. For example, is the examinee consistently slower or less accurate with orthographic stimuli (e.g., the numbers on the WJ III COG Visual Matching test) than with pictures and shapes (e.g., the WJ III Decision Speed stimuli)?

The evaluation of a student's written syntax, or ability to write sentences, should begin with comparison of his/her oral syntax abilities on the WJ III ACH Listening Comprehension cluster to his/her Writing Fluency cluster and Writing Samples test responses. Errors that might be red flags for possible difficulty with syntax would include word omissions, word order problems, incorrect subject–verb agreement, pronoun usage problems, and word-ending errors (Gregg & Hafer, 2001). Psycholinguists suggest that the breakdown of written syntax can be the result of weaknesses in any of several cognitive and linguistic abilities such as inductive reasoning, lexical knowledge, monitoring, and interference control (Butterworth & Howard, 1987). Therefore, a student's performance on the WJ III ACH Writing Fluency and Writing Samples tests might be compared to his/her performance on WJ III COG Comprehension–Knowledge, Processing Speed, Short-Term Memory, Cognitive Fluency, Cognitive Efficiency, Working Memory, and Executive Processes clusters. Examiners may also wish to perform a qualitative analysis of writing errors.

The ability to revise one's own writing requires many linguistic and executive functioning abilities (De La Paz, Swanson, & Graham, 1998; Graham, 1997). Interestingly, Graham, Schwartz, and MacArthur (1993) found that when writers with learning disabilities were asked to revise their written products, 80% of their time was spent on mechanics rather than on organization and/or ideation. The WJ III ACH provides two important tests, Editing and Punctuation and Capitalization, that can help examiners evaluate the revising skills of writers in a context that is isolated from the actual production of text and organization of ideas.

The WJ III ACH Writing Samples test provides a limited but adequate screening of text production. It is suggested that the examiner attempt to elicit longer writing samples of different genres (e.g., narrative, expository) to explore the full impact of cognitive and linguistic difficulties on written expression. The relationship among executive functioning, attention, working memory, and text production has only recently begun to be addressed in the literature (Berninger, 1999; Englert, 1990; Graham & Harris, 1999). Text construction does require the ability to employ self-regulatory processes governing skills such as planning, monitoring, evaluating, and revising, and many students with learning disabilities demonstrate difficulty in accessing and employing these executive functions (Englert et al., 1988; Graham & Harris, 1997, 1999). Therefore, it would be important for an examiner to compare a student's performance on the Writing Samples test (and any other writing samples) to his/her performance on the WJ III COG Executive Processes cluster.

The role of working memory in text construction has received little attention. Perfetti (1985) and Stanovich (1980), discussing working memory as it relates to text comprehension, suggested that word decoding contributes to an overload in working memory, leading to (receptive) text structure difficulties. However, Kintsch (1998) hypothesized that long-term memory plays a greater role in text comprehension. Whether the findings from research on the comprehension of text can be applied to the construction of text is uncertain. Because the debate over the cognitive and linguistic processes involved in the comprehension/construction of text remains unresolved, it is suggested that examiners consider the WJ III COG Comprehension–Knowledge, Cognitive Efficiency, Thinking Ability, Processing Speed, Cognitive Fluency, Executive Processing, Oral Expression, Oral Language, Listening Comprehension, Broad Reading, and Reading Comprehension clusters in interpreting WJ III ACH Writing Samples responses. Finally, a comparison should be made between a student's Academic Skills, Academic Fluency, and Academic Applications clusters to determine whether a breakdown might be primarily a skill issue, an application problem, or a (possibly residual) fluency issue.

SUMMARY

The National Joint Committee on Learning Disabilities (NJCLD), in its May/June 1997 report *Operationalizing the NJCLD Definition of Learning Disabilities for Ongoing Assessment in Schools*, provided a well-thought-out critique of the use of clinical judgment in the diagnostic process (see report for in-depth discussion). Learning disabilities are presented as a multidimensional construct, changing in manifestation across age, experiences, and ability. The NJCLD report concludes that "significant difficulty cannot be determined solely by a quantitative test score" (p. 6), and the report encourages use of both qualitative and quantitative data in decision-making. In fact, the report stresses that a "learning disability can exist when a numerical discrepancy does not" (p. 6).

Professionals participating in the diagnosis of learning disabilities have often put too much faith in test instruments at the expense of their own professional judgment. However, it is important to remember Mather's (1993) caution that "test results assist with judgment; they are not a substitute" (p. 188). Given the lack of empirically driven theoretical constructs underlying selection criteria for the diagnosis of learning disabilities, the professional judgment of evaluators is integral to decision-making. As Smith (1988) stated, "where there is no need for professional judgment, there is no need for professionals" (p. 62). The WJ III COG and WJ III ACH provide a technically, theoretically, and practically driven instrument to be used in the diagnosis of learning disabilities. Yet, in the end, the instrument is dependent upon the judgment, knowledge, and interpretations of the examiner.

REFERENCES

Aaron, P. G., & Joshi, R. M. (1992). *Reading problems: Consultation and remediation*. New York: Guilford.

American Psychiatric Association (1994). *Diagnostic and statistical manual of mental disorders (4th ed.)*. Washington, DC: Author.

Andrews, S. (1982). Phonological recoding: Is the regularity effect consistent? *Memory and Cognition, 10*, 565–575.

Ayers, J. (1975). *Southern California sensory integration tests*. Los Angeles: Western Psychological Services.

Baddeley, A. D. (1986). *Working memory*. Oxford, England: Clarendon Press.

Baddeley, A. D., & Hitch, G. (1974). Working memory. In G. H. Bower (Ed.), *The psychology of learning and motivation: Advances in research and theory* (Vol., 8, pp. 47–89). New York: Academic Press.

Badian, N. A. (1983). Dyscalculia and nonverbal disorders of learning. In H. R. Myklebust (Ed.), *Progress in learning disabilities* (Vol. V, pp. 235–264). New York: Grune & Stratton.

Barkley, R. A. (1996). Linkages between attention and executive functions. In G. R. Lyon & N. A. Krasneger (Eds.), *Attention, memory, and executive function* (pp. 307–325). Baltimore: Paul H. Brookes.

Barkley, R. A. (1997). Behavioral inhibition, sustained attention, and executive functions: Constructing a unifying theory of ADHD. *Psychological Bulletin, 121*, 65–94.

Barsch, R. H. (1967). *Achieving perceptual motor efficiency.* Seattle, WA: Special Child Publications.

Bell, L. C., & Perfetti, C. A. (1994). Reading skill: Some adult comparisons. *Journal of Educational Psychology, 86*, 244–255.

Berninger, V. W. (1996). *Reading and writing acquisition: A developmental neuropsychological perspective.* NY: Westview Press.

Berninger, V. W. (1999). Coordinating transcription and text generation in working memory during composing: Automatic and constructive processes. *Learning Disabilities Quarterly, 22*, 99–112.

Berninger, V. W., & Abbott, R. D. (1994). Redefining learning disabilities: Moving beyond aptitude–achievement discrepancies to failure to respond to validated treatment protocols. In G. R. Lyon (Ed.), *Frames of reference for the assessment of learning disabilities: New views on measurement* (pp. 163–183). Baltimore: Paul H. Brookes.

Bigler, E. D. (1992). The neurobiology and neuropsychology of adult learning disorders. *Journal of Learning Disorders, 25*(8), 488–506.

Bocian, K. M., Beebe, M. E., MacMillan, D. L., & Gresham, F. M. (1999). Competing paradigms in learning disabilities classification by schools and the variations in the meaning of discrepant achievement. *Learning Disabilities Research & Practice, 14*(1), 1–14.

Butterworth, B., & Howard, D. (1987). Paragrammatisms. *Cognition, 26*, 1–37.

Bruck, M. (1992). Persistence of dyslexics' phonological awareness deficits. *Developmental Psychology, 28*(5), 874–886.

Bruck, M. (1993). Word recognition and component phonological processing skills of adults with childhood diagnosis of dyslexia. *Developmental Review, 13*, 258–268.

Colarusso, R., Keel, M. C., & Dangel, H. L. (2001). A comparison of eligibility criteria and their impact on minority representation in LD programs. *Learning Disabilities Research & Practice, 16*(1), 1–7.

Coleman, C., Gregg, N., & Davis, J. M. (2001, June). *Analysis of word knowledge in the expository essays of college students with and without disabilities.* Paper presented at the meeting of the Society for the Scientific Study of Reading, Boulder, CO.

Cunningham, A. E., Perry, K. E., & Stanovich, K. E. (2001). Converging evidence for the concept of orthographic processing. *Reading and Writing, 14*, 549–568.

Cunningham, A. E., Stanovich, K. R., & Wilson, M. R. (1990). Cognitive variation in adult college students differing in reading ability. In T. H. Carr & B. A. Levy (Eds.), *Reading and its development: Component skills approaches* (pp. 129–159). San Diego: Academic Press.

Daneman, M., & Carpenter, P. A. (1980). Individual differences in working memory and reading. *Journal of Verbal Learning and Verbal Behavior, 19*, 450–466.

Danks, J. H., & End, L. J. (1987). Processing strategies for reading and listening. In R. Horowitz & S. J. Samuels (Eds.), *Comprehending oral and written language* (pp. 1–50). San Diego, CA: Academic Press.

Davis, H., Bryson, S., & Hoy, C. (1992). Case study of language and numerical disability: A sequential processing deficit? *Annals of Dyslexia, 42*, 69–89.

De La Paz, S., Swanson, P., & Graham, S. (1998). The contribution of executive control to the revising of students with writing and learning disabilities. *Journal of Educational Psychology, 89*, 203–222.

Decker, S. N. (1989). Cognitive processing rates among disabled and normal reading young adults: A nine year follow-up study. *Reading and Writing, 2*, 123–134.

DeFries, J. C., Plomin, R., Vandenberg, S. D., & Kuse, A. R. (1981). Parent-offspring resemblence for cognitive abilities in the Colorado Adoption Project: Biological, adoptive, and control parents and one-year-old children. *Intelligence, 5*, 245–277.

Dempster, F. N. (1992). The rise and fall of the inhibitory mechanism: Toward a unified theory of cognitive development and aging. *Developmental Review, 72*, 45–75.

Dempster, F. N. (1995). Interference and inhibition in cognition: An historical perspective. In K. N. Dempster & C. J. Brainwerd (Eds.), *Interference and inhibition in cognition* (pp. 3–26). San Diego, CA: Academic Press.

Denckla, M. B. (1998, November). *Understanding the role of executive function in language, academics and daily life.* Paper presented at American International College, Springfield, MA.

Denckla, M. B., & Reader, M. J. (1993). Education and psycho-social interventions: Executive dysfunction and its consequences. In R. Kurlan (Ed.), *Handbook of Tourette's Syndrome and related tic and behavioral disorders* (pp. 431–451). New York: Marcel Dekker.

Douglas, V., & Peters, K. G. (1979). Toward a clearer definition of the attentional deficit of hyperactive children. In G. A. Hale & M. Lewis (Eds.), *Attention and the development of cognitive skills* (pp. 173–247). New York: Plenum.

Dykman, R. A., Ackerman, P. T., & Oglesby, D. M. (1979). Selective and sustained attention in hyperactive, learning-disabled and normal boys. *Journal of Nervous and Mental Disease, 167*, 288–297.

Ehri, L. C. (1997). Learning to read and learning to spell are one and the same, almost. In C. A. Perfetti, L. Rieben, & M. Fayol (Eds.), *Learning to spell: Research, theory, and practice across languages* (pp. 237–270). Mahwah, NJ: Erlbaum.

Ehri, L. C. (1998). Grapheme–phoneme knowledge is essential for learning to read words in English. In J. L. Metsala & L. C. Ehri (Eds.), *Word recognition in beginning literacy* (pp. 3–39). Mahwah, NJ: Erlbaum.

Engle, R. W., & Cantor, J. (1992). Individual differences in working memory and comprehension: A test of four hypotheses. *Journal of Experimental Psychology: Learning, Memory, and Cognition, 18*, 972–992.

Englert, C. S. (1990). Unraveling the mysteries of writing through strategy instruction. In T. E. Scruggs & B. Y. L. Wong (Eds.), *Intervention research in learning disabilities* (pp. 186–223). New York: Springer-Verlag.

Englert, C. S., & Raphael, T. E. (1988). Constructing well-formed prose: Process, structure and metacognitive knowledge. *Exceptional Children, 54*, 513–520.

Englert, C. S., Raphael, T. E., Fear, K. L., & Anderson, M. (1988). Students' metacognitive knowledge about how to write informational text. *Learning Disabilities Quarterly, 11*, 18–46.

Evans, J. E., Floyd, R. G., McGrew, K. S., & Leforgee, M. H. (2002). The relations between measures of Cattell–Horn–Carroll (CHC) cognitive abilities and reading achievement during childhood and adolescence. *School Psychology Review, 1131*, 246–262.

Ewws, J. T., & Cameron, S. (1987). Selective attention in young children: The relations between visual search, filtering, and priming. *Journal of Experimental Child Psychology, 44*, 38–63.

Felton, R. H., & Wood, F. B. (1992). A reading-level match study of nonword reading skill in poor readers with varying IQ. *Journal of Learning Disabilities, 25*, 318–326.

Flanagan, D., McGrew, K., & Ortiz, S. (2000). *The Wechsler Intelligence Scales and Gf–Gc Theory: A contemporary approach to interpretation.* Boston: Allyn & Bacon.

Foorman, B. R. (1994). Phonological and orthographic processing: Separate but equal? In V. W. Berninger (Ed.), *The varities of orthographic knowledge* (pp. 321–357). The Netherlands: Kluwer Academic Press.

Frances, D. J., Shaywitz, S. E., Stuebing, K. K, Shaywitz, B. A., & Fletcher, J. M. (1994). Measurement of change: Assessing behavior over time and with a developmental context. In G. R. Lyon (Ed.), *Frames of reference for the assessment of learning disabilities: New views on measurement* (pp. 29–58). Baltimore: Paul H. Brookes.

Frith, U. (1985). Beneath the surface of developmental dyslexia. In K. E. Patterson, J. C. Marshall, & M. Coltheart (Eds.), *Surface dyslexia* (pp. 310–330). Hillsdale, NJ: Erlbaum.

Fuchs, L. S., Fuchs, D., Hosp, M. K., & Jenkins, J. R. (2001). Oral reading fluency as an indicator of reading competence: A theoretical, empirical, and historical analysis. *Scientific Studies of Reading, 5*(3), 239–256.

Fuchs, L. S., Fuchs, D., & Maxwell, L. (1988). The validity of informal reading comprehension measures. *Remedial & Social Education, 9*, 20–28.

Gaddes, W. (1980). *Learning disabilities and brain function: Neuropsychological approach.* New York: Springer-Verlag.

Geary, D. C. (1993). Mathematical disabilities: Cognitive, neuropsychological, and genetic components. *Psychological Bulletin, 114*(2), 345–362.

Geary, D. C. (2000). Mathematical disorders: An overview for educators. *Perspectives, 23*(3), 6–9.

Gough, P. B., & Tumner, W. E. (1986). Decoding, reading and reading disability. *Remedial and Special Education, 7*, 6–10.

Graham, S. (1997). Executive control in the revising of students with learning and writing difficulties. *Journal of Educational Psychology, 89*, 223–234.

Graham, S., Berninger, V., Abbott, R., Abbott, S., & Whitaker, D. (1997). The role of mechanics in composing of elementary school students: A new methodological approach. *Journal of Educational Psychology, 89*, 170–182.

Graham, S., & Harris, K. R. (1997). The role of self-regulation in the writing process. In D. Schunk & B. Zimmerman (Eds.), *Self-regulation of learning and performance: Issues and educational applications* (pp. 203–228). Hillsdale, NJ: Erlbaum.

Graham, S., & Harris, K. R. (1999). Assessment and intervention in overcoming writing difficulties: An illustration from the self-regulated strategy developmental model. *Language, Speech and Hearing Services in Schools, 30*, 255–264.

Graham, S., Schwartz, S., & MacArthur, C. (1993). Knowledge of writing and the composing process, attitude toward writing, and self-efficacy for students with and without learning disabilities. *Journal of Learning Disabilities, 26*, 237–249.

Gregg, N. (1994). Eligibility for learning disabilities rehabilitation services: Operationalizing the definition. *Journal of Vocational Rehabilitation, 4*, 86–95.

Gregg, N. (1995). *Written expression disorders.* The Netherlands: Kluwer Academic Press.

Gregg, N., & Coleman, C. (2001). *WJ III Preliminary Studies.* College Board Annual Reviewers Workshop, Saratoga Springs, NY, July 19, 2001.

Gregg, N., Coleman, C., & Davis, M. (2002). Discourse complexity of college writers with and without disabilities. *Journal of Learning Disabilities, 35*, 23–38.

Gregg, N., Coleman, C., Stennett, R., Davis, M., Nielsen, D., Knight, D., & Hoy, C. (2002). Sublexical and lexical processing of young adults with learning disabilities and attention deficit/hyperactivity. In E. Witruk & T. Lachbach (Eds.), *Basic functions of language and language disorders* (pp. 329–358). The Netherlands: Kluwer Academic Press.

Gregg, N., & Hafer, T. (2001). Disorders of written expression. In A. M. Bain, L. L. Bailet, & L. C. Moats (Eds.), *Written language disorders: Theory into practice, second edition.* Austin, TX: Pro-Ed.

Gregg, N., & Jackson, R. (1989). Dialogue patterns of the nonverbal learning disabilities population: Mirrors of self-regulation defaults. *Learning Disabilities: A Multidisciplinary Journal, 2*, 63–71.

Gregg, N., & Mather, N. (2002). School is fun at recess: Informal assessment of written language. *Journal of Learning Disabilities, 35*, 2–22.

Gregg, N., & Scott, S. (2000). Definitions and documentation: Theory, measurement, and the courts. *Journal of Learning Disabilities, 33*(1), 5–13.

Gregg, N., Scott, S., McPeek, D., & Ferri, B. (1999). Definitions and eligibility criteria applied to the adolescent and adult populations with learning disabilities across agencies. *Learning Disabilities Quarterly, 22*(3), 213–223.

Gregg, N., Stennett, R., & Coleman, C. (2001). *The WJ III Phonemic Awareness Cluster and the college population with learning disabilities.* Unpublished manuscript.

Gregg, N., Stennett, R., Coleman, C., Hoy, C., & Davis, M. (2001, June). *Contributions of working memory, fluency, lexical knowledge, phonology and orthography to the decoding and spelling of college students with and without dyslexia.* Paper presented at the meeting of the society for the Scientific Study of Reading, Boulder, CO.

Gresham, F. (2001, August 27–28). *Responsiveness to intervention: An alternative approach to the identification of learning disabilities.* Paper presented at the Learning Disabilities Summit: Building a Foundation for the Future, Washington, DC. Abstract retrieved February 14, 2002 from http://www.air.org/ldsummit/.

Gross-Tsur, V., Manor, O., & Shalev, R. S. (1996). Developmental dyscalculia: Prevalence and demographic features. *Developmental Medicine and Child Neurology, 38*, 25–33.

Hanich, L. G., Jordan, N. C., Kaplan, D., & Dick, J. (in press). Performance across different areas of mathematical cognition in children with learning disabilities. *Journal of Educational Psychology.*

Hayes, S. C., Gifford, E. V., & Ruckstuhl, L. E. (1996). Relational frame theory and executive function: A behavioral approach. In G. R. Lyon & N. A. Kraswegor (Eds.), *Attention, memory, and executive function* (pp. 279–305). Baltimore: Paul H. Brookes.

Hildyard, A., & Olson, D. R. (1978). Memory and inference in the comprehension of oral and written discourse. *Discourse, 1*, 99–119.

Holmes, V. M., & Castles, A. E. (2001). Unexpectedly poor spelling in university students. *Scientific Studies of Reading, 5*(4).

Horn, J. L., & Noll, J. (1997). Human cognitive capabilities: *Gf–Gc* theory. In D. Flanagan, J. L. Genshaft, & P. L. Harnsaw (Eds.), *Contemporary intellectual assessment: Theories, tests, and issues* (pp. 53–91). New York: Guilford.

Hoy, C., & Gregg, N. (1994). *Assessment: The special educator's role.* Pacific Grove, CA: Brooks/Cole.

Hoy, C., Gregg, N., Wisenbaker, J., Sigalas-Bonaham, S., King, M., & Moreland, C. (1996). Clinical model versus discrepancy model in determining eligibility for learning disabilities services at a rehabilitation setting. In N. Gregg, C. Hoy, and A. Gay (Eds.), *Adults with learning disabilities: Theoretial and practical perspectives* (pp. 55–67). New York: Guilford Press.

Johnson, D. J., & Myklebust, H. R. (1967). *Learning disabilities: Educational principles and practices.* New York: Grune & Stratton.

Just, M. A., & Carpenter, P. A. (1992). A capacity theory of comprehension. *Psychological Review, 99*, 592–599.

Kame'enui, E. J., & Simmons, D. C. (2001). Introduction to this special issue: The DNA of reading fluency. *Scientific Studies of Reading, 5*(3), 203–210.

Kavale, K. A. (1987). Theoretical issues surrounding severe discrepancy. *Learning Disabilities Research, 3*, 12–20.

Kavale, K. (2001, April 27–28). Discrepancy models in identification of learning disability. Paper presented at the Learning Disabilties Summit: Building a Foundation for the Future, Washington, DC. Abstract retrieved February 14, 2002 from http://www.air.org/ldsummit.

Kavale, K. A., & Forness, S. R. (2000). What definitions of learning disability say and don't say: A critical analysis. *Journal of Learning Disabilities, 33*(3), 239–256.

Keogh, B. K. (1994). A matrix of decision points in the measurement of learning disabilities. In G. R. Lyon (Ed.), *Frames of references for the assessment of learning disabilities* (pp. 15–26). Baltimore: Paul H. Brookes.

Kephart, N. C. (1960). *The slow learner in the classroom.* Columbus, OH: Merrill.

Kinberg, D. Y., & Farah, M. J. (1993). A united account of cognitive impairments following frontal lobe damage: The role of working memory in complex, organized behavior. *Journal of Experimental Psychology: General, 122*, 411–428.

Kintsch, W. (1998). *Comprehension: A paradigm for cognition.* Cambridge, England: Cambridge University Press.

Kirk, S. A., McCarthy, J. J., & Kirk, W. D. (1968). *Illinois tests of psycho-linguistic abilities* (rev. ed.). Urbana, IL: University of Illinois Press.

Knight, D. S. (2000). *A cognitive and linguistic model of individual differences in the reading comprehension of college students with and without learning disabilities.* University of Georgia, unpublished dissertation.

Kosc, L. (1974). Developmental dyscalculia. *Journal of Learning Disabilities, 7*(3), 164–177.

Kulak, A. G. (1993). Parallels between math and reading disability: Common issues and approaches. *Journal of Learning Disabilities, 26*(10), 666–673.

Landerl, K., Frith, U., & Wimmer, H. (1996). Intrusion of orthographic knowledge on phoneme awareness: Strong in normal readers, weak in dyslexic readers. *Applied Psycholinguistics, 17*, 1–14.

Lyon, G. R. (1994.). Critical issues in the measurement of learning disabilities. In G. R. Lyon (Ed.), *Frames of reference for the assessment of learning disabilities: New views on measurement* (pp. 3–14). Baltimore: Paul H. Brookes.

Lyon, G. R., & Krasnegor, N. A. (1996). *Attention, memory, and executive function.* Baltimore: Paul H. Brookes.

MacMillan, D. L., & Speece, D. L. (2000). Utility of current diagnostic categories for research and practice. In R. Gallimore, L. Bernheimer, D. MacMillan, D. Speece, & S. Vaughn (Eds.), *Developmental perspectives on children with high-incidence disabilities.* Mahwah, NJ: Erlbaum.

Marolda, M. R., & Davidson, P. S. (2000). Mathematical learning profiles and differentiated teaching strategies. *Perspectives, 23*(3), 10–15.

Mather, N. (1993). Critical issues in the diagnosis of learning disabilities addressed by the Woodcock–Johnson Psycho-Educational Battery—Revised. *Journal of Psychoeducational Assessment* [Monograph Series: WJ-R Monograph], 103–122.

Mather, N., & Gregg, N. (2001). Assessment with the Woodcock–Johnson III. In J. W. Andrews, H. Janzen, & D. Saklofske (Eds.), *Ability, achievement and behavior assessment: A practical handbook* (pp. 133–165). New York: Academic Press.

Mather, N., & Woodcock, R. W. (2001). Examiner's Manual. *Woodcock–Johnson III Tests of Cognitive Abilities.* Itasca, IL: Riverside Publishing.

McGrew, K. S., & Flanagan, D. P. (1998). *The intelligence test desk reference: Gf–Gc Cross-Battery Assessment.* Boston: Allyn & Bacon.

McGrew, K. S., Woodcock, R. & Ford, L. (2002). The Woodcock–Johnson Battery—Third Edition (WJ III). In A. S. Kaufman, & E. O. Lichtenberger (Eds.), *Assessing adolescent and adult intelligence* (2nd ed.) (pp. 561–628). Needham Heights, MA: Allyn & Bacon.

McGrew, K. S., & Woodcock, R. W. (2001). WJ III technical manual. *Woodcock–Johnson III.* Itasca, IL: Riverside Publishing.

Mercer, C. D., Jordan, L., Allsop, D. H., & Mercer, A. R. (1996). Learning disabilities definitions and criteria used by state education departments. *Learning Disability Quarterly, 19,* 217–232.

Meyer, G., Finn, S. E., Eyde, L. D., Kay, G. G., Moreland, K. L., Dies, R. R., Eisman, E. J., Kubiszyn, N., & Reed, G. M. (2001). Psychological testing and psychological assessment: A review of evidence and issues. *American Psychologist, 56*(2), 128–165.

Moats, L.C. (1995). *Spelling: Development, disability and instruction.* Baltimore: York Press.

Naglieri, J. A., & Reardon, S. M. (1993). Traditional IQ is irrelevant to learning disabilities—intelligence is not. *Journal of Learning Disabilities, 26,* 127–133.

National Joint Committee on Learning Disabilities. (1997). *Operationalizing the NJCLD definition of learning disabilities for ongoing assessment.* Http://www.ldonline.org/Njcld/operationalizing.html.

National Reading Panel. (2000). *Report of the National Reading Panel teaching children to read: An evidence-based assessment of the scientific research literature on reading and its implications for reading instructions.* Washington, DC: National Institute of Child Health and Human Development.

Oakhill, J., Cain, K., & Yill, N. (1998). Individual differences in children's comprehension skills: Toward an integrated model. In C. Hulme & R. M. Joshi (Eds.), *Reading and spelling: Developmental disorders* (pp. 342–367). Mahwah, NJ: Erlbaum.

Padget, S. Y. (1998). Lessons from research in dyslexia: Implications for a classification system for learning disabilities. *Learning Disabilities Quarterly, 21*(2), 167–178.

Pennington, B. F., Bennetto, Z., McAleer, D., & Roberts, R. J. (1996). Executive functions and working memory: Theoretical and measurement issues. In G. R. Lyon & N. A. Krasnegor (Eds.), *Attention, memory, and executive function* (pp. 327–348). Baltimore: Paul H. Brookes.

Perfetti, C. A. (1985). *Reading ability: Cognitive and psycholinguistic perspectives.* London: Oxford University Press.

Perfetti, C. A., Marron, M. A., & Foltz, P. W. (1996). Sources of comprehension failure: Theoretical perspectives and case studies. In C. Cornoldi & J. Oakhill (Eds.), *Reading comprehension difficulties: Processes and intervention* (pp. 137–165). Mahwah, NJ: Erlbaum.

Rabbitt, P. (1997). Introduction: Methodologies and models in the study of executive function. In P. Rabbitt (Ed.), *Methodology of frontal and executive function* (pp. 1–60). U.K.: Psychology Press.

Rack, J. P., Snowling, M. J., & Olson, R. K. (1992). The nonword reading deficit in developmental dyslexia. A Review. *Reading Research Quarterly 27*(1), 29–53.

Reynolds, C. R. (1984–1985). Critical measurement issues in learning disabilities. *Journal of Special Education, 18,* 451–475.

Richardson, J. T. E. (1996). Evolving concepts of working memory. In J. T. E. Richardson, R. W. Engle, L. Hasher, R. H. Logie, E. R. Stoltzfus, & R. T. Zacks (Eds.), *Working memory and human cognition* (pp. 3–24). New York: Oxford.

Roberts, R., & Mather, N. (1997). Orthographic dyslexia: The neglected subtype. *Learning Disabilities Research & Practice, 12,* 236–250.

Rock, I., Gopovik, A., & Hall, S. (1994). Do young children reverse ambiguous figures? *Perceptions, 23,* 635–644.

Rourke, B. P. (1993). Arithmetic disabilities, specific and otherwise: A neuropsychological perspective. *Journal of Learning Disabilities, 26(4),* 214–226.

Rourke, B. P., & Conway, J. A. (1998). Disabilities of arithmetic and mathematical reasoning: Perspectives from neurology and neuropsychology. In D. P. Rivera (Ed.), *Mathematics education for students with learning disabilities* (pp. 59–79). Austin, TX: Pro-Ed.

Schrank, F. A., & Woodcock, R. W. (2002). Report Writer for the WJ III. [Computer software]. Itasca, IL: Riverside Publishing.

Seidel, W. T., & Joschko, M. (1990). Evidence of difficulties in sustained attention in children with AD/HD. *Journal of Abnormal Child Psychology, 18,* 217–229.

Seidenberg, M. S., Waters, G. S., Barnes, M. A., & Tanenhaus, M. K. (1984). When does irregular spelling or pronunciation influence word recognition? *Journal of Verbal Learning and Behavior, 23,* 383–404.

Sharma, M. C. (1986). Progress of Dr. Ladislav Kosc's work on dyscalculia. *Focus on Learning Problems in Mathematics, 8*(3 & 4), 47–119.

Shaywitz, B. A., & Shaywitz, S. E. (1994). Measuring and analyzing change. In G. R. Lyon (Ed.), *Frames of reference for the assessment of learning disabilities: New views on measurement* (pp. 59–68). Baltimore: Paul H. Brookes.

Sheen, V. S., & Heerman, C. E. (1985). Intercorrelations of measures of reading and writing: Implications for college research on reading and writing. *Perceptual and Motor Skills, 60,* 677–678.

Siegel, L. (1989). IQ is irrelevant to the definition of learning disabilities. *Journal of Learning Disabilities, 22,* 469–486.

Siegel, L. S., & Ryan, E. B. (1988). Development of grammatical sensitivity, phonological, and short-term memory in normally achieving and learning disabled children. *Developmental Psychology, 24,* 28–37.

Simmons, D. C., Kame'enui, E. J., Good, R. H. III, Harn, B. A., Cole, C., & Braun, D. (2000). Building, implementing and sustaining a beginning reading model: School by school and lesson learning. *Oregon School Study Council (OSSC) Bulletin, 43*(3), 3–30.

Smith, F. (1988). *Professional judgment in the diagnosis of specific learning disabilities.* In Georgia Learning Resource System (Ed.), *Learning Disabilities and Eligibility Criteria* (pp. 88–95). Atlanta, GA: Metro East and West Learning Resources System.

Stanovich, K. E. (1980). Toward an interactive–compensatory model of individual differences in the development of reading fluency. *Reading Research Quarterly, 16,* 32–71.

Stanovich, K. E. (1991). Discrepancy definitions of reading disability: Has intelligence led us astray? *Reading Research Quarterly, 26,* 1–29.

Stoltzfus, E. R., Hasher, L., & Zacks, R. T. (1996). Working memory and aging: Current status of the inhibitory view. In J. T. E. Richardson, R. W. Engle, L. Hasher, R. H. Logie, E. R. Stoltzfus, & R. T. Zacks (Eds.), *Working memory and human cognition* (pp. 66–88). New York: Oxford.

Stothard, S. E., & Hulme, C. (1996). A comparison of reading comprehension and decoding difficulties in children. In C. Cornoldi & J. Oakhill (Eds.), *Reading comprehension difficulties: Processes and intervention* (pp. 93–112). Mahwah, NJ: Erlbaum.

Stricht, T. G., & James, J. H. (1984). Listening and reading. In P. D. Pearson, R. B. Barr, M. L. Kamil, & P. Mosenthal (Eds.), *Handbook of reading research* (Vol. 1, pp. 293–317). New York: Longman.

Torgesen, J. K. (1987). Thinking about the future by distinguishing between issues that have resolutions and those that do not. In S. Vaughn, & C. Bos (Eds.), *Research in learning disabilities: Issues and future directions* (pp. 55–68). Boston: Little, Brown.

Uhry, J. K., & Shepherd, M. J. (1993). Segmentation/spelling instruction as part of a first-grade reading program: Effects on several measures of reading. *Reading Research Quarterly, 28*, 219–233.

van der Meere, J., van Baal, M., & Sergeant, J. (1989). The additive factor method: A differential diagnostic tool in hyperactivity and learning disabilities. *Journal of Abnormal Child Psychology, 17*(4), 409–422.

Vellutino, F. R., Scanlon, D. M., & Lyon, G. R. (2000). Differentiating between difficult-to-remediate and readily remediated poor readers: More evidence against the IQ-discrepancy definition of reading disability. *Journal of Learning Disabilities, 33*, 223–228.

Vellutino, F. R., Scanlon, D. M., & Taneman, M. S. (1994). Components of reading ability: Issues and problems in operationalizing word identification, phonological coding, and orthographic coding. In G. R. Lyon (Ed.), *Frames of references for the assessment of learning disabilities: New views on measurement issues* (pp. 279–332). Baltimore: Paul H. Brookes.

Vgotsky, I. V. (1962). *Thought and language*. Cambridge, MA: MIT Press.

Wagner, R.K., Torgesen, J. K., & Rashotte, C. A. (1994). Development of reading-related phonological processing abilities: New evidence of bi-directional causality from a latent variable longitudinal study. *Developmental Psychology, 30*, 73–87.

Wagner, R. K., Torgesen, J. K., & Rashotte, C. A. (1999). *Comprehensive Test of Phonological Processing*. Austin, TX: Pro-Ed.

Wechsler, D. (1997a). *Wechsler Adult Intelligence Scale—Third Edition*. San Antonio, TX: The Psychological Corporation.

Wechsler, D. (1997b). *Wechsler Memory Scale—Third Edition*. San Antonio, TX: The Psychological Corporation.

Wertsch, J. V. (1998). *Mind as action*. New York: Oxford University Press.

Willows, D. M., & Terepocki, M. M. (1993). The relation of reversal errors to reading disabilities. In D. M. Willows, R. S. Kruk, & E. Corcos (Eds.), *Visual processes in reading and reading disabilities* (pp. 31–56). Hillsdale, NJ: Erlbaum.

Wolf, M., Bowers, P. G., & Biddle, K. (2000). Naming-speed processes, timing, and reading: A conceptual review. *Journal of Learning Disabilities, 33*, 387–407.

Wolf, M., & Katzir-Cohen, T. (2001). Reading fluency and its intervention. *Scientific Studies of Reading, 5*(3), 211–238.

Woodcock, R. W. (1993). An informational processing view of *Gf–Gc* theory. *Journal of Psychoeducational Assessment* [Monograph Series: WJ-R Monograph], 80–102.

Woodcock, R. W. (1997). The Woodcock–Johnson Tests of Cognitive Ability—Revised. In D. P. Flanagan, J. L. Genshaft, & P. L. Harrison (Eds.), *Contemporary intellectual assessment: Theories, tests and issues* (pp. 230–246). New York: Guilford.

Woodcock, R. W., & Johnson, M. B. (1977). *Woodcock–Johnson Psycho-Educational Battery*. Allen, TX: DLM.

Woodcock, R. W., & Johnson, M. B. (1989). *Woodcock–Johnson Psycho-Education Battery—Revised*. Itasca, IL: Riverside Publishing.

Woodcock, R. W., McGrew, K. S., & Mather, N. (2001). *Woodcock–Johnson III*. Itasca, IL: Riverside Publishing.

Zelazo, P. D., Carter, A., Reznick, J. S., & Frye, D. (1997). Early development of executive function: A problem-solving framework. *Review of General Psychology, 1*, 198–226.

Zelazo, P. D., & Jacques, S. (1997). Children's rule use: Representation, reflection, and cognitive control. In R. Vasta (Ed.), *Annals of Child Development, 12*, 119–176. London: Jessica Kingsley Press.

Zimmerman, B. J. (1989). A social cognitive view of self-regulated academic learning. *Journal of Educational Psychology, 81*, 329–339.

5

USING THE

WOODCOCK–JOHNSON III

DISCREPANCY PROCEDURES

FOR DIAGNOSING LEARNING

DISABILITIES

NANCY MATHER

The University of Arizona, Tuscon, Arizona 85721

FREDRICK A. SCHRANK

The Woodcock–Muñoz Foundation, Olympia, Washington 98501

The Woodcock–Johnson III consists of two assessment instruments: the *Woodcock–Johnson III Tests of Cognitive Abilities* (WJ III COG) and the *Woodcock–Johnson III Tests of Achievement* (WJ III ACH). The WJ III COG and WJ III ACH were normed together; this feature allows the batteries to function together and provides the examiner with several procedures for evaluating the presence and severity of discrepancies among scores. The WJ III discrepancy procedures are psychometrically valid because they are actual, not estimated, discrepancies that are obtained from direct comparisons of actual scores between measures.

The WJ III discrepancy procedures are psychometrically preferable to estimated discrepancies for two reasons. First, the WJ III discrepancies do not contain the errors associated with estimated discrepancies. Unlike the WJ III discrepancy procedures, estimated discrepancy procedures do not control for unknown differences that exist when comparing two tests that are based on different norming samples. Second, the discrepancy procedures used by the WJ III incorporate specific correlation coefficients between all predictor and criterion variables at each age level to provide the best estimates of the population characteristics. These correlation coefficients are based on a large, representative national sample of 8,818 subjects. In contrast, estimated discrepancy procedures are typically based on small samples (often less than 100) that have limited validity because the samples are often restricted in range of ability (demonstrated by standard deviations of less than 15).

The different types of discrepancies associated with the WJ III can help inform the diagnosis of a learning disability. In this chapter, the term *learning disability* is used as a general category. It is important to recognize that a diagnosis needs to be about a specific type of learning disability, such as a reading disability. The specific disability could be caused by some underlying condition (such as poor phonological awareness or poor memory) and may affect other areas as well (e.g., memorization of math facts). Instead of the vague, generic term *learning disability*, domain-specific labels such as *reading disability*, *math disability*, or *language impairment* are more descriptive of the problem. Specifying the domain of deficit helps reduce heterogeneity and makes the concept of the disability more coherent (Stanovich, 1993).

This chapter begins with a detailed discussion of the two fundamentally different types of discrepancy procedures for the WJ III: intra-ability and ability/achievement. Next, a case study provides an example of the different types of information from the discrepancies. In the final section there is a discussion of the limitations of various discrepancy procedures, and cautions with regard to interpretation.

INTRA-ABILITY DISCREPANCIES

The WJ III intra-ability discrepancy procedures were specifically designed to help identify an individual's strengths and weaknesses and to reveal factors that are intrinsic or related to learning processes. Because of the breadth of cognitive and academic abilities covered, the WJ III is well suited for this type of analysis. This type of careful examination of test performance is frequently recommended, as suggested by the following excerpt from the *Standards for Educational and Psychological Testing* (AERA, APA, & NCME, 1999):

> Because each test in a battery examines a different function, ability, skill, or combination thereof, the test taker's performance can be understood best when scores are not combined or aggregated, but rather when each score is interpreted within the context of all other scores and assessment data. For example, low scores on timed tests alert the examiner to slowed responding as a problem that may not be apparent if scores on different kinds of tests are combined. (p. 123)

As a reflection of the changing conceptualizations of the nature and identification of learning disabilities, the WJ III includes three alternatives for determining the presence and severity of intra-ability discrepancies: intra-cognitive, intra-achievement, and intra-individual. Information on the presence of any intra-cognitive discrepancies can be obtained by administering specific tests from the WJ III COG. Information on any discrepancies among areas of achievement can be obtained by administering specific tests from the WJ III ACH. These two procedures can be used separately or together. In addition, the intra-individual discrepancy procedure uses cognitive and achievement measures conjointly.

The three intra-ability discrepancies are bidirectional comparisons; that is, each ability is compared to the average of all of the other abilities in the comparison. For example, equal interest exists for an individual who demonstrates a strength in fluid reasoning but a weakness in short-term memory, and for an individual who has a strength in short-term memory but a weakness in fluid reasoning. Similarly, equal interest exists for the child who has a strength in mathematics but a weakness in reading, and for the child who has a strength in reading but a weakness in mathematics. Figure 5-1 displays the nature of the bidirectional comparisons used in the three intra-ability discrepancy procedures.

The intra-ability discrepancy procedures can help an evaluator explain how the abilities measured by the WJ III are related to learning difficulties. Any of the intra-ability discrepancy procedures can also be used to substantiate the "unexpectedness" of a difficulty by comparing and contrasting a person's performance in one area to the average of his or her performance in the other areas included in the procedure. Because they recognize the limitations of sole reliance on ability/achievement discrepancies, many evaluators in the United States use alternatives to the traditional ability/achievement discrepancy model for establishing the presence of a learning disability. The intra-ability discrepancy procedures can help professionals develop a solid case for identifying a learning disability in the absence of an ability/achievement discrepancy or to corroborate a diagnosis made on the basis of an ability/achievement discrepancy.

INTRA-COGNITIVE DISCREPANCIES

The WJ III COG includes clusters of abilities that are grouped categorically by defined kinds of tasks. A comparison of an individual's strengths and weaknesses among these abilities can be diagnostic. The WJ III COG Standard Battery includes cluster scores for three categories of intellectual abilities: Verbal Ability, Thinking Abilities, and Cognitive Efficiency. These cluster scores can be evaluated in the WJ III COG Standard Battery intra-cognitive discrepancy procedure. The WJ III COG Extended Battery includes the Cattell–Horn–Carroll (CHC) factors (Comprehension–Knowledge, Long-Term Retrieval, Visual-Spatial Thinking, Auditory Processing, Fluid Reasoning, Processing Speed, and Short-Term Memory) as well as two other categories of special intellectual abilities (Phonemic Awareness and Working Memory) that can be evaluated in the WJ III COG Extended Battery intra-cognitive discrepancy procedure. In the intra-cognitive discrepancy procedure, each cluster score is compared to the average of all of the other clusters in the comparison. For each of the intra-cognitive

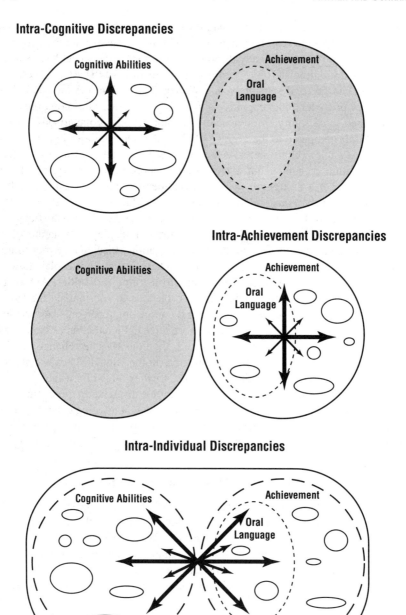

FIGURE 5-1   Bidirectional comparisons used in the intra-ability discrepancy procedures.

discrepancy options, the tests that comprise the interpretive cluster must be administered to obtain intra-cognitive discrepancies. Table 5-1 outlines the clusters that are included in the intra-cognitive discrepancy procedure when using either the Standard or Extended Battery and when using the *Woodcock–Johnson III Diagnostic Supplement to the Tests of Cognitive Abilities* (Woodcock, McGrew, Mather, & Schrank, 2003).

The intra-cognitive discrepancy procedure is particularly useful in identifying information-processing strengths and weaknesses. This type of analysis is consistent with Brackett and McPherson's (1996) suggestion that a "major value of detecting severe discrepancies within and between areas of cognition is the focus on cognitive processing components of learning disabilities (p. 79)." The intra-cognitive discrepancy procedure is most appropriate when the purpose of the assessment is to determine if certain cognitive factors are affecting academic performance. For example, the National Association of School Psychologists' statement (2002) on the Individuals with Disabilities Education Act (IDEA), *Learning Disabilities Criteria: Recommendations for Change in IDEA Reauthorization*, suggests that school psychologists should use cognitive assessment measures for

TABLE 5-1   WJ III Intra-Cognitive Discrepancies

Standard	Extended
Verbal Ability	Comprehension–Knowledge (*Gc*)
Thinking Ability	Visual-Spatial Thinking (*Gv*)
Cognitive Efficiency	Auditory Processing (*Ga*)
	Fluid Reasoning (*Gf*)
	Processing Speed (*Gs*)
	Short-Term Memory (*Gsm*)
	Phonemic Awareness[a]
	Working Memory[a]
	Visual-Spatial Thinking 3[a]
	Fluid Reasoning 3[a]
	Associative Memory[a]
	Visualization[a]
	Sound Discrimination[a]
	Auditory Memory Span[a]
	Numerical Reasoning[a]
	Perceptual Speed[a]

[a]These cluster scores are not required for calculation of intra-cognitive discrepancies. Details may be found in the manual for the *Diagnostic Supplement to the WJ III Tests of Cognitive Abilities* (Woodcock, McGrew, Mather, & Schrank, 2003).

"identifying strengths and weaknesses on marker variables (e.g., phonological processing, verbal short-term memory) known to be related to reading or other academic areas" (p. 1). Similarly, the American Academy of School Psychology (AASP, 2002) stated, "Rather than testing solely to obtain an IQ score, cognitive assessments should more appropriately be used to identify the core processes or functions causing an academic problem that are amendable to intervention or that require educational accommodations" (p. 2). The intra-cognitive discrepancy procedure may be particularly useful in the early identification of a learning difficulty, because it is possible to identify a cognitive processing disability as early as first grade rather than waiting for this disability to manifest itself in the form of failing grades several years later. As suggested by the AASP, "cognitive tests are useful for early identification of information-processing weaknesses (such as a delay in auditory processing or phonological awareness) that can lead to academic failure if left untreated" (p. 2).

Many states and school districts in the United States require documentation of a processing disorder in order to provide learning disabilities services. The intra-cognitive discrepancy procedure can be used for this purpose. For example, students with learning disabilities often have adequate scores on measures of verbal comprehension, but low scores on tests that measure processing speed (Morgan et al., 2000). Although the nature of various types of learning disabilities is still not fully understood, the practical and theoretical viability of including information-processing deficits in the criterion for diagnosing these disorders has improved considerably since the dissemination of federal guidelines (Shaw et al., 1995).

INTRA-ACHIEVEMENT DISCREPANCIES

Like the intracognitive discrepancy procedure, the intra-achievement discrepancy procedure allows an evaluator to examine strengths and weaknesses among areas of achievement. Table 5-2 defines the two sets of clusters that can be included in the intra-achievement discrepancy procedure options. Monroe (1932) explained that it was necessary to discriminate between a true case of reading disability and the child whose reading is poor for his or her age but who is nevertheless reading as well as would be expected based upon his or her other achievements. In other words, the problem is circumscribed and does not affect all areas of academic functioning. Similarly, Shaw et al. (1995) recommend that the first step for diagnosing learning disabilities should be to identify intra-individual discrepancies within achievement. This process involves identifying areas of difficulty as well as areas of strength.

Reading, math, and written language are made up of dissociable components (e.g., math basic skills and math reasoning). Aaron, Joshi, and Williams (1999) found that four different types of poor readers can be identified: (a) those with problems in decoding only, (b) those with problems in comprehension only, (c) those with a combination of poor decoding and comprehension, and (d) those

TABLE 5-2   WJ III Intra-Achievement Discrepancies

Standard	Extended
Broad Reading	Basic Reading Skills
Broad Math	Reading Comprehension
Broad Written Language	Math Calculation Skills
Oral Language—Standard	Math Reasoning
	Basic Writing Skills
	Written Expression
	Oral Expression
	Listening Comprehension
	Academic Knowledge

with poor reading speed and orthographic processing (measured by irregular word reading on a homophonic word and nonword identification task [e.g., identify the nonword—hear, here, heer]). Once the evaluator has determined the nature of the reading problem, he or she can then recommend specific strategies for building phoneme awareness, decoding, vocabulary, specialized knowledge, or comprehension, depending on the area or areas that are weak. The intra-achievement discrepancy procedure is useful for this purpose.

INTRA-INDIVIDUAL DISCREPANCIES

In some cases, the intra-individual discrepancy procedure can be useful for diagnosis and instructional planning. This combined procedure allows examiners to analyze an individual's cognitive and academic scores across the clusters of the WJ III COG and WJ III ACH and to view the pattern of covarying cognitive and achievement strengths and weaknesses. Like the other intra-ability discrepancy procedures, the intra-individual discrepancy procedure involves comparing each cognitive ability and achievement area of interest to the average of all other abilities.

The intent of the intra-individual discrepancy procedure is to focus attention on a person's differences among abilities across developmental and academic domains (Shaw et al., 1995). The procedure can be used with several combinations of clusters from the WJ III COG and WJ III ACH. Figure 5-2 shows how these abilities are analyzed together in the intra-individual discrepancies section of the *Report Writer for the WJ III* (Schrank & Woodcock, 2002). This example uses the set of clusters from the WJ III COG and WJ III ACH Extended Batteries.

The intra-individual discrepancy procedure is appropriate when the purpose of the assessment is to determine why the student has had difficulty, explain how the

DISCREPANCIES	STANDARD SCORES			DISCREPANCY		Significant at
	Actual	Predicted	Difference	PR	SD	+ or - 1.50 SD (SEE)
COMP-KNOWLEDGE (Gc)	97	85	12	88	+1.16	No
L-T RETRIEVAL (Glr)	66	91	-25	5	-1.63	Yes
VIS-SPATIAL THINK (Gv)	72	95	-23	4	-1.70	Yes
AUDITORY PROCESS (Ga)	96	92	4	63	+0.34	No
FLUID REASONING (Gf)	89	89	0	49	-0.01	No
PROCESS SPEED (Gs)	80	93	-13	16	-1.01	No
SHORT-TERM MEM (Gsm)	109	90	19	93	+1.45	No
PHONEMIC AWARE	96	91	5	65	+0.37	No
WORKING MEMORY	106	89	17	93	+1.45	No
BASIC READING SKILLS	80	88	-8	21	-0.82	No
READING COMP	99	88	11	95	+1.68	Yes
MATH CALC SKILLS	106	90	16	93	+1.50	No
MATH REASONING	72	90	-18	2	-2.11	Yes
BASIC WRITING SKILLS	92	89	3	63	+0.33	No
WRITTEN EXPRESSION	100	88	12	86	+1.07	No
ORAL EXPRESSION	85	89	-4	37	-0.34	No
LISTENING COMP	94	87	7	74	+0.63	No
ACADEMIC KNOWLEDGE	81	88	-7	21	-0.81	No

FIGURE 5-2 Intra-individual discrepancies from the *Report Writer for the WJ III* Table of Scores.

difficulty relates to academic performance, and select appropriate interventions. For example, this discrepancy procedure can help an examiner detect a pattern of cognitive/linguistic weaknesses that are reflected in an individual's listening comprehension, reading comprehension, and written expression. At the same time, a pattern of strengths may be noted in fluid reasoning, math calculation, and math reasoning.

One caution is in order with regard to the intra-individual discrepancy procedure. If an individual's achievement scores are significantly lower than his or her cognitive abilities, the intra-individual discrepancy procedure may mask significant intra-cognitive discrepancies because it is based on a larger mix of abilities (i.e., cognitive and achievement combined). It is possible that strengths or weaknesses that were found in the intra-cognitive or intra-achievement discrepancy procedures may become attenuated in the intra-individual discrepancy procedure. When an individual's cognitive and academic scores are combined in one statistical mix, the magnitude of differences between test scores will be different from what may have been observed in the separate intra-cognitive and intra-achievement discrepancy procedures. Low achievement scores will have the effect of lowering the predicted score (the score that is based on performance on all administered clusters). Consequently, the intra-individual discrepancy analysis may hide a significant cognitive weakness. In cases in which an individual's achievement scores are significantly lower than his or her cognitive scores, and in cases in which identification of a weakness in cognitive processing is required for identification of a learning disability, it is preferable to select the intra-cognitive and intra-achievement discrepancy procedures separately rather than relying solely on the intra-individual discrepancy procedure.

ABILITY/ACHIEVEMENT DISCREPANCIES

The WJ III also provides procedures for evaluating three types of ability/achievement discrepancies: (a) general intellectual ability/achievement, (b) predicted achievement/achievement, and (c) oral language ability/achievement. These discrepancy procedures are unidirectional—that is, only certain abilities are used to predict achievement. Figure 5-3 displays the nature of the uni-directional comparisons used in the WJ III ability/achievement discrepancy procedures.

The WJ III ability/achievement discrepancy procedures can be thought of as providing unique comparisons between certain categories of an individual's cognitive or oral language abilities and his or her levels of academic achievement. Each of the three ability/achievement discrepancy procedures is based on a different conceptualization of ability. The general intellectual ability/achievement discrepancy model is most similar to the concept of an ability/achievement discrepancy that was articulated in the Individuals with Disabilities Education Act. The predicted achievement/achievement discrepancy procedure provides the examiner with a more sophisticated tool for determining if an individual's current levels of achievement in each academic area would be predicted by his or her levels of associated cognitive abilities. The oral language ability/achievement discrepancy procedure allows the examiner to determine if an individual's levels of academic performance are consistent or inconsistent with his or her measured oral language proficiency. Information from one or more ability/achievement discrepancy procedure can also provide information about variability within an individual. Additionally, when more than one procedure for determining an ability/achievement discrepancy is used, the information can be compared and contrasted because each of the three ability/achievement discrepancy procedures is based on a different conceptualization of ability.

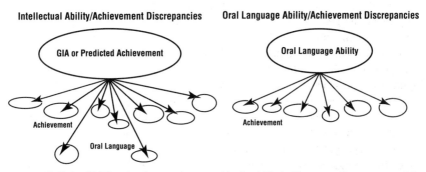

FIGURE 5-3   Unidirectional comparisons used in the ability/achievement discrepancy models in the WJ III.

GENERAL INTELLECTUAL ABILITY/
ACHIEVEMENT PROCEDURE

In 1975, when the Education for all Handicapped Children Act (Public Law [PL] 94-142) was first enacted in the United States, many states reported problems with establishing objective criteria for identifying a learning disability. The U.S. Office of Education adopted the concept of a discrepancy between intellectual ability and achievement with the goal of establishing guidelines for identifying children eligible for educational services. The difficulty in developing a qualitative definition of learning disability, combined with the need to make funding decisions, prompted school districts to use statistical methods to identify this group of children (Silver & Hagin, 1990). Because of state rules and regulations and the definition of learning disabilities provided in PL 94-142 as well as the subsequent reauthorizations (IDEA), the discrepancy procedure most often used is a comparison between an intelligence test score and an achievement test score. The WJ III general intellectual ability/achievement discrepancies were developed, in part, to address the language in the federal legislation that refers to this type of discrepancy.

The intellectual ability/achievement procedure on the WJ III uses a general intellectual ability (g) score as the predictor across achievement domains. The General Intellectual Ability (GIA) scores are the first principal component (g) measures obtained from principal component analyses. Either the General Intellectual Ability—Standard (GIA—Std) or General Intellectual Ability—Extended (GIA—Ext) score can be used as the ability measure. The GIA—Std is derived from the first seven tests in the WJ III COG. Each of the seven tests represents a different ability within one of seven broad CHC factors. The GIA—Ext score is derived from the 14 tests that constitute the broad CHC factors. Each GIA score is a weighted combination of cognitive tests that varies marginally by age, accounting for the largest portion of variance in the component tests. The GIA score represents a common ability underlying all intellectual performance.

Computer scoring makes calculation of g possible. Each test included in the GIA score is weighted to provide the best estimate of g. In contrast, tests such as the Wechsler intelligence scales weight all subtests equally, a procedure that does not provide the best estimate of g. In general, the tests that measure Gc (Verbal Comprehension and General Information) and Gf (Concept Formation and Analysis Synthesis) are among the highest g-weighted tests, a finding that is consistent with the extant factor-analytic research on g (e.g., Carroll, 1993). Figure 5-4 represents the average test weights for the GIA—Std scale. Figure 5-5 provides the average test weights for the GIA—Ext scale.

General intellectual ability (g) is a theoretical postulate. The little g represents a distillation of cognitive abilities represented by a common factor underlying all test performance (Jensen, 1998). The general factor is also identified in Carroll's three-stratum model of human cognitive abilities (Carroll, 1993). The psychological nature of g is uncertain because it cannot be defined by test content. However,

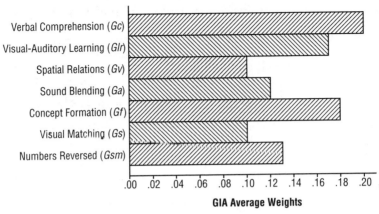

FIGURE 5-4   General Intellectual Ability—Standard average test weights.

g scores have broad practical utility, because they are often the best single-score predictors of various global criteria, such as overall school achievement or other life outcomes that have some relationship to cognitive ability.

The WJ III GIA scores have high correlations with other measures of intelligence. These correlations provide support for the use of the WJ III GIA scores in intellectual ability/achievement discrepancy evaluations. Table 5-3 contains

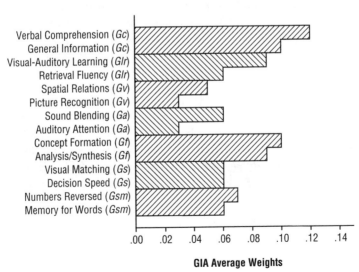

FIGURE 5-5   General Intellectual Ability—Extended average test weights.

TABLE 5-3   Observed and Corrected Correlations from Three Criterion Validity Studies for the WJ III COG GIA Score

| | Median correlation | | | |
| | GIA—Std | | GIA—Ext | |
Criterion	Observed	Corrected	Observed	Corrected
Differential Ability Scales	.72	.82	.74	.82
Stanford–Binet Intelligence Scale— Fourth Edition	.76	.82	.71	.80
Wechsler Intelligence Scale for Children— Third Edition	.72	.86	.76	.89

the obtained correlations from three criterion validity studies for the WJ III COG GIA scores. Details of these studies can be found in the *WJ III Technical Manual* (McGrew & Woodcock, 2001). For the WJ III COG, scores were compared with performances on other intellectual measures appropriate for individuals at the ages tested. Correlations with the *Differential Ability Scale* (DAS) General Conceptual Ability (GCA) score are reported as .72 for GIA—Std and .74 for GIA—Ext. Results of a study with the *Stanford–Binet Intelligence Scale— Fourth Edition* at the preschool level show correlations with the overall composite score to be .76 for GIA—Std and .71 for GIA—Ext. Correlations with the *Wechsler Intelligence Scale for Children—Third Edition* are reported as .71 for GIA—Std and .76 for GIA—Ext. Because the sample variances are somewhat truncated, as indicated by the standard deviations, a correction for restriction in range was applied to obtain better approximations of the values for the population parameters defined by each set of measures (Guilford & Fruchter, 1978). Table 5-3, therefore, also shows the corrected correlations between pairs of variables. Corrected correlations with the *Differential Ability Scale* General Conceptual Ability score are .82 for both GIA—Std and GIA—Ext. Corrected correlations with the *Stanford–Binet Intelligence Scale—Fourth Edition* are .82 for GIA—Std and .80 for GIA—Ext. Corrected correlations with the *Wechsler Intelligence Scale for Children—Third Edition* are .86 for GIA—Std and .89 for the GIA—Ext.

PREDICTED ACHIEVEMENT/ ACHIEVEMENT PROCEDURE

The name of this discrepancy procedure conveys its purpose: to predict an individual's academic performance in the near term, based on his or her current levels of associated cognitive abilities. The predicted achievement option is empirically—rather than theoretically—derived. Each predicted achievement score is based on test weights that vary developmentally. The weights represent the best statistical relationship between the cognitive abilities most related to an area of academic achievement at any given point in development. In the prediction of reading, the abilities weighted the most at the first-grade level differ from the abilities weighted the most during the secondary years. For example, in the early grades, Sound Blending (a measure of phonetic coding) is weighted more heavily than are some other cognitive abilities. As students advance in school years, Verbal Comprehension (a measure of vocabulary knowledge) increases in importance and is more heavily weighted.

One procedure for identifying a learning disability is to determine whether there is a discrepancy between ability (described as potential for school success) and achievement (equated with present levels of academic performance). In other words, a specific learning disability is sometimes characterized as "unexpected" or "unexplained" poor performance based on observations of the child's other capabilities and is not necessarily predicted by general intellectual competence. Although the WJ III predicted achievement clusters were not designed to estimate a student's "potential" for future school success, they can be useful for documenting "expected" good or poor academic performance by predicting academic functioning in each curricular area. This prediction is accomplished by including a mix of the cognitive tasks statistically associated with performance in the particular academic area and most relevant to the specific achievement domain. The intent of the predicted achievement/achievement discrepancy procedure is to determine if the person is performing as well as one would expect, *given his or her measured levels of associated cognitive abilities.*

Consider a child with poor basic reading skills who also has low scores on the Sound Blending and Visual Matching tests. In this case, the predicted achievement score for reading will reflect the low Sound Blending and Visual Matching scores, and the child may not show a discrepancy between predicted and actual achievement. This example shows how this discrepancy procedure predicts that the child will struggle with reading, and he or she does.

On the other hand, when a significant discrepancy exists between predicted achievement and actual achievement, the observed difference suggests that the measured abilities related to the cognitive domain are not the principal factor or factors inhibiting performance. In some cases, extrinsic factors (e.g., lack of proper instruction, economic disadvantage, lack of opportunity to learn, lack of interest, poor instruction, or poor motivation) may be responsible for the observed discrepancy.

ORAL LANGUAGE ABILITY/ACHIEVEMENT PROCEDURE

The WJ III ACH also contains an ability/achievement discrepancy procedure whereby the Oral Language—Extended cluster is used as the measure of ability. In the field of reading disabilities, one commonly proposed discrepancy model is to compare oral language abilities to specific domains of academic performance (Aaron, 1997; Badian, 1999; Spring & French, 1990). Betts (1946) suggested comparing listening comprehension (which he referred to as hearing capacity) to basic reading skills to help identify the level of expected reading competence, as well as to determine goals for remedial instruction. Spring and French (1990) argued that using discrepancies between listening comprehension and reading, rather than discrepancies between intelligence and reading, is advantageous for two reasons: (a) the concept of a discrepancy between reading and listening can be easily understood by parents and other laypersons, and (b) the discrepancy is more related to a variety of remedial strategies.

A substantial number of poor readers are deficient in decoding skills, but have adequate comprehension as determined by measures of listening comprehension (Aaron et al., 1999). This discrepancy between oral and written language is what makes the diagnosis "specific"; the difficulties are circumscribed and do not extend into many domains of functioning. Children with dyslexia are often described as having deficient decoding skills with adequate comprehension. Comprehension is viewed as a generic process that is common to both reading and listening and it is thought to be mediated at a deeper level by the same cognitive mechanisms (Aaron, 1997). For normally developing readers, levels of reading and listening comprehension are typically similar. For example, Palmer et al. (1985) obtained a correlation of .82 between listening comprehension and reading comprehension in a sample of college students. What distinguishes the individual with a reading disability from other poor readers is that their listening comprehension ability is higher than their ability to decode words (Rack, Snowling, & Olson, 1992), and thus the difficulty is "unpredicted" and specific to reading. If students perform poorly in both listening comprehension and reading, their problem is neither unexplained nor unexpected (Carroll, 1977).

Several studies have revealed that students identified as having learning disabilities differ from peers on many cognitive and academic measures, but not on oral language abilities. For example, a study examining the cognitive, linguistic, and achievement abilities of 200 college students with and without learning disabilities identified significant differences between the groups on phonological/ orthographic processing, cognitive efficiency, working memory, and academic fluency (McGrew et al., 2001). The significant differences between these groups can logically be linked to these specific underlying cognitive and linguistic deficits that are common to individuals with learning disabilities. In contrast, no significant differences in oral language measures were noted between the groups. Similarly, Morgan et al. (2000) found that individuals with learning disabilities had adequate scores on "power" measures of achievement, but poor performance on measures sensitive to speed, fluency, and efficiency. Spring and French (1990) found that children with reading disabilities scored significantly higher on listening comprehension tasks than on measures of reading comprehension.

Montani, Frawley, and Smith (2000) compared the performance of 30 third- and fourth-grade students with learning disabilities to 30 students without learning disabilities on the *Woodcock Diagnostic Reading Battery* (Woodcock, 1997a). The students who were diagnosed with learning disabilities scored lower than grade-mates on seven of the ten tests that involved phonological awareness (Sound Blending and Incomplete Words), processing speed (Visual Matching), and print (Letter–Word Identification, Word Attack, Reading Vocabulary, and Passage Comprehension). These groups exhibited no differences on the three tests measuring oral language (Oral Vocabulary, Listening Comprehension, and Memory for Sentences).

These findings suggest that many students with learning disabilities do not differ from peers on measures of oral language, but rather on specific cognitive and academic variables. One important goal of a learning disability evaluation is to distinguish children whose problems are specific to one or more cognitive domains from those whose problems result from a more pervasive impairment in language skills (which may be more appropriately classified as an oral language disorder) (Fletcher et al., 1998). Children who struggle with most aspects of language, as well as with many other cognitive abilities, may be more appropriately classified as having some degree of mental impairment (e.g., mild to moderate mental retardation).

The oral language ability/achievement procedure has particular relevance for helping evaluators distinguish between individuals with adequate oral language capabilities, but poor reading and writing abilities (i.e., specific reading disabilities), and individuals whose oral language abilities are commensurate with present levels of reading and writing performance. In the first case, when oral language performance is higher than reading ability, instructional recommendations focus on reading and writing development. In the second case, instructional recommendations are directed to all aspects of language development.

Stanovich (1991a,b) noted that using an oral language measure to predict reading and writing achievement is often preferable to using a general intelligence score because it is more consistent with the concept of "potential" and "unexpected" failure. He explained that using oral language ability as the aptitude measure moves us closer to a more principled definition of reading disability because it provides a more accurate estimate of what the person could achieve if the reading problem were entirely resolved. In addition, Stanovich (1993) argues that verbal aptitude measures help to isolate a more circumscribed disability or modular deficit.

COMPARATIVE INFORMATION OBTAINED FROM THE WJ III DISCREPANCY PROCEDURES

The following example illustrates how comparative information can be obtained from the intra-ability discrepancies and the various ability/achievement discrepancies. Ann, a third-grade student, was referred for evaluation by her teacher because of difficulties in reading. The goals of the assessment were to determine the extent of her reading difficulties and to identify the factors that had contributed to her slow reading development. When administered the WJ III COG, Ann had difficulty blending sounds orally (Sound Blending) and identifying the whole word when hearing only part of a word (Incomplete Words). She also scored in the low-average range on a processing speed test in which she had to rapidly locate the matching numbers in a row (Visual Matching). Performances on all other cognitive tests fell within the average range for her age and grade level.

Ann did not demonstrate a significant predicted achievement/achievement discrepancy in reading. Because of her low scores on phonological and processing speed tasks, her predicted reading achievement was low and her actual basic reading skills were also low. In other words, Ann's reading ability was within the predicted range for others who possess similar cognitive abilities. This lack of discrepancy does not rule out the existence of a specific reading disability, it merely shows that her present difficulties with reading are expected based upon the cognitive abilities most related to early reading performance.

On the intra-individual discrepancy procedure, Ann demonstrated significant weaknesses in Auditory Processing and Processing Speed, as well as weaknesses in Basic Reading and Writing Skills. Within the WJ III ACH, Ann's performance on tests of basic reading and writing skills were significantly lower than her performance on tests involving higher level oral language abilities and mathematics. This intra-achievement discrepancy was not surprising because problems with phonological processing have a greater impact on the development of literacy than on oral language and mathematics performance.

Significant discrepancies existed when Ann's GIA and oral language ability scores were compared to her scores for basic reading and writing skills. Her overall average abilities, as well as her average oral language abilities, suggested that Ann should have higher scores on reading tests.

As noted from this case, the lack of a predicted achievement/achievement discrepancy suggested that Ann's reading difficulties were not unexpected. Her cognitive abilities related to reading were at a low level. The intra-ability discrepancies, as well as the general intellectual ability/achievement and oral language ability/achievement discrepancies, helped to substantiate the diagnostic hypothesis that Ann's difficulties with reading were not due to a generalized language impairment but could be more accurately described as a "specific reading disability."

LIMITATIONS OF ABILITY/ACHIEVEMENT DISCREPANCY PROCEDURES

Identification of a learning disability has often—unfortunately—been predicated on the existence of an ability/achievement discrepancy. All ability/ achievement discrepancy procedures have inherent limitations. Over the past two decades, the use of an ability/achievement discrepancy model as the sole or determining criterion for the diagnosis of dyslexia and/or a learning disability has been questioned and criticized.

From the outset, the concept of an ability/achievement discrepancy was controversial. As Berninger (2001) pointed out:

> The definitions in the original federal legislation were also more influenced by the prevailing assessment practices of the time than by scientific research knowledge. The major assessment tool of the school psychologist was the IQ test, and the major diagnostic question was whether a student was mentally retarded (IQ below the normal range) or was underachieving relative to IQ (considered a yardstick for potential or expected achievement). For nearly a quarter of a century, IQ retained its prominent role as a cutoff criterion for mental retardation or as a criterion for evaluating whether achievement was discrepant from expected performance. (p. 25)

Although this practice no longer seems reasonable, Lyon et al. (2001) pointed out that the idea of using this type of discrepancy model was "probably reasonable at the time" (p. 266), primarily because many people in the 1970s viewed global IQ scores as good predictors of the ability to learn.

Despite a plethora of criticisms and concerns, in the United States most state and district identification guidelines continue to rely on such formulas (Frankenberger & Fronzaglio, 1991). Additionally, some local education agency practices continue to stipulate that an ability/achievement discrepancy must exist in order to diagnose a learning disability, despite the fact that alternatives to learning disability identification and diagnosis exist in most, if not all, state guidelines. Although this criterion is still used widely in school settings, it has been described as both unnecessary (Mather & Healey, 1990) and invalid (Lyon, 1995). The American Academy of School Psychology (2002) has issued a position statement recommending that use of an ability/achievement discrepancy formula as the sole or determining criterion of a specific learning disability should be discouraged. The existence of an ability/achievement discrepancy, in and of itself, is not sufficient to determine a specific learning disability or to be used as the sole or determining criterion for selecting children for instructional services. The problems in using a formula to categorize children are many, serious, and too often disregarded (Bateman, 1992). As stated by Berninger (2001), Lyon and Fletcher (2001), Scarborough (1989), and Vellutino, Scanlon, and Lyon (2000), an IQ/achievement discrepancy is not a valid way to identify children with learning disabilities in school settings. When used appropriately, however, the various WJ III ability/achievement discrepancy procedures can provide important *comparative* information.

Although most professionals agree that learning disabilities are characterized by unexpected poor performance in relation to other abilities, few support the procedure of using a numerical formula as the sole basis for a diagnosis. The concept of unexpected underachievement is relatively clear, but the way to operationalize these diagnostic criteria is problematic (MacMillan, Gresham, & Bocian, 1998). Monroe (1932) discussed the use of a discrepancy between ability and achievement as an indicator of reading disability in her book, *Children Who Cannot Read*. Monroe was one of the first researchers to distinguish between the child with a specific reading disability and the "generally subnormal child" who could not be regarded as a case of special disability because his or her other achievements would be similarly low.

Another major problem with ability/achievement discrepancy procedures is that they reveal little about the nature or causes of the learning difficulties. Assessments that focus solely on eligibility criteria are limited because they do not explore how and why a child learns in a particular way (Meltzer, 1994). These types of discrepancies may predict, but they do not diagnose. Vellutino et al. (2000) advised that "measures of general intelligence do not reliably discriminate between disabled and nondisabled readers and contribute little to clarifying the underlying causes of reading impairment" (p. 236). Furthermore, a discrepancy does not provide guidance for making decisions regarding remedial instruction (Aaron, 1997).

Another concern is that some students with specific learning disabilities will not exhibit an ability/achievement discrepancy because a weak cognitive ability or abilities will attenuate the prediction of achievement. Consequently, any identified deficiencies in cognitive abilities can result in lowered predictor scores and could lead to misdiagnosis if one were to rely solely on an ability/achievement discrepancy as the basis for the diagnosis. Many intelligence tests contain measures of cognitive abilities that are required when learning to read (Vellutino et al., 2000). Additionally, any measured discrepancy may be the result of factors other than "a disorder in one or more of the basic psychological processes," as suggested by the IDEA.

Still another serious limitation of a sole reliance on either the intellectual ability/ achievement procedure or the oral language ability/achievement procedure is that a student with a learning disability may or may not exhibit either type of discrepancy. Absence of a discrepancy should not be used as the sole criterion to exclude children from services (Dumont, Willis, & McBride, 2001). The relationship between intelligence measures and reading ability is reciprocal in that reading experience influences intelligence test scores, whereas cognitive and academic tests assess many of the same abilities (e.g., vocabulary, general information) (Aaron, 1997). Good readers tend to have large vocabularies and show gains in verbal abilities, whereas older students with reading difficulties may have depressed performance in oral language because of limited experience with text. Strang (1964) summarized this problem:

> Intelligence tests are not a sure measure of innate ability to learn. They measured "developed ability," not innate or potential intelligence. Previous achievement affects the test results. The poor reader is penalized on the verbal parts of the test. The fact that his store of information is limited by the small amount of reading he has done also works against him. (p. 212)

Lack of exposure to print contributes to reduced knowledge and vocabulary. With intellectual and oral language measures, deficiencies in language-based abilities may increase over time because of the prolonged difficulties with reading (Vellutino et al., 2000). This phenomenon has been described as the "Matthew effect," a biblical reference to the idea that the rich get rich and the poor get poorer (Stanovich, 1986; Walberg & Tsai, 1983). These Matthew effects alter the course of development in education-related cognitive skills (Stanovich, 1993). Furthermore, Berninger and Abbott (1994) point out that listening comprehension may not be a viable alternative because the expected level of achievement may be underestimated for students with attentional or language-processing problems, as well as for students for whom English is a second language.

Perhaps the most damaging aspect of the use of an ability/achievement discrepancy approach is that the procedure is predicated on failure. As Fletcher (1998) stated succinctly, "discrepancy prevents prevention" (p. 11). Children must fall behind their predicted level of performance to be deemed "technically eligible" for services. The result is that services are delayed until third grade and beyond. In fact, some school districts will not even evaluate children for eligibility for services under the learning disability category until after first grade. By preventing early intervention, discrepancy formulas are inconsistent with educational goals in the United States (Dickman, 2001). Fletcher et al. (1998) describe how discrepancy models preclude early intervention:

> The treatment implications of discrepancy models are perhaps the most serious limitations. The average age of identification of children with LD [learning disabilities] is about 10 years of age. This is partly an effect of the need for children who are struggling with academic skills to stay at the floor of the achievement tests as they fail to master skills to obtain a sufficiently low score to obtain a discrepancy. The use of discrepancy clearly moves the identification and intervention component to the later part of elementary school. Unfortunately, it is also clear that severe RD [reading disabilities] identified after age 8 may be more refractory to intervention, reflecting observations made many years ago. (p. 197)

Reading disabilities in particular are persistent and chronic. Without early intervention, the gap in reading ability that separates these children from typically developing readers becomes greater over time (Aaron, 1997). Many students who are struggling in school are found to be ineligible for services because they do not meet formal criteria, resulting in "persistent and often pernicious educational and psychological consequences" (Morgan et al., 2000, p. 489). More than a decade of research has undermined the practice of using an ability/achievement discrepancy as the sole criterion for learning disabilities (Stanovich, 1994). By combining an understanding of the manifestations and symptomatology of domain-specific learning disabilities in a practical model with common sense (otherwise known as professional judgment), examiners and other professionals can help make the shift from an approach based on school failure to one based on early intervention and prevention (Mather & Goldstein, 2001).

Simpson and Buckhalt (1990) stated: "Though the formula method may have some appeal because it requires less clinical competence and judgment, the fact remains that reducing an important diagnostic decision to a mathematical equation gives a false sense of objectivity to a contrived procedure that is still essentially

subjective" (p. 274). Many evaluators often apply regional definitions mechanis-
tically, based upon their version of the federal regulations (Shaw et al., 1995).
In other words, as noted by Willis and Dumont (2002), the determination of a
disability is an exercise in arithmetic, rather than a team decision. Furthermore,
the criterion set for the size of the discrepancy varies from region to region and
even among districts within the same region (Berninger, 1996).

Although all of the WJ III discrepancy procedures can provide useful and comparative information for determining the presence of a learning disability, no
discrepancy procedure should be used as the sole or determining criterion for
making a definitive diagnosis or negation of a learning disability. Accurate identification of a learning disability is a multidimensional procedure that involves
interpreting quantitative data, gathering qualitative information, reviewing educational history, considering familial factors, and analyzing the results of informal
assessments. Parent, teacher, and student reports, as well as classroom and test
session observations, must be included in the decision-making process. Trained
educational personnel make good decisions, and people—not test scores or
formulas—make accurate diagnoses and placement decisions. Two individuals
could have identical test scores, but only one may have a learning disability. The
first individual may have had many years of intensive educational therapy to
account for his or her present levels of achievement, whereas the second student
may have progressed through school with no additional assistance.

The WJ III discrepancy procedures are merely tools—they do not think or
diagnose. Clinical judgment is the mainstay of accurate diagnosis. The worth of
a test tool cannot be separated from the clinician who interprets the findings and
draws inferences (Meyer et al., 2001). As Batemen (1992) noted:

> The key to preventing further overidentification and misidentification is to exercise trained
> professional judgment. Our widespread reluctance to use this essential professional
> judgment in determining eligibility has been due not only to the eligibility teams' lack of
> experience, but also to a fear that courts expect objective quantification as the sole or major
> basis for decision making. Nothing could be further from the truth. The courts show the
> highest respect for professional judgment, originally of medical doctors and now of most
> other qualified experts, too. (p. 29)...First, if not foremost, it is a violation of law to rely
> on anything other than professional judgment. (p. 32)

CONCLUSIONS

Today, conceptualizations of the presence and nature of specific learning disabilities are changing. These changes are likely to be reflected in the reauthorization of IDEA which will alter national policy and procedures for identification
and eligibility. Careful identification of a significant, specific intra-ability weakness or weaknesses can provide examiners with important information for documentation of a specific learning disability. This type of identification is most
appropriately accomplished with the WJ III intra-cognitive, intra-achievement, or

intra-individual discrepancy procedures. The WJ III oral language/achievement discrepancy procedure is useful in many applications because the evaluator can determine if a student's oral language abilities differ significantly from performance in specific academic domains. Importantly, the lack of an ability/achievement discrepancy does not necessarily mean that the individual does not have a specific learning disability. In the case of the WJ III predicted achievement/achievement discrepancy procedure, it may mean that the individual is performing as well as can be expected given his or her current performance on relevant cognitive abilities.

Because the intent of each of the WJ III discrepancy procedures differs, experienced clinicians can use the different discrepancy procedures to provide comparative information to address the referral question. Most evaluators understand the limitations of ability/achievement discrepancy procedures, and use tests as tools to inform the decision-making process. These evaluators strive to identify the source of the problem and select strategies that will best meet a student's needs; they understand that remedial instruction addressing the source of the problem will be more effective than global approaches that do not address differential treatments (Aaron, 1997). In discussing the definition of learning disabilities, Doris (1993) emphasized the need for consensus in the field on specific criteria to use for learning disability identification. Although the problems appear formidable, he stated that "one wonders if the real progress will not come from disentangling groups of children from the huge conglomerate mass, rigorously specifying the nature of their difficulties, and systematically exploring appropriate educational interventions for these subgroups" (p. 112). The WJ III intra-ability discrepancy procedures are particularly useful for that purpose.

Most current theories of learning disabilities focus on domain-specific processes and, as a result, highlight the assessment of multiple abilities and how they vary (e.g., intra-ability discrepancies). The goals of a learning disability evaluation are therefore to (a) determine the factors, both intrinsic and extrinsic, that have caused the student to have difficulties; (b) explain how the observed difficulties relate to academic performance; and (c) select appropriate interventions. The purpose should be to diagnose the problem or problems, not to determine an IQ score (American Academy of School Psychology, 2002; Woodcock, 1997b). The WJ III is based on the belief that the diagnosis of learning disabilities needs to be multidimensional in nature—not solely determined by the findings of one single discrepancy procedure or one definitive score. Most importantly, the diagnosis must be informed by sound professional judgment.

REFERENCES

Aaron, P. G. (1997). The impending demise of the discrepancy formula. *Review of Educational Research, 67,* 461–502.

Aaron, P. G., Joshi, M., & Williams, K. A. (1999). Not all reading disabilities are alike. *Journal of Learning Disabilities, 32,* 120–137.

American Academy of School Psychology (AASP) (2002, September). *Response to the Report of the President's Commission on Excellence in Special Education.* Author.

American Educational Research Association (AERA), American Psychological Association (APA), & National Council on Measurement in Education (NCME). (1999). *Standards for educational and psychological testing.* Washington, DC: AERA.

Badian, N. A. (1999). Reading disability defined as a discrepancy between listening and reading comprehension: A longitudinal study of stability, gender differences, and prevalence. *Journal of Learning Disabilities, 32,* 138–148.

Bateman, B. (1992). Learning disabilities: The changing landscape. *Journal of Learning Disabilities, 25,* 29–36.

Berninger, V. W. (1996). *Reading and writing acquisition: A developmental neuropsychological perspective.* Boulder, CO: Westview Press.

Berninger, V. W. (2001). Understanding the 'lexia' in dyslexia: A multidisciplinary team approach to learning disabilities. *Annals of Dyslexia, 51,* 23–46.

Berninger, V. W., & Abbott, R. D. (1994). Redefining learning disabilities: Moving beyond aptitude–achievement discrepancies to failure to respond to validated treatment protocols. In G. R. Lyon (Ed.), *Frames of reference for the assessment of learning disabilities: New views on measurement issues* (pp. 163–183). Baltimore: Paul H. Brookes.

Betts, E. A. (1946). *Foundations of reading instruction.* New York: American Book.

Brackett, J., & McPherson, A. (1996). Learning disabilities diagnosis in postsecondary students: A comparison of discrepancy-based diagnostic models. In N. Gregg, C. Hoy, & A. F. Gay (Eds.), *Adults with learning disabilities: Theoretical and practical perspectives* (pp. 68–84). New York: Guilford.

Carroll, J. B. (1977). Developmental parameters of reading comprehension. In J. T. Guthrie (Ed.), *Cognition, curriculum, and comprehension* (pp. 1–15). Newark, DE: IRA.

Carroll, J. B. (1993). *Human cognitive abilities: A survey of factor-analytic studies.* Cambridge, UK: Cambridge University Press.

Dickman, G. E. (2001). Dyslexia and the aptitude–achievement discrepancy controversy. *Perspectives, 27,* 24–28.

Doris, J. L. (1993). Defining learning disabilities: A history of the search for consensus. In G. R. Lyon, D.B. Gray, J. F. Kavanagh, & N. A. Krasnegor (Eds.), *Better understanding learning disabilities: New views from research and their implications for education and public policies* (pp. 97–115). Baltimore: Paul H. Brookes.

Dumont, R., Willis, J., & McBride, G. (2001). Yes, Virginia there is a severe discrepancy clause, but it is too much ado about something? *The School Psychologist, 55*(1), 1, 4–13, 15.

Fletcher, J. M. (1998). IQ-discrepancy: An inadequate and iatrogenic conceptual model of learning disabilities. *Perspectives, 24*(1), 9–10.

Fletcher, J. M., Francis, D. J., Shaywitz, S. E., Lyon, G. R., Foorman, B. R., Stuebing, K. K., & Shaywitz, B. A. (1998). Intelligent testing and the discrepancy model for children with learning disabilities. *Learning Disabilities Research and Practice, 13,* 186–203.

Frankenberger, W., & Fronzaglio, K. (1991). A review of states' criteria and procedures for identifying children with learning disabilities. *Journal of Learning Disabilities, 24,* 495–500.

Guilford, J. P., & Fruchter, B. (1978). *Fundamental statistics in psychology and education.* New York: McGraw-Hill.

Jensen, A. R. (1998). *The g factor: The science of mental ability.* Westport, CT: Praeger.

Lyon, G. R. (1995). Toward a definition of dyslexia. *Annals of Dyslexia, 45,* 3–27.

Lyon, G. R., & Fletcher, J. M. (2001, Summer). Early warning system. *Education Matters,* 22–29.

Lyon, G. R., Fletcher, J. M., Shaywitz, S. E., Shaywitz, B. A., Torgesen, J. K., Wood, F. B., Schulte, A., & Olson, R. (2001). Rethinking learning disabilities. In C. E. Finn, A. J., Rotherham, & C. R. Hokanson, Jr. (Eds.), *Rethinking special education for a new century.* Dayton, OH: Thomas B. Fordham Foundation.

MacMillan, D. L., Gresham, F. M., & Bocian, K. M. (1998). Discrepancy between definitions of learning disabilities and school practices: An empirical investigation. *Journal of Learning Disabilities, 31,* 314–326.

Mather, N., & Goldstein, S. (2001). *Learning disabilities and challenging behaviors: A guide to intervention and classroom management.* Baltimore: Paul H. Brookes.

Mather, N., & Healey, W. C. (1990). Deposing aptitude–achievement discrepancy as the imperial criterion for learning disabilities. *Learning Disabilities: A Multidisciplinary Journal, 1,* 40–48.

McGrew, K., Gregg, N., Hoy, C., Stennett, R., Davis, M., Knight, D., Coleman, C., & Ford, L. (2001). *CHC Confirmatory factor analyses of WJ III, WAIS-III, WMS-III and KAIT—University Students with and without LD.* Manuscript submitted for publication.

McGrew, K. S., & Woodcock, R. W. (2001). *Woodcock–Johnson III. Technical Manual.* Itasca, IL: Riverside Publishing.

Meltzer, L. J. (1994), Assessment of learning disabilities: The challenge of evaluating cognitive strategies and processes underlying learning. In G. R. Lyon (Ed.), *Frames of reference for the assessment of learning disabilities: New views on measurement issues* (pp. 571–606). Baltimore: Paul H. Brookes.

Meyer, G. J., Finn, S. E., Eyde, L. D., Kay, G. G., Moreland, K. L., Dies, R. R., Eisman, E. J., Kubiszyn, T. W., & Reed, G. M. (2001). Psychological testing and psychological assessment: A review of evidence and issues. *American Psychologist, 56*(2), 128–165.

Monroe, M. (1932). *Children who cannot read.* Chicago: University of Chicago Press.

Montani, T. O., Frawley, P., & Smith, L. F. (2000). Differences in reading performance between students with and without learning disabilities using the *Woodcock Diagnostic Reading Battery. Diagnostique, 25,* 99–110.

Morgan, A. E., Singer-Harris, N., Bernstein, J. H., & Waber, D. P. (2000). Characteristics of children referred for evaluation of school difficulties who have adequate academic achievement scores. *Journal of Learning Disabilities, 33,* 489–500.

National Association of School Psychologists (NASP) (2002). *Position Statement. Learning Disabilities Criteria: Recommendations for Change in IDEA Reauthorization,* (p. 1). Retrieved November 20, 2002 from NASP website: http://www.nasponline.org/advocacy/NASP_IDEA.html

Palmer, J., McCleod, C., Hunt, E., & Davidson, J. (1985). Information processing correlates of reading. *Journal of Memory and Language, 24,* 59–88.

Rack, J. P., Snowling, M. J., & Olson, R. K. (1992). The nonword reading deficit in developmental dyslexia: A review. *Reading Research Quarterly, 27*(1), 28–53.

Scarbourough, H. S. (1989). Prediction of reading disability from familial and individual differences. *Journal of Educational Psychology, 81,* 101–108.

Schrank, F. A., & Woodcock, R. W. (2002). *Report Writer for the WJ III* [computer software]. *Woodcock–Johnson III.* Itasca, IL: Riverside Publishing.

Shaw, S. F., Cullen, J. P., McGuire, J. M., & Brinckerhoff, L. (1995). Operationalizing a definition of learning disabilities. *Journal of Learning Disabilities, 28,* 586–597.

Silver, A. A., & Hagin, R. A. (1990). *Disorders of learning in childhood.* New York: Wiley.

Simpson, R. G., & Buckhalt, J. A. (1990). A non-formula discrepancy model to identify learning disabilities. *School Psychology International, 11,* 273–279.

Spring, C., & French, L. (1990). Identifying children with specific reading disabilities from listening and reading discrepancy scores. *Journal of Learning Disabilities, 23,* 53–58.

Stanovich, K. E. (1986). Matthew effects in reading: Some consequences of individual differences in the acquisition of literacy. *Reading Research Quarterly, 21,* 360–407.

Stanovich, K. E. (1991a). Conceptual and empirical problems with discrepancy definitions of reading disability. *Learning Disability Quarterly, 14,* 269–280.

Stanovich, K. E. (1991b). Discrepancy definitions of reading disability: Has intelligence led us astray? *Reading Research Quarterly, 26,* 7–29.

Stanovich, K. E. (1993). The construct validity of discrepancy definitions of reading disability. In G. R. Lyon, D. B. Gray, J. F. Kavanagh, & N. A. Krasnegor (Eds.), *Better understanding learning disabilities: New views from research and their implications for education and public policies* (pp. 273–307). Baltimore: Paul H. Brookes.

Stanovich, K. E. (1994). Are discrepancy-based definitions of dyslexia empirically defensible? In K. P. van den Bos, L. S. Siegel, D. J. Bakker, & D. L. Share (Eds.), *Current directions in dyslexia research* (pp. 15–30). Alblasserdam, The Netherlands: Swets & Zeitlinger.

Strang, R. (1964). *Diagnostic teaching of reading.* New York: McGraw-Hill.

Vellutino, F. R., Scanlon, D. M., & Lyon, G. R. (2000). Differentiating between difficult-to-remediate and readily remediated poor readers: More evidence against the IQ–achievement discrepancy definition of reading disability. *Journal of Learning Disabilities, 33,* 223–238.

Walberg, H. J., & Tsai, S. (1983). Matthew effects in education. *American Educational Research Journal, 20,* 359–373.

Willis, J. O., & Dumont, R. P. (1998). *Guide to identification of learning disabilities* (3rd ed.). Peterborough, NH: Authors.

Woodcock, R. W. (1997a). *Woodcock diagnostic reading battery.* Itasca, IL: Riverside Publishing.

Woodcock, R. W. (1997b). The Woodcock–Johnson tests of cognitive ability—revised. In D. P. Flanagan, J. L. Genshaft, & P. L. Harrison (Eds.), *Contemporary intellectual assessment: Theories, tests, and issues* (pp. 230–246). New York: Guilford.

Woodcock, R. W., McGrew, K. S., Mather, N., & Schrank, F. A. (2003). *Woodcock–Johnson III diagnostic supplement to the tests of cognitive abilities.* Itasca, IL: Riverside Publishing.

6

USE OF THE WOODCOCK–JOHNSON III WITHIN THE CONTEXT OF A MODERN OPERATIONAL DEFINITION OF LEARNING DISABILITY

DAWN P. FLANAGAN

Department of Psychology, St. John's University,
Jamaica, New York 11439

The Woodcock–Johnson III (WJ III) measures a wide range of theory-based abilities and processes and therefore can be used effectively to evaluate individuals suspected of having a learning disability (LD) (Flanagan, Ortiz, Alfonso, & Mascalo, 2002). Although the WJ III provides many of the tools that are necessary for conducting the type of comprehensive evaluation of functioning that is required to identify and diagnose LDs, the manner in which these tools are used varies widely. Having reliable and valid theory-based measures, such as those that comprise the WJ III, is only part of the LD evaluation equation. In the LD field, it has long been recognized that such tools must be used within the context of an operational definition of LD (Kavale & Forness, 2000).

Considerable controversy surrounds the methods and procedures used in LD identification. Some practitioners support the approach known as the ability/achievement discrepancy model and base their diagnosis on criteria regarding the statistical rarity of an identified discrepancy. Other practitioners

base LD diagnoses on qualitative indicators (e.g., observations of test performance, work samples, teacher reports, and self-reports) and give little value to the
results of standardized testing. Sole reliance on either of these methods is problematic. Attempts to evaluate LDs may be hampered significantly by problems
that are inherent in the specific approach used in the course of assessment and
interpretation (Brackett & McPherson, 1996). Adherence to the best practices in
assessment is critical to the reliable and valid identification of LDs; this includes
not only selecting which tests should be used but also knowing *how* to use them
(Flanagan & Ortiz, 2002).

The purpose of this chapter is to demonstrate the use of the WJ III within the
context of an operational definition of LD. In this chapter a comprehensive
framework is presented for assessment that (a) follows established principles for
valid assessment and (b) incorporates a modern, theory-based operational definition of LD. Specifically, how practitioners can make decisions relevant to the
identification of LDs is illustrated, in particular those decisions related to the suf-
ficiency of a WJ III evaluation: normative versus deficit functioning, attributions
of performance, evaluations of potential mitigating factors, and evaluations of
underachievement. The information presented in this chapter can serve as one
model for completing LD referrals using the WJ III.

USING THE WJ III TO ASSESS INDIVIDUALS
REFERRED FOR LEARNING DIFFICULTIES

Figure 6-1 depicts the operational definition of LD developed by Flanagan et al.
(2002). This operational definition may be useful for applying the WJ III within the
context of an LD referral. The essential elements in defining LD, as illustrated in the
figure, include (a) inter-individual academic ability analysis, (b) evaluation of mitigating and exclusionary factors, (c) inter-individual cognitive ability analysis,
(d) integrated ability analysis, and (e) evaluation of interference with learning.
These elements are depicted as distinct levels in Figure 6-1 and together form an
operational definition of LD. The WJ III can be used effectively to gather information and test hypotheses at each level of this operational definition.

It is assumed that the levels of evaluation depicted in Figure 6-1 are undertaken
after prereferral assessment activities have been conducted and when a focused
evaluation of specific abilities and processes through standardized testing is
deemed necessary. Evaluation of the presence of a learning disability is based on
the assumption that an individual has been referred for testing specifically because
of observed learning difficulties, and that these difficulties have undergone an
appropriate remedial prereferral intervention or accommodation process with little
or no apparent success. Moreover, prior to beginning LD assessment with the WJ
III, other significant data sources could have (and probably should have) already
been uncovered within the context of these intervention activities. These data
may include results from informal testing, direct observation of behaviors, work

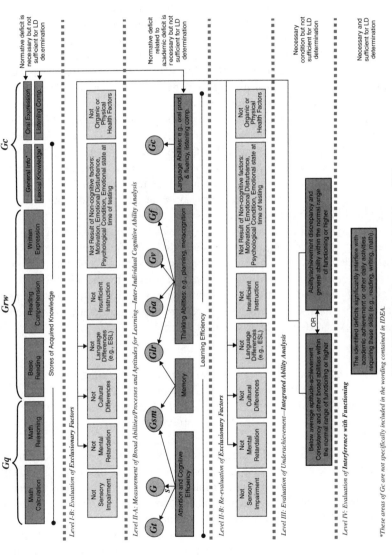

FIGURE 6-1   Operational definition of LD.

*These areas of Gc are not specifically included in the wording contained in IDEA.

samples, reports from people familiar with the individual's difficulties (e.g., teachers, parents), and information provided by the individual. In principle, Level I-A assessment should begin only after the scope and nature of an individual's learning difficulties have been documented (Flanagan et al., 2002).

It is important to note that before beginning Level I-A assessment with the WJ III, practitioners should decide what type of analysis will be conducted at Level III. For example, many practitioners in the United States are constrained by school district or state departmental regulations that necessitate an ability/achievement discrepancy analysis in the process of LD determination. Numerous procedures for discrepancy analysis are offered by the WJ III, only some of which may be relevant within the context of individual district and state criteria. Table 6-1 provides a brief description of and purpose for each discrepancy analysis offered by the WJ III. A review of Table 6-1 shows that only some of the WJ III discrepancy procedures are relevant to Flanagan et al.'s (2002) operational definition of LD. Therefore, if the WJ III is used within the context of this operational definition (see Figure 6-1), practitioners should first review Table 6-1 and select a priori the type of discrepancy analysis most appropriate for their purposes. Table 6-1 shows, for example, that if practitioners are required by law or circumstance to engage in ability/achievement discrepancy analysis for LD referrals, they should select the General Intellectual Ability (GIA)/achievement and intra-individual discrepancy procedures for data analysis at Level III. Selecting these analyses a priori guards against the unsupported practice of running multiple discrepancy analyses in an attempt to find a significant discrepancy for the purpose of satisfying existing criteria. In addition, when discrepancy analyses are selected a priori, practitioners can ensure that the tests necessary to run these analyses are included at Levels I-A and II-A of the assessment process.

LEVEL I-A: INTER-INDIVIDUAL ACADEMIC ABILITY ANALYSIS WITH THE WJ III— PERFORMANCE IN ACADEMIC SKILLS AND ACQUIRED KNOWLEDGE

Level I-A focuses on the basic concept of LD: that learning is somehow disrupted from its normal course on the basis of some type of internal dysfunction. Although the specific mechanism that inhibits learning is not directly observable, one can proceed on the assumption that it does manifest itself in observable phenomena, particularly academic achievement. Thus, the first component of the operational definition of LD involves documenting that some type of *learning dysfunction* exists. According to Flanagan et al. (2002), in the absence of academic weaknesses or deficits, the issue of LD is moot because such dysfunction is a necessary component of the definition. Therefore, in the Flanagan et al. (2002) method, the presence of a *normative deficit* established either through standardized testing, or through other means such as clinical observations of academic performance and work samples (or some combination thereof), is a necessary but insufficient condition for LD determination. Level I-A represents the first of what are, in effect, "tests" of the conditions necessary for determining the presence of a learning disability. When the "tests" at each of the four levels are passed, practitioners can be reasonably confident that a diagnosis of LD is appropriate.

The process at Level I-A involves comprehensive measurement of the major areas of academic achievement (e.g., reading, writing, and math abilities) or any subset of abilities that is the focus and purpose of the evaluation. The academic abilities depicted at this level in the operational definition are organized according to the seven areas of achievement specified in the federal definition of LD as outlined in the Individuals with Disabilities Education Act (IDEA) (Public Law [PL] 105-17). These seven areas are math calculation, math reasoning, basic reading, reading comprehension, written expression, listening comprehension, and oral expression (see Figure 6-1). Flanagan et al.'s (2002) rationale for using the IDEA labels was based primarily on the fact that these learning domains are included in most prevailing definitions of LD. They argue, however, that such definitions are not based on any particular theoretical formulation and thus are generally vague and nonspecific. Also, the labels may not be practical or sufficient. For example, the category of basic writing skills is omitted even though this is an area in which an individual's learning disability can be manifested. Therefore, for theoretical and psychometric reasons, the academic abilities depicted at Level I-A in Figure 6-1 are also organized according to the broad CHC abilities that encompass these achievement domains (i.e., *Gq*, *Grw*, and *Gc*).

Figure 6-1 shows that Level I-A abilities represent an individual's stores of acquired knowledge (Carroll, 1993; Woodcock, 1993). These specific knowledge bases (i.e., *Gq*, *Grw*, and *Gc*) develop almost exclusively as a function of formal instruction, schooling, and educationally related experiences. *Gc* is somewhat of an exception to this rule. According to Flanagan et al. (2002), the abilities that comprise *Gc* include examples not only of repositories of learned material (e.g., lexical knowledge, general information, and information about culture), but also abilities that reflect the processing of information, such as oral production, oral fluency, and listening ability. Consequently, a slight distinction is made between the narrow *Gc* abilities in Level I-A and those in Level II-A (see Figure 6-1). Flanagan and colleagues (2002) reasoned that the *Gc* abilities representing the stores of acquired knowledge are those that are likely to be of primary interest at Level I-A, whereas any assessment that progresses to Level II-A will likely focus more on the process-oriented abilities that comprise *Gc*. The dual nature of *Gc* is illustrated by the two-way arrows in Figure 6-1 that link *Gc* (and its narrow abilities) at Level I-A and Level II-A (see Flanagan et al., 2002, for a more detailed discussion).

The Flanagan et al. (2002) operational definition for LD evaluation is driven by presumptions of normalcy rather than preconceptions of dysfunction. Consequently, in the absence of any gross physiological trauma or developmental dysfunction, and given a history of appropriate and sufficient instruction and

TABLE 6-1 Types of Discrepancy Options Offered by the WJ III and Their Relevance to an Operational Definition of LD

Type of WJ III discrepancy analysis	Description	Correspondence to Flanagan et al.'s (2002) operational definition of LD	Comments
Intra-ability discrepancy options			
Intra-achievement	This discrepancy allows comparison of one area of academic achievement to the examinee's average performance in other achievement areas. An intra-achievement discrepancy is present within individuals who have specific achievement strengths or weaknesses. This type of information is an invaluable aid in instructional planning. Intra-achievement discrepancies can be calculated on four broad curricular areas or nine specific areas of academic performance	Level I-A	May be selected in combination with intra-cognitive discrepancy analysis
Intra-cognitive	This discrepancy is present within individuals who have specific cognitive strengths or weaknesses. Equal interest exists in either a strength or a weakness in one ability relative to the average of all other cognitive abilities. This profile of discrepancies can document areas of strength and weakness, provide insights for program planning, and contribute to a deeper understanding of the types of tasks that will be especially easy or difficult for an individual compared to his or her other abilities	Level II-A	May be selected in combination with intra-achievement discrepancy analysis
Intra-individual	This discrepancy reflects the amount of disparity among all cognitive and academic abilities. In this bidirectional comparison, the simultaneous relationships among various cognitive and academic skills are examined. This procedure provides a more complete picture of an examinee's functioning, which, in turn, could lead to the selection of the most appropriate service delivery and intervention options	Level III	If chosen, then selection of intra-achievement and/or intra-cognitive is not recommended unless the rationale for doing so is stated a priori

Ability/achievement discrepancy options

GIA/ACH (Std); GIA/ACH (Ext)	The General Intellectual Ability/achievement discrepancies are based on the first principal component (*g*) of the tests included in the GIA—Standard and the GIA—Extended scores. Use of these scores provides a generalized index of intellectual ability as the predictor measure	Level III	If selected, results of intra-individual analysis should also be considered
Oral Language/ Achievement	This discrepancy procedure compares oral language ability and academic performance and may be used to help substantiate the existence of a specific reading, math, or writing disability. Subjects with a significant negative discrepancy between oral language ability and achievement exhibit relative strengths in oral language with weaknesses in one or more areas of achievement	Level III	If selected, results of intra-individual analysis should also be considered
Predicted Achievement/ Achievement	This discrepancy procedure can be used in each academic area to determine if a subject is achieving commensurate with his or her current levels of associated cognitive abilities. This procedure uses differentially weighted composites to provide the best predictor of a given area of achievement at a given period of development	None	If selected, results of intra-ability analysis should also be considered. Within the context of the LD operational definition, the GIA/ACH and intra-ability analyses are recommended over this type of analysis

opportunity to learn, it is expected that an individual undergoing LD assessment will perform within normal limits (high- to low-average range of functioning) on WJ III tests (i.e., standard scores of 85 to 115, inclusive[1]). This is true for all the areas depicted at Level I-A in Figure 6-1 that may have been assessed. Testing this hypothesis involves comparing an examinee's performance to the WJ III standardization sample.

Table 6-2 provides a framework of norm-referenced score performances that may be used as a guide in interpreting WJ III standard scores. In general, the classifications provided in Table 6-2 closely approximate the classification schemata that are commonly used in assessment-related fields. For example, the descriptive classifications of performance are similar to those used in school and clinical psychology, whereas the normative classifications are typically used in the neuropsychology field. The Standard Score range and Percentile Rank range in Table 6-2, as well as their corresponding classifications, are provided as a means for establishing the criteria necessary to test a priori and a posteriori hypotheses that guide the interpretation process (Flanagan & Ortiz, 2002; Lezak, 1995). In the operational definition presented in Figure 6-1, the criterion for rejecting the hypothesis that performance is within normal limits is set at a level of greater than $+1$ SD and less than -1 SD from the mean. Adoption of such a range specifies that performance can be considered exceptional only when it falls either significantly above or significantly below the mean, indicating either normative strengths or normative weakness in functioning, respectively.

In essence, the first test in the operational definition (Level I-A in Figure 6-1) involves answering the following question: "Is performance on the WJ III ACH within normal limits relative to same-age peers in the general population?" Figure 6-2 shows the decision process that is involved in Level I-A assessment. Note that the comparison is not based on performance within the examinee, but rather on the examinee's individual performance against other individuals included in the WJ III standardization sample (see Table 6-2). Person-relative (or intra-individual) discrepancies, no matter how large, should not be interpreted as indicators of dysfunction unless one or more of the examinee's scores fall below the normal range of functioning (i.e., Standard Score < 85).

The *intra-ability* analyses of the WJ III (e.g., intra-achievement, intra-cognitive, and intra-individual) reflect statistical rarity in score differences as compared to the general population (based on actual discrepancy norms). However, it is important to remember that statistical rarity (which is associated with the term *abnormal*) is not synonymous with impairment or deficiency. Indeed, some deviations from normal or average are *valuable* deviations, and not all rarities are abnormal in the negative sense. Differences between test scores may be statistically significant

---

[1]Plus and minus 1 standard deviation of the normative mean (85–115, inclusive) for a test having a mean of 100 and a standard deviation of 15 is widely recognized as the range in which most people fall (i.e., 68% of the general population; see Lezak, 1995).

TABLE 6-2 Standard Scores, Percentile Ranks, and Corresponding Performance Classifications

Result		Classification of performance	
Standard Score range	Percentile Rank range	Descriptive	Normative
≥131	98 to 99+	Very superior	Normative strength, 16% of population (> +1 standard deviation)
121 to 130	92 to 97	Superior	
116 to 120	85 to 91	Above average	
111 to 115	76 to 84	High average	Normal limits, 68% of population (≤ +1 and ≥ −1 standard deviation)
90 to 110	25 to 75	Average	
85 to 89	16 to 24	Low average	
80 to 84	9 to 15	Below average	Normative weakness, 16% of population (< −1 standard deviation)
70 to 79	3 to 8	Deficient	
≤69	≤2	Very deficient	

Note: Some of these classifications are based in part on those described in Flanagan and Ortiz (2001), and Flanagan, Ortiz, Alfonso, and Mascolo (2002). The classifications in this table are recommended for use with Flanagan et al.'s operational definition of LD.

and rare, but they are not always or necessarily clinically meaningful. Practitioners should always seek to establish meaningful clinical significance as well as statistical significance. "The major weakness of the statistical rarity approach is that it has no values; it lacks any system for differentiating between desirable and undesirable behaviors. Of course, most users of the statistical rarity approach acknowledge that not all rarities should be identified as abnormal" (Alloy, Acocella, & Bootzin, 1996, p. 6).

The WJ III's intra-achievement discrepancy analysis can be used most effectively to identify an individual's *relative* strengths and weaknesses. The information generated from this type of person-relative analysis can be used to develop remedial strategies, educational plans, and specific academic interventions based on the data gathered at Level I-A. In addition to the intra-academic discrepancy procedure, the WJ III offers criterion-referenced scores (i.e., Instructional Range, Developmental Level Band, and Relative Proficiency Index) that also may be used in developing educational plans and interventions. However, population-relative data are necessary in evaluating an individual's performance in the domains assessed at Level I-A relative to a representative sample of same-age peers from the general population. The population-relative information offered by the WJ III includes standard scores, percentiles, *T*-scores, normal curve equivalents, and stanines. Information from these scores provides the necessary data to determine whether performance is within or outside of

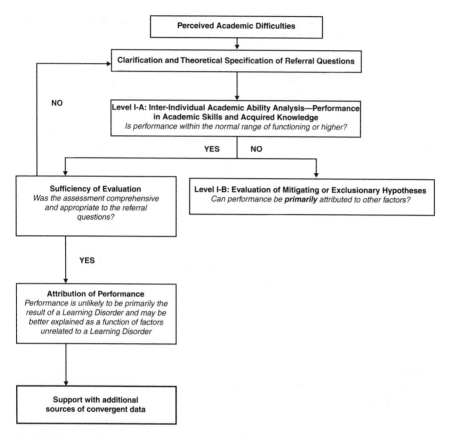

FIGURE 6-2   Decision flowchart for Level I-A of Flanagan et al.'s (2002) operational definition of LD. Adapted from Flanagan, Ortiz, Alfonso, and Mascolo (2002).

normal limits (i.e., ±1 SD from the normative mean) or any other range of ability (e.g., average, high average). Overall, the most information from an assessment can be derived when the results of both intra- and inter-individual ability analyses are considered. The latter is most useful for diagnostic purposes, and the former is most useful for instructional purposes (see Flanagan & Ortiz [2001] and Flanagan et al. [2002, 2003] for a more detailed discussion). Because the WJ III provides a range of criterion-referenced and norm-referenced scores, practitioners must understand their purposes and uses in order to realize the benefits and meaning of derived score information. Table 6-3 shows the tests of the WJ III that correspond to the Cattell–Horn–Carroll (CHC) abilities and LD areas listed in Level I-A of the operational definition. This table shows that all academic domains can be assessed with the WJ III, and some more comprehensively than others.

It is important to distinguish between adequate assessment or representation of a CHC broad ability, such as *Grw*, *Gc*, or *Gq*, and adequate assessment of federally specified academic achievement area, such as Basic Reading, Math Computation, or Listening Comprehension, within the context of LD determination. For example, Table 6-3 shows that the WJ III measures many qualitatively different aspects of *Grw*. The Letter–Word Identification and Passage Comprehension tests provide adequate representation of *Grw* because they assess two qualitatively different narrow abilities, namely, Reading Decoding (RD) and Reading Comprehension, Cloze Ability (CZ), respectively. However, using the WJ III subtests in this manner (e.g., to represent broad CHC abilities) provides a *sampling* of functioning in broad ability domains, as opposed to an *in-depth* assessment (see McGrew, Ford, & Woodcock, 2001). This sampling of functioning provides important baseline information that can be used to draw inferences about performance within a broad ability domain.

For example, if performance on the RD and CZ tests falls within normal limits, it may be reasonable to conclude that broad *Grw* ability is within normal limits, despite the fact that *Grw* encompasses more than RD and CZ abilities. However, a below-average *Grw* cluster (e.g., *Grw* scores between 80 and 84 on the RD and CZ tests) may be sufficient to conclude that the individual is limited in the broad *Grw* domain but may be insufficient to conclude that an individual is limited in either Basic Reading Skills or Reading Comprehension, which are two of the seven areas listed in the federal definition of LD. This outcome is possible because a single test (a) may not be sufficiently reliable to draw such conclusions, and (b) typically underrepresents the construct of interest (e.g., Basic Reading Skills). Thus, although adequate (or in-depth) assessment of *Grw* and *Gq* may be accomplished by administering two or more WJ III tests listed in the *Grw* and *Gq* columns in Table 6-3, adequate or in-depth assessment of the LD areas (e.g., Basic Reading Skills) requires that two or more tests that comprise the rows in Table 6-3 be administered.

To document that an individual has a deficit in Basic Reading Skills, for example, it is necessary to assess more than RD ability via the Letter–Word Identification test. Several other narrow CHC abilities measured by the WJ III contribute to an understanding of Basic Reading Skills. The first row in Table 6-3 shows that Word Attack (a measure of RD and PC:A), Sound Awareness (a measure of PC), and Reading Fluency (a measure of RS) may be administered in addition to Letter–Word Identification to achieve a more comprehensive evaluation of this academic domain. Therefore, when documentation of an individual's Basic Reading Skills is warranted, a test of RD (i.e., Letter–Word Identification) should be augmented with one or more qualitatively different tests of other basic reading skills (e.g., Reading Fluency, Word Attack). The same holds true for each LD academic assessment area. Therefore, prior to concluding that an individual has a deficit in one of the academic areas of LD from the federal definition, practitioners should ensure that the specific area in question is assessed adequately. That is, at least two CHC narrow abilities that correspond to an LD area (see Table 6-3)

TABLE 6-3 Representation of WJ III CHC Academic Abilities by LD Area

	CHC abilities listed at Level I-A of the operational definition of LD (Figure 6-1)				Other CHC abilities important in the assessment of LD		
LD areas listed in IDEA definition	Grw Reading^a	Grw Writing^a	Gq	Gc	Ga	Gs
Basic Reading Skills	L–W Identif. (RD) Word Attack (RD, PC:A)	—	—	—	Word Attack (RD, PC:A) *Sound Awareness* (PC)	Rdng. Fluency (RS)
Reading Comprehension	Pass. Comp. (RC, CZ) Rdng. Vocab (V, VL)	—	—	Rdng. Vocab (V, VL)	—	Rdng.—Fluency (RS)
Math Calculation	—	—	Calculation (A3)	—	—	Math Fluency (N, A3)
Math Reasoning	—	—	App. Problems (A3, KM, RQ) Quant. Concepts (KM, RQ)	—	—	—
Written Expression	—	Spelling (SG) Wrtg. Samples (WA) Editing (MY, EU) Punct. & Capit. (EU) *Spelling of Sounds* (SG, PC:A, PC:S)	—	Editing (MY, EU)	*Spelling of Sounds* (SG, PC:A, PC:S)	Writing Fluency (R9)
Oral Expression	—	—	—	Story Recall (LS; *Glr*-MM) Picture Vocab. (LD, VL)	—	—
Listening Comprehension	—	—	—	Understanding Direct. (LS, *Gsm*-MW) Oral Comp. (LS)	—	—

Other areas to consider at Level I

General Knowledge   —

  —   —   —

Verb. Comp. (VL, LD)   —
Gen. Info. (K0)
  Acad. Knwldg.
    (K0, K1, K2, A5)

Note: Story Recall–Delayed (*Glr*-MM) and Handwriting Legibility Scale are two supplemental measures on the WJ III ACH not included in this table. Test names appearing in italics are supplemental measures. Tests in boldface type are from the WJ III COG; all other tests listed are from the WJ III ACH. A3 = Math Achievement; A5 = Geography Achievement; EU = English Usage Knowledge; K0 = General (Verbal) Information; K1 = General Science Information; K2 = Information about Culture; KM = Math Knowledge; LD = Language Development; LS = Listening Ability; MM = Meaningful Memory; N = Number Fluency; PC:A = Phonetic Coding: Analysis; PC:S = Phonetic Coding: Synthesis; RC = Reading Comprehension; RD = Reading Decoding; RQ = Quantitative Reasoning; RS = Reading Speed; SG = Spelling Ability; V = Verbal (Printed) Language Comprehension; VL = Lexical Knowledge; WA = Writing Ability; WS = Writing Speed.

[a]The Reading and Writing (*Grw*) factor has been split in this table. This semantic distinction is intended to be congruent with the federal (United States) definition, which treats these abilities as distinct academic areas (e.g., basic reading, reading comprehension, written expression). This distinction was made for practical reasons and is not supported by current theory and research.

should be included in an assessment of that academic skill, particularly when other corroborating data are not available (see Flanagan et al., 2002, for an in-depth treatment of LD assessment).

The specific purpose for using the WJ III in the assessment of academic performance will determine whether the assessment should be organized in accordance with either the broad CHC academic abilities (*Grw*, *Gq*, etc.), or one or more of the seven areas of academic ability listed in the federal definition. It is likely that assessment of broad academic ability domains (e.g., *Grw*, *Gq*) will remain focused on ensuring adequate or in-depth representation of CHC abilities for practitioners who are either familiar with the WJ III or who are interested in directly comparing broad CHC academic abilities with broad CHC cognitive abilities (e.g., Flanagan et al., 2002; Flanagan & Ortiz, 2001). For example, the operational definition of LD presented in Figure 6-1 requires an evaluation of the relationship between functioning in specific academic skills and underlying cognitive processes and abilities. Organizing assessments according to broad CHC academic and cognitive ability domains would facilitate this process. Practitioners who engage in the assessment of both academic and cognitive abilities, therefore, would benefit from organizing their WJ III assessment in accordance with the broad CHC domains (Flanagan et al., 2002).

Not all practitioners, however, are involved in assessment of both academic and cognitive abilities. Many practitioners focus exclusively on either one or the other. For those practitioners who focus mainly on the assessment of academic abilities, it is likely that a focus on the seven academic areas of LD (as opposed to the CHC domains) would be desirable. For example, learning disability specialists, educational evaluators, reading specialists, and similar personnel involved in activities related to academic assessment may work as part of a multidisciplinary team in which their contribution focuses on assessment and evaluation of one or more academic ability domains, particularly in referrals of individuals with learning difficulties. When the focus of assessment is related primarily to academic abilities, organization of the WJ III tests according to commonly accepted academic ability domain labels, such as those listed in the federal definition of LD, may be more appropriate (see Table 6-3).

In addition to deciding on how to organize an academic assessment (i.e., by CHC or LD area), practitioners should decide whether a given assessment initially warrants a sampling of functioning in a given area or whether a more in-depth assessment of a particular academic skill area is warranted. This decision will affect how an initial WJ III assessment is organized. As stated previously, sampling functioning in a given CHC broad ability domain (such as *Grw* or *Gq*) would require selecting two qualitatively different measures of the broad ability listed in the corresponding column. In-depth assessment in either a CHC broad ability domain or LD area would require additional testing. The more qualitatively different aspects of the ability or academic skill that are measured, the better the estimate of functioning in that area (Messick, 1995).

In summary, practitioners may find it necessary to either sample functioning in a given domain (i.e., CHC broad academic ability or LD area) or conduct more in-depth or comprehensive assessments in one or more domains, depending on the purpose of evaluation. When either method is deemed necessary, Table 6-3 is useful for identifying the most appropriate WJ III measures to assess academic functioning.

LEVEL I-B: EVALUATION OF MITIGATING OR EXCLUSIONARY HYPOTHESES

At Level I-B, practitioners should evaluate whether a documented academic skill or knowledge deficit identified through Level I-A analysis of WJ III ACH data is *primarily* the result of individual noncognitive factors (e.g., motivation) or other "facilitator/inhibitor" factors that are external to the individual (e.g., inadequate instruction; see Information Processing Model [IPM] and related text in the WJ III COG *Examiner's Manual* [Mather & Woodcock, 2001]). According to Flanagan et al. (2002), because identified deficits do not automatically reflect an actual manifestation of LD, practitioners should refrain from ascribing causal links to LDs and instead develop alternative hypotheses related to other potential causes. For example, cultural or language differences are two common factors that can adversely affect test performance and result in data that appear to suggest LDs. In addition, lack of motivation, emotional disturbance, performance anxiety, psychiatric disorders, sensory impairments, medical conditions (e.g., hearing or vision problems), and so forth need to be ruled out as potential explanatory correlates to the deficiencies identified at Level I-A. The test at Level I-B involves answering the following question: "Are one or more external factors the primary reason for the deficit in academic performance uncovered at Level I-A?" Results of the WJ III Test Session Observations Checklist may be used, along with other data gathered at this level, to assist in answering this question.

The Test Session Observations Checklist, found on the WJ III Test Records, is a brief behavior rating scale that can be used to document pertinent examiner observations following testing. This seven-category rating scale provides information relating to an examinee's level of (a) conversational proficiency, (b) cooperation, (c) activity, (d) attention and concentration, (e) self-confidence, (f) care in responding, and (g) response to difficult tasks. Information from this checklist can help describe observed behaviors that may have facilitated or hindered an examinee's performance.

If the answer to the question at Level I-B is "yes" (meaning external factors are the primary cause of academic skill deficits), then the operational definition of LD is not met and assessment should not proceed to the next level. Assessment may proceed to Level II-A only when there is sufficient evidence and data to conclude confidently that the observed pattern of learning difficulties is not due primarily to exclusionary factors, even if they are contributory (Flanagan & Ortiz, 2001).

According to Flanagan et al. (2002), one of the major reasons for placing evaluation of exclusionary factors at this point in the assessment process is to provide a mechanism that is efficient in both time and effort and that may prevent the unnecessary administration of tests or imposition of further invasive and unneeded evaluative procedures. Use of standardized tests, such as the WJ III, cannot be considered a benign process. The implications and ramifications that can result from their use demands that they be carefully and selectively applied. Of course, it may not be possible to rule out completely and convincingly all of the potential factors at this stage in the assessment process. Indeed, many possibilities may explain poor performance on any given test of achievement. Therefore, proper assessment should seek to uncover and evaluate as many possibilities as is practical or necessary (Brackett & McPherson, 1996; Flanagan & Ortiz, 2001; Wilson, 1992).

It is possible that some relevant and important factors may not be apparent until later in the assessment process (i.e., following Level II-A assessment). For example, it may not be possible to rule out mild mental retardation or low general ability, because identification of these conditions are based, to a large extent, on data gathered at Level II-A of the operational definition. Evaluation of exclusionary factors, therefore, should be regarded as a recursive activity, occurring throughout the evaluation process. The process of ruling out external factors that contribute significantly to poor academic achievement, including psychological conditions, pervasive low ability, and so forth, begins early in the evaluation process and continues through the final level of analysis (Flanagan et al., 2002).

LEVEL II-A: INTER-INDIVIDUAL COGNITIVE ABILITY ANALYSIS WITH THE WJ III— PERFORMANCE IN ABILITIES/PROCESSES AND LEARNING EFFICIENCY

The test at Level II-A in Figure 6-1 is similar to the one at Level I-A, except that it is conducted with mostly cognitive (as opposed to academic) ability data from the WJ III. In general, the process of assessment at Level II-A, as with the measurement of abilities at Level I-A, proceeds with the expectation that an individual will perform within the general range of functioning (i.e., Standard Scores of 85 to 115, inclusive) in each of the areas represented in Level II-A (see Figure 6-1). The test at this level involves answering the question: "Is performance on the WJ III COG within normal limits relative to same-age peers in the general population?" The need to establish the presence of a deficiency in a particular cognitive ability or process that is either empirically or logically related to and the presumptive cause of the observed academic deficits (e.g., from Level I-A analysis and other data) is perhaps the most salient aspect of an operational definition of LD (Flanagan et al., 2002). This condition has historically been ill conceived and vague. A primary reason for the lack of clarity with regard to the *cognitive ability* or *processing deficiency* component of LD definitions may be the lack of a guiding theory to define this component. Clinicians have long understood the need to identify some sort of psychological dysfunction as an explanatory mechanism for deficient academic performance—yet there has been little if any theoretical specification to guide or support this practice; hence, a myriad of illogical assumptions are often made (Flanagan et al., 2002).

The cognitive abilities depicted at Level II-A in the operational definition of LD (see Figure 6-1) are organized in Table 6-4 according to their representation on the WJ III (i.e., *Gs, Gsm, Glr, Ga, Gv, Gf*, and *Gc*). Table 6-4 further organizes these CHC abilities according to the processes they represent primarily within an information-processing perspective, including attention and cognitive efficiency, memory, "thinking abilities," executive processes, and language abilities (e.g., Woodcock, 1993; Dean & Woodcock, 1999). The latter category represents the collection of *Gc* narrow abilities that, according to Flanagan et al. (2002), more accurately reflect processing skills as opposed to the abilities that represent stores of acquired knowledge that were evaluated at Level I-A.

Generally speaking, the abilities depicted at Level II-A provide valuable information about an individual's *learning efficiency*. Development of the cognitive abilities represented at this level tends to be less dependent on formal classroom instruction and schooling as compared to the academic abilities presented at Level I-A. Furthermore, specific or narrow abilities across many of the CHC areas listed in Level II-A may be combined to yield specific aptitudes for learning in different areas (e.g., reading, math, writing). These aptitudes are expected to be consistent with their respective academic areas measured at Level I-A (Flanagan et al., 2002).

Table 6-5 provides a summary of the recent literature on the relationship between cognitive abilities and specific academic achievements (Flanagan et al., 2002). For example, narrow abilities subsumed by *Gc* (lexical knowledge, language development, listening ability), *Gsm* (working memory), *Ga* (phonetic coding), *Glr* (naming facility), and *Gs* (perceptual speed) have been found to be related significantly to reading achievement. Similarly narrow abilities within these broad CHC domains have been identified as related to writing achievement. With the exception of *Glr, Ga*, and *Gv*, narrow abilities within the areas of *Gf, Gc, Gsm*, and *Gs* have demonstrated significant relationships with math achievement, and *Gf* (induction and general sequential reasoning) in particular has shown a stronger relationship to this academic area compared to its connections with areas of reading and writing. The information in Table 6-5 can be used to identify those CHC abilities that should receive primary consideration in the design of WJ III assessments for individuals referred for reading, math, or writing difficulties. Tables 6-3 and 6-4 may be used to help identify the WJ III tests that assess these abilities. The information in Table 6-5 can be used to determine whether the data support a relationship between academic and cognitive deficits that may have been uncovered at Levels I-A and II-A.

It is important to note that deficiency in a cognitive ability or process may be established through means other than standardized test performance.

TABLE 6-4 Representation of WJ III CHC Cognitive Abilities by Information-Processing Area

CHC ability	Attention and cognitive efficiency	Memory	Metacognition: Thinking abilities and executive processes	Language abilities
Gs	Visual Matching (P) Decision Speed (R4)[a] **Pair Cancellation** (R9, AC)[b]			
Gsm		Numbers Reversed (MW)[b] Memory for Words (MS) Auditory Working Mem. (MW)[b]		
Glr		Visual–Aud. Lrn. (MA) Retrieval Fluency (FI)[a] Visual–Aud. Lrn.—Delayed (MA) Rapid Picture Naming (NA)[a]	Visual–Aud. Lrn. (MA) Retrieval Fluency (FI)[a] Visual–Aud. Lrn.—Delayed (MA) Rapid Picture Naming (NA)[a]	
Ga			Sound Blending (PC:S) Auditory Attention (US, UR)[b] Incomplete Words (PC:A)	
Gv			Spatial Relations (Vz, SR) Picture Recog. (MV) **Planning** (SS[c], Gf-RG)	
Gf			**Concept Form.** (I) Analysis–Synthesis (RG)	

Gc

Verbal Comp. (VL, LD^c)
Understndg. Dir. (LS, LD^c)
Oral Comp. (LS)
Reading Vocab. (V, VL)
Picture Vocab. (LD,^{c} VL)

Note: In the last column, tests in italics are from the WJ III ACH; all other tests listed in the table are from the WJ III COG. Tests in boldface type comprise the Executive Processing Cluster on the WJ III. AC = Attention/Concentration; FI = Ideational Fluency; I = Induction; K0 = General (Verbal) Information; LD = Language Development; MA = Associative Memory; MS = Memory Span; MV = Visual Memory; MW = Working Memory; NA = Naming Facility; P = Perceptual Speed; PC:A = Phonetic Coding: Analysis; PC:S = Phonetic Coding: Synthesis; R4 = Semantic Processing Speed; RG = General (Sequential) Reasoning; SR = Spatial Relations; SS = Spatial Scanning; US = Speech/Sound Discrimination; UR = Resistance to Auditory Distortion; Vz = Visualization; VL = Lexical Knowledge.

^{a}This test contributes to the Cognitive Fluency Cluster.

^{b}This test contributes to the Broad Attention Cluster.

^{c}In Tables 6-3–6-5 only, LD = Language Development. Elsewhere in text, LD = Learning Disability. In this table only, SS = Spatial Scanning (elsewhere, SS = standard score).

TABLE 6-5 Relations between CHC Cognitive Abilities and Academic Achievement

CHC ability	Reading achievement	Math achievement	Writing achievement
Gf	Inductive (I) and general sequential reasoning (RG) abilities play a moderate role in reading comprehension	**Inductive (I) and general sequential (RG) reasoning abilities are consistently very important at all ages**	Inductive (I) and general sequential reasoning abilities are related to basic writing skills primarily during the elementary school years (e.g., ages 6 to 13) and are consistently related to written expression at all ages
Gc	**Language development (LD), lexical knowledge (VL), and listening ability (LS) are important at all ages. These abilities become knowledge increasingly more important with age**	**Language development (LD), lexical knowledge (VL), and listening abilities (LS) are important at all ages. These abilities become knowledge increasingly more important with age**	**Language development (LD), lexical knowledge (VL), and general information (K0) are important primarily after age 7. These abilities become increasingly more important with age**
Gsm	**Memory span (MS) is important especially when evaluated within the context of working memory**	Memory span (MS) is important especially when evaluated within the context of working memory	Memory span (MS) is important to writing, especially spelling skills, whereas working memory has shown relations with advanced writing skills (e.g., written expression)
Gv		May be important primarily for higher level or advanced mathematics (e.g., geometry, calculus)	
Ga	**Phonetic coding (PC) or "phonological awareness/processing" is very important during the elementary school years**		**Phonetic coding (PC), or "phonological awareness/processing," is very important during the elementary school years for both basic writing skills and written expression (primarily before age 11)**

Glr	Naming facility (NA), or "rapid automatic naming," is very important during the elementary school years. Associative memory (MA) may be somewhat important at select ages (e.g., age 6)	Naming facility (NA), or "rapid automatic naming," has demonstrated relations with written expression, primarily the fluency aspect of writing
Gs	Perceptual speed (P) abilities are important during all school years, particularly the elementary school years	Perceptual speed (P) abilities are important during all school years for basic writing and are related to written expression at all ages

Note: The absence of comments for a particular CHC ability and achievement area (e.g., *Ga* and mathematics) indicates that the research reviewed either did not report any significant relations between the respective CHC ability and the achievement area, or if findings were reported, they were weak and were for only a limited number of studies. Comments in boldface type represent the CHC abilities that showed the strongest and most consistent relations with the respective achievement domain.

From D.P. Flanagan, S.O. Ortiz, V.C. Alfonso, J.T. Mascolo. Achievement Test Desk Reference (ATDR): Comprehensive Assessment and Learning Disabilities. Published by Allyn and Bacon, Boston, MA. Copyright © 2002 by Pearson Education. Reprinted by permission of the publisher.

For example, deficient orthographic processing may not manifest itself on standardized tests of ability in the form of low score performance simply because no existing, valid measures have been designed specifically to assess this skill. However, difficulties with orthographic processing may be documented through appropriate, supported, error-analysis procedures and clinical observations that are consistent with current research. Data generated from Level II-A analyses, like those generated at Level I-A, also provide input for Level III analyses, should the process advance to this level. Typically, in addition to data on specific cognitive abilities and processes, a global ability score (e.g., WJ III General Intellectual Ability) is derived for later use in ability/achievement discrepancy analyses, if necessary and appropriate (see Flanagan et al., 2002). Regardless of the specific nature of the data gathered, the test at Level II-A is passed only when two specific criteria are met: (a) identification of deficiency in at least one area of cognitive ability or processing and (b) identification of logical, theoretically specified, or empirical links between at least one area of cognitive deficiency and the academic skill(s) deficiency identified in the Level I-A analyses (see Table 6-5).

The first criterion is necessary to establish the presence of a psychological processing disorder or dysfunction as defined by the literature pertaining to LD (see Flanagan et al., 2002, for a discussion). Poor achievement performance, in the absence of any cognitive impairment, does not meet any existing operational definition of LD, including the one proposed here (Flanagan et al., 2003, 2002). In addition, as was the case at Level I-A, person-relative (e.g., intra-cognitive) discrepancies, no matter how large, should not be interpreted as indicators of dysfunction unless one or more of the examinee's scores falls below and outside the normal limits of functioning (i.e., Standard Score [SS] < 85). Results of the WJ III intra-cognitive discrepancy analysis provide valuable information regarding whether an individual is functioning as well as could be expected given his or her present cognitive abilities. However, the WJ III intra-ability discrepancy procedure (i.e., cognitive and academic) was not designed for identifying a specific LD (McGrew et al., 2001). Because results from intra-cognitive analyses may or may not reveal dysfunction, it is necessary to evaluate any and all scores used in intra-ability analyses in terms of where they fall relative to the general population (see Flanagan & Ortiz, 2001).

The second criterion is necessary to establish a valid basis for linking the cognitive deficiency with the academic deficiency. For example, when an individual is referred for reading difficulties, it is reasonable to assume that manifest reading difficulties would emerge via Level I-A assessment and, if the reading difficulties are not the primary result of exclusionary factors (Level I-B assessment), then one or more cognitive abilities or processes underlying reading achievement may emerge as weaknesses following Level II-A assessment. This assumption is supported by theory-based research (see Table 6-5).

LEVEL II-B: REEVALUATION OF MITIGATING
OR EXCLUSIONARY FACTORS

Determining the presence of a cognitive deficiency that is empirically or logi-cally related to the deficiency identified at Level I-A is the core of the test at Level II-A, but it is not the only consideration. Although the absence of a defensible relationship between Level I-A and Level II-A deficiencies may eliminate the need to advance to Level III assessment, the process can also be halted or redi-rected through reevaluation of mitigating or exclusionary hypotheses as identified in Level II-B (see Figure 6-1). The presence of verifiable cognitive deficiencies that are directly related to academic performance difficulties is fundamental to the operational definition of LD. However, it is necessary to determine once again whether such deficiencies are primarily the result of mitigating or exclusionary factors. Hypotheses regarding reasonable explanations for observed cognitive deficiencies must be tested to ensure that the data accurately reflect true ability. Reevaluation of these mitigating and exclusionary factors illustrates the recursive and iterative nature of the LD evaluation process. Reliable and valid measurement of LD depends on being able to exclude the many factors that could negatively affect performance on standardized tests. When such factors have been evaluated carefully and excluded as the primary reason for the observed cognitive deficien-cies at this level, and when the two necessary criteria for the test at Level II-A have been met, the process may advance to Level III (Flanagan et al., 2002). Figure 6-3 shows the decision process that is involved in Level II-A and Level II-B assessment.

LEVEL III: INTEGRATED ABILITY ANALYSIS
WITH THE WJ III—EVALUATION
OF UNDERACHIEVEMENT

Advancement to Level III automatically implies that three necessary condi-tions for determination of LD have already been met: (a) one or more inter-individual academic ability deficits have been identified from WJ III (or other) data at Level I-A, (b) one or more inter-individual cognitive ability or processing deficiencies have been identified from WJ III (or other) data at Level II-A, and (c) the academic and cognitive deficiencies are related, either logically or empir-ically, and have been determined not to be the primary result of exclusionary factors (Levels I-B and II-B). What has not been yet determined, however, is whether the pattern of results (from Level I-A and Level II-A assessments) sup-ports either (a) the notion of underachievement in the manner that might be expected in cases of suspected LD or (b) the notion of underachievement caused by low overall ability, mild mental retardation, or other factors known to have an adverse impact on both academic and cognitive performance (e.g., sensory-motor

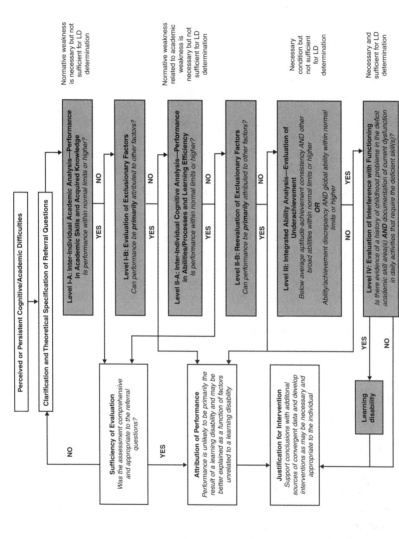

FIGURE 6-3   Decision flowchart for assessment of Flanagan et al.'s (2002) operational definition of LD. Adapted from Flanagan, Ortiz, Alfonso, and Mascolo (2002).

handicaps, lack of English language proficiency). Thus, the test at Level III involves answering the following question: "Does the examinee possess specific, circumscribed, and related academic and cognitive deficiencies that exist within an otherwise normal ability profile?" Answering "yes" to this question satisfies the Level III criterion of underachievement. According to Flanagan et al. (2002), the process of determining whether the criterion of underachievement is met at Level III can take one of two forms: analysis of below-average aptitude–achievement consistency, or analysis of ability/achievement discrepancy.

Flanagan et al.'s (2002) below-average aptitude–achievement consistency analysis is conceptually similar to the WJ III's intra-individual discrepancy analysis. However, evaluation at Level III does not necessarily seek to find only statistically significant, person-relative (intra-individual) discrepancies within the context of an examinee's own pattern of cognitive or academic abilities (although this information is useful). Rather, the nature of intra-individual analysis (called *integrated ability analysis* in Figure 6-1) at this point is concerned more specifically with evaluating whether a circumscribed set of related cognitive and academic deficiencies, relative to same-age peers in the general population, exists within an otherwise normal ability profile. In order to evaluate whether this condition of underachievement exists, in addition to evaluating results from the WJ III intra-individual discrepancy analysis, it is necessary to consider performance in all of the areas included in this analysis from a population-relative (interindividual) perspective.

Table 6-6 includes the results of a WJ III intra-individual discrepancy analysis; it is used here to demonstrate how practitioners can integrate person-relative and population-relative data. A review of the last column in Table 6-6 shows that Working Memory and Math Calculation emerged as significant intra-individual weaknesses (see bold-face entries in Table 6-6). This finding is supported by the extant literature on the relationship between cognitive functions and math achievement (see Table 6-5). However, an examination of the second column in Table 6-6 shows that, in addition to the actual standard scores for the Working Memory and Math Calculation Skills clusters (71 and 66, respectively), there are also similar deficiencies in the areas of Basic Writing Skills (74) and Written Expression (78; see italic entries in Table 6-6). Not only are Basic Writing Skills and Written Expression considered deficient relative to that of same-age peers in the general population (Table 6-2), but there is also an empirically supported relationship between working memory and writing achievement (see Table 6-5). In addition, a review of the actual standard scores in Table 6-6 shows that this case has a number of cognitive and academic abilities that are within the general range of functioning relative to those of same-age peers (e.g., *Gc, Gv, Ga, Gs,* Oral Expression, and Listening Comprehension). This example shows that when both person-relative information and population-relative information are considered conjointly, a complete picture of an individual's circumscribed (or domain specific) levels of function and dysfunction emerges. In summary, the data presented in Table 6-6 demonstrate consistency between a specific aptitude for

TABLE 6-6   Example of Intra-Individual Discrepancy Analysis from the WJ III Compuscore
and Profiles Program

Intra-individual discrepancies	Actual	Predicted	Difference	PR	SD	Significant at ±1.50 SD (SEE)
Comp–Knowledge (*Gc*)	93	85	+8	78	+0.77	No
Long-Term Retrieval (*Glr*)	86	88	−2	43	−0.17	No
Vis-Spatial Think (*Gv*)	96	93	+3	58	+0.19	No
Auditory Process (*Ga*)	95	91	+4	61	+0.28	No
Fluid Reasoning (*Gf*)	87	88	−1	47	−0.06	No
Process Speed (*Gs*)	106	91	+15	88	+1.15	No
Short-Term Mem (*Gsm*)	86	90	−4	37	−0.33	No
Phonemic Aware	108	90	+18	91	+1.36	No
Working Memory	**71**	**90**	**−19**	**5**	**−1.63**	**Yes**
Basic Reading Skills	85	87	−2	41	−0.24	No
Reading Comp	85	88	−3	40	−0.26	No
Math Calc Skills	**66**	**91**	**−25**	**2**	**−1.99**	**Yes**
Math Reasoning	80	87	−7	21	−0.81	No
Basic Writing Skills	*74*	*89*	*−15*	*9*	*−1.36*	*No*
Written Expression	*78*	*90*	*−12*	*17*	*−0.96*	*No*
Oral Expression	100	88	+12	85	+1.05	No
Listening Comp	98	87	+11	84	+0.99	No
Academic Knowledge	94	88	+6	73	+0.60	No

learning (i.e., Working Memory) and actual achievement in the areas of math and writing, which constitutes a circumscribed and related set of deficiencies within an otherwise normal ability profile. Such a finding passes the Level III test and thus meets the Level III criterion that is necessary for an LD diagnosis.

When the assessment activities at Level II-A are designed in a manner that generates broad CHC ability clusters and a WJ III GIA cluster, it is possible to engage in ability/achievement discrepancy analyses. If the academic and cognitive deficiencies identified at Levels I-A and II-A are logically or empirically related to one another and are both outside and below normal limits *and* lower than most remaining broad CHC ability clusters, and if the measures of the specific ability deficiencies identified at Level II-A are not included in the GIA, it would then be logical to expect that global ability will be within the general range of functioning and significantly discrepant from the identified academic deficiencies. A discrepancy occurs in this case primarily because the global ability composite contains few, if any tests on which the individual has difficulties; therefore, expectation of consistency is unwarranted. If, on the other hand, the global ability score was derived using one or more measures in which the individual demonstrated a deficiency, then the global ability estimate may be attenuated to such an extent that it is not significantly discrepant from the academic area(s) of deficiency. In this situation evaluation of consistency becomes salient, and if practitioners use the WJ III, they must examine functioning across the broad CHC clusters to determine whether some (but not necessarily all) broad abilities fall within or above the normal range of functioning.

Although the criterion of a below-average aptitude–achievement consistency within an otherwise normal ability profile represents a reasonable and research-based method for evaluating underachievement, the same cannot be said for discrepancy analysis. Discrepancy analysis should not be used as the sole or primary criterion for LD determination (Flanagan et al., 2002, 2003; Fletcher et al., 1998; Heath & Kush, 1991; McGrew, Ford, & Woodcock, 2001; Siegel, 1999; Stanovich, 1991). In the operational definition of LD proposed by Flanagan et al. (2002), identification of an ability/achievement discrepancy is accommodated in light of existing laws and state regulations, but it is neither a necessary nor sufficient condition for determination of LD. The aptitude–achievement consistency analysis, however, when conducted within the context of the operational definition of LD presented in Figure 6-1, may be used to diagnose LD because it is both psychometrically and theoretically defensible and it is supported by the domain specific LD literature (Flanagan et al., 2002).

LEVEL IV: EVALUATION OF INTERFERENCE WITH LEARNING

When the LD determination process reaches this point, presumably the criteria at each previous level were met. Additional gathering and analysis of data hardly seem necessary. But an operational definition of LD based only on the criteria of previous levels would be incomplete. This is because one of the basic eligibility requirements contained in both the legal and clinical prescriptions for diagnosing LD refers to whether the suspected learning problem(s) actually results in significant or substantial academic failure or other restrictions or limitations in daily life functioning.

The legal and diagnostic specifications of LD necessitate that practitioners review the whole of the collected data and make a professional judgment about the extent of the negative impact that any measured deficit has on an individual's performance in one or more areas of learning or academic achievement. Essentially, Level IV analysis serves as a kind of quality-control test designed to prevent the application of an LD diagnosis in cases in which "real-world" functioning is not in fact impaired as compared to same-age peers in the general population, regardless of the patterns seen in the data.

This final criterion requires practitioners to take a very broad survey not only of the entire array of data collected during the course of the assessment but also of the real-world manifestations and practical implications of any presumed disability. In general, if the principles inherent in Levels I-A through III have been adhered to and the criteria have been met, it is likely that in the vast majority of cases, Level IV analysis serves only to confirm conclusions that have already been drawn. However, in cases in which data may be equivocal or when procedures other than those specified in the comprehensive framework proposed herein have been utilized, Level IV analysis becomes an important safety valve, ensuring that any representations of an LD suggested by the data are indeed manifest in observable impairments in one or more areas of functioning in real-life settings. Level IV analysis helps to guard against the tendency to identify LDs on the basis of insufficient data or inappropriate criteria.

Space limitations preclude the inclusion of lengthy case illustrations of how the WJ III may be used within the context of Flanagan et al.'s operational definition of LD. Therefore, the reader is referred to Flanagan et al. (2002, 2003) for step-by-step examples and case presentations that demonstrate how the operational definition is used in practice. Prior to reading these cases or implementing the operational definition of LD, the reader may wish to review the decision flowchart in Figure 6-3. This flowchart will familiarize the reader with the various decision points that practitioners may face throughout the course of gathering data in cases of suspected LD.

CONCLUSIONS

When the criteria at each level of the operational definition are met, it may be concluded that the WJ III (and all other) data gathered are sufficient to support a diagnosis of LD. The operational definition presented in this chapter provides a guide to the process of using and interpreting the WJ III effectively within the context of LD referrals. Because the specifications and procedures implied by this definition are grounded in the same theory and research that guided the development of the WJ III, this instrument is particularly well suited for use in LD evaluations that subscribe to Flanagan et al.s' (2002) operational definition.

REFERENCES

Alloy, L. B., Acocella, J., & Bootzin, R. R. (1996). *Abnormal psychology*: *Current perspectives* (7th ed.). New York: McGraw-Hill.
Brackett, J., & McPherson, A. (1996). Learning disabilities diagnosis in postsecondary students: A comparison of discrepancy-based diagnostic models. In N. Gregg, C. Hoy, & A. F. Gay (Eds.), *Adults with learning disabilities: Theoretical and practical perspectives* (pp. 68–84). New York: Guilford.
Carroll, J. B. (1993). *Human cognitive abilities: A survey of factor-analytic studies*. Cambridge, UK: Cambridge University Press.

Dean, R., & Woodcock, R. (1999). *The WJ-R and Bateria-R in neuropsychological assessment (Research Report No. 3)*. Itasca, IL: Riverside Publishing.

Flanagan, D. P., & Ortiz, S. O. (2001). *Essentials of cross-battery assessment*. New York: John Wiley & Sons.

Flanagan, D. P., & Ortiz, S. O. (2002). Best practices in intellectual assessment: Future directions. In A. Thomas & J. Grimes (Eds.), *Best practices in school psychology–Fourth edition* (pp. 1351–1372). Washington DC: The National Association of School Psychologists.

Flanagan, D. P., Keiser, S., Bernier, J., & Ortiz, S. O. (2003). *Diagnosing learning disability in adulthood*. Boston: Allyn & Bacon.

Flanagan, D. P., McGrew, K. S., & Ortiz, S. O. (2000). *The Wechsler intelligence scales and Gf–Gc theory: A contemporary approach to interpretation*, Boston: Allyn & Bacon.

Flanagan, D. P., Ortiz, S. O., Alfonso, V., & Mascolo, J. (2002). *The achievement test desk reference (ATDR): Comprehensive assessment and learning disabilities*. Boston: Allyn & Bacon.

Fletcher, J. M., Francis, D. J., Shaywitz, S. E., Lyon, G. R., Foorman, B. R., Stuebing, K. K., & Shaywitz, B. A. (1998). Intelligent testing and the discrepancy model for children with learning disabilities. *Learning Disabilities Research & Practice, 13*(4), 186–203.

Heath, C. P., & Kush, J. C. (1991). Use of discrepancy formulas in the assessment of learning disabilities. In J. E. Obrzut & G. W. Hynd (Eds.), *Neuropsychological foundations of learning disabilities: A handbook of issues, methods and practice* (pp. 287–307). New York: Academic Press.

Individual with Disabilities Education Act (IDEA) amendments, Public Law 105-17, 11 stat. 37, 20 U.S.C. (26) (1997) § 1401.

Kavale, K. A., & Forness, S. R. (2000). What definitions of learning disability say and don't say: A critical analysis. *Journal of Learning Disabilities, 33*, 239–256.

Lezak, M. D. (1995). *Neuropsychological assessment* (3rd ed.). New York: Oxford University Press.

Mather, N., & Woodcock, R. W. (2001). Examiner's manual. *Woodcock–Johnson III Tests of Achievement*. Itasca, IL: Riverside Publishing.

McGrew, K. S., Ford, L., & Woodcock, R. W. (2002). The Woodcock–Johnson Battery—Third Edition (WJ III). In Alan S. Kaufman and Elizabeth O. Lichtenberger (authors), *Assessing adolescent and adult intelligence* (2nd ed., pp. 561–627). Boston: Allyn & Bacon.

McGrew, K. S., & Flanagan, D. P. (1998). *The intelligence test desk reference (ITDR): Gf–Gc cross-battery assessment*. Boston: Allyn & Bacon.

Messick, S. (1995). Validity of psychological assessment: Validation of inferences from persons' responses and performances as scientific inquiry into score meaning. In A.E. Kazdin (Ed.), *Methodological issues and strategies in clinical research* (2nd ed., pp. 241–261). Washington, DC: American Psychological Association.

Siegel, L. S. (1999). Issues in the definition and diagnosis of learning disabilities: A perspective on Guckenberger v. Boston University. *Journal of Learning Disabilities, 32*, 304–319.

Stanovich, K. (1991). Discrepancy definitions of reading disability: Has intelligence led us astray? *Reading Research Quarterly, 26*, 7–29.

Wilson, B. C. (1992). The neuropsychological assessment of the preschool child: A branching model. In I. Rapm & S. I. Segalowitz (Eds.), *Handbook of neuropsychology: Child neuropsychology* (Vol. 6, pp. 377–394).

Woodcock, R. W. (1993). An information processing view of Gf–Gc theory. *Journal of Psychoeducational Assessment* [Monograph Series: WJ-R Monograph], 80–102.

Woodcock, R. W., McGrew, K. S., & Mather, N. (2001). *Woodcock–Johnson III tests of achievement*. Itasca, IL: Riverside Publishing.

7

USING THE WOODCOCK–JOHNSON III TESTS OF ACHIEVEMENT WITH THE WISC-III AND WAIS-III TO DETERMINE A SPECIFIC LEARNING DISABILITY

LEADELLE PHELPS

State University of New York at Buffalo, Buffalo, New York 14260

KEVIN S. MCGREW

The University of Minnesota, Minneapolis, Minnesota 55455

The current procedure most frequently used for diagnosing a specific learning disability is based on the discrepancy model wherein a child must demonstrate a significant difference between her or his ability (as measured by an intelligence test) and achievement (as measured by an individually administered standardized assessment tool). A few assumptions are implicit in this model: (a) achievement and ability are highly correlated such that *expected achievement* is predicted by IQ; (b) the ability/achievement discrepancy denotes a disability whereas comparable scores signify functioning at or near capacity; and (c) scores on a variety of intelligence and achievement tests are equivalent and stable across time (e.g., testing completed 3 months later with different IQ and achievement measures will yield comparable discrepancy results) (Bocian, Beebe, MacMillan, & Gresham, 1999; Fletcher et al., 1998).

ABILITY/ACHIEVEMENT
DISCREPANCY CALCULATIONS

The ability/achievement discrepancy model has its roots in the original definition utilized in Public Law 94-142 (U.S. Office of Education, 1977) and continues via reauthorization in the Individuals with Disabilities Education Act (IDEA) of 1990. There is, however, a lack of consensus on how such a discrepancy should be calculated. Three methods of calculation are frequently employed: (a) using an IQ score to predict *expected grade level* of achievement, (b) using a *simple comparison* of IQ and achievement standard scores, and (c) utilizing *regression calculations* that adjust the standard score comparisons by the observed correlation between the IQ and achievement measures (Evans, 1990). The use of real discrepancy norms, which is possible only when the ability and achievement tests are conormed *and* the regression-adjusted discrepancy scores obtained in the standardization sample are converted to normative scores, represents a fourth method (McGrew, 1994). This fourth method is demonstrated in the ability/achievement discrepancy procedures that are available when the *Woodcock–Johnson III Tests of Cognitive Abilities* (WJ III COG) and *Woodcock–Johnson III Tests of Achievement* (WJ III ACH) are used together.

The first two methods exhibit difficulties that are inherent in their application. First, any formula that uses *expected grade level* is inherently flawed because grade formulas are uneven metrics that have considerable variability across ages (Reynolds, 1984). Second, the simple comparison of standard scores between two tests is problematic because (a) the correlation between achievement and IQ is far from perfect, a condition that necessitates a correction for regression to the mean, and (b) mean IQ scores increase at a rate of approximately three points per decade, an occurrence known as the Flynn effect (Flynn, 1984). Illustrations of these issues follow.

First, a one-point drop or increase in IQ does not result in a corresponding one-point drop or increase in achievement. For this phenomenon to occur, the correlation between ability and achievement measures must be a perfect one-to-one relationship. Such is never the case. The imperfect ability/achievement correlation results in *regression to the mean*, the phenomenon wherein a high score on one test will, on average, be accompanied by a lower score on the second test, and vice versa (Reynolds, 1984). The lack of a one-to-one ability/achievement score correspondence results in the simple difference method overidentifying high-ability individuals and underidentifying low-ability individuals as having a significant discrepancy. Finally, because achievement measures do not evidence the Flynn effect that is so apparent in cognitive tests (Gaskill & Brantley, 1996; Truscott & Phelps, 2002), a significant discrepancy is more likely to occur if an outdated IQ test is utilized. To avoid the further confoundment of the Flynn effect, examiners should utilize ability and achievement tests that are normed simultaneously or in close time proximity.

A less statistically flawed approach for determining an ability/achievement discrepancy is to use a regression formula that corrects for regression to the mean (Evans, 1993). The equation to correct for regression to the mean and compute the predicted achievement score is calculated by the following formula (Reynolds, 1990):

$$Y = r_{xy} (X - 100) + 100,$$

where Y = predicted achievement score, r_{xy} = correlation of the administered ability and achievement measures, and X = score obtained on the ability measure.

The actual discrepancy is then determined by comparing the *predicted* achievement score to the *actual* achievement score. Utilizing a point-difference criterion (e.g., 15-point difference) for the determination of learning disability (LD) eligibility requires the use of the standard error of estimate (SEE), *not* the actual standard deviation (SD). The SEE is the standard deviation of the actual achievement test around the predicted achievement score. The higher the correlation between the ability and achievement measures, the lower the SEE. It is the SEE, not the actual SD, that is used to determine if the discrepancy is significant (Pedhazur, 1997). This last point is critical to note because a +1 SEE value typically ranges from 10 to 12 standard score points—*not* 15 standard score points (McGrew, Werder, & Woodcock, 1991; McGrew & Woodcock, 2001). When using the regression model, the sample upon which the observed correlations were calculated should be sizeable and representative of the population at large. Finally, correlations should be obtained at different developmental (age or grade) levels, given that the relationship between ability and achievement varies developmentally (McGrew, 1994).

WJ III ABILITY/ACHIEVEMENT DISCREPANCY OPTIONS

The highest level of technical adequacy for ability/achievement discrepancy scores is present when (a) ability and achievement tests are normed on the same nationally representative sample, (b) the correlations used to adjust for regression effects vary as a function of ability and developmental level (age or grade) and curriculum area (e.g., reading, math), and (c) the actual regression-adjusted ability/achievement discrepancy scores are calculated in the norm sample and then used to construct actual discrepancy norms. Because the WJ III ability/achievement discrepancy procedure meets these conditions for optimal technical adequacy, the resulting WJ III norm-based ability/achievement discrepancies are the best possible estimates of discrepancies when using the WJ III COG and WJ III ACH batteries.

However, due either to tradition, preference, and/or guidelines, assessment professionals may choose not to use the WJ III COG as their measure of ability. One of the most frequent practices is the use of one of the Wechsler batteries as the measure of cognitive ability together with the WJ III ACH. In this situation, given that the ability and achievement measures are not conormed (which results in the inability to calculate developmental- and curriculum-sensitive regression-adjusted discrepancy scores), it is necessary to use the regression calculation procedures outlined above.

Using a sample ($N = 252$) of nonreferred individuals aged 6 to 16 years, Schrank, Becker, and Decker (2001) developed a regression table that outlines the expected achievement scores on various tests and cluster scores of the WJ III ACH battery given the *Wechsler Intelligence Scale for Children—Third Edition* (WISC-III) Full-Scale IQ score (Wechsler, 1991). The calculations in this table correct for regression to the mean and are accompanied by a worksheet that uses the SEE to determine significance. These materials are provided in Appendices B and C of this volume. Table 7-1 provides the obtained and corrected correlations between the WISC-III and WJ III ACH clusters and the SEE for the sample. Table 7-2 contains similar data for the *Wechsler Adult Intelligence Scale—Third Edition* (WAIS-III) (Wechsler, 1994) and the W-J III ACH clusters ($N = 89$). Caution should be exercised when using the WAIS-III/WJ III data for ability/achievement discrepancy calculations because (a) the sample size is somewhat small and (b) the WAIS-III Full-Scale IQ mean was 113.00, suggesting that the sample may not be representative of the population at large. Furthermore, caution must be exercised given that the calculations underlying the tables use a single correlation in each curriculum area for all possible age or grade levels. Therefore, the resultant expected scores do not account for any developmental changes in the correlations between the Wechsler ability measure and WJ III ACH measures. If developmental considerations of ability/achievement discrepancy calculations are deemed important, users are strongly encouraged to use the WJ III COG together with the WJ III ACH and interpret the discrepancy scores provided by the WJ III scoring software.

TABLE 7-1 Obtained and Corrected Correlations between the WJ III ACH Scores and the WISC-III Full-Scale IQ Score ($N = 252$)

WJ III Cluster	WISC-III Full-Scale IQ[a]		Mean	SD	SEE
	Obtained	Corrected			
Broad Reading	.61	.72	105.24	12.95	10.47
Broad Math	.60	.70	106.72	13.44	10.77
Broad Written Language	.43	.57	104.85	12.12	12.35

[a]WISC-III Full-Scale IQ Score Mean = 103.87, SD = 12.90.

TABLE 7-2 Obtained and Corrected Correlations between the WJ III ACH Scores and the WAIS-III Full-Scale IQ Score ($N = 89$)

WJ III Cluster	WAIS-III Full-Scale IQ[a]		Mean	SD	SEE
	Obtained	Corrected			
Broad Reading	.53	.60	106.16	13.01	12.03
Broad Math	.62	.67	107.35	13.53	11.10
Broad Written Language	.56	.64	108.66	12.44	11.50

[a]WAIS-III Full-Scale IQ Score Mean = 113.00, SD = 14.58.

ALTERNATIVES TO THE ABILITY/ ACHIEVEMENT DISCREPANCY MODEL

Even when the more statistically sound ability/achievement regression model is employed, considerable debate remains regarding the appropriateness of the discrepancy model. Because numerous studies utilizing traditional IQ tests (e.g., WISC-III; *Stanford–Binet Intelligence Scale—Fourth Edition* [SB-IV]) (Thorndike, Hagen, & Sattler, 1986) have failed to find a distinct cognitive profile for children classified as having an LD, many researchers have advocated that an assessment of ability (i.e., administration of an IQ test) is irrelevant (Fletcher et al., 1994, 1998; Gresham & Witt, 1997; Reschly & Ysseldyke, 1995; Vellutino, Scanlon, & Lyon, 2000). Other researchers have recommended either constructing new cognitive measures that are more sensitive to specific processing domains (Daniel, 1997; Wilson & Reschly, 1996) or developing new theoretical approaches for interpreting existing measures (Flanagan, McGrew, & Ortiz, 2000; McGrew & Flanagan, 1998).

Flanagan (2000) advocates that IQ tests must be theory based in order for the relationship between unique cognitive processes (e.g., fluid reasoning, short-term memory) and specific academic skills (e.g., reading comprehension) to be clearly understood and translated into related treatment procedures. Although "assessment for intervention" has long been a tenet of school psychology training, it has seldom been translated into practice (Wilson & Reschly, 1996). When a test is atheoretical in nature, it greatly constrains and limits any inferences that can be drawn from subtest, factor, or composite score analyses, especially as to how scores are related to processing competencies or treatment planning (Flanagan et al., 2000; Keith & Witta, 1997).

Alternative definitions of LD explored in the literature include (a) low achievement in and of itself (e.g., scoring at, or below, 1 standard deviation on an achievement measure) and (b) failure to respond to treatment (Hoskyn & Swanson, 2000; Iversen & Tummer, 1993; Stanovich & Stanovich, 1997; Vellutino et al., 2000; Wasik & Slavin, 1993). Depending on the definition of "low achievement" (e.g., 1 standard deviation below the normative mean), the first alternative would mean that approximately 16% of the population would be classified as having an LD, a figure that would bankrupt federal and state funding sources. Lowering the cutoff score (e.g., using the bottom 8% rather than the bottom 16% of the population) would be one alternative to this option. The second definition assumes that "children who are difficult to remediate may be accurately classified as disabled readers, whereas many, or most, children who are readily remediated may not be accurately classified as disabled learners" (Vellutino et al., 2000, p. 228). The second definition further assumes that school districts provide quality, individualized instruction that accurately separates children whose poor reading is a function of lack of opportunity from those who cannot perform in spite of receiving appropriate tutoring (Pressley, 1998).

A third alternative is the identification of processes that are specific to children with reading disorders (i.e., skills that reliably differentiate children with reading disorders from children who are low achievers). It is evident that global IQ scores, in isolation, predict neither reading success nor response to treatment for children experiencing delays in reading acquisition (Siegel, 1992; Vellutino et al., 2000). Specific cognitive processes that do provide assistance in identification of such children include language-based competencies such as phonemic awareness (knowledge of letter/sound relationships); rapid automatized naming of letters, symbols, and familiar words; and the decoding of more difficult words and pseudowords (Fletcher et al., 1994, 1998: Hoskyn & Swanson, 2000; Lyon & Moats, 1997; Stanovich & Siegel, 1994; Stanovich & Stanovich, 1997).

The primary impetus for evaluating relevant processing deficits specific to reading disorders comes from the Phonological-Core-Difference Model advocated by Stanovich and Siegel (e.g., Stanovich, 1988; Stanovich & Siegel, 1994). The assumptions of this model are (a) that specialized processes (such as phonological competencies) are not closely related to global functioning (such as composite IQ) yet underlie reading failure; (b) that both slow learners and children with reading disorders share a common phonological core deficit that is the source of their reading problems; and (c) that slow learners (comparable IQ/achievement scores) exhibit a flat cognitive profile (e.g., below-average visual-spatial, verbal, and nonverbal problem-solving skills) and multiple academic skill deficits (all academic areas are deflated), whereas children with reading disorders (average IQ but below-average reading) perform much better on nonverbal cognitive measures and display far more variability in their academic skill competencies (e.g., above-average performance in math but below-average functioning in reading comprehension). A recent meta-analysis confirmed these findings and indicated that verbal IQ was a strong mediating variable (Hoskyn & Swanson, 2000). The researchers found that the higher the verbal IQ, the more likely cognitive processing differences existed between the two groups. That is, children who were slow learners exhibited a flat cognitive processing profile and lower verbal IQ, whereas children with reading disabilities displayed marked variability in cognitive processing profiles and higher verbal IQs.

Until federal and state requirements for a significant discrepancy in determining a specific learning disability are altered, many professionals must continue the existing procedures, however flawed. It is advocated, therefore, that practitioners (a) determine the ability/achievement discrepancy via procedures that calculate standard score differences with correction for regression to the mean (i.e., use of regression tables such as those provided in Appendix B or actual discrepancy norms); (b) administer ability and achievement measures that are normed simultaneously or in close time proximity; (c) utilize ability tests that are theory based; and (d) assess processing skills that are related specifically to the disability in question (e.g., phonological awareness in the evaluation of a reading disorder). It should be noted that when assessing processing skills for determining a learning disability, if the processing skills are both deficient and part of a global ability cluster, then the ability/achievement cluster may not emerge as significant, a finding that, in and of itself, does not negate a diagnosis of LD. These recommendations are illustrated in the following case study.

CASE STUDY

Approximately 80% of children classified as having an LD evidence reading impairment (Meyer, 2000). Numerous research groups (e.g., Bowman Gray School of Medicine, Florida State University, Johns Hopkins University, University of Colorado, University of Houston, University of Miami, Yale University) funded by the National Institute of Child Health and Human Development have concluded that robust predictors of reading comprehension difficulties include deficits in (a) phonological awareness (knowledge of sound/letter relationships), (b) rapid automatized naming of letters and highly familiar simple words, and (c) decoding or "sounding out" more difficult words and pseudowords (Fletcher et al., 1998; Hoskyn & Swanson, 2000; Lyon & Moats, 1997; Stanovich & Siegel, 1994; Stanovich & Stanovich, 1997). For older students, the best prognostic indicator for *continued* reading problems is the inability to rapidly recognize and name words (sight word vocabulary) (Badian, 1999; Meyer et al., 1998). Given these data, analyses of phoneme competencies (knowledge of sound–symbol correspondence, decoding of words and pseudowords, sound blending) and basic reading skills (letter–word identification, rapid reading of simple words and sentences, sight word vocabulary) are appropriate and should be completed *in addition to* the customary assessment for the determination of an ability/achievement discrepancy.

BACKGROUND INFORMATION

Zachary P. (a pseudonym), a 7-year-old male, was referred for psychological testing at the end of the first grade. School records indicated that at the end of his kindergarten year, Zachary's teacher reported that he had gained few reading readiness skills and recommended retention at the kindergarten level. Because he was one of the oldest children in his class and was large for his age, both the school and his parents decided to promote him to the first grade. He was, however, targeted to receive remedial reading services throughout the first grade. These services consisted of small-group (three to four students) instruction three times a week.

In spite of the remedial reading services, Zachary continued to make inadequate progress in reading, and at the end of first grade, both the remedial reading and regular classroom teachers referred him to the Committee on Special Education for consideration of LD services. Both teachers noted that Zachary could not decode new words, read simple sentences very slowly, and exhibited poor reading comprehension.

A developmental history completed by Mrs. P. indicated that Zachary was a full-term baby and weighed 8 pounds, 7 ounces at birth. His medical history was unremarkable except for numerous episodes of acute otitis media (middle ear infections) that lasted until he was approximately 5 years old. Medical treatment included amoxicillan (an antibiotic) and several sets of ventilating tubes.

Developmental milestones were within the normal range except for speech acquisition. At age 3 years, Zachary's vocabulary was so limited that his pediatrician requested an evaluation be completed at a speech and language clinic affiliated with the local university. At the time, Mrs. P. estimated that Zachary's vocabulary was approximately 100 words, with most vocalizations being one word (e.g., wa-wa, go, no). He communicated primarily with gestures. Because the speech and language assessment results indicated significant delays in receptive and expressive language, Zachary was referred for, and received, speech therapy at the clinic until he entered kindergarten. These services were discontinued at that time when a reevaluation by the school indicated he no longer qualified for services.

ASSESSMENT RESULTS

Table 7-3 presents Zachary's results for the WISC-III. Using the Cattell–Horn–Carroll (CHC) theoretical framework to interpret the WISC-III (refer to Flanagan et al., 2000 for a complete discussion), it appears that Zachary's crystallized abilities (*Gc*; Information, Similarities, Vocabulary, Comprehension) are somewhat weak. Given his medical history of recurrent otitis media and early language impairment, his continued difficulties in language-related processing are to be expected (for a review, refer to Phelps, 1998). In comparison, his visual processing (*Gv*; Block Design, Object Assembly) and processing speed (*Gs*; Coding, Symbol Search) are more normalized.

Applying the Phonological-Core-Difference Model discussed earlier (Stanovich, 1988; Stanovich & Siegel, 1994), Zachary would appear to have a classic reading disorder. That is, he performs better on nonverbal tasks and

TABLE 7-3   WISC-III Subtest and Index Scores for Zachary P.

Verbal Subtest	Standard Score	Performance Subtest	Standard Score
Information	8	Picture Completion	11
Similarities	7	Coding	12
Arithmetic	10	Picture Arrangement	10
Vocabulary	11	Block Design	10
Comprehension	8	Object Assembly	11
Digit Span	9	Symbol Search	12

Factor Indices	Standard Score	Percentile
Verbal Comprehension	92	30
Perceptual Organization	104	61
Freedom from Distractibility	98	45
Processing Speed	112	79

IQ Indices	Standard Score	Percentile
Verbal IQ	93	32
Performance IQ	106	68
Full-Scale IQ	99	47

displays variability in his cognitive processing profile. Likewise, following the Phonological-Core-Difference Model, Zachary's WISC-III Verbal IQ score would suggest that he could benefit from, and respond well to, individualized reading instruction (Hoskyn & Swanson, 2000).

The results in Table 7-4 from the WJ III ACH validate the presence of a reading disorder. Zachary has notable difficulty with phonological processing. His ability to decode/encode pseudowords (Word Attack, Spelling of Sounds) is

TABLE 7-4   WJ III ACH Test and Cluster Results for Zachary P.

Test	Standard Score	Percentile
Letter–Word Identification	85	17
Reading Fluency	86	18
Passage Comprehension	89	23
Word Attack	83	13
Spelling of Sounds	78	7
Sound Awareness	76	6

Cluster Scores	Standard Score	Percentile
Broad Reading	84	15
Phoneme/Grapheme Knowledge	81	11

impaired. His sound–letter knowledge and auditory processing (Sound Awareness, Letter–Word Identification) are very weak. As a result, he cannot rapidly recognize and read simple words (Reading Fluency). In spite of receiving remedial reading instruction for one academic year, his reading comprehension (Passage Comprehension) is notably below average. These data demonstrate that the primary cause of Zachary's reading difficulties is a core phonological processing deficit.

Zachary's WISC-III Full-Scale IQ and WJ III ACH Broad Reading cluster are applied to the "WISC-III/WJ III Ability/Achievement Discrepancy Calculation Worksheet" (Appendix C) provided with the regression table in Appendix B. Using the regression table, Zachary's expected achievement is a standard score of 99 (based on an IQ score of 99 with the correction for regression to the mean). The resulting standard score discrepancy between the *actual* achievement score and the *predicted* achievement score is 15 points. The discrepancy is 18 points when using the WJ III Phoneme/Grapheme Knowledge cluster. Using the standard error of estimate provided in the calculation worksheet (SEE = 10.47 for Broad Reading cluster), Zachary has a 1.43 standard deviation achievement–achievement discrepancy.

The testing suggests that Zachary would likely benefit from daily individualized instruction in basic sound–letter correspondence, sound blending, and word attack. In addition, Zachary should practice spelling words that have dissimilar spelling yet are phonetically similar (e.g., bee, sea, key) and words that have disparate spelling and meaning yet are phonologically identical (e.g., there, their, they're; too, to, two). Academic instruction reflecting empirically supported cognitive strategies and directed practice in phonetic decoding and drilling are essential. Refer to Swanson, Carson, & Sachse-Lee (1996) and Chapter 3, this volume, for recommended instructional procedures appropriate for students with learning disabilities.

CONCLUSIONS

Most psychological assessments completed in school systems are intended to substantiate learning difficulties evidenced in the classroom. Special education services typically cannot be mandated until an individually administered battery of tests verifies a significant discrepancy between ability and achievement. Selection of the ability and achievement scales is an important decision for psychologists. The discrepancy is meaningless unless scores on a variety of intelligence and achievement tests are relatively equivalent and stable across time. In considering assessment options, professionals are well advised to select batteries that are current (i.e., normed within the last decade); have excellent standardization, reliability, and validity data; and were normed simultaneously or in close time proximity to one another. In addition, examiners should choose tests that are theoretically sound and sensitive to specific processing domains. Such data will greatly aid in the interpretation and translation of results into related intervention procedures.

The discrepancy model for determining a specific learning disability is fraught with debate. Nonetheless, a best-practices model dictates that grade-level differences should not be utilized for determining a learning disability because of the inherent variability across age groupings. Likewise, the simple standard score difference procedure is an unsound practice because of regression to the mean. Therefore, when assessment professionals choose not to use the WJ III COG together with the WJ III ACH, but instead select a different measure of cognitive functioning to combine with the WJ III ACH, utilization of a regression formula that corrects for regression to the mean and computes predicted achievement scores is the most statistically sound practice.

In addition to assessment for the determination of a significant ability/achievement discrepancy, examiners should also evaluate specific processing domains directly related to the disability. Although there is a paucity of data for math disorders, there is considerable empirically supported data regarding reading deficits. An evaluation of these critical competencies is essential for guiding subsequent intervention procedures.

REFERENCES

Badian, N. A. (1999). Reading disability defined as a discrepancy between listening and reading comprehension: A longitudinal study of stability, gender differences, and prevalence. *Journal of Learning Disabilities, 32*, 138–148.

Bocian, K. M., Beebe, M. E., MacMillan, D. L., & Gresham, F. M. (1999). Competing paradigms in learning disabilities classification by schools and the variations in the meaning of discrepant achievement. *Learning Disabilities Research, 14*, 1–14.

Daniel, M. H. (1997). Intelligence testing: Status and trends. *American Psychologist, 52*, 1038–1045.

Evans, L. D. (1990). A conceptual overview of the regression discrepancy model for evaluating severe discrepancy between IQ and achievement scores. *Journal of Learning Disabilities, 22*, 406–412.

Evans, L. D. (1993). A comparison of the impact of regression and simple difference discrepancy models on identification rates. *Journal of School Psychology, 30*, 17–29.

Flanagan, D. P. (2000). Wechsler-based CHC cross-battery assessment and reading achievement: Strengthening the validity of interpretations drawn from the Wechsler test scores. *School Psychology Quarterly, 15*, 295–329.

Flanagan, D. P., McGrew, K. S., & Ortiz, S. O. (2000). *The Wechsler intelligence scales and Gf–Gc theory: A contemporary approach to interpretation.* Boston: Allyn & Bacon.

Fletcher, J. M., Francis, D. J., Shaywitz, S. E., Lyon, G. R., Foorman, B. R., Studbing, K. K., & Shaywitz, B. A. (1998). Intelligence testing and the discrepancy model for children with learning disabilities. *Learning Disabilities Research and Practice, 13*, 186–203.

Fletcher, J. M., Shaywitz, S. E., Shankweiler, D. P., Katz, L., Liberman, I. Y., Stuebing, K. K., Francis, D. J., Fowler, A. E., & Shaywitz, B. A. (1994). Cognitive profiles of reading disability: Comparisons of discrepancy and low achievement definitions. *Journal of Educational Psychology, 86*, 6–23.

Flynn, J. R. (1984). The mean IQ of Americans: Massive gains 1932 to 1978. *Psychological Bulletin, 95*, 29–51.

Gaskill, F. W., & Brantley, J. C. (1996). Changes in ability and achievement scores over time: Implications for children classified as learning disabled. *Journal of Psychoeducational Assessment, 14*, 220–228.

Gresham, F. M., & Witt, J. C. (1997). Utility of intelligence tests for treatment planning, classification, and placement decisions: Recent empirical findings and future directions. *School Psychology Quarterly, 12*, 220–228.

Hoskyn, M., & Swanson, H. L. (2000). Cognitive processing of low achievers and children with reading disabilities: A selective meta-analytic review of the published literature. *School Psychology Review, 29*, 102–119.

Iversen, S., & Tummer, W. (1993). Phonological processing skills and the reading recovery program. *Journal of Educational Psychology, 85*, 112–126.

Keith, T. Z., & Witta, E. L. (1997). Hierarchical and cross-age confirmatory factor analysis of the WISC-III: What does it measure? *School Psychology Quarterly, 12*, 89–107.

Lyon, G. R., & Moats, L. C. (1997). Critical conceptual and methodological considerations in reading intervention research. *Journal of Learning Disabilities, 30*, 578–588.

McGrew, K. S. (1994). *Clinical interpretation of the Woodcock–Johnson Tests of Cognitive Ability—Revised*. Boston: Allyn & Bacon.

McGrew, K. S., & Flanagan, D. P. (1998). *The intelligence test desk reference (ITDR): A Gf–Gc cross-battery approach to intelligence test interpretation*. Boston: Allyn & Bacon.

McGrew, K. S., Werder, J. K., & Woodcock, R. W. (1991). *WJ-R technical manual*. Itasca, IL: Riverside Publishing.

McGrew, K. S., & Woodcock, R. W. (2001). Technical manual. *Woodcock–Johnson III*. Itasca, IL: Riverside Publishing.

Meyer, M. S. (2000). The ability/achievement discrepancy: Does it contribute to an understanding of learning disabilities? *Educational Psychology Review, 12*, 315–357.

Meyer, M. S., Wood, F. B., Hart, L. A., & Felton, R. H. (1998). Selective predictive value of rapid automatized naming in poor readers. *Journal of Learning Disabilities, 31*, 106–117.

Pedhazur, E. J. (1997). *Multiple regression in psychology and education*. New York: McGraw-Hill.

Phelps, L. (1998). Utility of the WISC-III for children with language impairments. In A. Prifitera & D. H. Saklofske (Eds.), *WISC-III clinical use and interpretation* (pp. 157–174). New York: Academic Press.

Pressley, M. (1998). *Reading instruction that works: The case for balanced teaching*. New York: Guilford Press.

Reschly, D. J., & Ysseldyke, J. E. (1995). School psychology paradigm shift. In A. Thomas & J. Grimes (Eds.), *Best practices in school psychology—III* (pp. 17–31). Washington, DC: National Association of School Psychologists.

Reynolds, C. R. (1984). Critical measurement issues in learning disabilities. *Journal of Special Education, 18*, 451–476.

Reynolds, C. R. (1990). Conceptual and technical problems in learning disability diagnosis. In C. R. Reynolds & R. W. Kamphaus (Eds.), *Handbook of psychological and educational assessment of children: Intelligence and achievement* (pp. 571–592). New York: Guilford Press.

Schrank, F. A., Becker, K. A., & Decker, S. (2001). *Calculating ability/achievement Discrepancies between the Wechsler intelligence scale for children—third edition and the Woodcock–Johnson III tests of achievement* (Assessment Service Bulletin No. 4). Itasca, IL: Riverside Publishing.

Siegel, L. S. (1992). An evaluation of the discrepancy definition of dyslexia. *Journal of Learning Disabilities, 25*, 618–629.

Stanovich, K. E. (1988). Explaining the differences between the dyslexic and the garden-variety poor reader: The phonological-core variable-difference model. *Journal of Learning Disabilities, 21*, 590–612.

Stanovich, K. E., & Siegel, L. S. (1994). Phenotypic performance profile of children with reading disabilities: A regression-based test of the phonological-core variable-difference model. *Journal of Educational Psychology, 86*, 24–53.

Stanovich, K. E., & Stanovich, P. J. (1997). Further thoughts on aptitude/achievement discrepancy. *Educational Psychology in Practice, 13,* 3–8.

Swanson, H. L., Carson, C., & Sachse-Lee, C. M. (1996). A selective synthesis of intervention research for students with learning disabilities. *School Psychology Review, 25,* 370–391.

Thorndike, R. L., Hagan, E. P., & Sattler, J. M. (1986). *Stanford–Binet intelligence test—fourth edition.* Itasca, IL: Riverside Publishing.

Truscott, S. D., & Phelps, L. (2002, February). *The Flynn effect changes IQ and influences special education classifications.* Symposium presentation at the National Association of School Psychologists, Chicago, IL.

United States Office of Education (1977). Assistance to states for education for handicapped children: Procedures for evaluating specific learning disabilities. *Federal Register, 42,* G1082–G1085.

Vellutino, F. R., Scanlon, D. M., & Lyon, G. R. (2000). Differentiating between difficult-to-remediate and readily remediated poor readers. *Journal of Learning Disabilities, 33,* 224–238.

Wasik, B. A., & Slavin, R. R. (1993). Preventing early reading failure with one-to-one tutoring: A review of five programs. *Reading Research Quarterly, 28,* 179–200.

Wechsler, D. (1991). *Wechsler intelligence scale for children—third edition.* San Antonio, TX: Psychological Corporation.

Wechsler, D. (1994). *Wechsler adult intelligence scale—third edition.* San Antonio, TX: Psychological Corporation.

Wilson, M. S., & Reschly, D. J. (1996). Assessment in school psychology training and practice. *School Psychology Review, 25,* 9–23.

8

ASSESSMENT WITH THE WOODCOCK–JOHNSON III AND YOUNG CHILDREN

MARY E. TUSING

Eau Claire Area School District
Eau Claire, Wisconsin 54701

DENISE E. MARICLE

Department of Education,
School of Counseling,
School Psychology
University of Wisconsin—Stout,
Menomonie, Wisconsin 54751

LAURIE FORD

Department of Educational and Counseling Psychology and Special Education
University of British Columbia
Vancouver, British Columbia, Canada V6T 1Z4

The level of expertise brought to the assessment process by an examiner can significantly impact the usefulness of child-specific information gained from any test (Flanagan, Mascolo, & Genshaft, 2000). This is particularly true for the Woodcock–Johnson III (WJ III) (Woodcock, McGrew, & Mather, 2001) when used with young children, given the test's comprehensiveness and complexity. Determining "where to begin" in an effort to use the WJ III effectively with young children (children 2 to 6 years of age) is dependent on a sound understanding of the psychometric and qualitative characteristics of the battery. In addition, it is necessary to have an understanding of the theoretical background of the WJ III, including the developmental nature of cognitive abilities measured by the battery and an understanding of how changes in these cognitive abilities are related to patterns of learning, preacademic growth, and academic growth. When used by an examiner with expertise in the assessment of young children and knowledge of the developmental nature of Cattell–Horn–Carroll (CHC) abilities, the WJ III can add to a comprehensive and meaningful evaluation of young children's abilities.

In the following chapter, the psychometric properties of the WJ III for young children are reviewed. Findings from research in developmental psychology, cognitive science, neuropsychology, and early education are incorporated to describe the developmental nature of abilities assessed by the WJ III and their relationship to early learning. Emphasis is placed on understanding the relationship between findings in research and issues in applied measurement practice. A rationale for test selection at various ages is provided along with illustrative case studies. The manner in which the WJ III Diagnostic Supplement contributes to an understanding of functioning in young children is also introduced.

A RATIONALE FOR NORM-REFERENCED ASSESSMENT WITH YOUNG CHILDREN

The ability to predict future academic or cognitive performance and to prescribe specific interventions from norm-referenced assessment tools for young children validly has been criticized (Bagnato & Neisworth, 1994; Barnett, Macmann, & Carey, 1992). Indeed, poor technical qualities of measures for children younger than 4 years and behavioral and linguistic challenges associated with completing standardized assessment tools limit the utility of norm-referenced assessment techniques with young children (Bracken, 1994; Flanagan & Alfonso, 1995). More recently, however, assessment with young children has been viewed as a "field in transition" (Meisels & Atkins-Burnett, 2001). Reviews of the technical adequacy of assessment tools for young children suggest continued improvement and increased sophistication in test construction (Bradley-Johnson, 2001; Flanagan & Alfonso, 1995). Further, efforts toward devising developmentally appropriate tasks to include on standardized assessment batteries have also increased (Coalson, Weiss, Zhu, Spruill, & Crockett, 2002; Korkman, Kirk, & Kemp, 1998; Mullen, 1995; Roid & Miller, 1997).

The trend toward improved assessment tools coincides with an ever-increasing need for reliable and valid assessment practices with young children. For example, in the United States, federal and state educational initiatives have led to the expansion of early childhood special education, early intervention, and school readiness programs in the public schools. Further, practitioners in clinical settings require assessment tools useful in the diagnosis and monitoring of acquired and neurodevelopmental disorders typically manifested prior to school age (i.e., Attention Deficit/Hyperactivity Disorder, brain injury, genetic abnormalities) (Espy, Kaufmann, Glisky, & McDiarmid, 2001; Hooper, 2000). As the relationships between specific cognitive abilities and later learning continue to be defined better (Evans, Floyd, McGrew, & Leforgee, in press; Konold, Juel, & McKinnon, 1999; Lonigan, Burgess, & Anthony, 2000; Whitehurst & Lonigan, 1998), it is anticipated that assessment tools for young children that reliably differentiate children's abilities into specific predictive domains, such as the WJ III, may also bridge the gap between assessment findings and treatment determination.

USING THE WJ III WITH YOUNG CHILDREN

The examiner interested in using the WJ III with young children should be well versed in the unique skills required for valid assessment of the young child. Young children often need additional time to warm up to the examiner and to separate from their caregiver. Further, given that young children are notorious for varying levels of motivation and attention, creating a testing environment in which the child is most likely to demonstrate his or her best effort is critical. Several features of the WJ III can facilitate this process. For example, test administration during standardization did not follow a set order of individual test presentation, which contributed to the strong stability of WJ III tests. This allows the user to administer tests out of sequence, if necessary. As a result, tests requiring only a pointing response can be administered first to children who are slow to warm up. Natural gaps between individual tests also allow the examiner to provide breaks during testing or to divide the assessment into several sessions if the child's attention or effort varies. Further, stimuli presented in the easels are child friendly and colorful, and young children tend to respond well to the use of a tape recorder for some tests. For users less experienced in testing young children, Chapter 3 of the Examiner's Manual (Mather & Woodcock, 2001) and Chapter 5 of the Diagnostic Supplement (Ford, 2003) provide additional administration considerations for young children.

CHANGES TO THE WJ III

Relative to the *Woodcock–Johnson Psychoeducational Battery—Revised* (WJ-R) (Woodcock & Johnson, 1989), the number of children age 5 years and younger included in the WJ III standardization sample was increased by over 40%. As a result, the standardization sample is more than adequate in size at each 1-year interval between ages 2:0 and 6:0. It is also representative of seven different demographic variables (gender, race, Hispanic origin, mother and father's level of educational experience, region, and community size) and five types of childcare settings (day care, home care, early learning center settings, preschools, and kindergartens). Test development for the WJ III also resulted in the addition of *early development* items on several tests, with the goal of enhancing usefulness of the battery at younger age ranges. Table 8-1 highlights the changes that were made to the WJ III that were intended to improve the utility of the battery with young children. The fact that tasks from each test are presented in a similar fashion across all age ranges allows for comparisons to be made across a child's performance at various stages of development. As a result, when the Relative Proficiency Index (RPI) and W Difference (W Diff) scores are examined, information useful for monitoring a child's progress in early intervention and primary grade settings can be determined.

In revising the WJ III, emphasis was also placed on creating a battery of tests with greater generalizability at the cluster score level, particularly the CHC cognitive ability clusters (McGrew & Woodcock, 2001). As a result, new tests were added to provide at least two qualitatively distinct measures for each cluster. This change has its greatest impact for those familiar with using the WJ-R Tests of Cognitive Abilities (COG) with young children. The WJ-R contained five early development tests, which were those tests with the best technical properties for children 5 years and younger (Schrank, 1991). These five tests then combined to produce an overall Broad Cognitive Ability: Early Development Scale score. As a result of the changes to the WJ III, three of the five early development tests were not retained on the WJ III COG Standard or Extended batteries, specifically Memory for Names, Memory for Sentences, and Visual Closure, and one is now included in modified form on both the cognitive and the achievement batteries, i.e., Picture Vocabulary. Therefore, the WJ III COG does not, by itself, provide an overall General Intellectual Ability (GIA) score specifically for young children, as the WJ-R did.

Although not included in the WJ III COG, data for the Memory for Names (*Glr*), Memory for Sentences (*Gsm*), and Visual Closure (*Gv*) tests were collected during standardization and are included in the recently published

TABLE 8-1   Changes to Enhance the Use of WJ III Tests with Young Children

Test	Description
Letter–Word Identification	Assesses child's letter and word identification skills. Initial items involve distinguishing letters from other pictures. Later items require the child to point to named letters and then to name letters. Word reading begins after item 15
Applied Problems	Assesses child's ability to analyze and solve math problems. Initial items assess the child's knowledge of number quantity and counting ability. Conceptual knowledge is also required, in that children must differentiate items to be counted from distracters (e.g., count number of circles present in a grouping of squares, rectangles, and circles)
Spelling	Assesses visual–motor integration, prewriting, and writing skills. Initial items require the child to copy shapes, trace lines, and copy letters. Items 8–14 ask the child to print letters after they are named; items 15 onward require the spelling of words
Picture Vocabulary	Assesses child's oral language development and word knowledge. Initial samples and items require receptive language skills; however, after item 2, children are to name the picture presented and it becomes an expressive language task
Academic Knowledge	Beginning items in each subtest require simple expressive (naming a picture) or receptive language (pointing to named picture) skills. Initial science items require knowledge of body parts, animals, and foods; initial social studies items require knowledge of clothing, household items, and occupations; initial humanities items require knowledge of art materials, colors, instruments, and basic features of common stories

Diagnostic Supplement (Woodcock, McGrew, Mather, & Schrank, 2003). When combined with tests from the WJ III COG, an Early Development GIA (EDev GIA) score can be generated. Table 8-2 identifies tests contributing to the EDev GIA score. It is a six-test cluster and, with the exception of Fluid Reasoning (*Gf*), includes one measure of each of the CHC broad ability factors. A Short-Term Memory (*Gsm*) cluster, Auditory Memory Span, can also be determined for young children when Memory for Sentences and Memory for Words are both administered. This cluster may be particularly useful with young children for early reading referrals because it provides a distinct measure of auditory, or phonological, memory ability.

Two early development achievement cluster scores can also be determined with WJ III ACH tests and the Diagnostic Supplement scoring program: a Pre-Academic Standard cluster, composed of Letter–Word Identification, Applied Problems, and Spelling, and a Pre-Academic Extended cluster, which adds Picture Vocabulary and Academic Knowledge (Table 8-3) (personal communication, Frederick Schrank, 2/13/02). Preliminary investigations of these achievement tests with young children suggest that the tasks, or at least their initial items, appear to be measuring pre-academic skills unique to younger children (McCullough, 2001), adding to the usefulness of the WJ III in decision-making regarding early school entrance, kindergarten screening efforts, or program evaluation.

TEST SELECTION

Practitioners must exercise reason when using the WJ III with young children because the scoring program will generate score profiles for half of the cognitive ability tests and at least 40% of the achievement tests for children as young as 24 months, and for all of the tests and composites by 5:0. As a result, the user must discern when the test is providing technically adequate and practically relevant information for the child being assessed. The decision tree for such choices is dependent on a number of factors including but not limited to the age of the child,

TABLE 8-2   Tests Contributing to the Early Development General Intellectual Ability

Test	Broad ability	Battery
Verbal Comprehension	*Gc*	WJ III Cognitive Standard Battery
Incomplete Words	*Ga*	WJ III Cognitive Standard Battery
Visual Matching	*Gs*	WJ III Cognitive Standard Battery
Memory for Names	*Glr*	Diagnostic Supplement
Visual Closure	*Gv*	Diagnostic Supplement
Memory for Sentences	*Gsm*	Diagnostic Supplement

TABLE 8-3   Tests Contributing to the Pre-Academic Clusters

Cluster/test	Battery
Pre-Academic Standard	
Letter–Word Identification	WJ III Achievement Standard Battery
Applied Problems	WJ III Achievement Standard Battery
Spelling	WJ III Achievement Standard Battery
Pre-Academic Extended	
Letter–Word Identification	WJ III Achievement Standard Battery
Applied Problems	WJ III Achievement Standard Battery
Spelling	WJ III Achievement Standard Battery
Picture Vocabulary	WJ III Achievement Extended Battery
Academic Knowledge	WJ III Achievement Extended Battery

the child's estimated level of ability, the purpose of assessment (i.e., determining eligibility for programs, assessing pre-academic skills, or supplementing other assessment data), and the technical properties of the test, specifically reliability and test floor.

Technical properties (Tables 8-4 and 8-5) of the WJ III COG and field studies with samples of developmentally delayed (Gelb & Alfonso, 2002) and speech/language-impaired preschoolers (Salava & Tusing, in preparation) indicate that the test does not function well as a stand-alone battery for all ability ranges until children are at least 4:0. Prior to this, several tests contributing to the overall GIA scores do not demonstrate adequate floor and/or internal consistency. In addition, many of the tests contain basic concepts that are beyond the grasp of young children, particularly those with developmental disabilities (Gelb & Alfonso, 2002). However, when the Diagnostic Supplement is utilized (i.e., Visual Closure, Memory for Names, and Memory for Sentences), which includes more developmentally appropriate tasks, the floor of the test is improved (Salava & Tusing, in preparation). This allows for Early Development GIA scores at least 2 SD below average for children as young as 2:0. Further, most of the tests contributing to the EDev GIA demonstrate adequate floor by 3:6, whereas some tests contributing to the GIA—Standard and GIA—Extended do not demonstrate adequate floor until 6:0 or 7:0 years of age.

Although not useful as a stand-alone battery for all young children, the WJ III COG can provide practical assessment information when it is used as a supplement to other tests, when information about specific cognitive abilities is desired, or when used with children with only mild developmental delays. Over one-third of the tests are adequate for use with children 3 to 4 years of age and nearly two-thirds are adequate for use with children under age 5. Further, cluster scores with acceptable internal consistency and floors can be determined for all but two of the CHC abilities by the age of 4 years. Several clusters demonstrate acceptable internal consistency at even younger ages, but will only produce scores as low as 1.5 SD below average.

TABLE 8-4   Internal Consistency and Age of Adequate Test Floor of WJ III Cognitive Clusters

Cluster	Consistency at age (years)[a]					Adequate floor[b]
	2	3	4	5	6	
General Intellectual Ability—Std	I	G	G	G	G	4 years, 2 months
General Intellectual Ability—Ext	I	I	G	G	G	3 years, 9 months
Brief Intellectual Ability	I	G	G	G	G	3 years, 11 months
Verbal Ability—Std	G	A	A	A	G	3 years, 2 months
Verbal Ability—Ext	G	G	G	G	G	3 years, 7 months
Thinking Ability—Std	I	G	G	G	G	4 years, 0 months
Thinking Ability—Ext	I	I	G	G	G	3 years, 7 months
Cognitive Efficiency—Std	I	G	G	G	G	5 years, 0 months
Cognitive Efficiency—Ext	I	I	G	G	G	4 years, 9 months
Comprehension–Knowledge (Gc)	G	G	G	G	G	3 years, 7 months
Long-Term Retrieval (Glr)	I	A	A	A	A	4 years, 0 months
Visual-Spatial Thinking (Gv)	A	G	A	A	I	3 years, 2 months
Auditory Processing (Ga)	I	G	G	G	A	3 years, 11 months
Fluid Reasoning (Gf)	I	A	G	G	G	6 years, 9 months
Processing Speed (Gs)	I	A	G	G	G	4 years, 3 months
Short-Term Memory (Gsm)	G	G	G	G	A	5 years, 0 months
Working Memory	I	I	G	G	G	6 years, 0 months
Broad Attention	I	I	G	G	G	5 years, 5 months
Cognitive Fluency	I	G	G	G	G	3 years, 6 months
Executive Processes	I	I	G	G	G	5 years, 2 months
Phonemic Awareness	G	G	G	G	A	4 years, 7 months

[a]Ratings for internal consistency reliability are based on Bracken's (1987) recommended standards: G (good) corresponds to $r > .90$, A (adequate) corresponds to $r > .80$ and $< .89$, and I (inadequate) corresponds to $r < .80$. Clusters not intended for a given age range were also rated as inadequate.

[b]Adequate floor represents the age at which a raw score of 1 is associated with a Standard Score at least 2 standard deviations below average.

Table 8-6 provides information on the internal consistency and test floors of WJ III Tests of Achievement (ACH). With young children, when considering the best tests to use from the WJ III ACH, again preference is given to tests included in the Diagnostic Supplement, because not all tests were designed to measure academic skills typically acquired before school entry. Both Pre-Academic clusters demonstrate adequate technical properties by 3:5 and 3:1, respectively. Further, a number of Oral Language tests (Understanding

TABLE 8-5 Internal Consistency and Age of Adequate Test Floor of WJ III Cognitive Tests

Test	Internal consistency[a]	Adequate test floor[b]
Verbal Comprehension	High at ages 2 and 6, medium at ages 3–5	3 years, 2 months
Picture Recognition	Low at ages 2, 5–6; medium at ages 3–4	3 years, 2 months
Auditory Attention	Medium at age 6, high at ages 3–5; not intended for age 2	3 years, 5 months
Memory for Words	Medium at ages 4–6, high at ages 2–3	3 years, 5 months
Retrieval Fluency	Low at ages 2–3, 6; medium at ages 4–5	3 years, 6 months
Rapid Picture Naming	High at ages 2–6	3 years, 6 months
Spatial Relations	High at ages 3–5, medium at age 6, low at age 2	3 years, 7 months
Visual Matching	High at ages 3–6; not intended for age 2	4 years, 2 months
General Information	Medium at ages 3–6, high at age 2	4 years, 2 months
Planning	Low at ages 4–6; not intended for ages 2–3	4 years, 6 months
Incomplete Words	Medium at ages 3–6, high at age 2	4 years, 8 months
Visual Auditory Learning	Medium at ages 3–6; not intended for age 2	4 years, 9 months
Concept Formation	High at ages 4–6, medium at age 3, low at age 2	5 years, 4 months
Decision Speed	Low at ages 3–4, medium at age 5, high at age 6; not intended for age 2	5 years, 4 months
Sound Blending	High at ages 2–5, medium at age 6	5 years, 6 months
Pair Cancellation	Medium at ages 5–6; not intended for ages 2–4	5 years, 8 months
Numbers Reversed	Medium at age 6, high at ages 3–5; not intended for age 2	6 years, 3 months
Auditory Working Memory	High at ages 4–6; not intended for ages 2–3	6 years, 5 months

(continues)

TABLE 8-5 *(continued)*

Test	Internal consistency[a]	Adequate test floor[b]
Analysis Synthesis	Medium at age 4, high at ages 5–6; not intended for ages 2–3	7 years, 5 months

[a]Ratings for internal consistency reliability are based on Bracken's (1987) recommended standards: "high" corresponds to $r \geq .90$, "medium" corresponds to $r > .80$ and $\leq .89$, and "low" corresponds to $r \leq .80$.

[b]Adequate floor represents the age at which a raw score of 1 is associated with a Standard Score at least 2 standard deviations below average.

Directions, Picture Vocabulary) are also psychometrically sound for use with children age 4 years and older and may provide useful information related to language development.

TEST VALIDITY

In general, the studies presented in the technical manual provide initial support for the use of the WJ III with young children. However, caution is warranted because the breadth and depth of information provided for children under the age of 6 are limited relative to data presented to support use of the WJ III with school-age children and adults. For example, although extensive developmental growth curve information is provided for children 5 years and older, similar information is not presented for younger children. This is unfortunate given that the youngest age ranges typically represent a period of significant growth in cognitive abilities. Similarly, test–retest reliabilities specific to young children are also difficult to ascertain from the technical manual, because findings are reported only for a sample of children 4 to 7 years of age.

Special studies focusing primarily on samples of young children are included in the technical manual (Mather & Woodcock, 2001); however, they include only typically developing children. Therefore, efficacy of the WJ III's use with special populations (e.g., developmentally delayed, language delayed, motorically impaired) is yet to be determined. Further, few studies examining the validity of the WJ III ACH for young children are currently available. Fortunately, studies (Gelb & Alfonso, 2002; Salava & Tusing, in preparation; Siders & Tusing, in preparation) are underway to investigate the use of the WJ III COG, WJ III ACH, and WJ III Diagnostic Supplement with special populations and to further examine the relationship of the WJ III with other preschool measures (e.g., intelligence tests, language proficiency measures, pre-academic skills measures).

TABLE 8-6 Internal Consistency and Age of Adequate Test Floor of Achievement Tests

Test	Internal consistency[a]	Adequate test floor[b]
Letter–Word Identification	High at ages 2–6	3 years, 4 months
Reading Fluency	Medium at age 6; not intended for ages 2–5	7 years, 5 months
Story Recall	Low at ages 2–5, medium at age 6	5 years, 7 months
Understanding Directions	Medium at ages 2–6	3 years, 11 months
Calculation	High at ages 5–6; not intended for ages 2–4	6 years, 10 months
Math Fluency	Not intended for ages 2–6	7 years, 4 months
Spelling	Low at age 3, medium at age 2; high at ages 4–6	3 years, 8 months
Writing Fluency	Not intended for ages 2–6	8 years, 4 months
Passage Comprehension	High at ages 2–6	5 years, 10 months
Applied Problems	Medium at age 6, high at ages 2–5	3 years, 6 months
Writing Samples	Low at age 5, medium at age 6; not intended for ages 2–4	6 years, 4 months
Story Recall—Delayed	Low at ages 3–6; not intended for age 2	Not applicable
Word Attack	High at ages 4–6; not intended for ages 2–3	6 years, 6 months
Picture Vocabulary	Low at ages 5–6, medium at ages 3–4, high at age 2	2 years, 8 months
Oral Comprehension	Medium at ages 4–6, high at age 2–3	5 years, 10 months
Editing	High at age 6; not intended for ages 2–5	9 years, 3 months
Reading Vocabulary	High at ages 5–6; not intended for ages 2–4	8 years, 5 months
Quantitative Concepts	Medium at ages 2–4, high at ages 5–6	4 years, 9 months
Academic Knowledge	Medium at age 6, high at ages 2–5	2 years, 8 months
Spelling of Sounds	Medium at age 6; not intended for ages 2–5	6 years, 1 month
Sound Awareness	Low at age 4, medium at age 5, high at age 6; not intended for ages 2–3	5 years, 10 months

(continues)

TABLE 8-6 *(continued)*

Test	Internal consistency[a]	Adequate test floor[b]
Punctuation and Capitalization	Low at age 6; not intended for ages 2–5	6 years, 2 months

[a]Ratings for internal consistency reliability are based on Bracken's (1987) recommended standards: "high" corresponds to $r \geq .90$, "medium" corresponds to $r > .80$ and $\leq .89$, and "low" corresponds to $r \leq .80$.

[b]Adequate floor represents the age at which a raw score of 1 is associated with a Standard Score at least 2 standard deviations below average.

Concurrent Validity

Special studies (McGrew & Woodcock, 2001) examined the relationship between the WJ III COG and the *Differential Ability Scale* (DAS) (Elliott, 1990), *Wechsler Preschool and Primary Scale of Intelligence—Revised* (WPPSI-R) (Wechsler, 1989), and the *Stanford–Binet Fourth Edition* (SB-IV) (Thorndike, Hagen, & Sattler, 1986) for samples of children 3 years of age and older. WJ III COG GIA scores were strongly correlated with composite scores from each of the tests (r values ranged from .67 to .76). Therefore, the WJ III COG appears to measure overall cognitive ability similar to other ability measures for young children despite different methods of task presentation. As expected, the WJ III Verbal Ability and Comprehension–Knowledge (*Gc*) clusters were strongly related to verbal ability clusters from the other batteries (r values ranged from .60 to .70), suggesting that the clusters measure similar constructs with regard to verbal abilities. Finally, discriminant validity was established for the WJ III Visual-Spatial Thinking (*Gv*) and Short-Term Memory (*Gsm*) clusters, as they were moderately related to the SB-IV Abstract/Visual Reasoning and Short-Term Memory clusters, respectively.

McCullough (2001) provided further support for the WJ III COG as a measure of overall intellectual ability; strong correlations between the WJ III GIA scores and the DAS and WPPSI-R composites were found for a sample of children 3:6 to 5:11 (r values ranged from .69 to .74). Oral language clusters from the WJ III ACH (i.e., Oral Language, Oral Expression, and Listening Comprehension) were also strongly related to the WPPSI-R and DAS verbal ability clusters. As a result, the WJ III ACH oral language tasks may also be interpreted as measures of Comprehension–Knowledge (*Gc*) for young children. Conversely, the WJ III ACH Academic Knowledge cluster demonstrated low to moderate correlations with the DAS and WPPSI-R. Thus, although it is often considered a measure of general knowledge for young children, Academic Knowledge appears to tap abilities different from those typically assessed by intelligence tests for young children.

Less differentiation existed among the remaining DAS, WPPSI-R, and SB-IV factor scores and WJ III COG clusters. As expected, the DAS Nonverbal Ability cluster and the WPPSI-R Performance Intelligence Quotient were most strongly related to the WJ III Thinking Ability clusters, for which the relationships were in the moderate range (r values ranged from .57 to .63). However, the DAS and WPPSI-R verbal ability clusters were moderately correlated with the WJ III Thinking Ability clusters (r values ranged from .60 to .63), the WJ III Verbal Ability and Gc clusters were moderately related to the WPPSI-R PIQ ($r = .62$), and the SB-IV Verbal Reasoning cluster was moderately related to the WJ III Thinking Ability and Cognitive Efficiency clusters (r values ranged from .61 to .67). This may be indicative of greater language demands on all types of intelligence test tasks for young children as well as less differentiation among cognitive abilities at this age range, because similar comparisons with school-age versions of the same tests demonstrate more distinct relationships among cluster scores (McGrew & Woodcock, 2001).

Construct Validity

Confirmatory factor analyses of the WJ III COG with standardization data for children under age 7 years indicate that although multiple cognitive ability factors were identified reliably for the samples, all seven CHC cognitive factors were not present (League, 2000; Teague, 1999). Teague (1999) determined that the WJ III data fit a five-factor model, including Comprehension–Knowledge (Gc), Auditory Processing (Ga), Visual Processing (Gv), Short-Term Memory (Gsm), and Long-Term Retrieval (Glr). Separate factors for Fluid Reasoning (Gf) and Processing Speed (Gs) did not emerge. This may be due to a lack of developmentally appropriate measures of reasoning and processing speed on the WJ III. This hypothesis is supported when the floors of tests contributing to each cluster are examined. Neither the Gsm nor the Gf clusters contain tests with adequate floors for children under 4 years.

Preliminary joint confirmatory factor-analytic studies that attempted to apply the CHC structure of cognitive abilities to tests from the WJ III COG, DAS, and WPPSI-R supported the findings of Teague (1999) and League (2000). Four, and in some cases six, CHC factors were identified, with crystallized ability, visual-spatial ability, auditory processing, and memory factors emerging most consistently (Ford, 2002). Interestingly, not only did fewer factors exist across the confirmatory factor analyses relative to similar analyses with school age children, but the factor loadings were weaker than those identified in analyses with older children. Accordingly, although the WJ III COG data demonstrate that multiple cognitive factors exist in young children, the nature of these factors and their relationships to one another appear to vary as a function of age.

Given the challenge in interpreting results from the first series of confirmatory factor-analytic studies, a series of exploratory factor analyses is currently underway to examine the unique relationships among WJ III COG tests for children age 5 years and younger (Ford, McGrew, & Tusing, in preparation). Again, multiple cognitive factors, not just a verbal/nonverbal ability dichotomy, are robust across the analyses and many of these factors appear consistent with CHC factors. However, it appears that some tests also tend to load on unexpected factors given the history of similar analyses with school age children. For example, tests not commonly interpreted as measures of crystallized ability tend to load more strongly on a *Gc* factor in this age range, perhaps due to a stronger linguistic demand of the tasks for young children. It may be that the placement of tests on CHC factors or the types of cognitive abilities present for young children is different from that established for school-age children and adults. The following section explores the developmental nature of CHC abilities in an effort to better understand the most effective ways to use the WJ III with young children.

UNDERSTANDING THE DEVELOPMENT OF COGNITIVE ABILITIES IN YOUNG CHILDREN USING CHC THEORY

Despite previous assertions that young children's cognitive abilities are less differentiated than those of older children (Garrett, 1946), new questions and approaches to developmental cognitive research (Grannot, 1998) have resulted in evidence for the presence of specific cognitive abilities at much younger ages than was once believed (Chen & Siegler, 2000). Further, although most psychometric research investigating the developmental nature of cognitive abilities has only included children 6 years of age and older, evidence from factor-analytic research for a greater differentiation of specific cognitive abilities in younger children exists (Horn & Noll, 1997). In fact, psychometric research has identified multiple latent factors, including reasoning, memory, processing speed, visual and auditory processing, and acquired knowledge, from preschool assessment tools for children as young as age 4 years (Hooper, 2000; League, 2000; Stone, Gridley, & Gyurke, 1991; Teague, 1999; Tusing & Ford, under review).

Accordingly, the ability to measure CHC abilities in young children is evident given appropriately designed measurement tools and stability in the ability domain to be measured. Nonetheless, developmental evidence for CHC theory also indicates that the broad cognitive abilities identified in the model, as well as the narrow abilities they subsume, follow different developmental patterns of growth and decline (Carroll, 1993; Horn, 1985, 1991) and therefore may be qualitatively different at various ages. As described previously, initial investigations of the factor structure of the WJ III for young children appear to support this notion.

Emerging from the literature are several general developmental trends that provide a greater understanding of young children's cognitive abilities as assessed by CHC measures. First, a strong relationship exists between neurobiological maturation and observed cognitive development. For young children, improvements in processing speed and cognitive efficiency appear to play a pivotal role in subsequent cognitive changes. Further, the use of strategies (e.g., rehearsal strategies to aid memory), which enhances cognitive efficiency and therefore higher level cognitive processing, also increases with age. Developmental growth in attention capabilities is vital as well (McDevitt & Ormrod, 2002). These developmental changes appear to impact the age by which some abilities can be reliably measured with current assessment techniques. Further, it is evident that several indicators of future academic learning can be measured reliably during the preschool age range, adding to the utility of applying CHC theory to the measurement of young children's cognitive abilities. Although the discussions here cannot alone adequately address the complexity of these findings, in the following sections the reader is provided with a framework to aid in making diagnostic decisions when using the WJ III with young children.

SPEED OF INFORMATION PROCESSING (*Gs*)

Research with adults indicates that age-related improvements in processing speed appear to continue well into adulthood. Further, response times for cognitive tasks decrease with age at a rate that is consistent across different types of tasks (e.g., motor, perceptual, or cognitive) (Kail, 1991; Hale, 1990). Findings have been extended to samples of children as young as age 4 years (Miller & Vernon, 1997). The consistency across patterns of developmental change has led researchers to conclude that a global mechanism exists that limits the speed with which children can process information, or limits the resources available for processing information, which in turn affects speed. Characteristics of the global mechanism are not clearly understood; however, hypotheses implicating age-related changes in myelination and in connections in the central nervous system have been forwarded (Kail, 2000). Myelination may have particular relevance for understanding the cognitive development of very young children, because the most significant changes in myelination occur between midgestation and 24 months of age (Sampaio & Truwitt, 2001). The importance of processing speed to cognitive development is best understood through an examination of concomitant age-related changes in reasoning and memory abilities. Referred to as "developmental cascade" (Fry & Hale, 1996), increased processing speed has been linked to improvements in attention and working memory, which are then related to increases in reasoning and problem solving. Thus speed of information processing is a key element in cognitive development and the relationship is evident early in life.

With the exception of subtests from the WPPSI-R (Wechsler, 1989) and NEPSY (Korkman et al., 1998), processing speed tasks for young children have not typically demonstrated adequate measurement properties for children younger than age 4 years. The WJ III includes several processing-speed tests, each thought to represent a different narrow ability under *Gs*. However, similar to other tests, two of the WJ III *Gs* tests do not demonstrate adequate floor or reliability with the youngest age ranges (Decision Speed, 5:4; Pair Cancellation, 5:8; see Table 8-5). One explanation for this may lie in the nature of the tasks.

It could be argued that traditional processing-speed tasks typically used with older children may not actually represent "simple cognitive tasks" for younger children. Siegler and Chen (Siegler, 1998; Chen & Siegler, 2000) argue this perspective for tasks requiring children to visually search a page to identify target stimuli within distracters, a common *Gs* task. Because young children have yet to develop efficient strategies for this type of task, their performance is not automatized, and therefore successful completion of the task requires greater attention and cognitive effort. As a result, the time required to complete the task also increases. Weinert and Schneider (1996) have also determined that the greater the differences across stimuli to be searched, the more effort required by young children for successful completion of the task, because the child must consciously evaluate whether each item matches the target stimuli. Successful completion of many processing-speed tasks also requires the ability to apply concepts such as "same" or to complete paper/pencil tasks, both of which may be difficult for young children (Bracken, 2000).

Visual Matching demonstrates somewhat greater measurement properties for young children, which is due in part to the specification of a separate task for young children that includes more developmentally appropriate stimuli. For Visual Matching 1, children must point to identical shapes in a row. All stimuli are the same color, and the number of distracters is lessened relative to Visual Matching 2. Rapid Picture Naming provides a type of processing-speed measure different from those described previously. For this task, children are to rapidly name objects that are presented in a row. This provides a measure of speed of lexical access or naming facility. Rapid Picture Naming has very strong measurement properties for young children as it demonstrates adequate floor by 3:6, which may be in part due to relatively simple directions and engaging picture stimuli.

MEMORY ABILITIES (*Gsm*, WORKING MEMORY, *Glr*)

Although research has historically suggested that memory abilities differ qualitatively from infant/toddler to preschool age ranges, contemporary findings suggest that early memory ability is considerably more robust than previously believed (Howe, 2000). In fact, the processes of memory appear to be quite similar across ages because much of the neurological hardware necessary for memory operations (encoding, storage, and retrieval) is in place early in life (Chen & Siegler, 2000). Another fundamental issue in the developmental memory literature is whether memory ability represents a unitary construct (Howe, 2000; Chuah & Maybery, 1999) or a set of multiple independent abilities (Eichenbaum & Cohen, 2001). The cognitive neuroscience literature supports the assertion of memory as a set of independent abilities, even at the youngest age ranges. CHC theory, and by association the WJ III COG, also represent memory as multiple independent abilities, namely Short-Term Memory (*Gsm*), *Gsm*'s narrow ability of Working Memory (*MW*), and Long-Term Retrieval (*Glr*). Consistent with neuropsychological research that localizes verbal memory and visuospatial memory to separate systems in the brain (Baddeley & Logie, 1999; Pickering, Gathercole, & Peaker, 1998) and contemporary research indicating a stronger relationship between visual memory tasks and spatial ability than between verbal memory tasks and verbal ability (Miyake, Friedman, Rettinger, Shah, & Hegarty, 2001), CHC theory also identifies visual memory under the broad ability of Visual Processing (*Gv*).

Controversy exists in the identification of processes responsible for growth in memory ability over time. However, as with other ability domains, neurobiological maturation, promoting increased processing speed and cognitive efficiency, as well as increased strategy use, appear to provide the best explanation for observed age-related improvements across all types of memory processes (Butler, Marsh, Sheppard, & Shappard, 1985; Cowan, Saults, Nugent, & Elliot, 1999; Damon, Kuhn, & Siegler, 1998; Miles & Morgan, 1996; Schneider & Pressley, 1997). For example, increases in the speed with which stimuli are encoded have been related to increases in the capacity of short-term memory stores (Weinert & Schneider, 1995) and working memory (Case, 1984; Gathercole & Hitch, 1993; Henry & Millar, 1993; Swanson, 1999; Towse, Hitch, & Hutton, 1998). Such findings are robust for older preschool children (Hulme & Roodenrys, 1994; Kail, 1997) and are indicated in research with children as young as 3 years old (Gathercole & Hitch, 1993). Age-related changes in memory abilities are also correlated with increased knowledge stores. It is well documented that young children can remember large amounts of information (to capacities similar to adult capacity) when the information is meaningful to them (Palmer, Weinhaus, & Pohlman, 2001). The relationship between stores of knowledge and processing speed appears complementary in that increased familiarity with information allows for enhanced processing speed and cognitive efficiency (Kuhn & Siegler, 1998), which in turn allows for greater learning. What develops in terms of memory abilities, then, at least across the youngest age ranges, is a general increase in the sophistication of memory processes, including strategy use, and the processing capacity of memory stores.

Short-Term Memory (*Gsm*)

Researchers are divided with regard to whether working memory is distinct or simply a narrow aspect of short-term memory (Baddeley & Hitch, 2000; Engle, Laughlin, Tuholski, & Conway, 1999; Richardson et al., 1996; Eichenbaum & Cohen, 2001). As a result, different models of working memory exist, each of which emphasize the importance of short-term memory span differently. CHC theory recognizes working memory as a narrow ability under *Gsm*. Thus, the WJ III *Gsm* cluster is identified by a verbal memory span task, Memory for Words, and a working memory task, Numbers Reversed. Memory for Words requires repeating lists of unrelated words in order. The Diagnostic Supplement includes an additional verbal memory span task, Memory for Sentences, which requires repeating word phrases of increasing lengths.

The development of memory span capacity throughout childhood is well documented. Through 4 years of age, the average child has a memory span of two to three items, about one-third of the average adult span. Research also suggests that young children are better able to remember words in a sentence than lists of unrelated words, further implicating the role of meaningfulness of stimuli in memory ability (Schneider & Pressley, 1997). Finally, the measurement of memory span appears to stabilize by 3 to 4 years of age (Pickering et al., 1998). Consistent with this pattern, Memory for Words and Memory for Sentences demonstrate adequate psychometric properties for use with young children at approximately 3:5 and 3:2, respectively. As a result, the Auditory Memory Span cluster of the Diagnostic Battery may be more appropriate when a measure of *Gsm* is desired for a young child.

Working Memory

Given increased recognition of the importance of working memory in cognitive development (Aylward, Gioia, Verhulst, & Bell, 1995; Case, 1984; Engle, Kane, & Tuholski, 1999), the WJ III provides an additional working memory cluster that includes Numbers Reversed and Auditory Working Memory. A critical feature of working memory is the maintenance of short-term stores of information during the processing of additional information (Case, 1984). It is argued that the capacity for working memory is present at young ages (Gathercole & Baddeley, 1993) and that it increases by one informational unit every 2 years until an adult capacity of about seven units at about 15 years of age is reached (Kemps, DeRammelaere, & Desmet, 2000). Similar to verbal memory span, working memory appears to improve with increases in processing speed. Assessment batteries for young children typically have not included working memory measures (McGrew & Flanagan, 1998), and although the WJ III includes two tests of working memory, neither demonstrates adequate measurement properties for children younger than age 6 years, primarily because of poor floor properties. This may, in part, be due to the nature of task presentation and the ability of young children to understand concepts such as "backwards." Nonetheless, use of the WJ III working memory tests with young children is limited.

Differences in the ability to adequately measure working memory versus memory span in young children may also be due in part to within-child variations in cognitive efficiency, because different brain regions are implicated in the maintenance (memory span) versus the processing (working memory) of information (Kail, 1993; Smith & Jonides, 1997). Functions associated with the processing aspect of working memory have been isolated to the prefrontal cortex, which is not fully mature until adult ages (Byrnes, 2001; Eichenbaum & Cohen, 2001), whereas memory span abilities appear to be mediated by regions that are developed by preschool ages (Smith & Jonides, 1997). Differences in the efficient use of memory strategies could also be implicated, because children younger than 6 years rarely rehearse to facilitate the remembering of orally presented stimuli (Gathercole & Baddeley, 1993). Research in cognitive psychology indicates still another aspect of frontal lobe functioning that may impact the measurement of working memory tasks for young children, namely attention (Eichenbaum & Cohen, 2001; Kane, Conway, Bleckley, & Engle,

2001; Tuholski, Engle, & Baylis, 2001). For adults, difficulties in changing attentional focus and inhibiting irrelevant input have been implicated in poorer working memory performance. Young children are even more suscepti- ble to interference during tasks requiring sustained attention (Schneider & Pressley, 1997).

Long-Term Storage and Retrieval (*Glr*)

Not to be confused with a child's overall store of knowledge, under CHC theory *Glr* abilities are those abilities influential in the storage and later acquisition of information (Horn, 1991). Currently, only the NEPSY and WJ III provide measures of *Glr* abilities for children younger than 5 years. On the WJ III, *Glr* abilities are indicated by the Visual Auditory Learning and Retrieval Fluency tests. These tests provide measures of the narrow abilities of associative memory and ideational flu- ency, respectively. The Diagnostic Supplement includes an additional measure of associative memory, Memory for Names. For young children, memory for paired associations is facilitated when the pairs are "accessible," that is, when pairs occur naturally or share semantic features. Therefore, tasks that include visual–verbal pairs with accessible features (e.g., the word cowboy and a picture resembling a man) are learned more easily by young children, whereas, those that are more sym- bolic in nature will be more difficult. Memory for associations is also dramatically impacted by the use of associative strategies (Reese, 1994). On Visual Auditory Learning, the child must name previously presented visual stimuli, whereas, on Memory for Names, the child must point to a previously pictured "space creature" when its name is presented orally by the examiner. Visual Auditory Learning is best used with children 4:0 and older; however, Memory for Names, which requires only a pointing response, demonstrates adequate measurement properties for children as young as 3:6.

For Retrieval Fluency, children are to name orally as many examples as possible from a given category within a 1-minute time period. The task measures fluency of retrieval of information from stored knowledge (Mather & Woodcock, 2001). The WJ III Retrieval Fluency test demonstrates adequate floor at 3:6; however, internal consistency is not adequate until at least 4 years of age. Similar findings are evident for a comparable test from the NEPSY (Ahmad & Warriner, 2001). As a result, tasks of verbal fluency in general appear to be best used with children at least 4:0 years of age. Research also suggests that older children are able to retrieve information from long-term memory much faster than younger children (McDevitt & Ormrod, 2002). One explanation for this is an increased use of strategies for encoding and retrieval of information by older children (Butler et al., 1985). This effect is also explained by age-related neurological maturation promoting increased processing speed, as well as age-related increases in knowledge. That is, a well-developed knowledge base facilitates the amount of information recalled and the speed of recall, because it allows for a greater degree of association among pieces of information (Schneider, 2000). Thus, in the case of Retrieval Fluency, developmental increases in vocabulary knowledge, particularly categorical knowledge, should be associated with greater fluency and performance on this task. Teague (1999) found just such a relationship with a sample of children 3 to 7 years of age, whereby the WJ III Retrieval Fluency task was more strongly related to measures of crystallized ability (*Gc*) than to measures of *Glr*.

VISUAL–SPATIAL THINKING (*Gv*)

An understanding of the development of *Gv* abilities requires an understanding of the development of the visual perception system, which has been studied extensively (Siegler, 1986). As a result of significant neurological growth in the visual systems during the first months of life, children reach adultlike levels of some aspects of perceptual functioning by 6 months of age. Further, the visual cortex of the brain reaches adultlike form by the later preschool years, and therefore visual perception appears to be fully developed by this time (McDevitt & Ormrod, 2001). As such, by 5 years of age, a child's ability to hold visual information in a visual sensory register is similar to that of adults (Dawson & Fischer, 1993; McDevitt & Ormrod, 2001). Consequently, perceptual skills are often viewed as the "launching pad from which other aspects of cognitive development take off" (Siegler, 1986, p. 135), which may explain why many intelligence tests for young children include several measures of visual processing. Visualization tasks, which require the ability to manipulate objects or visual patterns to form new representations, follow a sequential pattern of growth. By 2 years of age, children can complete simple board puzzles; four- or five-piece puzzles with multiple visual features are often accomplished by 3 years of age, 4-year-olds can typically complete puzzles of eight to ten pieces, and 5-year-olds will rely on visual features including color, shape, and size to complete puzzles (Dunn, 1999).

As mentioned previously, tasks of visual memory are strongly related to visual-spatial skills, such that children who score higher on visual-spatial tasks demonstrate better visual memory ability (Miles & Morgan, 1996). Typically developing young children also demonstrate consistently better visual memory than verbal memory (Schneider & Pressley, 1997). In fact, visual recognition memory appears to be present within days after birth (Slater, Morison, & Rose, 1982). At approximately 30 months, object permanence occurs such that children demonstrate the ability reliably to remember a visual stimulus after it is removed. Further, 3-year-olds can reliably identify a missing stimulus from a previously viewed set (Dunn, 1999). Similar to verbal memory, at the later preschool ages visual memory span is approximately three to four items. Verbal labeling, and consequently phonological or verbal memory, play a unique role in the visual memory of older preschoolers and primary grade children. That is, when children generate names for visual stimuli, recall is dramatically improved and rapid increases in visual memory occur (Kemps, DeRammelaere, & Desmet, 2000). This effect does not hold for older children, nor does labeling appear to promote memory capacity for children younger than 5 years. Further, when rehearsal becomes a regularly used strategy for remembering (at about 10 years), labeling is actually found to interfere with the memory process (Henry & Millar, 1993).

The WJ III *Gv* cluster includes a measure of visual memory and a measure of the ability to mentally manipulate visual patterns. The Diagnostic Supplement also includes a measure of visual closure. Picture Recognition requires the ability to form and store a mental representation of a visual stimulus and then recall or recognize it later, providing a measure of visual recognition memory. Spatial Relations involves perceiving and analyzing visual stimuli, and Visual Closure involves correctly identifying a picture that has been distorted or altered. An advantage in using the WJ III *Gv* tasks with young children is the lack of a motor requirement. As expected, given evidence for the measurement of both visual-processing and visual memory abilities at very young ages, the tests demonstrate strong measurement properties for children age 3 years and younger (Visual Closure, 2:7; Picture Recognition, 3:2; Spatial Relations, 3:7). The lack of a requirement for recalling pictures in serial order (relative to verbal span tasks, for which items must be recalled sequentially), as well as the use of a pointing versus oral response, may explain the relatively stronger measurement properties for Picture Recognition versus Memory for Words at the youngest ages. Noteworthy is the fact that some inconsistency in measurement across *Gv* tasks is evident for children 6 years of age (Table 8-4).

FLUID REASONING (*Gf*)

Theories of cognitive development suggest that young children's reasoning skills are qualitatively different from those of school-age children. That is, the nature of children's thinking and reasoning abilities change with age (McDevitt & Ormrod, 2002). However, when presented with appropriate wording and in developmentally appropriate forms, young children are capable of completing more advanced reasoning tasks than historically believed. For example, young children are more likely to demonstrate concrete operational thinking rather than preoperational thought when they are familiar with the stimuli presented (Ceci & Roazzi, 1994). Siegler (1996) has suggested that the aspect of reasoning ability that tends to change during the course of development is the range of situations in which a particular strategy or way of thinking is used. As a result, some strategies become more stable or prevalent at certain ages than others. As mentioned previously, changes in other cognitive abilities, particularly processing speed and working memory, appear to be closely related to improvements and increased sophistication of reasoning abilities (Fry & Hale, 1996). The automatization of cognitive abilities appears important as this allows for a greater working memory capacity for more complex thinking tasks. Others have argued that increases in processing speed can be traced to the discovery of new rules and strategies for reasoning (Chen & Siegler, 2000) or an improvement in the selection of existing strategies for problem solving (Amsel, Goodman, Savoie, & Clark, 1996). Development of the most sophisticated reasoning (e.g., abstract reasoning) appears to be related to maturation of the frontal lobes in the brain, which typically is not complete until adult ages.

Although *Gf* is one of the strongest indicators of general intellectual ability (*g*), few standardized tests of intelligence measure the ability adequately and even fewer batteries for young children provide psychometrically sound measures of *Gf*. Consistent with developmental theories of cognitive development, tasks designed to assess reasoning skills in young children need to be developmentally appropriate for the age with which they will be utilized. As a result, those tests for young children that successfully measure reasoning skills typically include *Gf* tasks that are qualitatively different in presentation than *Gf* tasks on school-age batteries. Typically these include measures of the narrow ability of Piagetian Reasoning (seriation, classification, conservation). For example, the *Leiter International Performance Scale—Revised* (Leiter-R) (Roid & Miller, 1997) has three *Gf* tests for children as young as age 2 years; however, the tests include sim-plified tasks of sequencing, classification, and matching. The WPPSI-III (Coalson et al., 2002) includes new measures of reasoning for young children as well. Descriptions of the new tests are also suggestive of qualitatively different tasks than are currently included on tests for older children. The WJ III includes two measures of *Gf*, Concept Formation and Analysis Synthesis, which are similar in presentation for all age ranges. Neither test appears adequate for young children (Concept Formation, adequate floor at 5:4; Analysis Synthesis, adequate floor at 7:5). Both require strong listening comprehension abilities and the instructions have linguistic concepts not typically understood by all young children (e.g., dif-ferent). Thus, the inability of the WJ III to adequately measure *Gf* abilities for young children appears to be a function of the developmental appropriateness of the task presented.

AUDITORY PROCESSING (*Ga*)

Auditory processing is a large domain within CHC theory, but can be summarized as abilities related to the localization of sounds; the processing of sound features such as tone, pitch, frequency, rhythm, and timing; and the processing of speech sounds (McGrew & Flanagan, 1998). As with *Gv*, understanding the developmental nature of auditory processing requires an understanding of the effects of neurologi-cal development on a child's ability to perform auditory tasks (Bellis, 1996). Sensitivity to sound patterns is present prenatally and infants can discriminate between subtle differences in sounds (Siegler, 1986). However, the efficiency and acuity of the auditory system continues to develop for several years following birth (Aoki & Siekevitz, 1988). Similar to processing speed, myelination of nerve fibers plays a critical role in developmental change (Sampaio & Truwitt, 2001). Typically, lower brain regions are myelinated within the first year, which leads to the ability to localize sounds, discriminate sounds from background noise, and perceive the temporal features of sounds. As a result, these are the auditory processing abilities that are the first to be measured reliably by researchers. As brain structures implicated in the efficient processing of verbal stimuli are myelinated, children are more capable of processing speech sounds. Studies of auditory processing also indicate that as stimuli increase in verbal complexity, so do the effects of age in the ability to process the information (Bellis, 1996). Both the WJ III COG and the WJ III ACH batteries provide tasks of auditory processing, all of which involve the processing of linguistic or verbal stimuli. Auditory Attention on the WJ III provides a unique measure of speech sound discrimination, particularly the ability to resist sensory distortion in understanding oral language. Consistent with developmental research, this demonstrates adequate internal consistency and test floor for children in the 3-year age range.

Phonological Awareness

Sound Blending and Incomplete Words from the WJ III COG and Sound Awareness from the WJ III ACH measure phonological awareness, a narrow ability of *Ga*. Phonological awareness is best understood as a general sensitivity to the sound structure of language. It is multidimensional in nature (Goswami & Bryant, 1992; Muter, Hulme, Snowling, & Taylor, 1997; Yopp, 1988) and includes the abilities to detect and produce rhymes, detect syllables and phonemes, blend phonemes to form words, and manipulate sounds within words (Lonigan, Burgess, & Anthony, 2000). Relative to school-age children, there has been significantly less study of preschool children's phonological awareness skills. However, the existing research suggests a stage-like process in the development of phonological awareness, because children are able to discriminate syllables and intrasyllabic units in words earlier than they are able to detect phonemes within words (Lonigan et al., 2000). Children as young as 3 years can detect rhymes in words (Bradley & Bryant, 1983), and most children can determine the syllables making up a word by the age of 4 years. By 4 to 5 years of age, children are better able to detect differences in sounds within a syllable. As sensitivity to oral language and vocabulary increases, so does the awareness of individual phonemes in words (Bryant, MacLean, Bradley, & Crossland, 1990; Metsala, 1999), such that children are able reliably to determine each individual phoneme within a spoken word around the age of 6 or 7 years (Goswami & Bryant, 1990).

In terms of measurement, phonological awareness skills appear to have greatest stability by the later preschool years (Byrne & Fielding-Barnsley, 1993; Wagner, Torgesen, & Rashotte, 1994). For example, Lonigan et al. (2000) found a high level of stability in a longitudinal measure of phonological awareness in which the performance of 5-year-old preschoolers on a series of tasks perfectly predicted the same children's performance on similar tasks in kindergarten and first grade. This prediction held despite significant growth across children's phonological awareness skill levels. However, the same measurement of phonological awareness was less stable during early preschool, particularly between 3 and 4 years of age. The authors suggest that this instability at younger ages is due to a significant and variable pattern of growth in phonological sensitivity between 3 and 4 years of age. The phonological awareness measures of the WJ III all measure sensitivity to speech sounds at the syllable and phoneme level, which may impact their measurement properties with young children. Each of the tests demonstrate adequate internal consistency across all preschool age ranges; however, Incomplete Words does not demonstrate adequate floor until 4:8; Sound Blending demonstrates adequate floor by 5:6 and Sound Awareness by 5:10.

COMPREHENSION–KNOWLEDGE (*Gc*)

Within CHC theory, *Gc* abilities include listening comprehension, general information, and many language-based skills, such as language development, lexical knowledge, communication ability, and oral fluency (Flanagan et al., 2000). As such, *Gc* tasks are more sensitive to cultural experiences than are other measures of cognitive ability. Developmentally, *Gc* shows a pattern of continued growth and integration throughout the life span. This is important because it provides a knowledge base upon which future learning and advanced reasoning can occur (McDevitt & Ormrod, 2002). At the youngest ages, there are important milestones that impact a child's ability to acquire and demonstrate knowledge. For example, two functionally separate memory systems are thought to exist for infants and toddlers. The first is present at birth and involves memories for social–emotional information. The second forms during the preschool years and consists of learned information. According to Pillemer and White (1989), it is only when the second system is in place, typically by the third year, that children are able to produce memories in response to situational demands and language-based prompting. Another important period of change related to the growth of *Gc* abilities occurs during language development. At about 18 months, children are first able to represent information symbolically. At 2 years of age, a vocabulary explosion typically occurs. Just prior to the vocabulary explosion, children's word retrieval abilities improve significantly, especially when aided by visual cues. During the vocabulary explosion, important neural changes occur that reorganize the child's language-based abilities (Dapretto & Bjork, 2000). As a result, children often make more word usage and retrieval errors during the vocabulary explosion than they do prior to this growth period (Gershkoff-Stowe & Smith, 1997).

Discussion of the growth of language abilities as related to *Gc* is important in understanding the measurement of *Gc* abilities in young children. This is because intelligence tests for young children typically assess vocabulary development and general knowledge with tasks requiring expressive and receptive language skills. This is true for the WJ III as well. On the cognitive battery, the Verbal Comprehension test provides a measure of the narrow abilities of language development and lexical knowledge. Children are to name pictures, provide synonyms and antonyms, and solve verbal analogies for this task. General Information also provides a measure of general knowledge, because children are to provide one-word responses to orally presented questions. It is noted that not all young children will be able to complete items from each subtest contributing to the overall raw score for the tests (e.g., Verbal Comprehension subtests B and C require knowledge of "synonyms" and "antonyms"); nonetheless, the initial subtests are appropriate for young children, allowing for adequate measurement properties at younger ages. Both tests demonstrate adequate internal consistency beginning at 2 years of age. Verbal Comprehension demonstrates adequate floor at 3:2 and General Information at 4:2. The achievement battery also provides measures of *Gc*. Understanding Directions and Picture Vocabulary are useful with children as young as 3:11 and 2:8, respectively. Story Recall and Oral Comprehension are better for use with older preschoolers. Each of these measures is strongly related to *Gc* measures on the cognitive battery (McCullough, 2001).

LINKING COGNITIVE ABILITIES AND EARLY LITERACY

Efforts to determine the precursors to reading prior to school age have greatly increased in the past decade, given findings of the devastating effect that poor early reading acquisition can have for later school success and behavior (Juel, 1988; Lentz, 1988). As a result, the field of early literacy has grown substantially. Early literacy involves the period of literacy development between birth and the time when children are exposed to traditional instruction in reading and written language (Lesiak, 1997). Research in this area is broad and encompasses many methodological perspectives. Nonetheless, findings generally suggest that learning to read results from a complex interaction of many different cognitive abilities (Lonigan et al., 2000; Muter & Diethelm, 2001; Stanovich, 1986). Further, different abilities are influential at different points in time during reading acquisition (Whitehurst & Lonigan, 1998) and weaknesses in any of the abilities can have multiplicative effects on the learning process (Konold, Juel, & McKinnon, 1999; Stanovich, 1986; Wolf & Bowers, 1999). In the following section, the organizational framework of the WJ III Cognitive Performance Model (Mather & Woodcock, 2001)[2] is used to link research on early literacy to the measurement of cognitive abilities for young children. When available, information on the multivariate nature of cognitive abilities in their relationship to early learning is provided.

COGNITIVE EFFICIENCY

One component of the learning process involves the efficiency with which children can perform cognitive tasks. As evidenced in the previous review of the developmental nature of CHC abilities, processing speed and cognitive efficiency play an important role in the development of young children's cognitive abilities.

---

[2]The Cognitive Performance Model is described in Chapter 1 of this volume.

A similar relationship is found between cognitive efficiency and nearly all areas of early learning (Fry & Hale, 1996).

Processing Speed

The ability to perform rapid naming tasks has received much attention in the reading acquisition literature (Denckla & Rudel, 1976; Torgesen et al., 1997; Wolf, Bowers, & Biddle, 2000), because a strong relationship between rapid naming tasks and later reading performance exists (Bowers, Steffy, & Tate, 1986). The relationship appears to be due to a shared automaticity in lower level processing, such that early breakdowns in the processes related to naming speed also disrupt reading acquisition, given that the perceptual, linguistic, and motor processes for both tasks are very similar (Wolf, 1991). Findings regarding the relationship between rapid naming tasks and reading have been extended to children as young as 3 years (Jackson & Myers, 1982; Scarborough, 1990; Wolf, Bally, & Morris, 1986), suggesting that naming-speed deficits can be identified well before reading is acquired. Wolf (1991) suggested that the relationship between naming speed and reading is actually developmental in nature. That is, in the "earliest developmental stages, all naming speed tasks predict all later reading abilities" (p. 131). However, as automaticity develops, automatized naming tasks involving symbols (i.e., letters or numbers) are better predictors of basic reading skills, whereas, object naming tasks, which require greater semantic processing, are better predictors of comprehension skills. Tests contributing to the WJ III Cognitive Fluency cluster (Rapid Picture Naming, Retrieval Fluency, and Decision Speed) all have a semantic load and therefore have the potential to provide meaningful information for the reading acquisition process of older preschool and primary grade children.

Short-Term Memory

Memory deficits have long been implicated in various forms of learning problems, although a causal relationship between memory and reading has not been established (Hulme & Roodenrys, 1994). Nevertheless, the indirect relationships between short-term memory and other abilities associated with reading may be meaningful for the practitioner attempting to relate cognitive ability profiles with predicted academic performance. For example, better performance on tasks involving short-term verbal or phonological memory and visual memory are associated with higher reading performance (Aylward et al., 1995; Kavale & Forness, 2000), and short-term memory deficits are identified as precursors to reading difficulties, including word recognition (Hulme & Roodenrys, 1994) and reading comprehension (Daneman & Merikle, 1996). Immediate memory for orally presented verbal stimuli has also been found to be related to the rate of vocabulary acquisition (Gathercole et al., 1992) and reading acquisition (Wagner et al., 1994). Further, working memory has been found to predict reading comprehension even better than traditional short-term memory tasks beginning at least at age 6 (Daneman & Merikle, 1996; Sternberg, 1994; Swanson & Berninger, 1996; Towse, Hitch, & Hutton, 1998), although the relationship appears to slowly decrease with age (Evans et al., in press).

THINKING ABILITIES

Another component of the learning process involves the application of various thinking abilities (i.e., auditory processing, visual processing, fluid reasoning, and long-term storage and retrieval) to new learning. Research on early literacy has implicated two important thinking abilities, namely, auditory processing and associative memory, in the reading acquisition process.

Auditory Processing

Phonological awareness has long been implicated in the acquisition of reading skills (Wagner et al., 1994). Children who are better able to detect syllables, rhymes, and phonemes are quicker at learning to decode words (Wagner & Torgesen, 1987). Further, although relationships between phonological awareness and language abilities exist, the connection between reading and phonological awareness is present even after skills related to receptive language, intelligence, memory, and socio-economic status are removed (Bryant et al., 1990). The relationship appears to be reciprocal, as phonological awareness influences reading acquisition, and increases in reading acquisition then improve phonological awareness (Lonigan & Whitehurst, 1998).

The above-mentioned findings are evident for preschool-age children as well. However, the predictive power of different phonological awareness tasks appears to change with age. For example, the ability to detect rhymes at age 3 years is predictive of stronger word recognition skills at age $4\frac{1}{2}$ (MacLean, Bryant, & Bradley, 1987). However, the ability to detect and manipulate sounds in words (blending and deletion) is a stronger predictor of reading at ages 4 and 5 years than is rhyming (Muter et al., 1997). Research with the WJ-R and WJ III provides evidence for the power of *Ga* tasks in predicting reading ability for children as young as 5 years (McGrew, Werder, & Woodcock, 1991; Evans et al., in press). Consistent with previous reading research, the WJ III Phonemic Awareness 3 cluster, which is a mixed measure of rhyming, phoneme deletion, substitution, and reversal tasks, predicted reading even better than the *Ga* or Phonemic Awareness cluster for children age 6 and older (Evans et al., in press).

Associative Memory

Perhaps one of the more important contributions from recent reading research with relevance for the understanding of relationships between thinking skills and reading acquisition is that of Windfuhr and Snowling (2001). They found that when tasks of phonemic awareness and short-term memory were considered with tasks of associative memory for children 6 to 11 years of age, the associative memory tasks provided unique contributions to the prediction of reading achievement beyond that of other tasks. Evans et al. (in press) also provide evidence from WJ III data for similar patterns of relationships between *Glr* tasks and reading abilities for children as young as 6 years. McCullough (2001) extended these findings for children as young as 3 years. In his research, the WJ III *Glr* and *Gsm* clusters were determined to be the best predictors of Basic Reading Skills as measured by the WJ III ACH. Part of this relationship appears to be due to contributions from the Visual–Auditory Learning test, a measure of visual–verbal paired associative learning. Given that the cognitive demands for this task are similar to those in early reading (i.e., learning and recalling words associated with symbols), the implications for using this test with young children are evident. Specifically, children with deficits in associative memory skills may demonstrate difficulties in learning to read that are independent of or in addition to difficulties with phonological awareness. Further research with children younger than age 6 is needed to determine whether this predictive relationship is evident prior to formal instruction in reading.

STORES OF ACQUIRED KNOWLEDGE

Knowledge of letters upon kindergarten entry is a strong predictor of short- and long-term reading success (Adams, 1990; Badian, 1995; Muter & Diethelm, 2001), which makes the WJ III Letter–Word Identification test useful with young children. The relationship between letter knowledge and reading is not causal, however, in that instruction in letter names alone does not affect future success in reading (Adams, 1990). Instead, the relationship between knowledge of letter names and later reading is most likely the result of broader language and literacy experiences on the part of the child (Lonigan et al., 2000). Indeed, children's language abilities have long been implicated in the acquisition of reading skills. For example, word retrieval difficulties, which can affect speeded naming tasks, are often present with more general- ized language disorders (German, 1990), and overall vocabulary knowledge and oral language skills during kindergarten are predictive of later reading skills (Butler et al., 1985; Muter & Diethulm, 2001; Scarborough, 1990, 1991). McCullough (2001) determined a similar pattern of relationship between the WJ III COG *Gc* cluster and reading, written language, and oral language clusters on the WJ III ACH.

Wagner et al. (1994) hypothesize that vocabulary knowledge provides a semantic representation of words to which phonological codes can be mapped. This relationship is evident in findings of significant concurrent and longitudinal correlations between measures of vocabulary and phonological awareness for preschool to early elementary age children (Lonigan et al., 2000). In fact, Lonigan et al. (2000) suggests that phonological awareness, oral language skills, and letter knowledge are all partially predictive of later increases in phonologi- cal awareness. Therefore, the assessment of abilities related to early reading acquisition should also take into account aspects of language development and vocabulary, as measured by the WJ III COG and ACH tests.

INTERRELATIONSHIPS AMONG ABILITIES

The WJ III Cognitive Performance Model highlights the importance of recognizing that a child's overall cognitive performance "results from a complex interaction of many components" (Mather & Woodcock, 2001, p. 78). A similar conception adds to one's understanding of the relationships between abilities and early reading acquisition. For example, Wolf and Bowers (1999) put forth the "Double-Deficit Hypothesis" to explain how deficits in both phonological awareness and naming speed put children at greater risk for poor reading acquisition. As indicated, some children identified with reading difficulties may demonstrate weaknesses in either phonological awareness or in naming speed during early development (McBride-Chang & Manis, 1996), and specific instruction to remediate these deficiencies is related to later improvements in academic achievement (Byrne & Fielding-Barnsley, 1993; O'Connor, Notari-Syverson, & Vadasy, 1996; Torgesen, Morgan, & Davis, 1993). However, children with combined phonological awareness and naming speed deficits are the most resistant to remediation efforts (Wolf et al., 2000). Further, children with "double deficits" often demonstrate identifiable reading problems earlier on in development. Konold et al. (1999) present similar findings for a sample of 5- to 10-year-old children. In their study, children who demonstrated weaknesses across all WJ-R measures of *Ga*, *Gc*, *Gs*, and *Gsm* had the poorest reading achievement. On the other hand, those who demonstrated a relative strength on at least one ability within these cognitive domains demonstrated relatively better reading skills. That is, children with a compensatory strength in either auditory processing, processing speed, crystallized ability, or short-term memory demonstrated equally better basic reading and reading comprehension skills than did those children without a relative strength.

CASE STUDIES/APPLICATIONS

Continued work is needed to better determine the empirical relationships between WJ III measures of cognitive ability and measures of academic achievement for young children. However, the preceding discussion highlighted the importance of understanding the developmental nature of CHC abilities when assessing young children. Assessment efforts that consider the complex interplay of cognitive abilities and early learning may lead to improvements in the identification of children in need of early intervention and/or remediation, thereby preventing later learning problems. The WJ III COG, WJ III ACH, and Diagnostic Supplement provide a number of tests valuable in this process. The following case studies highlight ways in which the instruments may be used with young children.

ALEX: AGE 5 YEARS, 7 MONTHS

This example illustrates the usefulness of the WJ III as a supplement to traditional assessment tools typically used with young children. It also highlights the importance of considering all levels of interpretive information when examining a child's overall performance on assessment tasks.

Case History

Alex is the first of two children and is in his second semester of kindergarten. He reportedly met all developmental milestones within average limits, and hearing and visual screening results indicate no difficulties. Throughout the school year, he has struggled with following classroom directions and sustaining attention in class. Academic performance also appears delayed. Behavioral assessment prior to the present referral indicated significant attention problems and withdrawn behavior in the classroom. Interventions resulted in behavioral improvements on Alex's part; however, academic progress remains a concern. According to teachers, Alex appears to be easily distracted in class, has difficulty organizing or initiating academic tasks, and is struggling in the current curriculum. While parents are fluent in English, the family speaks Tagali at home.

Assessments

The DAS, *Bracken Basic Concepts Scale—Revised* (BBCS-R), and an informal prereading inventory were administered. Also, select tests from the WJ III COG and WJ III ACH were administered to further assess oral language skills and to provide information regarding auditory processing and phonemic awareness skills. A summary of Alex's scores is provided in Table 8-7.

Interpretations

A significant discrepancy between Alex's performance on verbal and non-verbal tasks existed on the DAS (Verbal Ability, Standard Score of 74; Nonverbal Ability, Standard Score of 101). Fine motor skills, as well as the ability to perceive and analyze visual information and reconstruct visually presented designs, were relative strengths for Alex; for these aspects his performance ranked at the 73rd percentile. However, his performance on tasks influenced by receptive language skills, including knowledge of relational concepts and the ability to follow oral directions, was significantly below average. Likewise, Alex had significant difficulty with the Early Number Concepts task, for which his performance was also in the below-average range. Observations during testing and an analysis of Alex's errors suggest that his poor performance was primarily related to difficulties with ordinal relationships and basic concepts such as "more," "less," and "same." His performance on the BBCS-R was similar to the DAS and also suggested difficulties in understanding vocabulary associated with relational concepts, as well as concepts involving time, sequence, quantity, and position. He did demonstrate adequate knowledge of basic school readiness skills, such as colors, letters, and numbers. Further, on the DAS, Alex demonstrated average vocabulary knowledge for nouns and expressive language skills relative to same-age peers.

TABLE 8-7   Score Profile: Alex

Test/cluster/subtest	Standard score	Percentile	RPI score
Differential Ability Scales[a]			
General Conceptual Ability	86	18th	
Verbal Ability	74	4th	
Nonverbal Ability	101	53rd	
Verbal Comprehension	27	1st	
Naming Vocabulary	42	21st	
Picture Similarities	41	18th	
Pattern Construction	56	73rd	
Copying	56	73rd	
Early Number Concepts	38	12th	
WJ III Tests of Cognitive Ability			
Phonemic Awareness III	85	15th	70/90
Oral Language Extended	87	19th	75/90
Oral Expression	92	30th	82/90
Listening Comprehension	85	16th	67/90
Sound Blending	103	57th	92/90
Incomplete Words	88	21st	68/90
Story Recall	91	27th	84/90
Understanding Directions	90	25th	73/90
Picture Vocabulary	94	34th	80/90
Oral Comprehension	87	19th	80/90
Sound Awareness	75	5th	36/90
Bracken Basic Concept Scale—Revised[b]			
Total Test Composite	83	13th	
School Readiness Composite	98	45th	
Direction/Position	5	5th	
Self/Social Awareness	4	2nd	
Texture/Material	9	37th	
Quantity	4	2nd	
Time/Sequence	6	9th	

[a]Differential Ability Scales subtest standard scores are expressed as T scores.
[b]Bracken subtest scores are expressed as scaled scores (M = 10, SD = 3).

Alex's performance on WJ III COG and ACH tests was commensurate with that reported above. His overall Listening Comprehension cluster score ranked at the 16th percentile in comparison to the Oral Expression cluster, which ranked at the 30th percentile, again suggesting a relative weakness in receptive language skills. Tasks contributing to the Oral Expression cluster required the naming of pictures and recall of details provided in an orally presented story, whereas, Listening Comprehension tasks required Alex to listen to and follow orally presented directions and to complete oral sentences by providing a missing key word. Considering all assessment tasks, it appears that Alex demonstrated weaknesses in language-laden tasks that involved more abstract linguistic concepts and conceptual knowledge, including those that were less related to direct classroom instruction and less influenced by associative memory or simple recall skills.

An examination of the proficiency scores associated with Alex's performance on WJ III tasks allows the examiner to better pinpoint Alex's educational needs. This is particularly true because the language skills under question are being measured during a period of typically rapid development given Alex's age. Although Alex's listening comprehension skills are in the low-average range relative to same-age peers (standard score of 85), the Relative Proficiency Index (RPI) scores associated with the listening comprehension tests (Understanding Directions, 73/90; Oral Comprehension, 60/90) suggest that he will find age-level receptive language demands difficult to very difficult. This weakness is likely related to limited English proficiency for academic tasks, given his home language background, because the overall Cognitive Academic Language Proficiency (CALP) score associated with his listening comprehension skills was 3.5. A score at this level suggests that Alex would be expected to find the English language demands for his age level difficult.

A final aspect of assessment examined Alex's early reading ability, because this was a major demand of the curriculum of his classroom. Norm-referenced comparisons on the BBCS-R suggest adequate letter knowledge. An informal assessment of prereading skills was consistent with the BBCS-R and indicated that Alex could visually identify all English alphabet letters and was able to name 24 of 26 letters accurately, which indicated mastery of this academic skill. He had much greater difficulty when asked to identify letters when provided with the sound and when asked to provide the sound represented by a particular letter. His accuracy for these phonetic awareness tasks was less than 70% and at the frustration level.

Assessment with the WJ III clarified Alex's weaknesses with regard to these tasks. He demonstrated average (57th percentile) blending and auditory closure skills, as he was able to synthesize orally presented syllables to form words on the Sound Blending test. However, Alex was unable to complete the Auditory Attention test despite adequate technical properties of the test for his age range, which suggests significant weaknesses in speech–sound discrimination. He also demonstrated relative weaknesses (low to low average standard scores) on additional phonemic awareness tasks, including the ability to identify words with missing phonemes, to rhyme words, and to use phoneme deletion, substitution, and reversals to make new words. RPI scores (Incomplete Words, 68/90; Sound Awareness, 36/90) suggest that Alex's proficiency with more advanced phonemic awareness skills is limited. Weaknesses in these areas are consistent with Alex's below-average early reading skills.

Implications and Recommendations

Alex's weaknesses in receptive language skills and home language background warrant consideration for support through the English as a Second Language (ESL) program. His weaknesses in sound discrimination and advanced phonemic awareness tasks may also be reflective of limited familiarity with English language phonemes. Alex should benefit from direct instruction in language concepts (e.g., temporal, directional, positional, relational, and quantity-related words) and linguistic concepts that are less contextually driven. Directions given in the classroom should be monitored for sentence length and complexity. Repetition and/or simplification of orally presented instructions may be required. Further, when new concepts are presented, the provision of examples of how the information relates to previously learned material and the use of visual stimuli or experiential activities will be helpful to Alex. Should difficulties continue despite the recommended supports, further assessment by a language specialist may be warranted.

Alex demonstrates adequate vocabulary development and initial phonological awareness skills, in that he was able to adequately blend syllables and some phonemes to form words. However, his weaknesses with more advanced phonemic awareness skills suggest that he may continue to encounter significant difficulty in learning to read. To further enhance reading acquisition and prevent later reading disabilities, Alex may benefit from a phonological reading program that specifically teaches letter/sound and grapheme/sound relationships, segmentation, and deletion skills. A variety of engaging activities can be utilized in the school or home setting to develop these skills (e.g., rhyming games or songs, clapping to segments in words, literature that plays with language sounds). Commercial programs are also available that provide an appropriate sequence of instruction in phonological awareness skills (e.g., Adams, Foorman, Lundberg, & Beeler, 1998). Alex's performance with these tasks should be monitored to determine growth over time.

RACHEL: 4 YEARS, 7 MONTHS

This case demonstrates how the tests from the Diagnostic Supplement allow for a measure of overall cognitive functioning (GIA : EDev) for a young child. The profile also illustrates how the WJ III can be used in a cross-battery approach to provide additional information on specific cognitive abilities.

Case History

Rachel was referred to determine her eligibility for early childhood special education services. She was born 7 weeks premature and had significant difficulties breathing at birth. Most developmental milestones have been somewhat delayed. Rachel received speech/language services through a birth to three program, from which she was dismissed after turning three. She has participated in Head Start programming since then, and speech/language services have continued. Rachel is an only child. Her mother is trained as a preschool teacher and her father is an elementary school teacher. Both parents are very supportive and have worked diligently with Rachel on language skills at home. Current teachers are concerned that Rachel does not appear to learn new material as quickly as her peers and has difficulty remembering directions. However, when routines are well established she does well. Social development also appears delayed, in that Rachel's play routines tend to be simplistic and lacking in imaginative play.

Assessments

The *Vineland Adaptive Behavior Scales* (VABS), *Battelle Developmental Inventory* (BDI), and DAS were administered. Select tests from the WJ III COG and Diagnostic Supplement were also administered to provide an overall Early Development General Intellectual Ability score.

Interpretations

The adaptive behavior interview completed with Rachel's mother suggests delays of more than 1.5 standard deviations in language comprehension and self-help skills. Teacher ratings on the VABS and findings from the BDI were consistent with parent ratings and also suggest significant delays in receptive language and cognition, and mild delays in daily living skills, including toileting, dressing, and personal responsibility. Interpersonal relationships were also noted as a concern. Rachel demonstrates age-appropriate fine and gross motor skills.

Consistent findings emerged across both cognitive ability measures (Table 8-8). Rachel's overall cognitive functioning is in the low range and ranks at the 3rd to 4th percentiles. The WJ III RPI score (60/90) associated with her overall performance suggests mildly delayed cognitive development. Rachel will likely find tasks geared toward children her age quite frustrating, whereas, tasks geared toward children approximately $2\frac{1}{2}$ years younger than her will likely be easy (Developmental Zone < 2:0 to 4:2 years). Her speed in processing simple cognitive tasks also appears to be mildly delayed and is in the low range relative to children of the same age. Verbal skills (low average to average range) are better developed than visual-spatial skills (very low to low range), and therefore appear to be an area of relative strength for Rachel.

Rachel's performance across verbal ability tasks was consistent with her enriched environment and speech/language experiences. She demonstrated adequate vocabulary knowledge and expressive language skills. Receptive language tasks and tasks involving verbal reasoning were more difficult for her. Contributing to her performance in this area was an observed weakness in retaining orally presented directions. Rachel often requested that directions be repeated on the DAS Verbal Comprehension and Early Number Concepts subtests. Across visual-spatial tasks, Rachel demonstrated adequate visual–closure skills and visual–motor integration skills. However, tasks requiring mental rotations of the visual stimuli presented, as well as those influenced by problem-solving skills such as hypothesis testing and the ability to reconstruct a visual stimulus from its parts, were significantly more challenging.

Rachel's visual memory skills were in the low-average range relative to same-age peers, which suggests mild delays in this area as well. Auditory memory skills were a greater weakness and in the low range relative to same-age peers. Rachel struggled with retaining and restating number and word series presented to her orally. However, her performance on the Memory for Sentences task was somewhat stronger and suggests somewhat better short-term memory skills when the information to be remembered is more meaningful. Further, although associative

TABLE 8-8   Score Profile: Rachel

Cluster/subtest	Standard score	Percentile	RPI score
DAS General Conceptual Ability	75	4th	
WJ III Early Development GIA	71	3rd	60/90
DAS Verbal Ability Cluster	90	25th	
WJ III Comprehension/Knowledge Cluster (*Gc*)	87	18th	71/90
DAS Nonverbal Ability Cluster	68	2nd	
WJ III Visual–Spatial Thinking III (*Gv*)	74	4th	40/90
WJ III Auditory Memory Span (*Gsm*)	79	8th	34/90
DAS Verbal Comprehension	41	18th	
DAS Naming Vocabulary	48	42nd	
WJ III Verbal Comprehension	80	9th	64/90
WJ III General Information	91	28th	76/90
DAS Early Number Concepts	34	5th	
DAS Pattern Construction	38	12th	
DAS Picture Similarities	20	1st	
DAS Copying	43	24th	
WJ III Visual Closure	104	59th	93/90
WJ III Spatial Relations	73	4th	36/90
WJ III Picture Recognition	81	10th	44/90
DAS Recognition of Pictures	39	14th	
DAS Recall of Objects	40	16th	
WJ III Memory for Names	85	15th	73/90
DAS Recall of Digits	35	7th	
WJ III Memory for Words	76	6th	12/90
WJ III Memory for Sentences	89	23rd	66/90
WJ III Visual Matching	75	4th	36/90
WJ III Incomplete Words	105	64th	93/90

Note: DAS subtests standard scores are expressed as *T* scores.

memory skills were also in the low-average range, Rachel's RPI scores (73/90) for Memory for Names relative to the Auditory Memory Span cluster (34/90) and Picture Recognition (44/90) suggest much greater proficiency with memory tasks when visual and verbal cues are paired.

Implications and Recommendations

Given moderate delays in self-help skills and cognitive development, Rachel appears to qualify for early childhood services as a student with a "Significant Developmental Delay" according to state criteria (i.e., delays greater than 1.5 SD relative to same-age peers in cognitive development and self-help skills). She will benefit from cognitive tasks that are geared toward an age range approximately 14 to 16 months younger than her current age and from additional time to complete tasks. Teaching skills through a scaffolding technique may also be beneficial for Rachel, because this will allow her to experience new learning that is built upon previously acquired skills. To improve visual-spatial skills, Rachel should be provided with more visual tasks involving manipulatives, such as puzzles or other activities requiring the construction of a whole from its parts, and hypothesis testing. Further practice with concepts such as "same" and "different" and classification tasks that require her to sort objects by visual characteristics should be encouraged.

Memory abilities are a significant concern for Rachel, particularly when she is required to comprehend and store new information. Her overall profile suggests greater efficiency when visual and verbal cues are paired or when information to be retained is more meaningful and is paired with contextual cues. Thus, when presenting classroom material it will be important to provide Rachel with visual cues as well as guided instruction so that she can experience successful completion of a task before being asked to repeat the task independently. Storyboards with meaningful visual cues depicting the steps in new routines may be a useful teaching strategy. Oral directions should be kept short and should include linguistic concepts that Rachel has mastered. It will be helpful to break multistep directions into smaller parts and then have Rachel complete each part before moving on to the next step. Having her paraphrase directions before beginning a task will also be helpful. Extra repetition and over learning of new routines may also be needed.

ACKNOWLEDGMENT

The authors thank Jennifer Salava for her assistance with library research and in calculating test floors.

REFERENCES

Adams, M. J. (1990). *Beginning to read: Thinking and learning about print.* Cambridge, MA: MIT Press.

Adams, M. J., Foorman, B. R., Lundberg, I., & Beeler, T. (1998). *Phonemic awareness in young children.* Baltimore: Paul H. Brookes.

Ahmad, S. A., & Warriner, E. M. (2001). Review of the NEPSY: A developmental neuropsychological assessment. *The Clinical Neuropsychologist, 15*(2), 240–249.

Amsel, E., Goodman, G., Savoie, D., & Clark, M. (1996). The development of reasoning about causal and noncausal influences of levers. *Child Development, 67*(4), 1624–1646.

Aoki, C., & Siekevitz, D. (1988). Plasticity and brain development. *Scientific American, 259*(6), 56–65.

Aylward, G. P., Gioia, G., Verhulst, S. J., & Bell, S. (1995). Factor structure of the Wide Range Assessment of Memory and Learning in a clinical population. *Journal of Psychoeducational Assessment, 13,* 132–142.

Baddeley, A. D., & Hitch, G. J. (2000). Development of working memory: Should the Pascual–Leone and the Baddeley and Hitch models be merged? *Journal of Experimental Child Psychology, 77,* 128–137.

Baddeley, A. D., & Logie, R. H. (1999). Working memory: The multiple-component model. In A. Miyake & P. Shah (Eds.), *Models of working memory: Mechanisms of active maintenance and executive control* (pp. 28–61). New York: Cambridge University Press.

Badian, N. A. (1995). Preschool prediction: Orthographic and phonological skills, and reading. *Annals of Dyslexia, 44*, 3–25.

Bagnato, S. J., & Neisworth, J. T. (1994). A national study of the social and treatment "invalidity" of intelligence testing for early intervention. *School Psychology Quarterly, 9*, 81–101.

Barnett, P. W., Macmann, G. M., & Carey, K. T. (1992). Early intervention and the assessment of developmental skills: Challenges and directions. *Topics in Early Childhood Special Education, 12*(1), 21–43.

Bellis, T. J. (1996). *Assessment and management of central auditory processing disorders in the educational setting: From science to practice.* San Diego: Singular Publishing Group.

Bowers, P., Steffy, R., & Tate, E. (1986). Naming speed, memory, and visual processing in reading disability. *Canadian Journal of Behavioral Science, 18*, 209–223.

Bracken, B. A. (1994). Advocating for effective preschool assessment practices: A comment on Bagnato and Neisworth. *School Psychology Quarterly, 9*(2), 103–108.

Bracken, B. A. (2000). *The Psychoeducational Assessment of Preschool Children.* Needham Heights, MA: Allyn & Bacon.

Bradley, L., & Bryant, P. (1983). Categorizing sounds and learning to read: A causal connection. *Nature, 301*, 419–421.

Bradley-Johnson, S. (2001). Cognitive assessment for the youngest children: A critical review of tests. *Journal of Psychoeducational Assessment, 19*, 19–44.

Bryant, P. E., MacLean, M., Bradley, L. L., & Crossland, J. (1990). Rhyme and alliteration, phoneme detection, and learning to read. *Developmental Psychology, 26*, 429–438.

Butler, S. R., Marsh, H. W., Sheppard, M. J., & Shappard, J. L. (1985). Seven-year longitudinal study of the early prediction of reading achievement. *Journal of Educational Psychology, 77*(3), 349–361.

Byrne, B., & Fielding-Barnsley, R. F. (1993). Evaluation of a program to teach phonemic awareness to young children: A 1-year follow-up. *Journal of Educational Psychology, 85*, 104–111.

Byrnes, J. P. (2001). *Minds, brains, and learning.* New York: Guilford Press.

Carroll, J. B. (1993). *Human cognitive abilities: A survey of factor-analytic studies.* Cambridge, England: Cambridge University Press.

Case, R. (1984). The process of stage transition: A neopiagetian view. In R. L. Sternberg (Ed.), *Mechanisms of cognitive development.* New York: Freeman.

Ceci, S. J., & Roazzi, A. (1994). The effects of context on cognition: Postcards from Brazil. In R. J. Sternberg & R. K. Wagner (Eds.), *Mind in context: Interactionist perspectives on human intelligence.* Cambridge, England: Cambridge University Press.

Chen, Z., & Siegler, R. S. (2000). Across the great divide: Bridging the gap between and understanding of toddlers and other children's thinking. *Monographs of the Society for Research in Child Development, 65*(2, Serial No. 261).

Chuah, Y. M., & Mayberry, M. T. (1999). Verbal and spatial short-term memory: Common sources of developmental change? *Journal of Experimental Child Psychology, 73*, 7–44.

Coalson, D., Weiss, L., Zhu, J., Spruill, J., & Crockett, D. (2002, February). Development of the WPPSI-III. Paper presented at the annual meeting of the National Association of School Psychologists, Chicago, IL.

Cowan, N., Saults, J. S., Nugent, L. D., & Elliot, E. M. (1999). The microanalysis of memory span and its development in childhood. *International Journal of Psychology, 34*(516), 353–358.

Damon, W., Kuhn, D., & Siegler, R. W. (Eds.). (1998). *Handbook of child psychology: Vol. 2. Cognition, perception, and language.* New York: John Wiley & Sons.

Daneman, M., & Merikle, P. M. (1996). Working memory and language comprehension: A meta-analysis. *Psychonomic Bulletin and Review, 3*(4), 422–433.

Dapretto, M., & Bjork, E. L. (2000). The development of word retrieval abilities in the second year and its relationship to vocabulary growth. *Child Development, 71*(3), 635–648.

Dawson, G., & Fischer, K. (1993). *Human development and the developing brain.* New York: Guilford Press.

Denckla, M., & Rudel, R. (1976). Rapid automatized naming (RAN): Dyslexia differentiated from other learning disabilities. *Neuropsychologia, 14*, 471–479.

Dunn, W. (1999). Assessment of sensorimotor and perceptual development. In E. V. Nuttall, I. Romero, & J. Kalesnik (Eds.), *Assessing and screening preschoolers: Psychological and educational dimensions* (2nd ed., pp. 240–261). Boston: Allyn & Bacon.

Eichenbaum, H., & Cohen, N. J. (2001). *From conditioning to conscious recollection.* Oxford: Oxford University Press.

Elliott, C. D. (1990). *Differential ability scale.* New York: Psychological Corporation.

Engle, R. W., Kane, M. J., & Tuholski, S. W. (1999). Individual differences in working memory capacity and what they tell us about controlled attention, general fluid intelligence, and functions of prefrontal cortex. In A. Miyake & P. Shah (Eds.), *Models of working memory: Mechanisms of active maintenance and executive control* (pp. 28–61). New York: Cambridge University Press.

Engle, R. W., Laughlin, J. E., Tuholski, S. W., & Conway, A. R. A. (1999). Working memory, short-term memory, and general fluid intelligence: A latent-variable approach. *Journal of Experimental Psychology: General, 128*(3), 309–332.

Espy, K. A., Kaufmann, P. M., Glisky, M. L., & McDiarmid, M. D. (2001). New procedures to assess executive functions in preschool children. *The Clinical Neuropsychologist, 15*(1), 46–58.

Evans, J. J., Floyd, R. G., McGrew, K. S., & Leforgee, M. H. (in press). The relations between measures of Cattell–Horn–Carroll (CHC) cognitive abilities and reading achievement during childhood and adolescence. *School Psychology Review.*

Flanagan, D. P., & Alfonso, V. C. (1995). A critical review of the technical characteristics of new and recently revised intelligence tests for preschool children. *Journal of Psychoeducational Assessment, 13*, 66–90.

Flanagan, D. P., Mascolo, J., & Genshaft, J. L. (2000). A conceptual framework for interpreting preschool intelligence tests. In B. A. Bracken (Ed.), *The Psychoeducational Assessment of Preschool Children* (pp. 428–473). Boston: Allyn & Bacon.

Flanagan, D. P., McGrew, K. S., & Ortiz, S. O. (2000). *The Wechsler intelligence scales and Gf–Gc theory: A contemporary approach to interpretation.* Boston: Allyn & Bacon.

Ford, L. (2002). Understanding cognitive abilities in young children: Exploring abilities beyond *g.* In R. Floyd (Chair). *Beyond g: Implications from research with contemporary tests of cognitive abilities.* Symposium presented at the annual meeting of the National Association of School Psychologists.

Ford, L. (2003). Assessing young children. In R. W. Woodcock, K. McGrew, N. Mather, & F. J. Schrank. *Diagnostic Supplement to the WJ III.* Itasca, IL: Riverside Publishing.

Ford, L., McGrew, K., & Tusing, M. E. (in preparation). Exploratory factor analysis of preschool tests using CHC theory.

Fry, A. F., & Hale, S. (1996). Processing speed, working memory, and fluid intelligence: Evidence for a developmental cascade. *Psychological Science, 7*, 237–241.

Garrett, H. E. (1946). A developmental theory of intelligence. *American Psychologist, 1*, 372–378.

Gathercole, S. E., & Baddeley, A. D. (1993). *Working memory and language.* Hove, United Kingdom: Erlbaum.

Gathercole, S. E., & Hitch, G. J. (1993). Developmental changes in short-term memory: A revised working memory perspective. In S. F. Collins, S. E. Gathercole, M. A. Conway, & P. E. Morris (Eds.), *Theories of memory*; Hillsdale, New Jersey: Erlbaum.

Gathercole, S. E., Willis, C., Emslie, H., & Baddeley, A. D. (1992). Differentiating phonological memory and awareness of rhyme: Reading vocabulary development in children. *British Journal of Psychology, 82*(3), 387–406.

Gelb, M., & Alfonso, V. C. (2002). *Utility of the Woodcock–Johnson III tests of cognitive abilities with preschoolers with developmental delays.* Paper presented at the Train the Trainers Meeting, Itasca, IL.

German, D. J. (1990). *National college of education test of adolescent/adult word finding.* Austin, TX: PRO-ED.

Gershkoff-Stow, N., & Smith, E. (1997). A curvilinear trend in naming errors as a function of early vocabulary growth. *Cognitive Psychology, 34*(1), 37–72.

Goswami, U., & Bryant, P. E. (1990). *Phonological skills and learning to read.* Hillsdale, NJ: Erlbaum.

Goswami, U., & Bryant, P. E. (1992). Rhyme, analogy, and children's reading. In P. B. Gough, L. C. Ehri, & R. Treiman (Eds.), *Reading acquisition* (pp. 49–62). Hillsdale, NJ: Erlbaum.

Grannot, N. (1998). A paradigm shift in the study of development: Essay review of *Emerging Minds* by R. S. Siegler. *Human Development, 41,* 360–365.

Hale, S. (1990). A global developmental trend in cognitive processing speed in children. *Child Development, 61,* 653–663.

Henry, L. A., & Millar, S. (1993). Why does memory span improve with age? A review of the evidence for two current hypotheses. *European Journal of Psychology, 5*(3), 241–287.

Hooper, S. R. (2000). Neuropsychological assessment of the preschool child. In B. A. Bracken (Ed.). *The psychoeducational assessment of preschool children* (pp. 383–398). Boston: Allyn & Bacon.

Horn, J. L. (1985). Remodeling old models of intelligence. In B. B. Wolman (Ed.), *Handbook of Intelligence* (pp. 267–300). New York: Wiley.

Horn, J. L. (1991). Measurement of intellectual capabilities: A review of theory. In K. S. McGrew, J. K. Werder, & R. W. Woodcock. *WJ-R technical manual* (pp. 197–232). Allen, TX: DLM.

Horn, J. L., & Noll, J. (1997). Human cognitive abilities: Gf–Gc theory. In D. P. Flanagan, J. L. Genshaft, & P. L. Harrison (Eds.), *Contemporary intellectual assessment* (pp. 53–91). New York: Guilford Press.

Howe, M. L. (2000). *The fate of early memories: Developmental science and the retention of childhood experiences.* Washington, DC: American Psychological Association.

Hulme, C., & Roodenrys, S. (1994). Practitioner review: Verbal working memory development and its disorders. *Journal of Child Psychology and Psychiatry and Allied Disciplines, 3,* 373–398.

Jackson, N., & Myers, M. (1982). Letter-naming time, digit span, and precocious reading achievement. *Intelligence, 6,* 311–329.

Juel, C. (1988). Learning to read and write: A longitudinal study of 54 children from first through 4th grades. *Journal of Educational Psychology, 80,* 437–447.

Kail, R. (1991). Developmental change in speed of processing during childhood and adolescence. *Psychological Bulletin, 109,* 490–501.

Kail, R. (1993). The role of a global mechanism in developmental change in speed of processing. In M. L. Howe & R. Pasnak (Eds.), *Emerging themes in cognitive development: Vol. 1. Foundations.* New York: Springer-Verlag.

Kail, R. (1997). Phonological skill and articulation time independently contribute to the development of memory span. *Journal of Experimental Child Psychology, 67,* 57–68.

Kail, R. (2000). Speed of information processing: Developmental change and links to intelligence. *Journal of School Psychology, 38*(1), 51–61.

Kane, M. J., Conway, A. R. A., Bleckley, M. K., & Engle, R. W. (2001). A controlled-attention view of working memory capacity. *Journal of Experimental Psychology: General, 130*(2), 169–175.

Kavale, K. A., & Forness, S. R. (2000). Auditory and visual perception processes and reading ability: A quantitative reanalysis and historical reinterpretation. *Learning Disabilities Quarterly, 23*(4), 253–270.

Kemps, E., DeRammelaere, S., & Desmet, T. (2000). The development of working memory: Exploring the complementarity of two models. *Journal of Experimental Child Psychology, 77,* 89–109.

Konold, T. R., Juel, C., & McKinnon, M. (1999). *Building an integrated model of early reading acquisition* (Tech. Rep. No. 1–003). Ann Arbor, MI: University of Michigan, Center for the Improvement of Early Reading Achievement. Retrieved January 17, 2002, from the CIERA Web site: http://www.ciera.org.

Korkman, M., Kirk, U., & Kemp, S. (1998). *NEPSY: A Developmental Neuropsychological Assessment.* San Antonio, TX: The Psychological Corporation.

Kuhn, D., & Siegler, R. S. (1998). Handbook of child psychology: Vol. 2. Cognition, perception, and language (5th Ed.). New York, NY: Wiley.

League, S. (2000). *Joint factor analysis of the Woodcock–Johnson III and the Wechsler preschool and primary scale of intelligence—Revised.* Unpublished doctoral dissertation. University of South Carolina.

Lentz, F. E. (1988). Effective reading interventions in the regular classroom. In J. L. Graden, J. E. Zins, & M. J. Curtis (Eds.), *Alternative educational delivery systems: Enhancing instructional options for all students* (pp. 351–373). Washington, DC: National Association of School Psychologists.

Lesiak, J. L. (1997). Research based answers to questions about emergent literacy in kindergarten. *Psychology in the Schools, 34*(2), 143–158.

Lonigan, C. J., Burgess, S. R., & Anthony, J. L. (2000). Development of emergent literacy and early reading skills in preschool children: Evidence from a latent-variable longitudinal study. *Developmental Psychology, 36*(5), 596–613.

Lonigan, C. J., & Whitehurst G. J. (1998). Relative efficacy of parent and teacher involvement in a shared reading intervention for preschool children from low income backgrounds. *Early Childhood Research Quarterly, 13*(2), 263–290.

MacLean, M., Bryant, P. E., & Bradley, L. (1987). Rhymes, nursery rhymes, and reading in early childhood. *Merrill-Palmer Quarterly, 33*, 255–282.

Mather, N., & Woodcock, R. W. (2001). Examiner's Manual. *Woodcock–Johnson III tests of cognitive abilities.* Itasca, IL: Riverside Publishing.

McBride-Chang, C., & Manis, F. (1996). Structural invariance in the associations of naming speed, phonological awareness, and verbal reasoning in good and poor readers: A test of the double deficit hypothesis. *Reading and Writing, 8*, 323–339.

McCullough, J. (2001). *Predictive and concurrent validity of the Woodcock–Johnson—third edition with preschool age children.* Unpublished master's thesis. University of South Carolina.

McDevitt, T. M., & Ormrod, J. E. (2002). *Child development and education.* Saddle River, NJ: Pearson Education.

McGrew, K. S., & Flanagan, D. P. (1998). *The intelligence test desk reference (ITDR): Gf–Gc cross-battery assessment.* Boston: Allyn & Bacon.

McGrew, K. S., Werder, J. K., & Woodcock, R. W. (1991). *WJ-R technical manual.* Allen, TX: DLM.

McGrew, K. S., & Woodcock, R. W. (2001). Technical manual. *Woodcock–Johnson III.* Itasca, IL: Riverside Publishing.

Meisels, S. J., & Atkins-Burnett, S. (2001). The elements of early childhood assessment. In J. P. Shonkoff and S. J. Meisels (Eds.). *Handbook of early childhood intervention (2nd Ed).* New York, NY: Cambridge Press.

Metsala, J. L. (1999). Young children's phonological awareness and nonword repetition as a function of vocabulary development. *Journal of Educational Psychology, 91*(1), 3–19.

Miles, C., & Morgan, M. J. (1996). Developmental and individual differences in visual memory span. *Memory, 15*(1), 53–68.

Miller, L. T., & Vernon, P. A. (1997). Developmental changes in speed of information processing in young children. *Developmental Psychology, 33*(3), 549–554.

Miyake, A., Friedman, N. P., Rettinger, D. A., Shah, P., & Hegarty, M. (2001). How are visual-spatial working memory, executive functioning, and spatial abilities related? A latent variable analysis. *Journal of Experimental Psychology, 130*(4), 621–640.

Mullen, E. M. (1995). *Mullen scales of early learning.* Circle Pines, MN: American Guidance Service.

Muter, V., & Diethelm, K. (2001). The contribution of phonological skills and letter knowledge to early reading development in a multilingual population. *Language and Learning, 51*(2), 187–219.

Muter, V., Hulme, C., Snowling, M., & Taylor, S. (1997). Segmentation, not rhyming, predicts early progress in learning to read. *Journal of Experimental Child Psychology, 65*, 370–398.

O'Connor, R., Notari-Syverson, A., & Vadasy, P. (1996). Ladders to literacy: The effects of teacher-led phonological activities for kindergarten children with and without disabilities. *Exceptional Children, 63*, 117–130.

Palmer, G. A., Weinhaus, D. N., & Pohlman, C. (2001). Test reviews: NEPSY. *Journal of Psychoeducational Assessment, 19*, 89–95.

Pickering, S. J., Gathercole, S. E., & Peaker, S. M. (1998). Verbal and visuospatial short-term memory in children: Evidence for common and distinct mechanisms. *Memory and Cognition, 25*(6), 1117–1130.

Pillemer, D. B., & White, S. H. (1989). Childhood events recalled by children and adults. In H. W. Reese (Ed.), *Advances in child development and behavior: Vol. 21.* (pp. 297–340). New York, NY: Academic Press.

Reese, H. W. (Ed). (1994). *Advances in child development and behavior* (Vol. 25). San Diego, CA: Academic Press.

Richardson, J. T. E., Engle, R. W., Hasher, L., Logie, R. H., Stoltzfus, E. R., & Zacks, R. T. (1996). *Working memory and human cognition.* New York: Oxford University Press.

Roid, G. H., & Miller, L. J. (1997). *Leiter international performance scale—Revised.* Wood Dale, IL: Stoelting.

Salava, J., & Tusing, M. E. (in preparation). Concurrent validity of the WJ III tests of cognitive ability and the differential ability scales for a sample of preschool children with language delays.

Sampaio, R. C., & Truwitt, C. L. (2001). Myelination in the developing human brain. In C. A. Nelson & M. Luciana (Eds.), *Handbook of developmental cognitive neuroscience.* Cambridge, Massachusetts: MIT Press.

Scarborough, H. (1990). Very early language deficits in dyslexic children. *Child Development, 61*(6), 1728–1744.

Scarborough, H. (1991). Early syntactic development of dyslexic children. *Annals of Dyslexia, 41,* 207–290.

Schneider, W. (2000). Research on memory development: Historical trends and current themes. *International Journal of Behavioral Development, 24*(4), 407–420.

Schneider, W., & Pressley, M. (1997). *Memory development between two and twenty* (2nd ed.). Mahwah, NJ: Erlbaum.

Schrank, F. A. (1991). Using the WJ–R in preschool assessment. *Psychoeducational Network Riverside Monograph, 2.*

Siders, J., & Tusing, M. E. (in preparation). Assessing the language proficiency of preschool-age ESL students.

Siegler, R. S. (1986). *Children's thinking.* Englewood Cliffs, New Jersey: Prentice Hall.

Siegler, R. S. (1996). *Emerging minds: The process of change in children's thinking.* New York: Oxford Press.

Siegler, R. S. (1998). *Children's thinking.* Englewood Cliffs, New Jersey: Prentice Hall.

Slater, A., Morison, V., & Rose, D. (1982). Visual memory at birth. *British Journal of Psychology, 73,* 519–525.

Smith, E. E., & Jonides, J. (1997). Working memory: A view from neuroimaging. *Cognitive Psychology, 33,* 5–42.

Stanovich, K. E. (1986). Matthew effects in reading: Some consequences of individual differences in the acquisition of literacy. *Reading Research Quarterly, 21,* 360–407.

Sternberg, R. J. (Ed.). (1994). *Encyclopedia of human intelligence* (Vol. 2). New York: MacMillan.

Stone, B., Gridley, B., & Gyurke, J. (1991). Confirmatory factor analysis of the WPPSI-R at the extreme end of the age range. *Journal of Psychoeducational Assessment, 9,* 263–270.

Swanson, H. L. (1999). What develops in working memory? A life span perspective. *Developmental Psychology, 33,* 5–42.

Swanson, H. L., & Berninger, V. W. (1996). Individual differences in children's working memory and writing skill. *Journal of Experimental Child Psychology, 63*(2), 358–386.

Teague, T. (1999). *Confirmatory analysis of Woodcock–Johnson—third edition and the differential abilities scale with preschool age children.* Unpublished doctoral dissertation. University of South Carolina.

Thorndike, R. L., Hagen, E. P., & Sattler, J. M. (1986). *Stanford–Binet intelligence scale: 4th edition.* Chicago, IL: Riverside.

Torgesen, J. K., Morgan, S. T., & Davis, C. (1993). Effects of two types of phonological awareness training on word learning in kindergarten children. *Journal of Educational Psychology, 84*(3), 364–370.

Torgesen, J. K., Wagner, R. K., & Rashotte, C. A. (1997). Approaches to the prevention of phonologically based reading disabilities. In B. A. Blachman (Ed.), *Foundations of reading acquisition and dyslexia: Implications for early intervention* (pp. 287–304). Mahwah, NJ: Erlbaum.

Towse, J. N., Hitch, G. J., & Hutton, U. (1998). A re-evaluation of working memory capacity in children. *Journal of Memory and Language, 39,* 195–217.

Tuholski, S. W., Engle, R. W., & Baylis, G. C. (2001). Individual differences in working memory capacity and enumeration. *Memory and Cognition, 29*(3), 484–492.

Tusing, M. E., & Ford, L. (under review). Linking ability measures for young children to contemporary theories of cognitive ability. *International Journal of Testing.*

Wagner, R. K., & Torgesen, J. K. (1987). The nature of phonological processing and its causal role in the acquisition of reading skills. *Psychological Bulletin, 101,* 192–212.

Wagner, R. K., Torgesen, J. K., & Rashotte, C. A. (1994). The development of reading-related phonological processing abilities: New evidence of bi-directional causality from a latent variable longitudinal study. *Developmental Psychology, 30,* 73–87.

Wechsler, D. (1989). *Wechsler preschool and primary scale of intelligence—revised.* San Antonio, TX: Psychological Corporation.

Weinert, F. E., & Schneider, W. (Eds.). (1995). *Memory performance and competencies: Issues in growth and development.* Mahwah, NJ: Erlbaum.

Whitehurst, G. J., & Lonigan, C. J. (1998). Child development and emergent literacy. *Child Development, 69,* 848–872.

Windfuhr, K. L., & Snowling, M. J. (2001). The relationship between paired associate learning and phonological skills in normally developing readers. *Journal of Experimental Child Psychology, 80*(2), 160–173.

Wolf, M. (1991). Naming speed and reading: The contribution of the cognitive neurosciences. *Reading Research Quarterly, 26*(2), 123–141.

Wolf, M., Bally, H., & Morris, R. (1986). Automaticity, retrieval processes, and reading: A longitudinal study in average and impaired readers. *Child Development, 57,* 988–1000.

Wolf, M., & Bowers, P. (1999). The "double-deficit hypothesis" for the developmental dyslexias. *Journal of Educational Psychology, 91,* 1–24.

Wolf, M., Bowers, P. G., & Biddle, K. (2000). Naming-speed processes, timing, and reading: A conceptual review. *Journal of Learning Disabilities, 33*(4), 387–407.

Woodcock, R. W., & Johnson, M. B. (1989). *Woodcock–Johnson psycho-educational battery—revised.* Itasca, IL: Riverside Publishing.

Woodcock, R. W., McGrew, K. S., & Mather, N. (2001). *Woodcock–Johnson III.* Itasca, IL: Riverside Publishing.

Woodcock, R. W., McGrew, K. S., Mather, N., & Schrank, F. A. (2003). *Diagnostic supplement to the Woodcock–Johnson III tests of cognitive abilities.* Itasca, IL: Riverside Publishing.

Yopp, H. K. (1988). The validity and reliability of phonemic awareness tests. *Reading Research Quarterly, 23*(2), 159–177.

9

ASSESSMENT OF GIFTED CHILDREN WITH THE WOODCOCK–JOHNSON III

BETTY E. GRIDLEY AND KIMBERLY A. NORMAN

Department of Educational Psychology
Ball State University
Muncie, Indiana 47306

MARY G. RIZZA

Educational Foundations and Inquiry
Bowling Green State University, Bowling Green, Ohio 43403

SCOTT L. DECKER

Riverside Publishing Company, Itasca, Illinois 60143

"The United States is squandering one of its most precious resources—the gifts, talents, and high interests of many of its students." (Ross, 1993, p. 3).
"We must acknowledge the potential contribution to society of particularly capable learners and provide nourishment for development of that potential."
(Gridley, 1990, p. 811)

Some readers of this book may be tempted to skip this chapter. After all, why would anyone write an entire chapter about assessing gifted students with the Woodcock–Johnson III (WJ III)? School psychologists might argue that gifted students are not included under the Individuals with Disabilities Education Act (IDEA) and are therefore not part of the usual caseload. However, Coleman and Cross (2001) asserted that the gifted *are* handicapped. First, these individuals are different from their peers (even though their differences can be described more readily by strengths than weaknesses), and second, general education has often proved inadequate in meeting their needs. Unfortunately, the education of highly able youngsters remains largely unchanged from the state described by Gridley

(1990) more than 10 years ago. The dialogue about the educational needs of gifted children has continued in the past decade with discussions by Ross (1993) and Callahan (2000). A major area of debate has centered around the definition of giftedness. The danger remains that children with high-level abilities who are not challenged appropriately will develop behavior or other problems and their gifts will not be used to benefit themselves or the rest of society.

Why a whole chapter on giftedness? A unique series of issues and concerns must be addressed for this population. Although educators of the gifted have discussed these concerns elsewhere, many psychologists have little experience in assessing gifted individuals or dealing with the general issues prevalent in the field. The purpose of this chapter is to provide information for professionals interested in best practice regarding assessment of gifted students. The first part of the chapter provides a definition of giftedness and some background on its development. A rationale for the value of the WJ III in providing relevant information is also discussed. Next, there is an outline of some characteristics of gifted students that have general implications for testing. Finally, there is a presentation of case studies that illustrate various aspects of using the WJ III with gifted students.

DEFINITIONS OF GIFTEDNESS

Many definitions of "gifted" have been offered and the topic is in constant debate (cf. Coleman & Cross, 2001; Pfeiffer, 2001). Experts in gifted education surveyed by Pfeiffer (2001) named lack of consensus on how to conceptualize or define gifted and talented under the category of "greatest identification, assessment, and definitional issues" in the gifted field. An entire issue of the *Journal for the Education of the Gifted* (1999) was devoted to defining the term. Definitions of giftedness could be classified in a myriad of ways (cf. Coleman & Cross, 2001) depending upon one's purpose. Organization of the following discussion is based upon Gallagher and Courtright's (1986) taxonomy, which classifies giftedness into two categories: educational and psychological.

EDUCATIONAL DEFINITIONS AND PRACTICE

Educational definitions are concerned with the behaviors and traits that guide educational practice—particularly the identification and promotion of talent in school settings (Gallagher & Courtright, 1986). Callahan (2000) concluded that, based on citations and a number of state policy documents such as regulations for gifted programs, the fairly broad definition offered by the United States Office of Education (Marland, 1972) remained the predominant one used in schools.

According to this definition, "gifted and talented children are those who demonstrate achievement and/or potential in any of the following areas: general intellectual ability, specific academic aptitude, creativity or productive thinking, leadership ability, visual and performing arts, and psychomotor ability" (Marland, 1972, p. 10). When this definition was revised in 1993 in the U.S.

Department of Education Report, *National Excellence: A Case for Developing America's Talent,* the categories remained essentially the same, with the omission of psychomotor ability. The term "gifted and talented" was replaced with "outstanding talent." The new definition reads as follows:

> Children and youth with outstanding talent perform or show potential for performing at remarkably high levels of accomplishment when compared with others of their age, experience, or environment. These children and youth exhibit high performance capability in intellectual, creative, and/or artistic areas, possess an unusual leadership capacity, or excel in specific academic fields. They require services or activities not ordinarily provided by schools. Outstanding talents are present in children and youth from all cultural groups, across all economic strata, and in all areas of human endeavor. (Ross, 1993, p. 4)

Although not mandated under IDEA, many states provide programming for students of high ability. Exactly because there is no federal mandate, identification of such students has been highly idiosyncratic, varying greatly depending on location. Although purporting a philosophy of recognition of and education for multiple aspects of ability, many schools focus their identification practices on the first two aspects of this definition—general intellectual ability and specific academic performance (Callahan, 2000). Indeed, when schools operationalize this definition, they most often use an IQ definition of giftedness based on the top 3–5% on intelligence tests (Abeel, Callahan, & Hunsaker, 1994; Stephens & Karnes, 2000). High-level ability and/or performance are almost always defined as high test scores—usually two or more standard deviations above the mean on group tests. In many cases, these group tests are followed up with additional information, but this first screening may systematically eliminate some students, such as children in certain ethnic or socioeconomic groups, those who are culturally or linguistically different, or those with learning disorders who traditionally fare poorly on group tests. Additional information gathered seldom includes individual evaluations. Individual assessments are the exception rather than the rule, occurring only when serious questions arise or when sought through private funding by parents. For an excellent description of identification processes and issues, see Clark (2002).

PSYCHOLOGICAL DEFINITIONS AND PRACTICE

Psychological definitions seek understanding of the underlying mental processes that influence behavior (Gallagher & Courtright, 1986). Psychological definitions have ranged from narrow views focused on psychometric IQ and cutoff scores on intelligence tests (e.g, Terman, 1925) to more broad-based multifaceted ones that involve multiple abilities (e.g., Gagné, 1999; Gardner, 1983; Renzulli, 1978; Sternberg, 1997c), including Clark's (2002) model, which reflects a neurophysiological viewpoint.

NARROW VIEWS OF GIFTEDNESS AND CUTOFF SCORES

Early studies of giftedness focused on general intellectual ability as measured by the global score on an IQ test (Terman, 1925). Terman's criterion of 2 or more standard deviations above the mean on an intelligence test is often still used as the defining characteristic of giftedness. Proponents cite literature indicating that the global IQ score is one of the best predictors of school success.

Indeed, some researchers (e.g., McDermott & Glutting, 1997; MacMann & Barnett, 1997) have argued that the only defensible score on an IQ test is the general one. Yet Hale and Fiorello (2001), based on the results of their regression analysis, "encourage practitioners to never interpret the global IQ score if there is significant scatter or score variability" (p. 133). As will be demonstrated herein, highly able youngsters, like a large proportion of the general population (Hale, Fiorello, McGrath, & Ryan, 2001), have a great deal of variability on their profiles and the global IQ may be invalid due to significant factor or test variability. This asynchrony of development for gifted students has been discussed by a number of researchers working in the gifted area (e.g., Silverman, 1993). When a single overall score is the sole or primary criterion for specialized programs, these youngsters may be denied opportunities designed to enhance their success.

When a single global IQ score is used, the designated cutoff tends to be rigid. For example, 2 or more standard deviations above the mean may be the cutoff, and children who score even one point below that single value are deemed ineligible to receive special programming. Examiners using these cutoffs seldom make allowances for standard errors of measurement or other factors that influence test behavior. Administrators appear to feel more comfortable in telling parents that their child does not qualify if he or she does not make the specified score than in making allowances for measurement error.

Any identification that relies on using a single cutoff score on an individual IQ test also ignores limitations of the measurement process. This is particularly true when dealing with scores at either end of the normal curve, where errors are greater than for students scoring in the middle (Salvia & Ysseldyke, 1988).

THEORIES FOCUSING ON MULTIDIMENSIONAL VIEWS

Renzulli (1978) has been critical of the U.S. Office of Education definition for a number of reasons, but particularly because it did not include nonintellective factors. Renzulli's (1978, 1986, 1994) theory of gifted behavior involves an interaction among three basic clusters: above-average general or specific intellectual ability, high levels of task commitment (motivation), and high levels of creativity. According to Renzulli, gifted and talented children are those who apply this composite of traits to any potentially valuable area of performance. In his model, educators are asked to give this potential a chance to grow through a "revolving door" model of gifted education that allows for inclusion of many children.

Gardner (1983) criticized models of intelligence that focused on a single ability and proposed a model of multiple intelligences that included linguistic, logical mathematical, spatial, musical, bodily-kinesthetic, interpersonal, and intrapersonal. Since that time he has expanded his theory and elaborated on how to link educational programs to the various intelligences (Chen & Gardner,

1997; Gardner, 1999). Although it appears that Gardner never really articulated a theory of giftedness within his model, educators of the gifted have embraced its precepts and have attempted to classify children into groups based on these various intelligences. However, many of the evaluations relied on performance assessments and teacher judgments that have not yet been truly validated.

At the heart of Clark's (2002) neurophysiological model of brain function is the idea that high levels of intelligence correspond with advanced and accelerated brain functions in cognitive, affective, physiological, and intuitive areas. She emphasized the interaction between biological inheritance and the environment and provided a great deal of information about how her theory relates to education—but offered little information about assessment.

Sternberg's (1985, 1997b) triarchic theory of intelligence may be described as one of the most aggressive investigations into human functioning and intelligence. He characterized his theory of intellectual giftedness as a special case of his more general triarchic theory (Sternberg, 1986, 1997a). According to this model, gifted students display advanced problem-solving abilities as well as the ability to process information rapidly with unusual insight. Drawing on the idea that giftedness is a type of mental self-management, he hypothesized three basic elements: adapting to environments, selecting new environments, and shaping environments. The key psychological bases of intellectual giftedness are insight skills, including (a) separating relevant from irrelevant information, (b) combining isolated pieces of information into a unified whole, and (c) relating newly acquired information to that acquired in the past. Much of Sternberg's discussion of giftedness has focused on novel tasks; individuals with higher levels of intelligence are more readily able to solve novel tasks and to identify when problems exist.

Tannenbaum (1996) and Gagné (1999) both distinguished between potential and developed talents. Tannenbaum (1996) defined giftedness as potential for becoming critically acclaimed producers. Factors he identified as linking promise with potential included superior general intelligence, exceptional special aptitudes, nonintellective factors (e.g., motivation and self-concept), environmental influences, and chance or luck. Gagné (1999) included intellectual, creative, socioaffective, and sensorimotor categories. He emphasized the difference between natural or untrained abilities that he termed "aptitudes" or "gifts," and "talents," which he described as an expression of systematically developed abilities or skills in at least one field of human activity. Arguing that some models are too restrictive in their cutoffs, Gagné chose as a threshold the top 15% (+1 SD) for each of these categories as basic giftedness or talent and also included three other levels: moderately (+2 SD), highly (+3 SD), and extremely (+4 SD) gifted.

SUMMARY OF EXISTING DEFINITIONS

Although there are many definitions of giftedness, there is an emerging consensus on some aspects (Callahan, 2000). Giftedness, like intelligence, is multidimensional. Nonintellective or broader views of intelligence must be taken into account to explain differences in productivity. When discussing development of these abilities, psychological and instructional interventions can have an impact. Many of the theorists mentioned previously have developed educational programs based on their definitions, but their assessment and identification methods have been found lacking (Gridley, 2002; Plucker, Callahan, & Tomchin, 1996). Their theories have found attention in the popular press and are discussed by educators of the gifted at great length. However, Flanagan, McGrew, and Ortiz (2000) concluded that Gardner's and Sternberg's theories were "data-poor." For example, Messick (1992) criticized both theories as selectively applying extant factor-analytic research and disregarding or minimizing findings that may be seen as contrary to their theories.

OUR DEFINITION

CATTELL–HORN–CARROLL THEORY AND GIFTEDNESS

The Cattell–Horn–Carroll (CHC) theory of intelligence is a "consensus" view that combines Cattell and Horn's (e.g., Horn & Noll, 1997) model of *Gf* (fluid) and *Gc* (crystallized) intelligence with Carroll's (1993, 1997, in press) standard multifactorial model. Based on factor analysis of hundreds of data sets containing a myriad of cognitive measures, Carroll (1993) proposed a model whereby cognitive abilities were conceptualized as existing at three levels or strata: (a) a first, lower order stratum comprised of 50 to 60 or more narrow abilities, (b) a second stratum comprised of 8 to 10 or more broad abilities, and (c) a third stratum comprised of a single general intellectual ability, commonly called *g*. Proposing that all cognitive abilities could be classified into one of the three strata, Carroll (1993) termed his taxonomy the "standard multifactorial" view of cognitive abilities.

The value of the CHC view in defining giftedness is in its multidimensional nature as well as in its empirical support. The three strata allow for identification of broad as well as specific abilities that have been well supported by data from nearly 100 years of study about the nature of cognitive abilities.

OUR DEFINITION WITHIN CHC THEORY

We recognize that multidimensional definitions of giftedness that include various nonintellective factors are legitimate, but it is nearly impossible to identify all possible areas with a single test. Therefore, for the purpose of this chapter, we have limited our definition to aspects of intellectual giftedness that can be measured by the WJ III.

Our model is similar to Gagné's (1999) and Tannenbaum's (1986) in that it describes potential and accomplishment both in a general sense and in a way that is specific to a single area. However, we do not focus on the genetic causes of "gifts" but focus on "gifts" as intellectual abilities and "talents" as special academic aptitudes being of equal value in their need for nurturing and development. We also discount models of intelligence that focus on a global score and ignore multiple abilities, particularly when those abilities are unevenly developed, as they are in many highly able youngsters. Therefore, we offer the following definition based on CHC theory:

"Intellectually Gifted Students" are those who have demonstrated

1. Superior potential or performance in general intellectual ability (Stratum III) and/or
2. Exceptional potential or performance in specific intellectual abilities (Stratum II) and/or
3. Exceptional general or specific academic aptitudes (Strata I and II).

Consequently, in order to develop these abilities into high-level performance, these students need to be fully challenged and care must be taken to provide further facilitation and enrichment beyond that generally provided within the regular curriculum.

Within our definition we define *superior* as the top 10% of the population and *exceptional* as the top 5% of the population. These estimates consider epidemiological evidence that points to 5–20% of the population as being gifted (Pfeiffer, 2001) and recognize the need to allocate scarce resources within educational systems. We also recognize the limitations of any tests and urge users to exercise caution in the interpretation of scores. Examiners should interpret scores within "bands of error," thereby making allowances for standard errors of measurement and calling attention to nonintellective factors such as behavioral and environmental variables—both facilitators and inhibitors—that may affect test scores.

THE VALUE OF THE WJ III FOR ASSESSING INTELLECTUALLY GIFTED STUDENTS

Although some researchers (e.g., Sternberg, 1991) have criticized cognitive tests for not adequately reflecting current theories, others have pointed to individualized measures as being among the best information available (Kaufman & Harrison, 1986). Individualized evaluations like those provided for other "special" students should be used for gifted students. The WJ III is particularly suited to assess students based on our definition and other multidimensional conceptions of giftedness. Based on the CHC model of cognitive abilities, the battery includes a wide range of tasks designed to tap multiple empirically supported cognitive abilities (McGrew & Woodcock, 2001). The standard battery of seven tests on the *Woodcock–Johnson Tests of Cognitive Abilities* (WJ III COG) provides for assessment of seven broad abilities (Stratum II): Long-Term Retrieval (*Glr*), Short-Term Memory (*Gsm*), Processing Speed (*Gs*), Auditory Processing (*Ga*), Visual-Spatial Thinking (*Gv*), Comprehension–Knowledge (*Gc*), and Fluid Reasoning (*Gf*). Each of the broad abilities can be measured by at least two tests in order to explore various narrow abilities. A broad coverage of all achievement areas, including many areas not usually tapped by other batteries, allows for exploring specific academic talents. Extended General Intellectual Ability measures (GIA—Ext) that are similar to traditional global IQ scores are also available with the WJ III. It is possible to obtain a cognitive ability score, the Brief Intellectual Ability (BIA), from administering three tests: Verbal Comprehension, a measure of acquired knowledge; Concept Formation, a measure of fluid reasoning; and Visual Matching, a measure of cognitive efficiency. The *WJ III COG Examiner's Manual* (Mather & Woodcock, 2001) suggests that this procedure might be useful for research purposes and one of the editors of this book suggested that it might be useful for screening purposes in the gifted population. We are reserving judgment about its use for that purpose until we have further data. In the final section of this chapter, the BIA is compared to the Standard GIA (GIA—Std) and GIA—Ext scores.

Unfortunately, the complexity of the battery may also be one of its weaknesses. The amount of written material on the WJ III is nearly overwhelming. For example, each test kit comes with three manuals. We would suggest that the uninitiated start with the *WJ III Technical Abstract* (Schrank, McGrew, & Woodcock, 2001), which provides an excellent general overview and description of the battery as well as a summary of normative and psychometric characteristics such as reliability and validity coefficients. The various manuals also provide a great deal of information about the test's development. We also found two books in the "Essentials of ..." series by Mather, Wendling, & Woodcock (2001) and Schrank, Flanagan, Woodcock, & Mascolo (2002) to be very practical in their suggestions for administration and of great help in interpretation.

TECHNICAL CHARACTERISTICS
OF THE WJ III

Some issues specific to instruments used to assess gifted individuals must be addressed. After examining the WJ III, it is clear that many of the concerns identified by those educators surveyed in Pfeiffer's (2001) study may be eliminated. These educators named inadequate ceilings, inadequate reliability and validity, and lack of the ability to identify specific talents in students as being particularly problematic for using existing instruments with gifted students.

The WJ III provides adequate ceilings for nearly every child of school age, having been normed across the entire age range from 2 to 90+ years. Indeed, when compared with the *Wechsler Intelligence Scale for Children—Third Edition* (WISC-III), in which a total score of 160 is the maximum, the WJ III standard scores can range as high as 200 (Flanagan, 2000).

Reliability is within acceptable ranges. Test reliabilities are reported in *Assessment Service Bulletin Number 2* (Schrank, McGrew, & Woodcock, 2001) as well as in the *WJ III Technical Manual* (McGrew & Woodcock, 2001). Median reliability coefficients for the tests ranged from .76 to .94, with 90% being .80 or higher and 36% being .90 and higher. Median cluster reliabilities are also given, ranging from .81 to .98, with most being .90 or higher.

Content and construct validity for the narrow and broad abilities are well documented and include evidence based on content, developmental pattern, and factor analyses. Preliminary concurrent and predictive validity studies are reported in the manual; however, no studies were conducted using a gifted sample. Traditional abilities in the academic areas of reading, math, and writing can be assessed using the WJ III ACH, which includes 22 tests that measure specific narrow abilities (Stratum I) and can be combined into five broad abilities (Stratum II). These broad abilities include measures such as academic fluency—not typically included on other batteries—that may prove valuable in identification of rate versus level of production.

Other advantages of using the WJ III include use of confidence intervals specific to ability levels, the availability of an overall ability score that is more empirically supportable than those from other measures, and the cautious use of timed tests. It is particularly important to use appropriate bands of error for students who might be expected to score at the upper (or lower) extremes of the score distribution, where errors are larger than in the middle (Salvia & Ysseldyke, 1988). The GIA score provides an overall ability measure for the WJ III. Unlike the general ability scores found for other tests, this score is unique in that it is not the arithmetic mean of the tests but is a weighted composite of each test included to provide the best estimate of g. In general, those tests that are better measures of g—such as Gc and Gf—are more heavily weighted than those that have been shown to be less highly related through earlier factor analytic research (Carroll, 1993).

Although some of the tests on the WJ III are timed, the purpose of these tests is most often to gauge rate rather than level of production. No bonuses for fast performance such as with the WISC-III are given. Also, the tests that are timed have relatively low weightings for the GIA such that the GIA is not overly influenced by speed of production. Lowered rate of production may be due to any number of nonintellective as well as cognitive factors. Expected patterns of students with high-level abilities are discussed following the next section.

ADMINISTRATION, SCORING, AND INTERPRETATION

Administration of the battery is straightforward, with most stimulus material presented in easel format. Training manuals are provided with the kits. Once raw scores are obtained, scoring of the battery must be completed using the *WJ III Compuscore and Profiles Program* (WJ III CPP) (Schrank & Woodcock, 2001) that is included with the test kits. Standard scores, percentile ranks, and confidence intervals (bands of scores) are provided along with a number of options for other scores, such as grade and age equivalents. One score that is not usually available on other tests is the Relative Proficiency Index (RPI), which allows for a criterion-referenced type of interpretation. Schrank et al. (2002) have provided tables to translate these into "nomenclature that provides a description of the quality of performance" (p. 107). These qualitative labels are available in three categories, (a) proficiency level (negligible to advanced), (b) developmental level (extremely delayed to advanced), and (c) functional level (severely impaired to advanced), depending on the purpose of assessment. Schrank et al. (2002) also provide predictive terminology (e.g., very easy to impossible) to translate these labels into expectations for classroom performance. The case studies in this chapter illustrate how this information might be used in a clinical setting.

Comparisons are easy to obtain using the WJ III CPP. The WJ III CPP provides a listing of scores, discrepancy analyses, a narrative report, and score profiles. The narrative portion of the report aids in explaining various aspects of the evaluation to parents and teachers. The profiles report is useful in determining significant differences between scores. Schrank et al. (2002) have provided descriptions and explanations of the various scores along with a suggested step-by-step outline for interpretation of results.

In addition to the various theory-based cluster scores, several clinical clusters may provide additional information. One may also obtain intra-ability discrepancies (i.e, intra-cognitive, intra-achievement, and intra-individual) that can be used to identify relative strengths and weaknesses. Because the WJ III includes both cognitive and achievement tests that have been conormed on the same population, when assessment in both areas is completed, ability/achievement discrepancies can be determined with more precision than with traditional methods (see Chapter 5, this volume).

CHARACTERISTICS OF GIFTED STUDENTS AND IMPLICATIONS FOR TESTING

Table 9-1 outlines some characteristics of gifted students and how they may affect test results. This table is by no means an exhaustive list; readers are urged to consult Clark (2002) for a much more comprehensive treatment. Clark has included characteristics in cognitive, affective, societal, and physical sensing areas along with examples of related needs and possible concomitant problems related to each of the characteristics. As might be expected, not all students display all of these characteristics—or even some of them. However, based on the experiences of examiners working with gifted children, these characteristics are prevalent enough among youngsters with high-level abilities as to constitute expected patterns. Astute examiners will be on the lookout for the effects of these characteristics and their influence on the scores obtained. We have also indicated when such characteristics were taken into account in the case studies we have provided.

Many researchers (cf. Gridley, 1987, 1990; Pfeiffer, 2001) have also questioned whether various measures work for culturally diverse students, those from families with low socioeconomic status, and students who do not have English as the

TABLE 9-1   Characteristics of Gifted Students and Implications for Testing

Characteristic	Implications
Reflective	Penalized by timed tests. May appear to be "slow"
Easily bored if not challenged	Gets "easy" items wrong and "hard" items correct; establishing correct basals and ceilings may be problematic
Perfectionistic	Sacrifices time for correctness—may not earn bonus points for speed
Creative/divergent thinking, flexible thought processes, and heightened capacity for seeing unusual and diverse relationships	Comes up with answers that are not on standard list, but may actually be superior to "acceptable" answers; may solve problems in unorthodox ways; may give answers that appear off the subject or bizarre without further questioning
Advanced ability to see alternatives, make generalizations, see consequences, and form conceptual frameworks	May consider linear tasks to be boring; omits details and assumes that others will follow his/her reasoning; conceptual frameworks do not always follow the expected
Focused intense interest and or strength	May not be able to establish ceiling in certain areas; inconsistent pattern of scores
Advanced sense of humor	May give "playful" answers that need to be explored further; may need to be reminded to provide "serious" responses
Vivid imagination	May elaborate on answers to the extent that they "spoil" correct responses already given; may need to explain answers in great detail even when prompted otherwise; gives answers that may seem strange or pathological until further probing
Concerned with justice/fairness	May not want to score better than their peers and may give incorrect answers intentionally; answers may be very involved and not focus on the intention of the question but rather its social implications
Judgmental	Intolerant of tasks seen as "too easy"
Attempt to hide "differentness" and camouflage competence	May intentionally sabotage their scores by answering incorrectly
Competitiveness; need to be right and/or best	May sacrifice correctness for time—races against clock without checking for correctness; compares self with others; needs reassurance for correct answers
Sensitive to expectations of others; parent/self pressures to succeed	Anxiety may interfere with optimal performance; looks for feedback about performance; unusually vulnerable to perceived criticism; may perseverate on prior task that was not understood
Asycronous development; low tolerance for lag between abilities and self-expectations	Wide variation in performance depending on area tested— evaluated by some as not being "really gifted"; anxieties, insecurities, behavioral problems stemming from student's inability to deal with not being excellent in all areas
Unusually intense and/or persistent	Refuses to progress even when time is up; becomes upset when pressured to "go on to the next item"
Need for precision in expression and thinking	May criticize examiner for incorrect pronunciation or usage; may argue about test items

primary language spoken in the home. Certainly all these factors need to be taken into account when interpreting any test results, but they can be particularly salient for assessing youngsters with high-level abilities because of the propensity to over- look these students due to lack of skills necessary to perform at the highest levels on standardized tests.

CASE STUDIES

We do not suggest using the WJ III to the exclusion of other instruments or information. We agree with Gallagher (1994), who advocated for using multiple measures to identify academically talented youngsters. Indeed, the following case studies use a number of different instruments and procedures to ensure appropri- ate explication of the abilities of these youngsters. However, the WJ III is at the core of these evaluations and provides essential information that does not appear to be available from other instruments, such as the WISC-III (Flanagan, 2000).

The following case studies were chosen to illustrate various aspects of evalu- ation wherein the WJ III may provide advantages over other choices, as well as to illustrate comparisons with other instruments. For example, whenever possible, both the WISC-III and the WJ III COG were administered. We realize that this is a luxury many examiners may not have. However, the WJ III is a somewhat unknown entity in schools in some regions and the WISC-III remains the most used individual test of intelligence for identification of gifted students. Therefore, we administered both tests in order to make comparisons and gather clinical data.

Although the WJ III might be used for identification, the focus of each of the reported evaluations was not necessarily identification, but rather explication of the unique abilities of each child in order to provide for appropriate program- ming. At this time, because of the newness of the WJ III and its complexity, we are still learning about the tests and what they measure. Therefore, we offer inter- pretations based on our knowledge, observations, and experience. Tables for the case studies are similar to score reports generated by the WJ III CPP.

CASE STUDY 1

This case study illustrates how the WJ III might be used to answer a referral question of whether acceleration (grade skipping) is warranted. Also, the parents and the teacher disagreed about the level of this child's abilities. Although Elena's abilities might have been recognized eventually, no specific programming for gifted students is provided in her district until the third grade. One danger for gifted students is that unless they are provided with challenges early enough, they may become bored and develop negative attitudes toward school (Gridley, 1987). Because all decisions about placement in gifted and talented programs in Elena's school district are made on the basis of teacher referral, Elena may have been overlooked by teachers because she appeared to be "normal" and somewhat shy.

Referral

Name: Elena A.

Date of Birth: 10/30/94

Age: 6 years, 7 months

Sex: Female

School: Smalltown Elementary

Grade: K

Teacher: Ms. Roberts

Examiner: B. Price

Reason for Referral

Elena A. was referred by her parents. She was just completing kindergarten and her parents were concerned that the time spent had not been very productive. Elena reported being "bored" and not having much to do. She also reported that she was anxious to return home each day where she could engage in activities that were challenging. Mr. and Mrs. A wondered whether they should suggest that the school place her in second grade in the fall.

Background Information

Elena resides with her parents and two older brothers, ages 8 and 11. Elena's father reported that Elena had met all developmental milestones early. Elena and her parents reported that Elena had learned to read when she was 3 years old. Her parents and teacher described her as "well-adjusted socially and emotionally." Elena and her parents stated that she prefers to play with children who are older than she, often becoming impatient with those her age who "don't follow the rules." The teacher expressed the concern to the examiner that Elena was a "perfectly normal" little girl whose parents were overly involved.

Procedures/Tests Administered

The WJ III COG Standard Battery was administered, along with selected achievement tests from the *Woodcock–Johnson III Tests of Achievement* (WJ III ACH) and the WISC-III. Both parents and the kindergarten teacher completed the Behavior Assessment System for Children (BASC) (Reynolds & Kamphaus, 1992) and the Social Skills Rating System (SSRS) (Gresham & Elliot, 1990). Because of the question of accelerated placement, the examiner administered the socioemotional instruments to determine whether such a placement might be predicted to be successful based on nonintellective as well as intellective factors.

Summary/Clinical Impressions

During testing, rapport was easily established and Elena was very focused and cooperative. She talked freely about her family and a number of outside activities in which she was involved, including soccer and piano lessons. She answered questions without hesitation, but also did not appear to rush her answers. Her vocabulary and use of language was very advanced for her age. She answered questions thoroughly and appeared to enjoy challenging tasks. For example, although she reported not knowing how to do some things, such as the operations of multiplication and division on written calculations, she was able to solve similar problems using repeated addition when they were presented orally. She also asked if she could use her fingers for computations. When Elena indicated that she did not like the man's voice on the tape and seemed to have difficulty attending to the voice, the examiner changed to oral administration. Because of Elena's apparent interest and good attention span, an examiner who lacked experience with highly able youngsters might have overestimated her ability to attend and consequently underestimated the detrimental effect of the tape.

Results and Interpretation

Tables 9-2 and 9-3 give the results of testing for Elena. The WJ III scores are as reported in the WJ III CPP, with confidence intervals at the 90% level given for Elena and subsequent case studies. All WJ III standard scores are based on grade placement because the school specifically asked that Elena be compared with others in kindergarten. Elena scored in the very superior range on two measures of cognitive ability. Her Full-Scale IQ score of 153 on the WISC-III (143–153) and corresponding percentile rank (>99.9) was somewhat higher than her global score (GIA—Std) of 137 on the WJ III COG (132–141), with a percentile rank of 99. Verbal scores were similar for the two tests, with

TABLE 9-2   Results of Testing with the WISC-III for Elena

Composite/index (mean = 100, standard deviation = 15)	SS	PR	SS (90% band)
Full Scale (FSIQ)	150	>99.9	143–153
Verbal (VIQ)	139	99.5	132–142
Performance (PIQ)	153	>99.9	141–155
Verbal Comprehension (VCI)	141	99.7	133–144
Perceptual Organization (PCI)	148	99.9	136–150
Freedom from Distractibility (FD)	121	92	111–126
Processing Speed (PS)	150	>99.9	134–151

Subtest scores (mean = 10, standard deviation = 3)			
Verbal scale	Scaled score	Performance scale	Scaled score
Information	19	Picture Completion	17
Similarities	16	Coding	19
Arithmetic	14	Picture Arrangement	17
Vocabulary	19	Block Design	19
Comprehension	15	Object Assembly	19
(Digit Span)	13	(Symbol Search)	19

TABLE 9-3 Scores for WJ III COG and WJ III ACH for Elena

Cluster/test	RAW	GE	Easy to difficult		RPI	PR	SS (90% band)	z
Clusters								
GIA	—	3.8	2.4	5.8	99/90	99	137 (132–141)	2.44
Verbal Ability	—	5.1	3.5	7.1	100/90	99	136 (128–144)	2.41
Thinking Ability	—	4.2	2.0	9.0	99/90	98	132 (126–139)	2.16
Cognitive Efficiency	—	3.0	2.3	3.8	100/90	99	133 (126–140)	2.18
Phonemic Aware	—	4.8	1.4	11.1	97/90	94	124 (113–134)	1.59
Working Memory	—	2.1	1.2	3.0	98/90	84	115 (107–123)	0.99
Broad Reading	—	4.5	3.7	5.5	100/90	>99.9	152 (150–155)	3.50
Academic Skills	—	3.1	2.6	3.7	100/90	>99.9	158 (153–163)	3.89
Test								
Verbal Comprehension	—	5.1	3.5	7.1	100/90	99	136 (128–144)	2.41
Visual–Auditory Learning	12-E	5.4	1.9	>18.0	99/90	98	130 (122–139)	2.01
Spatial Relations	63-D	4.6	1.4	11.8	97/90	86	117 (110–123)	1.10
Sound Blending	19	5.4	1.9	10.2	98/90	95	124 (111–137)	1.62
Concept Formation	19-D	3.4	2.3	5.1	100/90	94	123 (116–130)	1.56
Visual Matching	31-2	2.9	2.4	3.6	100/90	99	138 (131–145)	2.54
Numbers Reversed	10	3.0	2.2	4.3	100/90	89	118 (110–126)	1.22
Incomplete Words	20	4.1	K.6	12.9	96/90	85	116 (104–128)	1.04
Auditory Work Memory	7	K.9	<K.0	1.9	90/90	50	100 (92–108)	−0.01
Vis-Aud Learn—Delayed	9	—	—	—	—	—	—	0.69
Form A of the following achievement tests was administered:								
Letter–Word Ident	51	4.4	3.7	5.2	100/90	>99.9	153 (149–156)	3.51
Reading Fluency	44	5.0	4.2	5.9	100/90	>99.9	157 (152–162)	3.80
Calculation	9	2.1	1.7	2.6	100/90	94	124 (115–132)	1.57
Spelling	25	2.6	2.1	3.3	100/90	99	133 (126–140)	2.21
Passage Comprehension	28	3.7	2.8	5.3	100/90	99.8	143 (137–148)	2.85
Applied Problems	29	3.1	2.5	3.9	100/90	99.6	140 (130–150)	2.69

	Standard scores			Discrepancy		
Discrepancies	Actual	Predicted	Difference	PR	SD	Significant at ±1.50 SD (SEE)
Intra-Cognitive						
Verbal Ability	136	123	+13	86	+1.09	No
Thinking Ability	132	130	+2	59	+0.23	No
COG Efficiency	133	119	+14	85	+1.05	No
Intellectual Ability/Achievement Discrepancies[a]						
Broad Reading	152	120	+32	99.8	+2.82	Yes

Note: Norms based on grade K.9.
[a]These discrepancies are based on GIA with ACH Broad Reading clusters.

a WISC-III Verbal IQ of 139 (132–142), with a percentile rank of 99.7, and a WJ III COG Verbal Ability of 136 (128–141), with a percentile rank of 99. The higher WISC-III score may be attributed to her higher performance score (i.e., Performance IQ [PIQ]).

On the WJ III COG, Elena's acquired knowledge and language comprehension (verbal ability), thinking ability (intentional cognitive processing), and automatic cognitive processing (cognitive efficiency) were all in the very superior range when she was compared with other children at her grade level. Although no significant discrepancies were found, relative to other cluster scores her lowest scores were for Phonemic Awareness, 124 (113–134), and Working Memory, 115 (107–123). Although these scores are in the superior and high average ranges, respectively, one might ordinarily be tempted to look for a lag in development of reading skills compared with other achievement areas. However, the scores on Sound Blending and Incomplete Words may have been lowered as a result of the problems encountered in using the taped administration. (We would caution against using the tape for younger students. The manual does suggest that these tests may be administered orally for younger students but does not indicate how young.)

Elena demonstrated extremely competent and advanced reading skills, scoring in the very superior range on Letter–Word Identification, Reading Fluency, and Passage Comprehension. Indeed, her Broad Reading score of 148 (145–151) at the >99.9th percentile was significantly higher (almost 3 standard deviations) than would be predicted based on the WJ III GIA—Std score of 134. Her mathematics abilities, although not as advanced as her language skills, were in the superior to very superior range. The examiner also noted unschooled but effective methods of solving problems, such as finger counting and repetitive addition for addition and multiplication, which were, as yet, unlearned skills.

All standardized testing and other information indicated overall cognitive ability in the very superior range as well as very advanced reading skills. Elena fits our definition in both categories, demonstrating superior overall cognitive abilities (GIA in the 99th percentile) as well as outstanding performance in specific achievement areas with Broad Reading at the >99.9th percentile (top <.1%) and Applied Problems at the 97th percentile (top 3%).

Social–emotional assessment indicated a child who was well adjusted with appropriate skills. Both parents rated Elena as having fewer behavior problems and more advanced social skills than others her age on the SSRS and within normal limits on the BASC, with adaptive skills as "high." On the SSRS, Elena's teacher rated her as "average" in both social skills and problem behaviors but also "average" as far as academic competence was concerned.

Recommendations

Elena appeared to be a good candidate for accelerated placement. The examiner suggested that Elena might be successful in second grade with appropriate instruction at her grade level in reading. The school agreed to the acceleration and currently Elena is enrolled in second grade and receiving instruction in reading with a third-grade group. Although Elena still reported that she is somewhat bored, 5 weeks into second grade her teacher noted that "Elena is doing very well academically and making friends rapidly." Her second-grade teacher rated her social skills and academic competence as "above average" on the SSRS.

CASE STUDY 2

Many gifted children present with multiple exceptionalities. Unfortunately, many people have difficulty accepting that a child can be both gifted and have learning disabilities. Whitmore (1981) described these children as being those who need special educational programming to accommodate one or more handicapping conditions while also needing special assistance to promote exceptional achievement in areas in which they may be gifted. These atypical students may assume that learning will be easy for them and may not be prepared for problems that arise from their disabilities. Because of this frustration, these students tend to be aggressive, careless, frequently off task, and may cause classroom disturbances (Beckley, 2002). Many of these children come to attention only because of behavioral problems that may either be the cause or the result of academic and social difficulties. A good review of issues in this area was provided by Brody and Mills (1997). This case study illustrates some of the difficulties faced by children who have outstanding intellectual potential but may have difficulties with behavior, achievement, and/or school production. In this case, school personnel were open to exploring beyond initial testing and the WJ III was used for additional assessment of information-processing abilities not available through use of a standard battery that included the WISC-III and achievement tests.

Referral

Name: Ryan M.
Date of Birth: 8/14/1993
Age: 8 years, 6 months
Sex: Male

School: Rural Elementary
Grade: 3
Teacher: Ms. Hector
Examiner: M. R.

Reason for Referral

Ryan was referred for follow-up testing to determine the nature of his continuing difficulties in reading and writing despite help through the Title One tutoring program and improved behavior. His tutor questioned whether there might be a learning disability that was interfering with Ryan's developing reading abilities. Additionally, Ryan's teacher reported that he seemed to be having difficulty in relating to his peers.

Previous Testing

Ryan was originally referred in second grade because of behavior problems. He was reported as "losing his temper" at school and home. He was noncompliant with the teacher and she reported that he often questioned her authority. He had difficulty in relating to his peers and was failing most subjects, obtaining Ds in Math and Fs in all other areas. His teacher reported that he often did not finish seatwork and that he commented, "the work was too difficult." She also noticed that Ryan took more time to complete assignments than the other students in her room and his papers were messy as a result of poor handwriting and numerous erasures.

Case conference notes indicated that participants, including Ryan's teacher and mother, were surprised by his WISC-III scores. His Full-Scale IQ (FSIQ) of 142 (136–145) was in the very superior range and in the top .3% when compared with his peers. Analyses did not find significant differences between his ability to reason with words and ideas and to visualize and manipulate objects in solving problems. Achievement in mathematics was in the high-average range, with achievement in reading and writing in the low to low-average range and not commensurate with predicted achievement based on the WISC-III score. Although his lowest score was on Processing Speed, this score was in the average range and did not provide adequate information to explain his academic difficulties.

The case conference committee formulated behavior programs for both home and school and recommended counseling to help Ryan develop his social skills and deal with his emotions in more positive ways. Although a significant discrepancy between expected and actual achievement was noted in reading and writing, the committee was undecided about eligibility for special education services due to the history of behavior problems and lack of specific evidence about processing difficulties. Therefore, eligibility for special education services was deferred and he was referred for tutoring in reading through the Title One program.

Background Information

By the time of the second testing, Ryan's mother and teacher reported a significant improvement in Ryan's behavior both at school and at home. His counselor also reported that he was making good progress but that he still had problems in understanding social relationships with other students. All participants were concerned about Ryan's continued difficulties with reading and writing. His Title One tutor reported that Ryan's progress was extremely slow despite her help. She indicated that Ryan had particular difficulties with phonics and seemed unable to use phoneme–grapheme relationships for decoding. She noted that he spent so much time trying to "sound out" words that he often missed the meaning of the story, although he appeared to comprehend when others read.

Procedures/Tests Administered

The WJ III COG Standard Battery, WJ III ACH Standard Battery, selected tests from both the WJ III COG and the WJ III ACH, a clinical interview, and BASC parent and teacher forms were administered.

Summary/Clinical Impressions

Many of Ryan's behaviors appeared to match those given in Table 9-1. Based on interviews and objective and projective personality/behavior measures, the examiner concluded that Ryan's problems with his peers may have been a result of his high expectations for their behavior. For example, Ryan informed the examiner that his friends often did not keep promises and sometimes invited others to play when he wanted their exclusive company.

During testing, Ryan seemed overly concerned about his performance, seeking assurance that his answers were correct and asking for answers to earlier questions. He also asked how he did in comparison with others who had taken the test. This constant need for reassurance and to be "right" appeared to affect his performance and may have lowered scores if he was afraid to take risks and guess when he was unsure about answers.

Results and Interpretation

Table 9-4 provides the results of evaluation with the WJ III COG and WJ III ACH for Ryan. Ryan's overall cognitive ability was in the superior range, with a GIA of 124 (117–130). This score was significantly lower than the FSIQ of 142 (136–145) obtained previously with the WISC-III. If a single cutoff score of 2 or more standard deviations above the mean were used, Ryan would have qualified for gifted programming based on his WISC-III score but not on his WJ III score. By using the band of scores for a 90% confidence interval, Ryan would still qualify under the former definition. However, Ryan's GIA of 124 (117–130) at the 94th percentile (top 6%) would have been well within the parameters of our definition of superior overall intellectual ability. However, if testing had not been completed, Ryan is one student who may have been overlooked for gifted placement because of his low achievement and behavior problems.

Ryan's performance on both the cognitive and achievement batteries reflected a great variability in performance and may help to explain his continued difficulties with reading. When his cognitive abilities are compared, Ryan's Verbal Ability of 131 (123–138) at the 98th percentile was a significant strength. Verbal Ability represents higher order, language-based acquired knowledge and the ability to communicate that knowledge. Ryan's Fluid Reasoning (*Gf*) and Comprehension–Knowledge (*Gc*) were 145 (135–138) at the 99.9th percentile and 131 (123–138) at the 98th percentile, respectively, and in the very superior range when compared with others his age. Comprehension–Knowledge refers to the breadth and depth of a person's acquired knowledge and the ability to communicate and reason using previously learned experiences or procedures. Fluid Reasoning involves reasoning, forming concepts, and solving problems using unfamiliar or novel procedures. Either of these broad abilities (Stratum II) would qualify Ryan as being gifted based on our definition. Ryan's Oral Language score of 121 (114–128) at the 92nd percentile was in the superior range when compared with others his age. Based on this information, it might be expected that Ryan would gain new knowledge and develop concepts much more rapidly than others his age.

Ryan's achievement scores were variable, ranging from limited to high average. The assessment found a significant discrepancy between predicted achievement based on Ryan's GIA and actual achievement in Broad Reading, Basic Reading, Broad Written Language, and Written Expression (see Table 9-4). The GIA was used for this comparison because it is common practice in his school district to use an IQ score to make eligibility determinations for students with learning

TABLE 9-4 Scores on WJ III COG and WJ III ACH for Ryan

Cluster/test	RAW	AE	Easy to difficult		RPI	PR	SS (90% band)		z
Cluster									
GIA	—	11-1	9-0	14-10	98/90	94	124	(117–130)	1.58
Verbal Ability (Ext)	—	13-3	11-0	16-2	99/90	98	131	(123–138)	2.04
Thinking Ability	—	11-9	8-6	20	96/90	88	118	(109–127)	1.19
COG Efficiency	—	9-3	8-4	10-4	96/90	70	108	(101–115)	0.52
Comp–Knowledge (*Gc*)	—	13-3	11-0	16-2	99/90	98	131	(123–138)	2.04
Fluid Reasoning (*Gf*)	—	>21	>21	>21	100/90	99.9	145	(135–154)	2.97
Phonemic Aware	—	5-8	4-5	7-7	68/90	7	78	(69–88)	−1.45
Phonemic Aware III	—	6-3	5-5	7-6	63/90	7	78	(72–84)	−1.46
Working Memory	—	8-0	6-11	9-6	86/90	42	97	(90–104)	−0.21
Exec Processes	—	17-4	12-8	>20	99/90	>99.9	148	(137–158)	3.18
Oral Language	—	13-7	8-11	>21	97/90	92	121	(114–128)	1.4
Total Achievement	—	7-10	7-4	8-6	75/90	25	90	(87–93)	−0.68
Broad Reading	—	7-4	7-1	7-8	29/90	12	82	(79–85)	−1.18
Broad Math	—	9-5	8-5	10-7	96/90	79	112	(106–118)	0.80
Broad Written Language	—	7-9	7-2	8-5	74/90	23	89	(84–94)	−0.75
Basic Reading Skills	—	7-3	7-0	7-6	14/90	12	83	(79–86)	−1.16
Math Calc Skills	—	10-0	8-9	11-8	97/90	90	119	(112–127)	1.28
Written Expression	—	7-3	6-6	8-4	71/90	15	84	(76–92)	−1.06
Academic Skills	—	8-0	7-7	8-5	71/90	32	93	(90–96)	−0.47
Academic Fluency	—	7-6	6-9	8-4	71/90	18	86	(82–91)	−0.91
Academic Apps	—	8-0	7-4	8-11	83/90	39	96	(92–100)	−0.28
Phoneme/Grapheme	—	7-0	6-7	7-5	35/90	12	83	(78–87)	−1.16
Test									
Verbal Comprehension	—	12-9	10-9	15-4	99/90	96	127	(118–136)	1.79
Visual–Auditory Learning	20-E	8-1	6-3	12-6	88/90	43	97	(90–105)	−0.18
Spatial Relations	67-D	12-0	7-7	>25	95/90	76	111	(102–119)	0.72
Sound Blending	12	5-10	4-8	7-6	64/90	16	85	(76–94)	−1.00
Concept Formation	39-E	>21	>21	>21	100/90	99.8	144	(130–158)	2.94
Visual Matching	33-2	8-10	8-3	9-6	94/90	63	105	(98–112)	0.33
Numbers Reversed	12	10-7	8-8	13-1	97/90	73	109	(99–119)	0.60
Incomplete Words	13	5-5	4-2	7-10	71/90	15	84	(74–94)	−1.05
Auditory Work Memory	7	6-3	5-3	7-5	54/90	12	83	(74–91)	−1.15
Vis-Aud Learn—Delayed	9	—	—	—	—	—	—		1.52
General Information	—	13-10	11-5	17-4	99/90	98	130	(119–141)	2.01
Analysis–Synthesis	30-E	>20	17-11	>20	100/90	99	137	(127–147)	2.46
Planning	—	>28	6-3	>28	95/90	99.5	138	(110–166)	2.55
Pair Cancellation	64	11-6	9-11	13-6	99/90	93	122	(118–127)	1.49
Form A of the following achievement tests was administered:									
Letter–Word Ident	30	7-3	7-1	7-5	4/90	9	80	(76–84)	−1.33
Reading Fluency	18	7-7	7-2	8-0	54/90	20	88	(84–92)	−0.82
Story Recall	—	12-6	6-10	>21	94/90	83	114	(105–123)	0.94
Understanding Directions	—	14-0	10-0	19	98/90	91	120	(112–129)	1.36
Calculation	18	10-5	9-5	11-10	99/90	93	122	(112–131)	1.45
Math Fluency	50	9-3	7-3	11-6	93/90	68	107	(102–112)	0.48
Spelling	26	8-1	7-9	8-7	78/90	37	95	(90–100)	−0.33

(continues)

TABLE 9-4 *(continued)*

Cluster/test	RAW	AE	Easy to difficult		RPI	PR	SS (90% band)	z
Writing Fluency	4	6-7	5-8	7-6	47/90	7	78 (69–88)	−1.45
Passage Comprehension	20	7-6	7-1	8-0	57/90	25	90 (85–95)	−0.67
Applied Problems	29	8-8	8-0	9-5	92/90	56	102 (93–111)	0.14
Writing Samples	15-B	8-2	7-1	10-9	87/90	43	97 (88–106)	−0.18
Word Attack	7	7-4	7-0	7-8	37/90	20	87 (82–93)	−0.84
Spelling of Sounds	10	6-4	5-11	6-11	33/90	4	74 (66–82)	−1.73
Sound Awareness	21	6-8	6-1	7-5	54/90	13	83 (77–88)	1.14
Handwriting	15	4-2	—	—	—	4	73 (59–88)	−1.80

	Standard scores			Discrepancy		
Discrepancies	Actual	Predicted	Difference	PR	SD	Significant at ±1.50 SD (SEE)
Intra-Cognitive						
Verbal Ability	127	109	+18	95	+1.60	Yes
Thinking Ability	118	114	+4	65	+0.37	No
COG Efficiency	108	112	−4	37	−0.34	
Intra-Achievement						
Broad Reading	82	107	−25	1	−2.53	Yes
Broad Math	112	98	+14	90	+1.29	No
Broad Written Language	89	105	−16	5	−1.64	Yes
Oral Language	121	96	+25	98	+2.04	Yes
Intellectual Ability/Achievement Discrepancies[a]						
Broad Reading	82	116	−34	0.3	−2.80	Yes
Basic Reading Skills	83	115	−32	0.4	−2.66	Yes
Broad Math	112	114	−2	42	−0.21	No
Math Calc Skills	119	113	+6	68	+0.47	No
Broad Written Language	89	115	−26	2	−2.13	Yes
Written Expression	84	115	−31	1	−2.38	Yes
Oral Language	121	116	+5	69	+0.49	No

Note: Norms based on age 8-6.
[a]These discrepancies are based on GIA with ACH Broad, Basic, and Applied clusters.

disabilities. Functionally, Ryan's reading skills are within the very limited to limited proficiency levels (RPIs from 4/90 to 34/90) and show that Ryan finds grade-level reading tasks to be very to extremely difficult. For example, when Ryan is asked to identify words, he might be expected to be 4% proficient, compared to an average student, who would be 90% proficient.

Because of Ryan's continuing difficulties with reading, particularly in sounding out words, measures of phonological processing were administered. Deficits in phonological skills have been linked to reading problems (e.g., Shankweiler & Liberman, 1989). Phonemic Awareness and Phonemic Awareness 3 are clinical clusters that measure knowledge and skills related to analyzing and synthesizing speech sounds. Phonemic Awareness consists of Sound Blending (students are required to synthesize words) and Incomplete Words (students analyze words with missing phonemes and are asked to identify complete words). Phonemic Awareness 3 consists of these tests from the WJ III COG plus Sound Awareness from the WJ III ACH, which provides additional measures of phonological awareness that include the abilities to rhyme words and manipulate phonemes. Relative weaknesses were found for Ryan in phonological awareness. Ryan's scores were in the limited range when compared with his age peers with an RPI of 63/90. This RPI means that Ryan would be predicted to complete tasks with 63% proficiency whereas others his age would be able to complete similar tasks with 90% proficiency. Two additional tests from the WJ III ACH, Word Attack and Spelling of Sounds, were administered to assess phoneme–grapheme knowledge (the understanding of sound–symbol relationships). Ryan also scored in the limited proficiency range on these tests. Ryan's working memory, although in the average range, was still a relative weakness and may be contributing to his learning problems.

Recommendations

A case conference committee that included the teacher of gifted students as well as the teacher for students with learning disabilities (LDs) was convened. Based on the additional information from the WJ III COG and WJ III ACH, the case conference committee determined that Ryan was a student with specific learning disabilities in reading and written language. These services were to be provided through the LD teacher within the regular education classroom in conjunction with Ryan's teacher. It was also recommended that Ryan be included in the program for gifted students. We suggested that Ryan remain in his regular classroom for most academic subjects, but be involved in a gifted program that consisted of one afternoon a week of enrichment activities. The teacher for the program for gifted students was somewhat reluctant about Ryan's inclusion but she agreed to "give it a try." She expressed concerns about whether he would be able to keep up with the other students given his difficulties in reading.

Comments

Many children such as Ryan, because of his behavior problems, would not be considered either for programs for children with high abilities or for programs for children with learning disabilities. In Ryan's case, it is probable that his behavior problems may actually have been partly the result of this dual exceptionality.

CASE STUDY 3

This case study illustrates where overall intellectual ability does not fall in the top 10% but specific cognitive and academic abilities fall above the 95th percentile. It also illustrates a case where extreme acceleration might be warranted based on demonstrated knowledge.

Referral

Name: Michele B.   **School:** Home schooled
Date of Birth: 9/20/1990   **Grade:** 6.0
Age: 11 years, 1 month   **Teacher:** Mr. & Mrs. B.
Sex: Female   **Examiner:** K. G.

Reason for Referral

Michele was referred by her parents to a clinic as part of a grant designed to evaluate students who were potentially gifted. Michele's parents had been home schooling her for the past year, but were concerned about lack of opportunities for interaction with her peers and development of appropriate social skills. They were considering whether to send her back to her previous school but wondered whether she would be adequately challenged, particularly in math and science.

Background Information

Michele attended a private parochial school for kindergarten through grade four. Her most recent group test scores on the Iowa Basic Skills test in March of her fourth-grade year ranged from the 72nd percentile in reading to the 99th percentile in math and science. Michele was scheduled to begin the sixth grade at the time of testing.

Mr. and Mrs. B. reported Michele was a quiet, well-behaved child interested in applying knowledge to everyday situations. Michele indicated that she enjoyed studying advanced mathematics, working on the computer, conducting science and chemistry experiments, and going to museums. Mr. and Mrs. B. said they recognized her advanced ability when she entered school, stating that she appeared better and quicker in academics than her peers and continually reported being bored. Therefore, after having tried a private school for the first few years, they decided on home schooling. Both parents described themselves as being very involved in teaching Michele. Their methods of teaching appeared quite flexible, with much of the instruction being experiential in nature. For example, they often took field trips and visited museums. They also acknowledged that Michele's greatest interest was in mathematics and science, with joint exploration of many advanced concepts in both areas. Michele brought to the testing sessions work samples that displayed complex chemical formulas and use of integral calculus and explained the principles illustrated. She also stated that she did not care for lessons in language arts and writing. Both parents reported Michele as being somewhat shy and hesitant to enter new situations. They said that they tried to provide opportunities for interaction with her peers, but that Michele appeared to be more comfortable around adults and did not seem to share interests with many children her own age. Michele reported that not many of the children she knew were very interested in the types of math and science projects that she liked to do.

Procedures/Tests Administered

The WJ III COG Standard Battery, WJ III ACH Standard Battery, WISC-III, a clinical interview, and BASC parent and teacher (fourth grade) forms were administered.

Summary/Clinical Impressions

Michele was tested on two separate occasions. At the first session, the WISC-III and the WJ III ACH were given at the request of the parents. At the request of the examiner, they agreed to return a month later for further testing with the WJ III COG. Michele approached the testing situation with some caution and initially appeared withdrawn and uncomfortable. However, rapport was gradually built and Michele reported liking home schooling—especially in mathematics and science— and playing video games. Michele often quickly replied, "don't know" and had to be encouraged to guess. However, when presented with mathematics and science questions, she answered readily, often elaborating beyond the parameters of the question. On some tasks it appeared that Michele was not motivated to perform her best. For example, on routine tasks she often stated that they were "too easy" despite performance that may have been less than optimal. She also did not appear concerned about time, working slowly and methodically on all tasks regardless of whether she was being timed or not.

Results and Interpretation

Tables 9-5 and 9-6 provide the results of testing for Michele. Michele's overall intellectual ability GIA of 117 (113–121) at the 87th percentile was in the high-average range and similar to her WISC-III FSIQ of 113 (104–113) at the 73rd

TABLE 9-5 Scores on WJ III COG and WJ III ACH for Michele

Cluster/test	RAW	AE	Easy to difficult	RPI	PR	SS (90% band)	z
Cluster							
GIA (Ext)	—	14-1	10-11	18-11	96/90	87	117 (113–121)	1.12
Verbal Ability (Ext)	—	18-8	15-2	24	99/90	98	132 (124–139)	2.10
Thinking Ability (Ext)	—	11-9	8-2	>22	91/90	58	103 (97–109)	0.21
Cognitive Efficiency (Ext)	—	12-3	10-7	14-7	95/90	70	108 (101–115)	0.53
Comp–Knowledge (*Gc*)	—	18-8	15-2	24	99/90	98	132 (124–139)	2.10
Long-Term Retrieval (*Glr*)	—	14-2	7-8	>22	92/90	70	108 (99–117)	0.53
Vis–Spatial Thinking (*Gv*)	—	6-6	5-0	9-5	67/90	7	77 (71–84)	−1.50
Auditory Process (*Ga*)	—	>25	11-3	>25	97/90	88	118 (108–127)	1.17
Fluid Reasoning (*Gf*)	—	13-2	9-11	17-7	94/90	67	106 (99–114)	0.43

(continues)

TABLE 9-5 *(continued)*

Cluster/test	RAW	AE	Easy to difficult		RPI	PR	SS (90% band)	z
Process Speed (*Gs*)	—	8-7	7-10	9-4	31/90	5	76 (71–81)	−1.60
Short-Term Memory (*Gsm*)	—	>22	>22	>22	100/90	99	134 (126–143)	2.27
Phonemic Aware	—	12-7	8-4	>28	92/90	62	105 (96–114)	0.31
Working Memory	—	20	15-9	>22	99/90	97	128 (121–135)	1.86
Knowledge	—	22	17-1	>37	100/90	99	136 (129–143)	2.41
Total Achievement	—	19	15-10	>22	100/90	99.8	142 (138–146)	2.81
Broad Reading	—	15-11	14-3	17-11	100/90	95	125 (121–129)	1.68
Broad Math	—	>22	>22	>22	100/90	>99.9	168 (160–177)	4.57
Broad Written Language	—	14-9	11-10	19	98/90	90	120 (113–126)	1.30
Math Calc Skills	—	>21	>21	>21	100/90	>99.9	170 (158–182)	4.65
Math Reasoning	—	>23	>23	>23	100/90	>99.9	159 (152–166)	3.94
Written Expression	—	13-1	10-9	18-1	96/90	81	113 (105–122)	0.89
Academic Skills	—	>22	>22	>22	100/90	>99.9	162 (154–170)	4.12
Academic Fluency	—	14-4	12-9	16-3	99/90	90	119 (116–123)	1.28
Academic Apps	—	23	15-4	>27	99/90	99	134 (127–141)	2.25
Academic Knowledge	—	32	20	>35	100/90	99.7	141 (132–150)	2.75
Test								
Verbal Comprehension	—	18-10	15-9	23	100/90	98	132 (123–141)	2.15
Visual–Auditory Learning	8-E	16-9	8-9	>19	94/90	68	107 (97–117)	0.47
Spatial Relations	61-D	8-9	6-3	16-8	84/90	33	93 (86–100)	−0.45
Sound Blending	22	15-1	10-6	>26	96/90	72	109 (100–117)	0.57
Concept Formation	28-E	12-3	9-6	16-5	93/90	58	103 (97–110)	0.21
Visual Matching	32-2	8-8	8-1	9-3	18/90	5	75 (69–81)	−1.69
Numbers Reversed	18	>22	17-7	>22	100/90	97	127 (118–136)	1.81
Incomplete Words	20	9-5	6-1	21	87/90	38	95 (83–107)	−0.32
Auditory Work Memory	28	17-10	13-5	>22	99/90	91	120 (113–128)	1.36
General Information	—	18-4	14-6	24	99/90	96	126 (116–136)	1.73
Retrieval Fluency	66	12-7	5-10	>30	91/90	64	106 (95–116)	0.37
Picture Recognition	25-C	5-1	3-11	6-10	45/90	3	73 (65–81)	−1.82
Auditory Attention	44	>20	13-1	>20	97/90	94	124 (109–138)	1.59
Analysis–Synthesis	25-D	14-0	10-6	>20	96/90	72	109 (97–121)	0.58
Decision Speed	23	8-5	7-5	9-7	48/90	12	82 (76–89)	−1.19
Memory for Words	21	>23	>23	>23	100/90	98	132 (121–144)	2.16
Form A of the following achievement tests was administered:								
Letter–Word Identification	72	21	18-8	>22	100/90	99.6	140 (132–147)	2.64
Reading Fluency	65	15-4	14-5	16-3	100/90	93	122 (118–126)	1.49
Story Recall	—	>21	14-2	>21	97/90	98	133 (119–146)	2.17
Calculation	44	>21	>21	>21	100/90	>99.9	189 (173–206)	5.95
Math Fluency	88	12-10	10-3	16-10	95/90	79	112 (108–117)	0.82
Spelling	45	17-1	14-7	19	99/90	92	121 (114–129)	1.43
Writing Fluency	22	13-2	11-6	15-8	98/90	84	115 (106–125)	1.01
Passage Comprehension	32	10-11	9-2	14-1	90/90	50	100 (90–110)	0.01
Applied Problems	60	>28	>28	>28	100/90	>99.9	156 (147–165)	3.73
Writing Samples	13-D	13-0	8-9	>23	93/90	69	108 (93–122)	0.51
Quantitative Concepts	—	>21	>21	>21	100/90	>99.9	171 (158–183)	4.72
Academic Knowledge	—	32	20	>35	100/90	99.7	141 (132–150)	2.75

Note: COG norms based on age 11-1; ACH norms based on age 10-11.

TABLE 9-6 WJ III Discrepancy Scores for Michele

Discrepancies	Standard scores			Discrepancy		
	Actual	Predicted	Difference	PR	SD	Significant at ±1.50 SD (SEE)
Intra-Cognitive						
Comp–Knowledge (*Gc*)	132	103	+29	99	+2.29	Yes
Long-Term Retrieval (*Glr*)	108	107	+1	53	+0.08	No
Visual–Spatial Thinking (*Gv*)	77	108	−31	2	−2.15	Yes
Auditory Process (*Ga*)	118	104	+14	85	+1.02	No
Fluid Reasoning (*Gf*)	106	107	−1	49	−0.03	No
Process Speed (*Gs*)	76	109	−33	1	−2.34	Yes
Short-Term Memory (*Gsm*)	134	102	+32	99.5	+2.57	Yes
Phonemic Aware	105	104	+1	52	+0.04	No
Working Memory	128	102	+26	98	+2.05	Yes
Predicted Achievement/Achievement Discrepancies[a]						
Broad Reading	125	108	+17	95	+1.68	Yes
Broad Math	168	105	+63	>99.9	+6.36	Yes
Math Calc Skills	170	99	+71	>99.9	+6.36	Yes
Math Reasoning	159	110	+49	>99.9	+5.05	Yes
Broad Written Language	120	105	+15	92	+1.38	No
Written Expression	113	103	+10	83	+0.95	No
Academic Knowledge	141	121	+20	99	+2.22	Yes

[a]These discrepancies are based on predicted achievement scores with ACH Broad, Basic, and Applied clusters.

percentile. Based on either test, Michele may not have qualified for gifted programs that use a single overall ability score (often 130 and above) to determine eligibility, nor would she fit our definition in the area of superior overall ability. However, on the WJ III COG, there was considerable variability among the abilities measured. Michele demonstrated significant strengths compared with the average of all her abilities in Comprehension–Knowledge (*Gc*), Short-Term Memory (*Gsm*), and Working Memory. These differences were also meaningful in that less than 1% of the standardization sample for Comprehension–Knowledge and .5% of the sample for Working Memory had differences this large. Michele demonstrated significant weaknesses in Visual-Spatial Thinking (*Gv*) and Processing Speed (*Gs*).

Overall, Michele's knowledge, academic skills, and ability to apply academic skills were all within the very superior range. When compared with others her age, Michele's performance in Math Calculation, with a Standard Score (SS) of 170 (158–182) and a percentile rank of >99.9, and Math Reasoning, with an SS of 159 (152–166) and a percentile rank of >99.9, were in the very superior range and considerably above (5 to 6 standard errors—see Table 9-6) those predicted based on her abilities. A difference this large was observed in less than one-tenth of 1% of the standardization sample (percentile rank [PR]of >99.9 under discrepancies). Indeed, in order to obtain those scores, Michele attempted all the mathematics examples; she made a single error on Calculation, wherein she was able to do a problem in integral calculus, missing only one problem involving trigonometric functions, and she made three errors on Applied Problems, wherein she appeared to understand the concepts but made calculation errors. Although the WJ III ACH was normed across the age range and for most individuals would have an adequate ceiling, because of Michele's unique abilities, there may not have been enough difficult items on these two tests to adequately assess Michele's knowledge. Her broad reading score of 125 (121–129) and a percentile rank of 95 was in the superior range and also above prediction, albeit by only about 2 standard errors. Her abilities in written language and written expression were high average and commensurate with expectations.

Recommendations

We worked with the school and they gave Michele a placement test to determine her skills. Based on our testing and theirs, Michele was placed in high school algebra and geometry and was very successful, receiving As in both classes. However, she continued to receive language arts and other instruction with her regular sixth-grade classroom. Michele, her parents, and her teachers also reported that Michele appeared to be much happier in her high school classes and that she was making friends there. She indicated that she felt more comfortable around her high school class mates than she did with those in sixth grade, indicating that they weren't as "silly" and could discuss important "stuff."

SUMMARY OF CASE STUDIES

Although the three case studies presented here are very different in their focus, there are some similarities. Scores varied within each profile. Generally, WJ III scores were lower than WISC-III scores. Although we found only a single study by Phelps (reported in the *WJ III Technical Manual* on page 71) with means for the WJ III and the WISC-III for the same children, the pattern was the same with our students. Although for her 150 students, Phelps found a difference of 3.6 points lower for the WJ III Standard Battery and 5.2 points lower for the WJ III Extended Battery, in some cases our differences were much larger. In all of our case studies, we found information about patterns of abilities not available from other tests. The use of the WJ III provided information that helped make some difficult decisions that were beneficial for these students.

POSTSCRIPT

We subsequently looked at the comparability of the WISC-III and the WJ III using a combined sample that consisted of the Phelps (*WJ III Technical Manual*, 2001) data as well as additional data on children from Canada. A description of the combined sample can be found on pages 21 and 22 of the *WJ III Report Writer Manual* (Schrank & Woodcock, 2002). Means for a subsample of 203 children who were administered the WJ III Standard Battery as well as the WISC-III were GIA—Std = 102.5 (SD = 11.91) and FSIQ = 104.3 (SD = 12.99). The correlation between the tests ($n = 144$) was $r = .70$ ($p < .001$). In that combined database, we identified another subsample of 114 individuals who were administered the WJ III Extended Battery and the WISC-III. Sample means for this group were GIA—Ext = 106.97 (SD = 12.35) and FSIQ = 105 (SD = 11.46). The correlation between the tests was $r = .77$ ($p < .001$).

Based on these data, we developed regression models to determine equivalency of cutoff scores. For the regression models, WJ III GIA—Std and GIA—Ext scores were regressed separately on the WISC-III FSIQ score. We found that FSIQ was significantly related to GIA—Std ($F[1,202] = 188.59$, $p < .001$) and accounted for 49% of the variance. The regression model for predicting GIA—Std scores was

$$\text{Predicted GIA—Std} = 35.97 + (.638)\text{FSIQ}.$$

We found that FSIQ was significantly related to GIA—Ext ($F[1,143] = 206.48$, $p < .001$) and accounted for 59% of the variance. The regression model for predicting GIA—Ext scores was

$$\text{Predicted GIA—Ext} = 28.77 + (.714)\text{FSIQ}.$$

Table 9-7 shows predicted equivalent scores for the WJ III Standard and Extended Batteries based on WISC-III FSIQ. Based on these comparisons, if a WISC-III cutoff score of 130 had been used, the corresponding cutoff score for the WJ III GIA—Std would more appropriately be around 118, with a comparable score of around 120 for GIA—Ext. Either of the WJ III scores would be within the parameters (using a band of scores) of our definition of superior general intellectual ability as the top 10% of the population.

We mentioned earlier that a Brief Intellectual Ability score is available with the WJ III COG. We scored the three required tests for all of our cases and

TABLE 9-7 Selected Predicted Equivalent WJ III GIA—Std and GIA—Ext Scores Based on WISC-III FSIQ

WISC-III FSIQ	WJ III GIA—Std[a]	WJ III GIA—Ext[b]
120	112.53	114.45
125	115.72	118.02
130	118.81	121.59
135	122.1	125.16
140	125.29	128.73

[a]Based on the regression formula: GIA—Std = 35.97 + (.638)FSIQ, $N = 203$.
[b]Based on the regression formula: GIA—Ext = 28.77 + (.714)FSIQ, $N = 144$.

TABLE 9-8   Comparison of Brief Intellectual Ability and General Intellectual
Ability for Case Studies

Student	BIA		GIA	
	SS (90% band)	PR	SS (90% band)	PR
Elena	134 (128–139)	99	137 (132-141)[a]	99
Ryan	133 (124–142)	99	124 (117-130)[a]	94
Michele	100 (95–104)	50	117 (113-121)[b]	87

[a]GIA—Std.
[b]GIA—Ext.

correlated the BIA and GIA. Table 9-8 presents the results of this analysis. Although the correlation between the BIA and GIA scores was $r = .75$ ($p = .14$), all except one of our students scored lower on the BIA than on the GIA. Using bands of scores results in somewhat better agreement, but these data provide little insight into the comparability of the scores for larger groups of children. Because of the possibility that such scores might eliminate children from consideration, at the present time we suggest that if the BIA were used for screening purposes that a generous cutoff score be established to help prevent eliminating students who might benefit from programming. For example, in our definition of giftedness that suggests the top 10% of students be considered, the cutoff score would be 120 on the GIA. Therefore, for screening purposes, we suggest setting the cutoff score lower on the BIA.

CONCLUSIONS

Why present an entire chapter on using the WJ III with the academically gifted? We trust that all will agree that the talents of children with high abilities are precious resources that would be unfortunate to waste. This population of children calls for a special set of talents and knowledge above and beyond those required to assess other exceptionalities. Instruments must be chosen carefully in order to address many of the concerns surrounding identification and programming. The argument about what constitutes giftedness has not been settled and little has been done to deal with aspects of giftedness such as creativity and task commitment. What we have done is offer a definition of giftedness within CHC theory that reflects current thought, and have looked at using one instrument—the WJ III—that is built on that theory to assess gifted youngsters.

Professionals have a great number of choices when selecting tests and other measures to use for identification and programming for gifted students. However, it is our opinion that the WJ III may be uniquely suited to accomplish this purpose both theoretically and empirically. Although no instrument is perfect, we are confident that we have provided a number of reasons for choosing the instrument. Whether there is agreement with our definition based on CHC theory, or not, consider that CHC theory is becoming widely accepted as one of the most viable ways of approaching intelligence and is well supported empirically. It might be expected that tests currently under revision, such as the *Stanford–Binet Intelligence Scale: Fourth Edition* (Thorndike, Hagen, & Sattler, 1986) and the WISC-III, may reflect the CHC theory to a greater degree than have past versions of the tests. However, the WJ III is the only currently available instrument that is well grounded in CHC theory. Furthermore, by judiciously using the various tests available in the battery, a broad variety of abilities may be tapped. The development of the WJ III seems to have addressed many of the issues raised by Pfeiffer (2001) and others (e.g., Callahan, 2000; Sternberg, 1982) about using intelligence tests for children with superior intellect.

Rizza, McIntosh, and McCunn (2001) were unable to identify a unique "gifted profile" that differentiated youngsters of high-level ability from matched controls; however, we found a great deal of variability within profiles. We therefore suggest adopting a broad view of intelligences within the CHC model that allows for identifying youngsters of outstanding specific as well as general ability. As a number of others have urged, it is time to dispense with the idea that giftedness is an all-or-nothing entity that is best measured by *g*. The idea of multiple abilities is not new, as Carroll's (1993) work so vividly displayed.

We encourage those who are involved in identification and programming for highly able youngsters to approach assessment in a thoughtful and reasoned manner by paying attention to those facilitators and inhibitors that may affect test performance. We have provided three case studies that have illustrated the WJ III use and interpretation with children with high academic abilities and aptitudes.

REFERENCES

Abeel, L. B., Callahan, C. M., & Hunsaker, S. L. (1994). *The use of published instruments in the identification of gifted students.* Washington, DC: National Association for Gifted Children.

Beckley, D. (2002). *Gifted and learning disabled: Twice exceptional students.* Retrieved February 1, 2002, from the LDOnline web site: http://www.ldonline.org/ld_indepth/gt_ld/nrcgt.html.

Brody, L. E., & Mills, C. J. (1997). Gifted children with learning disabilities: A review of the issues. *Journal of Learning Disabilities, 30*(3), 282–286.

Callahan, C. M. (2000). Intelligence and giftedness. In R. Sternberg (Ed.), *Handbook of Intelligence.* New York: Cambridge University Press.

Carroll, J. B. (1993). *Human cognitive abilities.* New York: Cambridge University Books.

Carroll, J. B. (1997). The three-stratum theory of cognitive abilities. In D. P. Flanagan, J. L. Genshaft, & P. L. Harrison (Eds.), *Contemporary intellectual assessment: Theories, tests, and issues* (pp. 122–130). New York: Guilford.

Carroll, J. B. (in press). The higher-stratum structure of cognitive abilities: Current evidence supports *g* and about ten broad factors. In H. Nyborg (Ed.), *The scientific study of general intelligence: Tribute to Arthur R. Jensen.* NY: Elsevier Science/Pergamon Press. Prepublication copy. Retrieved February 14, 2002, from http://www.iapsych.com/Carroll1b.pdf.

Chen, J. Q., & Gardner, H. (1997). Alternative assessment from a multiple intelligences perspective. In D. P. Flanagan, J. L. Genshaft, & P. L. Harrison (Eds.), *Contemporary intellectual assessment: Theories, tests, and issues* (pp. 105–121). New York: Guilford.

Clark, B. (2002). *Growing up gifted* (6th ed.) Columbus, OH: McMillan.

Coleman, L. J., & Cross, T. L. (2001). *Being gifted in school.* Waco, TX: Prufrock Press.

Flanagan, D. P. (2000). *Comparative features of major intelligence batteries: Content, administration, technical features, interpretation, and theory* (Assessment Service Bulletin No. 1). Itasca, IL: Riverside Publishing.

Flanagan, D. P., McGrew, K. S., & Ortiz, S. O. (2000). *The Wechsler Intelligence Scales and Gf–Gc theory: A contemporary approach to interpretation.* Boston: Allyn & Bacon.

Gagné, F. (1999). My convictions about the nature of abilities, gifts, and talents. *Journal for the Education of the Gifted, 22,* 109–136.

Gallagher, J. J. (1994). Current and historical thinking on education for gifted and talented students. In P. Ross (Ed.), *National excellence: An anthology of readings* (pp. 83–107). Washington, DC: U.S. Department of Education.

Gallagher, J. J., & Courtright, R. D. (1986). The educational definition of giftedness and its policy implications. In R. J. Sternberg & J. E. Davidson (Eds.), *Conceptions of giftedness* (pp. 93–111). New York: Cambridge University Press.

Gardner, H. (1983). Frames of mind: *The theory of multiple intelligences.* New York: Basic Books.

Gardner, H. (1999). *Intelligence reframed: Multiple intelligences for the 21st century.* New York: Basic Books.

Gresham, F. M., & Elliott, S. N. (1990). *Social skills rating system.* Circle Pines, MN: American Guidance Service.

Gridley, B. E. (1987). Children and giftedness. In J. Grimes & A. Thomas (Eds.), *Children's needs: Psychological perspectives* (pp. 234–241). Kent, OH: National Association of School Psychologists.

Gridley, B. E. (1990). Working with gifted children. In A. Thomas & J. Grimes (Eds.), *Best practices in school psychology, II* (pp. 811–821). Kent, OH: National Association of School Psychologists.

Gridley, B. E. (2002). In search of an elegant solution: Reanalysis of Plucker, Callahan & Tomechin (1996) with respects to Pyrt (2000). *Gifted Child Quarterly, 46,* 224–234.

Hale, J. B., & Fiorello, C. A. (2001). Beyond the academic rhetoric of 'g": Intelligence testing guidelines for practitioners. *The School Psychologist, 55*(4), 113–117, 131–135, 138–139.

Hale, J. B., Fiorello, C. A., McGrath, M., & Ryan, K. A. (2001, August). *WISC-III commonality analysis with typical and clinical populations.* Poster presented at the 109th annual convention of the American Psychological Association, San Francisco, CA.

Horn, J. L., & Noll, J. (1997). Human cognitive capabilities: *Gf–Gc* theory. In D. P. Flanagan, J. L., Genshaft, & P. L. Harrison (Eds.), *Contemporary intellectual assessment: Theories, tests, and issues* (pp. 53–91). New York: Guilford.

Journal for the Education of the Gifted, 22(2) (1999).

Kaufman, A. S., & Harrison, P. L. (1986). Intelligence tests and gifted assessment? What are the positives? Special issue: The IQ controversy. *The Roeper Review, 8,* 154–159.

Macmann, G. M., & Barnett, D. W. (1997). Myth of the master detective: Reliability of interpretations of Kaufman's "intelligence testing" approach to the WISC-III. *School Psychology Quarterly, 12,* 197–234.

Marland, S. P. (1972). *Education of the gifted and talented, Vol. 1. Report to the Congress of the United States by the U.S. Commissioner of Education.* Washington, DC: Department of Health, Education and Welfare.

Mather, N., Wendling, B. J., & Woodcock, R. W. (2001). *Essentials of WJ III tests of achievement assessment.* New York: Wiley.

Mather, N., & Woodcock, R. W. (2001). Examiner's manual. *Woodcock–Johnson III tests of cognitive abilities.* Itasca, IL: Riverside Publishing.

McDermott, P. A., & Glutting, J. J. (1997). Informing stylistic learning behavior, disposition, and achievement through ability tests—or more illusions of meaning? *School Psychology Review, 26,* 163–175.

McGrew, K. S., & Woodcock, R. W. (2001). Technical manual. *Woodcock–Johnson III*. Itasca, IL: Riverside Publishing.

Messick, S. (1992). Multiple intelligences or multilevel intelligence? Selective emphasis on distinctive properties of hierarchy: On Gardner's *Frames of Mind* and Sternberg's *Beyond IQ* in the context of theory and research on the structure of human abilities. *Psychological Inquiry, 3*(4), 365–384.

Pfeiffer, S. L. (2001). Professional psychology and the gifted: Emerging practice opportunities. *Professional Psychology, Research and Practice, 32*(2), 175–180.

Plucker, J. A., Callahan, C. M., & Tomchin, E. M. (1996). Wherefore art thou, multiple intelligences? Alternative assessments for identifying talent in ethnically diverse and low income families. *Gifted Child Quarterly, 40,* 81–92.

Renzulli, J. (1978). What makes giftedness? Reexamining a definition. *Phi Delta Kappan, 60,* 18–24.

Renzulli, J. (1986). The three ring conception of giftedness: A developmental model for creative productivity. In R. J. Sternberg & J. E. Davidson (Eds.), *Conceptions of giftedness* (pp. 53–92). New York: Cambridge University Press.

Renzulli, J. S. (1994). *Schools for talent development: A practical plan for total school improvement.* Mansfield Center, CT: Creative Learning Press.

Reynolds, C. R., & Kamphaus, R. W. (1992). *Behavior rating system for children.* Circle Pines, MN: American Guidance Service.

Rizza, M. G., McIntosh, D. E., & McCunn, A. (2001). Profile analysis of the *Woodcock–Johnson III Tests of Cognitive Abilities* with gifted students. *Psychology in the Schools, 38*(5), 447–455.

Ross, P. O. (1993). *National excellence: A case for developing America's talent.* Washington, DC: U. S. Government Printing Office. Retrieved January 25, 2002, from http://www.ed.gov/pubs/DevTalent/intro.html.

Salvia, J., & Ysseldyke, J. E. (1988). *Assessment in special and remedial education (5th ed.).* Boston: Houghton Mifflin.

Schrank, F. A., Flanagan, D. P., Woodcock, R. W., & Mascolo, J. T. (2002). *Essentials of WJ III cognitive abilities assessment.* New York: Wiley.

Schrank, F. A., McGrew, K. S., & Woodcock, R. W. (2001). *Technical abstract* (Assessment Service Bulletin No. 2). Itasca, IL: Riverside Publishing.

Schrank, F. A., & Woodcock, R. W. (2001). *WJ III compuscore and profiles program* [computer software]. Itasca, IL: Riverside Publishing.

Schrank, F. A., & Woodcock, R. W. (2002). *Manual and checklists. Report writer for the WJ III.* Itasca, IL: Riverside Publishing.

Shankweiler, D., & Liberman, I. Y. (1989). *Phonology and reading disability.* Ann Arbor, MI: University of Michigan Press.

Silverman, L. K. (1993). *Counseling the gifted and talented.* Denver, CO: Love Publishing.

Stephens, K. R., & Karnes, F. A. (2000). State definitions for the gifted and talented revisited. *Exceptional Children, 66,* 219–238.

Sternberg, R. J. (1982). Lies we live by: Misapplication of tests identifying the gifted. *Gifted Child Quarterly, 26*(4), 157–161.

Sternberg, R. J. (1985). *Beyond IQ: A triarchic theory of human intelligence.* London: Cambridge University Press.

Sternberg, R. J. (1986). A triarchic theory of intellectual giftedness. In R. J. Sternberg & J. E. Davidson (Eds.), *Conceptions of giftedness* (pp. 223–243). London: Cambridge University Press.

Sternberg, R. J. (1991). Death, taxes, and bad intelligence tests. *Intelligence, 15*(3), 257–269.

Sternberg, R. J. (1997a). A triarchic view of giftedness: Theory and practice. In N. Colangelo & G. A. Davis (Eds.), *Handbook of gifted education* (pp. 43–53). Needham Height, MA: Allyn & Bacon.

Sternberg, R. J. (1997b). The triarchic theory of intelligence. In D. P. Flanagan, J. L. Genshaft, & P. L. Harrison (Eds.), *Contemporary intellectual assessment: Theories, tests, and issues* (pp. 94–104). New York: Guilford.

Sternberg, R. J. (1997c). Intelligence and life-long learning: What's new and how do we use it? *American Psychologist, 52*(10), 1134–1139.

Tannenbaum, A. J. (1996). The IQ controversy and the gifted. In C. Benbow & D. Lubinski (Eds.), *Intellectual talent* (pp. 44–77). Baltimore: Johns Hopkins University Press.

Terman, L. M. (1925). *Genetic studies of genius: Vol. 1. Mental and physical traits of a thousand gifted children.* Stanford, CA: Stanford University Press.

Thorndike, R. L., Hagen, E. P., & Sattler, J. S. (1986). *Stanford–Binet Intelligence Scale: Fourth Edition.* Itasca, IL: Riverside Publishing.

Whitmore, J. R. (1981). Gifted children with handicapping conditions: A new frontier. *Exceptional Children, 48,* 106–113.

10

USING THE WOODCOCK–JOHNSON III TESTS OF COGNITIVE ABILITIES WITH STUDENTS WITH ATTENTION DEFICIT/HYPERACTIVITY DISORDER

LAURIE FORD

Department of Educational and
Counseling Psychology and
Special Education
University of British Columbia
Vancouver, British Columbia
Canada V6T 1Z4

TIMOTHY Z. KEITH

Department of Educational Psychology
The University of Texas at Austin
Austin, Texas 78712

RANDY GRANVILLE FLOYD

The University of Memphis
Memphis, Tennessee 38152

CHERYL FIELDS

Department of Psychology
University of South Carolina
Columbia, South Carolina 29208

FREDRICK A. SCHRANK

The Woodcock–Muñoz Foundation
Olympia, Washington 98501

319

Psychologists and other professionals often assess students who exhibit overactivity, poor impulse control, and attention or concentration problems. Students who display excessive levels of these characteristics may have Attention Deficit/Hyperactivity Disorder (AD/HD), a condition that affects nearly 5% of the school-age population (Barkley, 1998; Hoff, Doepke, & Landau, 2002). Although the prior editions of the *Woodcock–Johnson III Tests of Cognitive Abilities* (WJ III) have not been widely used in published studies with this population, the WJ III includes tests and clusters that may measure several associated cognitive character-istics of AD/HD, such as deficits in executive functioning, attention, and/or working memory. Additionally, *Report Writer for the WJ III* (Report Writer) (Schrank & Woodcock, 2002) includes several checklists that may be sensitive to the behaviors often exhibited by individuals with AD/HD. When used in conjunction with the WJ III, the checklists may assist a clinician in a diagnosis of AD/HD.

This chapter includes four parts. The first part includes a brief summary of the most frequently used diagnostic criteria and approaches to diagnosing AD/HD, and suggests use of a behavioral–cognitive model that includes assessment of behavioral characteristics as well as certain cognitive functions that may be sen-sitive to the condition, as suggested by prior research. The second part contains a description of extant research about use of the prior and current editions of the Woodcock–Johnson with individuals who have AD/HD. The third and major part of this chapter presents the results of a study of utility of the WJ III tests that com-prise the Executive Processes, Working Memory, and Broad Attention clusters and selected checklists from Report Writer in prediction of AD/HD. The fourth and final part of this chapter includes a discussion of the clinical applications of the WJ III and Report Writer for assessment of individuals who may have AD/HD. A case illustration completes the section.

DIAGNOSTIC CRITERIA AND A BEHAVIORAL–COGNITIVE APPROACH TO DIAGNOSING AD/HD

AD/HD is a neurobehavioral condition characterized by difficulty with attention, high activity levels, and impulsivity (American Psychiatric Association, 2000). Although there are many commonalities across definitions of AD/HD, the criteria used to diagnose the disorder may vary by diagnostic system. For example, although the 1997 reauthorization of the Individuals with Disabilities Education Act (IDEA) does not identify AD/HD as a stand-alone diagnosis in the definition of a "child with a disability," students with AD/HD may be served under the category of other health impairments (OHI). Some, but not all, children with AD/HD are eligible to receive special education and related services. To be eligible for services under IDEA the student must (a) have a condition that meets one of the disability categories listed in the regulations and (b) need special education and related ser-vices because of that disability. IDEA—Part B Final Regulations (1997) indicates that children with AD/HD are a diverse group of learners with a possible chronic or acute health problem that may result in eligibility in the OHI category. Some children with AD/HD may be eligible under other disability categories if they meet the criteria for those disabilities, whereas other students may not be eligible under Part B but may qualify for services under Section 504 of the Rehabilitation Act. (For additional information on the requirements for eligibility for services under IDEA, the reader is referred to Telzrow and Tankersly [2000].)

Professionals who work in nonpublic school settings frequently use the criteria found in the *Diagnostic and Statistical Manual of Mental Disorders* (DSM-IV) (American Psychiatric Association, 2000) or *International Classification of Diseases* (ICD 10) (World Health Organization, 1994) to identify AD/HD, whereas professionals working in settings such as universities, community colleges, and mental health centers may use criteria such as that specified in Section 504 of the Rehabilitation Act. The DSM-IV criteria, the most widely used in the diagnosis of AD/HD, specify three categories of symptoms: inattention, impulsivity, and overactivity (see Table 10-1). Barkley (1990) coined the term "holy trinity" of AD/HD to describe these categories of symptoms. These characteristics can result in observable behaviors for which presence and severity can be documented by informants, such as parents and teachers.

During the past two decades, understanding of the symptoms and associated features of AD/HD has increased (Barkley, 1997, 1998; Jensen & Cooper, 2002). As a result, well-designed assessment instruments, such as rating scales, self-report forms, observational techniques, and standardized ability tests, have been developed that target both the behavioral symptoms and associated cognitive characteristics of the disorder. (For a comprehensive overview of recent developments in assessment of AD/HD, see Barkley [1998], DuPaul & Stoner [1994], or Jensen & Cooper [2002].) Although the symptoms of AD/HD are typically descriptions of observable behaviors (see Table 10-1), and many assessment instruments that provide the most well-validated measures of AD/HD symptoms are based on ratings of behavior, a growing body of research has focused on use of standardized tests that measure cognitive ability and executive functioning deficits associated with AD/HD symptoms (e.g., Barkley & Grodzinsky, 1994; Barkley, Grodzinsky, & DuPaul, 1992; Hinshaw, 2002; Hinshaw, Carte, Sami, & Treuting, 2002; Perugini, Harvey, Lovejoy, Sandstrom, & Webb, 2000; Shallice et al., 2002; Willcutt et al., 2001). Research now supports the efficacy of cognitive tests for discriminating between individuals with AD/HD from those without the disorder (Assesmany, Mcintosh, Phelps, & Rizza, 2001; Gibney, Mcintosh, Dean, & Dunham, 2002; Dean & Woodcock, 1999; Prifitera & Dersh, 1993; Schwean, Saklofske, Yackulic, & Quinn, 1995).

Barkley's (1997) neuropsychological model of AD/HD may be of particular interest to examiners who use the *Woodcock–Johnson Tests of Cognitive Abilities* (WJ III COG) (Woodcock, McGrew, & Mather, 2001a). He proposed that executive functioning and working memory deficits may be associated with the characteristic features of AD/HD, including lack of behavioral self-control and

TABLE 10-1   DSM-IV TR Criteria for Attention Deficit/Hyperactivity Disorder

---

Either A OR B:

(A) Six (or more) of the following symptoms of **inattention** have persisted for at least 6 months to a degree that is maladaptive and inconsistent with developmental level:

- Fails to give close attention to details or makes careless mistakes in schoolwork, work, or other activities
- Has difficulty sustaining attention in tasks or play activities
- Does not seem to listen when spoken to directly
- Does not follow through on instructions and fails to finish schoolwork, chores, or duties in the workplace
- Has difficulty organizing tasks and activities
- Avoids, dislikes, or is reluctant to engage in tasks that require sustained mental effort
- Loses things necessary for tasks or activities
- Is easily distracted by extraneous stimuli
- Is forgetful in daily activities

(B) Six (or more) of the following symptoms of **hyperactivity–impulsivity** have persisted for at least 6 months to a degree that is maladaptive and inconsistent with developmental level:

Hyperactivity

- Fidgets with hands or feet or squirms in seat
- Leaves seat in classroom or in other situations in which remaining seated is expected
- Runs about or climbs excessively in situations in which it is inappropriate
- Has difficulty playing or engaging in leisure activities quietly
- Is often "on the go" or often acts as if "driven by a motor"
- Talks excessively

Impulsivity

- Blurts out answers before questions have been completed
- Has difficulty awaiting turn
- Interrupts or intrudes on others

AND

Some hyperactive–impulsive or inattentive symptoms that caused impairment were present before age 7 years

AND

Some impairment from the symptoms is present in two or more settings (e.g., at home, school, or work)

AND

There must be clear evidence of clinically significant impairment in social, academic, or occupational functioning

AND

The symptoms do not occur exclusively during the course of a Pervasive Developmental Disorder, Schizophrenia, or other Psychotic Disorder and are not better accounted for by another mental disorder (e.g., Mood Disorder, Anxiety Disorder, or Personality Disorder)

Note: Adapted from *Diagnostic and Statistical Manual of Mental Disorders.* (4th ed.), Text Revision (2000), Washington, DC, American Psychiatric Association, pp. 92–93.

inattention or distractibility. The WJ III COG includes tests and clusters that purport to measure these constructs. Consequently, a behavioral–cognitive assessment of children and adults with AD/HD would include (a) a set of criterion-referenced procedures for measuring the behavioral symptoms of AD/HD and

(b) a set of norm-referenced tests sensitive to the cognitive or neuropsycholog-ical deficits associated with the disorder. The WJ III COG, when combined with a set of checklists included in Report Writer, may include several components of such an assessment. Specifically, the Report Writer Parent, Teacher, Classroom Observation, and Test Session Observation checklists can be used to document, in different settings, the presence of behavioral characteristics and associated features of AD/HD. The WJ III COG can be used to assess a vari-ety of cognitive abilities and executive functions that may be relevant in the assessment of AD/HD.

USE OF THE WOODCOCK–JOHNSON IN THE ASSESSMENT OF AD/HD

There has been prior research examining the validity of measures from the *Woodcock–Johnson Psycho-Educational Battery—Revised* (WJ-R) (Woodcock & Johnson, 1989) and WJ III in the diagnosis of AD/HD, including two unpub-lished studies of individuals with AD/HD and using the WJ-R. As part of a much larger study of individuals with clinical diagnoses, Dean and Woodcock (1999) reported the cluster and test score patterns for a group of 494 patients diagnosed with AD/HD. The results indicate a pattern of lower Processing Speed (*Gs*) scores with stronger scores in Visual Processing (*Gv*). The lowest scores were on the WJ-R Visual Matching test and the highest scores were on the WJ-R Visual Closure test. Wasserman and Becker (2000) compared 102 individuals with AD/HD to a demographically matched sample from the WJ-R standardization sample. They suggested that Long-Term Retrieval (*Glr*) and Auditory Processing (*Ga*) abilities differentiated children with AD/HD from those without.

Two studies using the WJ III with individuals who have AD/HD are reported in the *WJ III Technical Manual* (McGrew & Woodcock, 2001). The first study was conducted by Barbara Vesley. The second study was conducted by David Yasutake and Janet Lerner. Vesley (2001) conducted a small study of students with learning disabilities (*n* = 29), students with AD/HD (*n* = 30), and regular classroom students (*n* = 31) ranging from 5 to 12 years of age. The assessment battery included 15 tests from the WJ III COG, 9 tests from the WJ III ACH (Woodcock, McGrew, & Mather, 2001b), 3 tests from the *Diagnostic Supplement to the WJ III Tests of Cognitive Abilities* (Woodcock, McGrew, Mather, & Schrank, 2003), the *Wechsler Intelligence Scale for Children—Third Edition* (WISC-III) (Wechsler, 1991), and the *Tests of Variables of Attention* (TOVA) (Greenberg, 1998). In addition, the *Behavior Assessment System for Children* (BASC) (Reynolds & Kamphaus, 1992) Teacher and Parent Rating Scales were also completed. Although there was evidence of restriction in the range of the variables in the analysis, several WJ III tests demonstrated evidence of external relations with measures of AD/HD characteristics. Concept Formation and Visual

Matching were significantly correlated with a composite score obtained from the TOVA. Several cognitive tests (Concept Formation, Visual Matching, Decision Speed, and Auditory Working Memory) and achievement clusters (Broad Reading and Broad Math) were significantly correlated with the School Problems composite from the BASC Teacher Rating Scale, which encompasses ratings on the Attention Problems and Learning Problems subscales. The WJ III ACH Broad reading cluster, four WJ COG tests, and one WISC-III subtest contributed to two composite variables (i.e., functions) that correctly classified 64% of these children. The WJ III COG tests included Concept Formation, Visual–Auditory Learning, Rapid Picture Naming, and Incomplete Words. Results indicated that the Concept Formation and Incomplete Words tests were the most important tests in the classification of AD/HD.

Lerner and Yasutake (2001) collected data on a sample of 48 children with AD/HD ranging from 6 to 17 years of age. Children were administered 18 tests from the WJ III COG and 8 tests from the WJ III ACH. One-sample *t*-tests were employed to determine if the mean score for each WJ III test was significantly lower than the population average. The WJ III COG Auditory Attention test and the WJ III ACH Oral Comprehension, Passage Comprehension, and Calculation tests were significantly lower than average when the level needed for significance was adjusted for multiple comparisons.

THE EXECUTIVE PROCESSES, BROAD ATTENTION, WORKING MEMORY, AND CHECKLIST STUDY

This section includes details of a discriminative validity study of the efficacy of the WJ III Executive Processes, Broad Attention, and Working Memory clusters, and the Report Writer Parent and Teacher checklists in the prediction of AD/HD. These clusters, tests, and checklists are described next.

WJ III CLUSTERS

Executive Processing

Three aspects of executive functioning are subsumed by the Executive Processing cluster, based on a logical task analysis of the information-processing requirements of the component tests. Concept Formation requires the ability to repeatedly shift one's mental set, Planning requires strategic thinking, and Pair Cancellation requires proactive interference control.

Broad Attention

Four aspects of attention are subsumed by the Broad Attention cluster, based on a logical task analysis of the information-processing requirements of the component tests. Numbers Reversed requires attentional capacity, Auditory

Working Memory requires the ability to divide one's attention, Auditory Attention requires selective attention, and Pair Cancellation requires sustained attention.

Working Memory

Tests of working memory require the individual to both hold information and perform mental operations with the information. The two tests that contribute to this cluster, Numbers Reversed and Auditory Working Memory, require the examinee to hold information in memory and then perform a mental operation before responding.

WJ III TESTS

Concept Formation

Concept Formation, a measure of Fluid Reasoning and the narrow ability of Induction, is a controlled learning task. Except for the last several items, examinees are given immediate feedback regarding the correctness of their response before a new item is presented. The test requires categorization and inductive reasoning. It is one type of an executive processing task that requires mental flexibility when shifting mental sets. The examinee is provided a complete set of the stimuli and must derive the rule for the item. After correctly completing an item, the examinee is presented with another set of stimuli and must shift their mental set to derive the rule for the new item.

Numbers Reversed

Numbers Reversed is a measure of Short-Term Memory. The task is for the examinee to hold a series of numbers in memory while performing a mental operation (reversing the number sequence); consequently, this task is defined as a measure of Working Memory. For example, the examinee is given the sequence 7-6-2-4 and then asked to repeat it backward (4-2-6-7).

Auditory Working Memory

Auditory Working Memory is also a measure of Short-Term Memory and Working Memory. Unlike the Numbers Reversed test, examinees are given a series of both numbers and objects. The examinee is asked to listen to the series, to hold them in immediate awareness, and then to repeat them back, providing the objects first (in sequence) and then the numbers (in sequence). For example, given the sequence cat–2–boat–7–5-orange, the examinee would repeat first the objects in sequence (cat–boat–orange) and then the digits (2-7-5).

Auditory Attention

Auditory Attention is a measure of Auditory Processing and the narrow ability Speech–Sound Discrimination. The task requires selective attention. The examinee must overcome the effects of auditory distractions to understand oral language. During the task, the examinee listens to a series of words presented amidst background noise and points to pictures that represent the words presented. The items increase in difficulty by (a) increased difficulty of the sound discriminations and (b) the background noise increases in intensity (with the intensity of the word presentation remaining at the same auditory level).

Planning

Planning is a measure that likely measures both the broad abilities of Fluid Reasoning (especially at younger ages) and Visual Processing. It measures the narrow abilities of Sequential Reasoning and Spatial Scanning. The test requires use of the mental processes involved in determining, selecting, and applying solutions using forethought. Examinees are presented with a drawing of a pattern. They must trace the pattern without removing the pencil from the paper or retracing any lines.

Pair Cancellation

Pair Cancellation measures Processing Speed and Attention and Concentration. The test provides information about interference control and sustained attention. The examinee is required to stay on task in vigilant manner. The examinee is given 3 minutes to locate and mark a repeated pattern as quickly as possible. The visual presentation of more than 200 images of soccer balls, dogs, and cups on one page may be distracting for many examinees, especially given the time pressure.

REPORT WRITER CHECKLISTS

The Report Writer Parent and Teacher checklists provide information about specific behaviors exhibited by the individual, as reported by an informant.

Teacher Checklist

The Teacher Checklist includes several sections, two of which were used in this study: Current Classroom Functioning and Problem Behaviors in the Classroom. In the Current Classroom Functioning section, the teacher is asked to categorize the individual's classroom behavior in several areas, including attention to detail, sustained attention, listening ability, follow-through on schoolwork, organization, response to academic tasks requiring sustained mental efforts, and response to extraneous stimuli, among other areas. In the Problem Behaviors in the Classroom section, the teacher is asked to indicate the presence and severity of any problem behaviors in eight broad categories of possible problem behaviors: inattentiveness, overactivity, impulsiveness, uncooperative behavior, anxiousness, withdrawal, aggressiveness, and other inappropriate (nonaggressive) behaviors. For each category, the teacher is asked to check "Yes" or "No." For each "Yes" response (indicating the student exhibits the problem behavior in the classroom), the teacher is asked to describe the behavior specifically, to rate how seriously the behavior impedes the student's opportunity to learn, and to rate how disruptive the behavior is to others.

Parent Checklist

The Parent Checklist also includes several sections, two of which were used in this study. In the Current Behaviors section, parents are asked to describe the child's attitude toward school, level of effort toward schoolwork, attention to details, attention span, listening ability, follow-through on homework, level of organization, response to difficult tasks, orderliness, response to distractions, remembering/forgetfulness, typical activity level at home and in social situations, ability to play quietly, style of motor activity, amount of talking, ability to take turns, and interaction with peers. The Behavior Problems at Home section includes eight categories of problem behaviors: inattentiveness, overactivity, impulsiveness, uncooperative behavior, anxiousness, withdrawal, aggressiveness, and other inappropriate (nonaggressive) behaviors. For each category, the parent is asked to check "Yes" or "No." For each "Yes" response (indicating the child exhibits the problem behavior at home), the parent is asked to describe the behavior and to rate its seriousness.

SAMPLE

Participants in the present study were 58 students with AD/HD, ages 6 years to 14 years, 10 months, and 51 students without AD/HD ages 6 years, 8 months to 12 years, 4 months. The difference in age between AD/HD students and those without AD/HD was not statistically significant. Students with AD/HD were selected based on the criteria that they met a physician's diagnosis of AD/HD. No attempt was made to exclude children with comorbid diagnoses such as reading disorder, oppositional defiant disorder, or conduct disorder (American Psychiatric Association, 2000). Students with AD/HD who were prescribed medication that demonstrated short-term therapeutic effects (e.g., stimulant medications) were retained in the study if parent or physician approval was obtained to withhold a morning, afternoon, or daily dose of the medication, as would be necessary per medication effects, to assess the students in a nonmedicated condition. Students who were prescribed medication that demonstrated long-term therapeutic effects (e.g., antidepressants and anxiolytics) were eliminated from the study. Students without AD/HD were included in the study if (a) they had not been diagnosed with AD/HD or any other behavioral, emotional, or learning disorder and (b) they were not prescribed psychotropic medications.

INSTRUMENTATION

Children completed the six WJ III tests (Concept Formation, Numbers Reversed, Auditory Working Memory, Auditory Attention, Planning, and Pair Cancellation). Parents or guardians completed the WJ III Parent Checklist and the Behavior Rating Inventory of Executive Functioning (BRIEF) (Gioia, Isquith, Guy, & Kenworthy, 2000) Parent Rating Scale. The children's regular education teacher completed the WJ III Teacher Checklist and the BRIEF

Teacher Rating Scale. The BRIEF rating scales consist of eight clinical scales and two validity scales, which combine to form three index scores.

PROCEDURE

Students were selected from public schools and nonresidential clinic settings at selected sites in the United States and Canada. Parents were contacted to request their consent for their student to participate in the study. In the school settings, permission forms were sent to both the parents of children with and without AD/HD in selected grades. Because more permission forms were returned than were needed for the non-AD/HD sample, participants were selected to match the demographics of the AD/HD sample to the degree possible (e.g., age, gender, ethnicity, and grade).

Selected items from the Current Behaviors of the WJ III Parent Checklist and WJ III Teacher Checklist were used in this study. Composite variables focusing on inattentive and overactive behavior were created for both the Parent Checklist and the Teacher Checklist. "I don't know" and "Does Not Apply" ratings were categorized as missing, and relevant items were averaged for each composite. Higher scores on the composite scores reflect greater levels of inappropriate behavior, whereas lower scores reflect lower levels of inappropriate behavior. The composites and items used to create each composite used in this study are shown in Table 10-2. More information about the items is shown in Tables 10-3 and 10-4. This study also included two indexes and one composite provided on both the BRIEF Parent Rating Scale and the BRIEF Teacher Rating Scale. The Behavioral Regulation Index (BRI) comprises the Inhibit, Shift, and Emotional Control scales. The Metacognition Index (MI) comprises the Initiate, Working Memory,

TABLE 10-2   Items and Composite Used to Create Composite Scores for the WJ III Parent and Teacher Checklists

Composite	Items or composite used
Parent Behavior Rating	Parent checklist items C through R
Parent Problem Behavior	Behavior problems at home, Inattentiveness, Overactivity, and Impulsiveness
Teacher Behavior Rating	Teacher checklist items C through T
Teacher Problem Behavior	Behavior problems in the classroom, Inattentiveness, Overactivity, and Impulsiveness
Classroom Observation	Totals of inattentive, overactive, and impulsive behaviors
Parent Composite	Mean of Parent Behavior Rating and Parent Problem Behavior, with each converted to z-scores prior to summing
Teacher Composite	Mean of Teacher Behavior Rating and Teacher Problem Behavior, with each converted to z-scores prior to summing

TABLE 10-3   WJ III Parent Checklist Items Useful in the Diagnosis of Children with AD/HD

Part I: Current Behaviors	Part II: Problem Behaviors at Home
C.3 Often fails to give close attention to details or makes careless mistakes	A.1 Inattentiveness (presence or absence)
D.3 Often has difficulty sustaining attention in tasks or play activities	B.1 Overactivity
E.3 Often does not seem to listen when spoken to directly	C.1 Impulsiveness
F.3 Often does not follow through on instructions and fails to finish homework	
G.3 Often has difficulty organizing his or her tasks and activities	
H.4 Often avoids, dislikes, or is reluctant to engage in tasks that are difficult	
I.3 Often loses personal belongings	
J.3 Often easily distracted	
K.3 Often forgets what he or she is supposed to do	
L.3 Often fidgets with hands or feet or squirms	
M.3 Often runs about or climbs excessively (inappropriately)	
N.2 Often has difficulty playing quietly	
O.4 Is often "on the go" or acts as if "driven by a motor"	
P.3 Often talks excessively	
Q.3 Often has difficulty awaiting turn	
R.3 Often interrupts or intrudes on others (butts into conversations)	

Plan/Organize, Organization of Materials, and Monitor scales. The Global Executive Composite (GEC) is a global composite that stems from ratings on each item or scale.

ANALYSES AND RESULTS

In the following discussions, the research questions and the analytic methods used to answer each question are described briefly, and are followed by a summary of the primary findings.

HOW WELL DO THE WJ III TESTS PREDICT AD/HD STATUS?

As the first step in these analyses, Analysis of Variance (ANOVA) was used to determine whether children with and without AD/HD performed at statistically significantly different levels on the selected WJ III tests and clusters derived from those clusters. Effect sizes (η^2) were also calculated and represent the variance explained

TABLE 10-4   WJ III Teacher Checklist Items Useful in the Diagnosis of Children with AD/HD

Part I: Current Classroom Functioning	Part II: Problem Behaviors in the Classroom
C.3 Often fails to give close attention to details or makes careless mistakes	A.1 Inattentiveness
D.3 Often has difficulty sustaining attention in tasks or play activities	B.1 Overactivity
E.3 Often does not seem to listen when spoken to directly	C.1 Impulsiveness
F.3 Often does not follow through on instructions and fails to finish homework	
G.3 Often has difficulty organizing his or her tasks and activities	
H.4 Often avoids, dislikes, or is reluctant to engage in tasks that are difficult	
I.3 Often loses personal belongings	
J.3 Often easily distracted	
K.3 Often forgets what he or she is supposed to do	
L.3 Often fidgets with hands or feet or squirms	
M.2 Often leaves seat in classroom	
N.3 Often runs about or climbs excessively (inappropriately)	
O.2 Often has difficulty playing quietly	
P.4 Is often "on the go" or acts as if "driven by a motor"	
Q.3 Often talks excessively	
R.5 Often blurts out answers before the questions have been completed	
S.3 Often has difficulty awaiting turn	
T.3 Often interrupts or intrudes on others (butts into conversations)	

in AD/HD status by each WJ III test. These analyses demonstrate the extent to which these tests, each in isolation, could separate children with and without AD/HD.

Table 10-5 shows the results of this analysis. The table shows the means and standard deviations for each WJ III test and cluster for the total sample, as well as for the AD/HD and non-AD/HD groups. The table shows the results of the Analyses of Variance, comparing performance on each test and cluster by AD/HD status. Each of the WJ III tests and clusters, with the exception of Auditory Attention, was statistically significantly related to the presence or absence of AD/HD. In all cases, students without AD/HD scored at a statistically significantly higher level than did students without the disorder. The final column shows the value of η^2 for each WJ test and cluster by AD/HD status. Again, η^2 represents the variance explained in each test or cluster by AD/HD status; a common rule of thumb is that η^2 values of .01, .15, and .25 represent small, medium, and large effect sizes, respectively (Cohen, 1992). The Concept Formation and Auditory Working Memory tests showed moderate to large effects, as did the Working Memory and Broad Attention Clusters.

TABLE 10-5 Means, Standard Deviations, F-Tests, and η^2 for WJ III Tests and Clusters for Total Sample, AD/HD, and Non-AD/HD Samples

WJ III test or cluster	Mean (M), n, SD	Total	AD/HD	Non-AD/HD	F	P	η^2
Concept Formation	M	96.63	90.78	103.29	27.02	<.001	.20
	n	109	58	51			
	SD	13.98	12.86	12.18			
Numbers Reversed	M	99.17	94.16	104.86	14.35	<.001	.12
	n	109	58	51			
	SD	15.61	14.55	14.92			
Auditory Working Memory	M	103.17	96.69	110.55	32.60	<.001	.23
	n	109	58	51			
	SD	14.38	13.05	12.17			
Auditory Attention	M	100.39	99.19	101.75	1.14	.29	.01
	n	109	58	51			
	SD	12.49	11.25	13.76			
Planning	M	106.44	102.59	110.82	17.53	<.001	.14
	n	109	58	51			
	SD	11.00	8.12	12.23			
Pair Cancellation	M	99.22	96.79	102.10	5.05	.03	.05
	n	105	57	48			
	SD	12.31	13.98	9.30			
Working Memory cluster	M	101.06	94.31	108.73	31.60	<.001	.23
	n	109	58	51			
	SD	15.13	12.72	14.05			
Broad Attention cluster	M	100.21	94.00	107.58	25.91	<.001	.20
	n	105	57	48			
	SD	15.17	14.00	13.16			
Executive Processes cluster	M	98.45	92.84	105.10	24.31	<.001	.19
	n	105	57	48			
	SD	14.05	13.67	11.43			

Results suggest that the WJ III tests and clusters may be useful in identifying AD/HD children. A number of tests (Concept Formation, Numbers Reversed, Auditory Working Memory, Planning, and Pair Cancellation) and clusters (Working Memory, Broad Attention, and Executive Processes) showed predictable and statistically significant differences for the sample of AD/HD in comparison with non-AD/HD children.

In the second step of these analyses, logistic regression was used to determine the extent to which the WJ III tests could predict AD/HD status, in combination. For these analyses, AD/HD status was regressed on scores of the six WJ III tests in a simultaneous (forced entry) logistic regression. Logistic regression is a method for predicting a single, categorical dependent variable (AD/HD versus non-AD/HD) from several independent variables (e.g., the WJ III tests). The χ^2 was used to determine the statistical significance of the prediction. A statistically significant χ^2 means that the independent variables predict AD/HD status successfully. A number of analogues to R^2 from multiple regressions have been developed for logistic regression; the Nagelkerke R^2 analogue was used to determine magnitude of the relation between AD/HD status and the WJ III tests in combination. (The Nagelkerke R^2 is one of several R^2 analogues available to estimate the variance explained by the predictor variables in logistic regression. It may slightly overestimate R^2 in comparison, for example, to η^2, but other R^2 analogues lead to the same conclusions noted below.) Finally, the unstandardized regression coefficients and their statistical significance were used to determine the relative importance of each WJ III test in predicting AD/HD status, with the other tests already controlled.

The six WJ III COG tests predicted AD/HD status at a statistically significant level ($\chi^2 = 42.32$ [df = 6], $p < .001$); furthermore, the six tests were strongly related to AD/HD versus non-AD/HD status ($R^2 = .44$). Table 10-6 shows the unstandardized coefficients (b) for each test, its standard error (SE), degrees of freedom (df), and statistical significance (probability, p). As shown in Table 10-6, the Auditory Working Memory and Planning tests were statistically significant predictors of AD/HD status, even with the other variables statistically controlled. In other words, these two tests explained a unique portion of the variation in AD/HD status beyond that explained by the other WJ tests. These findings further suggest the utility of the WJ III tests in separating AD/HD from non-AD/HD children, and that Auditory Working Memory and Planning may be particularly useful in such a diagnosis.

HOW WELL DOES THE WJ III CHECKLIST PREDICT AD/HD STATUS?

These analyses paralleled those for the WJ III tests. ANOVAs and effect sizes were calculated for each of the Checklist Composite variables to determine the

TABLE 10-6 Results of Logistic Regression Using WJ III Tests to Predict AD/HD Classification Status

WJ III test	b	SE	df	p
Concept Formation	−.03	.02	1	.16
Numbers Reversed	−.03	.02	1	.18
Auditory Working Memory	−.06	.03	1	.02
Auditory Attention	.03	.02	1	.22
Planning	−.07	.03	1	.048
Pair Cancellation	.00	.02	1	.99

Note: $\chi^2 = 42.23$; df = 6; $p = .001$; Nagelkerke $R^2 = .44$.

extent to which each could be used in isolation to separate AD/HD and non-AD/HD children. As shown in the top portion of Table 10-7, both the WJ III parent checklist and the teacher checklist were statistically significantly related to AD/HD status. Children with AD/HD scored statistically significantly higher on both checklists than did those without AD/HD, meaning that they were rated by parents and teachers as having more problems with inattention, overactivity, and impulsiveness. Both effect sizes were quite large, and the Parent responses—with an effect size of .66—were particularly predictive of AD/HD status.

Sequential (hierarchical) logistic regression was used to predict AD/HD status from both checklist composites. For this analysis, the Teacher Composite was first entered into the regression, and then the Parent Composite was added in a separate block. This procedure was used to determine the extent to which the teacher and parent checklists, in combination, were useful in predicting AD/HD status. Because it may be more difficult to obtain parent as compared to teacher ratings, these variables were added in sequential fashion to determine whether parent

TABLE 10-7   Means, Standard Deviations, F-Tests, and Effect Sizes (η^2) for WJ III Rating Scale Composites and BRIEF Composites for Total Sample, AD/HD, and Non-AD/HD Samples

Rating scale score	Mean (M), n, SD	Total	AD/HD	Non-AD/HD	F	P	η^2
WJ III Parent	M	.00	.73	−.83	204.32	<.001	.66
Composite	n	109	58	.51			
	SD	.96	.63	.49			
WJ III Teacher	M	.01	.46	−.50	36.24	<.001	.26
Composite	n	107	57	50			
	SD	.95	.81	.85			
BRIEF BRI—Parent	M	57.13	65.09	48.24	62.34	<.001	.37
	n	108	57	51			
	SD	13.89	11.91	10.05			
BRIEF MI—Parent	M	58.29	67.04	48.51	101.34	<.001	.49
	n	108	57	51			
	SD	13.29	9.75	9.32			
BRIEF GEC—Parent	M	58.29	67.16	48.37	96.71	<.001	.48
	n	108	57	51			
	SD	13.64	10.06	9.74			
BRIEF BRI—Teacher	M	59.35	65.63	52.32	17.07	<.001	.14
	n	106	56	50			
	SD	17.77	17.40	15.55			
BRIEF MI—Teacher	M	60.18	68.28	50.94	32.83	<.001	.24
	n	107	57	51			
	SD	17.81	16.56	14.46			
BRIEF GEC—Teacher	M	60.19	67.95	51.34	29.67	<.001	.22
	n	107	57	50			
	SD	17.74	16.01	15.42			

ratings improved the prediction of AD/HD status above and beyond that of teacher ratings. In addition to the statistics previously discussed, change in χ^2 ($\Delta\chi^2$) was used to determine the statistical significance of the improvement in prediction, and ΔR^2 was used to describe the magnitude of the improvement in prediction.

Table 10-8 shows the results of these analyses. The table shows the variable entered at each block, the resulting R^2, change in R^2, χ^2 (and $\Delta\chi^2$), and the level of statistical significance of χ^2. Both steps of this sequential logistic regression were statistically significant. The overall composite from the teacher checklist was strongly related to AD/HD status, as was the overall composite from the parent checklist. The WJ checklists appear quite successful at predicting AD/HD versus non-AD/HD status. We should note, however, that once the parent checklist entered the logistic regression, the teacher checklist was no longer statistically significant, meaning its information was redundant when considered with the parent information. Nevertheless, these findings suggest that the WJ III checklists may be very useful in the identification of AD/HD.

HOW DO THE WJ III CHECKLISTS COMPARE WITH THE BRIEF IN PREDICTING AD/HD?

The BRIEF is a commonly used, standardized behavioral rating scale for the diagnosis of AD/HD. Because the BRIEF is norm referenced, it seemed worthwhile to compare the BRIEF with the criterion-referenced Report Writer checklists in their ability to predict AD/HD status. AD/HD status was regressed on the BRIEF Parent and Teacher Behavioral Regulation indexes and Metacognition indexes in the first block of a sequential logistic regression, with the teacher and parent checklists added in a second block to determine whether the checklists improved the prediction of AD/HD status beyond the BRIEF scales. The results of this logistic regression are shown in Table 10-9. This procedure was then reversed in a second logistic regression to determine whether the BRIEF scales improved the prediction of AD/HD status beyond the checklists (see Table 10-10). The statistical significance and importance of step two in each analysis were determined using $\Delta\chi^2$ and ΔR^2. The purpose of these analyses was to determine

TABLE 10-8 Results of Sequential Logistic Regression Using the WJ III Teacher and Parent Checklist Composites to Predict AD/HD Classification

Variables entered by block	Nagelkerke R^2	ΔR^2	χ^2	df	p
Block 1 WJ III Teacher Composite	.33	—	30.48	1	<.001
Block 2 WJ III Parent Composite	.77	.44	61.20	1	<.001

Note: The value shown for χ^2 for block 1 is the χ^2 for that block; all subsequent χ^2 values (and degrees of freedom and probabilities) are changes in χ^2 from the previous block.

TABLE 10-9 Results of Sequential Logistic Regression Using BRIEF BRI and MI Scores and WJ III Parent and Teacher Checklist Composites to Predict AD/HD Classification

Variables entered by block	Nagelkerke R^2	ΔR^2	χ^2	df	p
Block 1	.68	—	74.11	4	<.001
BRIEF BRI—Parent					
BRIEF MI—Parent					
BRIEF BRI—Teacher					
BRIEF MI—Teacher					
Block 2	.79	.11	18.91	2	<.001
WJ III Parent Composite					
WJ III Teacher Composite					

Note: BRI, Behavioral Regulation Index; MI, Metacognition Index. The value shown for χ^2 for block 1 is the χ^2 for that block; all subsequent χ^2 values (and degrees of freedom and probabilities) are changes in χ^2 from the previous block.

whether the Report Writer checklists and the BRIEF scales added anything unique to the prediction of AD/HD status above that of the other instrument. As shown in the tables, the Report Writer checklists improved the prediction of AD/HD status beyond that of the BRIEF scales ($\Delta\chi^2$ [2] = 18.91, $p < .001$, $\Delta R^2 = .11$), but the BRIEF scales did not improve prediction beyond that of the checklists ($\Delta\chi^2$ [4] = 5.27, $p = .26$, $\Delta R^2 = .03$). Although not shown here, the same pattern of results was shown when the BRIEF global composite (GEC) scores were used. These findings further support the utility of the Report Writer checklists as a tool in the identification of AD/HD. Furthermore, at least in the current study, the Report Writer checklists offered something unique beyond the BRIEF scales in making such decisions, but the reverse was not the case. That is, the

TABLE 10-10 Results of Sequential Logistic Regression Using WJ III Parent and Teacher Checklist Composites and BRIEF BRI and MI Scores to Predict AD/HD Classification

Variables entered by block	Nagelkerke R^2	ΔR^2	χ^2	Δdf	p
Block 1	.76	—	87.76	2	<.001
WJ III Parent Composite					
WJ III Teacher Composite					
Block 2	.79	.03	5.27	4	.26
BRIEF BRI—Parent					
BRIEF MI—Parent					
BRIEF BRI—Teacher					
BRIEF MI—Teacher					

Note: BRI, Behavioral Regulation Index; MI, Metacognition Index. The value shown for χ^2 for block 1 is the χ^2 for that block; all subsequent χ^2 values (and degrees of freedom and probabilities) are changes in χ^2 from the previous block.

ability of the BRIEF scales to separate AD/HD from non-AD/HD children was captured equally well by the Report Writer checklists.

HOW WELL DO THE WJ III TESTS AND CHECKLISTS PREDICT AD/HD STATUS, IN COMBINATION?

In typical clinical practice, one would not make a diagnosis of AD/HD based only on test scores or checklists. To determine whether the Report Writer checklists provide useful prediction above that provided by the WJ III tests, a sequential logistic regression was conducted in which the WJ tests were added in one block, the WJ Teacher Composite was added in a second block, and the WJ Parent Composite was added in a third block. In this determination, $\Delta\chi^2$ was used to determine whether the variables added in each block were statistically significant, and ΔR^2 was used to determine the unique increase in prediction at each step.

As shown in Table 10-11, the prediction of AD/HD status improved at a statistically significant level for each additional block added to the equation, and there were substantial improvements in the R^2 analogue at each step as well. This finding means that although the WJ III tests used may be useful in the identification of AD/HD, the Report Writer checklists add considerably to that identification. When used in combination, the WJ III tests and checklists may be useful adjuncts in the assessment and identification of AD/HD.

STUDY SUMMARY

The WJ III Executive Processes, Broad Attention, and Working Memory clusters, as well as their component tests, and the Report Writer Parent and

TABLE 10-11   Results of Sequential Logistic Regression Using WJ III Tests and WJ III Teacher and Parent Checklist Composites to Predict AD/HD Classification

Variables entered by block	Nagelkerke R^2	ΔR^2	χ^2	Δdf	p
Block 1	.47	—	44.67	6	<.001
Concept Formation					
Numbers Reversed					
Auditory Working Memory					
Auditory Attention					
Planning					
Pair Cancellation					
Block 2	.53	.06	6.81	1	.009
WJ III Teacher Composite					
Block 3	.84	.32	51.15	1	<.001
WJ III Parent Composite					

Note: The value shown for χ^2 for block 1 is the χ^2 for that block; all subsequent χ^2 values (and degrees of freedom and probabilities) are changes in χ^2 from the previous block.

Teacher Checklists may be useful in the identification of children with AD/HD. Although the tests and checklists may be useful in isolation, these findings suggest that they may be especially useful when used in combination. Children with AD/HD, other things being equal, will likely score lower on the Concept Formation, Numbers Reversed, Auditory Working Memory, Planning, and Pair Cancellation tests, and on the Working Memory, Broad Attention, and Executive Processes Clusters of the WJ III. Such children may also demonstrate elevated ratings by parent and teachers on items of the WJ III checklists that contain critical diagnostic criteria, as defined by DSM-IV, on inattention, overactivity, and impulsivity. Finally, children with AD/HD are likely to show these characteristics in combination. When AD/HD is the relevant referral question, a pattern of lower scores on the indicated tests and clusters and endorsement of critical items on the checklists should provide satisfactory evidence for an AD/HD diagnosis.

CLINICAL APPLICATIONS AND CASE ILLUSTRATION

As described in this study, the parent and teacher checklists from the *Report Writer for the WJ III* are useful in identifying the behaviors associated with AD/HD. Results of this study lend support to the suggestion made by Schrank & Woodcock (2002) that the checklists can provide documentation to support or contradict a clinical hypothesis of AD/HD. That is, as part of a comprehensive assessment, these checklists can alert clinicians to the symptoms of AD/HD, confirm a hypothesis, or rule out AD/HD as a consideration. Other checklists may also provide useful information. For example, the Test Session Observation Checklist is provided on the front cover of both the WJ III COG and WJ III ACH Test Records. This checklist provides an opportunity to record overall observations of behavior during the test session. Of particular relevance to an AD/HD referral are questions regarding attention and concentration, activity level, care in responding, and response to difficult tasks as observed during testing.

When used in conjunction with these checklists, the WJ III includes some tests that may be sensitive to the cognitive determinants, correlates, or effects of AD/HD. Table 10-12 summarizes the tests that have been found to be useful for this purpose. The table is based on the research discussed in this chapter. A logical analysis of the tests included in Table 10-12 suggests that many, if not all, of the tests on the list require moderate to high levels of attention and concentration.

Depending on the nature of the referral question, a number of WJ III COG tests and clusters may be useful in the diagnosis of AD/HD, based on the study documented in this chapter. The task requirements for each of these tests can be examined to confirm one or more clinical hypotheses for an individual. Concept Formation may be sensitive to any difficulties in shifting response patterns. Attentional capacity, or the ability to hold information while performing some

TABLE 10-12 WJ III Tests That May Be Sensitive to AD/HD

Test	Source[a]				
	1	2	3	4	5
COG Test 2: Visual–Auditory Learning		■	■		
COG Test 4: Sound Blending		■			
COG Test 5: Concept Formation			■		■
COG Test 6: Visual Matching	■		■		
COG Test 7: Numbers Reversed					■
COG Test 8: Incomplete Words		■	■		
COG Test 9: Auditory Working Memory			■		■
COG Test 14: Auditory Attention				■	
COG Test 16: Decision Speed			■		
COG Test 18: Rapid Picture Naming			■		
COG Test 19: Planning					■
COG Test 20: Pair Cancellation					■
COG Test 21: Memory for Names		■			
COG Test 26: Cross Out	■				
ACH Test 5: Calculation				■	
ACH Test 9: Passage Comprehension				■	
ACH Test 15: Oral Comprehension				■	

[a]Source: 1, Dean & Woodcock (1999); 2, Wasserman & Becker (2000); 3, Vesley (2001); 4, Lerner & Yasutake (2001); 5, Ford (2003).

action on the information, is required by Numbers Reversed. Auditory Attention may also be of clinical interest, particularly if there are issues concerning selective attention and/or concentration abilities amid auditory distractions. Auditory Working Memory may be useful for determining an individual's ability to divide information that is held in short-term memory. Planning may be useful in describing the individual's ability to use forward thinking, or forethought, with a defined task. This test may also be sensitive to the ability to inhibit impulsive responses. Pair Cancellation may be used to assess the individual's ability to stay on task in a vigilant manner, or capacity to sustain attention for a brief period of time. These tests combine to create the Broad Attention, Working Memory, and Executive Processes clusters that provide the benefits of increased reliability and greater validity when making generalizations about an individual because each cluster score is based on more than one test.

Several of the tests that were found to differentiate AD/HD individuals from non-AD/HD individuals in the other cited studies may be similarly clinically useful for hypothesis generation. For example, some WJ III tests may be used to examine a hypothesis that the individual may be experiencing difficulties with fluency and efficiency. Decision Speed is a measure of cognitive automaticity, requiring the individual to make quick conceptual decisions. Rapid Picture Naming may be particularly sensitive to the speed, consistency, and accuracy of naming facility. Additionally, Visual Matching and Cross Out are each measures of perceptual speed. Low scores in these tests may be reflective of limitations in attention; low scores on these two tests and other tests requiring high levels of attention (e.g., Memory for Names) have been shown to be related to neurological disorders (Dean & Woodcock, 1999).

As demonstrated in the following case illustration, a number of the WJ III tests and clusters, when used conjointly with selected checklists of Report Writer, can contribute to a behavioral–cognitive assessment of an individual with AD/HD.

CASE ILLUSTRATION

Jeff, an 18-year-old student attending his first year of college at a large, state-supported university, is taking a typical first-year course load of Chemistry, Psychology, English, and Sociology. Most of his classes consist of lectures delivered to a large group of 200 to 300 students. The only exception is a small Chemistry lab.

Recently, Jeff referred himself to the university disability resource center with the hope of receiving some academic support due to increasing levels of difficulty completing assignments and paying attention in class. He reported being forgetful, disorganized, and restless. Recently, he failed several examinations. During a recent visit to his physician, a clinical interview was completed and Jeff was subsequently given a preliminary diagnosis of AD/HD and prescribed Concerta.

As evidenced on the Report Writer Adolescent and Adult Self-Report Checklist, Jeff has demonstrated characteristic AD/HD symptoms for over 6 months (in some cases over 10 years), including a failure to give close attention to details, resulting in careless mistakes in schoolwork, work, and other activities; difficulty sustaining attention in tasks; restlessness, lack of follow-through on instructions, and failure to finish schoolwork; difficulty organizing tasks and activities; losing things; a reluctance to engage in tasks that require sustained mental effort; and distractibility and forgetfulness. Some of the inattentive symptoms were present before the age of 7 years. The symptoms are present in multiple settings, such as in the classroom, at home, and at work. The behaviors are adversely impacting his social, academic, and occupational functioning and no other mental disorders are evidenced.

The checklist also provided documentation that Jeff has had a long history of attention and concentration problems, so a clinical interview was conducted that yielded the following information: In prior years of schooling, some of Jeff's teachers expressed concerns about these behaviors, but no formal referrals for special assistance were made, possibly because his overall academic performance was consistently average or above average. His measured performance on the yearly group-administered achievement tests, however, was typically below his classroom performance. His SAT scores were low average. Jeff was admitted to college based largely on his reference letters and prior academic performance.

Because no prior psychoeducational evaluation had been conducted previously, one was completed by the resource center staff. In addition to the Adolescent and Adult Self-Report Checklist, selected tests from the WJ III COG and WJ III ACH were administered. (The Report Writer Executive Processes and Cognitive Fluency Checklist and the Test Session Observation Checklists were also completed as part of the cognitive portion of the assessment.) Additionally, the examiner was able to complete the Classroom Behavior Observation Checklist through an observation of Jeff during his chemistry lab.

During the observation during Chemistry lab, Jeff was rated off-task on 85% of intervals recorded. This amount of off-task behavior is qualitatively different from a comparison peer. Inattentive, overactive, and impulsive behaviors were observed. Although Jeff was recently prescribed medication for possible AD/HD, he had not taken the medication for over a week prior to the observation. A conversation with both the lab instructor and Jeff confirmed that the observation was characteristic of Jeff's typical lab performance. The classroom observation was consistent with Jeff's self report.

In order to gain an understanding of Jeff's intellectual ability, the seven tests in the General Intellectual Ability (GIA—Std) cluster were administered. His overall general intellectual ability falls in the average to above-average range. His Cognitive Efficiency score is lower (below average) than his Verbal Ability (superior) and Thinking Ability (above average) scores.

During the examination, Jeff appeared at ease but appeared fidgety or restless at times. He became distracted often. Although, at times, he appeared to respond too quickly to the tasks, he generally persisted when tasks became difficult.

Given the focus of the referral, tests used to form the Executive Processing, Working Memory, Cognitive Fluency, and Broad Attention clinical clusters were also administered. Results indicate significantly lower scores on all tests and clusters that comprise these clusters, with all scores falling in the below-average range of functioning. Test session observations support this interpretation of his test scores. On the Concept Formation test, he appeared to demonstrate some difficulty shifting concepts. He did not appear to benefit from or use the feedback that was provided to improve his performance. On the Planning test, he demonstrated an impulsive style when he appeared to "jump right in" without scanning or studying the items. On the Pair Cancellation test, he periodically lost focus and began looking for targets unsystematically.

Selected tests from the WJ III ACH (those forming the Academic Fluency cluster) were also administered. All Academic Fluency tests and the resulting cluster score fall in the below-average range. Test session observations verify his below-average performance on these tests. He provided answers slowly on the Retrieval Fluency test. On the Decision Speed test, he made conceptual decisions at an inconsistent rate and sometimes was inaccurate in decision-making. His rate was also inconsistent on the Rapid Picture Naming test, on which he showed instances of naming inaccuracy. These scores are significantly lower than his overall GIA score and are commensurate with the Executive Processes, Broad Attention, Working Memory, and Cognitive Efficiency cluster scores. A comparison of Jeff's test and cluster standard scores is provided below:

Test	Standard Scores		Standard Scores
WJ III COG tests		**WJ III clusters**	
Verbal Comprehension	121	General Intellectual	111
Visual–Auditory Learning	112	Ability (GIA)	
Spatial Relations	115	Verbal Ability	121
Sound Blending	102	Thinking Ability	108
Concept Formation	98	Cognitive Efficiency	90
Visual Matching	101	Executive Processing	84
Numbers Reversed	81	Working Memory	81
Auditory Working Memory	79	Broad Attention	81
Retrieval Fluency	82	Cognitive Fluency	83
Auditory Attention	83	**WJ III ACH clusters**	
Decision Speed	83	Academic Fluency	82
Rapid Picture Naming	82		
Planning	75		
Pair Cancellation	80		
WJ III ACH tests			
Reading Fluency	85		
Math Fluency	83		
Writing Fluency	78		

A review of Jeff's developmental and academic history and current problems, as provided by the Report Writer checklists and clinical interview, and the classroom observation in his Chemistry lab all indicate that Jeff meets the qualifying criteria for a diagnosis of AD/HD according to the *Diagnostic and Statistical Manual of Mental Disorders* (American Psychiatric Association, 2000). His performance on selected tests from the WJ III COG and WJ III ACH indicate that his AD/HD behavioral symptoms coexist with relative executive processing, working memory, attention, and fluency weaknesses.

SUMMARY

The goal of this summary of the existing research using the WJ-R and WJ III is to help better understand validity of the WJ III for assessment of individuals with AD/HD. A study of the diagnostic utility of several of the WJ III COG tests and clusters, as well as selected criterion-referenced checklists from Report Writer has been presented. Analysis of these data provides validity evidence for the Report Writer parent and teacher checklists and the WJ III Broad Attention, Working Memory, and Executive Processes clusters, and the Auditory Working Memory, Planning, Pair Cancellation, Numbers Reversed, and Concept Formation tests in the diagnosis of AD/HD. An example of a clinical application has been provided.

Diagnostic criteria for AD/HD are primarily behavior based. The parent and teacher checklists in Report Writer are shown to be useful for gathering and documenting behavioral manifestations of AD/HD, such as restlessness, poor concentration, distractibility, and high levels of activity. Additionally, the WJ III COG may be useful for describing the executive processing characteristics of an individual who has AD/HD, such as any concomitant limitations in working memory capacity and/or inattention to cognitive task demands. This type of cognitive processing information can be used to support a diagnosis of AD/HD and may assist in identifying needed services and interventions.

ACKNOWLEDGMENTS

The authors thank Carla Merkel for her assistance in the preparation of this chapter and Erica LaForte, Edward Kirby, and Krista Smart for their assistance with data collection.

REFERENCES

American Psychiatric Association (2000). *Diagnostic and statistical manual of mental disorders* (4th ed., text revision). Washington, DC: Author.

Assesmany, A., McIntosh, D. E., Phelps, L., & Rizza, M. G. (2001). Discriminant validity of the WISC-III with children classified as AD/HD. *Journal of Psychoeducational Assessment, 19,* 137–147.

Barkley, R. A. (1990). *Attention-deficit hyperactivity disorder: A handbook for diagnosis and treatment.* New York: Guilford Press.

Barkley, R. A. (1997). *AD/HD and the nature of self-control.* New York: Guilford.

Barkley, R. A. (1998). *Attention deficit hyperactivity disorder: A handbook for diagnosis and treatment* (2nd ed.). New York: Guilford.

Barkley, R. A., & Grodzinsky, G. M. (1994). Are tests of frontal lobe functions useful in the diagnosis of attention deficit disorders? *Clinical Neuropsychologist, 8,* 121–139.

Barkley, R. A., Grodzinsky, G. M., & DuPaul, G. J. (1992). Frontal lobe functions in attention deficit disorder with and without hyperactivity: A review and research report. *Journal of Abnormal Child Psychology, 20,* 163–188.

Cohen, J. (1992). A power primer. *Psychological Bulletin, 112*, 155–159.

Dean, R. S., & Woodcock, R. W. (1999). *The WJ–R and Bateria–R in neuropsychological assessment* (Research Report No. 3). Riverside Publishing.

DuPaul, G. J., & Stoner, G. (1994). *AD/HD in the schools: Assessment and intervention strategies.* New York: Guilford.

Ford, L. (2003). Assessing preschool children. In R. W. Woodcock, K. S. McGrew, N. Mather, & F. A. Schrank. Woodcock–Johnson III Diagnostic Supplement. Itasca IL: Riverside Publishing.

Gibney, L. A., McIntosh, D. E., Dean, R. S., & Dunham, M. (2002). Diagnosing attention disorders with measures of neurocognitive functioning. *International Journal of Neuroscience, 112*, 539–564.

Gioia, G. A., Isquith, P. K., Guy, S. C., & Kenworthy, L. (2000). *Behavior rating inventory of executive function.* Odessa, FL: Psychological Assessment Resources.

Greenberg, L. M. (1998). *Tests of variables of attention.* Los Alamitos, CA: Attention Disorders Inc.

Hinshaw, S. P. (2002). Preadolescent girls with attention-deficit/hyperactivity disorder: I. Background characteristics, comorbidity, cognitive and social functioning, and parenting practices. *Journal of Consulting and Clinical Psychology, 70*, 1086–1098.

Hinshaw, S. P., Carte, E. T., Sami, N., Treuting, J. J., & Zupan, B. A. (2002). Preadolescent girls with attention-deficit/hyperactivity disorder: II. Neuropsychological performance in relation to subtypes and individual classification. *Journal of Consulting and Clinical Psychology, 70*, 1099–1111.

Hoff, K. E., Doepke, K., & Landau, S. (2002). Best practice in the assessment of children with attention deficit/hyperactivity disorder: Linking assessment to intervention. In J. Grimes and A. Thomas (Eds.). *Best practices in school psychology IV. Vol. II* (pp. 1224–1251). Bethesda, MD: National Association of School Psychologists.

Individuals with Disabilities Education Act Amendments of 1997 (Public Law No. 105-17), U.S.C. §§ 33–1400 et seq. (statute).

Jensen, P. S., & Cooper, J. R. (Eds.) (2002). *Attention deficit hyperactivity disorder: State of the science. Best practices.* Kingston, NJ: Civic Research Institute.

Lerner, J., & Yasutake, D. (2001). School-age AD/HD sample. In K. S. McGrew, & R. W. Woodcock. *Technical manual. Woodcock–Johnson III.* Itasca, IL: Riverside Publishing.

McGrew, K. S., & Woodcock, R. W. (2001). *Technical manual. Woodcock–Johnson III.* Itasca, IL: Riverside Publishing.

Perugini, E. M., Harvey, E. A., Lovejoy, D. W., Sandstrom, K., & Webb, A. H. (2000). The predictive power of combined neuropsychological measures for attention-deficit/hyperactivity disorder in children. *Child Neuropsychology, 6*, 101–114.

Prifitera, A., & Dersh, J. (1993). Base rates of WISC-III diagnostic subtest patterns among normal and learning disabled, and AD/HD samples. *Journal of Psychoeducational Assessment, WISC-III Monograph Series*, 43–55.

Reynolds, C. R., & Kamphaus, R. (1992). *Behavior assessment system for children.* Circle Pines, MN: American Guidance Service.

Schrank, F. A., & Woodcock, R. W. (2002). *Report writer for the WJ III compuscore and profiles program* [computer software]. Itasca, IL: Riverside Publishing.

Schwean, V. L., & Saklofske, D. H., Yackulic, R.A., & Quinn, D. (1995). Aggressive and nonaggressive AD/HD boys: Cognitive, intellectual, and behavioral comparisons. *Journal of Psychoeducational Assessment. Special AD/HD Issue Monograph*, 6–21.

Shallice, T., Marzocchi, G. M., Coser, S., Del-Savio, M., Meuter, R. F., & Rumiati, R. I. (2002). Executive function profile of children with attention deficit hyperactivity disorder. *Developmental Neuropsychology, 21*, 43–71.

Telzrow, C. F., & Tankersly, M. (2000). *IDEA amendments of 1997: Practice guidelines for school-based teams.* Bethesda, MD. National Association of School Psychologists.

Vesley, B. (2001). Grades 1 through 6 normal, LD, AD/HD sample. In K. S. McGrew & R. W. Woodcock (Eds.), *Technical manual. Woodcock–Johnson III.* Itasca, IL: Riverside Publishing.

Wasserman, J. D., & Becker, K. A. (2000). *Clinical application of the Woodcock–Johnson Tests of cognitive ability—revised with children diagnosed with attention-deficit/hyperactivity disorders.* Itasca, IL: Riverside Publishing.

Wechsler, D. (1991). *The Wechsler intelligence scale for children—Third edition.* San Antonio, TX: Psychological Corporation.

Willcutt, E. G., Pennington, B. F., Boada, R., Ogline, J. S., Tunick, R. A., Chhabildas, N. A., & Olson, R. K. (2001). A comparison of the cognitive deficits in reading disability and attention-deficit/hyperactivity disorder. *Journal of Abnormal Psychology, 110,* 157–172.

Woodcock, R. W., & Johnson, M. B. (1989). *Woodcock–Johnson psycho-educational battery— revised.* Itasca, IL: Riverside Publishing.

Woodcock, R. W., McGrew, K. S., & Mather, N. (2001a). *Woodcock–Johnson III: Tests of cognitive abilities.* Itasca, IL: Riverside Publishing.

Woodcock, R. W., McGrew, K. S., & Mather, N. (2001b). *Woodcock–Johnson III: Tests of achievement.* Itasca, IL: Riverside Publishing.

Woodcock, R. W., McGrew, K. S., Mather, N., & Schrank, F. A. (2003). *Woodcock–Johnson III diagnostic supplement.* Itasca, IL: Riverside Publishing.

World Health Organization (1994). *International classification of diseases* (10th ed.). Geneva: Switzerland.

11

A COGNITIVE

NEUROPSYCHOLOGY

ASSESSMENT SYSTEM

RAYMOND S. DEAN

Neuropsychology Laboratory
Ball State University
Muncie, Indiana 47306

RICHARD W. WOODCOCK

Vanderbilt University
Nashville, Tennessee 37235

SCOTT L. DECKER

Riverside Publishing Company
Itasca, Illinois 60143

FREDRICK A. SCHRANK

The Woodcock–Muñoz Foundation
Olympia, Washington 98501

INTRODUCTION

The relationship between human behavior and brain function has intrigued scholars for centuries, yet our knowledge of the relationship between behavior and the integrity of the central nervous system owes more to the research vigor of the past 30 years than to any other time in history. Of continuing interest is the relationship between areas of the brain and cognitive, sensorimotor, and affective functioning. This body of knowledge has become known as neuropsychology and seeks to relate behavior to brain functioning. Neuropsychological assessment has evolved as a method of defining the functional integrity of the brain by observing behavior under standardized conditions. In North America, neuropsychological assessment generally involves administration of standardized test batteries (e.g., the Halstead–Reitan Neuropsychological Test Battery [Reitan & Halstead, 1955] and the Luria–Nebraska Neuropsychological Test Battery [Golden, Purish, & Hammeke, 1985]).

Dean (1989) argued in favor of a neuropsychological perspective for understanding and diagnosis of neurological, psychiatric, and educational disorders.

The ideas discussed in this chapter are an outgrowth of this perspective. This perspective provides the theoretical framework for the Dean–Woodcock Neuropsychological Assessment System (D-WNAS) that utilizes the Woodcock–Johnson III (WJ III) (Woodcock, McGrew, & Mather, 2001a), the Dean Woodcock Sensory-Motor Battery (D-WSMB), the Dean–Woodcock Structured Interview (D-WSI), and the Dean–Woodcock Emotional Status Examination (D-WESE) as parts of an interpretive system in which both neurological and psychological data are integrated into a comprehensive view of an individual's cognitive, academic, sensory, motor, and emotional functioning.

This chapter begins with an historical overview of the quantitative and qualitative approaches to neuropsychological assessment; these approaches are contrasted to the functional approach utilized by the D-WNAS. Cattell–Horn–Carroll (CHC) theory provides the theoretical basis and the WJ III provides the assessment tools for determining an individual's functional levels of cognitive abilities. A cognitive neuropsychology model, based on the WJ III, is presented. The model may be useful for understanding cognitive strengths and weaknesses from a neuropsychological perspective. Next, the D-WSMB is described in detail, as well as the D-WSI and D-WESE. Finally, two case illustrations are presented to illustrate the utility of the D-WNAS for describing functional levels of cognitive, academic, and sensory-motor performance.

HISTORICAL OVERVIEW

Ultimately, all voluntary human behavior may be traced to brain functioning. Although nineteenth century research—which based conclusions about normal brain functioning on case studies of patients with diseased brains—has been criticized (Reitan, 1974), early investigations led to our present understanding of the relationship between behavioral defects and cerebral impairment. The idea of one-to-one correspondence between behavior and localized microstructures of the brain seems naive by today's standards. It is now recognized that the location, magnitude, and chronicity of a brain lesion interact with developmental history and individual differences in such a way to make microlocalization of a specific function tenuous. Although rather clear knowledge of the location of a lesion may be available for a patient, rarely is it possible for the neurosurgeon or neurologist to make specific predictions about the patient's behavioral functioning.

As in most areas of measurement, neuropsychological assessment has grown out of a need in an applied area. In the case of neuropsychology, the most salient influence has been the desire on the part of the medical community to more fully describe the behavioral effects of brain damage. Neuropsychological assessment has often been considered an adjunct to the neurological examination. Basically a noninvasive technique, neuropsychological assessment was seen as a viable alternative to physical diagnostic procedures that held a mortality probability in themselves (e.g., the angiogram). Administration of experimental and standardized psychological measures to patients with documented structural brain lesions gave rise to a database that allowed investigation of the sensitivity of these measures to brain damage (Reitan, 1966). In the post-World War II years, these data were expanded with a relatively large number of patients with documented brain lesions resulting from head wounds. Such events, when combined with the growing empirical emphasis beginning in the decade just prior to World War II, nurtured a quantitative approach that continues to characterize neuropsychological assessment in North America (Reitan, 1955). Moreover, theoretical notions concerning brain function mattered less than the utility of assessment procedures in predicting and localizing cortical damage (Reitan, 1955).

Current neuropsychological assessment practices represent an interaction between behavioral neurology, experimental psychology, and advances in psychometric theory (Dean, 1987). With few exceptions, current batteries in North America are either versions of preexisting clinical procedures or clinical adaptations of laboratory procedures. Early on, the specific procedures included in test batteries were based more on their ability to predict the presence of brain damage than any underlying theoretical notion of the functioning of the brain, and testing procedures were included or excluded based on their ability to localize and/or predict the presence of neuropathology (Reitan, 1955).

The major focus of the North American quantitative approach has been development of test batteries that allow identification of aberrant neurological conditions from a structural standpoint using standardized methods and comparisons with normative samples. This point of view is exemplified by Reitan (1955, 1966) and reflected in the construction of the Halstead–Reitan Neuropsychological Test Battery (H-RNTB) (Reitan & Wofson, 1993). Because the methods of the quantitative orientation have been adopted on the bases of predictive efficiency, this approach, which provides continuous predictive validation, is most frequently faulted as being atheoretical and lacking data necessary to understand and document the loss of individual functions (Luria & Majovski, 1977).

In contrast, Luria (1966) proposed a more qualitative approach that focused on pathognomonic signs deemed to be useful in understanding a patient's functioning. Luria's theoretical view of cortical functioning rested on the development of specific assessment techniques that would lead to rehabilitation strategies. Consistent with many of Luria's (1966) arguments, a number of neuropsychologists have stressed methods that view neuropsychological assessment as a dynamic, interactive process. From this point of view, the importance of diagnosis is subserved by the concern for providing a comprehensive view of a patient's cognitive and sensorimotor functioning.

As opposed to other theorists who have argued that functions are discretely localized in specific areas of the brain, Luria (1970) and proponents of the qualitative school maintained that higher forms of human cognitive activity (e.g., memory) are based on the participation of all levels of cerebral activity and, as such, are more heuristically organized into functional systems of the brain. The crux of Luria's observation-based approach was a syndrome analysis or qualification of the symptom in which examiners described behaviors and formulated hypotheses regarding the dysfunction of the brain. Based on such an evaluation of the patient's symptoms, specific assessment techniques were developed to test early hypotheses (Luria, 1973). Hence, data resulting from the assessment were not viewed in terms of quantitative norms but instead were considered in terms of patterns of functioning (Luria, 1973). The techniques used in this approach change from patient to patient as well as for the cerebral function being considered. The flexibility during evaluation seems more indicative of a behavioral neurologist than what Western practitioners would consider neuropsychological assessment (Dean, 1987). As such, Luria's strategy is most often criticized as employing a far too subjective approach with few opportunities to validate procedures or establish norms other than clinical norms (see Luria, 1973).

Today, medical advances are changing the nature of neuropsychological assessment. The sophistication of radiological diagnostic techniques has grown geometrically in the past 20 years. The new generation of computer tomography (CT) scanning equipment, magnetic resonance imaging (MRI), and recent advances in positron emission tomography and functional MRI hold clear implications for the diagnosis and localization of neurological dysfunction. In the past, the noninvasive nature of neuropsychological assessment and the lack of radiological techniques to portray soft tissue made obvious the utility of neuropsychological assessment as a diagnostic tool. Continued refinement of radiological procedures will reduce the dependence on neuropsychological assessment in diagnosis and localization of brain damage per se. As a result, increasing importance has been placed on outlining a functional impairment as well as defining the adaptive behavior remaining following brain damage (Dean & Gray, 1990). Although definitive knowledge concerning the anatomical integrity of the brain may be available, rarely is the neurologist or neurosurgeon in a position to predict the behavioral expression of a given lesion in the patient's postmorbid environment. This prediction is even less accurate in childhood because brain development must also be taken into account (Dean, 1987).

Modern neuropsychological assessment practices will increasingly be influenced by the need to understand the patient's behavioral deficits and plan rehabilitation. Neuropsychological assessment can offer a heuristic framework in which components of the patient's emotional, cognitive, and physical functioning can provide rehabilitation specialists an in-depth view of the patient (see Boll, 1987). However, few attempts have been made to interface presently available measures with rehabilitation strategies. An implicit assumption in the past has been that diagnosis or syndrome identification is heuristic enough to allow for differential treatment and convey an understanding at a functional level. For many neurological diagnoses, little is gained in our appreciation of the individual patient's functional capabilities or, in fact, the patient's needs in rehabilitation planning. Because most neuropsychological test batteries are merely a collection of tests that have been shown to predict brain damage, the underlying functions measured by these tests are obscure. The future of neuropsychological assessment would seem to rest on the ability to go beyond a simple "brain damage/no brain damage" decision. However, the test user has few available measures that offer both the power to predict diagnostic outcomes and an unambiguous functional profile. The D-WNAS focuses on empirically derived single-function measures, based on current neuropsychological and information-processing theory. This approach departs from the traditional atheoretical approach seen in many of our presently available batteries.

THEORETICAL FOUNDATIONS OF THE DEAN–WOODCOCK NEUROPSYCHOLOGY MODEL

The assessment of cognitive abilities, or intelligence, is an integral part of the neuropsychological examination. As such, the Dean–Woodcock Neuropsychological Assessment System integrates the assessment of cognitive abilities with assessment of sensory-motor functions. The system integrates Cattell–Horn–Carroll theory within a broader interpretation of an individual's neuropsychological functioning. An appreciation of the model aids in interpreting the impact of functional deficits on the observed performance of an individual.

Cattell (1941) first proposed "fluid and crystallized intellectual abilities" (Gf–Gc) theory in reaction to the nonheuristic contemporary theories of intelligence of his time. Cattell postulated that two major classes of influences affected the normal development of cognitive abilities. The first class, fluid intelligence, was related to biological influences such as genetic, physiological, and neurological factors. The second class, crystallized intelligence, was developed through educational and cultural opportunities and influences.

During the same decade, neuropsychologists were developing similar theories of intelligence. Ward Halstead (1947) made the distinction between psychometric and biological intelligence. In his scheme, psychometric intelligence incorporated aspects of learned or cultural knowledge and was primarily measured by formal intelligence tests. Biological intelligence was less influenced by cultural factors and memorized learning. It involved behavioral functions that were more sensitive to brain damage, which included aspects of novel problem solving (e.g., Category Test). Donald Hebb was one of the first researchers to notice that standard intelligence tests are not highly sensitive to brain lesions (Hebb, 1942). Hebb (1949) proposed a theory of intelligence that distinguished between type A and type B intelligence. According to Hebb, intelligence type A was a biologically based form of intelligence that represented the capacity to reason whereas intelligence type B was more reflective of cultural learning. Halstead's biological intelligence and psychometric intelligence and Hebb's type A and type B intelligence are very similar to Cattell's fluid and crystallized intelligence. The similarities in these theories suggest that research at the time was converging on similar conceptions of intelligence. Despite these similarities, little formal research has been done to investigate and synthesize these theoretical perspectives, because

Gf–Gc theory predominantly stayed in psychometrics, and neuropsychologists, being less interested in theory, maintained an actuarial perspective (Decker et al., in preparation).

Although Cattell originally postulated two types of intellectual ability, this two-factor model of human cognitive abilities has not been the view of either Horn or Cattell for nearly 30 years (Horn, 1988). Cattell and Horn expanded the initial *Gf–Gc* theory to incorporate four additional abilities: short-term memory, long-term memory, visual perception, and speed of information processing. Through subsequent research, predominantly through the use of factor analysis, the basic two-factor theory was extended to encompass as many as 8 to 10 broad dimensions of intellectual functioning.

Carroll's (1993) seminal work provided additional specification and verification to the broad cognitive abilities identified by Horn and Cattell. Carroll's theory was derived from the statistical and logical analysis of hundreds of data sets that included various collections of published and unpublished tests. The results led Carroll to suggest an empirically derived three-stratum theory of intelligence that approximately corresponded to Horn and Cattell's extended *Gf–Gc* model. Carroll's theory consists of eight broad abilities that have a commonality through *g*. Carroll's model can be described as a hierarchy of abstractions, with the first-stratum traits being the most specific, the second-stratum traits (i.e., broad abilities; see below) being more general, and the third-stratum trait being the most general. The third-stratum variable, also known as *g*, represents general intelligence. The second-stratum factors represent broad categories of individual abilities, which Carroll called fluid intelligence, crystallized intelligence, general memory and learning, broad visual perception, broad auditory perception, broad retrieval ability, broad cognitive speediness, and processing speed. Specific, or first-stratum, cognitive abilities are narrow expressions of one of these broad categories of abilities.

The major distinction between the two models is the third-stratum ability, or *g* factor. Carroll includes a higher order *g* factor in his model whereas Horn has stated that convincing construct validity evidence for existence of a singular *g* has not been established (Horn, 1991; Horn & Noll, 1997). Despite this difference, most researchers agree that the models are more similar than different. As such, the model is often referred to as the Cattell–Horn–Carroll model. More complete descriptions of how CHC theory is operationalized in the WJ III can be found in McGrew & Woodcock (2001) and Schrank, Flanagan, Woodcock, & Mascolo (2002). The D-WNAS assesses the CHC broad abilities directly from the WJ III.

DESCRIPTION OF THE DEAN–WOODCOCK NEUROPSYCHOLOGY MODEL

Although not included in traditional discussions of cognitive abilities, there are other stores of knowledge and skills that are important for the assessment of neuropsychological functioning, including sensory and motor functioning.

In fact, the assessment of sensory and motor functions is frequently the initial phase of the neuropsychological examination. The evaluation of basic sensory input and motor output provides information on the integrity of these systems and establishes the patient's ability to participate reliably in tests of cognitive abilities. Even more broadly stated, "sensorimotor functions have long been shown to have a powerful relationship to a broad range of human adaptive abilities" (Hom & Reitan, 1984, p. 266).

The integration of assessment of sensory-motor functioning with empirically validated cognitive abilities provides the basis for the Dean–Woodcock Neuropsychology Model. The model has been adapted for neuropsychology from the *Gf–Gc* Information-Processing Model (Woodcock, 1993, 1998). Figure 11-1 portrays the interaction of various cognitive and noncognitive factors in the production of cognitive and motor performance.

Most models provide a simplified representation of the relationships among the components of a complex process. Though there may be some correlation, a model of cognition does not necessarily represent the underlying physical components and their connections. The Dean–Woodcock Neuropsychology Model (Figure 11-1) was derived from combining CHC theory with information processing theory. The model will be presented here in a stepwise manner to aid the reader in its application. Before reading the explanation that follows, however, the reader should consider certain features of the model:

1. The model in Figure 11-1 indicates whether a process or pathway involves the peripheral nervous system, the central nervous system, or both.
2. The arrow in the lower left-hand corner of Figure 11-1 represents the input of physical stimuli from external or internal sources.
3. The right-hand, or output, side of the model includes cognitive and motor outcomes.
4. The horizontal dimension of Figure 11-1 represents a single cycle of cognitive processing, including input, processing, and output. The right-hand, or output side, of the model serves as the input for the next cycle. (The model may be perceived as being wrapped into a cylinder, with the output of one cycle becoming the input for the next cycle.)
5. The vertical dimension of the model represents the level of cognitive processing. Reflexive processes are represented in the lowest portion of the model. Above this level, automatic processes are represented. The upper region of the model includes the thinking and reasoning processes.
6. The model recognizes that cognitive performance and motor performance are not determined by cognitive abilities alone, but also by the influence of noncognitive factors, called facilitators–inhibitors.

Although this model may appear complex at first, reading the following sections will provide an appreciation of how cognitive and noncognitive influences interact to produce cognitive and motor performance. This, in turn, may contribute to a more insightful interpretation of neuropsychological information.

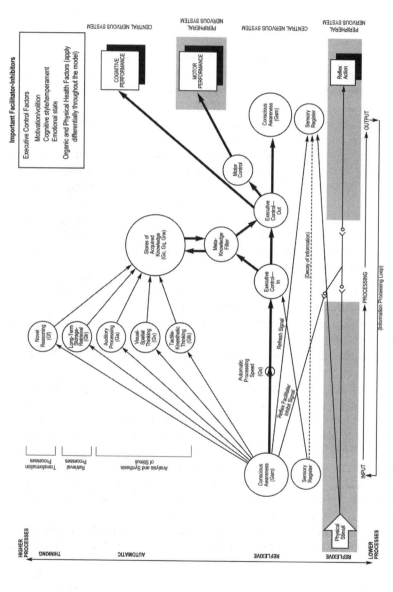

FIGURE 11-1   Dean–Woodcock Neuropsychology Model. Reproduced from *Research Report Number 3: The WJ-R and Bateria-R in Neuropsychological Assessment* by Raymond S. Dean and Richard W. Woodcock, with permission of the publisher. Copyright © 1999 by The Riverside Publishing Company, Itasca, Illinois. All rights reserved.

Reflexive Level

The lowest level in the cognitive neuropsychology model represents one of the most fundamental neurological functions, the reflex arc (Figure 11-2). For example, unexpectedly touching a very hot object (physical stimuli) will elicit a response of rapid retraction of the hand (reflex action). This process is represented in Figure 11-2 by the line extending from physical stimuli to reflex action. Note that the reception of physical stimuli and motor response are located in the peripheral nervous system, but that part of the reflex arc takes place in the spinal cord portion of the central nervous system. The protective reflex action occurs quickly, even before there is any conscious awareness of heat or pain.

While the reflex action is underway, a signal is traveling to the appropriate sensory register in the brain (Figure 11-3). Recall that because the horizontal dimension of the model represents only a single cycle of functioning, the contents of the sensory register on the right side of the model are simultaneously acting upon the contents of the sensory register represented on the left side. The dotted line between the sensory register on the left and the sensory register on the right indicates that the sensory information will rapidly decay if there is no further input.

Figure 11-4 introduces the concept of conscious awareness. The information that has reached the sensory register is routed through executive control into conscious awareness. There is now an awareness of having touched the hot object. Executive control operates as a traffic director in the cognitive system, allocating attentional resources, directing automatic and nonautomatic activity, and monitoring operations. Though it is in the stream of conscious awareness, executive control usually performs its responsibilities automatically.

Conscious awareness, in concert with executive control, can exercise limited control over some reflex and sensory registers (Figure 11-5). At least four types of controlling actions may be initiated from conscious awareness. First, an inhibit signal can moderate the normal action of the reflex arc. For example, if an object that is suspected of being hot must be touched, conscious awareness can suppress operation of the reflex arc, allowing handling of the object even though it is painful. Second, a facilitative signal to the reflex arc can enhance its proclivity to initiate a reflex action even if the object is only slightly warm. The third controlling action can signal the sensory register to recycle its stored information through conscious awareness, a type of review process that is available only for a second or two. For example, if a sound is not immediately recognized, conscious awareness may transmit a refresh signal to the sensory register and then its contents back into conscious awareness, thus providing a short-lived opportunity to "rehear" the sound. A similar function of the refresh signal facilitates the rehearsal of auditory stimuli. If the stimulus is a telephone number that must be remembered long enough to dial, the refresh signal allows rehearsing that number. Baddely (1994) refers to this process as the "phonological loop." The fourth type of controlling action allows conscious awareness to attend to the contents of sensory registers that are being ignored. For example, typically a conscious effort must be made to attend to the feeling of pressure exerted on the feet by properly fitted shoes.

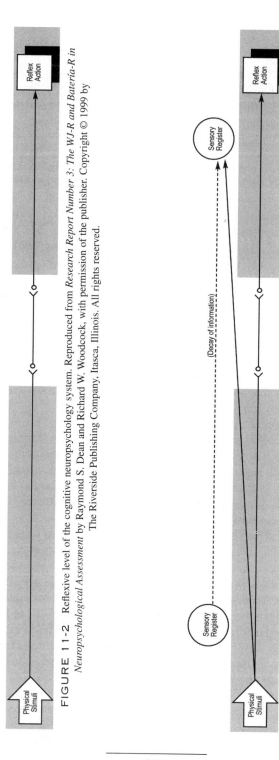

FIGURE 11-2 Reflexive level of the cognitive neuropsychology system. Reproduced from *Research Report Number 3: The WJ-R and Batería-R in Neuropsychological Assessment* by Raymond S. Dean and Richard W. Woodcock, with permission of the publisher. Copyright © 1999 by The Riverside Publishing Company, Itasca, Illinois. All rights reserved.

FIGURE 11-3 Input to sensory registers. Reproduced from *Research Report Number 3: The WJ-R and Batería-R in Neuropsychological Assessment* by Raymond S. Dean and Richard W. Woodcock, with permission of the publisher. Copyright © 1999 by The Riverside Publishing Company, Itasca, Illinois. All rights reserved.

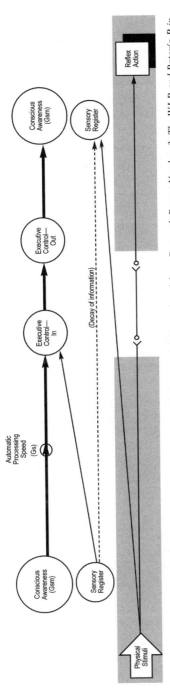

FIGURE 11-4   Automatic level of the cognitive neuropsychology model. Reproduced from *Research Report Number 3: The WJ-R and Bateria-R in Neuropsychological Assessment* by Raymond S. Dean and Richard W. Woodcock, with permission of the publisher. Copyright © 1999 by The Riverside Publishing Company, Itasca, Illinois. All rights reserved.

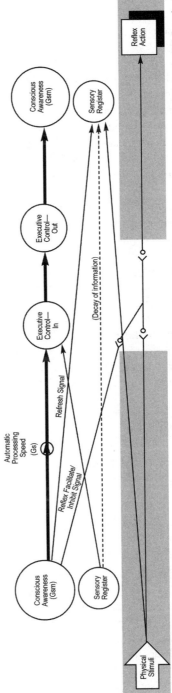

FIGURE 11-5   Influence of conscious awareness upon reflex arcs and sensory registers. Reproduced from *Research Report Number 3: The WJ-R and Bateria-R in Neuropsychological Assessment* by Raymond S. Dean and Richard W. Woodcock, with permission of the publisher. Copyright © 1999 by The Riverside Publishing Company, Itasca, Illinois. All rights reserved.

Note that the path from conscious awareness through executive control, and to certain other areas in the complete model (Figure 11-1), is represented by a broad line, indicating that this is the "freeway" of cognitive functioning. Most of the activity at this level is automatic. Two CHC broad abilities, Short-Term Memory (*Gsm*) and Processing Speed (*Gs*), and certain facilitator–inhibitors, play important roles along this freeway. These abilities reflect an individual's capacity to hold information in conscious awareness and to perform automatic tasks rapidly. If the individual has a processing-speed limitation, this operates as if a partially closed valve is reducing the flow of information along the automatic pathway.

Figure 11-6 adds a large circle to the model that represents the stores of declarative and procedural knowledge. In the pathway between executive control and these stores of knowledge lies the metaknowledge filter. This portion of the model decides, more or less imperfectly, whether the declarative and/or procedural knowledge is known and available. If not, executive control may attempt to generate a strategy to solve the problem. The model, as described in Figure 11-6, can be used to explain recognition of familiar stimuli, such as your name when you are called, or the face of a friend.

Neuropsychologists are also concerned with other types of processing, particularly motor, tactile, and kinesthetic. Such processing represents a complex interaction of cortical and subcortical functions as well as pathways in the spinal cord and the peripheral nervous system. Figure 11-7 adds motor and cognitive performance to the model. Note that motor performance is moderated by motor control that is part of the central nervous system. The wish to write down a telephone number that is currently in conscious awareness would involve central and peripheral nervous system pathways.

Now suppose the stimulus in conscious awareness was the question, "How do you spell your name?" We have already described the path that this stimulus (the question) would follow, from the arrow representing physical stimuli into conscious awareness, with executive control operating as a traffic director. The question, "How do you spell your name?" is routed through the metaknowledge filter by executive control into the stores of knowledge. Assuming that the individual knows how to spell his or her name, the retrieval of the spelling is automatic. Upon returning to executive control, the output goes to cognitive performance and to a motor representation in either speech or writing. Of course, if the individual has not learned to spell his or her name, there is no store of that knowledge, and the individual could not provide a correct response. Note that the stores of declarative and procedural knowledge include three of the previously described CHC abilities—Comprehension–Knowledge (*Gc*), Quantitative Knowledge (*Gq*), and Reading–Writing (*Grw*).

Further suppose that the stimulus (question) changes and the task is to spell your name backward (as a personal experiment, try it!). The response no longer requires a simple automatic recall from stored knowledge but, rather, requires thinking. Figure 11-8 adds the thinking abilities to the model. These include the CHC abilities of Visual-Spatial Thinking (*Gv*), Auditory Processing (*Ga*), Long-Term

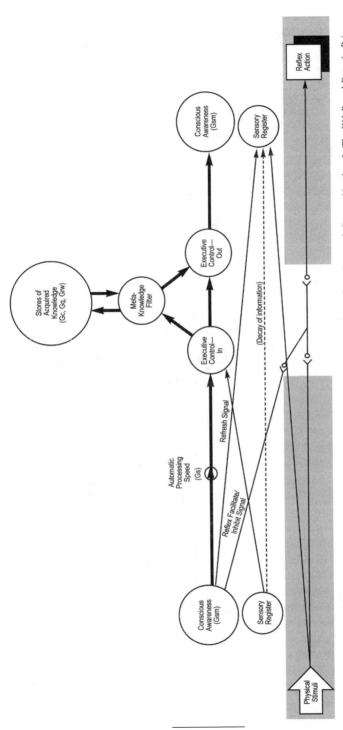

FIGURE 11-6 The metaknowledge filter and stores of acquired knowledge. Reproduced from *Research Report Number 3: The WJ-R and Batería-R in Neuropsychological Assessment* by Raymond S. Dean and Richard W. Woodcock, with permission of the publisher Copyright © 1999 by The Riverside Publishing Company, Itasca, Illinois. All rights reserved.

357

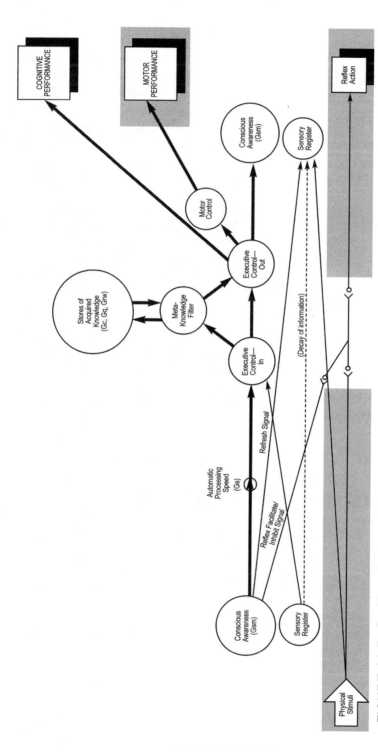

FIGURE 11-7 Cognitive performance and motor performance components of the cognitive neuropsychology model. Reproduced from *Research Report Number 3: The WJ-R and Bateria-R in Neuropsychological Assessment* by Raymond S. Dean and Richard W. Woodcock, with permission of the publisher. Copyright © 1999 by The Riverside Publishing Company, Itasca, Illinois. All rights reserved.

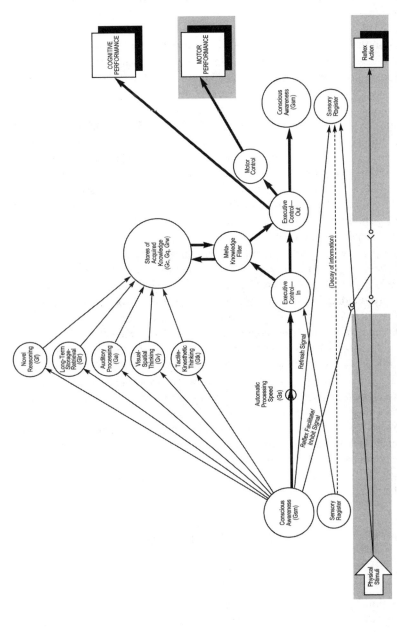

FIGURE 11-8 The thinking abilities added to the cognitive neuropsychology model. Reproduced from *Research Report Number 3: The WJ-R and Batería-R in Neuropsychological Assessment* by Raymond S. Dean and Richard W. Woodcock, with permission of the publisher. Copyright © 1999 by The Riverside Publishing Company, Itasca, Illinois. All rights reserved.

Retrieval (*Glr*), and Fluid Reasoning (*Gf*). Neuropsychologists are also concerned with other types of processing, particularly motor, tactile, and kinesthetic processing (*Gtk*). Such processing represents a complex interaction of cortical and subcortical functions as well as pathways in the spinal cord and the peripheral nervous system.

Because the attempt to spell a name backward has likely not previously been made, there is no direct stored knowledge to draw upon. As a result, the cognitive system must produce a strategy for attacking that problem. That strategy, along with the question, enters conscious awareness. Most people solve this problem by visualizing their name in the "mind's eye" and then spelling it backward. Because this process is executed through the use of one of the thinking abilities (i.e., Visual-Spatial Thinking), the result flows through the stores of knowledge, through executive control, and on to cognitive and motor performance. The reversed spelling of a name, on its way through the stores of knowledge, leaves a trace in the memory systems. If this process is repeated enough times, that trace grows and becomes part of stored knowledge. Subsequently, at the request to spell a name backward, that information can be retrieved automatically and reported without invoking the previously required thinking process.

At this point, except for the facilitator–inhibitors, we are now back to the complete model as represented in Figure 11-1. Note the box in the upper right-hand corner of Figure 11-1. That box lists some of the facilitator–inhibitors that can exert a profound influence on cognitive and motor performance. Facilitator–inhibitors primarily operate on executive control in this model and include, for example, motivation/volition, cognitive style or temperament, and emotional state. In addition, various organic factors operate as facilitator–inhibitors and apply differentially throughout the model. The input of physical stimuli may be especially impacted by organic factors such as impaired vision or hearing.

When considering this model, two caveats are in order. First, as complex as this model may appear, it is an oversimplification of the neurological bases of cognitive processing. Most cognitive processing requires the interaction of many components and, further, requires many cycles for completion. Second, the model represents functional relationships among the components and there is not necessarily specific neuroanatomical correspondence that can be said to underlie a particular component or pathway.

THE DEAN–WOODCOCK NEUROPSYCHOLOGICAL ASSESSMENT SYSTEM

Some time ago, Boll (1987) and others pointed out that a neuropsychological assessment offers the most complete psychological picture of a subject's cognitive, sensory-motor, and emotional status. The Dean–Woodcock Neuropsychological Assessment System relies extensively upon the WJ III Tests of Cognitive Abilities

(WJ III COG) (Woodcock, McGrew, & Mather, 2001c) for assessment of cognitive functions and the WJ III Tests of Achievement (WJ III ACH) (Woodcock, McGrew, & Mather, 2001b) for assessment of areas of academic achievement. The Diagnostic Supplement to the WJ III Tests of Cognitive Abilities (Woodcock, McGrew, Mather, & Schrank, 2003) also provides supplemental cognitive tests that can be incorporated into a cognitive neuropsychological assessment. In addition, the Dean–Woodcock Sensory-Motor Battery (Dean & Woodcock, 2003a) and the Dean–Woodcock Structured Interview and Dean–Woodcock Emotional Status Exam (Dean & Woodcock, 2003b,c) round out assessment of the functions shown in Figure 11-1. When a broad-based consideration of the neurological implications of a subject's performance is desired, the D-WSMB offers information concerning the peripheral and central nervous system functions not measured directly by the WJ III. The D-WSI and D-WESE each provide a formal assessment of important "facilitator–inhibitors" of cognitive, academic, and sensory-motor performance. Table 11-1 presents an outline of the D-WNAS by the major function measured. The table also identifies the sources for each component.

An individual's performance on the tests of the D-WNAS may be interpreted in a number of ways. For many applications in neuropsychology, information on the individual's functional level may provide the most useful interpretation of the individual's test performance. The Rasch-derived (Rasch, 1960) W scale that underlines the D-WNAS allows the clinician to provide a criterion-referenced interpretation of the individual's functional level, including the presence and severity of any impairment. The functional levels defined by the D-WNAS are based on actual task proficiency, not just relative standing in a group.

On the D-WNAS, the difference between an individual's ability on each scale and the difficulty of the task is directly translated into a set of probabilistic implications about the individual's expected level of success with tasks similar to those on the scale (Woodcock, 1999). The difference between an individual's ability and the ability of the average person at his or her age or grade is called the W Diff. The W Diff is similar to the decibel (dB) scale, which is often used as an index of hearing acuity. Normal hearing is referenced at zero on the dB scale. If an individual has a hearing loss of −40 dB, this indicates the additional amplitude necessary for that individual to hear a standard signal that a normal hearing person would hear at 0 dB. A person with a hearing problem is usually classified as handicapped or in need of special services because he or she has a significant deficit in the quality of their aural performance, not because he or she falls below some point on a norm-referenced scale.

If an individual is presented with tasks that have a difficulty level on the W Diff scale that is of the same value as the person's ability, then there is a 50% probability that the individual will succeed with those tasks. If the individual is presented with tasks that are lower on the W Diff scale than his or her ability, then the probability of success is greater than 50%. On the other hand, if the tasks are above the individual's ability on the scale, the probability of success is less than 50%. In psychometrics, the W Diff is an example of the person-characteristic

TABLE 11-1   Outline and Component Sources of the Dean–Woodcock Neuropsychological Assessment System

Outline	Component source[a]
I. General Intellectual Ability (GIA—Standard)	WJ III COG
II. Broad Abilities	
Comprehension–Knowledge	WJ III COG
Long–Term Retrieval	WJ III COG
Visual-Spatial Thinking	WJ III COG
Auditory Processing	WJ III COG
Fluid Reasoning	WJ III COG
Processing Speed	WJ III COG
Short-Term and Working Memory	WJ III COG
Quantitative Ability	WJ III ACH
Reading and Writing Ability	WJ III ACH
III. Sensory Assessment	
Visual Acuity	D-WSMB
Visual Confrontation	D-WSMB
Naming Pictures of Objects	D-WSMB
Auditory Acuity	D-WSMB
Tactile Perception	D-WSMB
IV. Motor Assessment	
Gait and Station	D-WSMB
Romberg (traditional, one foot, heel to toe)	D-WSMB
Coordination/Gross Cerebellar Assessment	D-WSMB
Construction	D-WSMB
Mime Movements	D-WSMB
Left–Right Movements	D-WSMB
Finger Tapping	D-WSMB
Grip Strength	D-WSMB
Lateral Preference	D-WSMB
Expressive Speech	D-WSMB
V. History/Emotional Status	
Structured Interview	D-WSI
History (medical, psychiatric, social, family)	D-WSI
Emotional Status	D-WESE

[a]WJ III COG, Woodcock–Johnson Tests of Cognitive Abilities; WJ III ACH, Woodcock–Johnson Tests of Achievement; D-WSMB, Dean–Woodcock Sensory-Motor Battery; D-WSI, Dean–Woodcock Structured Interview; D-WESE, Dean–Woodcock Emotional Status Examination.

function defined by Carroll (1987, 1990). This function predicts the individual's probability of success as items or tasks increase in difficulty. Carroll referred to this concept as "behavioral scaling." Figure 11-9 illustrates the relationship between a person's ability and task difficulty on the W Diff scale.

Because the W Diff scale is an equal-interval scale of measurement, any given distance between two points on the W Diff scale has the same interpretation for any area measured by the D-WNAS. This is true whether the W Diff represents a person's ability to solve problems involving novel reasoning or the person's grip

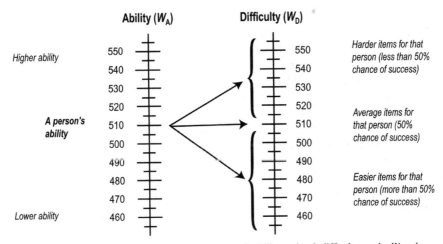

FIGURE 11-9 Relationship between a person's ability and task difficulty on the W scale. Reproduced from Manual and Checklists for the *Report Writer for the WJ III* by Fredrick A. Schrank and Richard W. Woodcock, with permission of the publisher. Copyright © 2002 by The Riverside Publishing Company, Itasca, Illinois. All rights reserved.

TABLE 11-2 Probability of Success Given the Difference on the W Scale between Ability and Difficulty[a]

Ability minus difficulty (W_{A-D})	Probability of success (P)	Ability minus difficulty (W_{A-D})	Probability of success (P)
+50	.996	0	.500
+45	.993	−5	.366
+40	.988	−10	.250
+35	.979	−15	.161
+30	.964	−20	.100
+25	.940	−25	.060
+20	.900	−30	.036
+15	.839	−35	.021
+10	.750	−40	.012
+5	.634	−45	.007
0	.500	−50	.004

[a] Reproduced from Manual and Checklists for the *Report Writer for the WJ III* by Fredrick A. Schrank and Richard W. Woodcock, with permission of the publisher. Copyright © 2002 by The Riverside Publishing Company, Itasca, Illinois. All rights reserved.

strength. Table 11-2 describes this probabilistic relationship between measured ability and task difficulty.

In the D-WNAS, the *W* Diff is used to identify the individual's functional level on reference tasks. For example, these broad categories of functional level, ranging from "Very Advanced" to "Severely Impaired," help describe how proficient the individual is with tasks that are of average difficulty for others of the same age or grade. Table 11-3 shows the functional levels used in the D-WNAS. Derivation of these labels is an automated option in the *WJ III Compuscore and Profiles Program, Version 2.0* (Schrank & Woodcock, 2003) and the *Report Writer for the WJ III* (Schrank & Woodcock, 2002).

Note that Table 11-3 identifies two categories that represent regions of uncertainty about the cut score: "Within Normal Limits to Advanced" and "Mildly Impaired to Within Normal Limits." In any system of classification characterized by one or more levels and attendant cutting scores, professionals may be uncomfortable when a patient's score is within a point or two of a predetermined criterion score. This is particularly critical when the scores are being used to make important decisions about the individual. One approach to this problem is to define "regions of uncertainty" about the cutting scores. These regions draw attention to marginal scores and set the stage for special consideration or further assessment before a decision is made. For most purposes in neuropsychology, the region of uncertainty between "Within Normal Limits" and "Mildly Impaired" is the most important, because many decisions hinge on whether the patient's ability is impaired.

Additionally, the *W* Diff allows the neuropsychologist to make criterion-referenced, probabilistic statements about the ease or difficulty with which the individual will find similar tasks. These probabilities range from "impossible" for individuals whose functional level is "Severely Impaired" (*W* Diff score, –51 and below), to "extremely easy" for individuals whose functional level is "Very Advanced" (*W* Diff score, +31 and above). Table 11-3 also contains the task

TABLE 11-3   Correspondence between *W* Diff, Reported RPI, Functional Level, and Implications for Performance

W Diff	Reported RPI	Functional level	Person will find age- or grade-level tasks
+31 and above	100/90	Very advanced	Extremely easy
+14 to +30	98/90 to 100/90	Advanced	Very easy
+7 to +13	95/90 to 98/90	Within normal limits to advanced	Easy
–6 to +6	82/90 to 95/90	Within normal limits	Manageable
–13 to –7	67/90 to 82/90	Mildly impaired to within normal limits	Difficult
–30 to –14	24/90 to 67/90	Mildly impaired	Very difficult
–50 to –31	3/90 to 24/90	Moderately impaired	Extremely difficult
–51 and below	0/90 to 3/90	Severely impaired	Impossible

implications that correspond to functional levels. For example, if a patient obtains a Relative Proficiency Index (RPI) score of 65/90 on the WJ III COG Concept Formation test, the neuropsychologist would interpret a mild impairment in inductive fluid reasoning ability, and could also predict that the patient will find age- or grade-level tasks involving categorical reasoning very difficult.

THE DEAN–WOODCOCK SENSORY-MOTOR BATTERY

A fundamental element of the overall interpretive system is the Dean–Woodcock Sensory-Motor Battery. The D-WSMB is a collection of tests drawn primarily from the traditional neurological examination to provide comprehensive coverage of basic sensory and motor functions, most of which have pathognomonic significance. Although used routinely across a variety of settings, pathognomonic signs have received little attention in terms of basic test development (Buchanan & Heinrichs, 1989).

The D-WSMB is composed of two major sections—sensory and motor. The sensory section consists of several tests that evaluate simple and complex visual, auditory, and tactile perception. Motor functions are assessed with nine individual tests. Three of the measures are standardized adaptations of neurological tests of subcortical functioning. The six remaining motor tests are predominantly meant to measure motor functioning at the cortical level. The assessment of subcortical motor functions is important because impairment at this level may often mimic cortical dysfunction. Table 11-4 presents an overview of each test and the function measured.

A number of specific inferential techniques have evolved in the interpretation of neuropsychological assessment findings (Reitan, 1974) and are incorporated in the D-WSMB. They include level of performance, left–right differences (i.e., lateralization), pathological signs, and complex pattern analyses. The first inferential technique focuses on the patient's level of performance on measures of individual abilities. Using normative data as a standard, the patient's results are compared to cutoff scores to determine whether performance is aberrant or normal. The second technique involves a comparison of the patient's left–right hemispheric abilities and is congruent with research outlining the cerebral lateralization of brain function (Reitan, 1974; Reitan & Davidson, 1974). Like the patient's level of performance, the functional efficiency of the left and right sides of his or her body is systematically examined with regard to sensory perception and motoric functions. The data obtained from this examination are often grouped into behavior constellations that may be compared to constellations that reflect neuropathology. Using this inferential technique, sensory-motor symptoms that rarely would be displayed in a patient without the presence of neurological dysfunction can be isolated. Signs of cerebral dysfunction reflect a combination of symptoms that have been shown to have diagnostic significance. The segmental (or pathognomonic) sign approach has been shown to produce errors in the conservative direction (false negatives). The fourth inferential technique, complex pattern analysis, is an integration of the level of performance, lateralization techniques, and segmental signs.

TABLE 11-4   Tests of the D-WSMB and Functions Measured

Sensory-motor category and subtest	Function or symptom assessed
Sensory tests	
Lateral Preference Scale	Laterality
Near-Point Visual Acuity	Visual acuity screening
Visual Confrontation	Peripheral visual field deficits
Naming Pictures of Objects	Screening for features of dynamic aphasia and visual dysgnosia for drawings
Auditory Acuity	Elements of vestibular and acoustic functions
Tactile examination	
Palm Writing	Sensory functioning associated with graphesthesia
Object Identification	Symptoms of astereognosia
Finger Identification	Errors associated with asomatognosia and tactile projection
Simultaneous Localization	Assesses positive signs of asomatognosia, tactile projection, and right–left confusion
Motor tests (subcortical)	
Gait and Station	Peripheral and central nervous system functioning, screening for ataxia, muscular weakness, and spasticity
Romberg	Unsteadiness associated with cerebellar or vestibular dysfunction
Coordination	Gross motor coordination and symptoms associated with ataxia, dyskinesia, and myoclonic jerks
Motor tests (cortical)	
Construction (Cross and Clock)	Visuconstructive ability or constructional paraxis
Mime Movements	Ideomotor functioning and signs of auditory vernal agnosia and ideokinetic apraxia
Left–Right Movements	Left–right confusion, including errors or perseveration and awkwardness
Finger Tapping	Manual dexterity of upper extremities
Grip Strength	Strength of upper extremities

DEAN–WOODCOCK STRUCTURED INTERVIEW AND DEAN–WOODCOCK MENTAL STATUS EXAM

The Dean–Woodcock Structured Interview and the Dean–Woodcock Emotional Status Examination provide pertinent information regarding the patient's history and current psychological and medical functioning. Further, they address the need in neuropsychological assessment to consider factors that may inhibit or facilitate a patient's performance.

The luxury of the control for facilitators and inhibitors of cognitive and sensorimotor functioning used in laboratory research is not possible in the clinical setting. Therefore, the interpretation of the data resulting from the neuropsychological examination must attempt to account for factors such as emotional state, motivation, temperament, and prior medical conditions that may influence performance. For example, attributing impaired cognitive functioning to brain injury in a patient with a long-standing psychiatric disorder is questionable. Similarly, although scores on measures of written language may well be similar to those for patients with known neurological conditions, facilitators and inhibitors must be ruled out prior to the diagnosis of neurologically related conditions. In addition, a patient's premorbid history, age at onset, and emotional reaction to an impairment all may interact to obscure diagnostic findings (see Dean, 1989).

As is true in other health sciences, a patient's presenting symptoms must be interpreted relative to his or her medical, social, and family history. The D-WSI and the D-WESE are structured interviews for this purpose. Each offers a systematic approach to collecting information concerning the patient's present state and history shown to be useful in the interpretation of the results of any psychological evaluation and in drawing conclusions about neuropsychological functioning (Dean & Gray, 1993). The D-WSI takes into account all relevant factors in the patient's background. The D-WESE allows the systematic collection of emotional/psychiatric data useful in understanding the patient. The neuropsychological examination involves the cooperation and concentration of the patient. Therefore, it is not unreasonable to consider a patient's level of emotional functioning as a potential moderating variable of neuropsychological functioning. For example, a number of studies have shown that when chronic schizophrenics are excluded from consideration, the accuracy rate of the neuropsychological examination in differentiating psychiatric patients is not significantly different than that found between normal and brain-damaged individuals. Although this conclusion seems robust, emotional disturbance exists in both psychiatric and neurological patients; therefore, the question arises as to the effects of emotional disturbance on neuropsychological findings.

Neuropsychological assessment has made its most significant contribution in psychiatric settings when equivocal evidence existed concerning the patient's neurological integrity. Neuropsychological assessment examines a comprehensive array of behaviors that are compared to normative standards and to those occurring in known, neurological conditions. Such information allows the examination of "minor" behavioral/cognitive impairment, which is often the early sign of neurologically related disorders. These data also provide the clinician information concerning the extent of a patient's behavioral impairment relative to normal cohorts and known pathological groups. For example, in evaluating psychiatric aspects of a closed-head injury, neuropsychological assessment provides information useful both in diagnosing and in understanding the severity of impairment in cognitive, sensorimotor, and emotional functioning. The extent to which the patient displays residual impairment relative to his or her premorbid state offers useful information in rehabilitation planning. Thus, an assessment of a patient's mental status at the time of the neuropsychological examination becomes crucial in our understanding of a patient's cognitive and sensorimotor functioning.

CLINICAL APPLICATION OF THE D-WNAS

In the following description of two clinical cases using the D-WNAS, a selected battery of WJ III tests was used to assess a broad array of cognitive functions. The neuropsychologist experienced with other batteries may find these cases of interest because they elucidate the breadth of cognitive processes measured by the WJ III and information concerning the peripheral and central nervous system measured by the D-WSMB—all expressed in terms of functional levels. Additionally, the cases illustrate inclusion of important information concerning facilitators and inhibitors of performance measured by the D-WSI and the D-WESE.

Case I: Richard M.

Richard M. is a 49-year-old, right-handed, married, male podiatrist. His chief complaints relate to a stroke that occurred 6 months prior to this appointment. According to a CT scan administered immediately following the cardiovascular accident (CVA), the patient showed a bleed in the right parietal area that involved the right ventricle. A more recent MRI showed an infarction in the right parietal area extending into the subcortical structures. The bleed, though, was resolved. His principal symptoms involved numbness, paresthesia, and a burning sensation on the left side of his body.

Richard's medical history is significant for uncontrolled hypertension and type II diabetes that was confirmed only at the time of his CVA. He denied a history of seizures, but admitted a concussion in 1980. Prior to his CVA, he denied a history of known chronic illness, surgery, accidents, or medical treatment. He admitted smoking 10+ cigars per day for 20 years and abusing ethanol for 15 years. He has had three citations for driving under the influence (DUI) of alcohol.

The Emotional Status Exam included reports of anxiety, depression, impulsivity, inattention, and hypomania. The patient had been taking an antidepressant prior to his CVA but reported that he "cut back on the medication due to sexual impotence."

His overall cognitive ability was found to be in the high-average range. However, assessment indicated functional variability among the patient's cognitive and motor abilities.

Comprehension–Knowledge. The patient's verbal comprehension, or knowledge and understanding of words, was within normal limits.

Long-Term Retrieval. When new visual symbols (rebuses) were associated with orally presented familiar words, the patient's recall of visual symbols was within normal limits. When recall was delayed by 3 days, the patient's performance was also within normal limits.

Visual-Spatial Thinking. The patient's ability to match and combine shapes necessary in solving abstract visual-spatial problems was mildly impaired. His visual short-term (less than 30 seconds) recognition memory was within normal limits.

Auditory Processing. The patient's ability to integrate, or blend, sounds into words was within normal limits. Auditory closure of incomplete words missing one or more phonemes was also within normal limits.

Fluid Reasoning. The patient's ability to learn and apply new concepts when given feedback was advanced. On a measure of analysis–synthesis, which involves analyzing components of an incomplete logic puzzle and providing the missing components, the patient's performance was also advanced.

Processing Speed. When required to scan and locate identical numbers in a row the patient was mildly impaired. His ability to quickly and correctly match items based on common conceptual associations was also mildly impaired.

Short-Term and Working Memory. The patient's short-term, or immediate, memory (less than 30 seconds) was within normal limits for unrelated words. His ability to manipulate and transform a series of numbers was mildly impaired. His auditory working memory capacity, requiring the ability to manipulate and transform numbers and words, was within normal limits.

Quantitative Ability. The patient's skill in performing mathematical calculations was within normal limits for an individual of similar age. The patient's skill in analyzing and solving practical mathematical problems was also within normal limits.

Reading and Writing Ability. The patient's performance in identifying isolated letters and words was within normal limits to advanced. His ability to comprehend written passages while he was reading was within normal limits. Spelling performance was within normal limits. The quality of the patient's writing samples was mildly impaired.

Motor Assessment. As shown in the summary of his results, his gait and station were impaired. Coordination and manual dexterity for the left side were moderately impaired. Handwriting (right hand) was in the impaired range. In addition, his Romberg test was positive and mild construction dyspraxia was present. Although bilateral problems existed, those functions most often interpreted as right hemispheric were more clearly indicated. Verbal expression was characterized by moderate dysarthria. A summary of this information is presented below:

Name: Richard M.	**Handedness:** Right
Gender: Male	**Diagnosis:** CVA
Education: DPM	**Time Since Onset:** 6 months

FUNCTION	RATING
GENERAL INTELLECTUAL ABILITY	
GIA (Standard)	113
COMPREHENSION–KNOWLEDGE	
Verbal Comprehension	WNL (within normal limits)
LONG-TERM RETRIEVAL	
Visual–Auditory Learning	WNL
Visual–Auditory Learning—	WNL
Delayed Recall	

VISUAL–SPATIAL THINKING
   Spatial Relations   Mildly impaired
   Picture Recognition   WNL

AUDITORY PROCESSING
   Sound Blending   WNL
   Incomplete Words   WNL

FLUID REASONING
   Concept Formation   Advanced
   Analysis–Synthesis   Advanced
   Planning   WNL

PROCESSING SPEED
   Visual Matching   Mildly impaired
   Decision Speed   Mildly impaired

SHORT-TERM AND WORKING MEMORY
   Memory for Words   WNL
   Numbers Reversed   Mildly impaired
   Auditory Working Memory   WNL

QUANTITATIVE ABILITY
   Calculation   WNL
   Applied Problems   WNL

READING AND WRITING ABILITY
   Letter Word Identification   WNL to advanced
   Passage Comprehension   WNL
   Spelling   WNL
   Writing Samples   Mildly impaired

SENSORY ASSESSMENT
   Visual Acuity   WNL
   Visual Confrontation   WNL
   Naming Pictures of Objects   WNL
   Auditory Acuity   WNL
   Tactile Perception   Mildly impaired

MOTOR ASSESSMENT
   Gait and Station   Moderately impaired
   Romberg (traditional, one foot,   Moderately impaired
      heel to toe)
   Coordination/Gross Cerebellar   Moderately impaired
      Assessment
   Construction   Mildly impaired
   Mime Movements   WNL
   Left–Right Movements   Mildly impaired

Finger Tapping	Moderately impaired (left)
Grip Strength	Moderately impaired (left)
Lateral Preference	Right
Expressive Speech	Mildly impaired

HISTORY/EMOTIONAL STATUS

Structured Interview	Long-term tobacco and alcohol use
History (Medical, psychiatric, social, family)	Hypertension; CVA; type II diabetes; medication: Paxil (40 mg, qhs) and Buspar (15 mg, bid); married, three adult children
Emotional Status	Anxiety, depression, inattention, hypomanic

These data are consistent with a cognitively gifted man who has suffered a CVA and has a number of areas of impairment, among them subcortical motor impairment, depression, inattention, and distractibility. Overall, the patient's neuropsychological functioning was in the mildly impaired range. Specifically, mild to moderate impairment will make motor performance very difficult to extremely difficult. Additionally, cognitive tasks requiring rapid processing of information will be very difficult for him. At this point in time, the patient is seen as being totally disabled from his practice as a podiatrist and is not capable of driving an automobile. However, the patient's CVA occurred only 6 months ago and, as such, further recuperation may be experienced. The patient's psychiatric medication should be reviewed in light of his presenting psychiatric features. Consideration of an alternative antidepressive/antianxietal medication may assist in reducing his concerns regarding sexual performance. He should be considered for neuropsychological evaluation in the next 3–6 months to monitor his recovery.

Case II: John M.

John is a 7-year-old, left-handed, white male who just completed the first grade. He was accompanied by his mother. His mother reported a number of disruptive behaviors, including hypermotor behavior, distractibility, and problems with concentration. He also stated that he "hears a little man's voice."

The patient lives with his mother, biological brother, and his stepfather. He sees his biological father on alternate weekends. His peer relationships are reported to be good. His mother reports that John's teacher had some difficulty with him during the past year, identifying him as "the class clown." He completed the first grade, receiving no special education services. His grades were fair.

Medically, the patient experienced significant perinatal distress. He was the product of a premature delivery, weighing 5 lb, 20 oz. An emergency cesarean section delivery was required, and he had significant respiratory distress that required considerable intervention with steroids. He continues to take steroids as needed for asthma. He has allergies for a number of airborne particles. The patient has diminished appetite. Sleep patterns are reported to be normal.

His mother saw developmental milestones as being normal. He has never been seen by a mental health professional. Two years ago, the chief complaints, as noted above, led his primary care physician to diagnose Attention Deficit/Hyperactivity Disorder, Combined Type. Recently, the physician referred him for a neuropsychological evaluation.

The patient's Emotional Status Examination indicated moderate maladjustment with reported anxiety, depression, hypermotor behavior, and inattention. He was not taking psychoactive medication when seen.

The patient's overall intellectual ability is in the average range. Most of his cognitive functions (comprehension–knowledge, long-term retrieval, visual-spatial thinking, auditory processing, and fluid reasoning) are within normal limits, although he demonstrated mild impairment on measures of processing speed and short-term memory. For example, when required to scan and locate identical numbers in a row the patient was mildly impaired. His ability to quickly and correctly match items based on common conceptual associations was also mildly impaired. His short-term, or immediate, memory (less than 30 seconds) and his auditory working memory capacity, requiring the ability to manipulate and transform numbers and words, were mildly impaired. Although most measured areas of academic functioning are also within normal limits, the patient demonstrated a mild impairment in the ability to comprehend written passages while reading.

The patient's sensory and motor assessment indicated that mild impairment was present for left-side tactile perception of upper extremities, left-hand finger agnosia, and balance/strength of the left leg. An overview of his cognitive, sensory, motor, and emotional assessment follows:

Name: John M.
Gender: Male
Education: Second grade, present

Handedness: Left
Diagnosis: AD/HD, Coordination
Time Since Onset: Congenital

FUNCTION	RATING
GENERAL INTELLECTUAL ABILITY	
GIA (Standard)	93
COMPREHENSION–KNOWLEDGE	
Verbal Comprehension	WNL (within normal limits)
LONG-TERM RETRIEVAL	
Visual–Auditory Learning	WNL
Visual–Auditory Learning— Delayed Recall	WNL

VISUAL–SPATIAL THINKING
    Spatial Relations   WNL
    Picture Recognition   WNL

AUDITORY PROCESSING
    Sound Blending   WNL
    Incomplete Words   WNL

FLUID REASONING
    Concept Formation   WNL
    Analysis–Synthesis   WNL
    Planning   WNL

PROCESSING SPEED
    Visual Matching   Mildly impaired
    Decision Speed   Mildly impaired

SHORT-TERM AND WORKING
MEMORY
    Memory for Words   Mildly impaired
    Numbers Reversed   WNL
    Auditory Working Memory   Mildly impaired

QUANTITATIVE ABILITY
    Calculation   WNL
    Applied Problems   WNL

READING AND WRITING ABILITY
    Letter–Word Identification   WNL
    Passage Comprehension   Mildly impaired
    Spelling   WNL
    Writing Samples   WNL

SENSORY ASSESSMENT
    Visual Acuity   WNL
    Visual Confrontation   WNL
    Naming Pictures of Objects   WNL
    Auditory Acuity   WNL
    Tactile Perception   Moderately impaired (left)

MOTOR ASSESSMENT
    Gait and Station   Mildly impaired (left leg)
    Romberg (traditional, one foot, heel to toe)   WNL
    Coordination/Gross Cerebellar Assessment   WNL
    Construction   WNL
    Mime Movements   WNL
    Left–Right Movements   WNL
    Finger Tapping   Mildly impaired (left)

MOTOR ASSESSMENT (*continued*)

Grip Strength	Mildly impaired (bilateral)
Lateral Preference	Left
Expressive Speech	WNL

HISTORY/EMOTIONAL STATUS

History (medical, psychiatric, social, family)	Premature, respiratory distress, emergency C-section; asthma; sees biological father every other week
Emotional Status	Hypermotor behavior, depression, inattention, anxiety

In summary, John M. is a young man of average cognitive ability with Attention Deficit/Hyperactivity Disorder, Combined Type. In addition, as often seen with AD/HD, he has comorbid anxiety and depression. In general, his neuropsychological functioning ranged from mildly impaired to within normal limits. Although most age-level cognitive and academic tasks should be manageable for John, tasks involving processing speed, auditory short-term memory, and reading comprehension will be very difficult for him. Mild impairments in these areas may be secondary effects of AD/HD. Consequently, the patient should be considered for a trial on both an antidepressant and stimulant medication. The patient also has a mild, left-side sensory-motor impairment; some motor tasks will be very difficult for him. Although the impairment is thought to be congenital in etiology, it should be reviewed by a neurologist so as to rule out any active neuropathology. Following a negative neurological examination, the patient should also be considered for occupational and physical therapy. The patient should be reevaluated following stabilization on medication and a neurological examination.

SUMMARY

Neuropsychological assessment in North America has often been faulted as being atheoretical and quantitative in approach. This reliance can be traced to the need for measures that would predict general brain damage and specificity of localization. A new generation of radiological diagnostic techniques has decreased the need for neuropsychological methods that would localize damage. However, rarely is the neurologist or neurosurgeon able to predict functional outcomes of localized brain damage; neuropsychological assessment is needed for this purpose.

The Dean–Woodcock Neuropsychological Assessment System, which includes the WJ III, is based on a cognitive neuropsychological assessment model. The complete D-WNAS, as described in this chapter, offers a unifying portrayal of human cognitive, sensory-motor, and affective functions and their assessment. The method of scaling utilized by the system may be especially useful for describing the presence and severity of functional impairments in neuropsychological assessment. The system was designed so that professionals can use one or more components, depending on the training of the examiner and the intended use of the results. The D-WNAS offers a neuropsychological interpretation of the WJ III. The broad and narrow abilities measured by the WJ III can be interpreted via a system of functional levels, ranging from advanced to severely impaired. The functional levels can be used to describe the ease or difficulty with which the patient will find similar, real-world, tasks.

REFERENCES

Baddely, A. (1994). *Working Memory*. Oxford: Clarendon Press.

Boll, T. J. (1987). The role of neuropsychology in the general practice of children and adolescent psychology. *Journal of Child and Adolescent Psychotherapy, 4*, 13–18.

Buchanan, R. W., & Heinrichs, D. W. (1989). The neurological evaluation scale (NES): A structured instrument for the assessment of neurological signs in schizophrenia. *Psychiatric Research, 27*, 335–350.

Carroll, J. B. (1987). New perspectives in the analysis of abilities. In R. R. Ronning, J. A. Glover, J. C. Conoley, & J. C. Witt (Eds.), *The influence of cognitive psychology on testing* (pp. 267–284). Hillsdale, NJ: Erlbaum.

Carroll, J. B. (1990). Factor analysis since Spearman: Where do we stand? What do we know? In R. Kanfer, P. L. Ackerman, & R. Cudek (Eds.), *Abilities, motivation and methodology* (pp. 43–67). Hillsdale, NJ: Erlbaum.

Carroll, J. B. (1993). *Human cognitive abilities: A survey of factor-analytic studies*. New York: Cambridge University Press.

Cattell, R. B. (1941). Some theoretical issues in adult intelligence testing. *Psychological Bulletin, 38*, 592.

Dean, R. S. (1987). Foundations of rationale for neuropsychological bases of individual differences. In L. C. Hartlage & C. F. Telzrow (Eds.), *The neuropsychology of individual differences: A development perspective*. New York: Plenum Press.

Dean, R. S. (1989). Perspectives on the future of neuropsychological assessment. In B. S. Plake and J. C. Witt (Eds.), *Buros-Nebraska Series on Measurement and Testing*. New York: Erlbaum.

Dean, R. S., & Gray, J. W. (1990). Traditional approaches to neuropsychological assessment. In T. B. Gutkin & C. Reynolds (Eds.), *The handbook of school psychology* (pp. 269–288). New York: John Wiley & Sons.

Dean, R. S., & Gray, J. W. (1993). Traditional approaches to neuropsychological assessment. In C. R. Reynolds and R. W. Kamphaus (Eds.), *Handbook of psychological and educational assessment of children* (pp. 371–388). New York: Guilford Publishers.

Dean, R. S., & Woodcock, R. W. (2003a). *Dean–Woodcock sensory-motor battery*. Itasca, IL: Riverside Publishing.

Dean, R. S., & Woodcock, R. W. (2003b). *Dean–Woodcock structured interview*. Itasca, IL: Riverside Publishing.

Dean, R. S., & Woodcock, R. W. (2003c). *Dean–Woodcock emotional status examination*. Itasca, IL: Riverside Publishing.

Decker, S. L., Hill, S. K., & Dean, R. S. (in preparation). Comparing tests of executive planning and abstract reasoning.

Golden, C. J., Purish, A. D., & Hammeke, T. A. (1985). *Luria–Nebraska neuropsychological battery*. Los Angeles: Western Psychological Services.

Halstead, W. C. (1947). *Brain and intelligence: A quantitative study of the frontal lobes*. Chicago: University of Chicago Press.

Hebb, D. O. (1942). *The organization of behavior: A neuropsychological theory*. New York: Science Editions.

Hebb, D. O. (1949). *The organization of behavior: A neuropsychological theory.* New York: John Wiley.

Hom, J., & Reitan, R. M. (1984). The Halstead–Reitan battery as a predictor of brain damage. In R. M. Reitan & L. M. Davidson (Eds.), *Clinical neuropsychology: Current status and applications.* New York: Wiley.

Horn, J. L. (1988). Thinking about human abilities. In J. R. Nesselroade & R. B. Cattell (Eds.), *Handbook of multivariate psychology—revised* (pp. 645–685). New York: Academic Press.

Horn, J. L. (1991). Measurement of intellectual capabilities: A review of theory. In K. S. McGrew, J. K. Werder, & R. W. Woodcock, *WJ-R Technical Manual* (pp. 197–232). Itasca, IL: Riverside Publishing.

Horn, J. L., & Noll, J. (1997). Human cognitive abilities: Gf–Gc theory. In D. P. Flanagan, J. L. Genshaft, & P. L. Harrison (Eds.), *Contemporary intellectual assessment: Theories, tests, and issues* (pp. 53–91). New York: Guilford Press.

Luria, A. R. (1966). *Higher cortical functions in man.* New York: Basic Books.

Luria, A. R. (1970). The functional organization of the brain. *Scientific American, 3,* 66–78.

Luria, A. R. (1973). *The working brain.* London: Penguin Press.

Luria, A. R., & Majovski, L. V. (1977). Basic approaches used in American and Soviet clinical neuropsychology. *American Psychologist, 32,* 959–968.

McGrew, K. S., & Woodcock, R. W. (2001). *Technical Manual. Woodcock–Johnson III.* Itasca, IL: Riverside Publishing.

Rasch, G. (1960). *Probabilistic models for some intelligence and attainment tests.* Copenhagen, Denmark: Danish Institute for Educational Research.

Reitan, R. M. (1955). An investigation of the validity of Halstead's measures of biological intelligence. *Archives of Neurology and Psychiatry, 73,* 28–35.

Reitan, R. M. (1966). Problems and prospects in studying the psychological correlates of brain lesions. *Cortex, 2,* 127–154.

Reitan, R. M. (1974). Methodological problems in clinical neuropsychology. In R. M. Reitan & L. A. Davidson (Eds.), *Clinical neuropsychology: Current status and applications.* New York: Wiley & Sons.

Reitan, R. M., & Davidson, L. A. (1974). *Clinical neuropsychology: Current status and applications.* New York: Wiley & Sons.

Reitan, R. M., & Halstead, W. C. (1955). *The Halstead–Reitan neuropsychological test battery.* Tucson, AZ: Neuropsychology Press.

Reitan, R. M., & Wolfson, D. (1993). *The Halstead–Reitan neuropsychological test battery.* Tucson, AZ: Neuropsychology Press.

Schrank, F. A., & Woodcock, R. W. (2002). *Report Writer for the WJ III* [Computer software]. Itasca, IL: Riverside Publishing.

Schrank, F. A., & Woodcock, R. W. (2003). *WJ III Compuscore and Profiles Program, Version 2.0* [Computer software]. Itasca, IL: Riverside Publishing.

Schrank, F. A., Flanagan, D. P., Woodcock, R. W., & Mascolo, J. T. (2002). *Essentials of WJ III cognitive abilities assessment.* New York: Wiley.

Woodcock, R. W. (1993). An information processing view of Gf–Gc theory. *Journal of Psychoeducational Assessment* [Monograph Series: WJ-R Monograph], 80–102.

Woodcock, R. W. (1998). *The WJ-R and Bateria-R in neuropsychological assessment: Research report number 1.* Itasca, IL: Riverside Publishing.

Woodcock, R. W. (1999). What can Rasch-based scores convey about a person's test performance? In S. E. Embretson & S. L. Hershberger (Eds.), *The new rules of measurement: What every psychologist and educator should know* (pp. 105–127). Mahwah, NJ: Erlbaum.

Woodcock, R. W., McGrew, K. S., & Mather, N. (2001a). *The Woodcock–Johnson III.* Itasca, IL: Riverside Publishing.

Woodcock, R. W., McGrew, K. S., & Mather, N. (2001b). *The Woodcock–Johnson III tests of achievement.* Itasca, IL: Riverside Publishing.

Woodcock, R. W., McGrew, K. S., & Mather, N. (2001c). *The Woodcock–Johnson III tests of cognitive abilities.* Itasca, IL: Riverside Publishing.

Woodcock, R. W., McGrew, K. S., Mather, N., & Schrank, F. (2003). *Diagnostic supplement to the Woodcock–Johnson III tests of cognitive abilities.* Itasca, IL: Riverside Publishing.

12

THE *WOODCOCK–JOHNSON III*
TESTS OF COGNITIVE
ABILITIES IN COGNITIVE
ASSESSMENT COURSES

JEFFERY P. BRADEN

School Psychology Program
Department of Educational Psychology
University of Wisconsin—Madison
Madison, Wisconsin 53706

VINCENT C. ALFONSO

Graduate School of Education
Fordham University
New York, New York 10023

The primary goal in this chapter is to help instructors of cognitive assessment to incorporate the new *Woodcock–Johnson III Tests of Cognitive Abilities* (WJ III COG) (Woodcock, McGrew, & Mather, 2001) in their courses. Professionals in the field who may be using the WJ III COG may also benefit from the material presented here. To assist instructors and practitioners alike, the following information, materials, and resources are presented: (a) data on the course in cognitive assessment and perceived reasons why previous editions of WJ III COG—the *Woodcock–Johnson Psycho-Educational Battery: Part One, Tests of Cognitive Ability* (WJ) (Woodcock & Johnson, 1977) and the *Woodcock–Johnson Tests of Cognitive Ability—Revised* (WJ-R) (Woodcock & Johnson, 1989, 1990)—have not been widely taught in graduate psychology programs; (b) discussions of various problems and issues in cognitive assessment courses; (c) a brief description of the unique features of the WJ III COG; and (d) a detailed explanation of best practices for preservice WJ III COG training, including several tools and activities.

SURVEYS OF CONTEMPORARY COGNITIVE
ASSESSMENT COURSE PRACTICES

The initial course on individual cognitive assessment forms an important foundation for the preparation and services of professional psychologists, especially those who work in schools (e.g., school psychologists). Most professional psychology programs (e.g., clinical, counseling, school) require their students to take at least one course on individual cognitive assessment (American Psychological Association, 1981; National Association of School Psychologists, 2000).

The assessment of cognitive abilities has been ranked as one of the most important and frequently provided services performed by professional psychologists (Alfonso & Pratt, 1997; Anderson, Cancelli, & Kratochwill, 1984; Goh, Teslow, & Fuller, 1981; Reschly & Wilson, 1995; Stinnett, Havey, & Oehler-Stinnett, 1994). In addition to learning how to administer, score, and interpret cognitive tests, the course on cognitive assessment usually provides training and education in interviewing, recording behavioral observations, developing and maintaining rapport, following standardized methods for collecting and scoring data, using established methods for interpreting data, and reporting findings in oral and written media (Alfonso, Oakland, LaRocca, & Spanakos, 2000).

Despite the apparent importance of cognitive assessment, few studies have investigated the nature and characteristics of courses that are designed to instruct students in this practice. However, two surveys conducted approximately 12 years apart provide substantial information on various components of the course in cognitive assessment, including tests that are taught, and other topics, activities, and time requirements. For the purpose of this chapter, we will focus on trends in the use of cognitive and intelligence tests only.

An early survey conducted by Oakland and Zimmerman (1986) of school psychology professors who taught a course on individual cognitive assessment provided information on a variety of characteristics associated with the course. For example, 90% of the respondents reported test administration, scoring, interpretation, and reporting of information from individually administered cognitive tests to be very important. The various *Wechsler Scales* and the *Stanford–Binet: Form LM* (SB: LM) were emphasized in the majority of courses. A typical course required students to submit seven protocols and practice tests. Course instructors, students, and teaching assistants committed an average of 14, 11, and 10 hours per week to the course, respectively.

Although the original survey results provided useful information on the course at that time, many changes in the field of cognitive assessment occurred in the ensuing years such that the results published in 1986 were rendered obsolete. Changes in the field included the publication of several new or revised cognitive tests, such as the *Differential Ability Scales* (DAS) and WJ-R, the introduction of new or reauthorization of federal mandates (e.g., Public Laws 99-457 and 105-17), and the publication of new comprehensive texts on cognitive assessment (e.g., Flanagan, Genshaft, & Harrison, 1997; Jensen, 1998; McGrew & Flanagan, 1998).

Therefore, Alfonso et al. (2000) conducted a subsequent survey to provide year-2000 data regarding the ways school psychology programs prepare their students in the area of cognitive assessment.

Consistent with results of most surveys on test use (e.g., Brown & McGuire, 1976; Kamphaus, Petoskey, & Rowe, 2000; Piotrowski & Keller, 1989), the various Wechsler Scales and *Stanford-Binet Intelligence Test* (SB) were the most emphasized tests taught in cognitive assessment courses in 2000. For example, 92% of the course instructors required at least one administered and scored *Wechsler Intelligence Scale for Children—Third Edition* (WISC-III) protocol, 80% of the course instructors required at least one *Wechsler Adult Intelligence Scale—Revised* (WAIS-R) protocol, and 74% required at least one SB protocol. Students were required to complete approximately five to six scored WISC-III protocols, three to four WISC-III reports, and one WISC-III competency exam. Students who were required to use the SB typically completed three to four scored protocols, two to three written reports, and one competency exam.

Less than 26% of course instructors required at least one administered and scored DAS or WJ-R protocol. On average, students were required to complete only two scored WJ-R protocols, two WJ-R reports, and one WJ-R competency exam. In Oakland and Zimmerman's (1986) original survey, only 6% of course instructors required at least one WJ administered and scored protocol. Thus, historically in school psychology programs the WJ and WJ-R tests were not taught or highlighted in the course on cognitive assessment. However, the proportion of instructors requiring students to administer at least one WJ or WJ-R was larger in the more recent study, suggesting greater acceptance and use of the WJ and WJ-R in cognitive assessment courses.

Course instructors indicated that they gave great or moderate consideration to factors such as frequency of use, validity across various populations, psychometric soundness, theoretical underpinnings, and field expectations when selecting tests to emphasize or teach. Availability of tests and instructor familiarity with specific tests were given limited consideration in test selection. Therefore, it is unclear as to why the WJ and WJ-R were not taught by more instructors, because they received positive reviews regarding their psychometric soundness and theoretical underpinnings. We explore this issue in greater detail in the following section.

WHY HAVE THE WJ AND WJ-R BEEN ABSENT FROM COGNITIVE ASSESSMENT COURSES?

Although the WJ-R COG (and its predecessor, the WJ) had strong psychological and psychometric integrity, positive scholarly reviews, and evidence of value, it was largely absent from the curricula of psychology training programs (Alfonso et al., 2000; Alfonso & Pratt, 1997). Much like the comic Rodney Dangerfield (who twists his tie, bugs out his eyes, and moans "I get no respect"), WJ advocates wondered why it received such limited respect from some psychology training programs. Consequently, the discrepancy between the status of the WJ among researchers versus instructors deserves attention.

We believe the limited respect the WJ series of tests has received among training programs, until just recently was largely undeserved. We suggest three factors that may have contributed to the relative absence of previous WJ tests in cognitive assessment courses: (a) the marketing history of the test; (b) test scoring and administration procedures; and (c) professional inertia.

MARKETING HISTORY

The original WJ (Woodcock & Johnson, 1977) and its revision, the WJ-R (Woodcock & Johnson, 1989, 1990), were published by DLM, Inc., of Allen, Texas. DLM was devoted to distributing instructional materials to special education teachers, and thus their marketing strategies tended to focus on teachers and professionals in special education. When they published the original WJ, and later the WJ-R, DLM was in the commercially understandable position of wanting to sell tests to their primary market base (i.e., special education). Thus, they tended to minimize the need for psychological training and certification, and sold tests to teachers, speech pathologists, and other nonpsychologists. This undoubtedly led many psychologists to assume that the test was not a bona fide test of cognitive abilities, because genuine intelligence tests are usually restricted to psychologists.

Historians of children's television may be interested in knowing that the immediate and immense success of *Barney & Friends* (a children's television show known for its insipid song lyrics and remarkable popularity among preschoolers) led DLM, Inc. to sell the WJ-R (and other DLM tests) to Riverside Publishing. The DLM children's television division owned *Barney & Friends*; the show was such a commercial success that DLM sold all of its other subsidiaries (including its test division) and retained only its children's television enterprise. Riverside Publishing, which publishes other psychological tests (including the *Stanford–Binet Intelligence Scale: Fourth Edition*), has a more traditional marketing approach. In other words, the WJ III COG, unlike the original WJ and WJ-R COG, is now marketed with the same user qualifications as those applied to other individually administered intelligence tests. However, because it was originally marketed to educational diagnosticians and other nonpsychologists, some psychologists may remain suspicious of its psychological integrity.

ADMINISTRATION AND SCORING PROCEDURES

The original WJ was notorious for the laborious computational procedures needed to derive cluster scores. For example, most other tests required examiners to simply sum test scores to yield clusters. However, the WJ required examiners to weight subtests differentially and required examiners to sum these weighted scores (some of which were negative) to yield clusters. These complex and lengthy computational requirements coexisted with other features that were very different compared to other tests (e.g., individual subtest standard scores were not available on the WJ; only clusters could be converted to standard scores). These differences discouraged widespread use of the WJ, especially when other tests with simpler scoring procedures were available. The WJ-R overcame some of these limitations (e.g., clusters were not based on differentially weighted scores), and a computerized scoring program was developed (i.e., WJ-R Compuscore) (Woodcock & Johnson, 1990) to reduce scoring demands. The WJ III has taken another step in the process of simplifying scoring, by distributing computer-scoring software with every kit (and requiring the software to produce scores). However, some current test users and instructors may not like the exclusive use of computers for scoring because they cannot "see" how scores are derived and must trust the program to be accurate.

The WJ and the WJ-R were also less popular than many other cognitive batteries because they were based exclusively on easel-driven administration. Easels are convenient for examiners because all test materials are contained in one place. The exclusive use of easels, however, may make a test less interesting to examinees, especially those who have difficulty sustaining attention across multiple tasks (e.g., young children, individuals with attention deficits or developmental delays) (Alfonso & Flanagan, 1999). A second reason why the WJ-R was less popular than other batteries may have been related to the required use of audiotapes for administration of certain tests (i.e., it was the only battery at the time that required use of audiotape administration). Unfortunately, for those who do not like the exclusive use of easel content and the use of taped tests, the WJ III COG maintains these features. However, there are important reasons for maintaining these features, particularly for audio tests (e.g., without audio equipment, examiners could not assess auditory processing abilities effectively).

PROFESSIONAL INERTIA

One of the biggest impediments to the popularity of any new (or substantially revised) test is the reluctance of professionals (i.e., examiners and instructors) to surrender their familiar tools. It is time consuming to learn new tests. Experienced examiners who are fluent in giving a particular test can attend to the examinee's behavior, recognize unusual responses, and use time efficiently. Why surrender these virtues unless the newer test offers compelling advantages? Scholars and researchers have found the advantages of the WJ and WJ-R (e.g., conormed cognitive and achievement batteries, adherence to cognitive theory, measurement of a broader range of cognitive factors) more compelling than their practitioner colleagues; course instructors may find themselves struggling to reconcile the scientific arguments that might support change with the practical arguments that argue against it. Finally, instructors of assessment courses frequently develop materials (e.g., videotapes, overheads, handouts, practice exercises, classroom tests) that support training for a particular instrument. Adding a new test to a course can mean weeks of work, requiring instructors to leave the comfort and command of a familiar test. These are not trivial changes, and so training—even more than practice—tends to replicate the familiar over the novel (Alfonso et al., 2000). It is interesting to note that tests and practices were stable despite the relatively limited influence instructors ascribed to personal familiarity with and availability of tests, suggesting that practitioners either are unaware of the degree to which professional inertia influences their instructional practices or that they have resisted including previous versions of the WJ III COG in their course for reasons other than those sampled.

THE INTERPRETATION OF THE COGNITIVE COMPOSITE

Some critics (Reeve, Hall, & Zarkeski, 1979; Shinn, Algozzine, Marston, & Ysseldyke, 1982; Ysseldyke, Shinn, & Epps, 1981) claimed the WJ and WJ-R produced a cognitive composite that was more achievement-loaded than composites produced by other tests. Although McGrew (1994a,b) offered a compelling response to these criticisms (cf. Willis & Dumont, 1994), the charge was effective in discouraging many practitioners from adopting the WJ and WJ-R. A related challenge was the issue of whether examiners should select specific or general aptitudes (i.e., ability estimates) for calculating ability/achievement discrepancies. Proponents of the Woodcock system (e.g., McGrew, 1986) advocated the use of specific aptitudes (i.e., a composite score drawn from four tests that best predict achievement in a given domain), because specific aptitude scores more accurately predict achievement. In contrast, critics argued that use of specific aptitudes is inappropriate, because the predictor tests confound ability with achievement (i.e., the cognitive tests are too similar to achievement tests to estimate cognitive ability independently). This debate remains unresolved, but has added to the perception that estimates of cognitive ability from the WJ and WJ-R were achievement loaded.

However, the differences between the WJ III COG and other popular cognitive batteries may be viewed as a virtue. Many of the novel features of the WJ series have now been incorporated into other batteries (e.g., differential weighting of tests to produce composite scores, use of computer-scoring programs, use of audiotapes, inclusion of fluid reasoning tasks). We believe that the WJ III deserves professional respect because it meets or exceeds the standards by which other tests are accepted and judged. Furthermore, we suspect that some of the "oddities" of the WJ III COG (e.g., tape-administered tests, battery complexity, selective testing) will become standards that will be emulated by other tests in the future. Given the relatively wide usage of the WJ III (which suggests its popularity among practitioners), and the involvement of professional training programs in the WJ III grants program (as discussed in the following paragraphs), the WJ III COG and its unique features may be gaining wider acceptance.

We also note that there have been supportive efforts to provide assistance to course instructors to encourage adoption of the WJ III COG. These resources include a CD ROM created by Riverside Publishing and a WJ III COG materials grant program sponsored and funded by The Woodcock–Munoz Foundation. As part of the grant program, psychology training programs may apply for and receive WJ III COG kits and related training materials for instructional purposes. This foundation also supports meetings of cognitive course instructors representing different training programs at professional conventions (e.g., the National Association of School Psychologists and the American Psychological Association) to exchange ideas such as course syllabi, activities, and teaching techniques. These activities serve multiple purposes, including the dissemination of scholarly information about the WJ III, professional networking, and dissemination of information about funding for research.

It appears that these efforts, along with continued research on the various editions of the WJ/WJ-R/WJ III COG, have achieved success in increasing the popularity of the WJ III COG in contemporary assessment courses. As of October 2002, 79 school psychology programs (more than one-third of all programs identified by the National Association of School Psychologists) have committed at least 35% of their assessment course to WJ III COG instruction (Fredrick Schrank, personal communication, October 23, 2002). This, accompanied with wide use of the WJ III COG in schools and other clinical settings, suggests that many instructors have decided that the WJ III COG is worth respect—and worthy of inclusion in cognitive assessment courses.

CHALLENGES IN TEACHING THE COURSE ON COGNITIVE ASSESSMENT

Instructors must confront three major challenges in a cognitive assessment course: (a) establishing the connection between specific instruments and contemporary psychological and scientific standards; (b) ensuring administration and scoring accuracy; and (c) deriving accurate interpretations of assessment results. The following comments are intended to help instructors meet these challenges with respect to the WJ III COG.

CONNECTING STANDARDS AND PRACTICE

Instructors must help students understand that assessment instruments must be used in the context of scientific and professional ethical standards. Explicit references and correspondence in assessment materials to scientific bases and professional standards, such as examiner and technical manuals, help students understand the connections. Some features of the WJ III COG aid in this process, whereas others hinder it.

One feature that supports the link between the WJ III and scientific standards is the synthesis of the work of Raymond Cattell, John Horn, and John Carroll. The integration of their work has come to be known as Cattell–Horn–Carroll

(CHC) theory (see the various WJ III manuals for reviews of the theory) as a basis for the WJ III COG. This work is extensive and provides a strong link between the assessment instrument and its scientific knowledge base. We consider the review and synthesis of CHC theory to be a strong demonstration of the link between cognitive science and assessment practice.

However, there are some points that inhibit the science/instrument connection. For example, the use of "multiple intelligences" to describe the second-order factors of the hierarchical CHC model (which are adequately explained in the WJ III manuals) can be easily confused with Gardner's (1999) work, who uses the term "multiple intelligences" in an entirely different framework. In addition, the scientific basis for the information-processing frameworks presented in the WJ III manuals to interpret test results is inadequately described (as will be discussed in greater detail later in this section).

Alignment of the test materials to professional standards is generally strong. The *Technical Manual* (McGrew & Woodcock, 2001) organizes the presentation of validity evidence in the framework outlined in the *Standards for Educational and Psychological Testing (3rd ed.)* (AERA, APA, NCME, 1999). That is, the validity evidence is divided into five sections corresponding to (a) test content, (b) response processes, (c) internal structure, (d) relationships to other variables, and (e) test consequences. The information related to internal structure is strong, particularly for the CHC factor and General Intellectual Ability (GIA) scores, and the evidence contained in the validity section on relationships to other variables is generally adequate. Instructors will find that the organization and content of this section generally help students see the links between the WJ III COG and contemporary assessment standards. (For detailed information regarding validity evidence for the WJ III COG in the context of the *Standards*, readers are directed to Chapter 1 of this volume.)

ADMINISTRATION AND SCORING ACCURACY

It is imperative that those who administer and score cognitive tests do so without making errors, because interpretation is based on accurate estimates of an individual's functioning. Moreover, diagnostic, educational placement, and intervention decisions are usually made, in part, with reference to the individual's performance on standardized, norm-referenced tests (e.g., cognitive tests). Although it is clear to most professionals and students-in-training that administration and scoring of cognitive tests should occur without error, the existing literature indicates that for the most part protocols are far from being error free.

For example, a recent literature review in conjunction with the extensive review conducted by Alfonso and Pratt (1997) regarding examiner administration and scoring errors revealed the following conclusions. First, whether the examiner is a professional psychologist or student-in-training, a significant number of errors are committed on protocols that are fabricated or are based on real examinees. Second, almost invariably these studies have investigated the Wechsler

Scales (e.g., WAIS-R, WISC-III). Only two studies investigated other tests, such as the SB and Kaufman Assessment Battery for Children (K-ABC). Third, it appears that a wide breadth of errors is committed, including incorrect addition, incorrect point assignment, failure to record responses verbatim, incorrect calculation of age, and inappropriate questioning or querying of responses. Fourth, although many errors are committed on verbal tests (e.g., Wechsler Vocabulary and Comprehension tests), errors are also committed on almost all other tests and at times they affect the various aggregate scores (e.g., IQ) to a large degree.

Although no studies have investigated examiner errors on the WJ series of tests, it is reasonable to believe that examiners do make errors on them, in light of the findings of the myriad of studies involving the Wechsler Scales. In addition, given that the WJ III COG is making its way into training programs and the field, it is incumbent upon the profession to begin to investigate examiner proficiency in administering and scoring this test. As a result, Schermerhorn and Alfonso (in preparation) are gathering data regarding graduate student proficiency in administering and scoring the core WJ III COG tests (i.e., Tests 1–7 and 11–17).

Initial data analyses of the performance of 22 graduate students across 78 WJ III COG protocols administered for practice indicate the following results. First, almost without fail, students completed all identifying information, the observations checklist, and additional questions on the cover sheet of the test record. Second, students administered the designated sample items on each protocol for each test with the exception of the Verbal Comprehension and Memory for Words tests, for which students did not administer sample items on 18% and 6% of the protocols, respectively. Students administered all subtests of tests (e.g., Verbal Comprehension and General Information), and correct versions of tests (e.g., Visual Matching) on all 78 protocols. Third, students committed many errors that may have significant effects on an individual's test and cluster scores. For example, students did not: (a) use suggested or correct starting points for the General Information test on as many as 10% of the protocols; (b) calculate raw scores correctly on the Spatial Relations test on 14% of the protocols; (c) encircle the correct raw score total on the scoring table for the Numbers Reversed test on 7% of the protocols; (d) enter the correct raw score into the scoring program for the Spatial Relations test on 14% of the protocols; and (e) record errors for the Concept Formation test on 22% of the protocols. Given these findings, instructors are encouraged to use Schermerhorn and Alfonso's checklist (see Figure 12-1).

DERIVING ACCURATE INTERPRETATIONS

Ideally, interpretation of test results is based on validity evidence. That is, the validity of an assessment is determined by the accuracy of the meaning the examiner assigns to the scores; accurate interpretations enhance validity, whereas inaccurate interpretations undermine validity (AERA, APA, NCME, 1999; Messick, 1989, 1995). Furthermore, the meaning of assessment results is determined by the arguments supporting—or refuting—various meanings based on available

ID #	P1	P2	P3
Signed consent form			
Handed in test record			
Handed in subject response form			
Handed in COMPUSCORE printout			

1 = YES	
2 = NO	
3 = DK	
4 = N/A	

TEST RECORD COVER SHEET:	P1	P2	P3
Completed identifying information			
Completed observations checklist			
Answered additional questions			

VERBAL COMPREHENSION (1):	P1	P2	P3
Administered all 4 subtests			
Used suggested starting points			
Correct basal (3 lowest correct)			
Correct ceiling (3 highest incorrect)			
Administered all sample items (1B, 1C, 1D)			
Tested by complete pages			
Accepted one-word responses unless noted			
Counted items below basal as correct			
Recorded errors			
Summed scores from all 4 subtests correctly			
Correct subtest raw score			
Encircled correct row for total number correct			
Entered correct raw score into software			

VISUAL–AUDITORY LEARNING (2):	P1	P2	P3
Correct basal (test story 1)			
Correct ceiling – cutoff scores			
Score based on number of errors			
Circled each word missed/told on test record			
Filled in date			
Filled in time			
Correct subtest raw score			
Encircled correct row for total number correct			
Filled in software score entry correctly			
Entered correct raw score into software			

SPATIAL RELATIONS (3):	P1	P2	P3
Administered sample items			
Correct basal (item 1)			
Correct ceiling – cutoff scores			
Correct subtest raw score			
Encircled correct row for total number correct			
Filled in software score entry correctly			
Entered correct raw score into software			

SOUND BLENDING (4):	P1	P2	P3
Administered sample items			
Correct basal (item 1)			
Correct ceiling (6 highest incorrect)			
Recorded errors			
Administered some items orally			
Correct subtest raw score			

CONCEPT FORMATION (5):	P1	P2	P3
Correct starting point			
Correct basal (intro 1 {pre &1st} or 2 {2nd +})			
Correct ceiling – cutoff scores			
Counted items 1 - 5 as correct if not admin.			
Accepted correct synonyms			
Recorded errors			
Correct subtest raw score			
Encircled correct row for total number correct			
Filled in software score entry correctly			
Entered correct raw score into software			

VISUAL MATCHING (6):	P1	P2	P3
Admin correct version (1=ages 2-4; 2=ages 5+)			
Used test record for version 2 only			
Completed sample items			
Completed practice exercises			
Recorded time to complete			
Correct basal (item 1)			
Correct ceiling – time limit (1=2 mn; 2=3 mn.)			
Scored 1 point for each correct pair			
Wrote in score next to each item			
Correct subtest raw score			
Encircled correct row for total number correct			
Filled in software score entry correctly			
Entered correct raw score into software			

NUMBERS REVERSED (7):	P1	P2	P3
Used suggested starting points			
Correct basal (3 lowest in group correct)			
Correct ceiling (3 highest in group incorrect)			
Counted all items below basal as correct			
Recorded errors			
Correct subtest raw score			
Encircled correct row for total number correct			
Entered correct raw score into software			

FIGURE 12-1 WJ III COG administration and scoring checklist. The protocol numbers (P1, P2, P3) allow instructors to determine if students make progress from one test administration to another. Instructors may reproduce this checklist for use in their courses.

GENERAL INFORMATION (11):	P1	P2	P3
Administered both subtests			
Used suggested starting points			
Correct basal (4 lowest correct)			
Correct ceiling (4 highest correct)			
Counted all items < basal in each subtest			
Recorded errors			
Summed scores from 2 subtests correctly			
Correct subtest raw score			
Encircled correct row for total number correct			
Entered correct raw score into software			

RETRIEVAL FLUENCY (12):	P1	P2	P3
Administered all items			
Used tally marks to record correct responses			
Summed tally marks correctly			
Summed scores from 3 subtests correctly			
Correct subtest raw score			
Encircled correct row for total number correct			
Entered correct raw score into software			

PICTURE RECOGNITION (13):	P1	P2	P3
Administered sample items			
Correct basal (item 1)			
Correct ceiling – cutoff scores			
Scored 1 pt. each picture recalled in any order			
Scored all items correctly (sum of each pict.)			
Correct subtest raw score			
Encircled correct row for total number correct			
Filled in software score entry correctly			
Entered correct raw score into software			

AUDITORY ATTENTION (14):	P1	P2	P3
Administered training items			
Retrained any missed items			
Correct basal (item 1)			
Correct ceiling (6 highest incorrect)			
Recorded errors			
Correct subtest raw score			
Encircled correct row for total number correct			
Entered correct raw score into software			

ANALYSIS-SYNTHESIS (15):	P1	P2	P3
Administered color pretest			
Marked level of performance on color pretest			
Started with sample items			
Correct basal (item 1)			
Correct ceiling – cutoff scores			
Recorded errors			
Correct subtest raw score			
Encircled correct row for total number correct			
Filled in software score entry correctly			
Entered correct raw score into software			

DECISION SPEED (16):	P1	P2	P3
Used subject response booklet			
Completed sample items			
Completed practice exercises			
Correct basal (item 1)			
Correct ceiling – time limit (3 minutes)			
Recorded exact time to complete			
Awarded pts only when both pictures marked			
Wrote in score next to each item			
Correct subtest raw score			
Encircled correct row for total number correct			
Entered correct raw score into software			

MEMORY FOR WORDS (17):	P1	P2	P3
Began with sample items			
Used suggested starting points			
Correct basal (all 3 in lowest group of 3 corr.)			
Correct ceiling (all 3 in high. group of 3 incor)			
Accepted words similar sound/rhyme w/target			
Counted items below basal as correct			
Recorded errors			
Correct subtest raw score			
Encircled correct row for total number correct			
Entered correct raw score into software			

Note: P = protocol number (P1, P2, P3) in order for instructors to determine if students make progress from one test administration to another. Instructors may reproduce this checklist for use in their courses.

FIGURE 12-1 (*Continued*)

evidence (Kane, 1992). For example, interpreting a cognitive composite score as evidence that an examinee "lacks the capacity to do grade-level work" would be invalid, because there is no evidence to support the argument that tests of intellectual ability measure intellectual capacity directly. In contrast, an interpretation that an examinee "has a low probability of doing grade-level work, particularly in the absence of strong instructional support" is more likely to be valid, because many tests provide evidence of relationships between global ability composites and achievement test scores, and because evidence shows individuals with low cognitive scores are unlikely to perform in the average range on achievement tests, particularly in the absence of intensive instruction. Thus, test evidence does not support a "capacity-based" argument for score interpretation, but would support a "probability-based" argument for score interpretation.

According to testing standards, instructors are obligated to help students understand—and evaluate—the claims made for any test score interpretation. The WJ III COG is no exception. The materials in the WJ III COG *Examiner's Manual* (Mather & Woodcock, 2001) suggest that the following claims should be invoked to interpret examinees' WJ III COG results:

1. WJ III scores are strongly linked to contemporary theories of cognitive abilities (i.e., hierarchical abilities as represented in the CHC model).
2. There are two distinct models (i.e., Cognitive Performance Model, Information Processing Model) and one implied model (Clinical Clusters and Tests) for interpreting second-order factor scores.
3. Differences among scores within an examinee are useful for identifying relative strengths and weaknesses.
4. Unusual scores (i.e., those that are unusually high, unusually low, or unusually different) imply psychoeducational diagnoses (e.g., high composite scores imply intellectual giftedness, low composite scores imply cognitive delay or disability, and an unusually high or low cluster score implies a strength or weakness in a given domain).

The first step to evaluate these claims is to have students read the materials in the WJ III COG manual. Exercises that can assist students in understanding these claims include inviting students to read and present sections of the manual to their peers, working individually or in small groups, and having instructors present information via lecture, perhaps also using materials developed by the test publisher (e.g., PowerPoint presentations, overheads, activities) to support learning.

The second step is to invite students to evaluate critically the claims made in the manual. Among the steps needed to prompt appropriate criticism is review of other works that are independent of the test manual (e.g., test critiques, research studies), and the application of general issues to specific instruments. Some of the issues important to any cognitive battery, including the WJ III COG, include the value of ipsative score interpretation (sometimes called "profile analysis"), the role of general intellectual ability versus second-order factors, and methods for selecting and using interpretive models to guide interventions. We recommend engaging students in active criticism via debates (with teams of students arguing for or against a particular perspective, but then inviting the teams to "switch sides" so that they ultimately argue both sides of the issue), critiques, and presentations.

Some resources to assist in these activities include scholarly works on ipsative score interpretation (cf. Kamphaus, Petoskey, & Morgan, 1997; Kaufman, 1994; Sattler, 2001), the role of general versus specific cognitive abilities in human performance (cf. Ceci & Williams, 1997; Horn & Noll, 1997; Jensen, 1998; Woodcock, 1997), and the use of interpretive models to guide interventions (e.g., Flanagan & Ortiz, 2001; cf. Gresham, 2001; Gresham & Witt, 1997; McGrew & Woodcock, 2001; Reschly, 1997; Reschly & Grimes, 1995). The last issue (i.e., whether cognitive tests have value for selecting interventions over other methods, such as empiric approaches) is particularly important for psychoeducational assessment, and students should be introduced to the concepts and arguments related to the "treatment utility" of cognitive assessment (e.g., Braden & Kratochwill, 1997; Hayes, Nelson, & Jarrett, 1987).

There are three other issues related to score interpretation unique to the WJ III COG that deserve mention. The first is an incongruity between the evidence presented in support of the WJ III COG model and the scores derived from the WJ III COG. That is, the manual invokes literacy (*Grw*) and quantitative reasoning (*Gq*) factors when presenting validity data. However, the WJ III COG battery does not produce *Grw* or *Gq* cluster scores. This creates a problem, in that the manual presents factor-analytic evidence that does not match the actual test outcomes. It is not possible to know to what degree the factor-analytic results might differ if *Grw* and *Gq* were removed from the analyses, and thus it is not possible to conclude whether the factor-analytic evidence supports the WJ III COG, because the available evidence supports a different model than is available to examiners using the WJ III COG (i.e., examiners do not have access to *Grw* and *Gq* scores, and therefore cannot invoke the interpretive model supported in the WJ III COG manual). We suggest that instructors should note the problem (i.e., that the model used in factor analyses is not reflected in the scores provided to examiners), and caution students to recognize this as an unresolved problem. Resolution of the problem would appear to take one of two forms; either factor-analytic data could be reanalyzed, omitting factors not reflected in scores, or protocols for deriving *Grw* and *Gq* scores could be provided so that the scores examiners obtain match the factor-analytic data presented in support of the CHC model.

The second feature unique to the WJ III COG is the "selective testing" principle. This principle recommends that examiners select only those tests needed to obtain the information relevant to the referral. Selective testing is unique to the WJ III COG (although the SB: IV provides limited selective testing), because the manuals of most other cognitive batteries direct examiners to give the same set of tests for every examinee. Instructors should note this feature of the WJ III COG as a positive one (after all, giving every test would be fatiguing for the examiner and examinee—and generally unnecessary). However, this positive feature also creates a problem for test administration. Different interpretive models require different tests, and so students must either select the model they plan to use before beginning the assessment (and give only those tests), or the students must give all but one of the WJ III COG tests to have the data they need to apply the three interpretive models. The latter option may be viewed as the safest (better to have too much information than need to go back and obtain more), but it undermines the utility of the selective testing principle. Instructors should highlight this dilemma for students, and could use this dilemma to invite further discussion of whether interpretive models should be identified a priori or post hoc (see Kamphaus et al., 1997). As is true for other cognitive batteries, the WJ III COG does not specifically recommend a priori versus post hoc model selection, nor does the manual provide guidance for how examiners would select an interpretive model a priori to guide selective testing.

The third feature unique to the WJ III COG is the availability of various methods to calculate scores and discrepancies. The *WJ III Compuscore and Profiles Program* (Schrank & Woodcock, 2001) requires examiners to select either age-based norms (the approach used in all other cognitive batteries) or grade-based norms (which are unique to the WJ series). Likewise, examiners may select GIA (Standard or Extended), "predicted achievement," or Oral Language scores as the basis for calculating ability/achievement discrepancies. The program then compares regressed ability scores to the scores obtained by the examinee to help the examiner determine whether the examinee's achievement scores are similar to, higher than, or lower than the score one would expect, given the selected predictor score. In the WJ-R COG, the use of selected cognitive subtests to predict achievement was known as "specific aptitudes"; in the WJ III COG, this option is labeled "predicted achievement."

Instructors should note that the use of a subset of cognitive tests to predict achievement is a controversial issue (as discussed earlier in this chapter in relationship to WJ/WJ-R history), and that the manual does not identify the weights given to specific tests used in calculating "predicted achievement" scores for various achievement clusters. Students should be helped to appreciate that the omission of this information may undermine independent evaluation of the validity of "predicted achievement" discrepancies (i.e., it is difficult to evaluate the validity of scores when origins are not specified completely), and may inhibit selective testing (e.g., it is not possible for students to anticipate the "weight" given to specific cognitive tests needed to predict reading achievement versus mathematics achievement). We address the issue of norms selection in the next section of this chapter. However, instructors should note that there are no data to show that the use of one set of norms, or one method of predicting discrepancies, is superior to any other method (Buckley, Schroeder, & Braden, 2000; Buckley, Schroeder, Potts, McGivern, & Braden, 2000).

We believe the WJ III COG provides rich opportunities to instructors to help students connect professional standards in educational and psychological testing to a specific cognitive battery. The WJ III COG manual is organized to respond to the new validity standards, and the availability of evidence (and occasionally, its omission) provides opportunities to engage students in applying standards to the WJ III. The availability of PowerPoint presentations, handouts, video clips, and other materials to support WJ III COG training will help instructors to ensure that students understand the claims and evidence available for the WJ III COG (see Appendix D, WJ III COG Teaching Resources, at the end of this volume). We argue that such understanding is a necessary condition for evaluating validity claims and drawing accurate interpretations. However, instructors must encourage students to fulfill their obligation to evaluate the WJ III COG (and other psychological tests) by identifying and applying key themes in the field (e.g., consequential validity, treatment utility) and by developing and responding to validity arguments (Kane, 1992). Polemic approaches, such as critiques, presentations, and debates, are useful devices to engage students in critically and carefully drawing accurate score interpretations.

UNIQUE ADMINISTRATION FEATURES OF THE WJ III COG

Although tests of cognitive ability are alike in many ways, the WJ III COG is unique in some respects that are relevant for professional training. Some of these features aid training. For example, the restricted range of examinee responses (i.e., most items request examinees to provide a single word or point to select a response) reduces the amount of learning needed to administer tests successfully, relative to other tests of cognitive ability that require examiners to anticipate a wider range of examinee responses. Likewise, a single, uniform battery that can be used with examinees who are from 2 to more than 90 years of age ("womb to tomb coverage") is unusual; the Wechsler Scales require students to learn three different batteries (preschool, child, and adult versions) to cover this same age range.

However, unique features can be confusing because they are unlikely to be familiar or learned in the context of other tests. Some students will inappropriately overgeneralize procedures and practices learned on other tests to the WJ III COG. We have identified some features on the WJ III COG that differ substantially from other tests; instructors may want to identify these features for themselves and their students to ensure appropriate discrimination and learning. We list these unique characteristics of the WJ III COG, and some suggested instructional activities or responses that may help students understand these features, in Table 12-1.

BEST PRACTICES FOR WJ III COG TRAINING

Training in the WJ III COG should preferably take place in the broader context of psychological and educational assessment. Otherwise, training becomes focused on the concrete features of assessment, such as handling materials, recording

TABLE 12-1 Unique Features of the WJ III and Suggested Instructional Responses to Support Learning

Feature	Instructional response
Test by complete pages	Provide multiple examples in which examinees must continue testing after obtaining the same number of consecutive incorrect responses required to discontinue, but that occur prior to the page being completed (e.g., *Examiner Training Workbook*; Wendling & Mather, 2001, p. 5)
Lack of manipulatives in the battery	Remind examiners to consider breaks, interspersing WJ III with other tests to alleviate fatigue and sustain attention
Taped tests	Demonstrate appropriate administration using headphones; obtain a headphone splitter (available from electronics stores for less than $5) to demonstrate how to connect two headsets into a single cassette tape player; remind students to distinguish clearly between headphone sets handed to examinees and that used by the examiner (to reduce head lice transmission); remind students to clean headphones after every use
Discrete, limited responses	Remind examiners to prompt examinees for one-word answers to open-ended items
Computer scoring and report profiling	Model use of computer scoring program, including how to set default values to correspond to local expectations (e.g., some states require a discrepancy $\geq$ [1.75] or [2.0] for a significant discrepancy; the WJ III scoring program default is [1.50]
Conormed achievement battery	Remind examiners that it is generally preferable to use conormed batteries for identifying ability/achievement discrepancies (e.g., WJ III COG/ACH, WISC-III/WIAT-II, CAS/WJ-R ACH, DAS/BASIS) than to use scores from tests normed at different times on different groups
Predicted achievement versus General Intellectual Ability	Discuss the relative merits of using GIA to predict academic performance versus specific cognitive aptitudes. Two of the benefits: (a) GIA uses the broadest estimate of ability (thus minimizing specific cognitive deficits) and is similar to how other tests (e.g., WISC-III/WIAT-II) determine discrepancies, but (b) The predicted achievement option is more efficient, and provides more accurate prediction of achievement. It is important to note that available data do not clearly identify either approach as superior for identifying ability/achievement discrepancies; both approaches identify similar, but not exactly the same, discrepancies. Also, discuss criticisms of the discrepancy approach in general
Age versus grade norms	Discuss relative merits of each type of norm: (a) age-based norms are more widely used (increasing comparability to scores from other tests); and (b) grade-based norms reflect the referral context more accurately in educational settings. Also note that the norms produced will differ little unless the student's age is markedly different than grade (e.g., retention, promotion), in which case careful consideration of the issues is warranted

(continues)

TABLE 12-1 (*continued*)

Feature	Instructional response
Age versus grade norms (*continued*)	(e.g., should a retained child's achievement be compared to students of the same age who have been exposed to more challenging material?)
"Womb to tomb" coverage	Require students to produce cases spanning the preschool, school, and adult age ranges to experience how the test session and content are similar and different across the developmental span
Relative Proficiency Index (RPI) scores	Explain these as an index of mastery (the WJ-R used "Relative Mastery Index," or RMI), in which the test difficulty is established so that a person at the center of the norm group (age or grade) will earn 90% correct; the examinee's score is then presented relative to this value (e.g., 35/90 may be interpreted as this examinee earning 35% correct on a test when the average student scores 90%). Note that RPIs are most valuable for identifying how far below proficiency an examinee is, but are relatively useless as indexes for individuals above proficiency (i.e., the range from 90 to 100 is limited by a ceiling effect). Also, note that RPIs offer a strong alternative to grade equivalents for explaining performance to individuals not familiar with standard scores
Rasch scale scores (*W* scores)	Explain that *W* scores are equal-interval scores that adequately approximate ratio-level measurement. As such, they can be interpreted as an "absolute," rather than relative, measure of cognitive performance (e.g., changes in standard scores reflect norm-referenced changes; changes in *W* scores reflect criterion-referenced changes). *W* scores are similar to "scale scores" commonly found on large-scale achievement tests, and could be used to establish proficiency level statements of performance
Feedback in testing, or "controlled learning" tests	Note that three WJ III tests (i.e., tests 2, 5, and 13) require examiners to provide feedback to examinees regarding the accuracy of their responses for some or all items other than sample items. This is a departure from most other tests, which restrict feedback only to sample items; emphasize this feature via modeling and practice
Delayed administration of long-term retrieval tests	Explain that two tests on the WJ III COG allow for delayed recall over multiple hours or days. Test 10 (Visual-Auditory Learning— Delayed) must be administered 30 minutes to 8 days after the first administration of Test 2 (Visual-Auditory Learning). Remind examiners to record exact time and date of administration for Test 2, and to ensure that Test 10 is completed within 192 hours of Test 2 administration

responses, and the like. Although these features are important and must be mastered, students may lose the focus on the broader context and purpose of assessment as they struggle to master administration and scoring procedures. Consequently, we recommend that training include active engagement in applying standards, exercises to establish administration and scoring accuracy, and opportunities to bridge science and practice in deriving valid interpretations of assessment results. We have already mentioned some activities intended to accomplish these goals; in this section, we make additional suggestions to assist instructors and students.

APPLYING STANDARDS

To use professional standards effectively and knowledgeably, students should use the standards to evaluate tests and construct new meanings. We recommend that students work individually or in teams to apply test standards (e.g., AERA, APA, NCME, 1999) to evaluate the tests they learn. We have included an exercise and a scoring rubric that guides students to apply validity standards to the evaluation of the WJ III (see Appendix D, at the end of this book). Again, we refer the reader to Chapter 1 (this volume) for an excellent discussion of professional standards and validity especially as it applies to the WJ III.

ENHANCING ADMINISTRATION AND
SCORING ACCURACY

Earlier in this chapter we reported information regarding examiner administration and scoring accuracy based on the extant literature and preliminary data from a study on the WJ III COG. This initial study with the WJ III indicated that students make administration and scoring errors on the WJ III COG, and that some of the errors are not trivial. For example, entering the wrong value in the scoring program software may have significant effects on General Intellectual Ability and cluster scores. When students do not record correct responses to test items, qualitative information regarding an individual's performance is lost, along with the ability to verify scoring decisions independently. The literature regarding training on administration and scoring of cognitive assessment instruments was reviewed by Alfonso and Pratt (1997) and is summarized here. In addition, we provide some concrete activities for instructors that can assist them in training professionals how to maximize administering and scoring accuracy of cognitive tests, including the WJ III COG.

Alfonso and Pratt (1997) concluded that having students administer and score many test protocols (e.g., 10) in and of itself does not necessarily improve administration and scoring accuracy, even when feedback is provided after each administration. Therefore, they suggested that a combination of methods should be used to decrease administration and scoring errors. These methods include the use of behavioral checklists, peer trainers, test manuals, videotapes, and administration and scoring checklists such as the one in Figure 12-1 or the one found in the *WJ III Examiner Training Workbook* (Wendling & Mather, 2001). This checklist contains items that are particular to each test (e.g., summing tally marks correctly on Retrieval Fluency) as well as some items that apply to most tests (e.g., recording examinee errors). Course instructors may want to use the checklist that appears in Figure 12-1 as a student handout, as a tool for assisting with grading protocols, or as a template for use in their own research.

In addition to the use of checklists, we believe that the culmination of training in test administration and scoring should be a competency exam wherein students are required to administer part or all of the WJ III COG to their instructor or to their instructor's assistant. Conversely, submission of a videotape by the student demonstrating successful WJ III COG administration could meet the competency exam requirement. Scoring of the test should also be included as part of the competency exam. Figure 12-2, a flowchart of activities designed to enhance administration and scoring accuracy, may be used by students in preparation for a competency exam.

INTERPRETING TEST RESULTS

Interpreting assessment results always takes place in a context. The same set of results may have dramatically different meanings for examinees in different contexts (e.g., low Comprehension–Knowledge composites may mean different things for examinees who have not been exposed to English and North American culture than for examinees who have). Consequently, we recommend that training in test interpretation reflect case-based instruction (see Merseth [1994] and Putnam and Borko [2000] for essential elements of case-based learning and professional development). These cases can come from the example provided in the WJ III COG training materials (Riverside, 2001) or from cases developed by the instructor and the students. Some instructors may want to develop a complete case of a client seeking services that demonstrates how the WJ III COG is used in the assessment process. Also, because students typically assess volunteers as part of their training, instructors should consider setting aside time for their students to present the results of these assessments.

To enhance case-based interpretation, we recommend that instructors first demonstrate interpretation using a complete case. The case should present the information in the sequence in which it was obtained (i.e., referral information, records review, observations, assessment, integration of data, validation of inferences, decisions and recommendations), with discussion of what the information means and how the information shapes decisions about what to do next at each juncture. We suggest a common set of questions (see Appendix D, at the end of this book, for an example of a set of questions) for all cases to help students internalize an interpretive framework that links the specifics of each case (e.g., context, results) to the scientific knowledge base of the profession, and in particular, the evidence supporting and limiting WJ III COG interpretations.

Also, we suggest that instructors require students to integrate multiple sources of information to provide effective interpretations. Students must draw

Step 1: Introduction

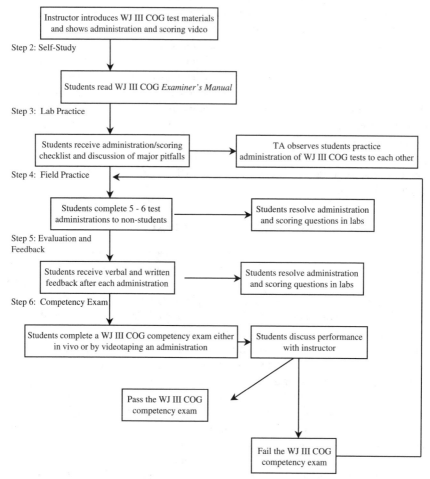

Step 2: Self-Study

Step 3: Lab Practice

Step 4: Field Practice

Step 5: Evaluation and Feedback

Step 6: Competency Exam

FIGURE 12-2   Step-by-step flowchart to prepare students for competency exams in cognitive assessment.

on psychometric and statistical principles to anticipate the role of measurement error in interpretation, theories of intelligence to attribute accurate meaning to scores, and a broad knowledge of professional psychology and psychological development to understand clients, their contexts, and their presenting problems. The following list provides some key issues that instructors should consider and address in preparing students to interpret results appropriately from any cognitive abilities test.

1. Fundamental assessment literacy. The key concepts in this domain include the ubiquitous nature of measurement error, reliability, validity, and steps professionals

can take to reduce error and increase the validity of their assessments (see Stiggins, 1995).

2. Theories of intelligence. The lack of attention to a fundamental understanding of the nature of the construct being measured (intelligence) can lead to inappropriate interpretations (e.g., beliefs that different cognitive factor scores reflect independent cognitive abilities). Unfortunately, most students spend much more time acquiring the skills needed to obtain scores than they do developing an understanding of the construct they are measuring. Courses emphasizing theories of intelligence, and their links to intelligence tests, can help ground interpretations in a sound theoretical basis and reduce inappropriate or inaccurate interpretations.

3. Fundamental quantitative literacy. Psychologists often make inappropriate interpretations of scores because they do not have a sound grasp of the quantitative principles that apply to measurement and assessment. A common example is inappropriately interpreting a reliable difference between two scores (e.g., one that exceeds a 68%, 90%, or 95% confidence threshold) as an unusual or rarely occurring score difference. Many reliable score differences (e.g., those exceeding a 90% or 95% threshold) occur often, yet students inaccurately presume a reliable difference is unusual. For example, a 15-point difference between PIQ and VIQ on the Wechsler Scales is reliable ($p < .05$), but fairly common (more than 30% of the normative population has a discrepancy of 15 points or more) (Wechsler, 1991). A second problem is inaccurately presuming that errors in measuring intelligence work only in one direction—that is, to lower obtained scores relative to "true" scores. In fact, errors that inflate scores are equally common (error is symmetrically distributed on both sides of a true score), but many students and psychologists fail to apply this understanding to score interpretation. Instead, students often suggest that an examinee's score may underestimate the examinee's ability due to fatigue, poor rapport, or dialect differences, yet they rarely if ever suggest that an examinee's score overestimates ability due to unusual energy, exceptional rapport, examiner bias, guessing, or luck. We recommend Salsberg (2001) for an entertaining and illuminating account of the principles relating to statistics and measurement.

4. Failing to apply critically general and specific knowledge to score interpretation. Remarkably, many students have relevant knowledge (e.g., they understand assessment and quantitative literacy, or theories of intelligence), but they fail to apply it to the score interpretation process. Instead, they may accept at face value test claims (e.g., that a test assesses "nonverbal ability"), or that a particular constellation of test scores argues in favor of or against a particular method of instruction for a client. This is unfortunate, and may be exacerbated when different faculty teach different courses (e.g., different faculty may teach cognitive theory and development, quantitative methods, measurement, and cognitive assessment courses). Consequently, students develop episodic, incomplete, or context-specific representations (e.g., statistical knowledge is important only in statistics, not in assessment contexts) of the knowledge needed to inform appropriate score interpretation. Coordinating and integrating instruction to include

interdisciplinary study and genuine application can help students develop a more integrated, generalized, and critical approach to test score interpretation (see Fenwick, 2000; Putnam & Borko, 2000 for methods to help students construct meaning from information).

Fortunately, the authors and publisher of the WJ III provide multiple resources to assist in generating accurate score interpretations. These resources include information in the WJ III manuals, scoring software, on-line resources, training videos, and *Report Writer for the WJ III* (Report Writer) (Schrank & Woodcock, 2002). The Report Writer allows examiners to incorporate information from multiple sources, which allows examiners to combine results from the WJ III tests with observations, structured checklist information (provided in the report writer manual), and data from other cognitive tests. The software includes multiple sources of data (e.g., test scores, teacher checklist data, examiner observations), but it leaves the interpretation of results to the examiner. These and other resources are listed in Appendix D at the end of this book. We have also included in Appendix D an example syllabus that incorporates many of the activities we recommend for teaching the WJ III COG. Note that the course syllabus does not include every activity; we have provided more activities and resources than may be reasonable to include in a single semester to give instructors choices that match their needs.

CONCLUSIONS

We close this chapter by noting that effective professional training in the WJ III COG entails procedures, concepts, and methods that are common to other tests of intelligence. Although we believe that the WJ III poses some training challenges, we also note that most of these challenges are also posed by other cognitive ability tests (often to a greater degree). Our chapter, then, is intended to illustrate some of the challenges and opportunities that the WJ III provides to professional educators. Specifically, we note that the WJ and WJ-R were underrepresented relative to other tests of cognitive ability in cognitive assessment courses. Our review of the literature suggests that this underrepresentation had less to do with particular weaknesses or problems, and more to do with historical effects (e.g., marketing history, inertia). We also note that the WJ III offers many links to professional standards, contemporary mental ability theory, and cognitive assessment. Additionally, we have highlighted some particular scoring challenges and unique features of the WJ III that require attention in cognitive assessment courses.

Although cognitive tests are only one part of a comprehensive assessment, tests often have significant influence in the outcomes and dispositions associated with assessments. Although these outcomes are not well understood (see our concerns regarding the dearth of consequential validity for all cognitive tests), we write from the perspective that strong training will reduce errors in administration, scoring, and interpretation of the WJ III COG. Additionally, we assume that well-trained examiners will be more likely to ensure that assessment produces beneficial effects for the examinee. We hope that this chapter will assist others in providing strong training, and in so doing, enhance examinees' welfare and professional assessment practices.

ACKNOWLEDGMENT

We thank the editors and Randy G. Floyd for their reviews and comments on earlier drafts of this manuscript.

REFERENCES

Alfonso, V. C., & Flanagan, D. P. (1999). Assessment of cognitive functioning in preschoolers. In E. Vazquez, I. Romero, & J. Kalesnik (Eds.), *Assessing and screening preschoolers: Psychological and educational dimensions* (2nd ed.) (pp. 186–217). Boston: Allyn & Bacon.

Alfonso, V. C., & Pratt, S. I. (1997). Issues and suggestions for training professionals in assessing intelligence. In D. P. Flanagan, J. L. Genshaft, & P. L. Harrison (Eds.), *Contemporary intellectual assessment: Theories, tests, and issues* (pp. 326–344). New York: Guilford.

Alfonso, V. C., Oakland, T. D., LaRocca, R., & Spanakos, A. (2000). The course on individual cognitive assessment. *School Psychology Review, 29,* 52–64.

American Educational Research Association, American Psychological Association, and National Council on Measurement in Education (AERA, APA, NCME) (1999). *Standards for educational and psychological testing* (3rd ed.). Washington, DC: Author.

American Psychological Association. (1981). *Specialty guidelines for the delivery of services by school psychologists.* Washington, DC: Author.

Anderson, T. K., Cancelli, A. A., & Kratochwill, T. R. (1984). Self-reported assessment practices of school psychologists: Implications for training and practice. *Journal of School Psychology, 22,* 17–29.

Braden, J. P., & Kratochwill, T. R. (1997). Treatment utility of assessment: Myths and realities. *School Psychology Review, 26,* 475–485.

Brown, W. R., & McGuire, J. M. (1976). Current psychological assessment practices. *Professional Psychology, 7,* 475–484.

Buckley, J. A., Schroeder, J. L., & Braden, J. P. (2000, March). *Woodcock–Johnson—Revised (WJ-R): Defining aptitude-achievement discrepancies in a sample of students with and without learning disabilities.* Poster presented at the National Association of School Psychologists Annual Meeting, New Orleans, LA.

Buckley, J. A., Schroeder, J. L., Potts, M. K., McGivern, J. E., & Braden, J. P. (2000, August). *Woodcock–Johnson—Revised (WJ-R): Defining aptitude-achievement discrepancies in a clinical versus nonclinical sample of adults.* Paper presented at the American Psychological Association annual meeting, Washington, DC.

Ceci, S. J., & Williams, W. M. (1997). Schooling, intelligence, and income. *American Psychologist, 52,* 1051–1058.

Fenwick. T. J. (2000). Expanding conceptions of experiential learning: A review of the five contemporary perspectives on cognition. *Adult Education Quarterly, 50,* 243–272.

Flanagan, D. P., Genshaft, J. L., & Harrison, P. A. (Eds.). (1997). *Contemporary intellectual assessment: Theories, tests, and issues.* New York: Guilford.

Flanagan, D. P., & Ortiz, S. O. (2001). *Essentials of cross-battery assessment.* New York: Wiley.

Gardner, H. (1999). *Intelligence reframed: Multiple intelligences for the 21st century*. New York: Basic Books.

Goh, D. S., Teslow, C. J., & Fuller, G. B. (1981). The practice of psychological assessment among school psychologists. *Professional Psychology, 12,* 696–706.

Gresham, F. M. (2001, August). Responsiveness to intervention: An alternative approach to the identification of learning disabilities. *Paper presented at the Learning Disabilities Summit: Building a Foundation for the Future.* Office of Special Education Programs, Washington, DC. Available at the web site: http://www.air.org/ldsummit/paper.htm.

Gresham, F. M., & Witt, J. C. (1997). Utility of intelligence tests for treatment planning, classification, and placement decisions: Recent empirical findings and future directions. *School Psychology Quarterly, 12,* 249–267.

Hayes, S. C., Nelson, R. O., & Jarrett, R. B. (1987). The treatment utility of assessment: A functional approach to evaluating assessment quality. *American Psychologist, 42,* 963–974.

Horn, J. L., & Noll, J. (1997). Human cognitive capabilities: *Gf–Gc* theory. In D. P. Flanagan, J. L. Genshaft, & P. L. Harrison (Eds.), *Contemporary intellectual assessment: Theories, tests, and issues* (pp. 53–91). New York: Guilford.

Jensen, A. R. (1998). *The g factor: The science of mental ability.* Westport, CN: Praeger.

Kamphaus, R. W., Petoskey, M. D., & Morgan, A. W. (1997). A history of intelligence test interpretation. In D. P. Flanagan, J. L. Genshaft, & P. L. Harrison (Eds.), *Contemporary intellectual assessment: Theories, tests, and issues* (pp. 32–47). New York: Guilford.

Kamphaus, R. W., Petoskey, M. D., & Rowe, E. W. (2000). Current trends in psychological testing of children. *Professional Psychology: Research and Practice, 31,* 155–164.

Kane, M. T. (1992). An argument-based approach to validity. *Psychological Bulletin, 112,* 527–535.

Kaufman, A. S. (1994). *Intelligent testing with the WISC-III.* New York: Wiley.

Mather, N., & Woodcock, R. W. (2001). *Examiner's manual. Woodcock–Johnson III Tests of Cognitive Abilities.* Itasca, IL: Riverside Publishing.

McGrew, K. S. (1986). *Clinical interpretation of the Woodcock–Johnson tests of cognitive ability.* Orlando, FL: Grune & Stratton.

McGrew, K. S. (1994a). The achievement content criticism of the Woodcock–Johnson and Woodcock–Johnson—Revised: A myth. *Communiqué, 22,* 13–14.

McGrew, K. S. (1994b). School psychologists vs. school proceduralists: A response to Willis and Dumont. *Communiqué, 22,* 13,15.

McGrew, K. S., & Flanagan, D. P. (1998). *The intelligence test desk reference: Gf–Gc cross-battery assessment.* Boston: Allyn & Bacon.

McGrew, K. S., & Woodcock, R. W. (2001). *Technical manual. Woodcock–Johnson III.* Itasca, IL: Riverside Publishing.

Merseth, K. K. (1994). Cases, case methods, and the professional development of educators. *ERIC Digest.* Washington, DC: ERIC Clearinghouse on Teaching and Teacher (ED 401272). Available at the web site: http://80orders.edrs.com.ezproxy.library.wisc.edu/members/sp.cfm?AN=ED401272.

Messick, S. (1989). Validity. In R. Linn (Ed.), *Educational measurement* (3rd ed.) (pp. 104–131). Washington, DC: American Council on Education.

Messick, S. (1995). Validity of psychological assessment: Validation of inferences from persons' responses and performances as scientific inquiry into score meaning. *American Psychologist, 50,* 741–749.

National Association of School Psychologists (2000). *Standards for training and field placement programs in school psychology. Standards for the credentialing of school psychologists.* Washington, DC: Author.

Oakland, T. D., & Zimmerman, S. A. (1986). The course on individual mental assessment: A national survey of course instructors. *Professional School Psychology, 1,* 51–59.

Piotrowski, C., & Keller, J. W. (1989). Psychological testing in outpatient mental health facilities: A national study. *Professional Psychology: Research and Practice, 20,* 423–425.

Putnam, R., & Borko, H. (2000). What do new views of knowledge and thinking have to say about research on teacher learning. *Educational Researcher, 29,* 4–15.

Reeve, R., Hall, R., & Zarkeski, R. (1979). The Woodcock–Johnson Tests of Cognitive Ability: Concurrent validity with the WISC-R. *Learning Disability Quarterly, 2,* 63–69.

Reschly, D. J. (1997). Utility of individual ability measures and public policy choices for the 21st century. *School Psychology Review, 26,* 234–241.

Reschly, D. J., & Grimes, J. P. (1995). Best practices in intellectual assessment. In A. Thomas & J. Grimes (Eds.), *Best practices in school psychology* (3rd ed.). Bethesda, MD: National Association of School Psychologists.

Reschly, D. J., & Wilson, M. S. (1995). School psychology faculty and practitioners: 1986 to 1991 trends in demographic characteristics, roles, satisfaction, and system reform. *School Psychology Review, 24,* 62–78.

Riverside Publishing (2001). *University training package.* Itasca, IL: Author.

Salsberg, D. L. (2001). *The lady tasting tea: How statistics revolutionized science in the twentieth century.* New York: W. H. Freeman.

Sattler, J. M. (2001). *Assessment of children: Cognitive applications* (4th ed.). San Diego: Jerome M. Sattler.

Schermerhorn, S. M., & Alfonso, V. C. (in preparation). *Graduate student administration and scoring errors on the Woodcock–Johnson III Tests of Cognitive Abilities.*

Schrank, F. A., & Woodcock, R. W. (2001). *WJ III compuscore and profiles program (version 1.1b).* Itasca, IL: Riverside Publishing.

Schrank, F. A., & Woodcock, R. W. (2002). *Report Writer for the WJIII.* Itasca, IL: Riverside Publishing.

Shinn, M., Algozzine, B., Marston, D., & Ysseldyke, J. (1982). A theoretical analysis of the performance of learning disabled students on the Woodcock–Johnson Psycho-Educational Battery. *Journal of Learning Disabilities, 15,* 221–226.

Stiggins, R. J. (1995). Assessment literacy for the 21st century. *Phi Delta Kappan, 77,* 238–245.

Stinnett, T. A., Havey, J. M., & Oehler-Stinnett, J. (1994). Current test usage by practicing psychologists: A national survey. *Journal of Psychoeducational Assessment, 12,* 331–350.

Wechsler, D. (1991). *Wechsler Intelligence Scale for Children—Third Edition.* San Antonio, TX: Psychological Corporation.

Wendling, B. J., & Mather, N. (2001). *Examiner training workbook. Woodcock–Johnson III Tests of Cognitive Abilities.* Itasca, IL: Riverside Publishing.

Willis, J., & Dumont, R. (1994). "In God we trust, all others bring your data." *Communiqué, 22,* 13–14.

Woodcock, R. W. (1997). The Woodcock–Johnson Tests of Cognitive Ability—Revised. In D. P. Flanagan, J. L. Genshaft, & P. L. Harrison (Eds.). *Contemporary intellectual assessment: Theories, tests, and issues* (pp. 230–246). New York: Guilford.

Woodcock, R. W., & Johnson, M. B. (1977). *Woodcock–Johnson Psycho-educational Battery.* Itasca, IL: Riverside Publishing.

Woodcock, R. W., & Johnson, M. B. (1989, 1990). *Woodcock–Johnson Psycho-educational Battery—Revised.* Itasca, IL: Riverside Publishing.

Woodcock, R. W., & Johnson, M. B. (1990). *Compuscore for the WJ-R.* Chicago: Riverside.

Woodcock, R. W., McGrew, K. S., & Mather, N. (2001). *Woodcock–Johnson III Tests of Cognitive Abilities.* Itasca, IL: Riverside Publishing.

Ysseldyke, J. E., Shinn, M., & Epps, S. (1981). A comparison of the WISC-R and the Woodcock–Johnson Tests of Cognitive Ability. *Psychology in the Schools, 18,* 15–19.

APPENDIX A

SOURCES CONTRIBUTING TO VALIDITY EVIDENCE

Type of Validity Evidence

#	Source	WJ (1978)	WJ-R (1989)	WJ III (2001)	Theory Development	Expert Review	Factor Analysis—Exploratory	Factor Analysis—Confirmatory	Cluster/Profile Analysis	Developmental	Criterion—Concurrent	Criterion—Predictive	Discriminative	Normal	LD	ADHD	Standardization Sample	Other	Preschool Age	School Age and Adolescence	Early Adulthood	Middle Adulthood	Late Adulthood
1	Algozzine & Ysseldyke (1981)	✓									✓		✓					✓		✓			
2	Algozzine, Ysseldyke, & Shinn (1982)	✓									✓		✓	✓	✓			✓		✓			
3	Aram & Ekelman (1988)	✓									✓		✓	✓				✓		✓			
4	Arffa, Rider, & Cummings (1984)	✓									✓							✓	✓				
5	Beden, Rohr, & Ellsworth (1987)	✓																					
6	Bickley, Keith, & Wolfle (1995)		✓					✓		✓					✓					✓	✓	✓	
7	Binks & Gold (1998)		✓		✓			✓			✓										✓	✓	
8	Bohline (1985)	✓									✓		✓	✓				✓		✓			
9	Bolen, Kimball, Hall, & Webster (1997)												✓	✓		✓		✓				✓	
10	Bracken, Prasse, & Breen (1984)	✓									✓		✓	✓	✓					✓			
11	Breen (1984)	✓									✓		✓		✓					✓			
12	Breen (1985)	✓											✓		✓					✓			
13	Breen (1986)	✓											✓		✓								
14	Buchanan & Wolf (1986)												✓	✓	✓					✓			
15	Buckhalt, McGhee, & Ehrler (2001)		✓								✓			✓							✓		
16	Burns, Nettelbeck, & Cooper (2000)		✓								✓			✓						✓			
17	Carroll (1993)	✓	✓		✓		✓							✓			✓		✓	✓	✓	✓	✓
18	Carroll (in press)				✓	✓	✓							✓			✓		✓	✓	✓	✓	✓
19	Casey, Cohen, Schuerholz, Singer, & Denckla (2000)		✓						✓		✓				✓			✓		✓		✓	✓
20	Coleman & Harmer (1985)	✓									✓			✓				✓		✓			✓

21	Cuenin (1990)
22	Cummings (1982)
23	Cummings & Sanville (1983)
24	Daleiden, Drabman, & Benton (2002)
25	Dalke (1988)
26	Dean & Woodcock (1999)
27	Dumont, Willis, Farr, McCarthy, & Price (2000)
28	Estabrook (1984)
29	Evans, Carlsen, & McGrew (1993)
30	Evans, Floyd, McGrew, & Leforgee (2002)
31	Flanagan (2000)
32	Flanagan, Kranzler, & Keith[a]
33	Flanagan & McGrew (1998)
34	Flanagan, McGrew, & Ortiz (2000)
35	Flanagan & Ortiz (2001)
36	Floyd, Evans, & McGrew (in press)
37	Floyd, Flanagan, Evans, & McGrew (2002)
38	Ford, Simmons, & North[a]
39	Ford, Teague, & Tusing[a]
40	Frattali, Liow, Craig, Korenman, Makhlouf, Sato, Biesecker, & Theodore (2001)
41	Garcia & Stafford (2000)
42	Gregg & Hoy (1985)
43	Gregg & Hoy[a]
44	Harrington, Kimbrell, & Dai (1992)
45	Horn (1991)
46	Horn & Noll (1997)
47	Hoy & Gregg (1986)
48	Hoy, Gregg, Jagota, King, Moreland, & Manglitz (1993)
49	Ingram & Hakari (1985)
50	Ipsen, McMillan, & Fallen (1983)
51	Jensen (1998)
52	Kaufman & O'Neal (1988a)
53	Kaufman & O'Neal (1988b)
54	Kaufman, Horton, Gott, Wolff, Nelson, Azen, & Manis (1995)
55	Keating, List, & Merriman (1985)
56	Keith (1999)

(continues)

Type of Validity Evidence

#	Source	WJ (1978)	WJ-R (1989)	WJ III (2001)	Theory Development	Expert Review	Factor Analysis—Exploratory	Factor Analysis—Confirmatory	Cluster/Profile Analysis	Developmental	Criterion—Concurrent	Criterion—Predictive	Discriminative	Normal	LD	ADHD	Standardization Sample	Other	Preschool Age	School Age and Adolescence	Early Adulthood	Middle Adulthood	Late Adulthood
					Content		Structural			External				Sample Description					Age of Participants				
57	Keith, Kranzler, & Flanagan (2001)			✓										✓						✓			
58	Konold, Glutting, & McDermott (1997)		✓						✓		✓			✓			✓			✓			
59	Laughon & Torgesen (1985)	✓									✓			✓						✓			
60	Laurent (1997)		✓								✓			✓		✓				✓	✓		
61	Lerner & Yasutake[a]			✓																✓			
62	List, Keating, & Merriman (1985)	✓								✓	✓			✓					✓	✓	✓		
63	Manis, Cohn, McBride-Chang, Wolff, & Kaufman (1997)		✓							✓									✓	✓			
64	Marston & Ysseldyke (1984)	✓							✓				✓		✓		✓	✓		✓			
65	Masterson (1993)		✓								✓			✓						✓			
66	Mather & Bos (1984)	✓											✓	✓						✓			
67	Mather & Burch (1986)	✓									✓		✓		✓			✓		✓			
68	Mather & Udall (1985)	✓											✓					✓		✓			
69	McArdle, Ferrer-Caja, Hamagami, & Woodcock (2002)		✓					✓		✓				✓					✓	✓	✓	✓	✓
70	McCallum & Hooper[a]			✓					✓					✓						✓	✓	✓	
71	McGhee (1993)		✓		✓			✓			✓			✓					✓	✓			
72	McGhee & Liberman (1994)		✓		✓			✓			✓			✓						✓			
73	McGrew (1983)	✓					✓								✓			✓		✓			
74	McGrew (1984)	✓					✓				✓			✓			✓			✓			
75	McGrew (1985)	✓					✓			✓				✓			✓			✓			
76	McGrew (1987a)	✓					✓							✓				✓		✓			
77	McGrew (1987b)	✓									✓						✓	✓		✓			

#	Citation	1	2	3	4	5	6	7	8	9	10	11	12	13	14	15	16	17	18	19	20	21	22	23	24	25	26	27	28
78	McGrew (1993)		✓							✓	✓			✓			✓			✓			✓		✓		✓		
79	McGrew (1997)		✓				✓							✓									✓		✓		✓		✓
80	McGrew & Flanagan (1998)		✓		✓	✓																	✓						
81	McGrew, Flanagan, Keith, & Vanderwood (1997)		✓					✓		✓		✓						✓			✓				✓		✓	✓	✓
82	McGrew & Hessler (1995)		✓							✓	✓						✓			✓			✓		✓		✓	✓	✓
83	McGrew & Knopik (1993)		✓							✓	✓						✓			✓			✓		✓		✓	✓	✓
84	McGrew & Knopik (1996)		✓					✓									✓			✓			✓						
85	McGrew & Murphy (1995)		✓			✓											✓			✓			✓		✓		✓	✓	✓
86	McGrew & Pehl (1988)	✓								✓	✓		✓							✓			✓		✓		✓	✓	✓
87	McGrew, Werder, & Woodcock (1991)		✓		✓	✓	✓	✓		✓	✓	✓	✓	✓	✓	✓	✓	✓	✓	✓	✓		✓	✓	✓		✓	✓	✓
88	McGrew & Woodcock (2001)			✓		✓		✓		✓	✓	✓	✓	✓	✓	✓	✓	✓	✓	✓	✓		✓	✓	✓		✓	✓	✓
89	McGrew, Woodcock, & Ford (2002)			✓						✓			✓		✓	✓	✓		✓				✓	✓	✓		✓	✓	✓
90	McGue, Shinn, & Ysseldyke (1982)	✓					✓			✓				✓									✓						
91	McIntosh & Dunham[a]			✓						✓			✓				✓						✓						
92	Meinhardt, Hibbett, Koller, & Busch (1993)		✓							✓									✓			✓			✓				
93	Merrell (1990)		✓									✓			✓				✓			✓							
94	Merrell & Shinn (1990)		✓									✓			✓				✓			✓							
95	Merriman, Keating, & List (1985)	✓						✓	✓				✓										✓			✓			
96	Noll & Horn (1998)				✓																				✓				
97	Norton[a]			✓						✓			✓												✓				
98	Patel, Seltzer, Wu, & Schupf (2001)		✓							✓							✓						✓		✓	✓			
99	Phelps[a]			✓						✓			✓								✓		✓						
100	Phelps & Ford[a]			✓						✓			✓								✓		✓						
101	Phelps & Rosso (1985)	✓								✓									✓			✓							
102	Phelps, Rosso, & Falasco (1984)	✓								✓					✓				✓			✓							
103	Phelps, Rosso, & Falasco (1985)	✓								✓			✓						✓			✓							
104	Reed & McCallum (1995)		✓							✓			✓									✓							
105	Reeve, Hall, & Zakreski (1979)	✓								✓				✓					✓			✓							
106	Reilly, Drudge, Rosen, Loew, & Fischer (1985)	✓								✓	✓		✓									✓							
107	Rizza, McIntosh, & McCunn (2001)		✓									✓	✓			✓	✓			✓			✓						
108	Rosso & Phelps (1988)	✓								✓									✓			✓							
109	Salthouse (1998)		✓					✓										✓				✓			✓	✓	✓	✓	
110	Santos (1989)	✓								✓		✓		✓	✓							✓							
111	Shinn, Algozzine, Martson, & Ysseldyke (1982)	✓						✓				✓	✓		✓							✓			✓	✓	✓		
112	Stormont-Spurgin & Zentall (1995)	✓									✓					✓		✓		✓		✓							
113	Strein (1990)	✓					✓	✓			✓			✓					✓		✓	✓	✓						
114	Teeter & Smith (1993)		✓							✓		✓		✓						✓		✓							

(*continues*)

Type of Validity Evidence

Source	Battery			Content		Structural			External				Sample Description					Age of Participants				
	WJ (1978)	WJ-R (1989)	WJ III (2001)	Theory Development	Expert Review	Factor Analysis—Exploratory	Factor Analysis—Confirmatory	Cluster/Profile Analysis	Developmental	Criterion—Concurrent	Criterion—Predictive	Discriminative	Normal	LD	ADHD	Standardization Sample	Other	Preschool Age	School Age and Adolescence	Early Adulthood	Middle Adulthood	Late Adulthood
115 Telzrow & Harr (1987)	✓									✓			✓	✓			✓		✓			
116 Thompson & Brassard (1984)	✓									✓							✓		✓			
117 Tupper (1990)	✓									✓									✓		✓	
118 Vesley[a]			✓							✓			✓	✓					✓	✓		
119 Walsh, Lowenthal, & Thompson (1989)	✓									✓				✓	✓		✓		✓			
120 Waschbusch, Daleiden, & Drabman (2000)		✓								✓	✓	✓		✓	✓		✓		✓			
121 Williams, McCallum, & Reed (1996)		✓			✓					✓			✓		✓		✓		✓			
122 Woodcock (1978)	✓				✓			✓	✓	✓			✓	✓			✓	✓	✓	✓	✓	✓
123 Woodcock (1990)		✓					✓			✓						✓			✓	✓	✓	
124 Woodcock (1998)		✓								✓		✓				✓		✓	✓	✓	✓	✓
125 Ysseldyke, Algozzine, & Shinn (1981)	✓									✓		✓		✓			✓		✓			
126 Ysseldyke, Algozzine, Shinn, & McGue (1982)	✓									✓		✓		✓			✓		✓			
127 Ysseldyke, Shinn, & Epps (1981)	✓									✓		✓		✓			✓		✓			

[a]Note: Study reported in the *WJ III Technical Manual* (McGrew & Woodcock, 2001).

Appendix B

Expected Achievement on the WJ III Given WISC-III Full-Scale IQ and Correction for Regression to the Mean

Source: Reproduced from the Woodcock–Johnson III Assessment Service Bulletin Number 4. Calculating Ability/Achievement Discrepancies between the *Wechsler Intelligence Scale for Children—Third Edition* and the *Woodcock–Johnson III Tests of Achievement* (Table 2, pp. 4–7), by Fredrick A. Schrank, Kirk A. Becker, and Scott Decker, with permission of the publisher. Copyright © 2001 by The Riverside Publishing Company, Itasca, Illinois. All rights reserved.

WISC-III FSIQ	Broad Reading	Basic Reading Skills	Reading Comp	Broad Math	Math Calculation Skills	Math Reasoning	Broad Written Language	Basic Writing Skills	Written Expression	Oral Expression	Listening Comp	Academic Knowledge
40	57	65	56	58	63	55	66	65	67	63	68	51
41	58	65	57	59	64	56	67	65	67	64	68	52
42	58	66	58	60	65	57	67	66	68	64	69	53
43	59	66	59	60	65	57	68	66	68	65	69	54
44	60	67	59	61	66	58	68	67	69	66	70	55
45	61	67	60	62	66	59	69	68	70	66	70	55
46	61	68	61	62	67	60	69	68	70	67	71	56
47	62	69	61	63	68	60	70	69	71	68	71	57
48	63	69	62	64	68	61	70	69	71	68	72	58
49	63	70	63	65	69	62	71	70	72	69	72	59
50	64	70	64	65	70	63	72	70	72	69	73	59
51	65	71	64	66	70	63	72	71	73	70	73	60
52	66	72	65	67	71	64	73	72	73	71	74	61
53	66	72	66	67	71	65	73	72	74	71	75	62
54	67	73	67	68	72	66	74	73	75	72	75	63
55	68	73	67	69	73	66	74	73	75	72	76	63
56	68	74	68	69	73	67	75	74	76	73	76	64
57	69	75	69	70	74	68	76	75	76	74	77	65
58	70	75	69	71	74	69	76	75	77	74	77	66
59	71	76	70	71	75	69	77	76	77	75	78	67
60	71	76	71	72	76	70	77	76	78	75	78	68
61	72	77	72	73	76	71	78	77	78	76	79	68
62	73	78	72	74	77	72	78	78	79	77	79	69
63	74	78	73	74	77	72	79	78	80	77	80	70
64	74	79	74	75	78	73	80	79	80	78	81	71
65	75	79	75	76	79	74	80	79	81	79	81	72
66	76	80	75	76	79	75	81	80	81	79	82	72
67	76	80	76	77	80	75	81	81	82	80	82	73
68	77	81	77	78	81	76	82	81	82	80	83	74
69	78	82	77	78	81	77	82	82	83	81	83	75
70	79	82	78	79	82	78	83	82	83	82	84	76
71	79	83	79	80	82	78	84	83	84	82	84	76
72	80	83	80	81	83	79	84	83	85	83	85	77
73	81	84	80	81	84	80	85	84	85	83	85	78
74	81	85	81	82	84	81	85	85	86	84	86	79
75	82	85	82	83	85	81	86	85	86	85	86	80
76	83	86	83	83	85	82	86	86	87	85	87	81
77	84	86	83	84	86	83	87	86	87	86	88	81
78	84	87	84	85	87	84	88	87	88	87	88	82
79	85	88	85	85	87	84	88	88	88	87	89	83
80	86	88	85	86	88	85	89	88	89	88	89	84
81	86	89	86	87	88	86	89	89	89	88	90	85
82	87	89	87	87	89	87	90	89	90	89	90	85
83	88	90	88	88	90	87	90	90	91	90	91	86
84	89	91	88	89	90	88	91	91	91	90	91	87
85	89	91	89	90	91	89	91	91	92	91	92	88
86	90	92	90	90	91	90	92	92	92	91	92	89
87	91	92	91	91	92	90	93	92	93	92	93	89
88	91	93	91	92	93	91	93	93	93	93	94	90
89	92	93	92	92	93	92	94	94	94	93	94	91

WISC-III FSIQ	Broad Reading	Basic Reading Skills	Reading Comp	Broad Math	Math Calculation Skills	Math Reasoning	Broad Written Language	Basic Writing Skills	Written Expression	Oral Expression	Listening Comp	Academic Knowledge
90	93	94	93	93	94	93	94	94	94	94	95	92
91	94	95	93	94	95	93	95	95	95	94	95	93
92	94	95	94	94	95	94	95	95	96	95	96	94
93	95	96	95	95	96	95	96	96	96	96	96	94
94	96	96	96	96	96	96	97	96	97	96	97	95
95	96	97	96	97	97	96	97	97	97	97	97	96
96	97	98	97	97	98	97	98	98	98	98	98	97
97	98	98	98	98	98	98	98	98	98	98	98	98
98	99	99	99	99	99	99	99	99	99	99	99	98
99	99	00	00	99	99	99	99	99	99	99	99	99
100	100	100	100	100	100	100	100	100	100	100	100	100
101	101	101	101	101	101	101	101	101	101	101	101	101
102	101	101	101	101	101	101	101	101	101	101	101	102
103	102	102	102	102	102	102	102	102	102	102	102	102
104	103	102	103	103	102	103	102	102	102	102	102	103
105	104	103	104	103	103	104	103	103	103	103	103	104
106	104	104	104	104	104	104	103	104	103	104	103	105
107	105	104	105	105	104	105	104	104	104	104	104	106
108	106	105	106	106	105	106	105	105	104	105	104	106
109	106	105	107	106	105	107	105	105	105	106	105	107
110	107	106	107	107	106	107	106	106	106	106	105	108
111	108	107	108	108	107	108	106	106	106	107	106	109
112	109	107	109	108	107	109	107	107	107	107	106	110
113	109	108	109	109	108	110	107	108	107	108	107	111
114	110	108	110	110	109	110	108	108	108	109	108	111
115	111	109	111	110	109	111	109	109	108	109	108	112
116	111	109	112	111	110	112	109	109	109	110	109	113
117	112	110	112	112	110	113	110	110	109	110	109	114
118	113	111	113	113	111	113	110	111	110	111	110	115
119	114	111	114	113	112	114	111	111	111	112	110	115
120	114	112	115	114	112	115	111	112	111	112	111	116
121	115	112	115	115	113	116	112	112	112	113	111	117
122	116	113	116	115	113	116	112	113	112	113	112	118
123	116	114	117	116	114	117	113	114	113	114	112	119
124	117	114	117	117	115	118	114	114	113	115	113	119
125	118	115	118	117	115	119	114	115	114	115	114	120
126	119	115	119	118	116	119	115	115	114	116	114	121
127	119	116	120	119	116	120	115	116	115	117	115	122
128	120	117	120	119	117	121	116	117	115	117	115	123
129	121	117	121	120	118	122	116	117	116	118	116	124
130	121	118	122	121	118	122	117	118	117	118	116	124
131	122	118	123	122	119	123	118	118	117	119	117	125
132	123	119	123	122	119	124	118	119	118	120	117	126
133	124	120	124	123	120	125	119	119	118	120	118	127
134	124	120	125	124	121	125	119	120	119	121	118	128
135	125	121	125	124	121	126	120	121	119	121	119	128
136	126	121	126	125	122	127	120	121	120	122	119	129
137	126	122	127	126	123	128	121	122	120	123	120	130
138	127	122	128	126	123	128	122	122	121	123	121	131
139	128	123	128	127	124	129	122	123	122	124	121	132
140	129	124	129	128	124	130	123	124	122	125	122	132
141	129	124	130	129	125	131	123	124	123	125	122	133
142	130	125	131	129	126	131	124	125	123	126	123	134
143	131	125	131	130	126	132	124	125	124	126	123	135
144	132	126	132	131	127	133	125	126	124	127	124	136

(continues)

WISC-III FSIQ	Broad Reading	Basic Reading Skills	Reading Comp	Broad Math	Math Calculation Skills	Math Reasoning	Broad Written Language	Basic Writing Skills	Written Expression	Oral Expression	Listening Comp	Academic Knowledge
145	132	127	133	131	127	134	126	127	125	128	124	137
146	133	127	133	132	128	134	126	127	125	128	125	137
147	134	128	134	133	129	135	127	128	126	129	125	138
148	134	128	135	133	129	136	127	128	127	129	126	139
149	135	129	136	134	130	137	128	129	127	130	127	140
150	136	130	136	135	130	137	128	130	128	131	127	141
151	137	130	137	135	131	138	129	130	128	131	128	141
152	137	131	138	136	132	139	130	131	129	132	128	142
153	138	131	139	137	132	140	130	131	129	132	129	143
154	139	132	139	138	133	140	131	132	130	133	129	144
155	139	133	140	138	134	141	131	132	130	134	130	145
156	140	133	141	139	134	142	132	133	131	134	130	145
157	141	134	141	140	135	143	132	134	132	135	131	146
158	142	134	142	140	135	143	133	134	132	136	131	147
159	142	135	143	141	136	144	133	135	133	136	132	148
160	143	135	144	142	137	145	134	135	133	137	132	149

Appendix C

Ability/Achievement
Discrepancy Worksheet

Source: Reproduced from the Woodcock–Johnson III Assessment Service Bulletin Number 4. Calculating Ability/Achievement Discrepancies between the *Wechsler Intelligence Scale for Children—Third Edition* and the *Woodcock–Johnson III Tests of Achievement* (Table 2, pp. 4–7), by Fredrick A. Schrank, Kirk A. Becker, and Scott Decker, with permission of the publisher. Copyright © 2001 by The Riverside Publishing Company, Itasca, Illinois. All rights reserved.

WISC-III/WJ III ACH Ability/Achievement Discrepancy Calculation Worksheet

Name_____   WISC-III FSIQ _____

WJ III Achievement Clusters	Column 2 Actual Achievement		Column 3 Predicted Achievement		Column 4 Ability/ Achievement SS Difference		Column 5 SEE		Column 6 Discrepancy SD
Broad Reading	☐	−	☐	=	☐	÷	10.47	=	☐
Basic Reading Skills	☐	−	☐	=	☐	÷	12.10	=	☐
Reading Comprehension	☐	−	☐	=	☐	÷	10.29	=	☐
Broad Math	☐	−	☐	=	☐	÷	10.77	=	☐
Math Calculation Skills	☐	−	☐	=	☐	÷	11.90	=	☐
Math Reasoning	☐	−	☐	=	☐	÷	9.94	=	☐
Broad Written Language	☐	−	☐	=	☐	÷	12.35	=	☐
Basic Writing Skills	☐	−	☐	=	☐	÷	12.11	=	☐
Written Expression	☐	−	☐	=	☐	÷	12.50	=	☐
Oral Expression	☐	−	☐	=	☐	÷	11.85	=	☐
Listening Comprehension	☐	−	☐	=	☐	÷	12.61	=	☐
Academic Knowledge	☐	−	☐	=	☐	÷	8.77	=	☐

Appendix D

WJ III COG Teaching Resources

RESOURCE LIST

Description	Source
A guide to recommending interventions drawn from WJ III COG and Achievement battery results	Mather, N., & Jaffe, L. E. (2002). *Woodcock–Johnson III: Reports, recommendations, and strategies.* New York: Wiley
A guide to WJ III COG administration, scoring, and interpretation	Schrank, F. A., Flanagan, D. P., Woodcock, R. W., & Mascolo, J. T. (2002). *Essentials of WJ III cognitive abilities assessment.* New York: Wiley
Institute for Applied Psychometrics (web site sponsored and populated by a WJ III test author for researchers and instructors supporting CHC theory); includes PowerPoint presentations, handouts, and articles	Web site: http://www.iapsych.com
Report-writing software, manual, and forms (generate technical data, text, and allow examiners to include data from a structured checklist, other tests, and comments)	Schrank, F. A., & Woodcock, R. W. (2002). *Report writer for the WJ III.* Itasca, IL: Riverside
Riverside Publishing provides training materials, including a CD-ROM (with slides and handouts), Self-Study Training Package (CD-ROM based), and VHS training videos	Web site: http://www.riverpub.com/products/clinical/wj3/materials.html
Training handouts, worksheets, and comments provided by Professors Dumont and Willis of Fairleigh Dickinson University	Web site: http://alpha.fdu.edu/psychology/woodcock_index.htm
Web site containing the full text of service bulletins and newsletters, and lists of supplemental resources (e.g., training events, books)	Web site: http://www.riverpub.com/products/clinical/wj3/resource.html

VALIDITY OF COGNITIVE TESTS

The validity—and value—of cognitive tests are questioned frequently in the popular media. This assignment will introduce you to the professional standards by which all educational and psychological tests should be judged. Then, you will apply those standards to the available evidence to judge the validity of intelligence tests—or more precisely, to the validity of scores (e.g., GIA, cluster) produced by the WJ III. You *must* consider the evidence contained in the test manuals (found in each test kit), and the readings required for the class, in your evaluation. You *may* consider other sources in your evaluation, including articles appearing in professional journals, test critiques, and the like. Your evaluation must weigh the available evidence in light of our professional standards. Organize standards and evidence ratings in a table, and be sure to include a summary paragraph stating and justifying your position on cognitive test score validity (see the scoring rubric provided in this Appendix for details).

Specifically, use the standards presented in Chapter 1 of *The Standards for Educational and Psychological Testing* (AERA, APA, NCME, 1999) to evaluate the WJ III COG. Follow the steps below:

1. Identify and evaluate the claims of the WJ III COG. You will need to understand the claims to rate the relevance of forms of evidence. Look for explicit and implicit claims (e.g., "examiners may find this test useful for..."). Note the source of the claim (e.g., page number in manual). Careful attention to the claims of the WJ III authors will help you decide what evidence is needed to support the intended uses and interpretations of test scores.

2. Sort the standards into categories reflecting the five areas of validity evidence identified in the *Standards*. Create a sixth category of standards that applies generally across all evidence domains (i.e., standards not linked to a particular form of validity evidence). Do your best to put a standard into only one of your six categories. For example, validity standards 1.8 and 1.9 could be put into a variety of categories, but probably best belong under the "Response Processes" heading.

3. List the Standards in tables reflecting each category of validity (see sample validity tables provided in this Appendix).

4. In the "Relevance" columns, rate from 0 to 4 ("not at all" to "essential") your judgment of the relevance of the standard for the WJ III COG. Some standards may be essential to justify WJ III COG claims; others may be irrelevant. The importance of the standards is determined by the nature of the claim!

5. In the "Evidence" columns, judge the adequacy of evidence from 0 to 4 ("none" to "exemplary"). Include notes in the "Comments" sections to justify your decisions.

6. Write a brief statement (one to two paragraphs; see the "Summary Comment" sample page, this Appendix) of your conclusions regarding the validity of the WJ III COG. Please consider the degree to which the evidence supports

the claims of the test, taking into account the relevance of the evidence (e.g., ample irrelevant evidence is less supportive than modest evidence supporting relevant domains). Also consider three types of decisions related to the validity claims of the WJ III: supported, lacking/not supported, or inconclusive (e.g., the available evidence is neither so deficient to warrant a "not supported" judgment, nor sufficient to demonstrate a judgment of "supported").

7. Finally, judge your work using the scoring rubric (see sample, next page). I will use the same rubric to evaluate your work; the final grade for the assignment is my rating. I will return the rubric and assignment to you with my comments. See me if you would like to discuss my ratings of your work.

Rubric for Evaluation of Cognitive Test Validity

Name: _____

Test: _____

Domain	Self-rating	Instructor
Clarity of evaluative framework (10 points possible)		
• Identifies test claims accurately (2) • Sorts and applies AERA, APA, NCME standards (3) • Rates importance of evidence accurately, given test claims (2) • Rates quality of evidence accurately (2) • Provides appropriate justifications for ratings (1)		
Position on validity (5 points possible)		
• Clearly stated position (1) • Position clearly linked to standards and evidence (2) • Identifies unclear, controversial, or unsupported claims (1) • Suggests evidence needed to clarify ambiguous areas (1)		
Total Rating (15 possible)		

Comments:

Validity of Cognitive Tests Claims and Evidence Table

| Test: |
| Student: |
| Date: |
| Author Claims for Intended Use of Test Results (include source) |
| |

Domain: Test Content

Standard	Relevance	Evidence
	0 1 2 3 4	0 1 2 3 4
	0 1 2 3 4	0 1 2 3 4
	0 1 2 3 4	0 1 2 3 4
	0 1 2 3 4	0 1 2 3 4
	0 1 2 3 4	0 1 2 3 4
	0 1 2 3 4	0 1 2 3 4
	0 1 2 3 4	0 1 2 3 4
	0 1 2 3 4	0 1 2 3 4
	0 1 2 3 4	0 1 2 3 4
	0 1 2 3 4	0 1 2 3 4
	0 1 2 3 4	0 1 2 3 4

Comments:

Domain: Response Processes

Standard	Relevance	Evidence
	0 1 2 3 4	0 1 2 3 4
	0 1 2 3 4	0 1 2 3 4
	0 1 2 3 4	0 1 2 3 4
	0 1 2 3 4	0 1 2 3 4
	0 1 2 3 4	0 1 2 3 4
	0 1 2 3 4	0 1 2 3 4
	0 1 2 3 4	0 1 2 3 4
	0 1 2 3 4	0 1 2 3 4
	0 1 2 3 4	0 1 2 3 4
	0 1 2 3 4	0 1 2 3 4
	0 1 2 3 4	0 1 2 3 4

Comments:

Domain: Internal Structure

Standard	Relevance	Evidence
	0 1 2 3 4	0 1 2 3 4
	0 1 2 3 4	0 1 2 3 4
	0 1 2 3 4	0 1 2 3 4
	0 1 2 3 4	0 1 2 3 4
	0 1 2 3 4	0 1 2 3 4
	0 1 2 3 4	0 1 2 3 4
	0 1 2 3 4	0 1 2 3 4
	0 1 2 3 4	0 1 2 3 4
	0 1 2 3 4	0 1 2 3 4
	0 1 2 3 4	0 1 2 3 4
	0 1 2 3 4	0 1 2 3 4

Comments:

Domain: Relations to Other Variables

Standard	Relevance	Evidence
	0 1 2 3 4	0 1 2 3 4
	0 1 2 3 4	0 1 2 3 4
	0 1 2 3 4	0 1 2 3 4
	0 1 2 3 4	0 1 2 3 4
	0 1 2 3 4	0 1 2 3 4
	0 1 2 3 4	0 1 2 3 4
	0 1 2 3 4	0 1 2 3 4
	0 1 2 3 4	0 1 2 3 4
	0 1 2 3 4	0 1 2 3 4
	0 1 2 3 4	0 1 2 3 4

Comments:

Domain: Test Consequences

Standard	Relevance	Evidence
	0 1 2 3 4	0 1 2 3 4
	0 1 2 3 4	0 1 2 3 4
	0 1 2 3 4	0 1 2 3 4
	0 1 2 3 4	0 1 2 3 4
	0 1 2 3 4	0 1 2 3 4
	0 1 2 3 4	0 1 2 3 4
	0 1 2 3 4	0 1 2 3 4
	0 1 2 3 4	0 1 2 3 4
	0 1 2 3 4	0 1 2 3 4
	0 1 2 3 4	0 1 2 3 4
	0 1 2 3 4	0 1 2 3 4

Comments:

Domain: General Standards

Standard	Relevance	Evidence
	0 1 2 3 4	0 1 2 3 4
	0 1 2 3 4	0 1 2 3 4
	0 1 2 3 4	0 1 2 3 4
	0 1 2 3 4	0 1 2 3 4
	0 1 2 3 4	0 1 2 3 4
	0 1 2 3 4	0 1 2 3 4
	0 1 2 3 4	0 1 2 3 4
	0 1 2 3 4	0 1 2 3 4
	0 1 2 3 4	0 1 2 3 4
	0 1 2 3 4	0 1 2 3 4
	0 1 2 3 4	0 1 2 3 4

Comments:

Summary Comment
Your Position Statement on the Validity of the WJ III COG

(Hint: List author claims and, based on your review and application of the standards and the available evidence, judge whether the available evidence supports, does not support, or is inconclusive regarding the author's claims.)

QUESTIONS TO GUIDE CASE-BASED
INTERPRETATION OF ASSESSMENT RESULTS

Identifying and Defining the Problem

Why is the individual being referred for assessment? What are the problems and who reports them? Are problem definitions shared among all relevant parties (e.g., teacher, parent, individual, spouse)? What are the expected outcomes of the assessment (e.g., intervention, diagnosis, placement, eligibility for services)?

Establishing the Context

How has the individual functioned in the past in similar settings? Are there unusual features in the developmental history that may be relevant to the problem? How long has the problem existed (duration), how severe is it (intensity), and how often does it appear (frequency)? What do independent observations, interviews, and other data suggest with respect to these issues? How might cultural, socioeconomic, and linguistic factors affect perceptions and behaviors across settings? Have there been efforts to solve the problem in the past? If so, what is the nature of those efforts (i.e., the quality of intervention and the integrity with which the intervention was applied)?

Identifying the Information Needed to Solve the Problem

What knowledge bases (e.g., cognitive abilities research, educational intervention research, developmental psychopathology) are relevant to the problem at hand? What are the plausible and relevant hypotheses for understanding the problem? What information is needed to assess these hypotheses or achieve the desired outcomes? What are the best methods to obtain the information? Is the WJ III a useful tool in this case, and if so, how?

Using WJ III COG Assessment Results to Understand the Problem

What is the individual's General Intellectual Ability score? Are cluster and other test scores congruent with this general level? Are the scores and clusters consistent? If not, are the differences among scores and clusters reliable? Are reliable differences also unusual? How can the similarities and differences among results lead to hypotheses regarding the nature of the problem? What evidence could refute or challenge these hypotheses? What scientific knowledge-base supports (or challenges) your interpretations?

Using Assessment Information to Resolve the Problem

Does information support, refute, or fail to clarify rival hypotheses regarding the initial problem or concern? How can the information be used to help resolve the problem (e.g., diagnosis, placement, intervention)? Is it possible to provide evidence-based recommendations (e.g., educational or psychological interventions supported by research) drawn from the assessment results? If so, what are they? What are the benefits of the use and interpretation of results you are presenting to the individual? What are the risks or dangers to the individual? How can the results best be presented to maximize benefits and minimize risks?

Sample Syllabus

Cognitive Ability Assessment

COURSE OVERVIEW

In this course, the participant will be introduced to individually administered tests of cognitive ability commonly used with school-age children and youth. Skills in test administration, scoring, interpretation, and report writing will be developed. The course includes lecture, discussion, demonstration, and supervised practice. In the course, general concepts and theories will be introduced as well as specific applications and technologies used to better understand cognitive abilities in children and youths. Primary emphasis will be placed on assessment procedures for use with school-age students and young adults. Supervised practicum is required. The course will focus on the context of using tests of cognitive abilities, theory, culture and other contextual factors, administration, and scoring. Initial skills in interpretation will be developed with more in-depth focus and practice on interpretation in the following term.

Prerequisites

- Statistics and Research Methods

Corequisites

- Introduction to Measurement
- Professional Issues and Ethics

Required Texts

Flanagan, D. P., Genshaft, J. L., Harrison, P. L. (Eds). (1997). *Contemporary intellectual assessment: Theories, tests, and issues.* New York: Guilford.

Kaufman, A. (1994). *Intelligent testing with the WISC-III.* New York: Wiley.

McGrew, K. S., and Flanagan, D. P. (1998). *The intelligence test desk reference (ITDR): Gf–Gc cross-battery assessment.* New York: Allyn & Bacon.

Schrank, F. A., Flanagan, D. P., Woodcock, R. J., & Mascola, J. (Eds). (2002). *Essentials of WJ III Cognitive Abilities Assessment.* New York: Wiley.

Recommended or Supplemental Texts

Schrank, F. A., & Flanagan, D. P. (Eds). (2003). *WJ III clinical use and interpretation: Scientist–practitioner perspectives.* San Diego: Academic Press.

Sattler, J. (2001). *Assessment of children: Cognitive applications* (4th ed). Jerome M. Sattler, Publisher.

Required Materials

- Stop watch
- Clip board
- Mechanical pencils with erasers
- Email address (check daily during the week)
- Positive attitude and strong work ethic!! (optional but of benefit)

Additional Requirement

All students are required to sign up for the IAP list serv. This list serve is devoted to understanding and interpreting tests of cognitive abilities according the CHC framework discussed in class. Students join the list serve by going to the IAP website at www.IAPsych.com. On occasion, recent activity on the list serve will be discussed in class. In addition, from time to time, new postings on the IAP web site may be assigned as readings for the entire class.

Objectives for the Course

Upon completion of the course, the student will

- Demonstrate an understanding of the historical foundations in assessment as it relates to the assessment of cognitive abilities.
- Demonstrate an understanding of both the historical and contemporary theories of cognitive ability.
- Demonstrate an understanding of issues related to the measurement of cognitive abilities.
- Demonstrate an understanding of and generate major arguments supporting and limiting the validity of tests of cognitive abilities.
- Demonstrate an understanding of historical and current research on the nature of cognitive abilities.
- Demonstrate an understanding of contextual variables (e.g., culture, standardization sample, and examiner) influencing performance on tests of cognitive abilities.
- Demonstrate an understanding of various controversies regarding the use of cognitive measures with school children and youth.
- Demonstrate a working knowledge of CHC theory and its application to current tests of cognitive abilities.
- Administer the *Woodcock–Johnson III: Tests of Cognitive Abilities* (WJ III COG), the *Wechsler Intelligence Scale for Children-III* (*WISC-III*), and the *Differential Ability Scales* (DAS) using standardized directions at a mastery level.
- Demonstrate proficiency for scoring (including computer scoring when applicable) the WJ III COG, WISC-III, DAS, KAIT, and WAIS-III using normative data and scoring procedures.
- Demonstrate beginning skills in interpreting the WJ III COG, WISC-III, and DAS.

- Recognize and apply major theories of cognitive abilities and measurement principles when selecting, using, and interpreting assessment information.
- Demonstrate preliminary report writing and case summary skills.
- Develop an appreciation and awareness for the uses and limitations that intelligence tests may have for persons from diverse ethnic, cultural, linguistic, and socioeconomic backgrounds.

COURSE REQUIREMENTS

Attendance and Participation

You are expected to not only attend class but also to be an *active* participant during class discussions. This means you must do the readings and assignments (when applicable) in advance of class and come prepared for class meetings. You should be on time (this means allow adequate morning travel time, because we start early) and plan to stay for the entire class session. Repeatedly being late for class will result in your grade being dropped one letter grade. **100 possible points (10% of total semester grade).**

Weekly Journal/Reading Summaries

You will keep a weekly journal with summaries of weekly readings and assignments. Each week you should bring to class a brief (one page or less) integrated summary of the readings and include comments and questions (if any) you have about the reading. You should organize your summary as follows:

1. Name and date at the top left
2. Key "take home" or summary points
3. Reactions/comments
4. Questions

Remember, keep the summary *under one page* if at all possible. In addition to the weekly summaries, you should include some periodic journaling on your test practices and other activities. Keep all returned summaries and activities in a paper notebook with your journaling. This is not graded beyond ensuring that you complete the summary each week and a review of your journal midway through and at the end of the term. However, you should make at least one additional entry beyond the weekly summary in your journal each week (ideally more). The entire journal file will be turned in at the end of the semester (in addition to the summaries each week). **100 possible points (10% of total semester grade).**

Protocols

You will complete a minimum of nine test practice test record forms or protocols that will be assessed for scoring accuracy. You must submit at least two WISC-III, two WJ III COG, and two DAS protocols that are free from major scoring errors. The test record scoring checklist will be distributed in class prior to the first protocol due date. All protocols must include a consent form and the computer scoring printout when applicable at the time they are due or you will not receive credit for the assignment. A participant cannot be assessed more than once with the same instrument, although it is acceptable to assess the same person with different instruments. *You are required to submit at least three protocols each on the WISC-III, WJ III COG, and DAS* but you may submit as many protocols as you need to meet this standard (i.e., some students may need to do more than three protocols per test to attain competency). You cannot pass the course without meeting this standard. The more you practice before turning a protocol in for a grade, the more likely you are to meet the course requirement with fewer administrations. **180 possible points (18% of total semester grade).**

Videotapes

You are required to submit two videotapes each for the WISC-III, WJ III COG, and DAS. You must earn 8 of 10 possible points for the videotape to demonstrate mastery of test administration (lower ratings will require you to submit another videotape). The videotape checklist will be distributed in class prior to the assignment due date. You must also self-rate your tape before you submit it for a grade. Tapes turned in for a grade must include a signed consent form, an original copy of the protocol for the taped session, and your self-rating/critique. The tapes should represent students of a variety of ages. At least one tape should be of a student under age 8 years and at least one of a student over age 16 years. **180 possible points (18% of total semester grade).**

Videotape Critique

Each student will find a partner, and will review and critique their partner's videotape. The student will (1) watch the videotape, (2) complete the videotape critique form, (3) write a one-paragraph reaction to the experience, (4) briefly discuss the critique with your partner, and (5) submit the critique to the course instructor for review. Details of the critique will be outlined in a separate handout. **30 possible points (3% of total course grade).**

Sample Write-Up

Each student will do one brief sample test write-up for each of the major tests reviewed during the semester (WJ III, WISC-III, and DAS). The instructor will provide the raw scores and chronological age and you will be responsible for completing the scoring, summarizing the scores, and briefly interpreting the results. Students will do one write-up each for the WISC-III, WJ III COG, and the DAS. Details will be provided in a separate handout. **60 possible points (6% of total semester grade).**

The Great IQ Debate

Each student will be assigned to a team that will either defend or attack the value of intelligence tests. You should address their value in general for school-age children and youth, and in particular for children from ethnic/cultural/linguistic minorities. Your team will then post a synopsis of the strongest points you believe will support *the other side of the case* (e.g., if you were attacking tests, you will defend them). This exercise will require you to work both with a group and alone, and it will require you to argue both sides of the issue before deciding which ones are the strongest arguments. When making points, citation of appropriate literature and respect for others is crucial. Dogmatic opinions prevent scholarly consideration of important issues. **150 possible points (15% of total semester grade).**

Final Semester Checkout

Each student will sign up for a 2-hour final checkout and oral final at the end of the semester. The first portion of the session will be for observation of test administration. During the second portion, the student will respond to questions covering readings and practice exercises from the semester. If the student does not demonstrate mastery on either component, the checkout must be repeated until mastery is attained. You could be required to repeat either or both portions of the "checkout" if mastery is not demonstrated. If you have to repeat either portion of the exam, the highest possible score you can obtain is a "B" (you cannot receive an "A" if you have to repeat the exam). **200 possible points (20% of total semester grade).**

Grading

• Attendance and Participation	100 points (10%)
• Journal and Reading Summaries	100 points (10%)
• Protocols (3 WISC-III; 3 WJ III COG; and 3 DAS minimum)	180 points (18%)
• Videotapes (2 WISC-III; 2 WJ III COG; and 2 DAS minimum)	180 points (18%)
• Peer Video Critique	30 points (3%)
• Sample Write-Ups (1 WISC; 1 WJ III; and 1 DAS minimum)	60 points (6%)
• The Great IQ Debate	150 points (15%)
• Fall Semester Checkout	200 points (20%)

Total: 1000 points (100%)

Testing Participants

While we will work to identify a pool of potential practice participants, you are also responsible for helping to locate participants. You are encouraged to work together to recruit participants. To complete the requirements for the course this semester, you must administer a minimum of nine tests. Some participants may be tested with more than one instrument. However, you must test at least one student younger than age 8 years and one older than age 16 years. Every effort should be made to include at least one participant who is bilingual or of minority ethnic status. You may test only people who fit within the age range of the test you are using. You must receive written consent from the participant and their parent/legal guardian. Consent forms must accompany protocols, reports, and videotapes. UNDER NO CIRCUMSTANCE SHOULD TEST RESULTS BE SHARED WITH PARENTS OR CLIENTS. This should be made clear before testing. You should avoid testing participants at high risk for learning difficulties and/or who have been identified as having disabilities (including those currently receiving special education services).

INDEX